EN: SECOND COMING. Contains material originally published in magazine form as SECOND COMING: PREPARE, X-MEN: SECOND COMING #1-2, UNCANNY X-MEN #523-525, NEW MUTANTS #12-14, X-MEN LEGACY 5-237 and X-FORCE #26-28. First printing 2010. ISBN# 978-0-7851-4678-0. Published by MARVEL WORLDWIDE, INC., a subsidiary of MARVEL ENTERTAINMENT, LLC. OFFICE OF PUBLICATION: 417 5th Avenue, New NY 10016. Copyright © 2010 Marvel Characters, Inc. All rights reserved. $39.99 per copy in the U.S. and $44.99 in Canada (GST #R127032852); Canadian Agreement #40668537. All characters featured in this issue and the active names and likenesses thereof, and all related indicia are trademarks of Marvel Characters, Inc. No similarity between any of the names, characters, persons, and/or institutions in this magazine with those of any living ead person or institution is intended, and any such similarity which may exist is purely coincidental. **Printed in the U.S.A.** ALAN FINE, EVP - Office of the President, Marvel Worldwide, Inc. and EVP & CMO Marvel Characters DAN BUCKLEY, Chief Executive Officer and Publisher - Print, Animation & Digital Media; JIM SOKOLOWSKI, Chief Operating Officer; DAVID GABRIEL, SVP of Publishing Sales & Circulation; DAVID BOGART, SVP of Business Affairs ent Management; MICHAEL PASCIULLO, VP Merchandising & Communications; JIM O'KEEFE, VP of Operations & Logistics; DAN CARR, Executive Director of Publishing Technology; JUSTIN F. GABRIE, Director of Publishing torial Operations; SUSAN CRESPI, Editorial Operations Manager; ALEX MORALES, Publishing Operations Manager; STAN LEE, Chairman Emeritus. For information regarding advertising in Marvel Comics or on Marvel.com, please ct Ron Stern, VP of Business Development, at rstern@marvel.com. For Marvel subscription inquiries, please call 800-217-9158. **Manufactured between 8/16/10 and 9/15/10 by R.R. DONNELLEY, INC., SALEM, VA, USA.**
? 7 6 5 4 3 2 1

X-MEN SECOND COMING

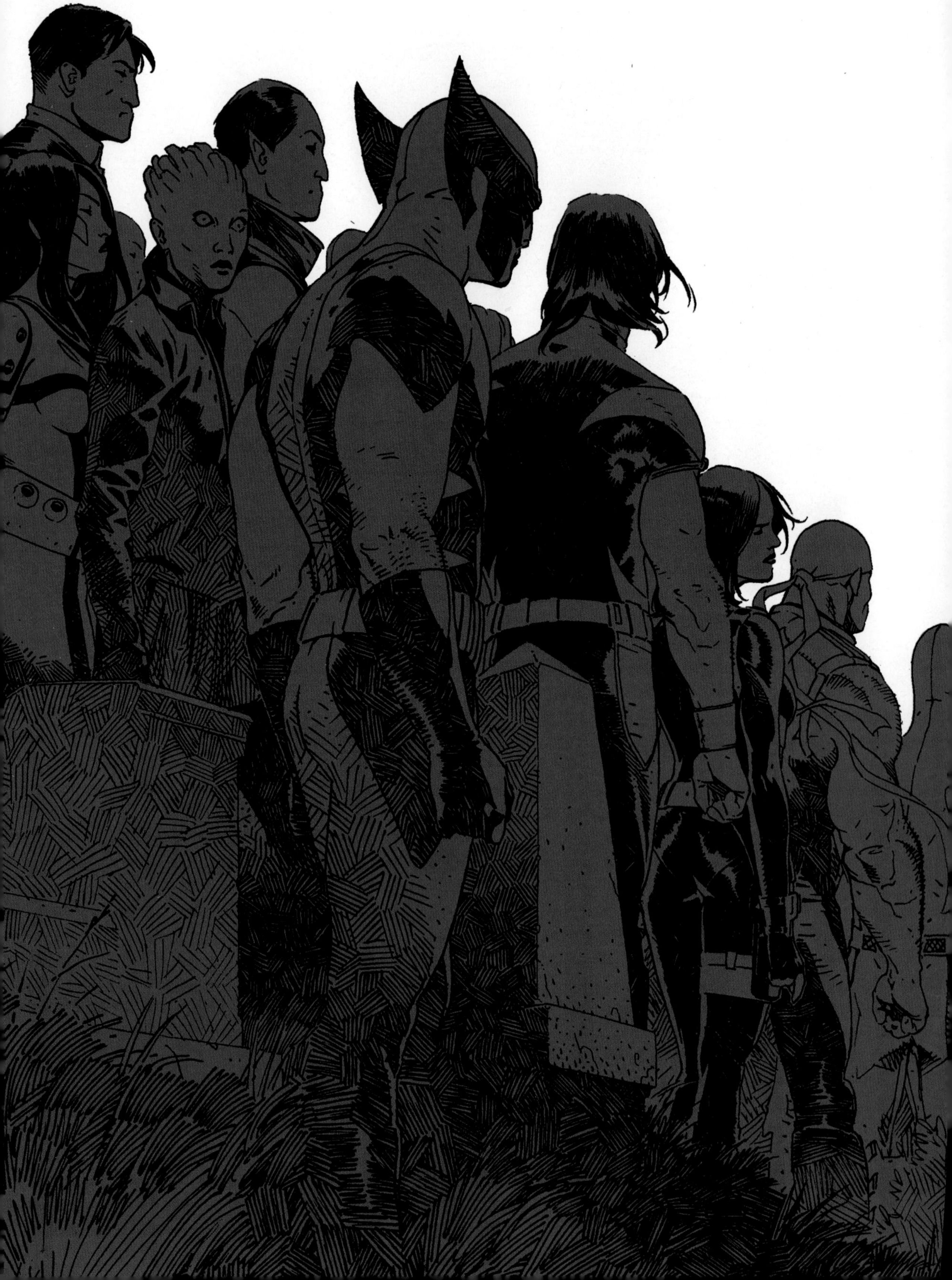

SECOND COMING: PREPARE
Writer: MIKE CAREY
Penciler: STUART IMMONEN
Inker: MICHAEL LACOMBE
Colorist: JUSTIN PONSOR

X-MEN: SECOND COMING #1
Writers: CRAIG KYLE & CHRIS YOST
Penciler: DAVID FINCH
Inker: BATT
Colorist: ASPEN'S
PETER STEIGERWALD

UNCANNY X-MEN #523-525
Writer: MATT FRACTION
Penciler: TERRY DODSON
Inker: RACHEL DODSON
Colorist: JUSTIN PONSOR

NEW MUTANTS #12-14
Writer: ZEB WELLS
Artist: IBRAIM ROBERSON with
LAN MEDINA & NATHAN FOX
Colorist: BRIAN REBER with
MATT MILLA & JOSE VILLARRUBIA

X-MEN: LEGACY #235-237
Writer: MIKE CAREY
Penciler: GREG LAND
Inker: JAY LEISTEN
Colorist: JUSTIN PONSOR

X-FORCE #26-28
Writers: CRAIG KYLE & CHRIS YOST
Penciler: MIKE CHOI
Colorist: SONIA OBACK

X-MEN: SECOND COMING #1
CHAPTER 1
Writer: ZEB WELLS
Artist: IBRAIM ROBERSON
Colorist: MATT MILLA
CHAPTER 2
Writer: MIKE CAREY
Artist: ESAD RIBIC
Colorist: MATT WILSON
CHAPTER 3
Writers: CRAIG KYLE & CHRIS YOST
Penciler: GREG LAND
Inker: JAY LEISTEN
Colorist: FRANK MARTIN
CHAPTER 4
Writer: MATT FRACTION
Penciler: TERRY DODSON
Inker: RACHEL DODSON
Colorist: BRAD ANDERSON

Cover Artists: DAVID FINCH & JASON KEITH and ADI GRANOV
Letterer: VC'S JOE CARAMAGNA & CORY PETIT with CLAYTON COWLES & JOE SABINO
Assistant Editor: JODY LEHEUP Associate Editor: DANIEL KETCHUM
Editors: NICK LOWE & JEANINE SCHAEFFER Executive Editor: AXEL ALONSO

Collection Editor: MARK D. BEAZLEY Editorial Assistants: JAMES EMMETT & JOE HOCHSTEIN
Assistant Editors: NELSON RIBEIRO & ALEX STARBUCK Editor, Special Projects: JENNIFER GRÜNWALD
Senior Editor, Special Projects: JEFF YOUNGQUIST Senior Vice President of Sales: DAVID GABRIEL
Production: JERRY KALINOWSKI Book Design: JEFF POWELL

Editor in Chief: JOE QUESADA
Publisher: DAN BUCKLEY
Executive Producer: ALAN FINE

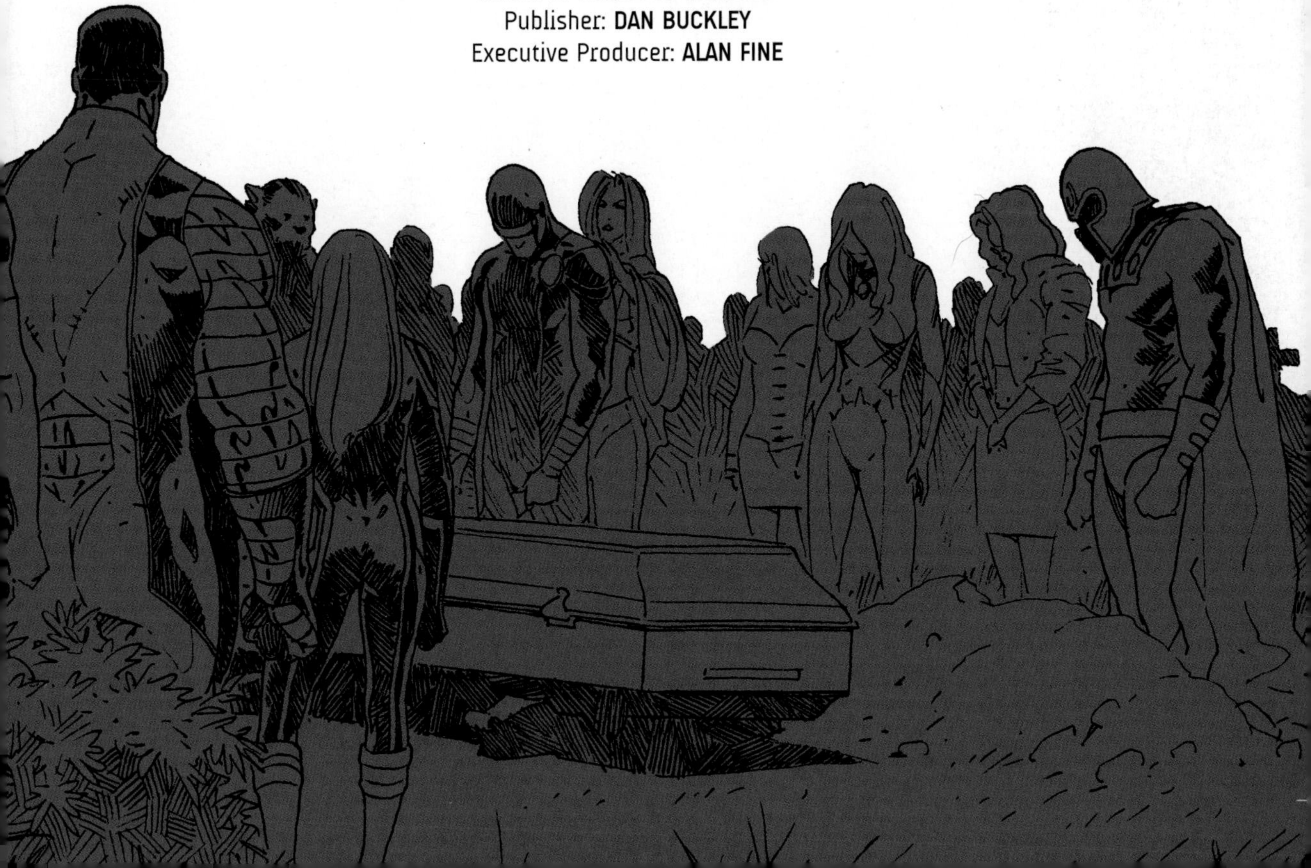

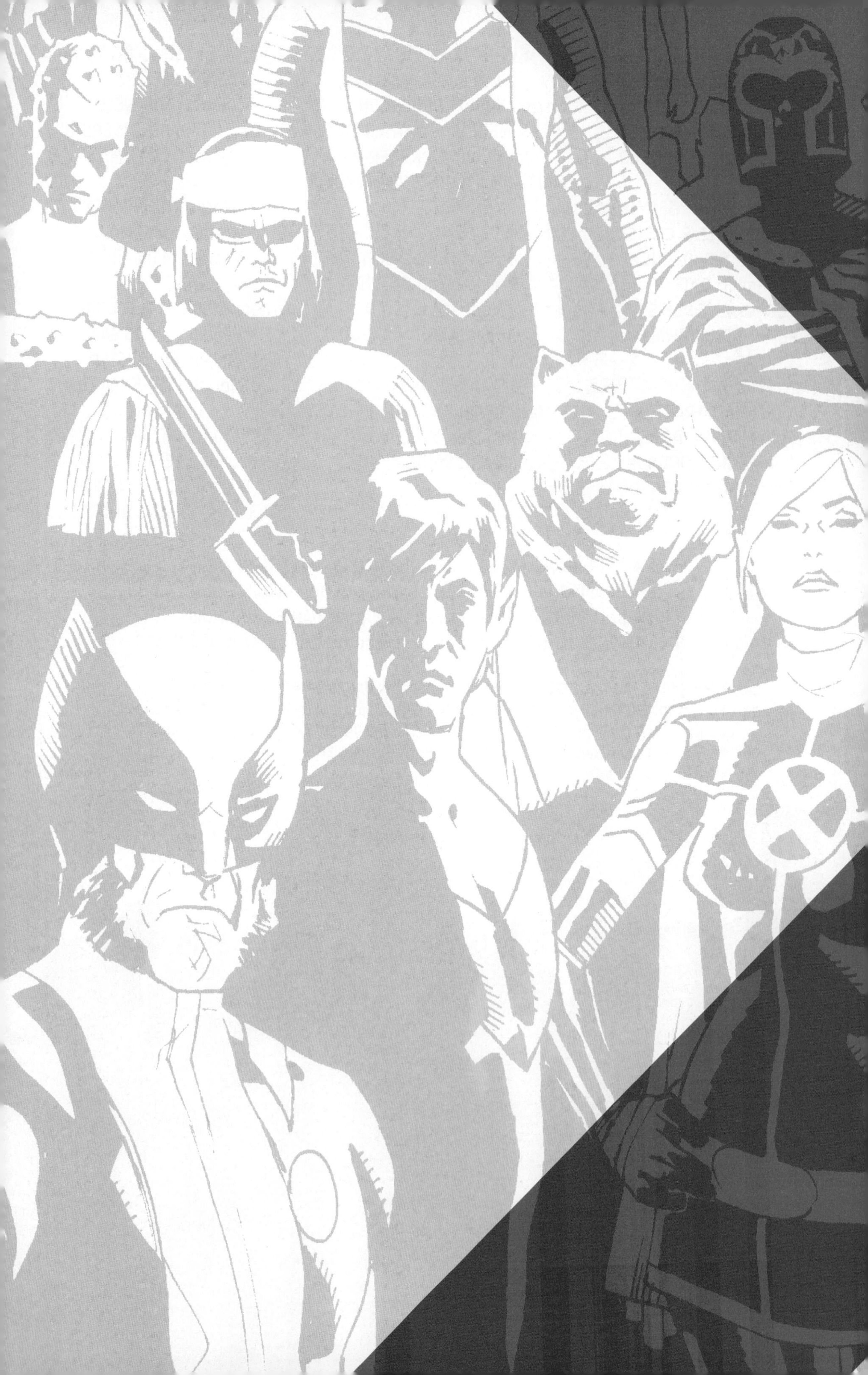

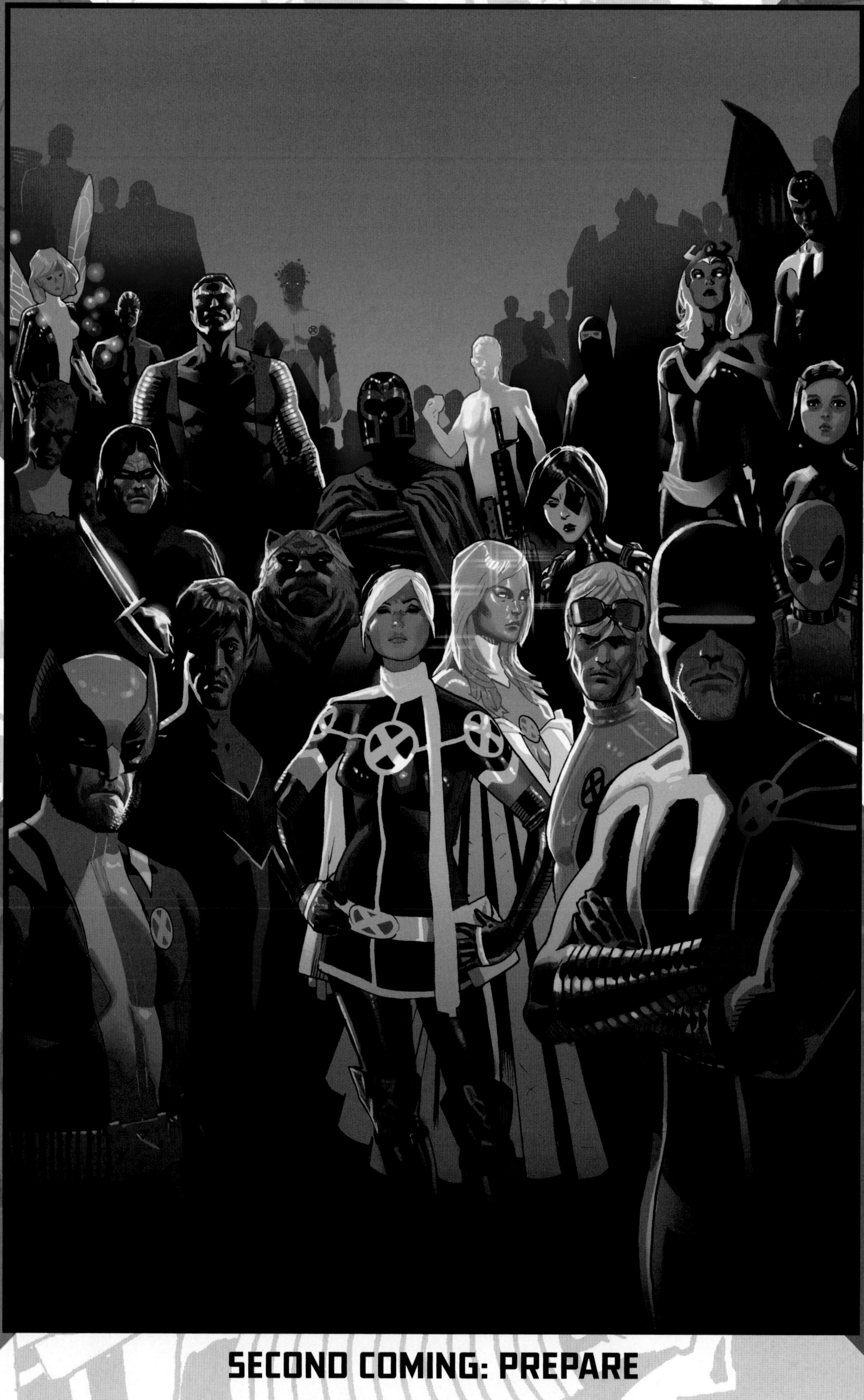

SECOND COMING: PREPARE

Previously...

In the blink of an eye, the mutant species went from a population of 16 million to 198. To make matters worse, the mutant gene had shut down and years passed with no new mutant activations. With extinction all but guaranteed, mutantkind's outlook was bleak.

Then, one morning, the impossible happened and a mutant baby was born. Her birth was greeted with carnage and death but her salvation came in the form of the X-Man Cable. Cable and the X-Men saved her from those who wanted to control or kill her, but, faced with the matter of her upbringing, chose to send her into the future with Cable as her caretaker. Thus, the X-Men were left to wait for this girl to hopefully become something that could save their species.

The future proved just as dangerous as the present, but Cable kept her safe and taught her to be a soldier like him. After 16 years in the future, she decided to come back. Her name is Hope Summers, and she has returned.

But the X-Men weren't the only ones waiting. This story takes place two days after Hope and Cable returned from the future.

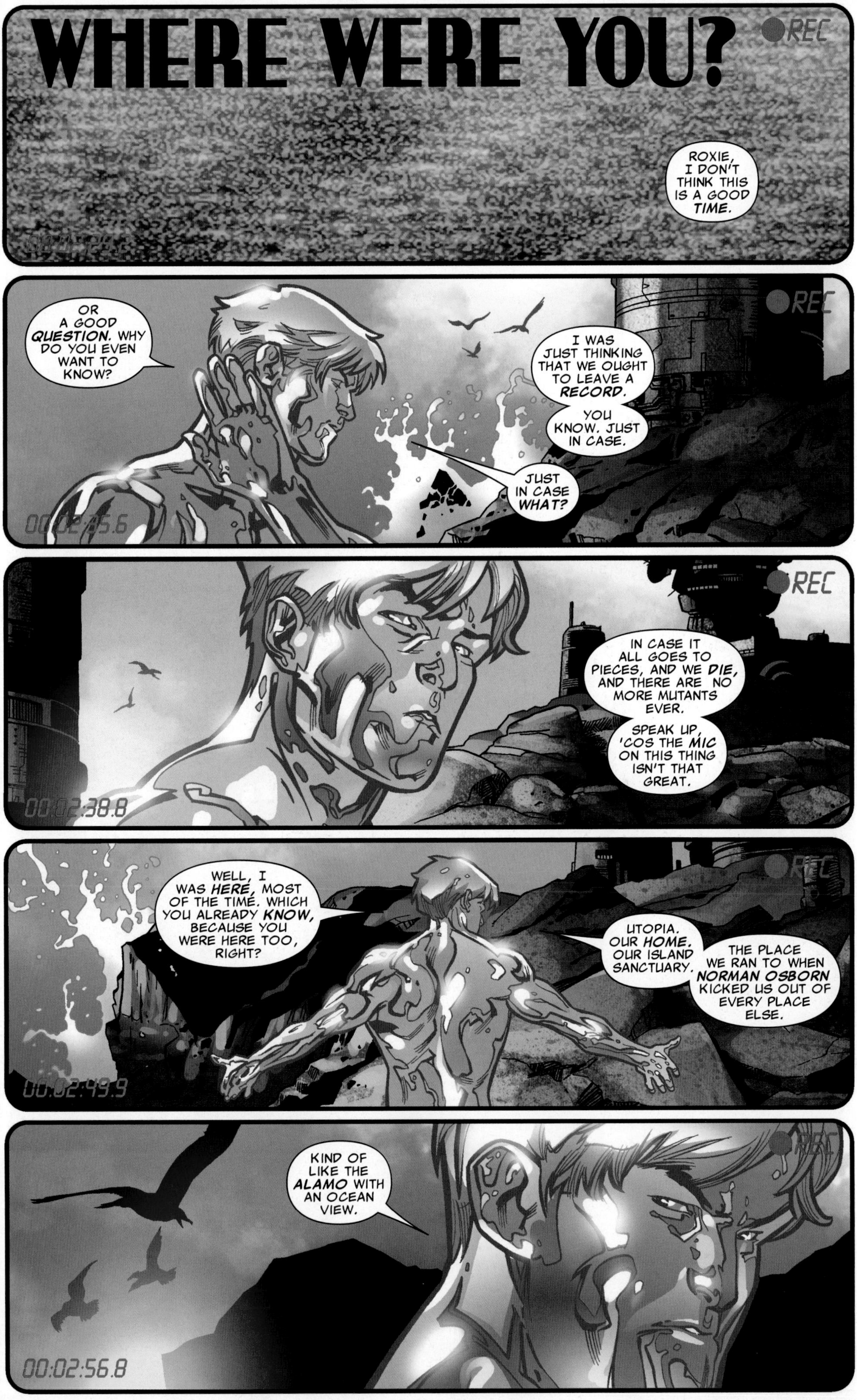
WHERE WERE YOU?
REC
ROXIE, I DON'T THINK THIS IS A GOOD TIME.
REC
OR A GOOD QUESTION. WHY DO YOU EVEN WANT TO KNOW?
I WAS JUST THINKING THAT WE OUGHT TO LEAVE A RECORD.
YOU KNOW. JUST IN CASE.
JUST IN CASE WHAT?
00:02:35.6
REC
IN CASE IT ALL GOES TO PIECES, AND WE DIE, AND THERE ARE NO MORE MUTANTS EVER.
SPEAK UP, 'COS THE MIC ON THIS THING ISN'T THAT GREAT.
00:02:38.8
REC
WELL, I WAS HERE, MOST OF THE TIME. WHICH YOU ALREADY KNOW, BECAUSE YOU WERE HERE TOO, RIGHT?
UTOPIA. OUR HOME. OUR ISLAND SANCTUARY.
THE PLACE WE RAN TO WHEN NORMAN OSBORN KICKED US OUT OF EVERY PLACE ELSE.
00:02:49.9
REC
KIND OF LIKE THE ALAMO WITH AN OCEAN VIEW.
00:02:56.8

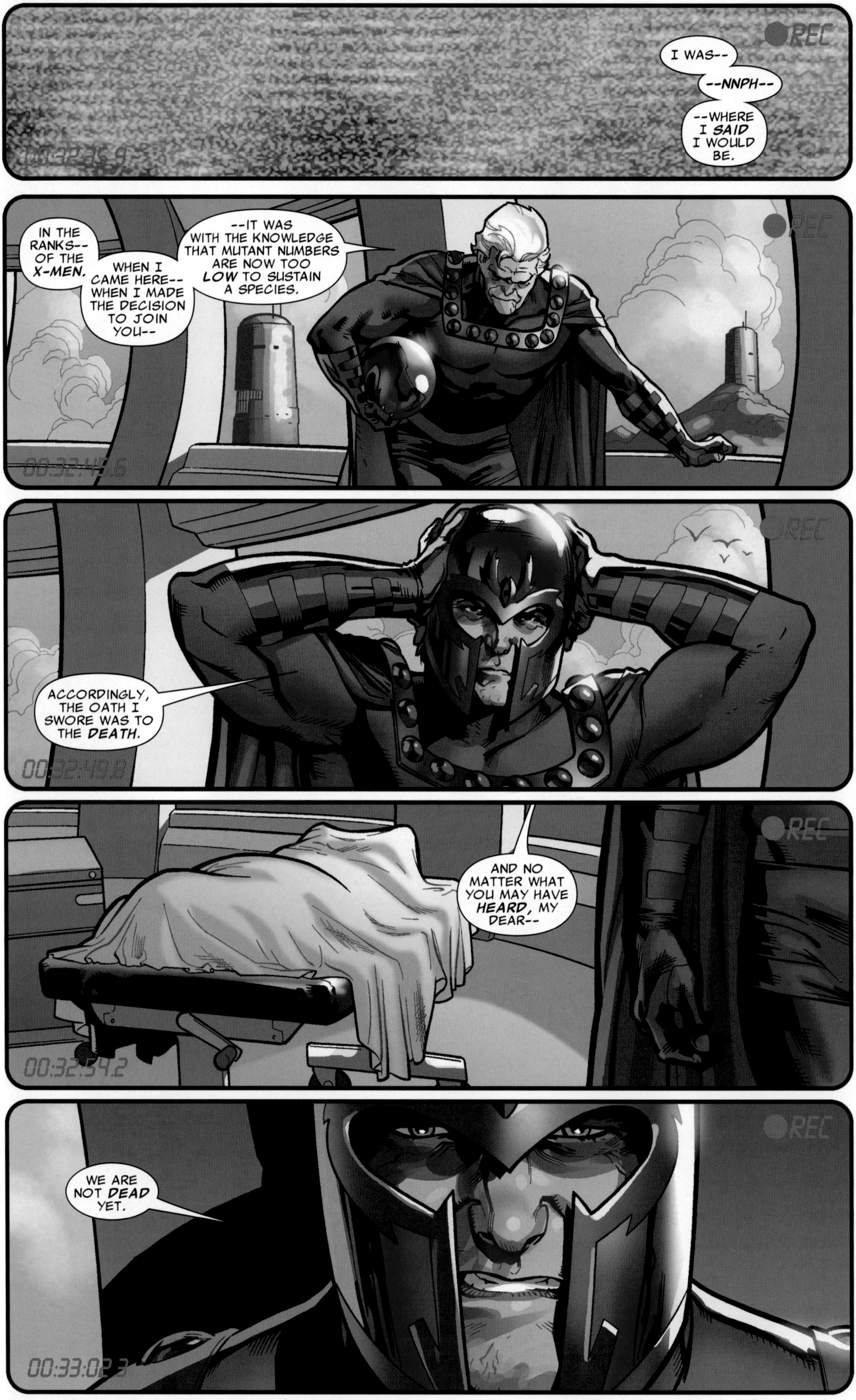
REC
00:32:35.9
I WAS--
--NNPH--
--WHERE I SAID I WOULD BE.
REC
00:32:45.6
IN THE RANKS-- OF THE X-MEN.
WHEN I CAME HERE-- WHEN I MADE THE DECISION TO JOIN YOU--
--IT WAS WITH THE KNOWLEDGE THAT MUTANT NUMBERS ARE NOW TOO LOW TO SUSTAIN A SPECIES.
REC
00:32:49.8
ACCORDINGLY, THE OATH I SWORE WAS TO THE DEATH.
REC
00:32:54.2
AND NO MATTER WHAT YOU MAY HAVE HEARD, MY DEAR--
REC
00:33:02.3
WE ARE NOT DEAD YET.

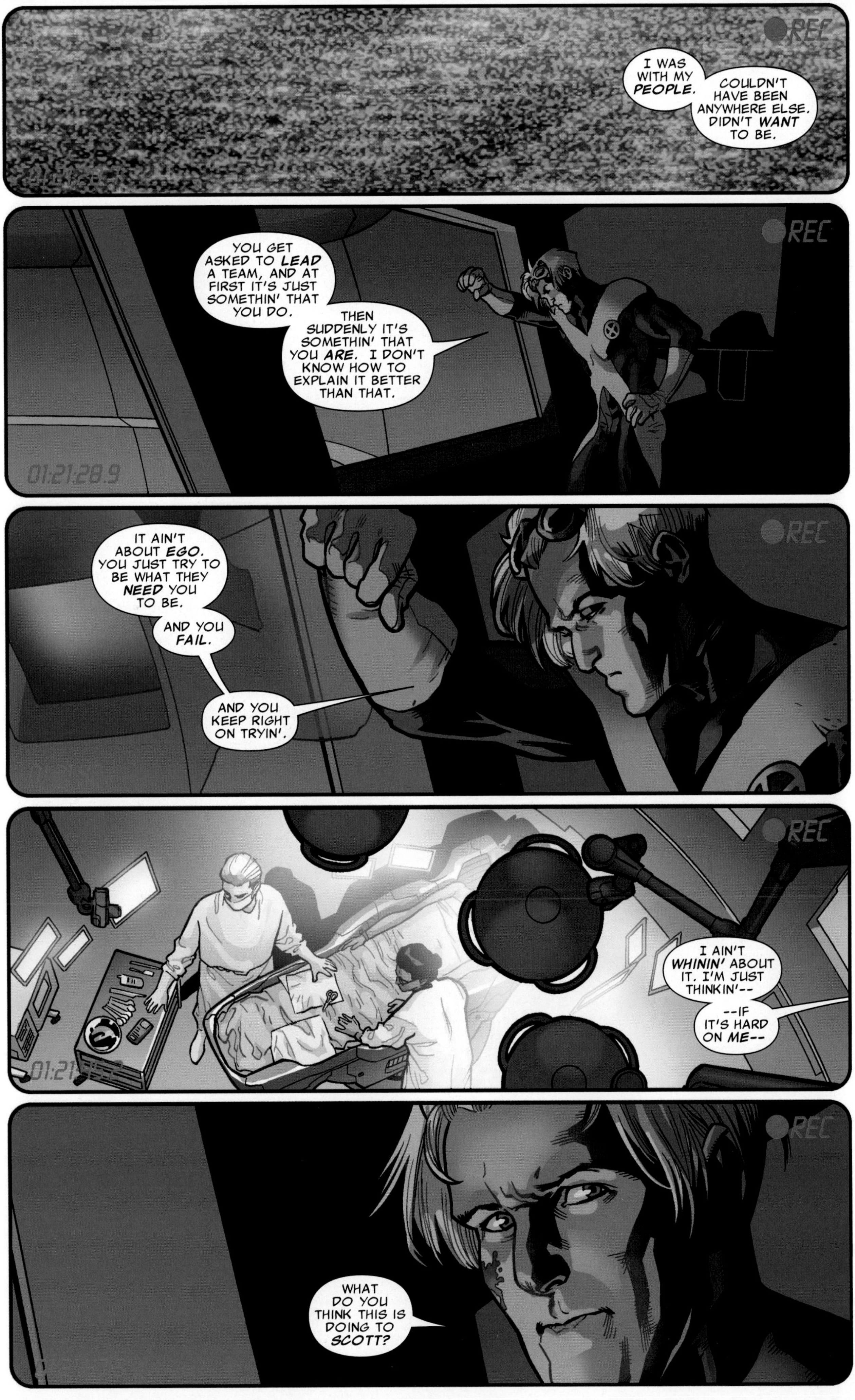
REC
I WAS WITH MY PEOPLE.
COULDN'T HAVE BEEN ANYWHERE ELSE. DIDN'T WANT TO BE.
REC
YOU GET ASKED TO LEAD A TEAM, AND AT FIRST IT'S JUST SOMETHIN' THAT YOU DO.
THEN SUDDENLY IT'S SOMETHIN' THAT YOU ARE. I DON'T KNOW HOW TO EXPLAIN IT BETTER THAN THAT.
01:21:28.9
REC
IT AIN'T ABOUT EGO. YOU JUST TRY TO BE WHAT THEY NEED YOU TO BE.
AND YOU FAIL.
AND YOU KEEP RIGHT ON TRYIN'.
REC
I AIN'T WHININ' ABOUT IT. I'M JUST THINKIN'--
--IF IT'S HARD ON ME--
REC
WHAT DO YOU THINK THIS IS DOING TO SCOTT?

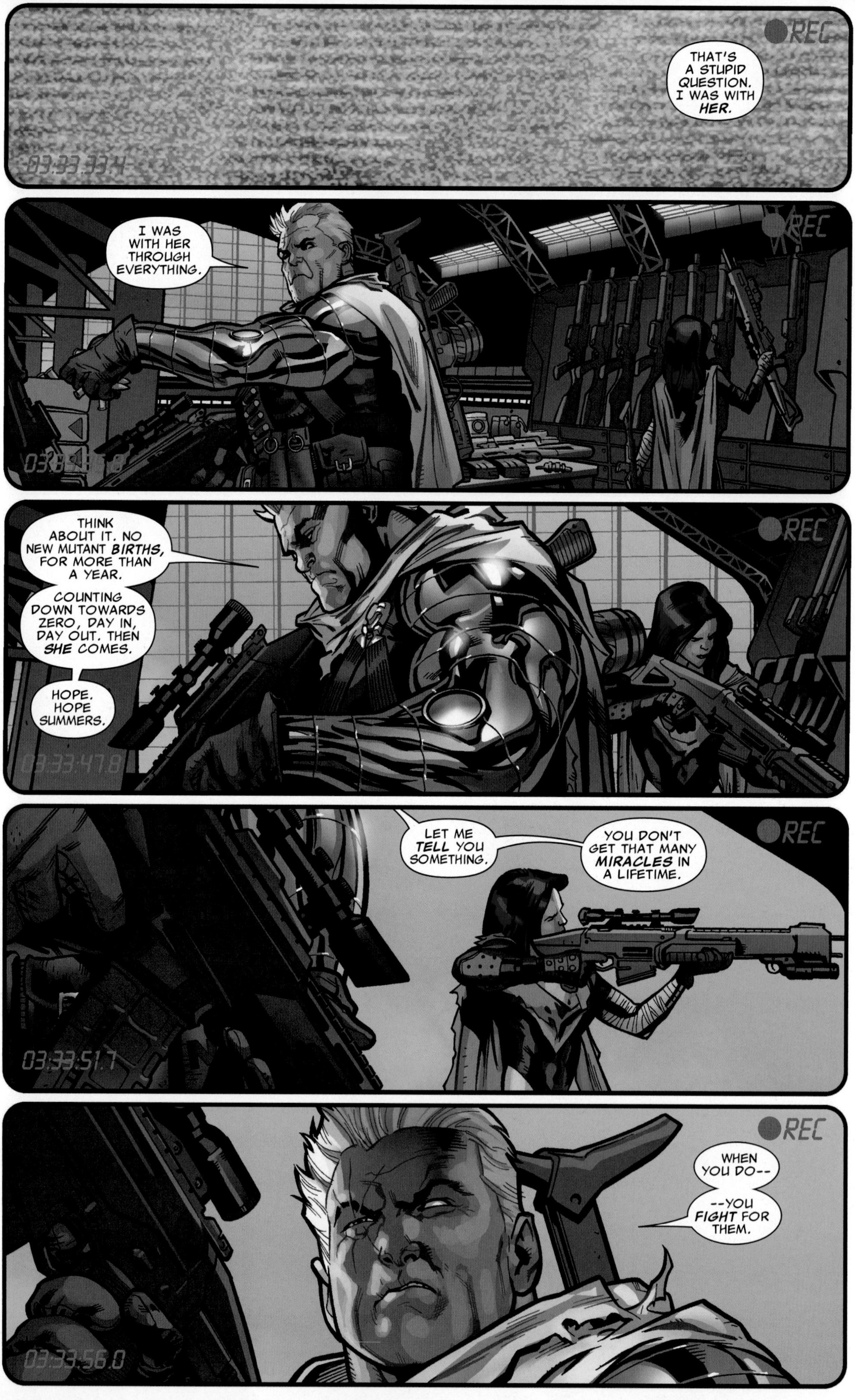
REC
THAT'S A STUPID QUESTION. I WAS WITH HER.
03:33:33.4
REC
I WAS WITH HER THROUGH EVERYTHING.
REC
THINK ABOUT IT. NO NEW MUTANT BIRTHS, FOR MORE THAN A YEAR.
COUNTING DOWN TOWARDS ZERO, DAY IN, DAY OUT. THEN SHE COMES.
HOPE. HOPE SUMMERS.
03:33:47.8
REC
LET ME TELL YOU SOMETHING.
YOU DON'T GET THAT MANY MIRACLES IN A LIFETIME.
03:33:51.7
REC
WHEN YOU DO--
--YOU FIGHT FOR THEM.
03:33:56.0

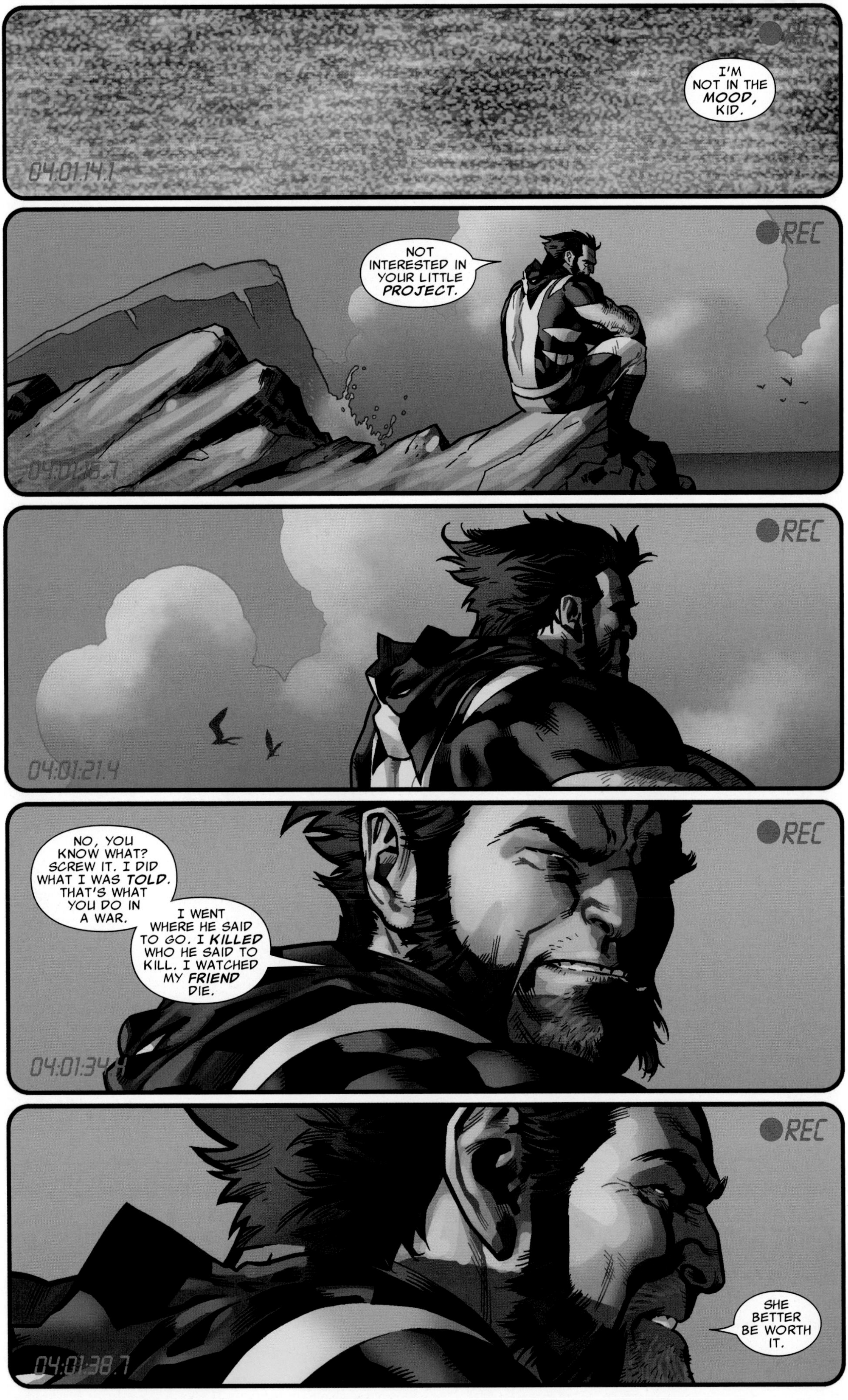

I'M NOT IN THE MOOD, KID.
04:01:14.1
REC
NOT INTERESTED IN YOUR LITTLE PROJECT.
REC
04:01:21.4
REC
NO, YOU KNOW WHAT? SCREW IT. I DID WHAT I WAS TOLD. THAT'S WHAT YOU DO IN A WAR.
I WENT WHERE HE SAID TO GO. I KILLED WHO HE SAID TO KILL. I WATCHED MY FRIEND DIE.
REC
SHE BETTER BE WORTH IT.
04:01:38.7

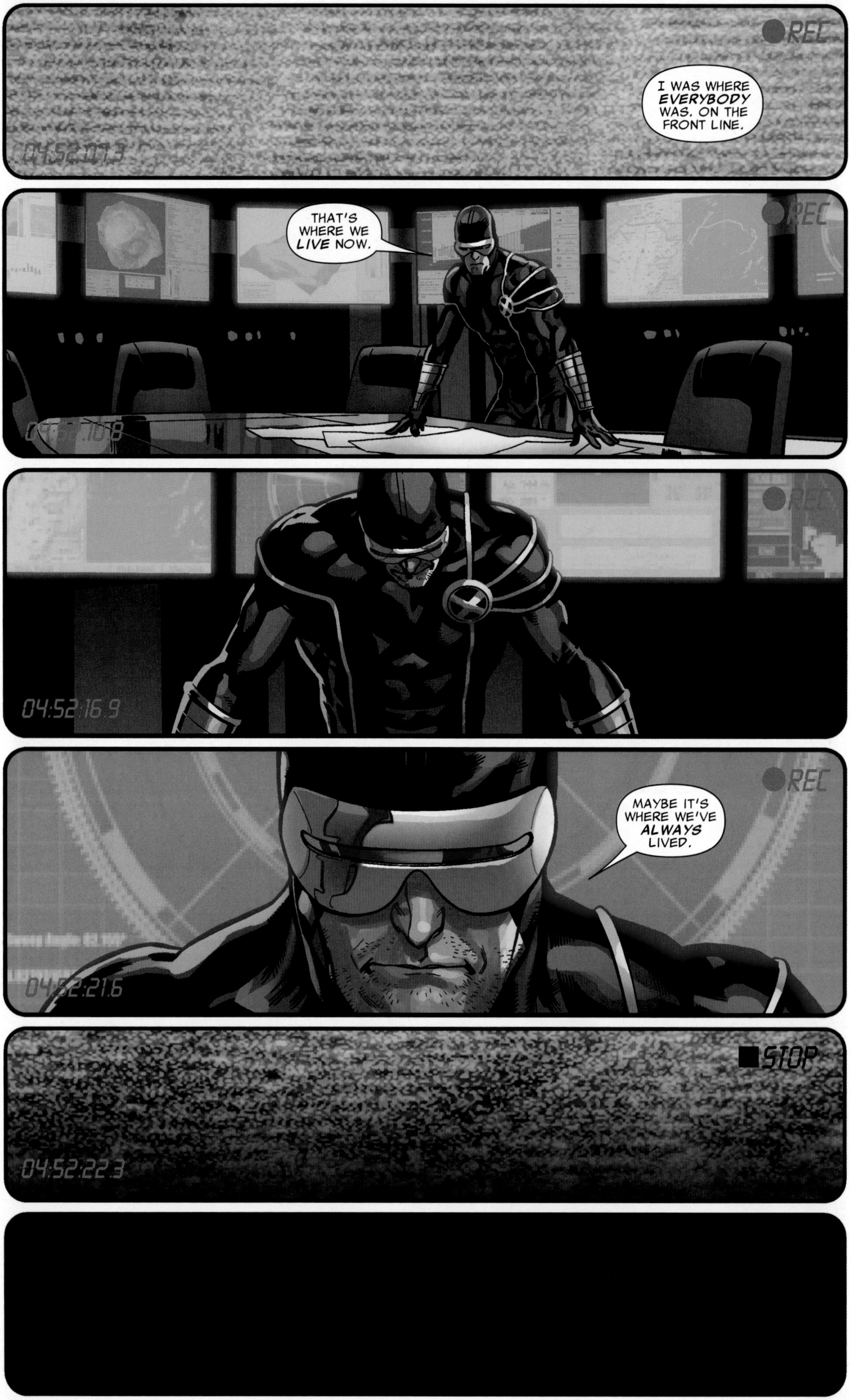
REC
I WAS WHERE EVERYBODY WAS. ON THE FRONT LINE.
REC
THAT'S WHERE WE LIVE NOW.
04:52:16.9
REC
MAYBE IT'S WHERE WE'VE ALWAYS LIVED.
STOP
04:52:22.3

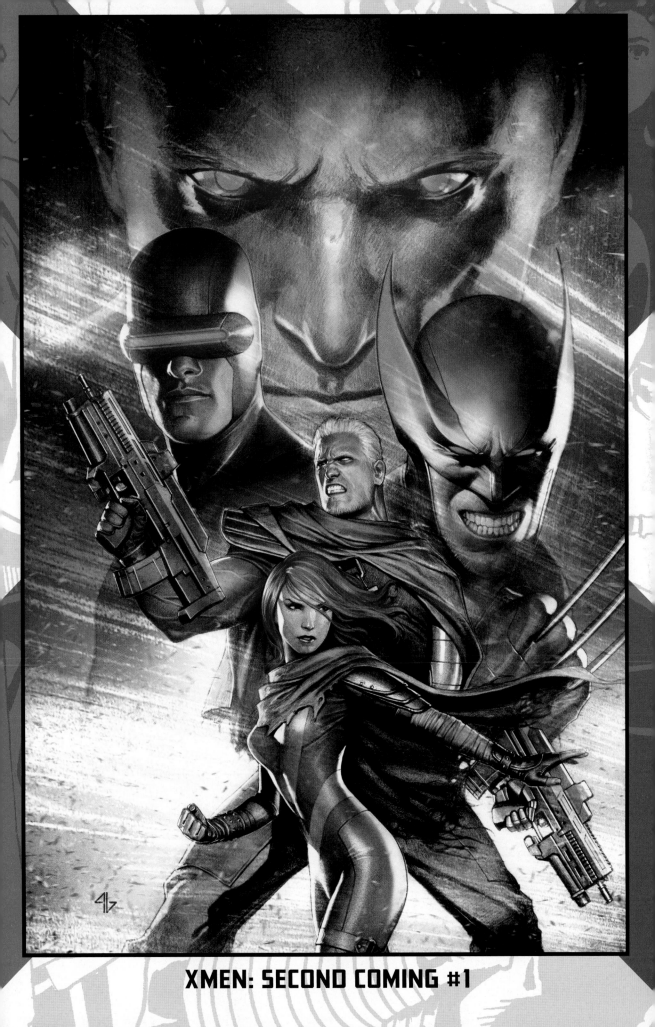

XMEN: SECOND COMING #1

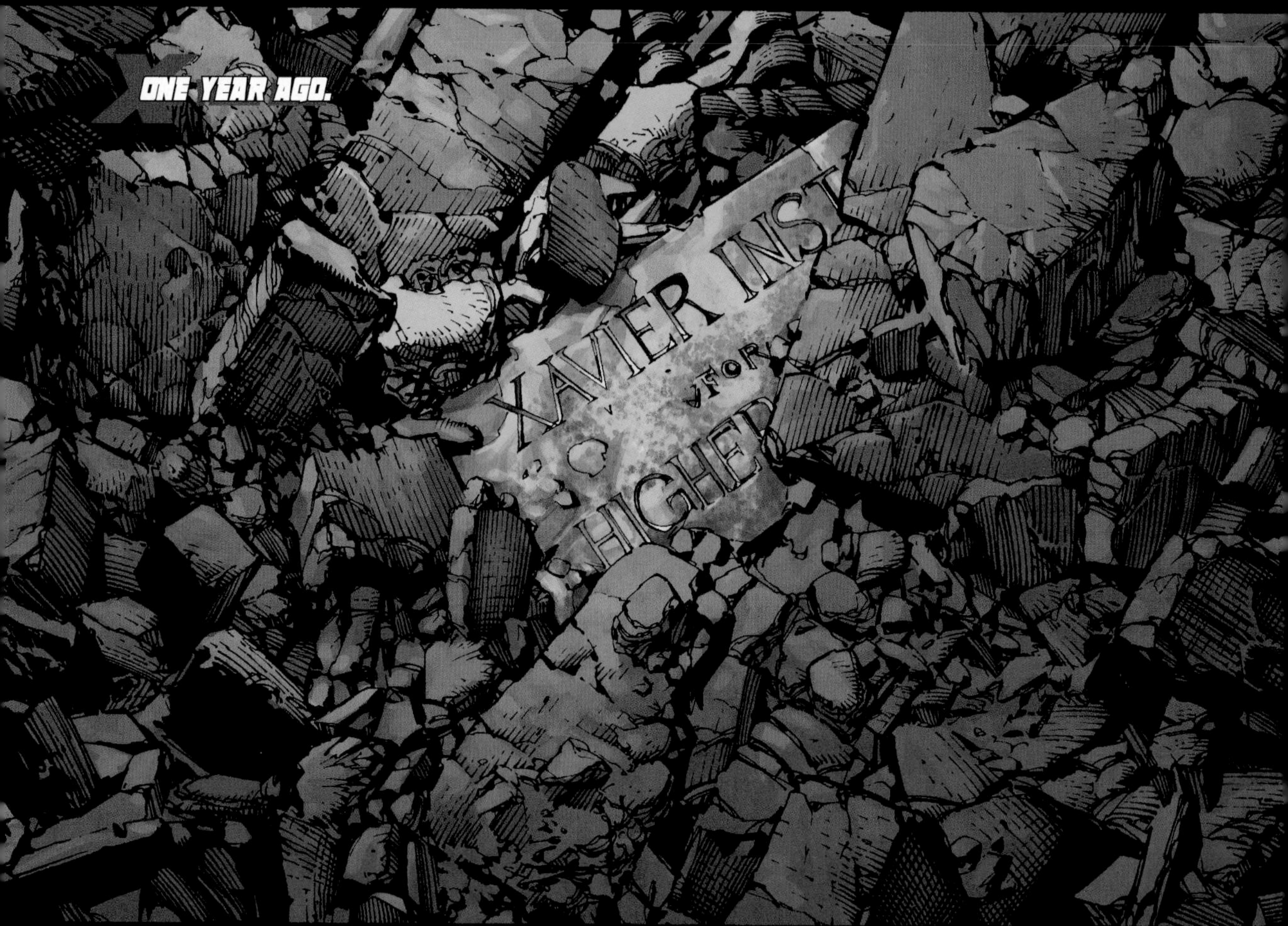
ONE YEAR AGO.
XAVIER INST
FOR
HIGHER

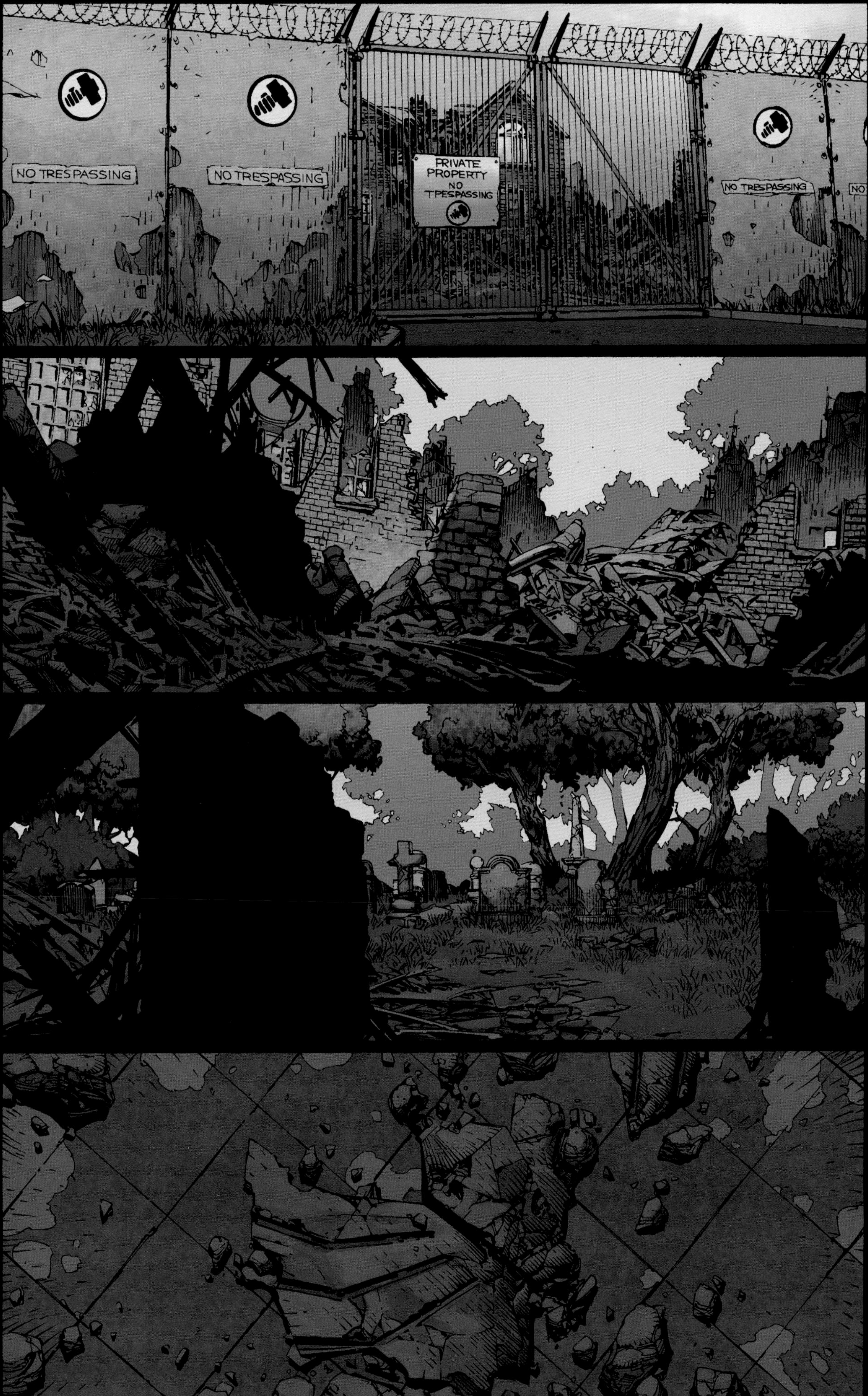
NO TRESPASSING
NO TRESPASSING
PRIVATE PROPERTY NO TPESPASSING
NO TRESPASSING

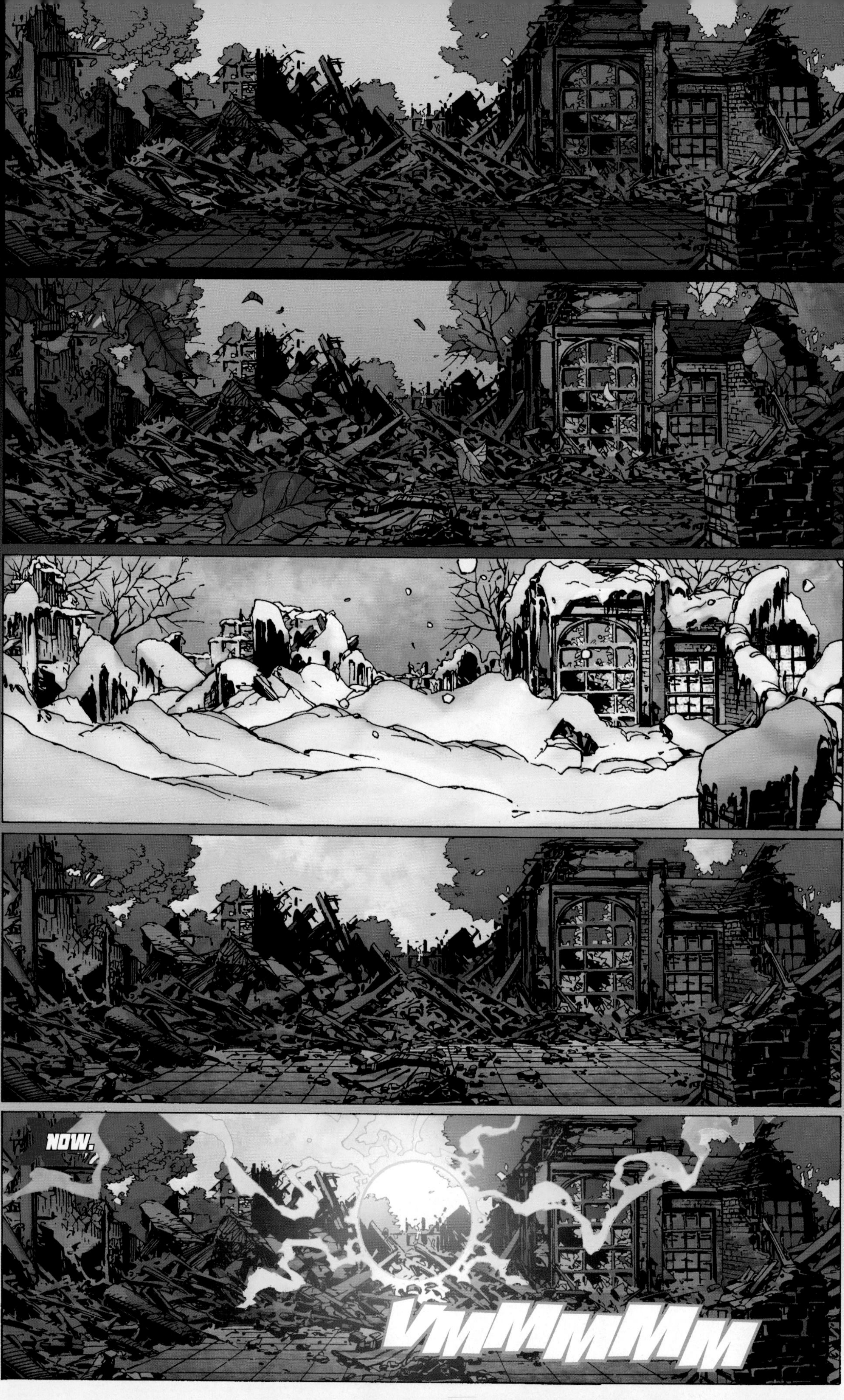
NOW.
VMMMMMM

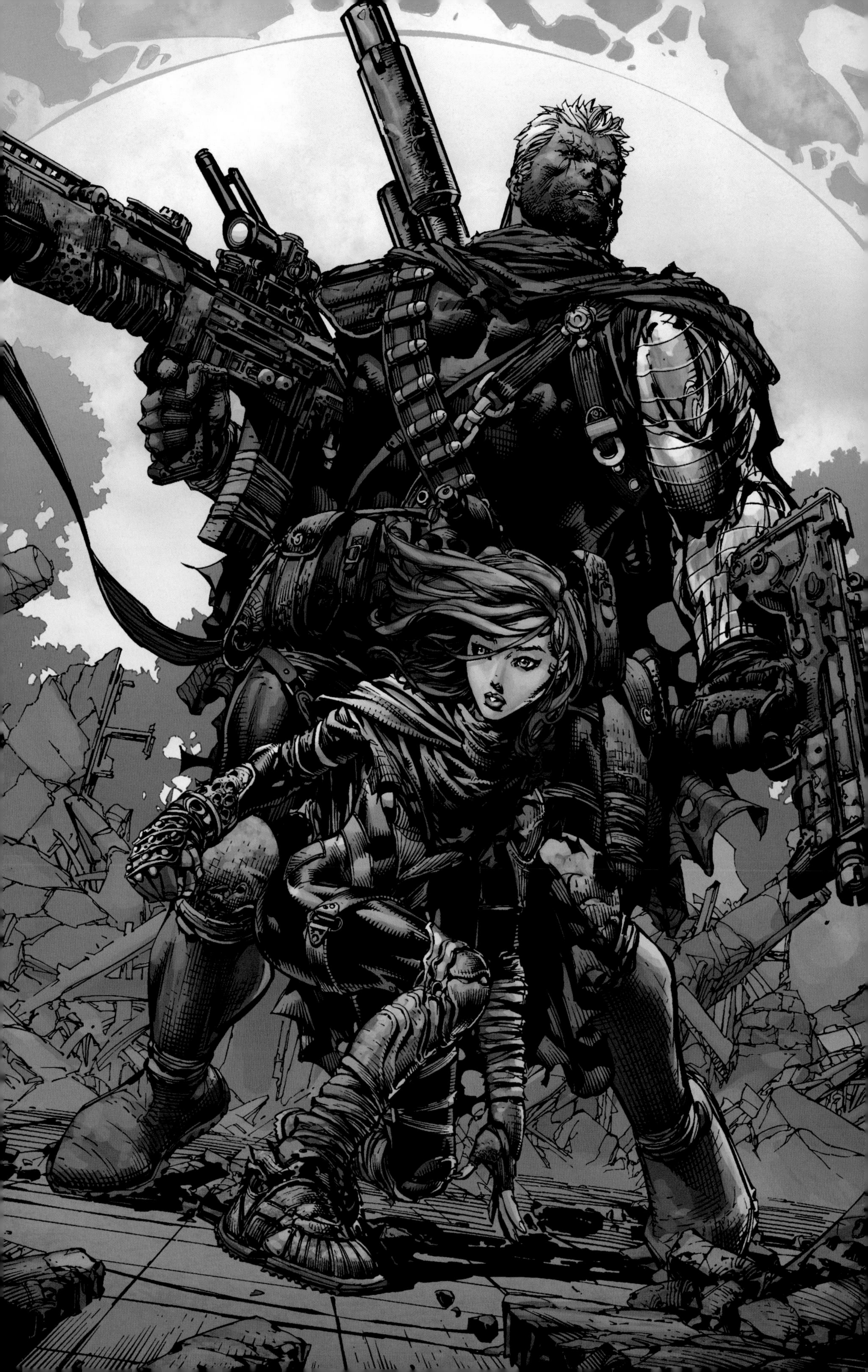

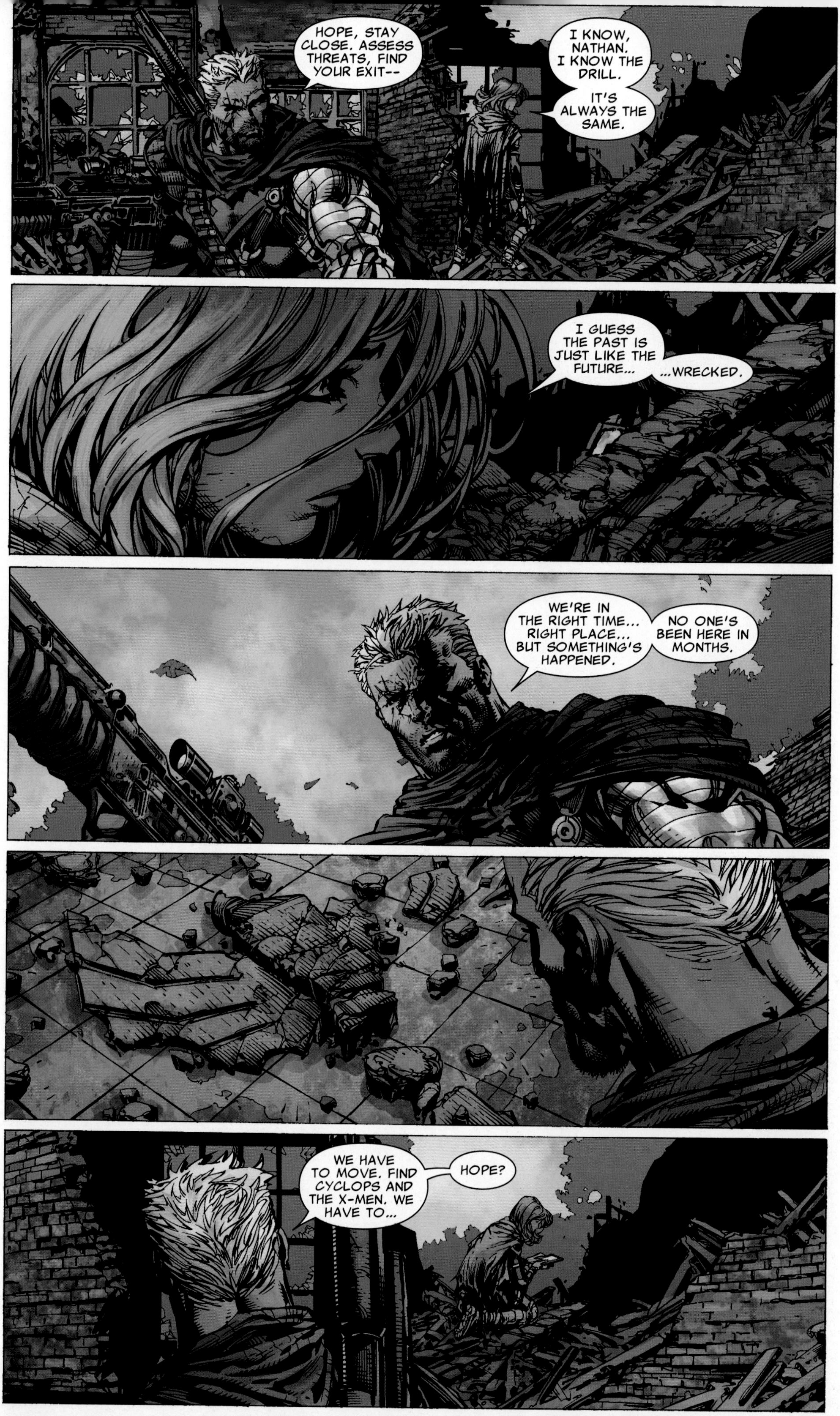
HOPE, STAY CLOSE. ASSESS THREATS, FIND YOUR EXIT--
I KNOW, NATHAN. I KNOW THE DRILL.
IT'S ALWAYS THE SAME.
I GUESS THE PAST IS JUST LIKE THE FUTURE...
...WRECKED.
WE'RE IN THE RIGHT TIME... RIGHT PLACE... BUT SOMETHING'S HAPPENED.
NO ONE'S BEEN HERE IN MONTHS.
WE HAVE TO MOVE. FIND CYCLOPS AND THE X-MEN. WE HAVE TO...
HOPE?

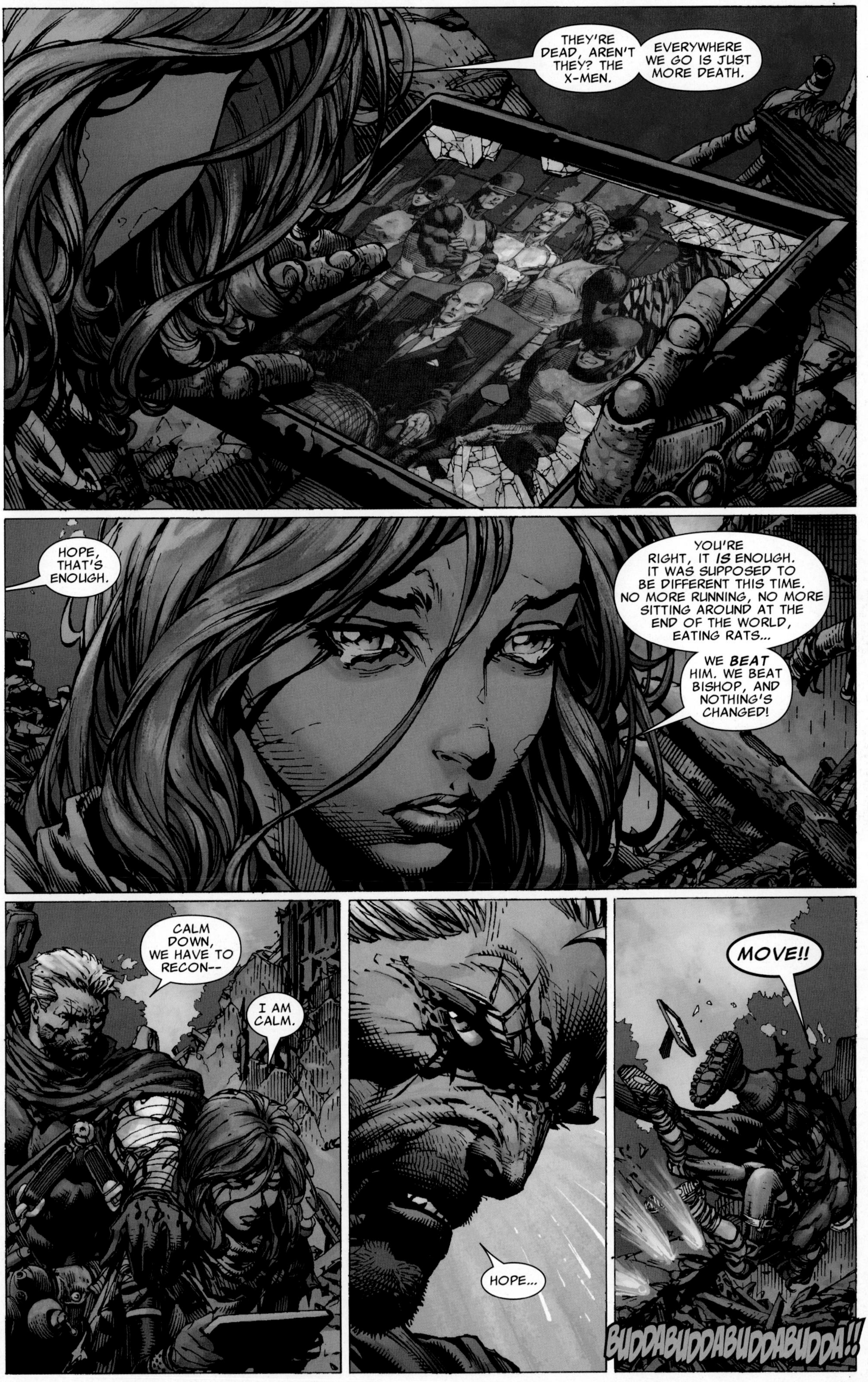
THEY'RE DEAD, AREN'T THEY? THE X-MEN.
EVERYWHERE WE GO IS JUST MORE DEATH.
HOPE, THAT'S ENOUGH.
YOU'RE RIGHT, IT IS ENOUGH. IT WAS SUPPOSED TO BE DIFFERENT THIS TIME. NO MORE RUNNING, NO MORE SITTING AROUND AT THE END OF THE WORLD, EATING RATS...
WE BEAT HIM. WE BEAT BISHOP, AND NOTHING'S CHANGED!
CALM DOWN, WE HAVE TO RECON--
I AM CALM.
HOPE...
MOVE!!
BUDDABUDDABUDDABUDDA!!

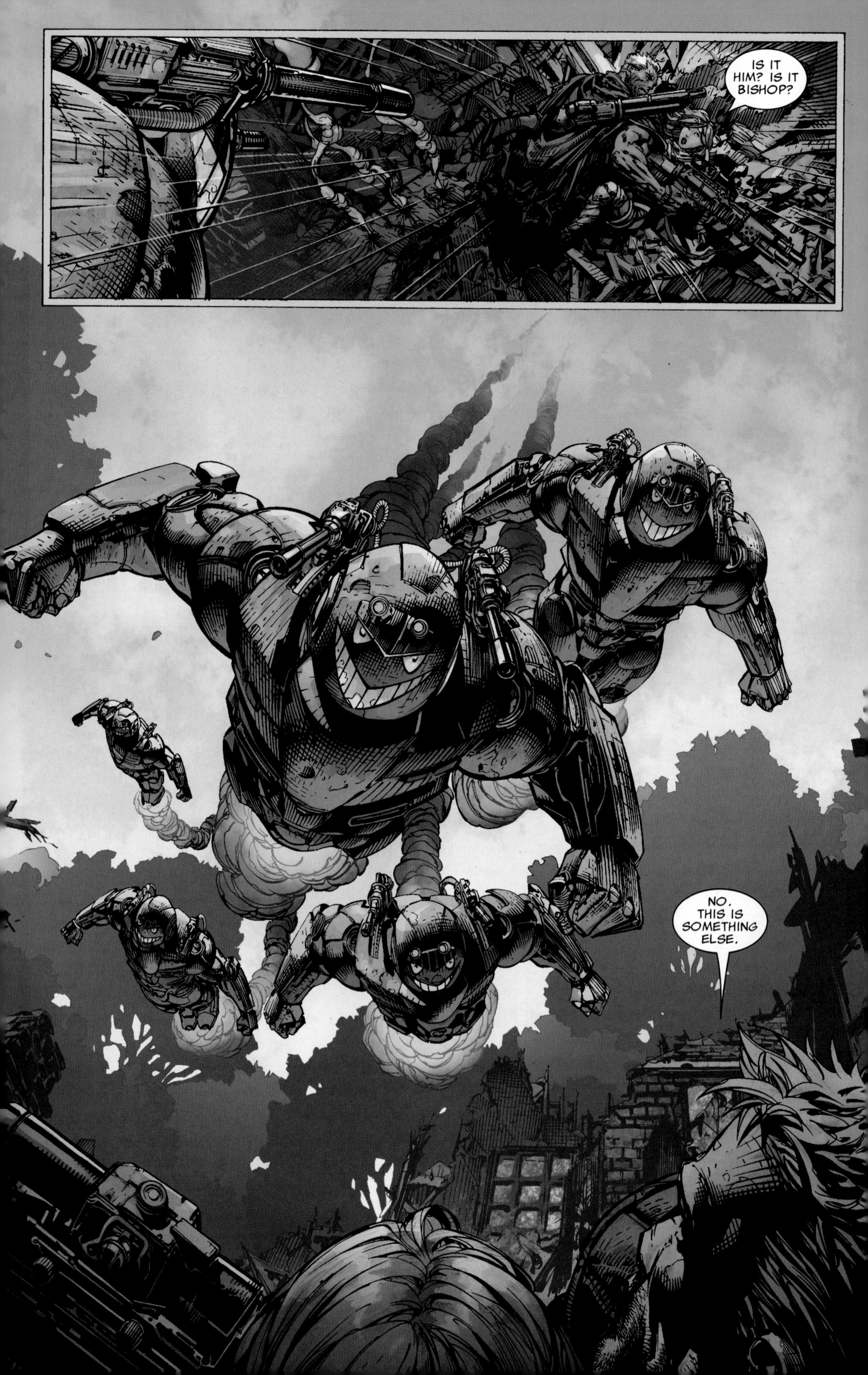
IS IT HIM? IS IT BISHOP?
NO. THIS IS SOMETHING ELSE.

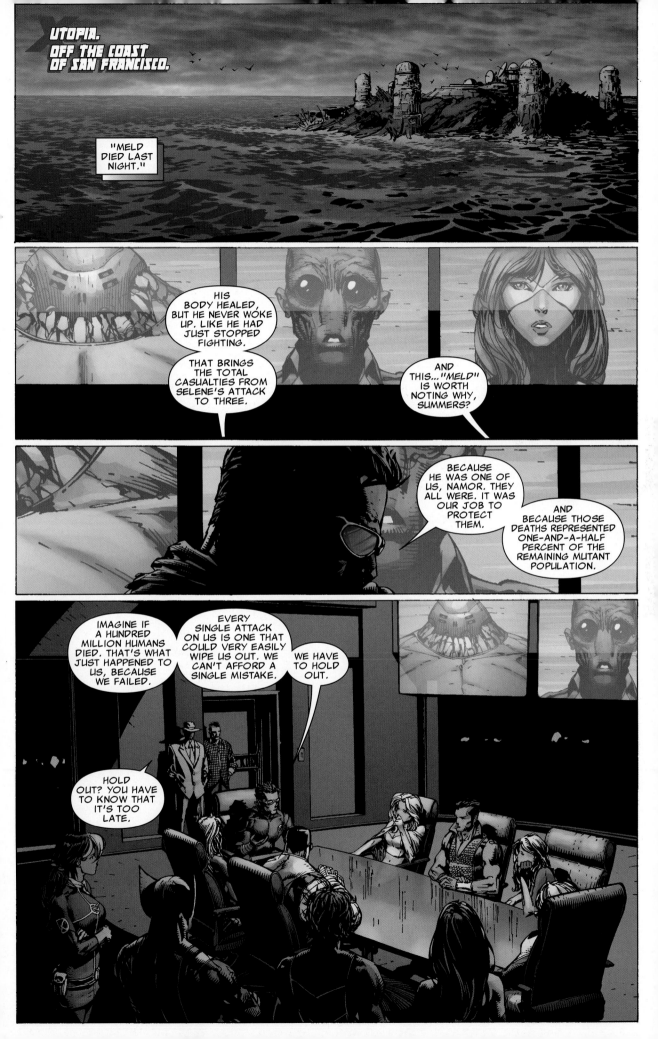

UTOPIA.
OFF THE COAST
OF SAN FRANCISCO.

"MELD DIED LAST NIGHT."

HIS BODY HEALED, BUT HE NEVER WOKE UP. LIKE HE HAD JUST STOPPED FIGHTING.

THAT BRINGS THE TOTAL CASUALTIES FROM SELENE'S ATTACK TO THREE.

AND THIS..."MELD" IS WORTH NOTING WHY, SUMMERS?

BECAUSE HE WAS ONE OF US, NAMOR. THEY ALL WERE. IT WAS OUR JOB TO PROTECT THEM.

AND BECAUSE THOSE DEATHS REPRESENTED ONE-AND-A-HALF PERCENT OF THE REMAINING MUTANT POPULATION.

IMAGINE IF A HUNDRED MILLION HUMANS DIED. THAT'S WHAT JUST HAPPENED TO US, BECAUSE WE FAILED.

EVERY SINGLE ATTACK ON US IS ONE THAT COULD VERY EASILY WIPE US OUT. WE CAN'T AFFORD A SINGLE MISTAKE.

WE HAVE TO HOLD OUT.

HOLD OUT? YOU HAVE TO KNOW THAT IT'S TOO LATE.

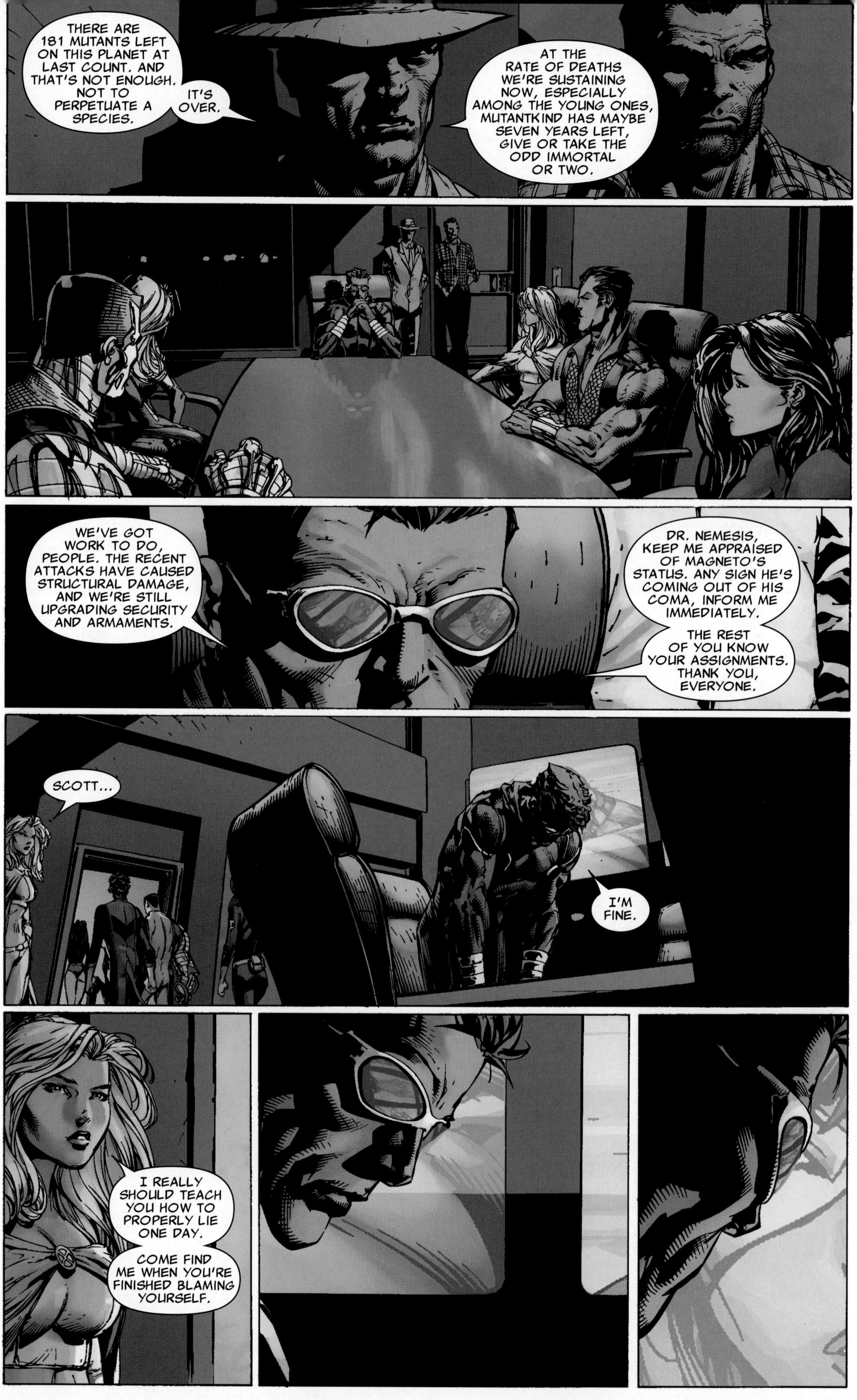
THERE ARE 181 MUTANTS LEFT ON THIS PLANET AT LAST COUNT. AND THAT'S NOT ENOUGH. NOT TO PERPETUATE A SPECIES.
IT'S OVER.
AT THE RATE OF DEATHS WE'RE SUSTAINING NOW, ESPECIALLY AMONG THE YOUNG ONES, MUTANTKIND HAS MAYBE SEVEN YEARS LEFT, GIVE OR TAKE THE ODD IMMORTAL OR TWO.
WE'VE GOT WORK TO DO, PEOPLE. THE RECENT ATTACKS HAVE CAUSED STRUCTURAL DAMAGE, AND WE'RE STILL UPGRADING SECURITY AND ARMAMENTS.
DR. NEMESIS, KEEP ME APPRAISED OF MAGNETO'S STATUS. ANY SIGN HE'S COMING OUT OF HIS COMA, INFORM ME IMMEDIATELY.
THE REST OF YOU KNOW YOUR ASSIGNMENTS. THANK YOU, EVERYONE.
SCOTT...
I'M FINE.
I REALLY SHOULD TEACH YOU HOW TO PROPERLY LIE ONE DAY.
COME FIND ME WHEN YOU'RE FINISHED BLAMING YOURSELF.

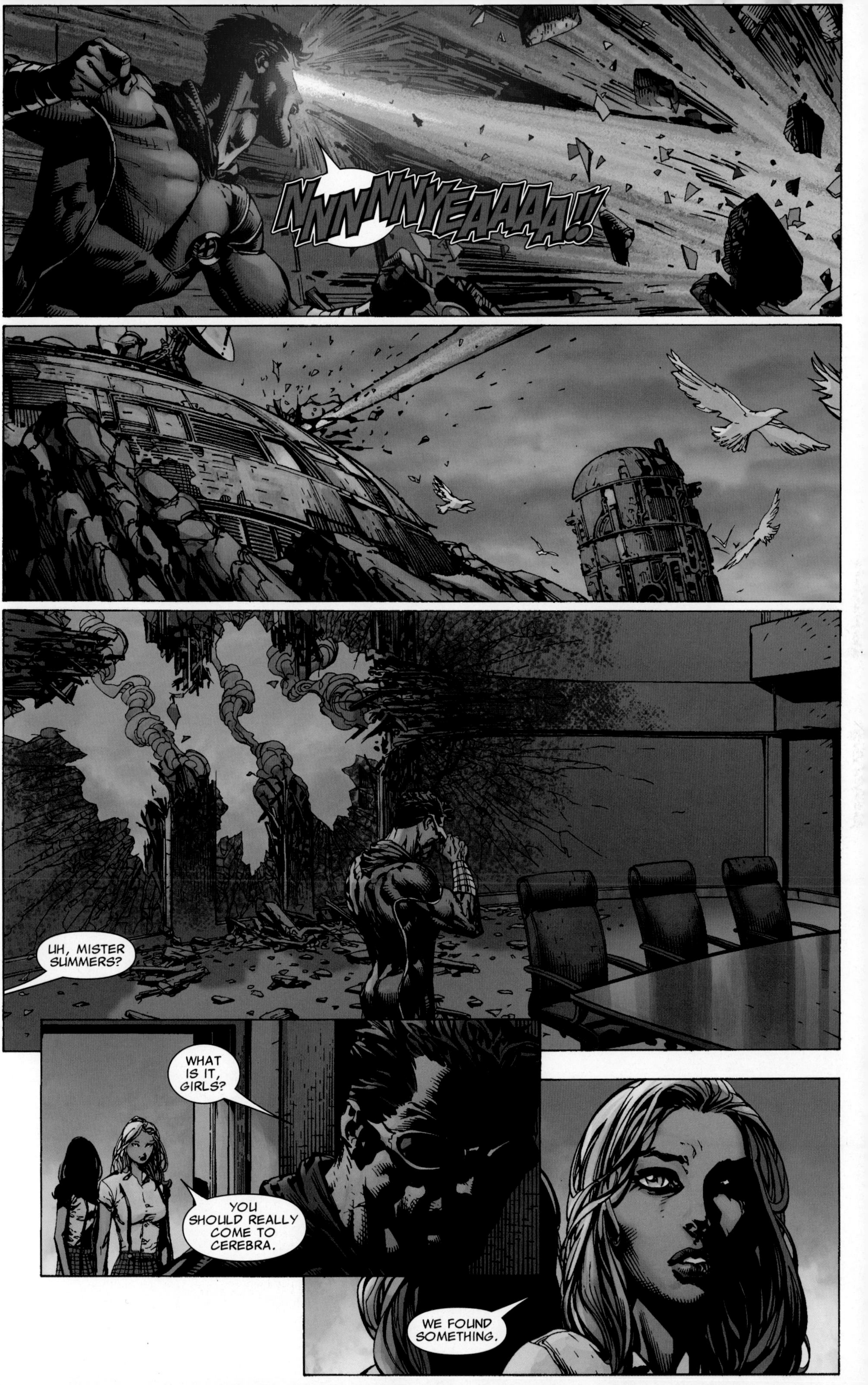
NNNNNYEAAAA!!
UH, MISTER SUMMERS?
WHAT IS IT, GIRLS?
YOU SHOULD REALLY COME TO CEREBRA.
WE FOUND SOMETHING.

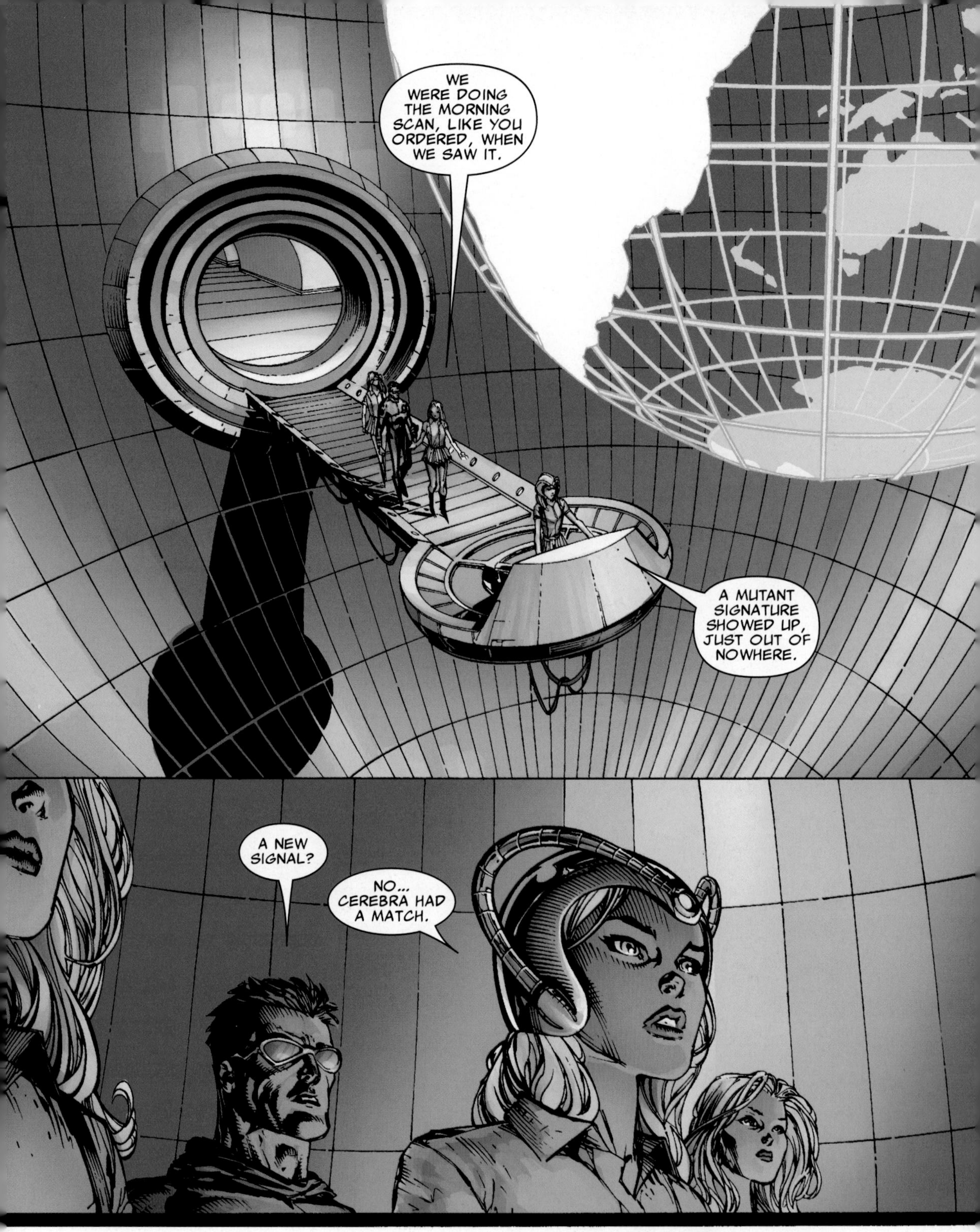
WE WERE DOING THE MORNING SCAN, LIKE YOU ORDERED, WHEN WE SAW IT.
A MUTANT SIGNATURE SHOWED UP, JUST OUT OF NOWHERE.
A NEW SIGNAL?
NO... CEREBRA HAD A MATCH.

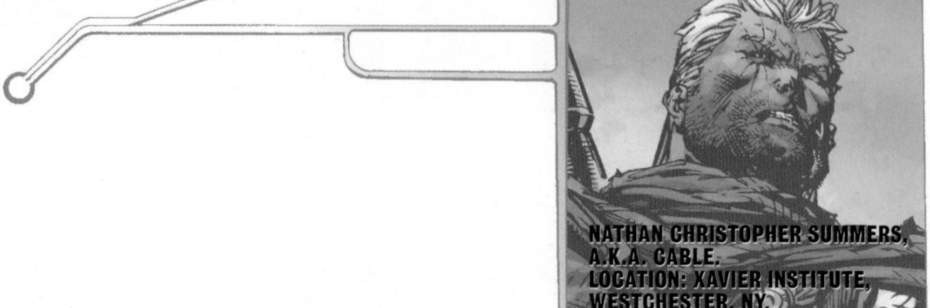
NATHAN CHRISTOPHER SUMMERS, A.K.A. CABLE.
LOCATION: XAVIER INSTITUTE, WESTCHESTER, NY.

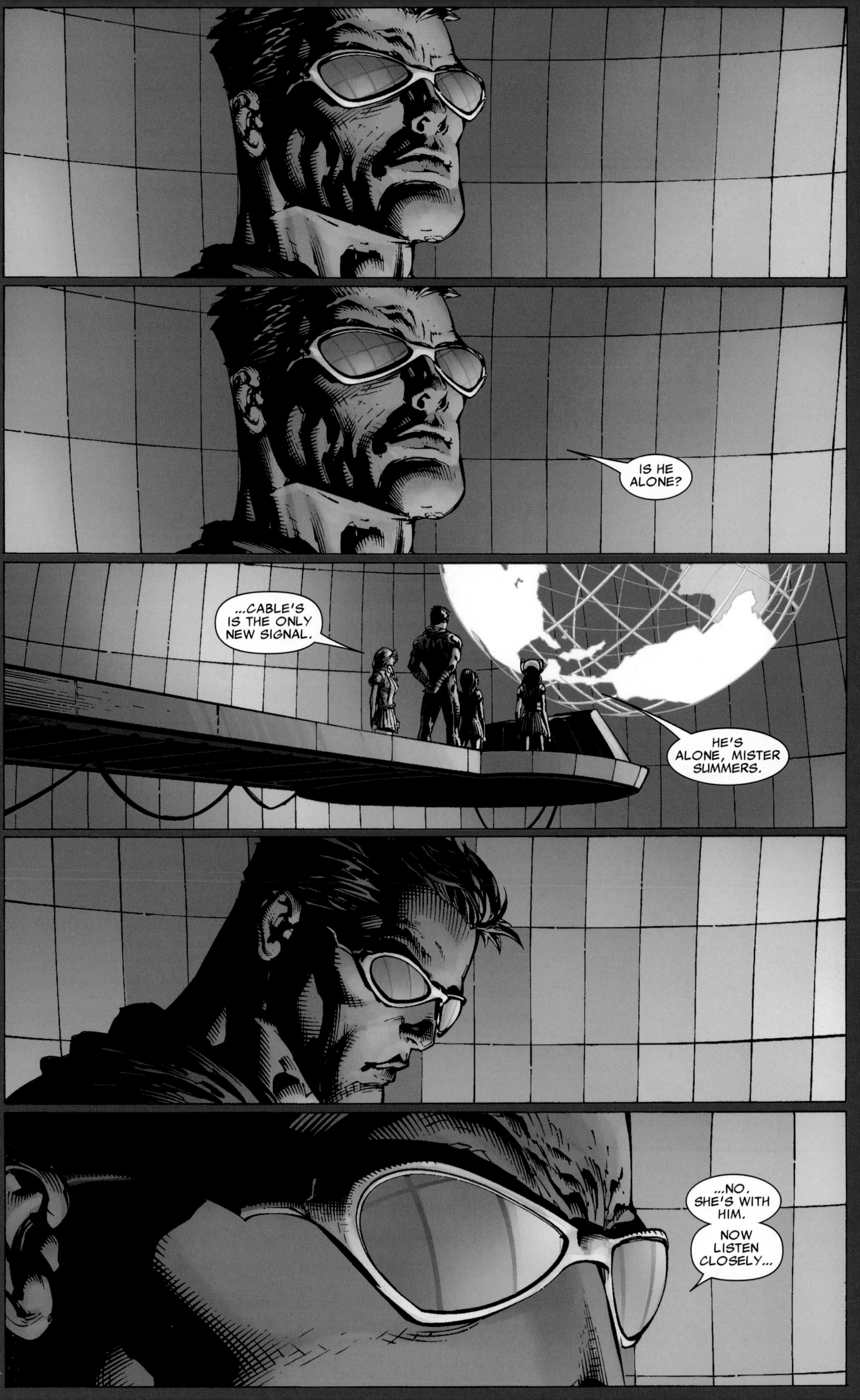
IS HE ALONE?
...CABLE'S IS THE ONLY NEW SIGNAL.
HE'S ALONE, MISTER SUMMERS.
...NO. SHE'S WITH HIM.
NOW LISTEN CLOSELY...

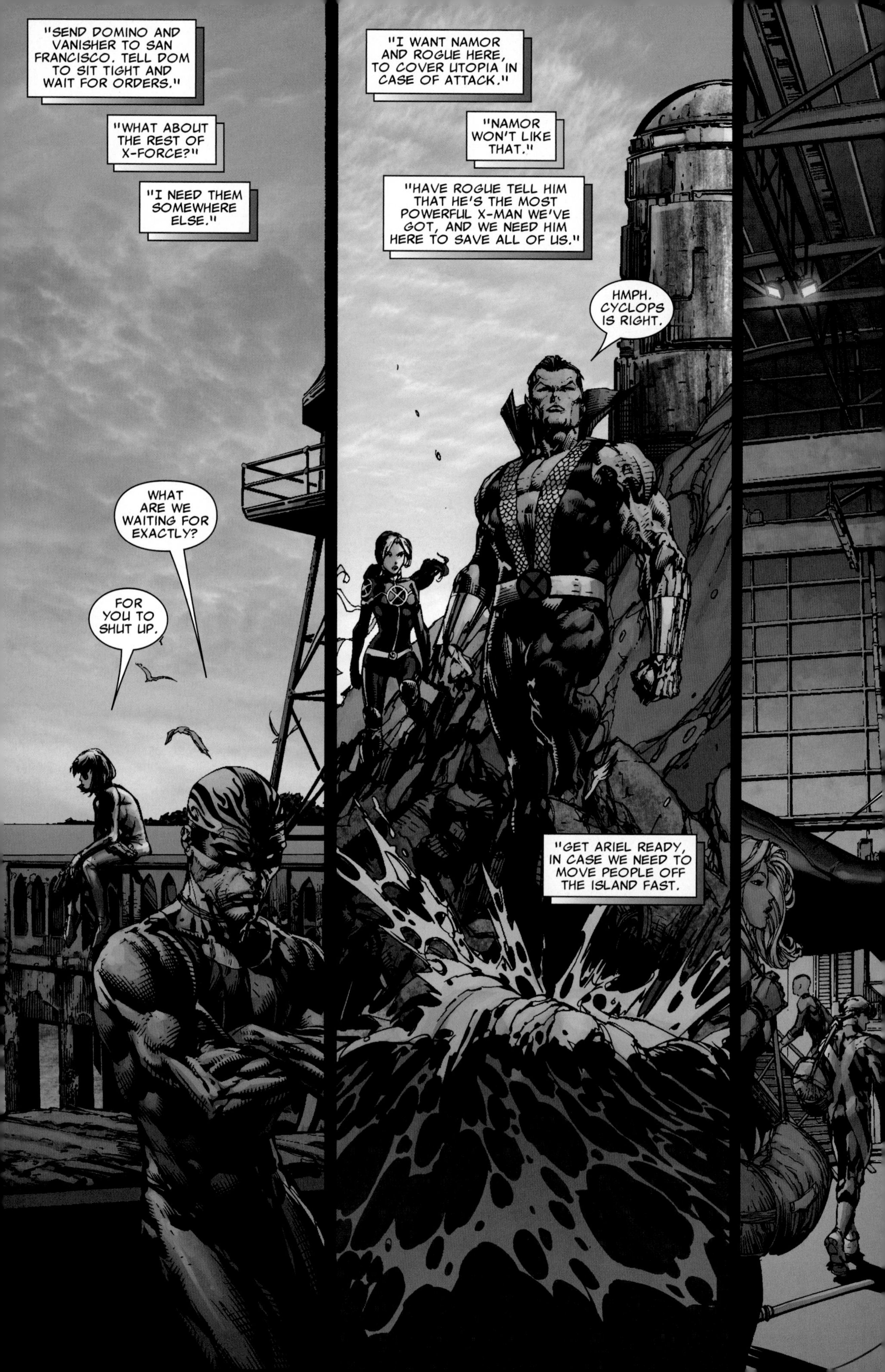
"SEND DOMINO AND VANISHER TO SAN FRANCISCO. TELL DOM TO SIT TIGHT AND WAIT FOR ORDERS."
"WHAT ABOUT THE REST OF X-FORCE?"
"I NEED THEM SOMEWHERE ELSE."
WHAT ARE WE WAITING FOR EXACTLY?
FOR YOU TO SHUT UP.
"I WANT NAMOR AND ROGUE HERE, TO COVER UTOPIA IN CASE OF ATTACK."
"NAMOR WON'T LIKE THAT."
"HAVE ROGUE TELL HIM THAT HE'S THE MOST POWERFUL X-MAN WE'VE GOT, AND WE NEED HIM HERE TO SAVE ALL OF US."
HMPH. CYCLOPS IS RIGHT.
"GET ARIEL READY, IN CASE WE NEED TO MOVE PEOPLE OFF THE ISLAND FAST.

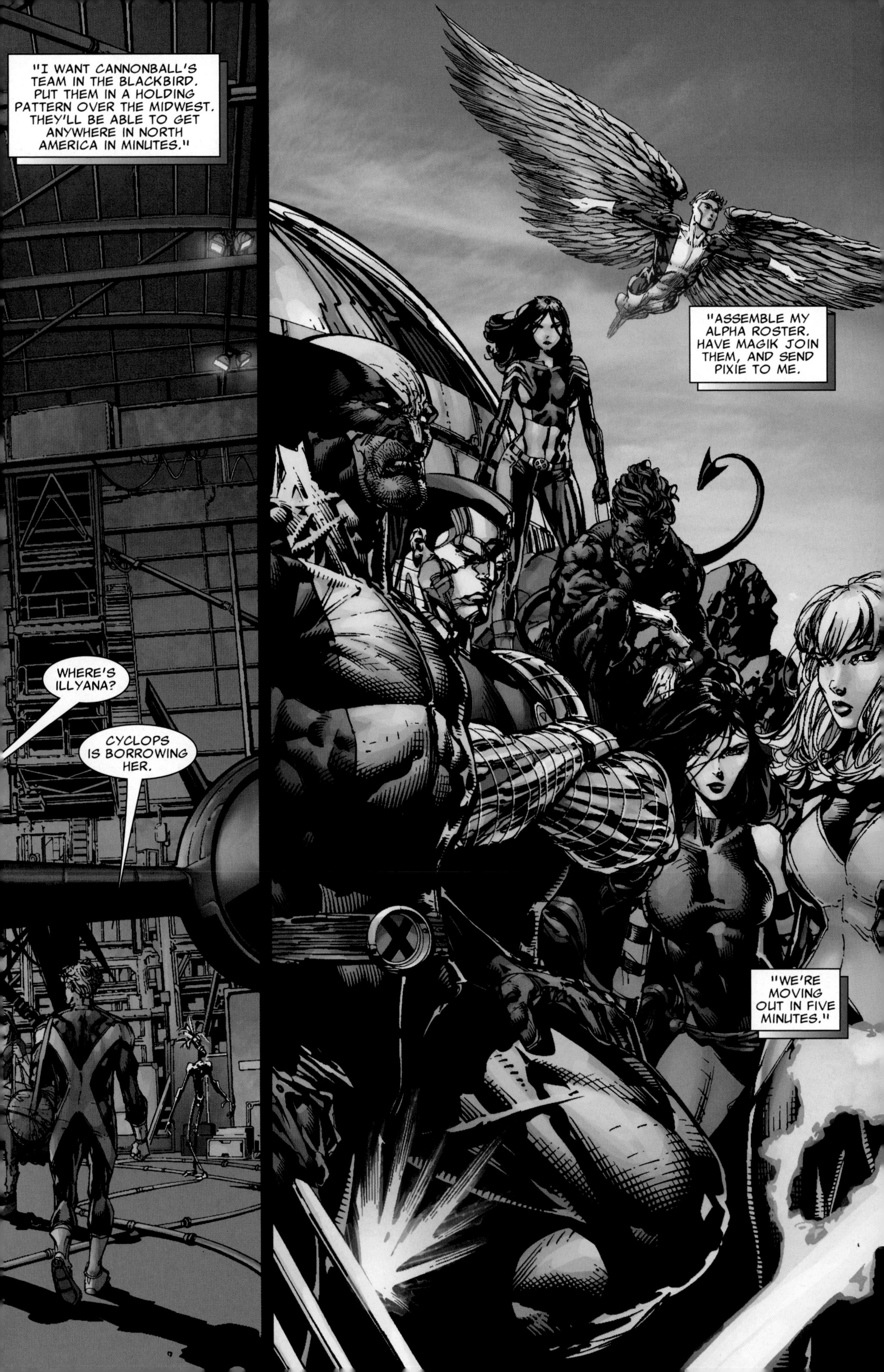
"I WANT CANNONBALL'S TEAM IN THE BLACKBIRD. PUT THEM IN A HOLDING PATTERN OVER THE MIDWEST. THEY'LL BE ABLE TO GET ANYWHERE IN NORTH AMERICA IN MINUTES."
WHERE'S ILLYANA?
CYCLOPS IS BORROWING HER.
"ASSEMBLE MY ALPHA ROSTER. HAVE MAGIK JOIN THEM, AND SEND PIXIE TO ME.
"WE'RE MOVING OUT IN FIVE MINUTES."

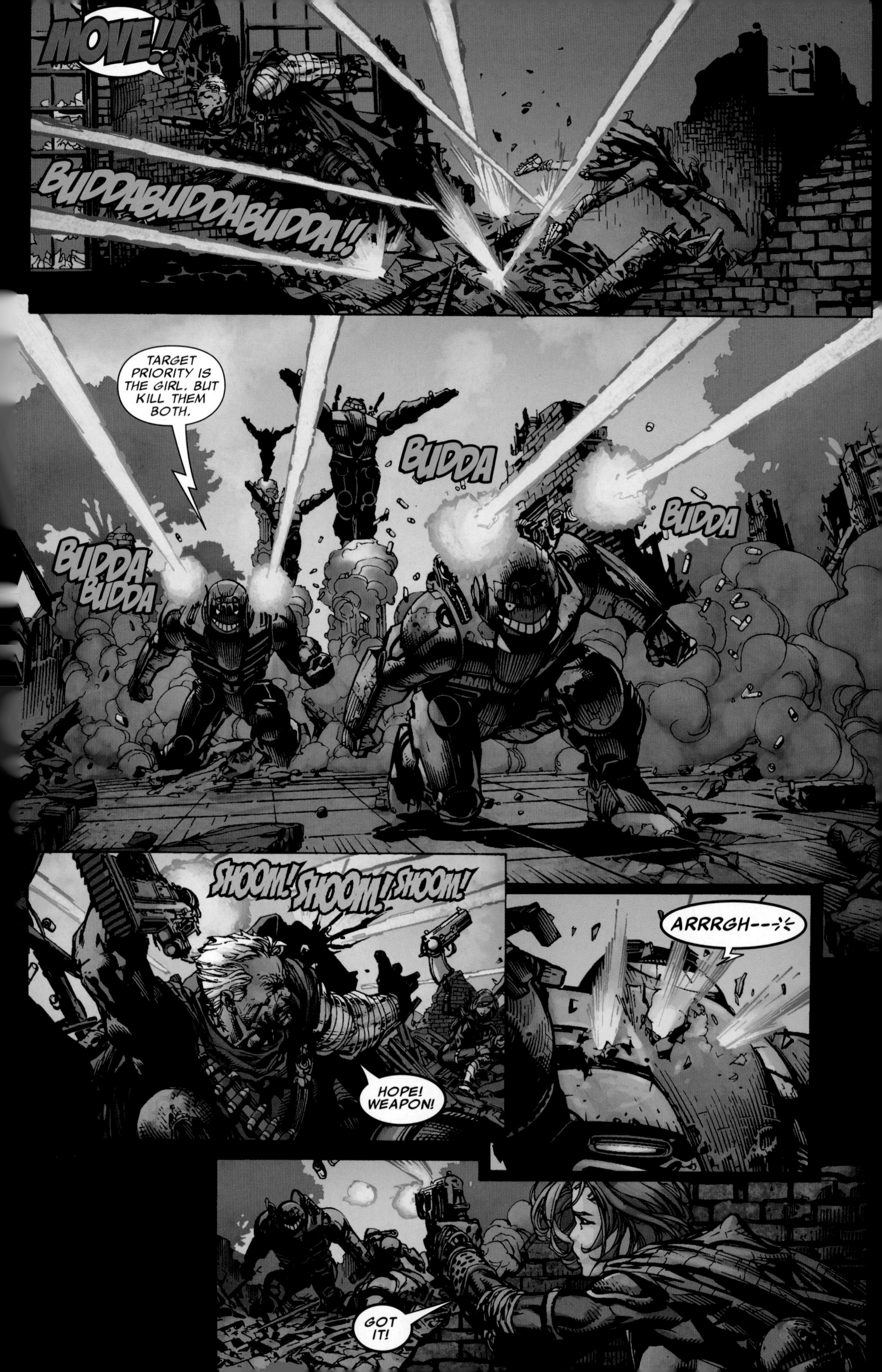
MOVE!!
BUDDABUDDABUDDA!!
TARGET PRIORITY IS THE GIRL. BUT KILL THEM BOTH.
BUDDA
BUDDA
BUDDA BUDDA
SHOOM! SHOOM! SHOOM!
HOPE! WEAPON!
ARRRGH--
GOT IT!

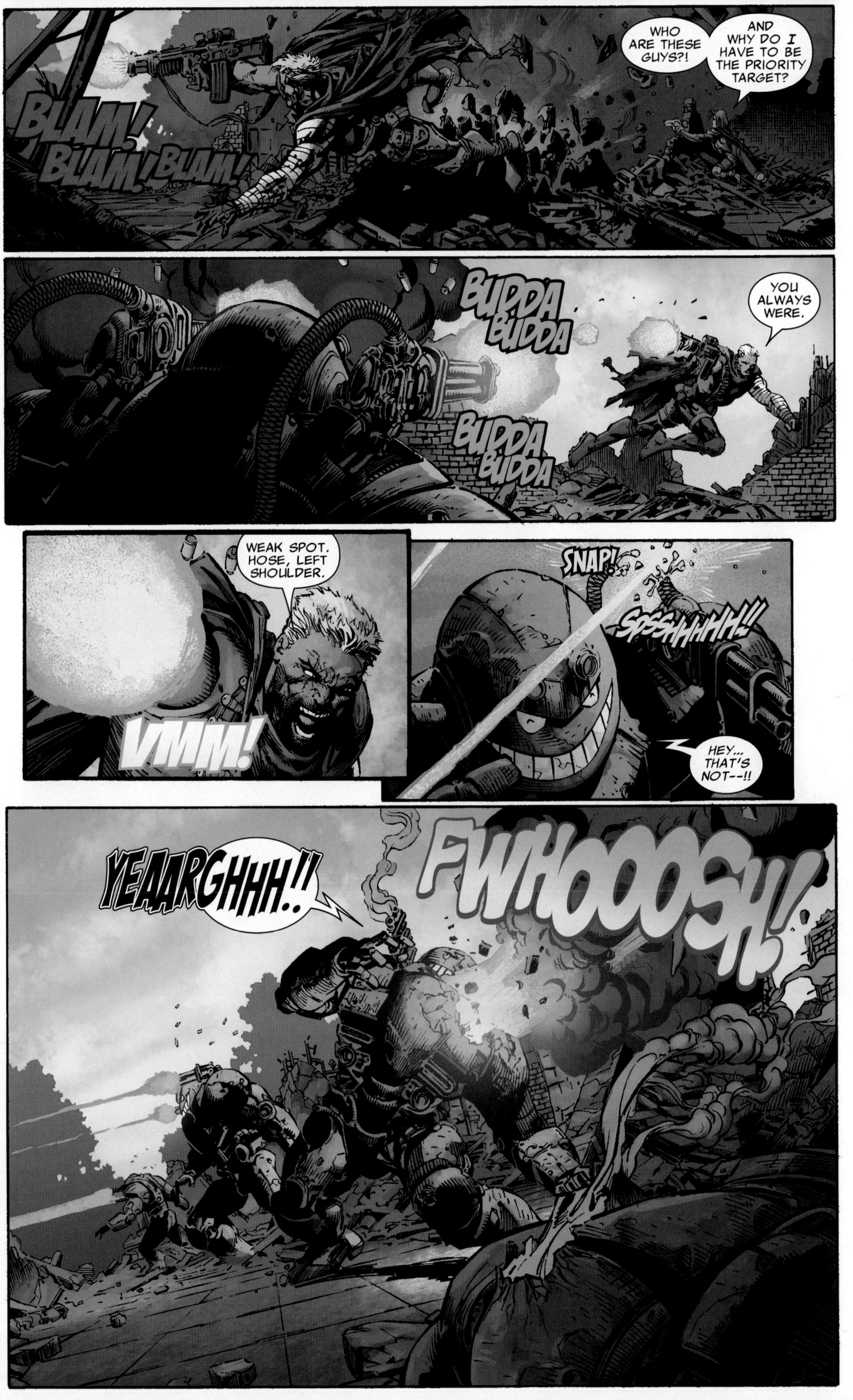
BLAM! BLAM! BLAM!
WHO ARE THESE GUYS?!
AND WHY DO I HAVE TO BE THE PRIORITY TARGET?
BUDDA BUDDA
BUDDA BUDDA
YOU ALWAYS WERE.
WEAK SPOT. HOSE, LEFT SHOULDER.
VMM!
SNAP!
SPSSHHHHH!!
HEY... THAT'S NOT--!!
YEAARGHHH!!
FWHOOOOSH!

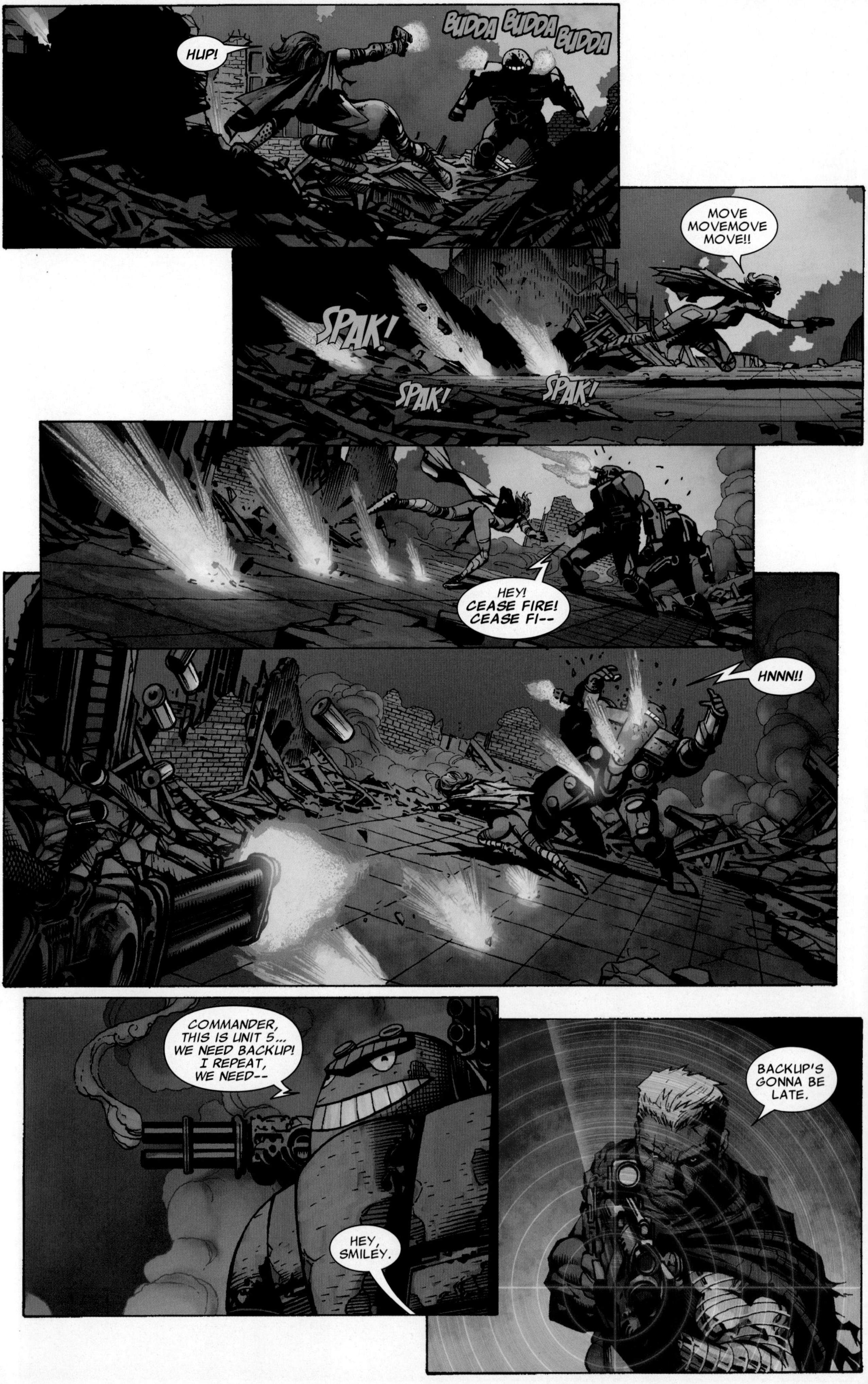
BUDDA BUDDA BUDDA
HUP!
MOVE MOVEMOVE MOVE!!
SPAK!
SPAK!
SPAK!
HEY! CEASE FIRE! CEASE FI--
HNNN!!
COMMANDER, THIS IS UNIT 5... WE NEED BACKUP! I REPEAT, WE NEED--
HEY, SMILEY.
BACKUP'S GONNA BE LATE.

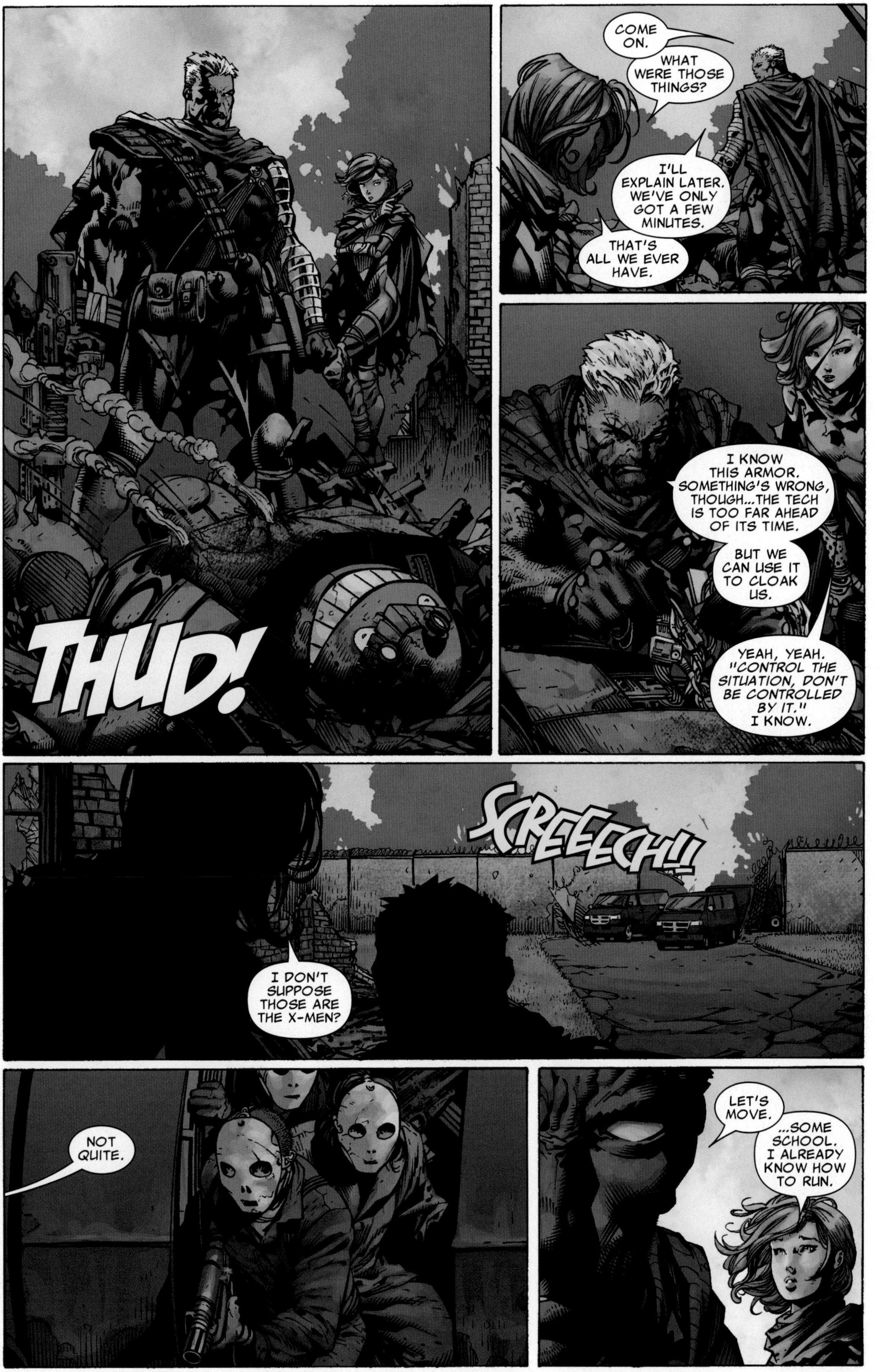

THUD!
COME ON.
WHAT WERE THOSE THINGS?
I'LL EXPLAIN LATER. WE'VE ONLY GOT A FEW MINUTES.
THAT'S ALL WE EVER HAVE.
I KNOW THIS ARMOR. SOMETHING'S WRONG, THOUGH...THE TECH IS TOO FAR AHEAD OF ITS TIME.
BUT WE CAN USE IT TO CLOAK US.
YEAH, YEAH. "CONTROL THE SITUATION, DON'T BE CONTROLLED BY IT." I KNOW.
SCREEECH!!
I DON'T SUPPOSE THOSE ARE THE X-MEN?
NOT QUITE.
LET'S MOVE.
...SOME SCHOOL. I ALREADY KNOW HOW TO RUN.

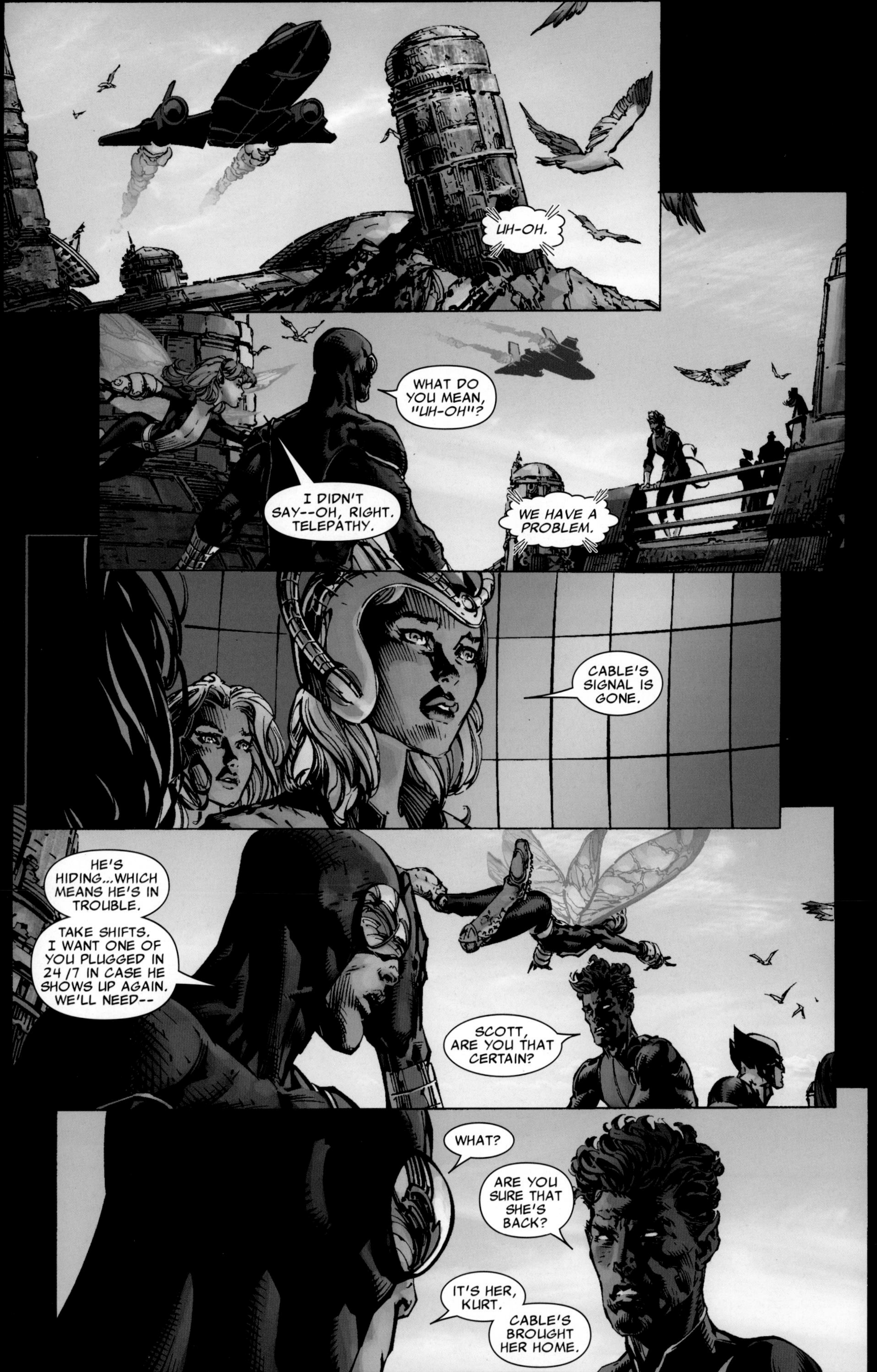
UH-OH.
WHAT DO YOU MEAN, "UH-OH"?
I DIDN'T SAY--OH, RIGHT. TELEPATHY.
WE HAVE A PROBLEM.
CABLE'S SIGNAL IS GONE.
HE'S HIDING...WHICH MEANS HE'S IN TROUBLE.
TAKE SHIFTS. I WANT ONE OF YOU PLUGGED IN 24/7 IN CASE HE SHOWS UP AGAIN. WE'LL NEED--
SCOTT, ARE YOU THAT CERTAIN?
WHAT?
ARE YOU SURE THAT SHE'S BACK?
IT'S HER, KURT.
CABLE'S BROUGHT HER HOME.

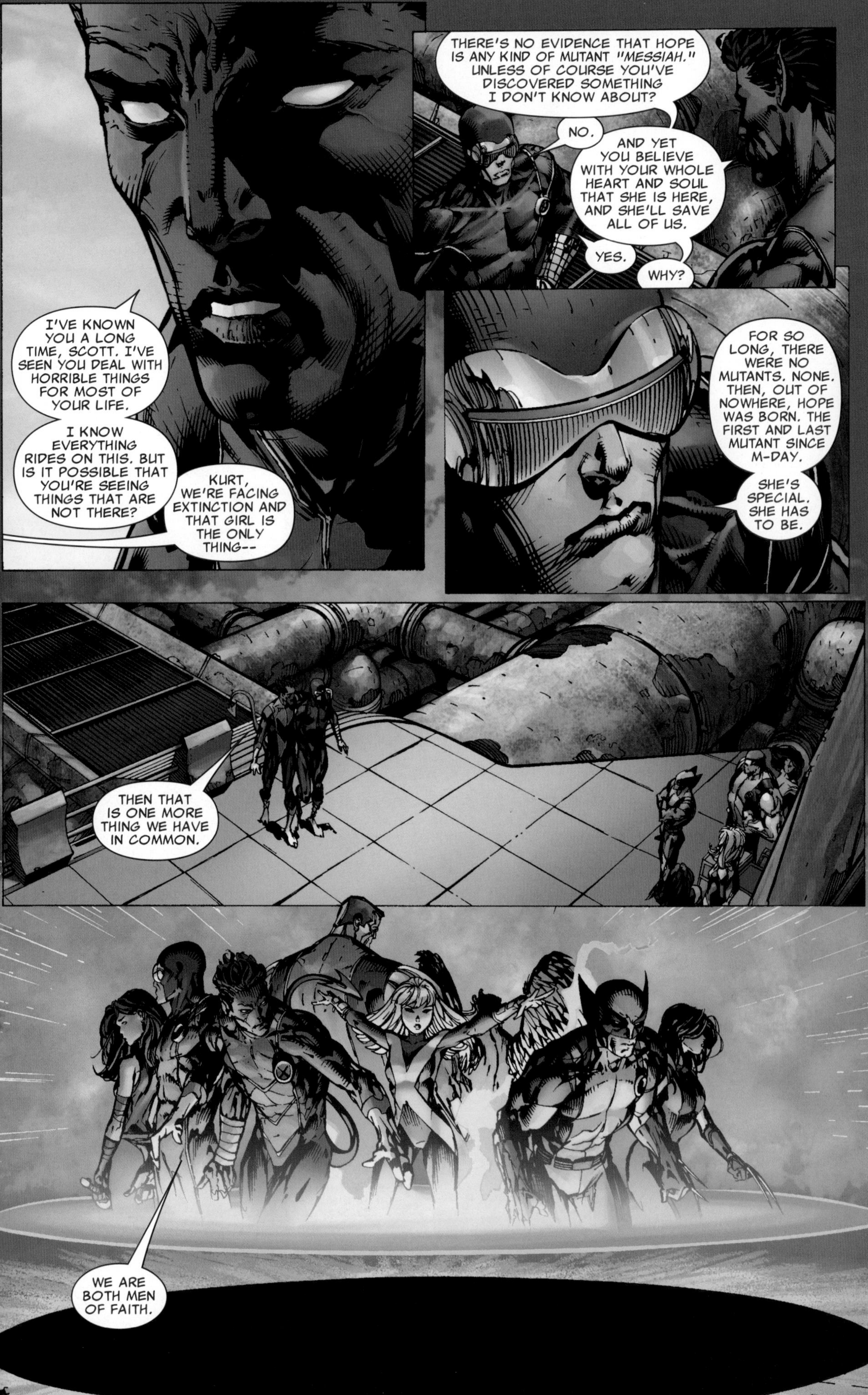
THERE'S NO EVIDENCE THAT HOPE IS ANY KIND OF MUTANT "MESSIAH." UNLESS OF COURSE YOU'VE DISCOVERED SOMETHING I DON'T KNOW ABOUT?
NO.
AND YET YOU BELIEVE WITH YOUR WHOLE HEART AND SOUL THAT SHE IS HERE, AND SHE'LL SAVE ALL OF US.
YES.
WHY?
I'VE KNOWN YOU A LONG TIME, SCOTT. I'VE SEEN YOU DEAL WITH HORRIBLE THINGS FOR MOST OF YOUR LIFE.
I KNOW EVERYTHING RIDES ON THIS. BUT IS IT POSSIBLE THAT YOU'RE SEEING THINGS THAT ARE NOT THERE?
KURT, WE'RE FACING EXTINCTION AND THAT GIRL IS THE ONLY THING--
FOR SO LONG, THERE WERE NO MUTANTS. NONE. THEN, OUT OF NOWHERE, HOPE WAS BORN. THE FIRST AND LAST MUTANT SINCE M-DAY.
SHE'S SPECIAL. SHE HAS TO BE.
THEN THAT IS ONE MORE THING WE HAVE IN COMMON.
WE ARE BOTH MEN OF FAITH.

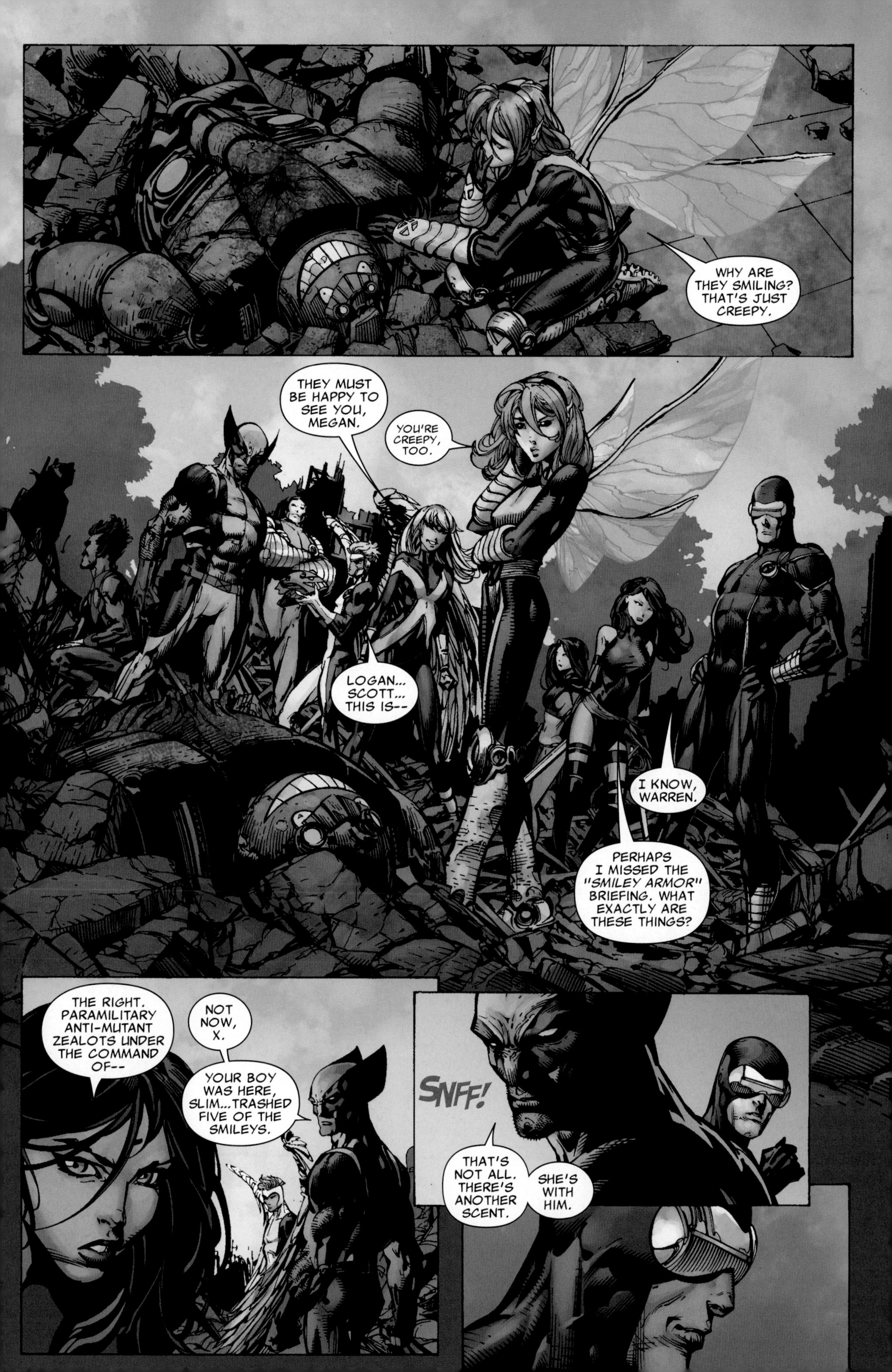
WHY ARE THEY SMILING? THAT'S JUST CREEPY.
THEY MUST BE HAPPY TO SEE YOU, MEGAN.
YOU'RE CREEPY, TOO.
LOGAN... SCOTT... THIS IS--
I KNOW, WARREN.
PERHAPS I MISSED THE "SMILEY ARMOR" BRIEFING. WHAT EXACTLY ARE THESE THINGS?
THE RIGHT. PARAMILITARY ANTI-MUTANT ZEALOTS UNDER THE COMMAND OF--
NOT NOW, X.
YOUR BOY WAS HERE, SLIM...TRASHED FIVE OF THE SMILEYS.
SNFF!
THAT'S NOT ALL. THERE'S ANOTHER SCENT.
SHE'S WITH HIM.

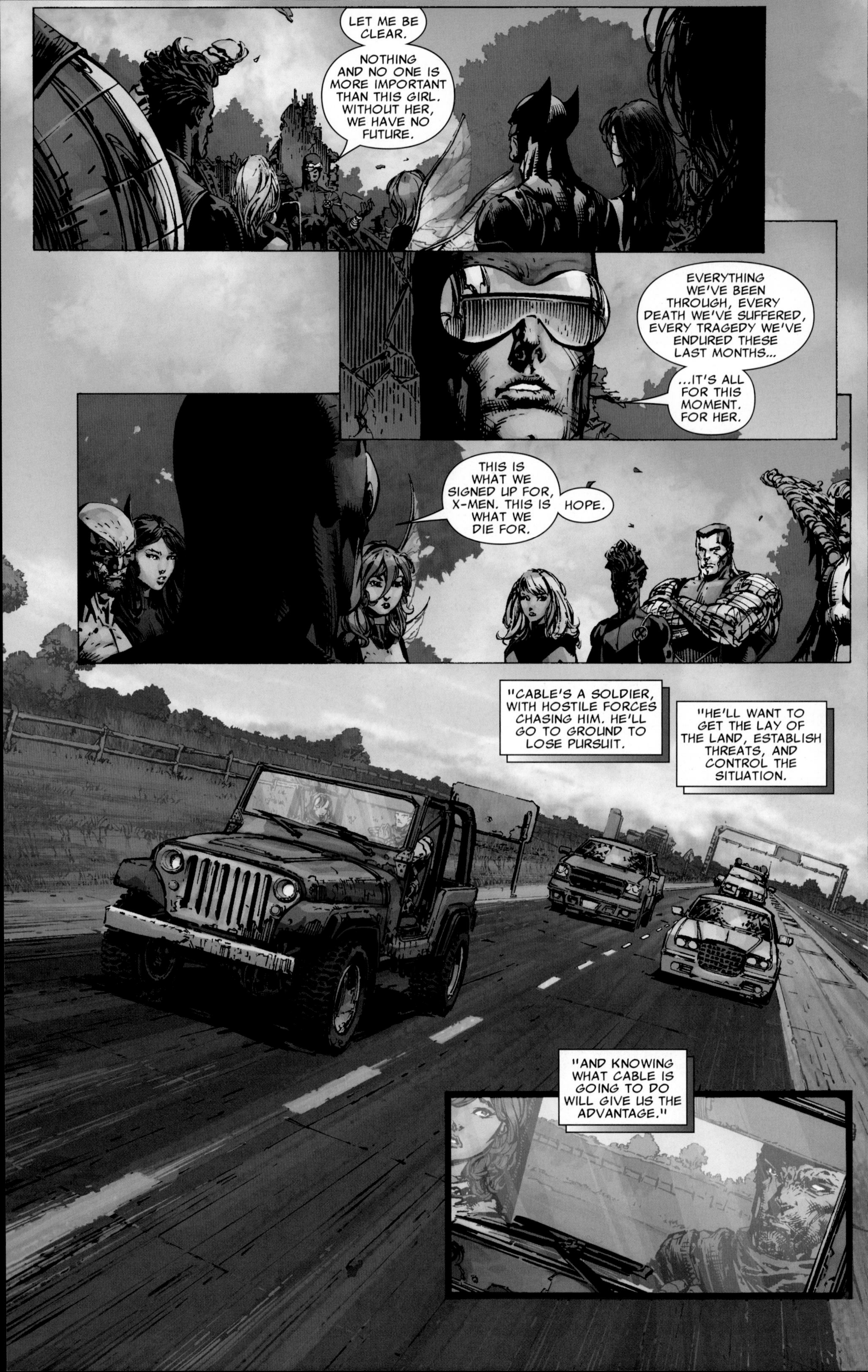
LET ME BE CLEAR.
NOTHING AND NO ONE IS MORE IMPORTANT THAN THIS GIRL. WITHOUT HER, WE HAVE NO FUTURE.
EVERYTHING WE'VE BEEN THROUGH, EVERY DEATH WE'VE SUFFERED, EVERY TRAGEDY WE'VE ENDURED THESE LAST MONTHS...
...IT'S ALL FOR THIS MOMENT. FOR HER.
THIS IS WHAT WE SIGNED UP FOR, X-MEN. THIS IS WHAT WE DIE FOR.
HOPE.
"CABLE'S A SOLDIER, WITH HOSTILE FORCES CHASING HIM. HE'LL GO TO GROUND TO LOSE PURSUIT.
"HE'LL WANT TO GET THE LAY OF THE LAND, ESTABLISH THREATS, AND CONTROL THE SITUATION.
"AND KNOWING WHAT CABLE IS GOING TO DO WILL GIVE US THE ADVANTAGE."

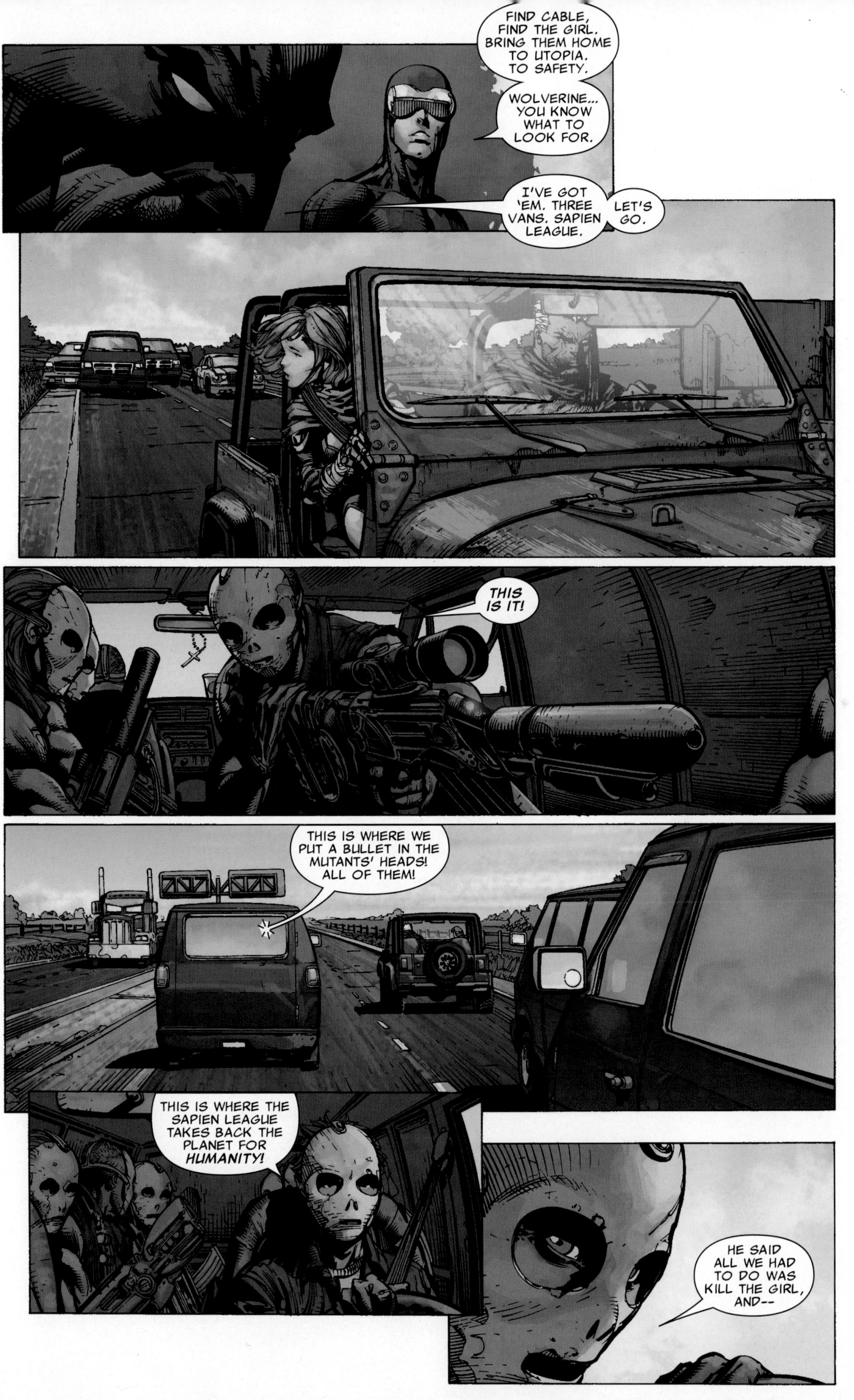
FIND CABLE, FIND THE GIRL. BRING THEM HOME TO UTOPIA. TO SAFETY.
WOLVERINE... YOU KNOW WHAT TO LOOK FOR.
I'VE GOT 'EM. THREE VANS. SAPIEN LEAGUE.
LET'S GO.
THIS IS IT!
THIS IS WHERE WE PUT A BULLET IN THE MUTANTS' HEADS! ALL OF THEM!
THIS IS WHERE THE SAPIEN LEAGUE TAKES BACK THE PLANET FOR HUMANITY!
HE SAID ALL WE HAD TO DO WAS KILL THE GIRL, AND--

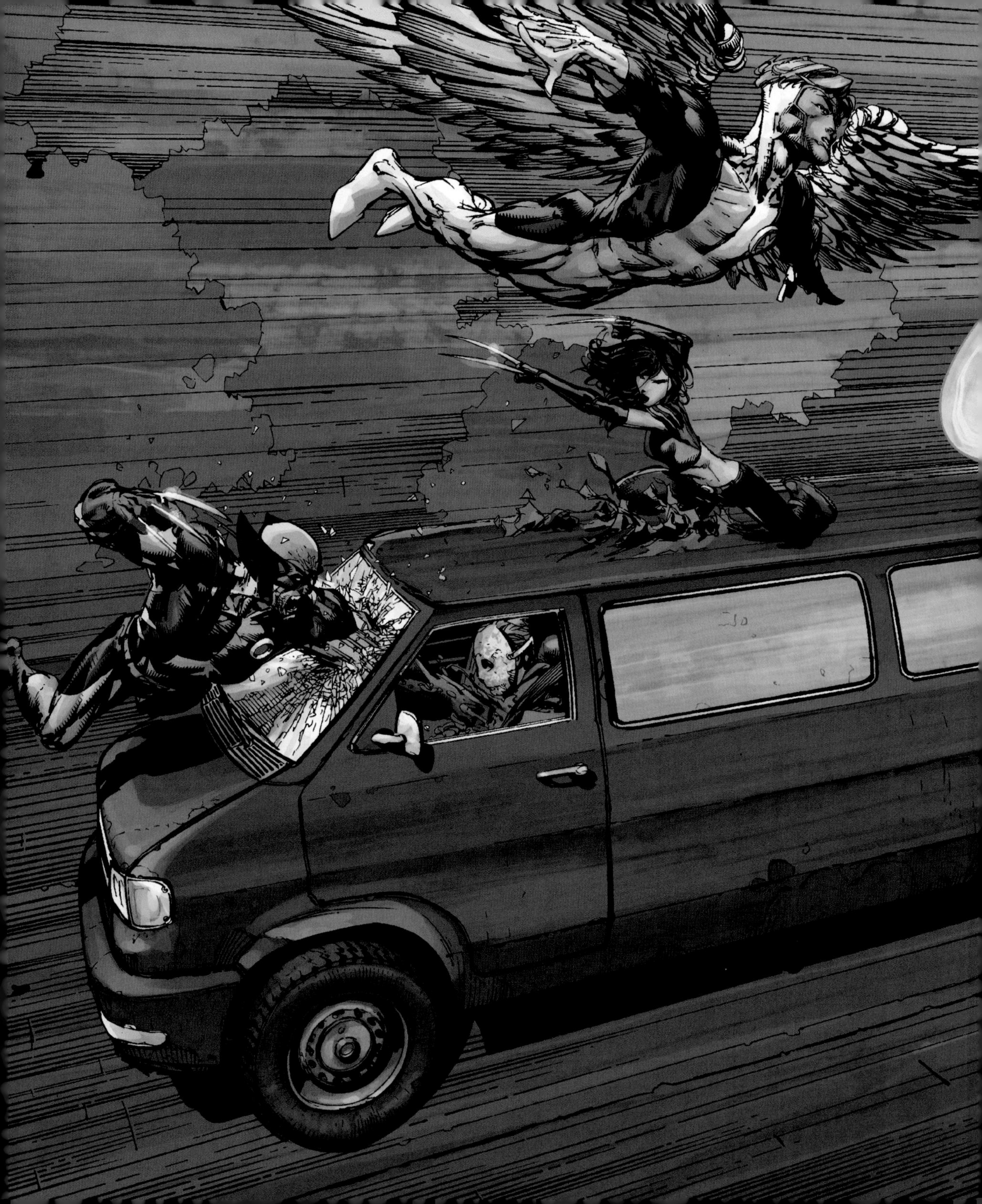

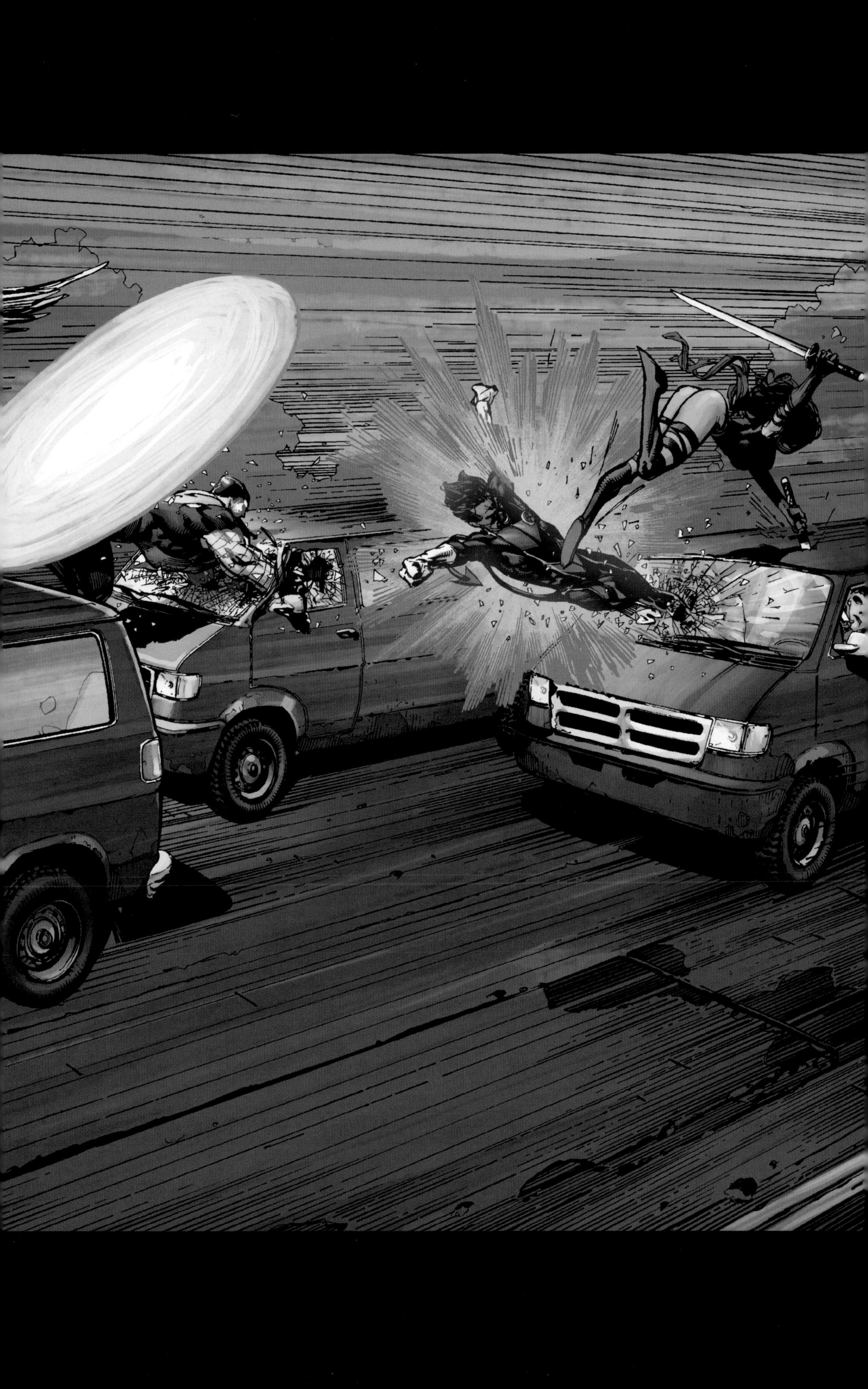

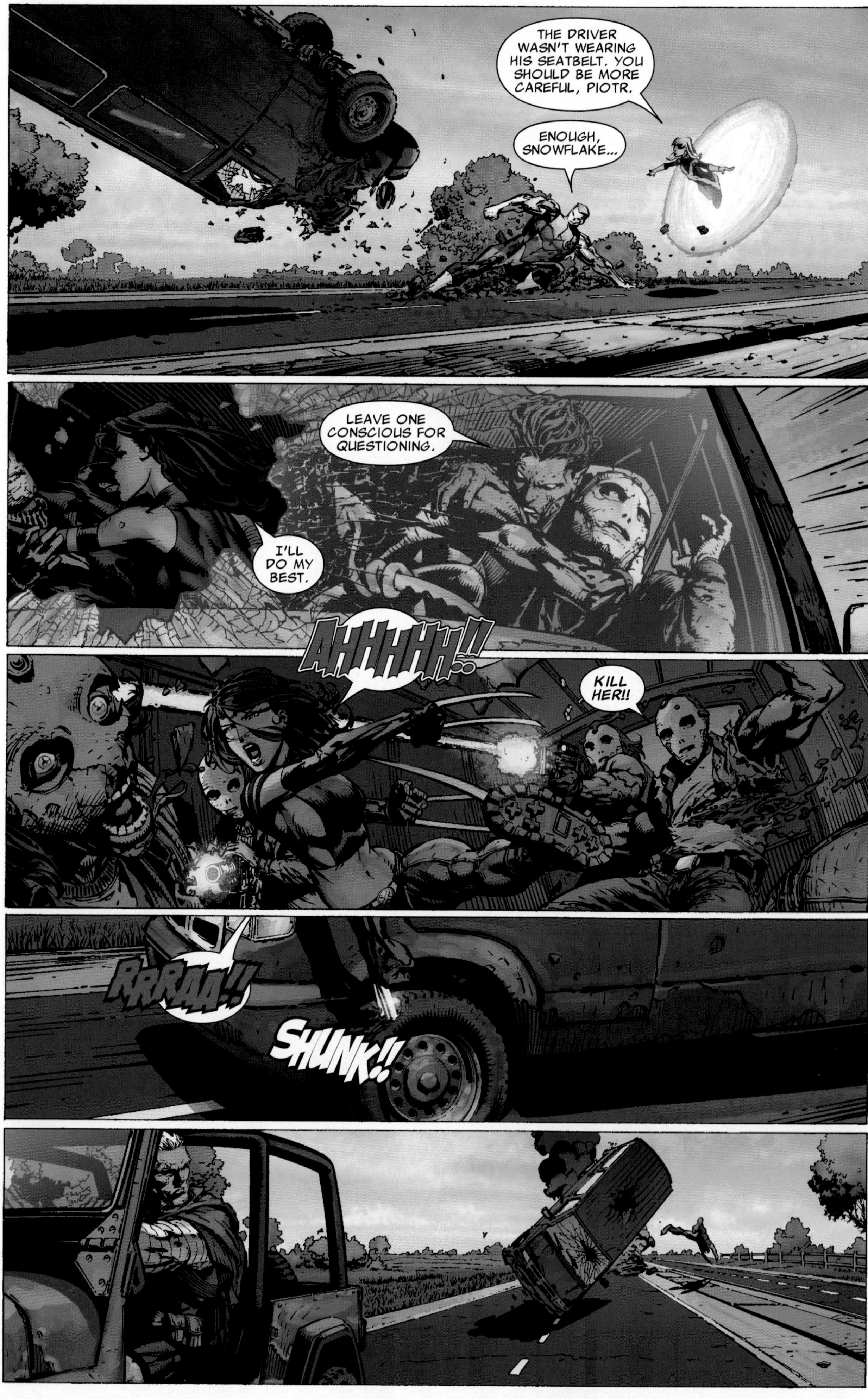
THE DRIVER WASN'T WEARING HIS SEATBELT. YOU SHOULD BE MORE CAREFUL, PIOTR.
ENOUGH, SNOWFLAKE...
LEAVE ONE CONSCIOUS FOR QUESTIONING.
I'LL DO MY BEST.
AHHHHH!!
KILL HER!!
RRRAA!!
SHUNK!!

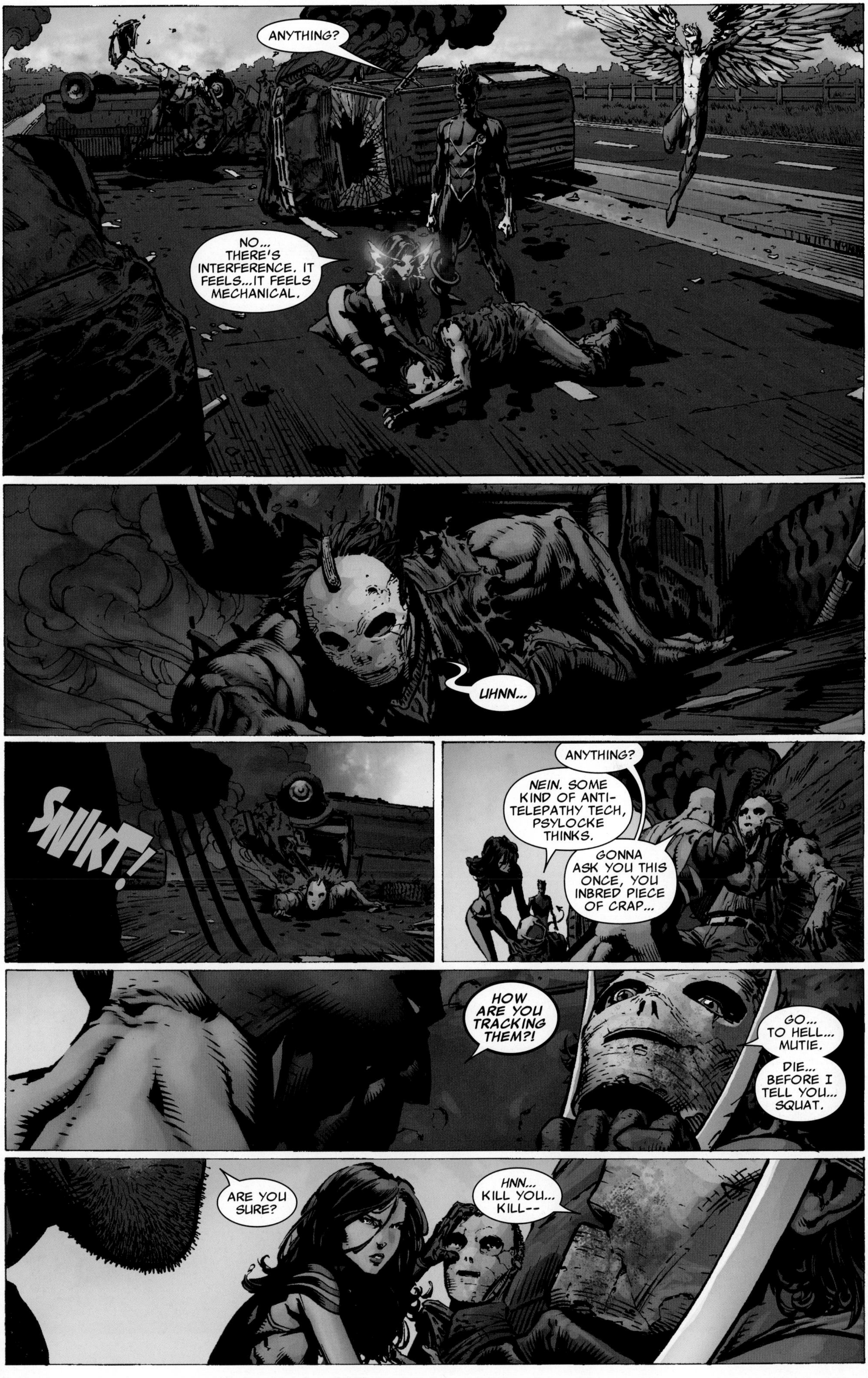
ANYTHING?
NO... THERE'S INTERFERENCE. IT FEELS...IT FEELS MECHANICAL.
UHNN...
SNIKT!
ANYTHING?
NEIN. SOME KIND OF ANTI-TELEPATHY TECH, PSYLOCKE THINKS.
GONNA ASK YOU THIS ONCE, YOU INBRED PIECE OF CRAP...
HOW ARE YOU TRACKING THEM?!
GO... TO HELL... MUTIE.
DIE... BEFORE I TELL YOU... SQUAT.
ARE YOU SURE?
HNN... KILL YOU... KILL--

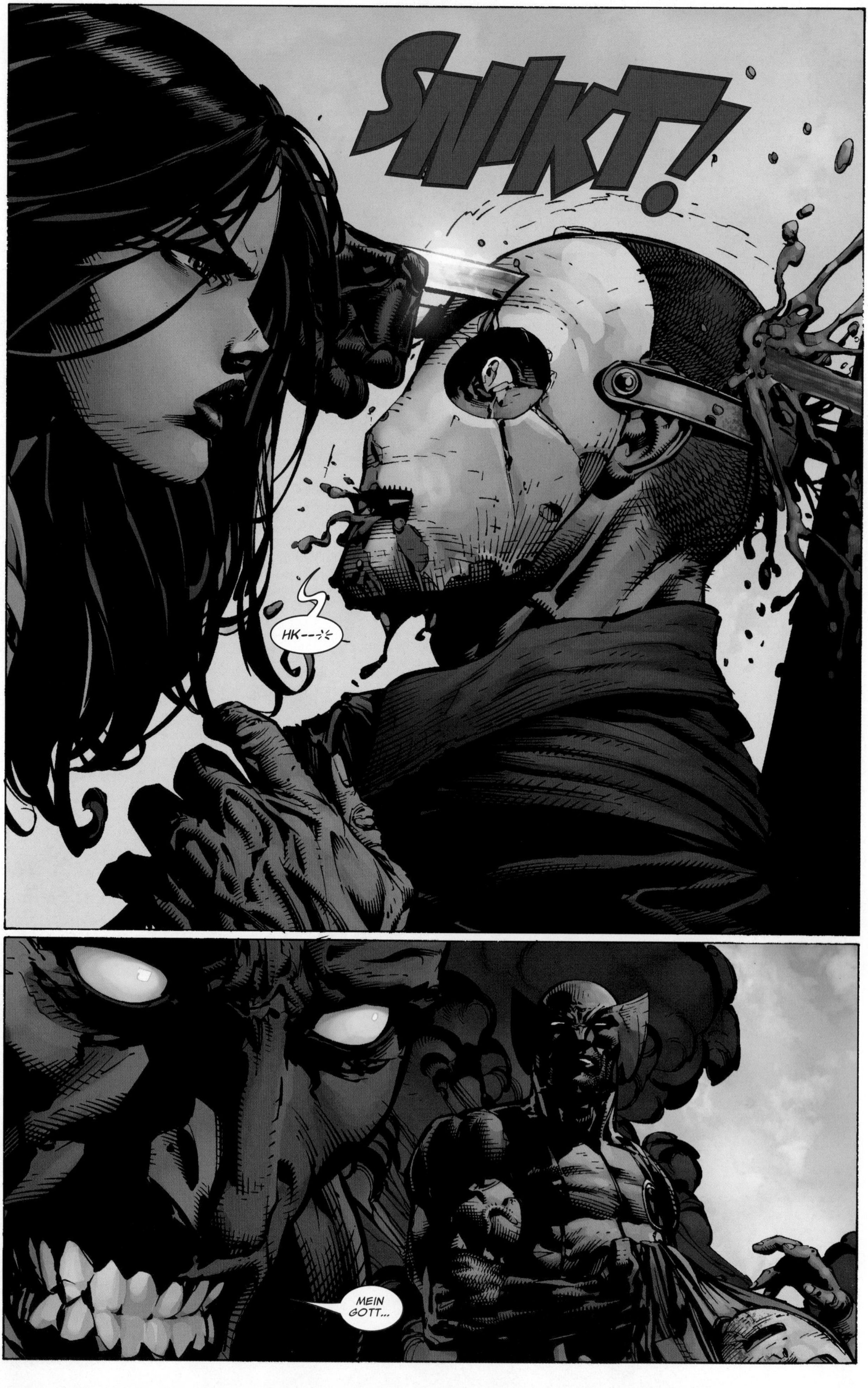
SNIKT!
HK--
MEIN GOTT...

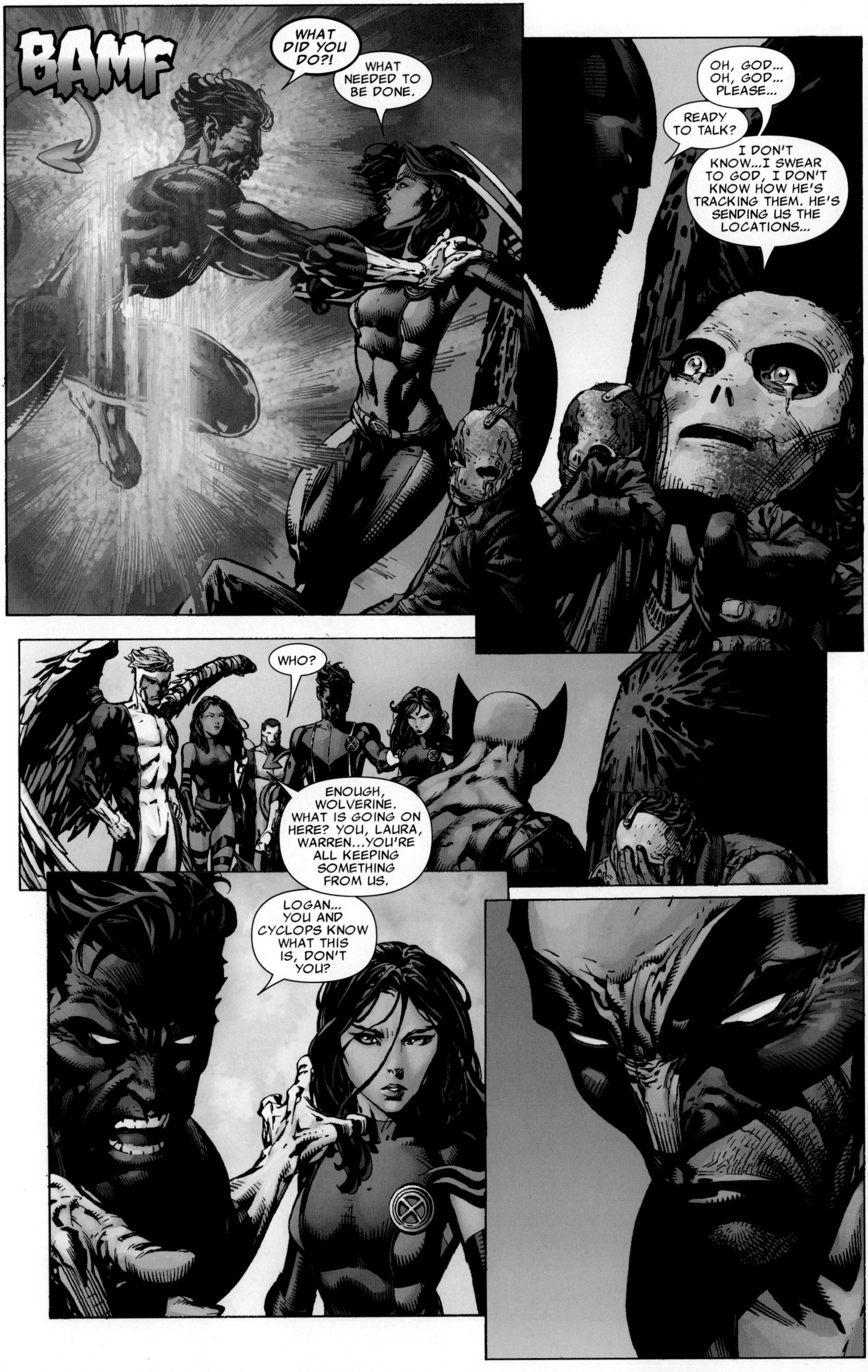
BAMF
WHAT DID YOU DO?!
WHAT NEEDED TO BE DONE.
OH, GOD... OH, GOD... PLEASE...
READY TO TALK?
I DON'T KNOW...I SWEAR TO GOD, I DON'T KNOW HOW HE'S TRACKING THEM. HE'S SENDING US THE LOCATIONS...
WHO?
ENOUGH, WOLVERINE. WHAT IS GOING ON HERE? YOU, LAURA, WARREN...YOU'RE ALL KEEPING SOMETHING FROM US.
LOGAN... YOU AND CYCLOPS KNOW WHAT THIS IS, DON'T YOU?

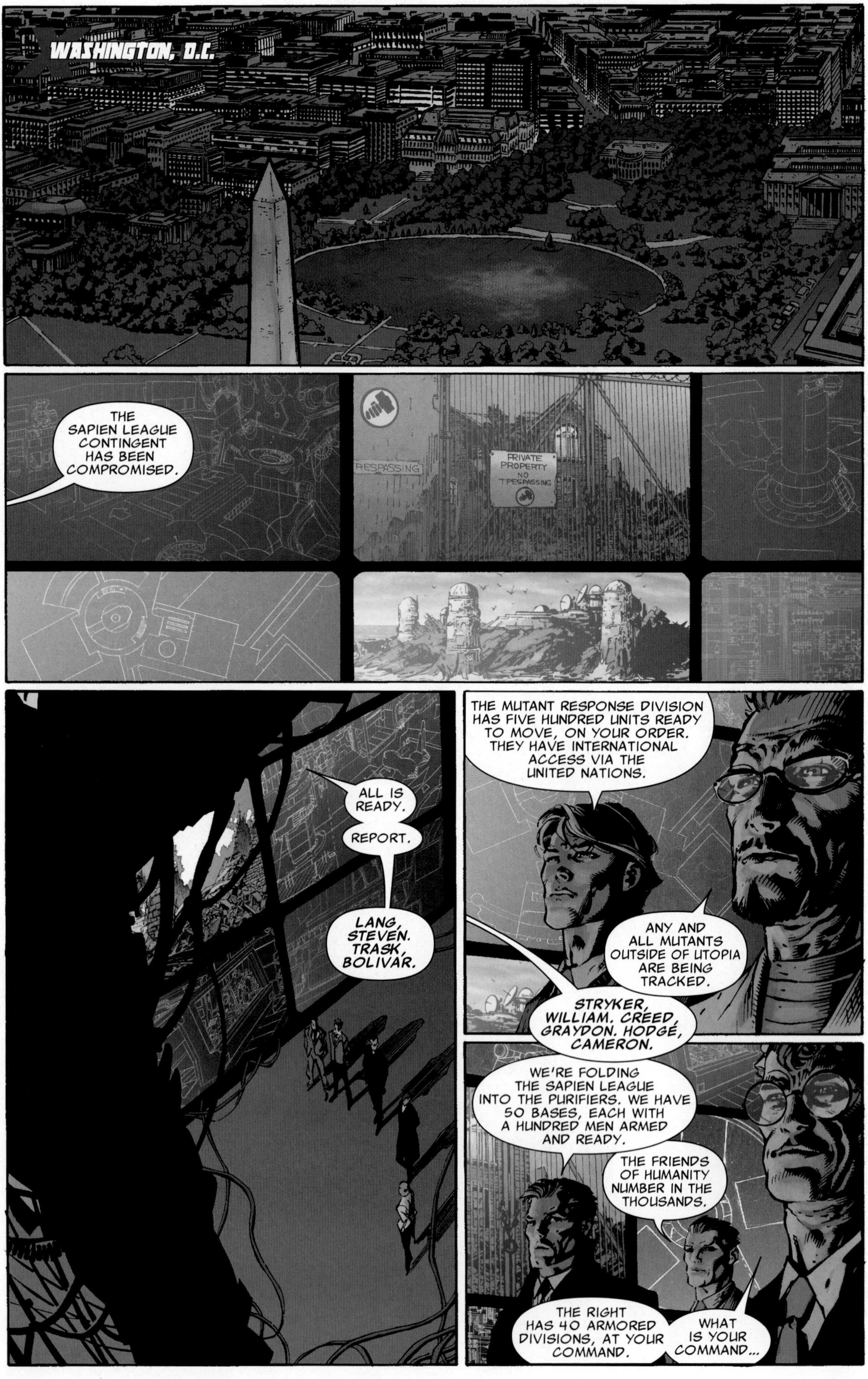
WASHINGTON, D.C.
THE SAPIEN LEAGUE CONTINGENT HAS BEEN COMPROMISED.
TRESPASSING
PRIVATE PROPERTY NO TRESPASSING
ALL IS READY.
REPORT.
LANG, STEVEN. TRASK, BOLIVAR.
THE MUTANT RESPONSE DIVISION HAS FIVE HUNDRED UNITS READY TO MOVE, ON YOUR ORDER. THEY HAVE INTERNATIONAL ACCESS VIA THE UNITED NATIONS.
ANY AND ALL MUTANTS OUTSIDE OF UTOPIA ARE BEING TRACKED.
STRYKER, WILLIAM. CREED, GRAYDON. HODGE, CAMERON.
WE'RE FOLDING THE SAPIEN LEAGUE INTO THE PURIFIERS. WE HAVE 50 BASES, EACH WITH A HUNDRED MEN ARMED AND READY.
THE FRIENDS OF HUMANITY NUMBER IN THE THOUSANDS.
THE RIGHT HAS 40 ARMORED DIVISIONS, AT YOUR COMMAND.
WHAT IS YOUR COMMAND...

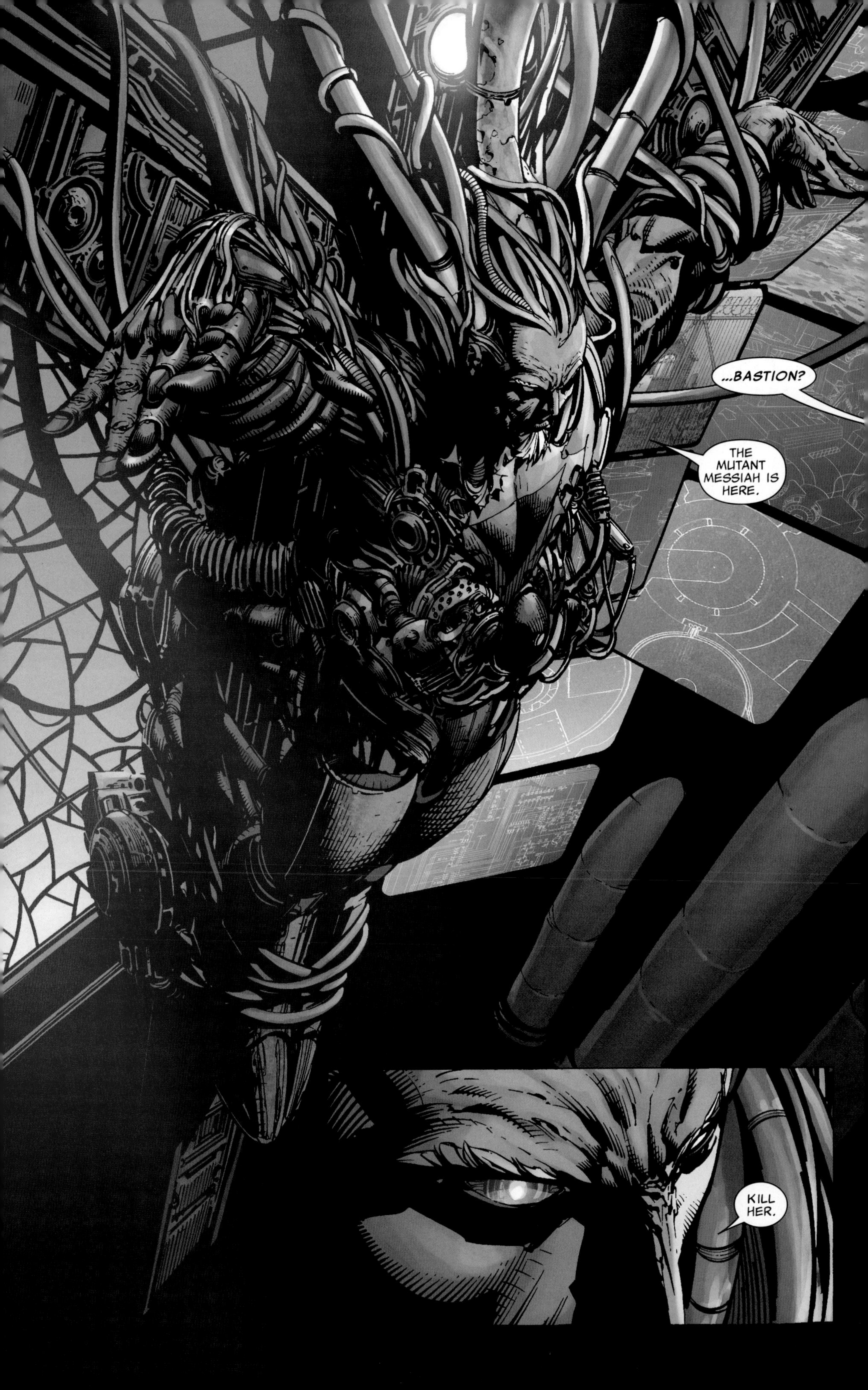
...BASTION?
THE MUTANT MESSIAH IS HERE.
KILL HER.

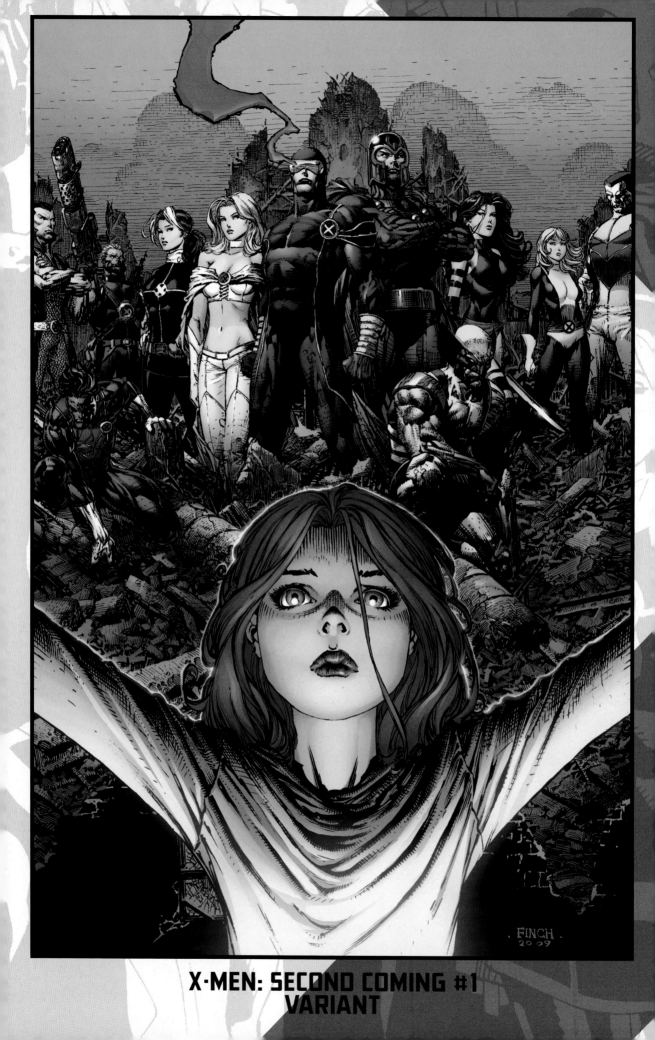

X-MEN: SECOND COMING #1
VARIANT

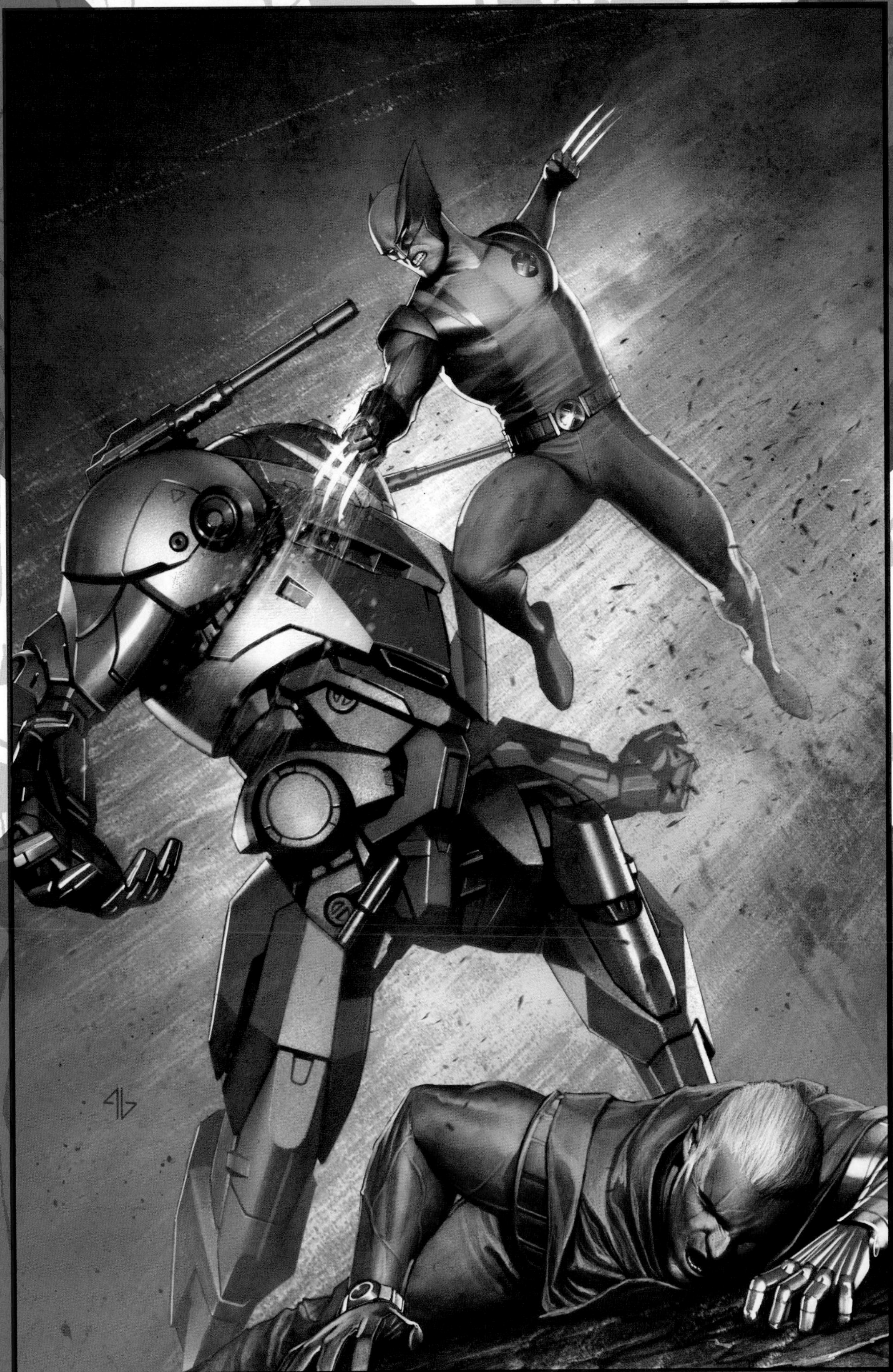

UNCANNY X-MEN #523

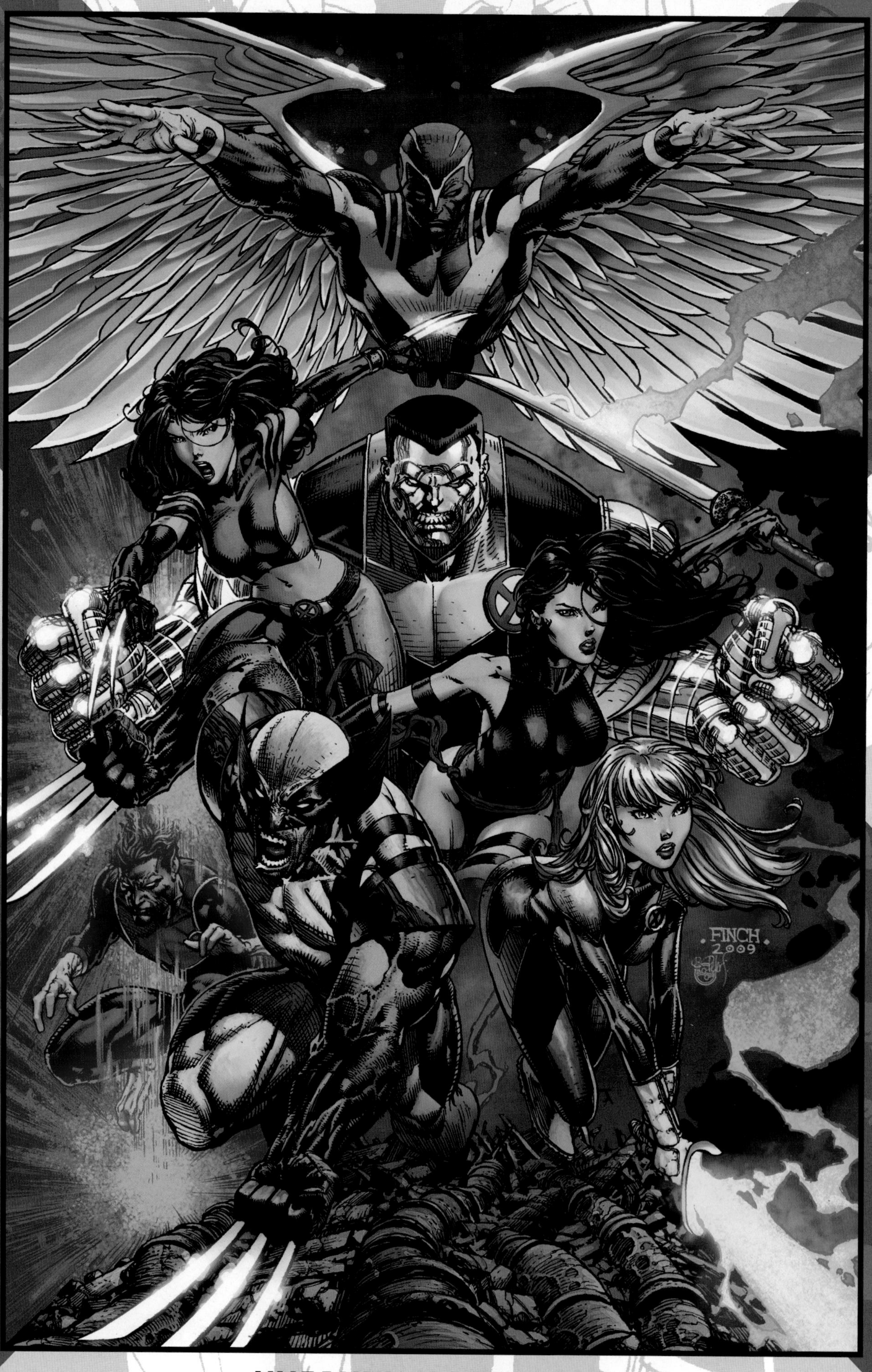
FINCH 2009

UNCANNY X-MEN #523
VARIANT

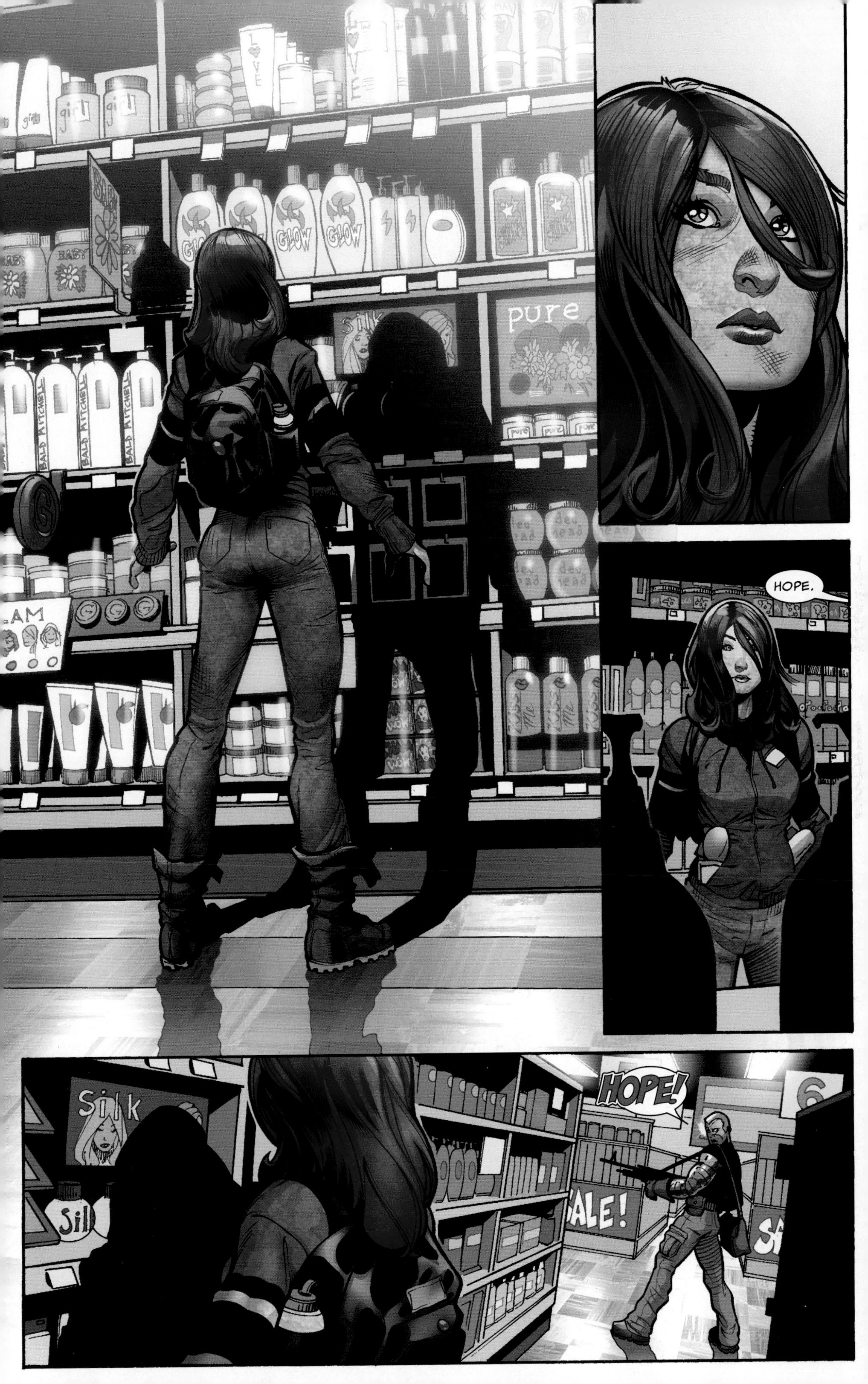
HOPE.
HOPE!

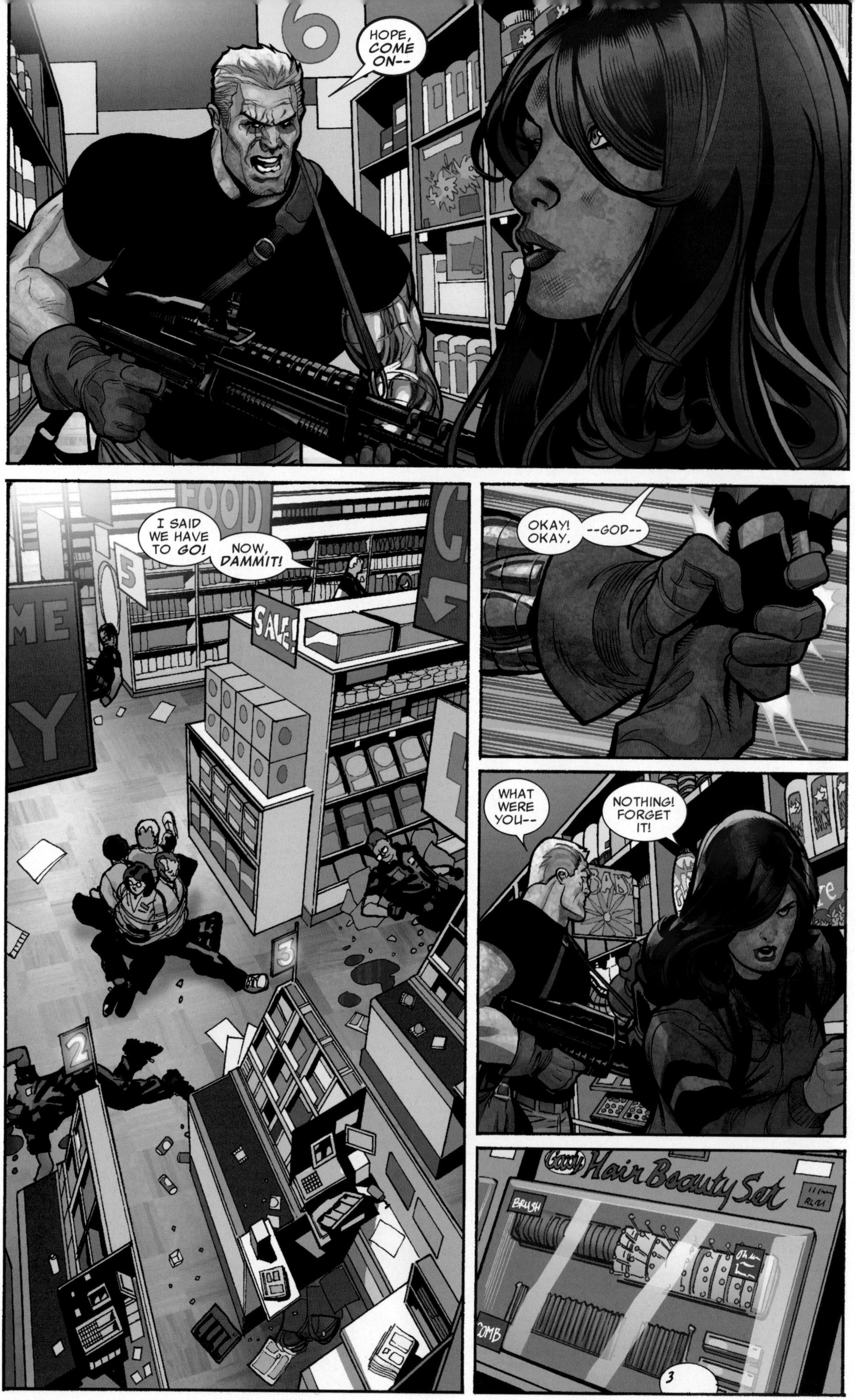
HOPE, COME ON--
I SAID WE HAVE TO GO!
NOW, DAMMIT!
OKAY! OKAY.
--GOD--
WHAT WERE YOU--
NOTHING! FORGET IT!
Hair Beauty Set
BRUSH
COMB

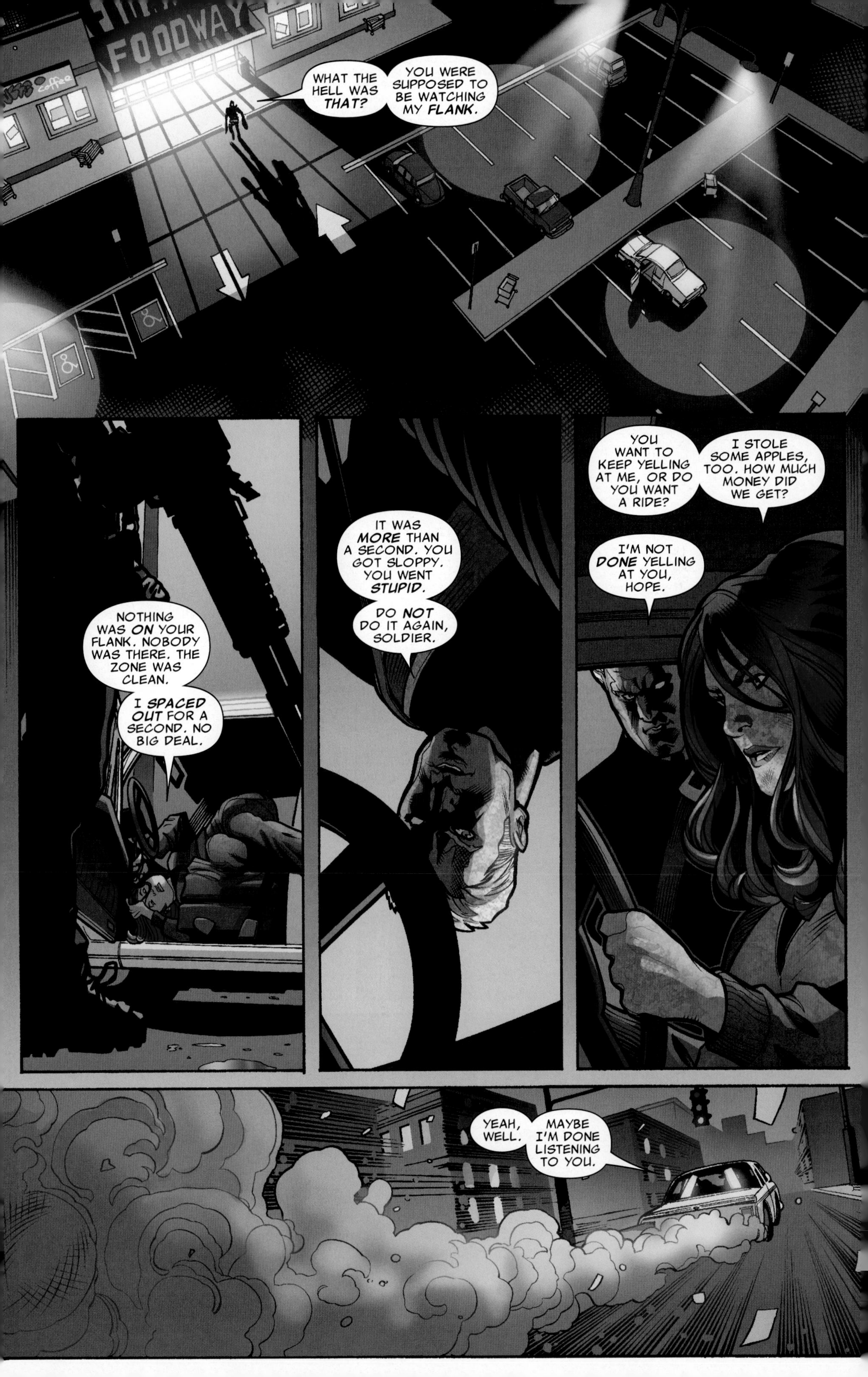
FOODWAY
coffee
WHAT THE HELL WAS THAT?
YOU WERE SUPPOSED TO BE WATCHING MY FLANK.
NOTHING WAS ON YOUR FLANK. NOBODY WAS THERE. THE ZONE WAS CLEAN.
I SPACED OUT FOR A SECOND. NO BIG DEAL.
IT WAS MORE THAN A SECOND. YOU GOT SLOPPY. YOU WENT STUPID.
DO NOT DO IT AGAIN, SOLDIER.
YOU WANT TO KEEP YELLING AT ME, OR DO YOU WANT A RIDE?
I STOLE SOME APPLES, TOO. HOW MUCH MONEY DID WE GET?
I'M NOT DONE YELLING AT YOU, HOPE.
YEAH, WELL.
MAYBE I'M DONE LISTENING TO YOU.

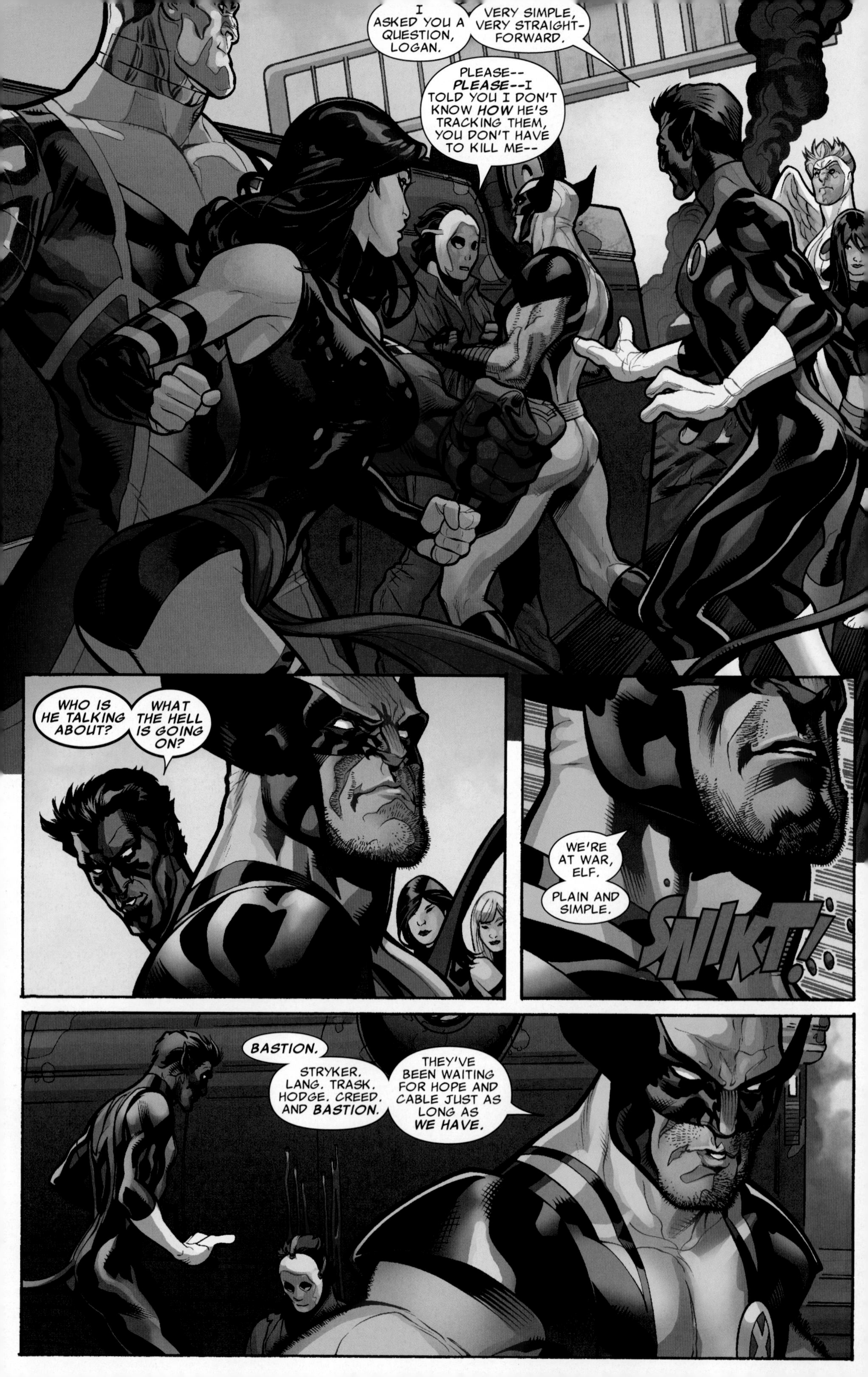
I ASKED YOU A QUESTION, LOGAN.
VERY SIMPLE, VERY STRAIGHT-FORWARD.
PLEASE-- PLEASE--I TOLD YOU I DON'T KNOW HOW HE'S TRACKING THEM, YOU DON'T HAVE TO KILL ME--
WHO IS HE TALKING ABOUT?
WHAT THE HELL IS GOING ON?
WE'RE AT WAR, ELF.
PLAIN AND SIMPLE.
SNIKT!
BASTION.
STRYKER. LANG. TRASK. HODGE. CREED. AND BASTION.
THEY'VE BEEN WAITING FOR HOPE AND CABLE JUST AS LONG AS WE HAVE.

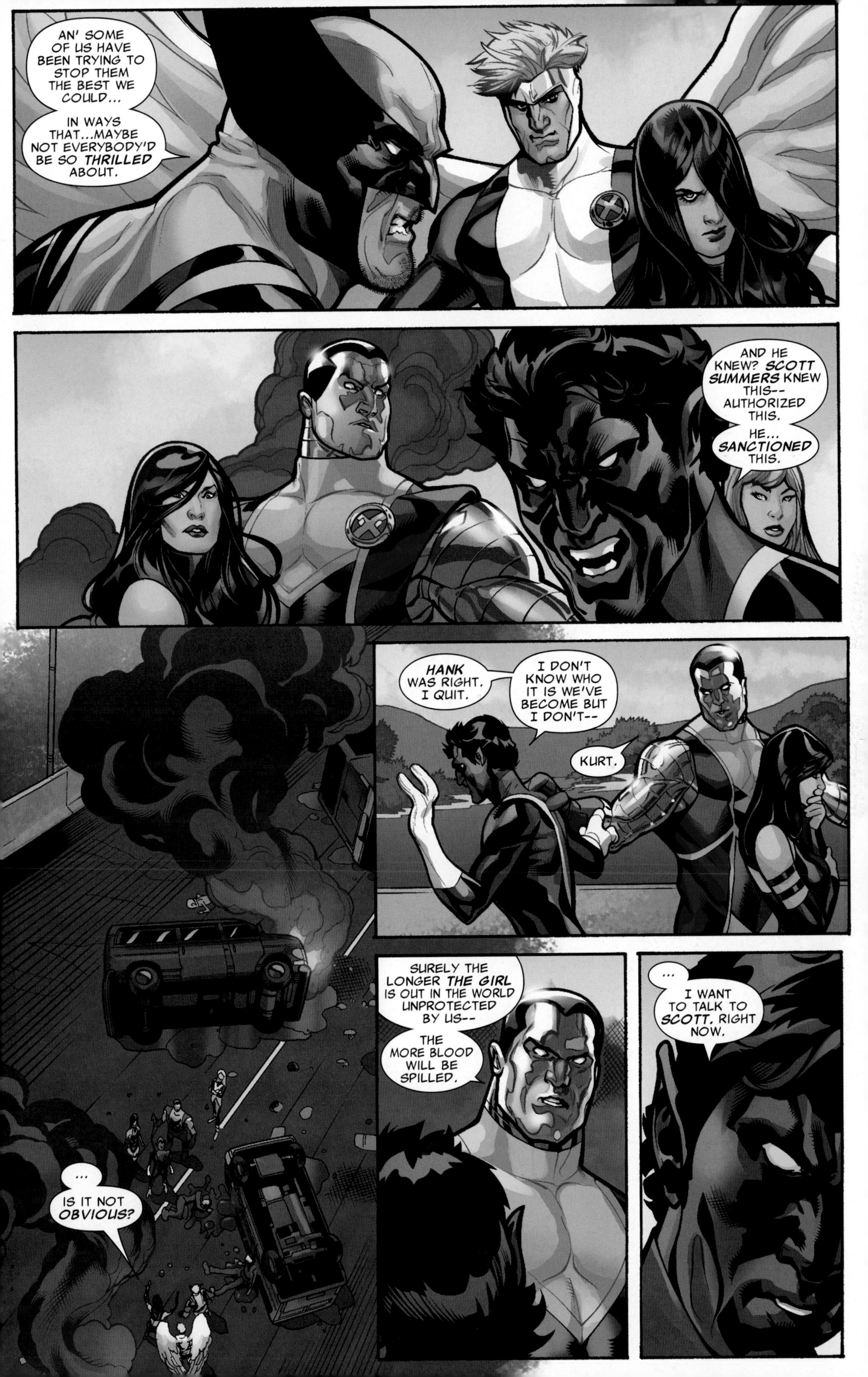
AN' SOME OF US HAVE BEEN TRYING TO STOP THEM THE BEST WE COULD...
IN WAYS THAT...MAYBE NOT EVERYBODY'D BE SO THRILLED ABOUT.
AND HE KNEW? SCOTT SUMMERS KNEW THIS-- AUTHORIZED THIS.
HE... SANCTIONED THIS.
HANK WAS RIGHT. I QUIT.
I DON'T KNOW WHO IT IS WE'VE BECOME BUT I DON'T--
KURT.
...
IS IT NOT OBVIOUS?
SURELY THE LONGER THE GIRL IS OUT IN THE WORLD UNPROTECTED BY US--
THE MORE BLOOD WILL BE SPILLED.
...
I WANT TO TALK TO SCOTT. RIGHT NOW.

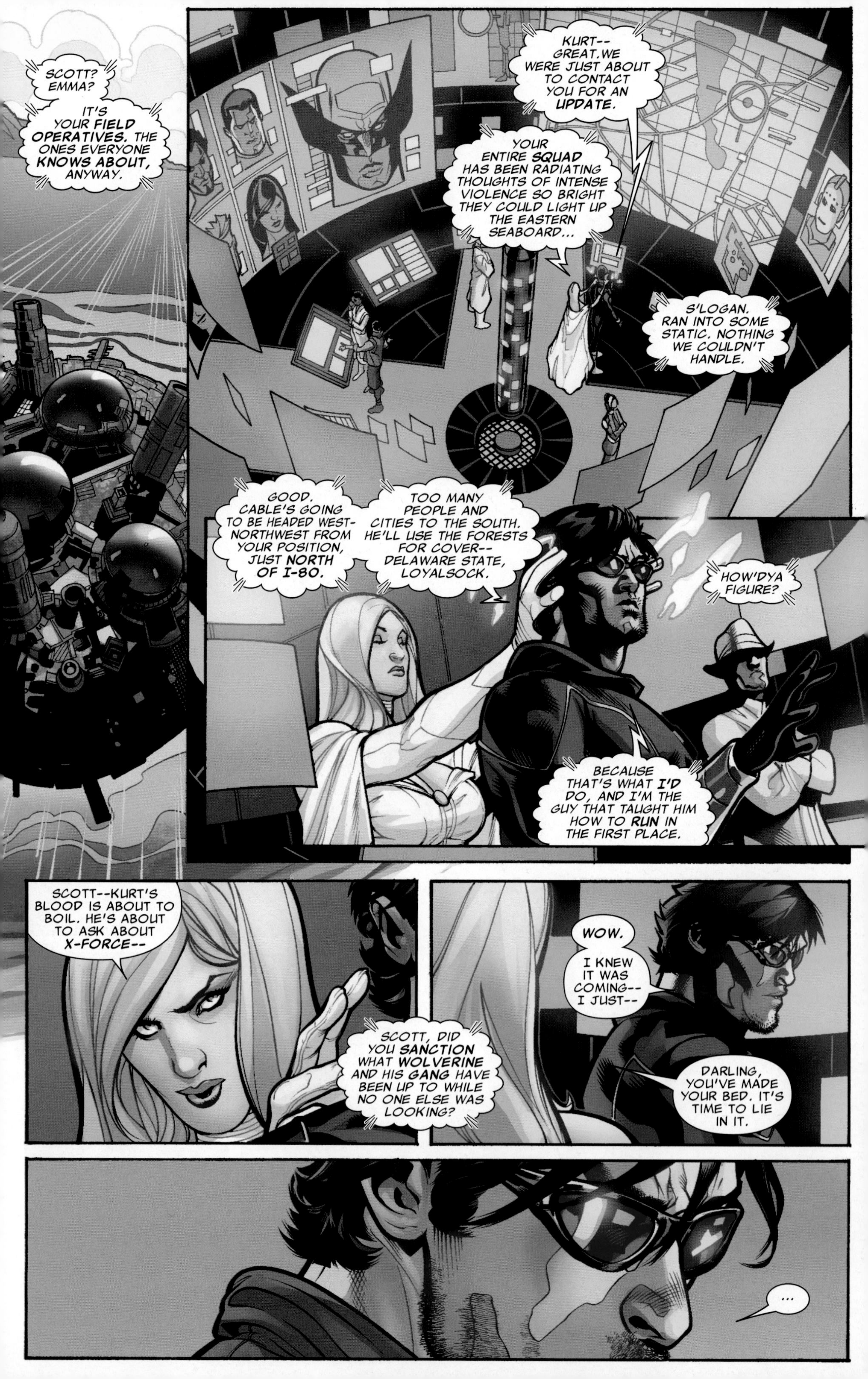
SCOTT? EMMA?
IT'S YOUR FIELD OPERATIVES. THE ONES EVERYONE KNOWS ABOUT, ANYWAY.
KURT-- GREAT. WE WERE JUST ABOUT TO CONTACT YOU FOR AN UPDATE.
YOUR ENTIRE SQUAD HAS BEEN RADIATING THOUGHTS OF INTENSE VIOLENCE SO BRIGHT THEY COULD LIGHT UP THE EASTERN SEABOARD...
S'LOGAN. RAN INTO SOME STATIC. NOTHING WE COULDN'T HANDLE.
GOOD. CABLE'S GOING TO BE HEADED WEST-NORTHWEST FROM YOUR POSITION, JUST NORTH OF I-80.
TOO MANY PEOPLE AND CITIES TO THE SOUTH. HE'LL USE THE FORESTS FOR COVER-- DELAWARE STATE, LOYALSOCK.
HOW'DYA FIGURE?
BECAUSE THAT'S WHAT I'D DO, AND I'M THE GUY THAT TAUGHT HIM HOW TO RUN IN THE FIRST PLACE.
SCOTT--KURT'S BLOOD IS ABOUT TO BOIL. HE'S ABOUT TO ASK ABOUT X-FORCE--
SCOTT, DID YOU SANCTION WHAT WOLVERINE AND HIS GANG HAVE BEEN UP TO WHILE NO ONE ELSE WAS LOOKING?
WOW.
I KNEW IT WAS COMING-- I JUST--
DARLING, YOU'VE MADE YOUR BED. IT'S TIME TO LIE IN IT.
...

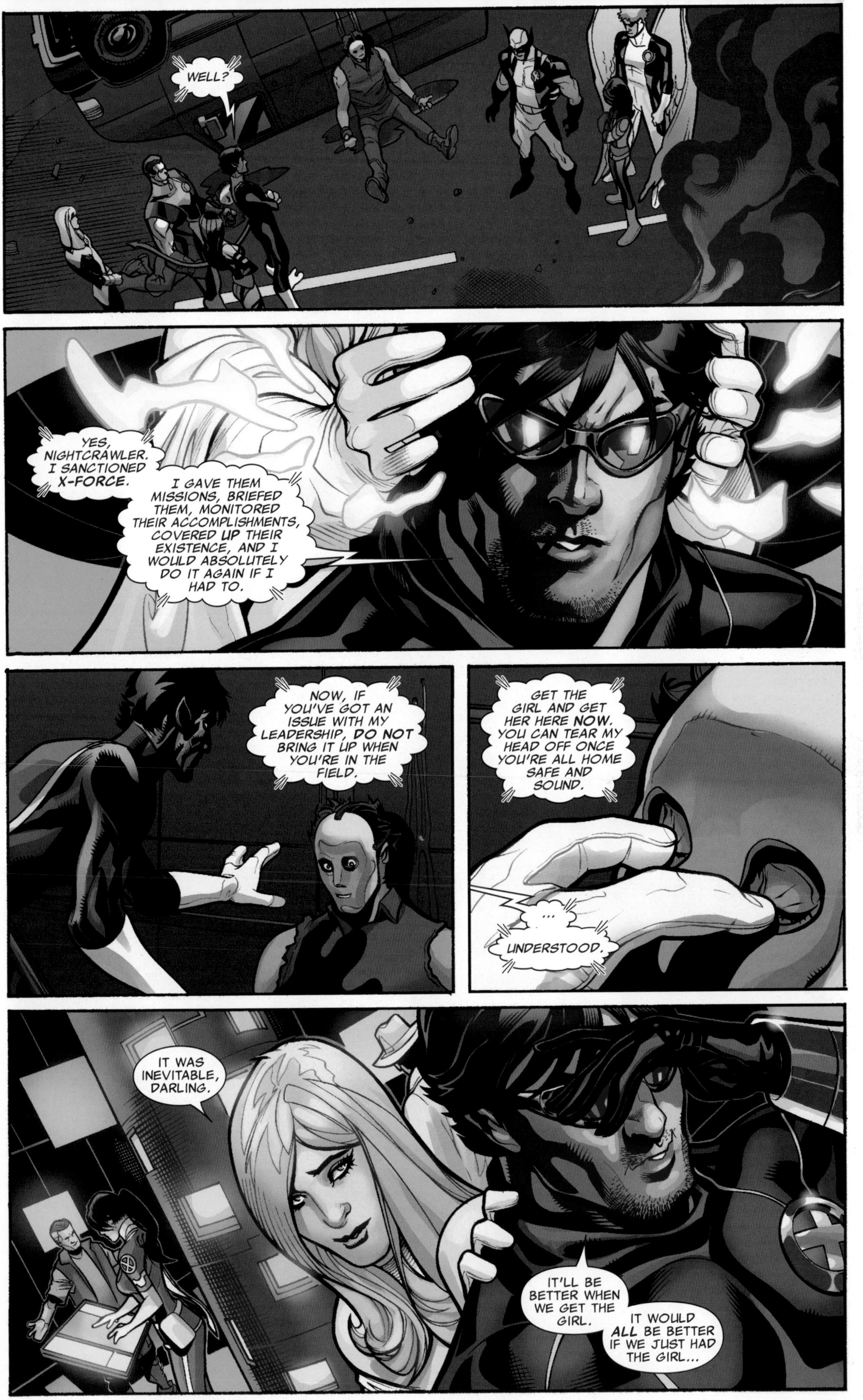

WELL?
YES, NIGHTCRAWLER. I SANCTIONED X-FORCE.
I GAVE THEM MISSIONS, BRIEFED THEM, MONITORED THEIR ACCOMPLISHMENTS, COVERED UP THEIR EXISTENCE, AND I WOULD ABSOLUTELY DO IT AGAIN IF I HAD TO.
NOW, IF YOU'VE GOT AN ISSUE WITH MY LEADERSHIP, DO NOT BRING IT UP WHEN YOU'RE IN THE FIELD.
GET THE GIRL AND GET HER HERE NOW. YOU CAN TEAR MY HEAD OFF ONCE YOU'RE ALL HOME SAFE AND SOUND.
...
UNDERSTOOD.
IT WAS INEVITABLE, DARLING.
IT'LL BE BETTER WHEN WE GET THE GIRL.
IT WOULD ALL BE BETTER IF WE JUST HAD THE GIRL...

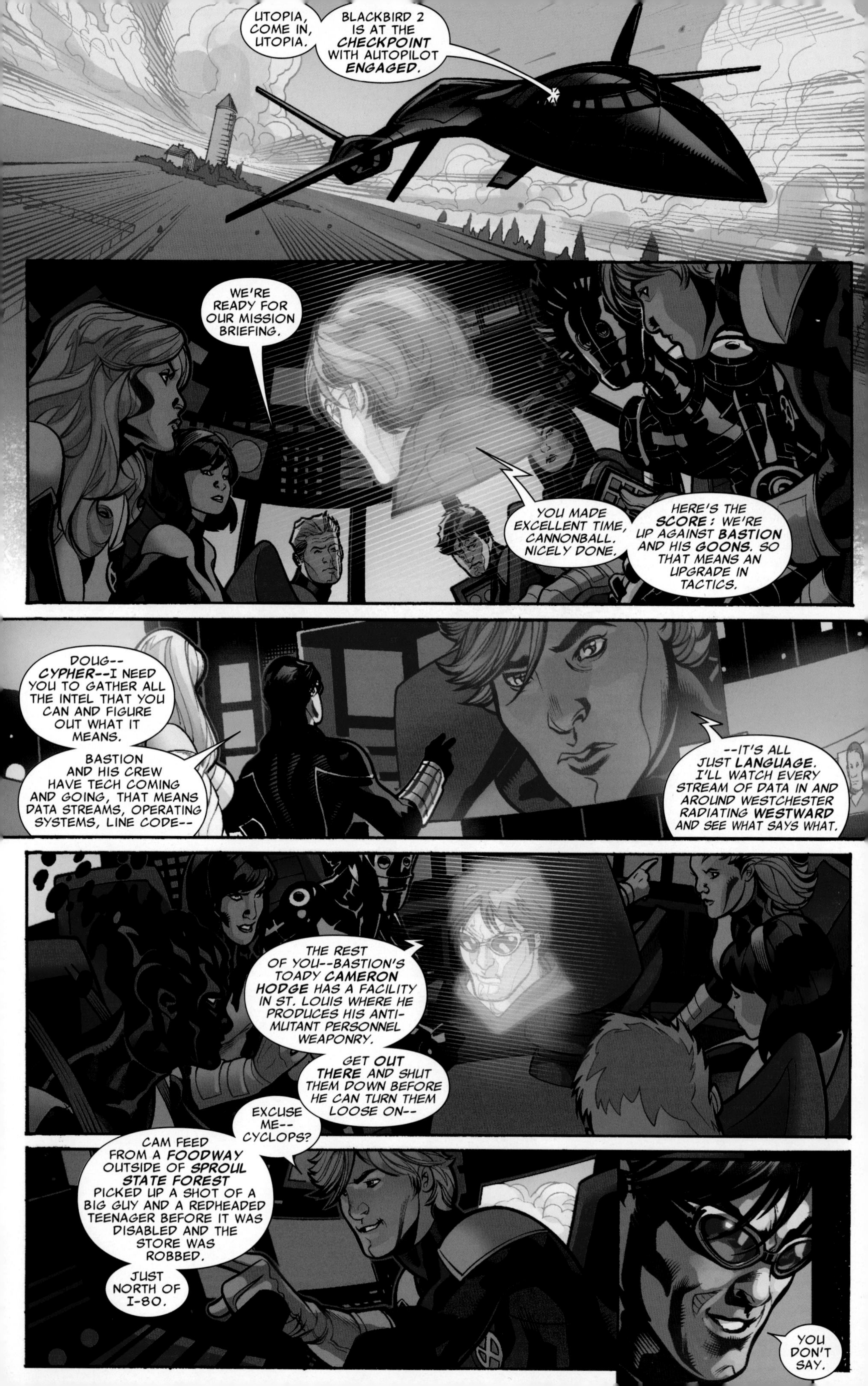
UTOPIA, COME IN, UTOPIA.
BLACKBIRD 2 IS AT THE CHECKPOINT WITH AUTOPILOT ENGAGED.
WE'RE READY FOR OUR MISSION BRIEFING.
YOU MADE EXCELLENT TIME, CANNONBALL. NICELY DONE.
HERE'S THE SCORE: WE'RE UP AGAINST BASTION AND HIS GOONS. SO THAT MEANS AN UPGRADE IN TACTICS.
DOUG--CYPHER--I NEED YOU TO GATHER ALL THE INTEL THAT YOU CAN AND FIGURE OUT WHAT IT MEANS.
BASTION AND HIS CREW HAVE TECH COMING AND GOING, THAT MEANS DATA STREAMS, OPERATING SYSTEMS, LINE CODE--
--IT'S ALL JUST LANGUAGE. I'LL WATCH EVERY STREAM OF DATA IN AND AROUND WESTCHESTER RADIATING WESTWARD AND SEE WHAT SAYS WHAT.
THE REST OF YOU--BASTION'S TOADY CAMERON HODGE HAS A FACILITY IN ST. LOUIS WHERE HE PRODUCES HIS ANTI-MUTANT PERSONNEL WEAPONRY.
GET OUT THERE AND SHUT THEM DOWN BEFORE HE CAN TURN THEM LOOSE ON--
EXCUSE ME--CYCLOPS?
CAM FEED FROM A FOODWAY OUTSIDE OF SPROUL STATE FOREST PICKED UP A SHOT OF A BIG GUY AND A REDHEADED TEENAGER BEFORE IT WAS DISABLED AND THE STORE WAS ROBBED.
JUST NORTH OF I-80.
YOU DON'T SAY.

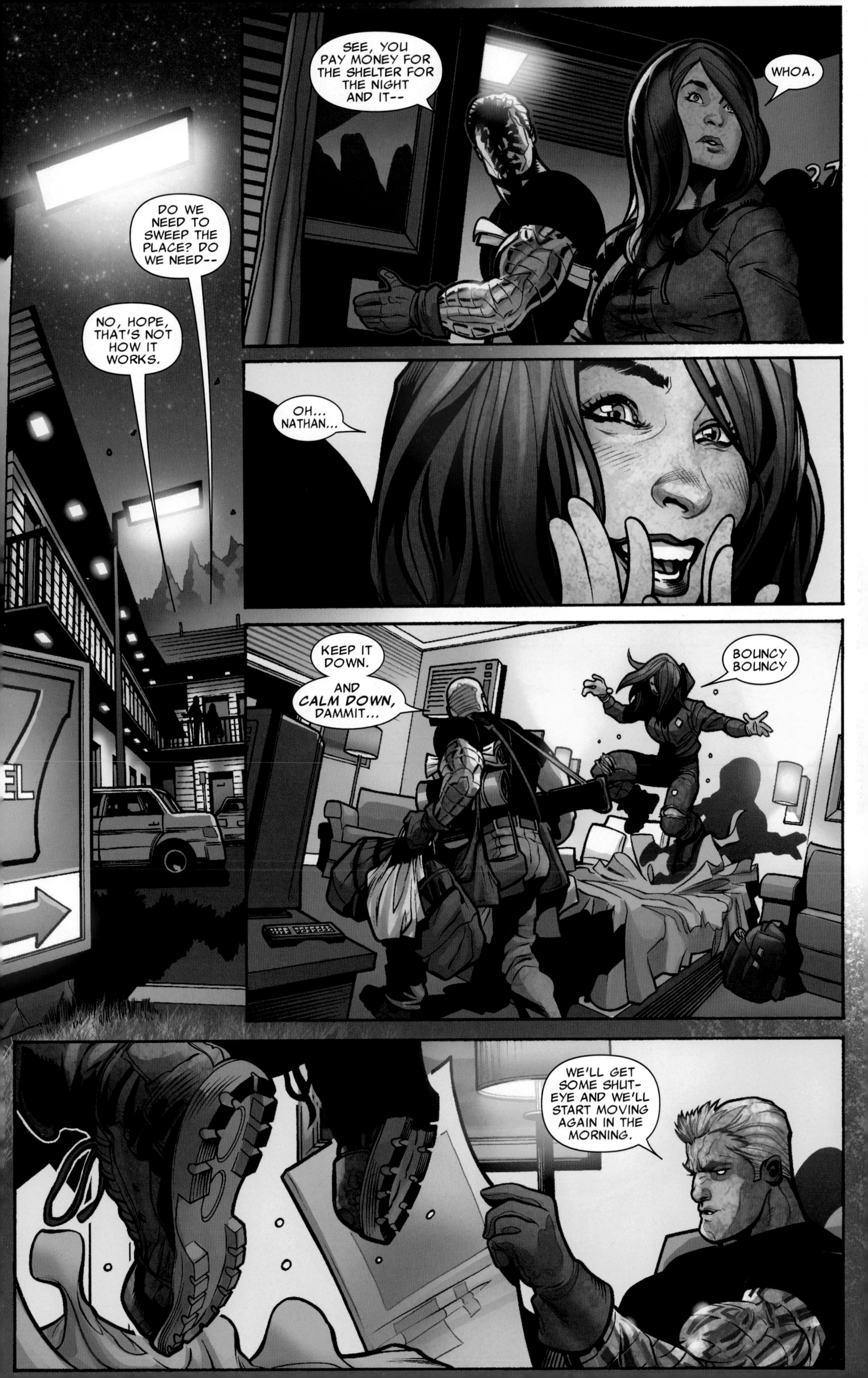
DO WE NEED TO SWEEP THE PLACE? DO WE NEED--
NO, HOPE, THAT'S NOT HOW IT WORKS.
EL
SEE, YOU PAY MONEY FOR THE SHELTER FOR THE NIGHT AND IT--
WHOA.
OH... NATHAN...
KEEP IT DOWN.
AND CALM DOWN, DAMMIT...
BOUNCY BOUNCY
WE'LL GET SOME SHUT-EYE AND WE'LL START MOVING AGAIN IN THE MORNING.

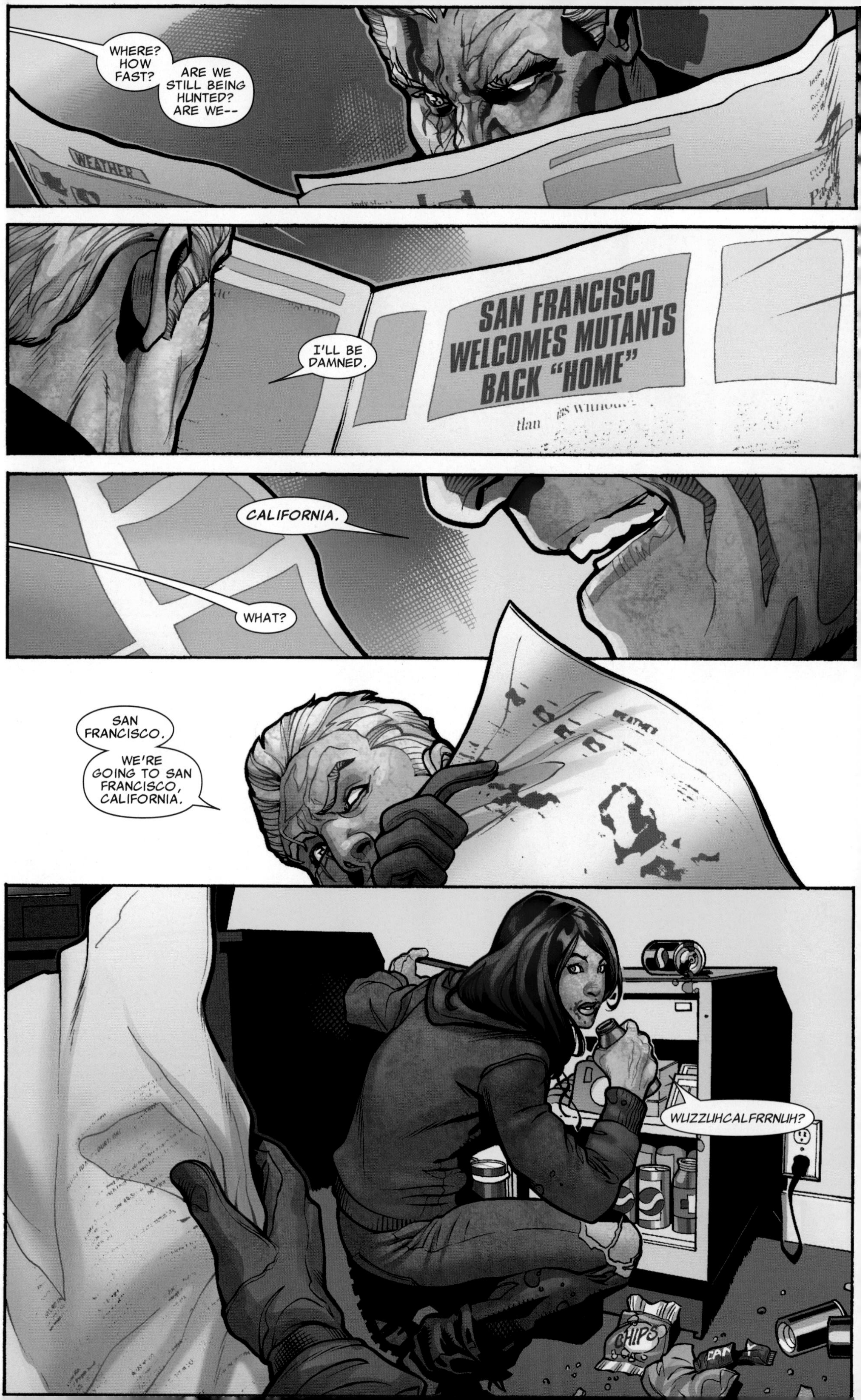
WHERE? HOW FAST?
ARE WE STILL BEING HUNTED? ARE WE--
WEATHER
SAN FRANCISCO WELCOMES MUTANTS BACK "HOME"
I'LL BE DAMNED.
CALIFORNIA.
WHAT?
SAN FRANCISCO.
WE'RE GOING TO SAN FRANCISCO, CALIFORNIA.
WUZZUHCALFRRNUH?
CHIPS

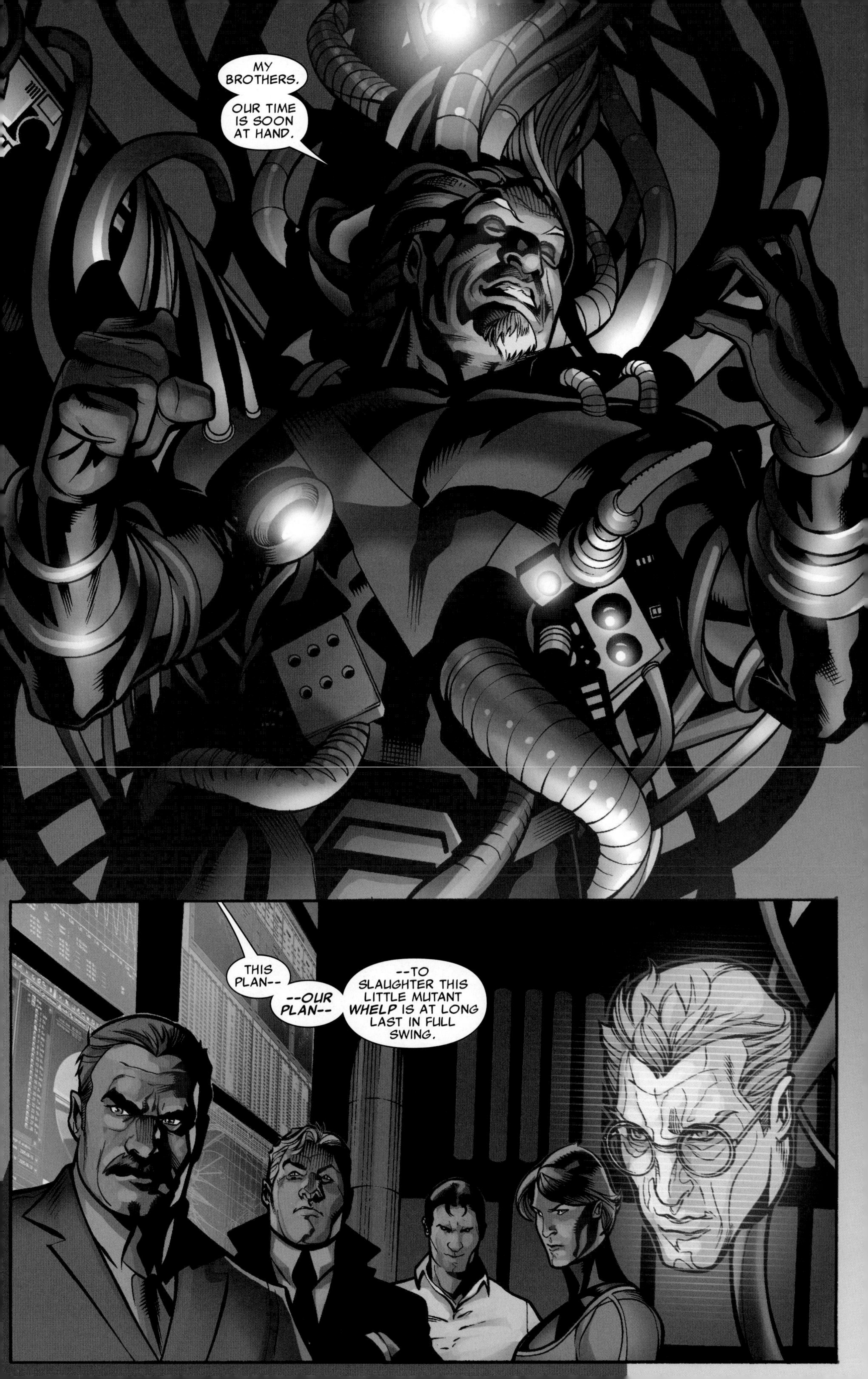
MY BROTHERS.
OUR TIME IS SOON AT HAND.
THIS PLAN--
--OUR PLAN--
--TO SLAUGHTER THIS LITTLE MUTANT WHELP IS AT LONG LAST IN FULL SWING.

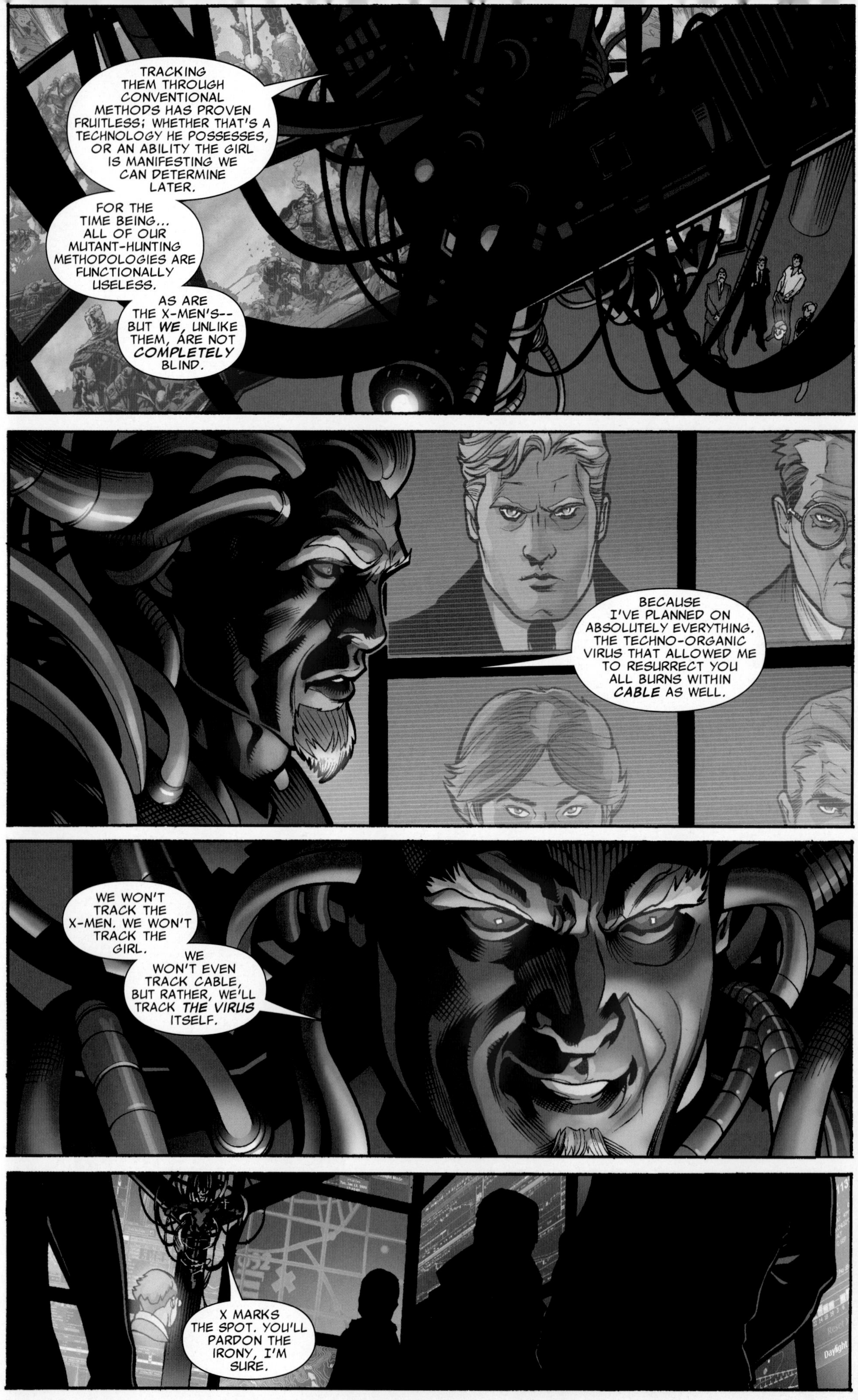
TRACKING THEM THROUGH CONVENTIONAL METHODS HAS PROVEN FRUITLESS; WHETHER THAT'S A TECHNOLOGY HE POSSESSES, OR AN ABILITY THE GIRL IS MANIFESTING WE CAN DETERMINE LATER.
FOR THE TIME BEING... ALL OF OUR MUTANT-HUNTING METHODOLOGIES ARE FUNCTIONALLY USELESS.
AS ARE THE X-MEN'S-- BUT WE, UNLIKE THEM, ARE NOT COMPLETELY BLIND.
BECAUSE I'VE PLANNED ON ABSOLUTELY EVERYTHING. THE TECHNO-ORGANIC VIRUS THAT ALLOWED ME TO RESURRECT YOU ALL BURNS WITHIN CABLE AS WELL.
WE WON'T TRACK THE X-MEN. WE WON'T TRACK THE GIRL.
WE WON'T EVEN TRACK CABLE, BUT RATHER, WE'LL TRACK THE VIRUS ITSELF.
X MARKS THE SPOT. YOU'LL PARDON THE IRONY, I'M SURE.

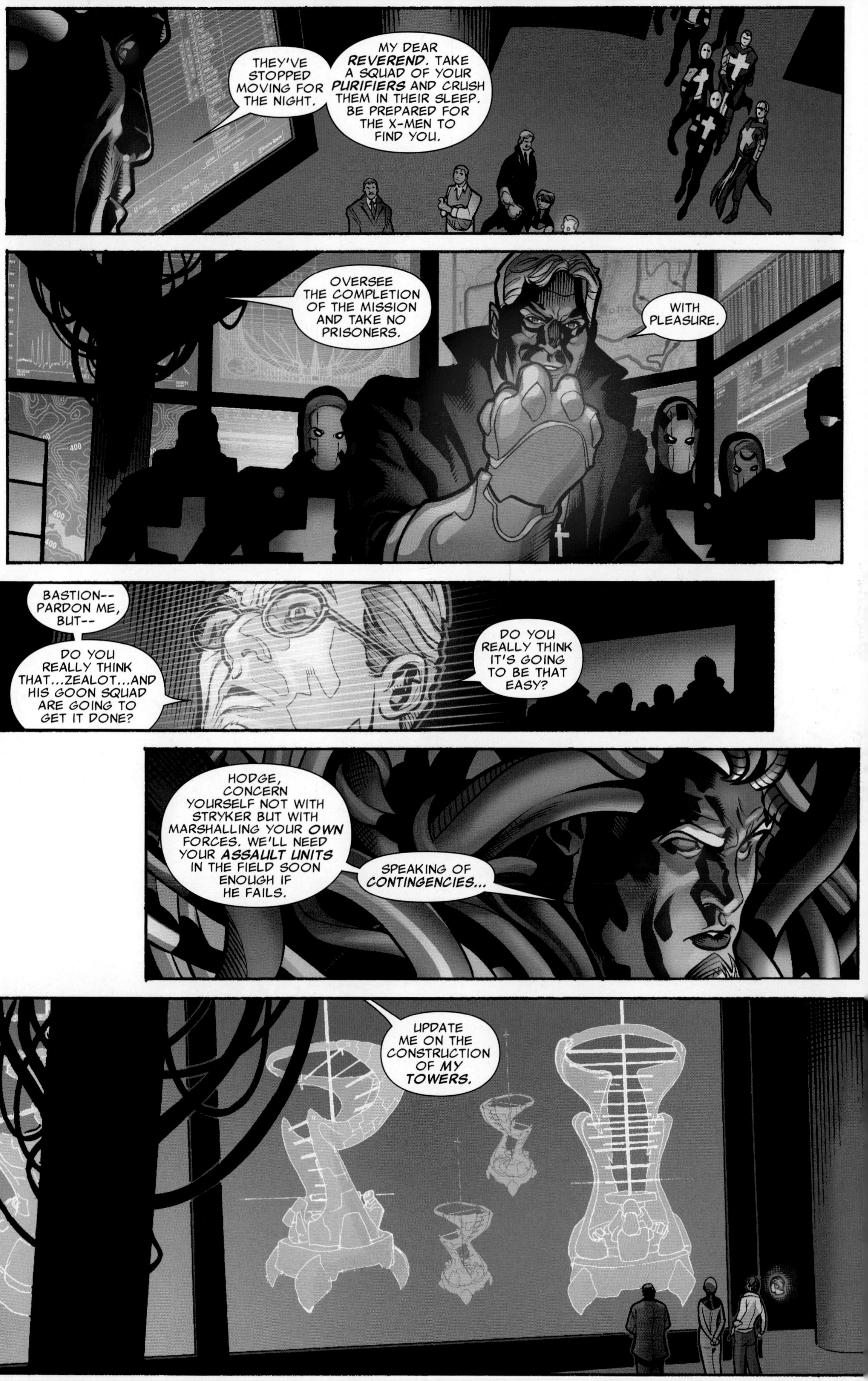

THEY'VE STOPPED MOVING FOR THE NIGHT.
MY DEAR REVEREND. TAKE A SQUAD OF YOUR PURIFIERS AND CRUSH THEM IN THEIR SLEEP. BE PREPARED FOR THE X-MEN TO FIND YOU.
OVERSEE THE COMPLETION OF THE MISSION AND TAKE NO PRISONERS.
WITH PLEASURE.
BASTION-- PARDON ME, BUT--
DO YOU REALLY THINK THAT...ZEALOT...AND HIS GOON SQUAD ARE GOING TO GET IT DONE?
DO YOU REALLY THINK IT'S GOING TO BE THAT EASY?
HODGE, CONCERN YOURSELF NOT WITH STRYKER BUT WITH MARSHALLING YOUR OWN FORCES. WE'LL NEED YOUR ASSAULT UNITS IN THE FIELD SOON ENOUGH IF HE FAILS.
SPEAKING OF CONTINGENCIES...
UPDATE ME ON THE CONSTRUCTION OF MY TOWERS.

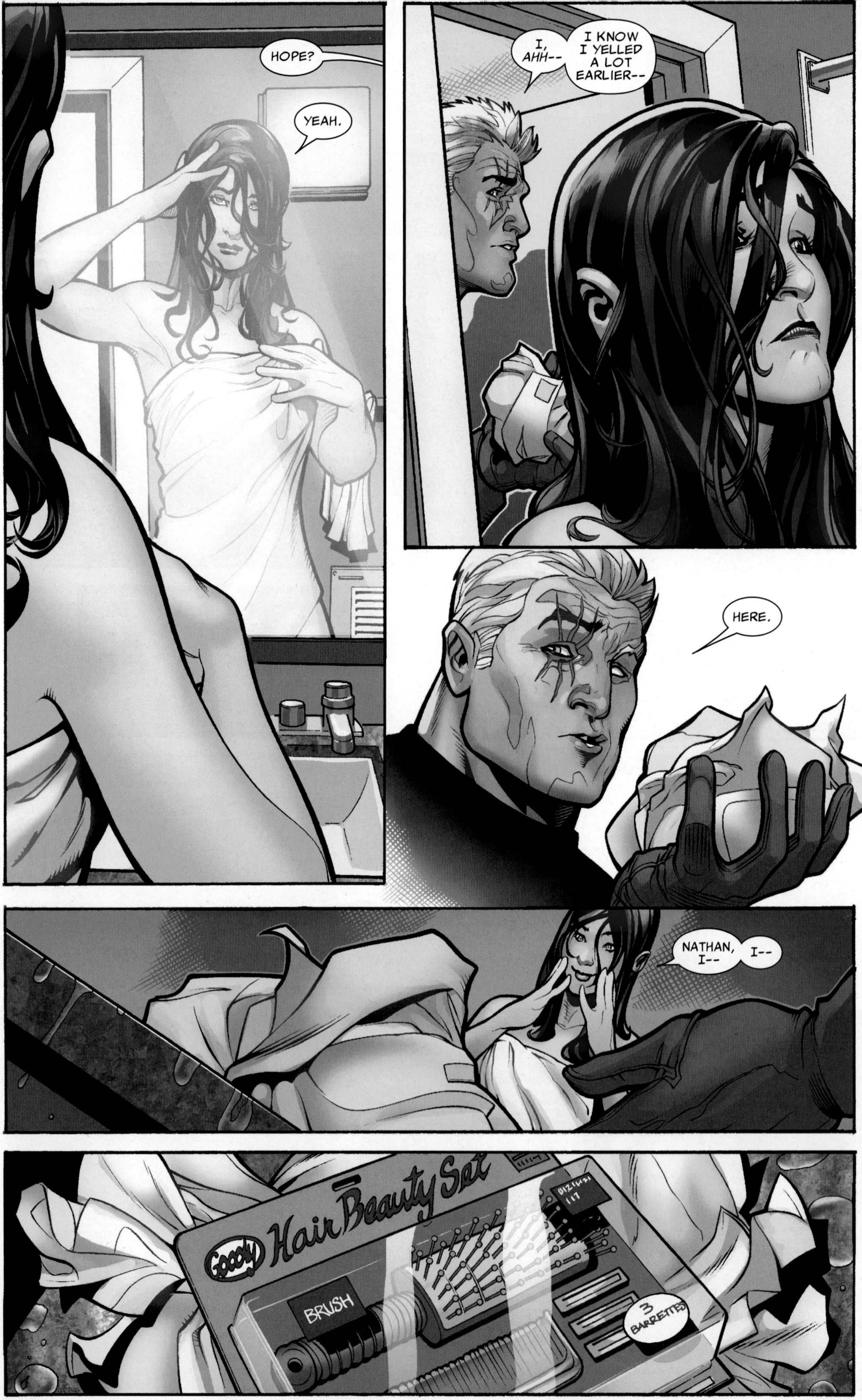
HOPE?
YEAH.
I, AHH--
I KNOW I YELLED A LOT EARLIER--
HERE.
NATHAN, I--
I--
Hair Beauty Set
BRUSH
3 BARRETTES

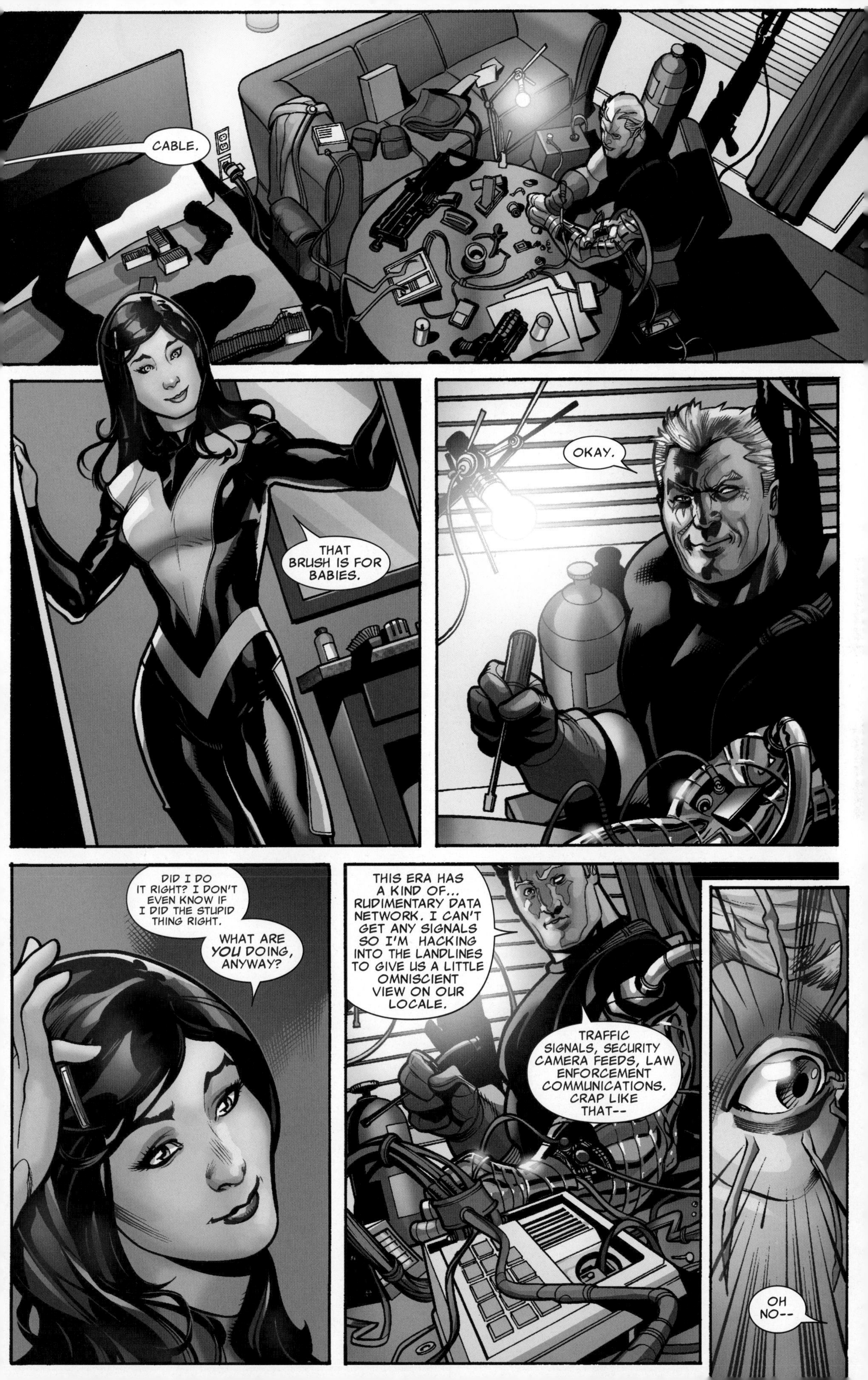
CABLE.
THAT BRUSH IS FOR BABIES.
OKAY.
DID I DO IT RIGHT? I DON'T EVEN KNOW IF I DID THE STUPID THING RIGHT.
WHAT ARE YOU DOING, ANYWAY?
THIS ERA HAS A KIND OF... RUDIMENTARY DATA NETWORK. I CAN'T GET ANY SIGNALS SO I'M HACKING INTO THE LANDLINES TO GIVE US A LITTLE OMNISCIENT VIEW ON OUR LOCALE.
TRAFFIC SIGNALS, SECURITY CAMERA FEEDS, LAW ENFORCEMENT COMMUNICATIONS. CRAP LIKE THAT--
OH NO--

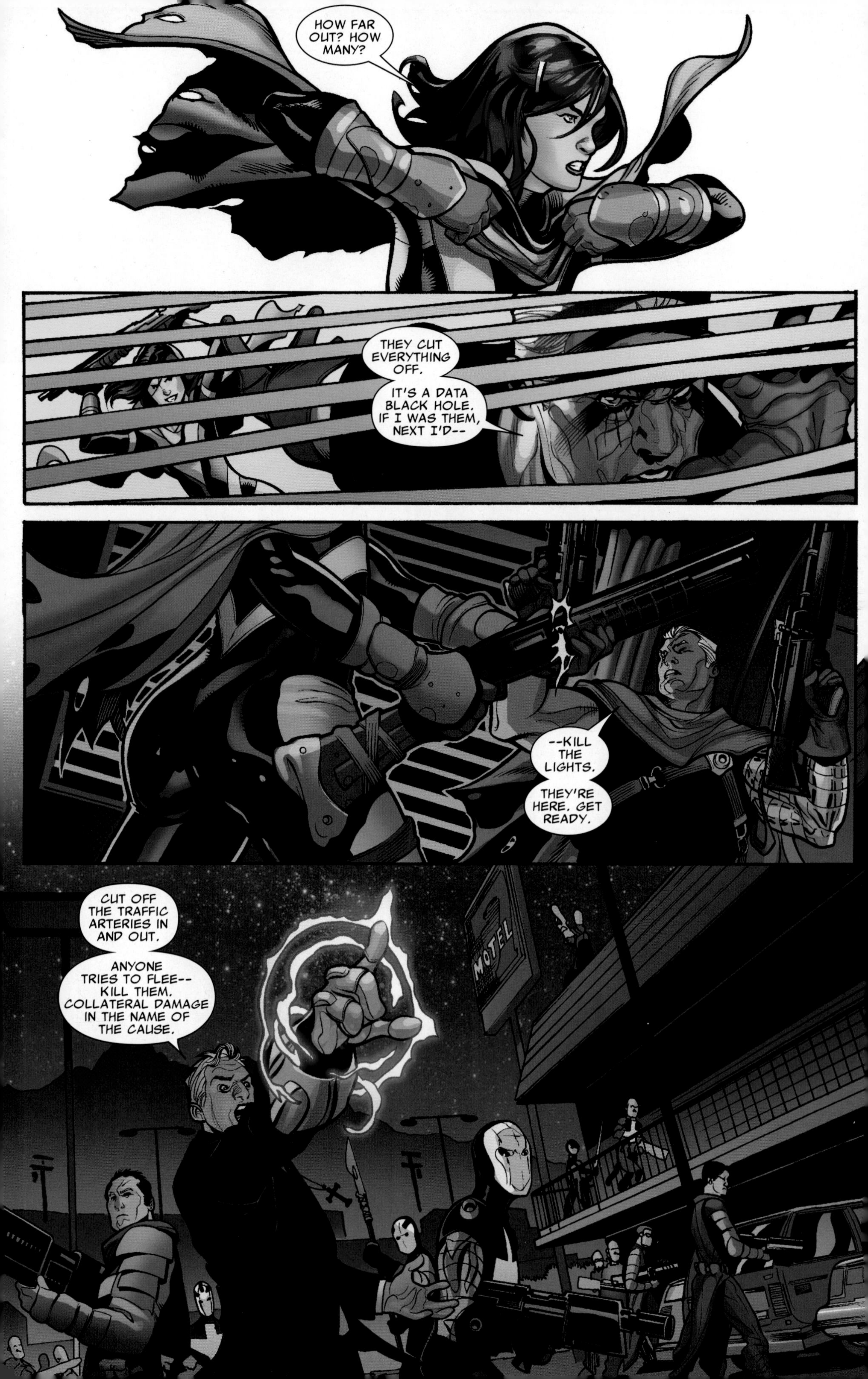
HOW FAR OUT? HOW MANY?
THEY CUT EVERYTHING OFF.
IT'S A DATA BLACK HOLE. IF I WAS THEM, NEXT I'D--
--KILL THE LIGHTS.
THEY'RE HERE. GET READY.
CUT OFF THE TRAFFIC ARTERIES IN AND OUT.
ANYONE TRIES TO FLEE--KILL THEM. COLLATERAL DAMAGE IN THE NAME OF THE CAUSE.
MOTEL

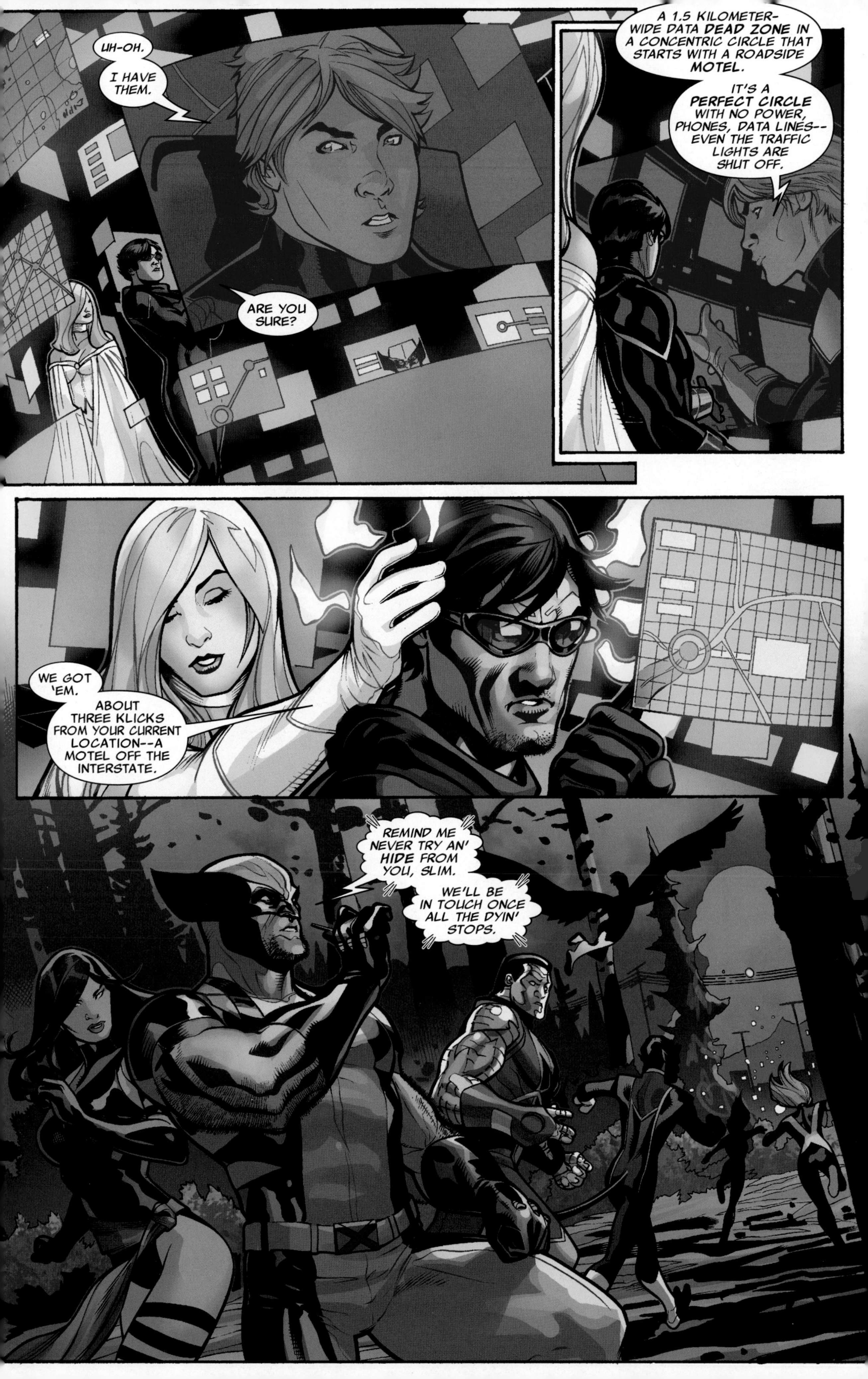
UH-OH.
I HAVE THEM.
ARE YOU SURE?
A 1.5 KILOMETER-WIDE DATA DEAD ZONE IN A CONCENTRIC CIRCLE THAT STARTS WITH A ROADSIDE MOTEL.
IT'S A PERFECT CIRCLE WITH NO POWER, PHONES, DATA LINES--EVEN THE TRAFFIC LIGHTS ARE SHUT OFF.
WE GOT 'EM.
ABOUT THREE KLICKS FROM YOUR CURRENT LOCATION--A MOTEL OFF THE INTERSTATE.
REMIND ME NEVER TRY AN' HIDE FROM YOU, SLIM.
WE'LL BE IN TOUCH ONCE ALL THE DYIN' STOPS.

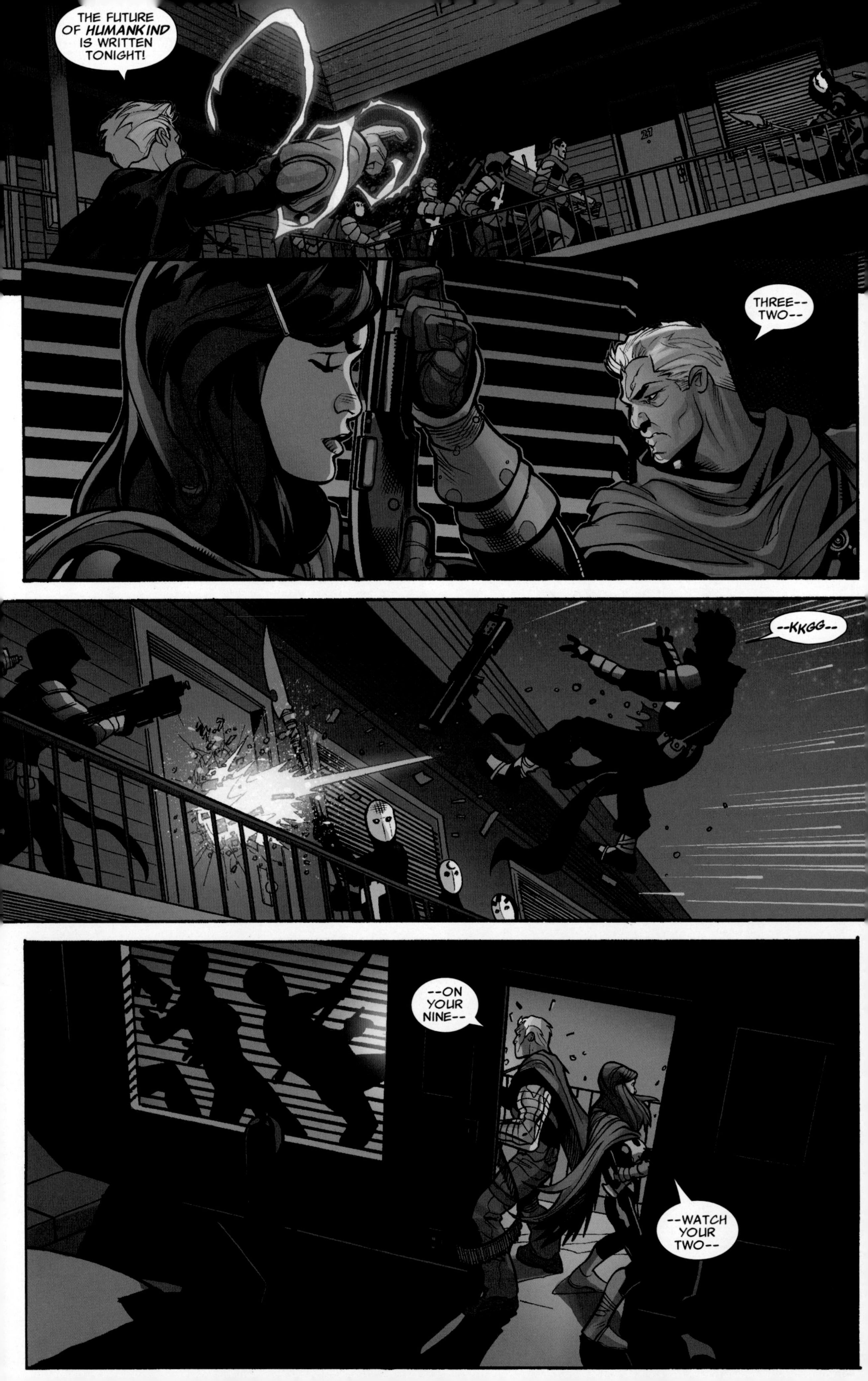
THE FUTURE OF HUMANKIND IS WRITTEN TONIGHT!
THREE-- TWO--
--KKGG--
--ON YOUR NINE--
--WATCH YOUR TWO--

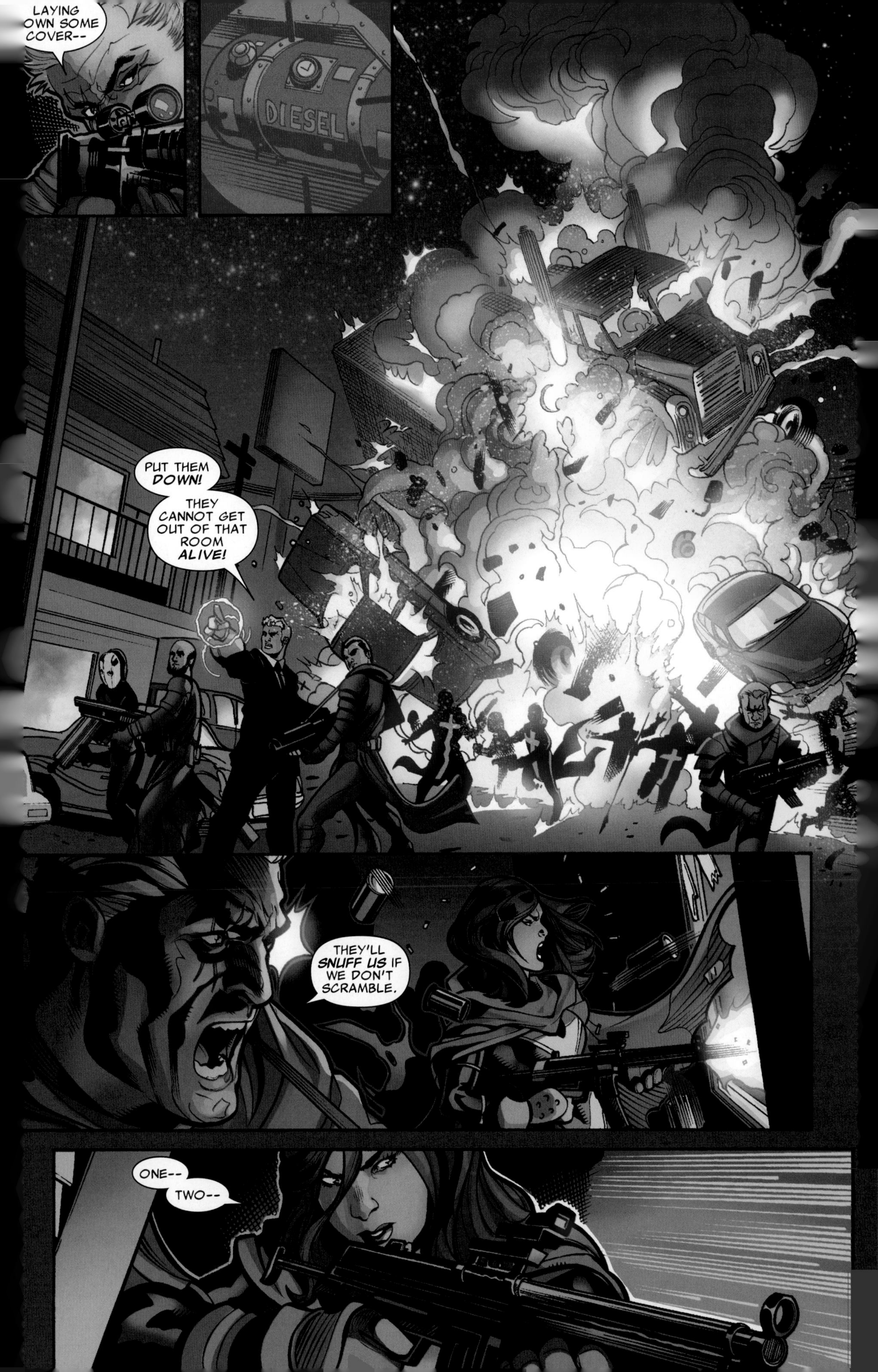
LAYING DOWN SOME COVER--
DIESEL
PUT THEM DOWN!
THEY CANNOT GET OUT OF THAT ROOM ALIVE!
THEY'LL SNUFF US IF WE DON'T SCRAMBLE.
ONE--
TWO--

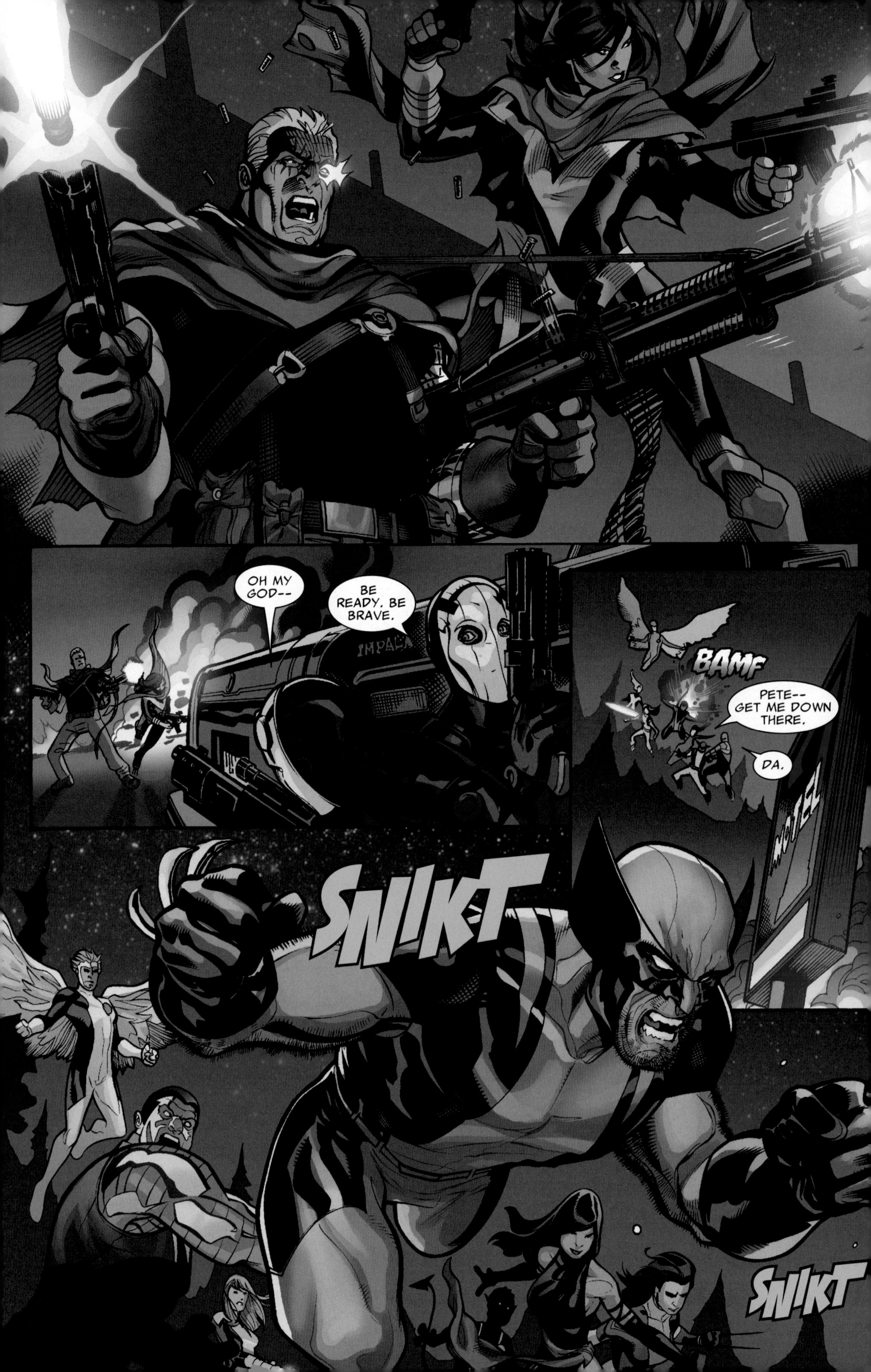
OH MY GOD--
BE READY. BE BRAVE.
IMPALA
BAMF
PETE-- GET ME DOWN THERE.
DA.
MOTEL
SNIKT
SNIKT

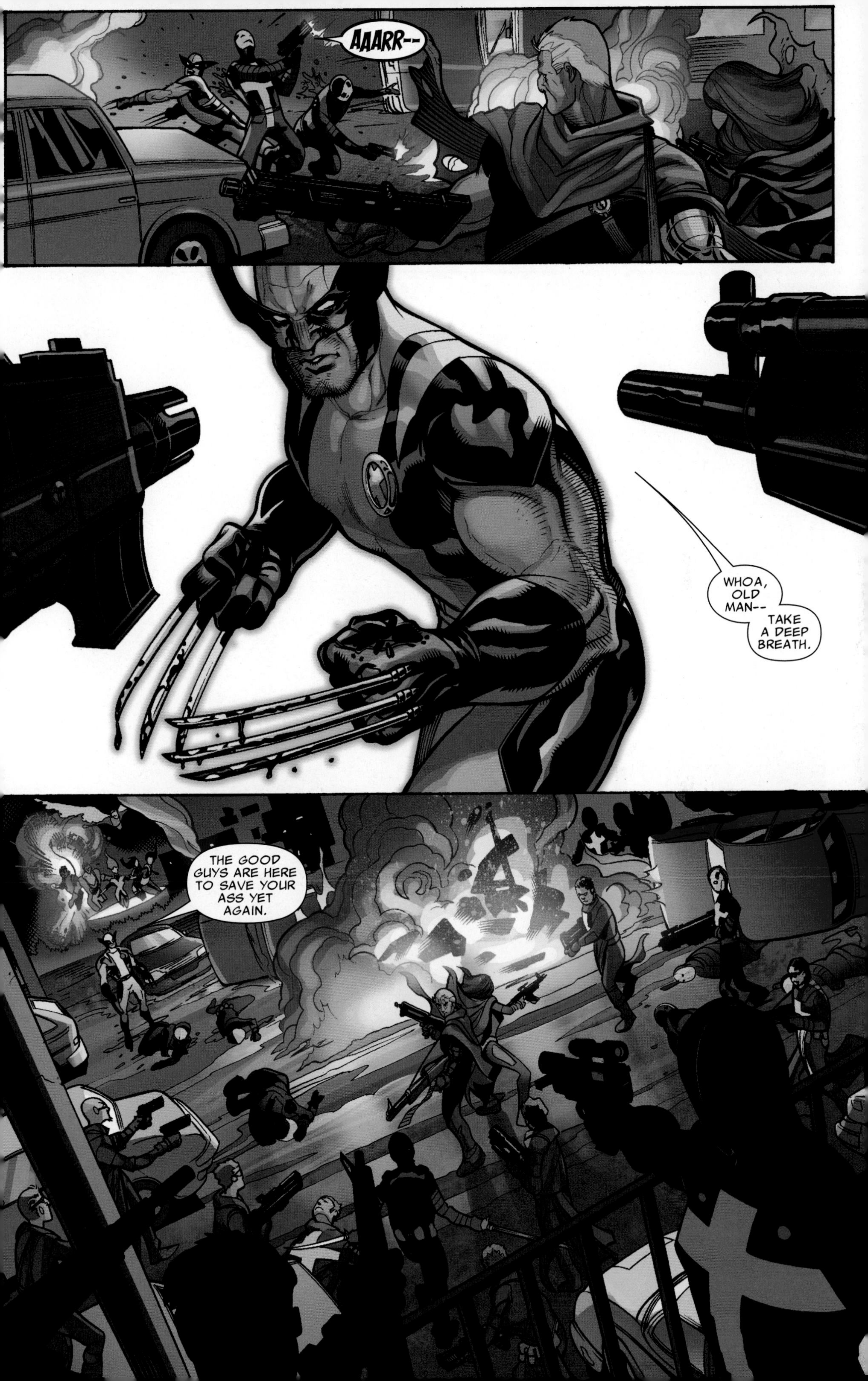
AAARR--
WHOA, OLD MAN-- TAKE A DEEP BREATH.
THE GOOD GUYS ARE HERE TO SAVE YOUR ASS YET AGAIN.

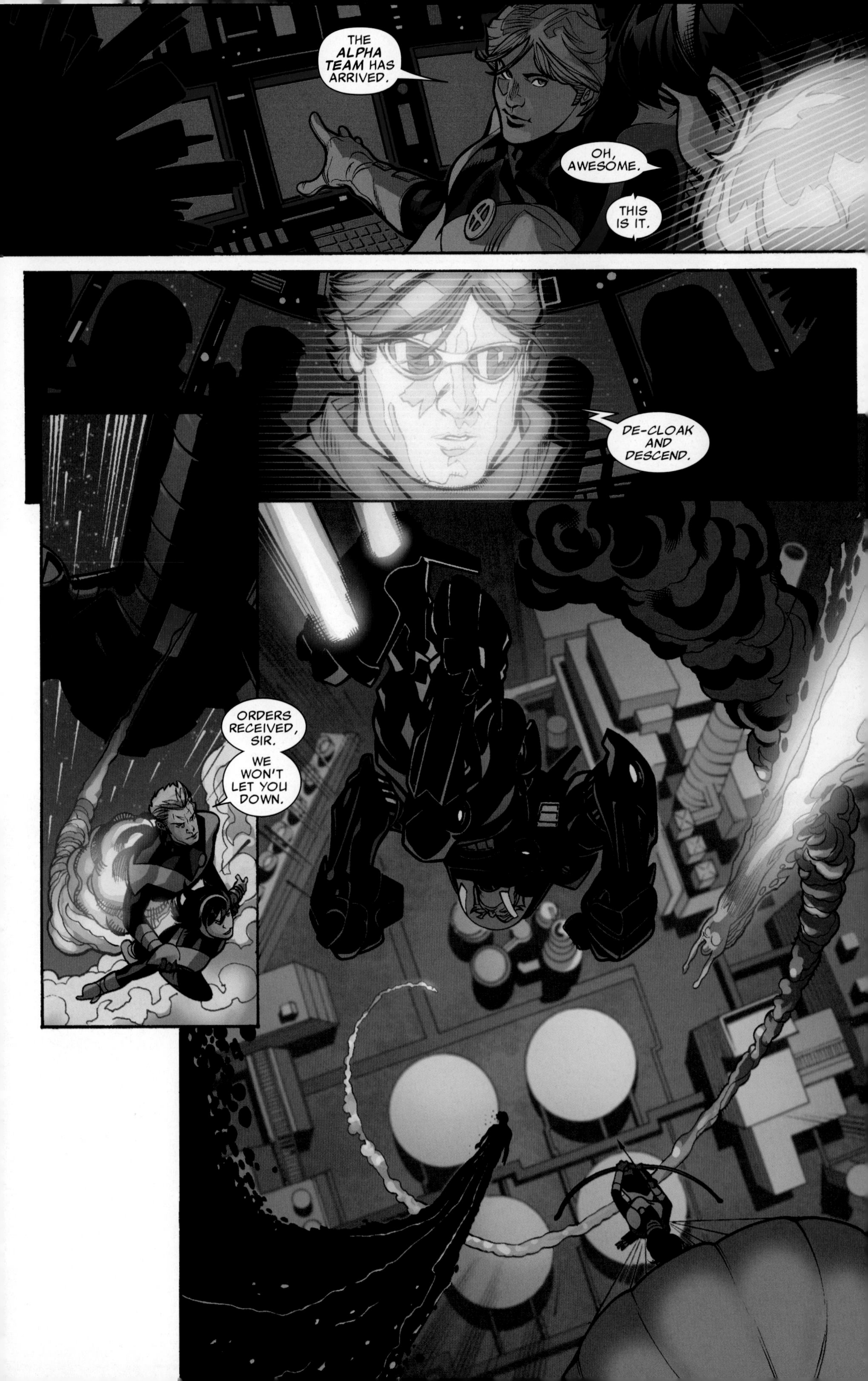
THE ALPHA TEAM HAS ARRIVED.
OH, AWESOME.
THIS IS IT.
DE-CLOAK AND DESCEND.
ORDERS RECEIVED, SIR.
WE WON'T LET YOU DOWN.

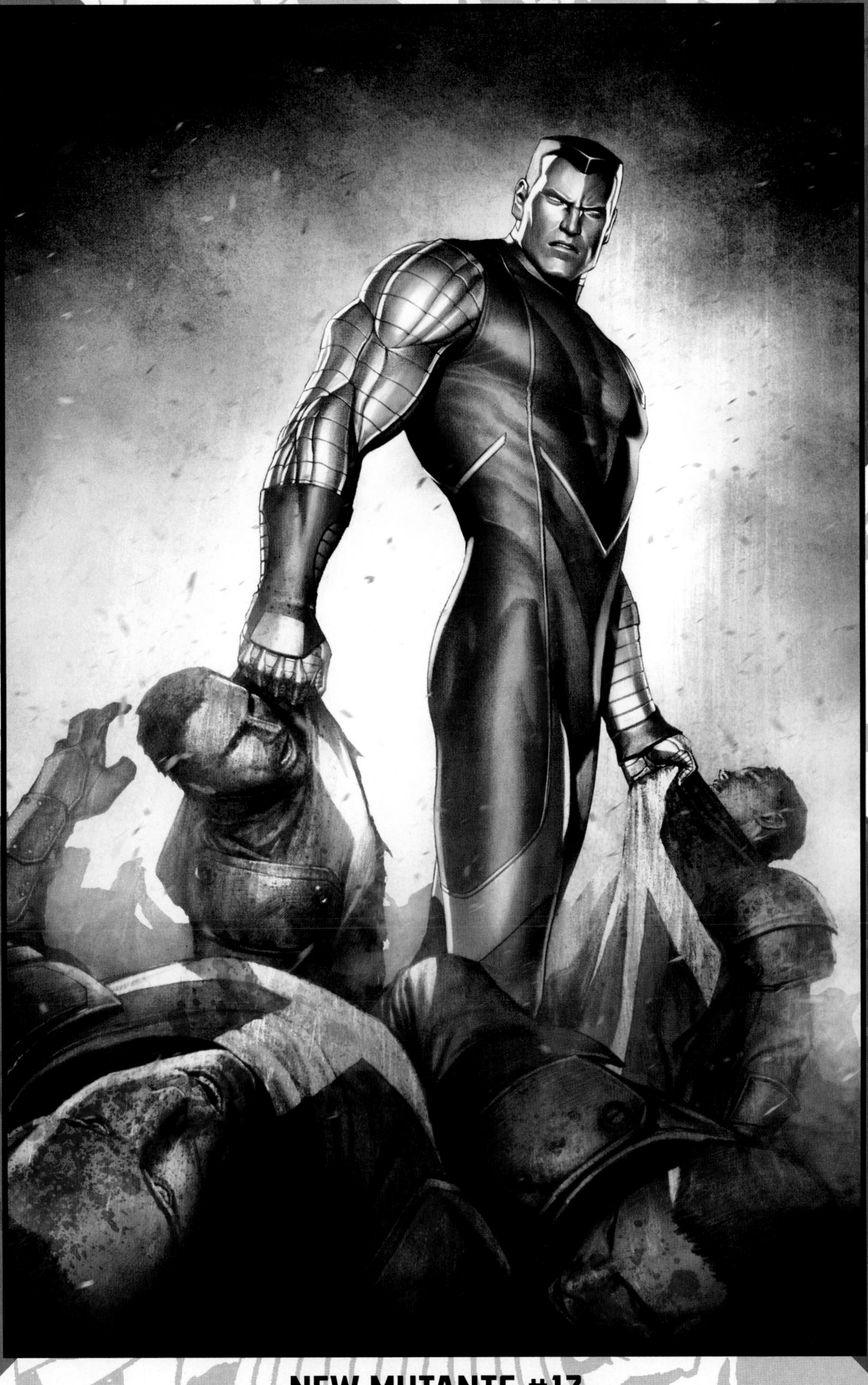

NEW MUTANTS #12

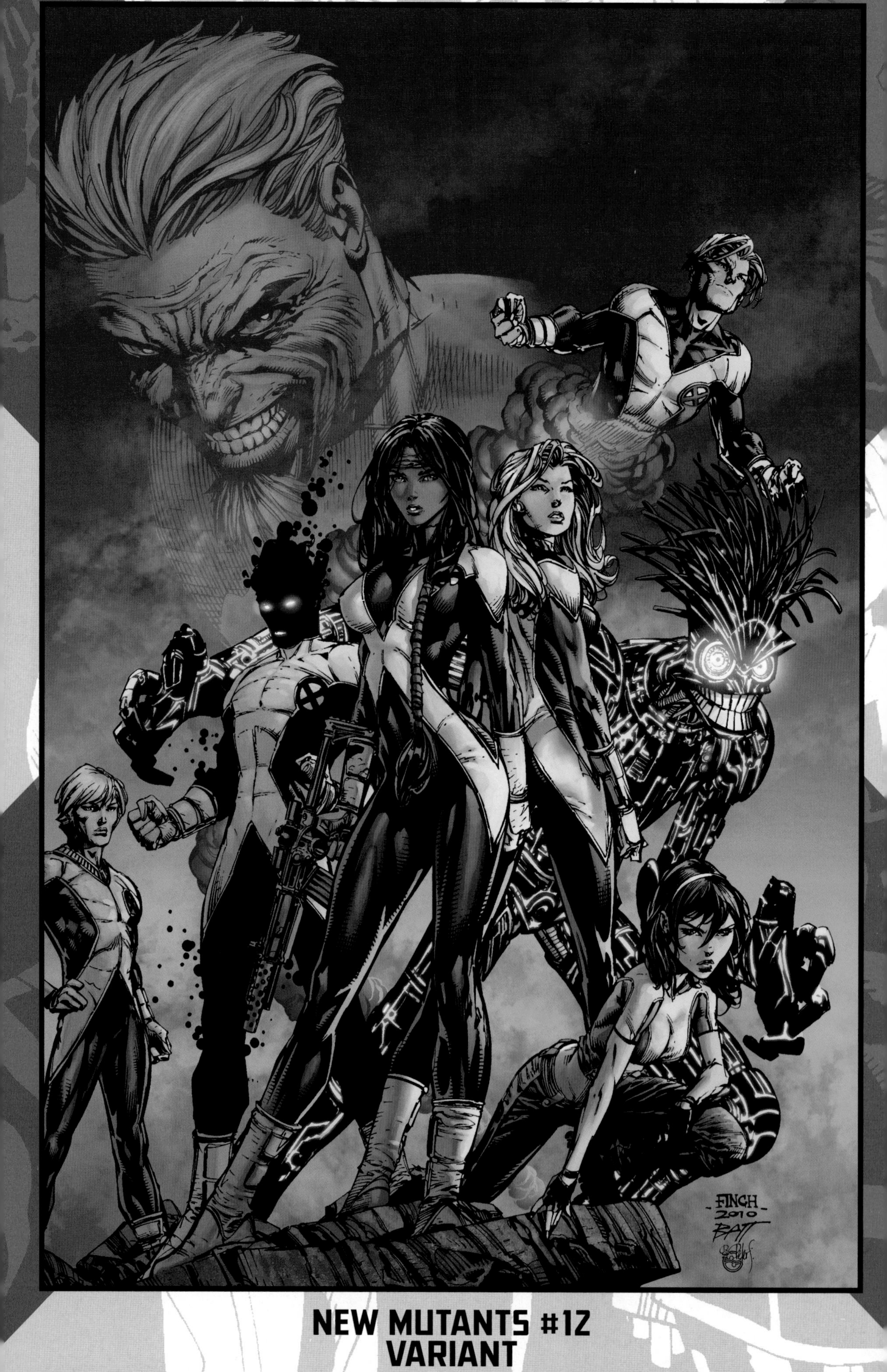
FINCH
2010
BATT

NEW MUTANTS #12
VARIANT

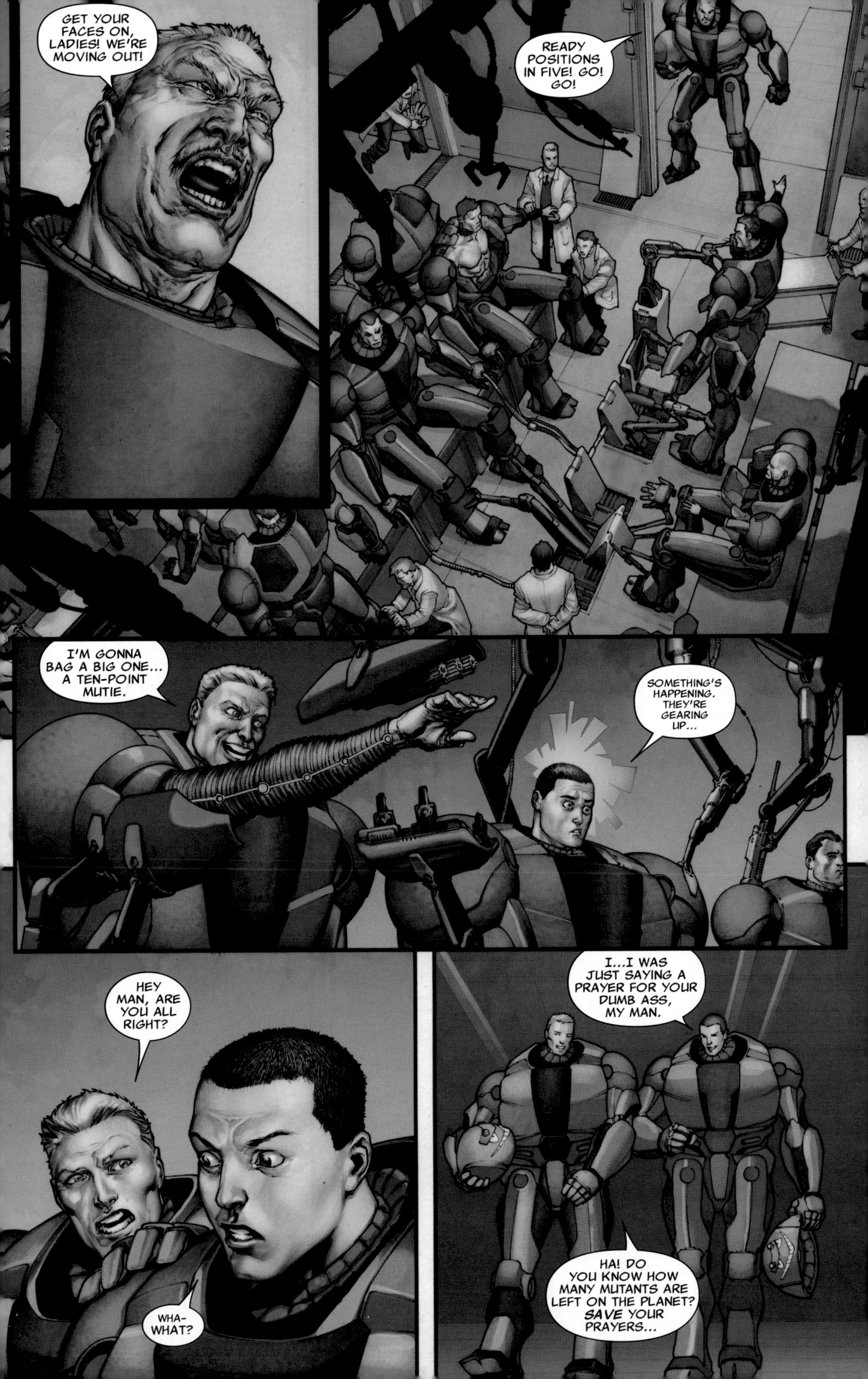
GET YOUR FACES ON, LADIES! WE'RE MOVING OUT!
READY POSITIONS IN FIVE! GO! GO!
I'M GONNA BAG A BIG ONE... A TEN-POINT MUTIE.
SOMETHING'S HAPPENING. THEY'RE GEARING UP...
HEY MAN, ARE YOU ALL RIGHT?
WHA-WHAT?
I...I WAS JUST SAYING A PRAYER FOR YOUR DUMB ASS, MY MAN.
HA! DO YOU KNOW HOW MANY MUTANTS ARE LEFT ON THE PLANET? SAVE YOUR PRAYERS...

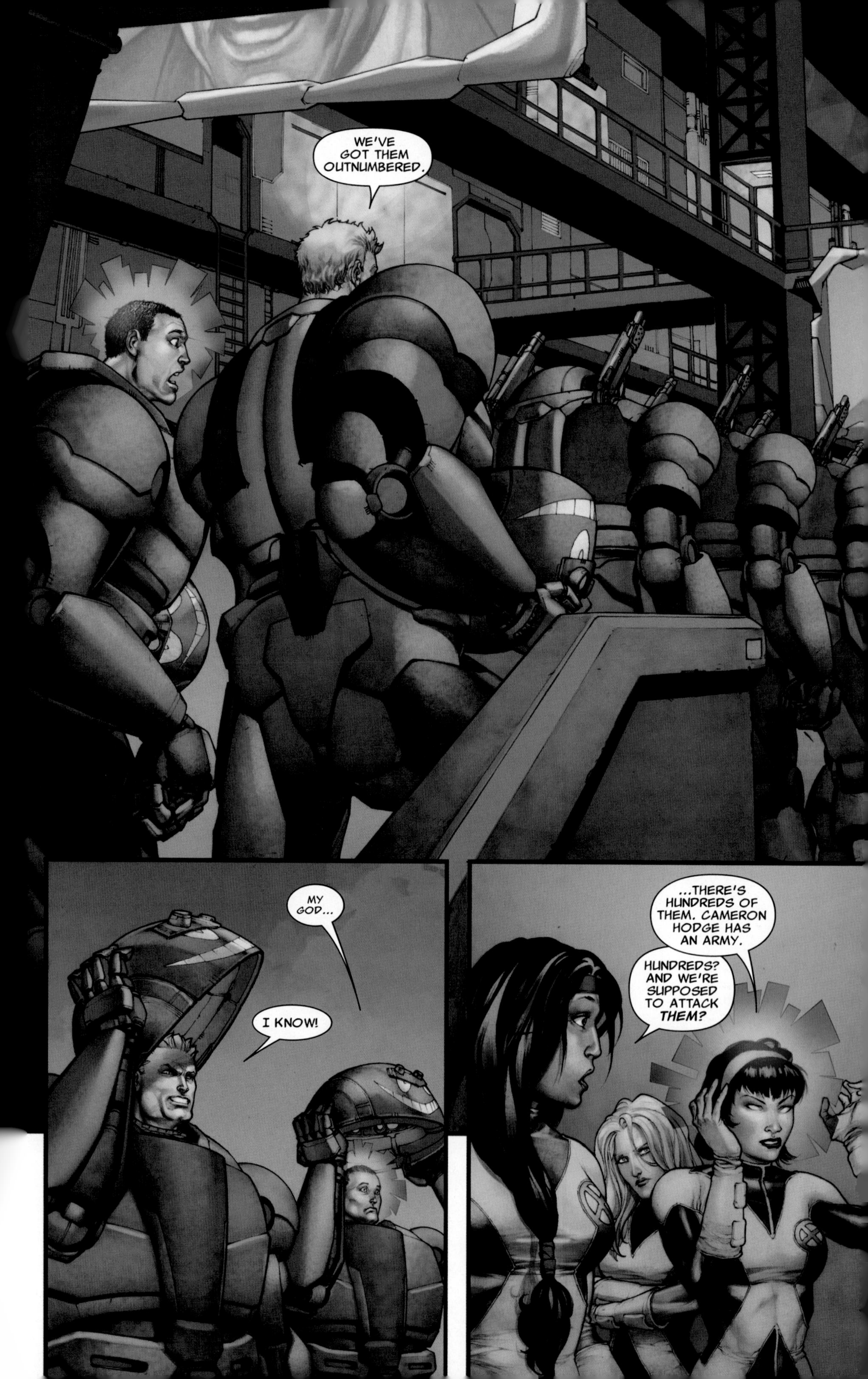
WE'VE GOT THEM OUTNUMBERED.
MY GOD...
I KNOW!
...THERE'S HUNDREDS OF THEM. CAMERON HODGE HAS AN ARMY.
HUNDREDS? AND WE'RE SUPPOSED TO ATTACK *THEM*?

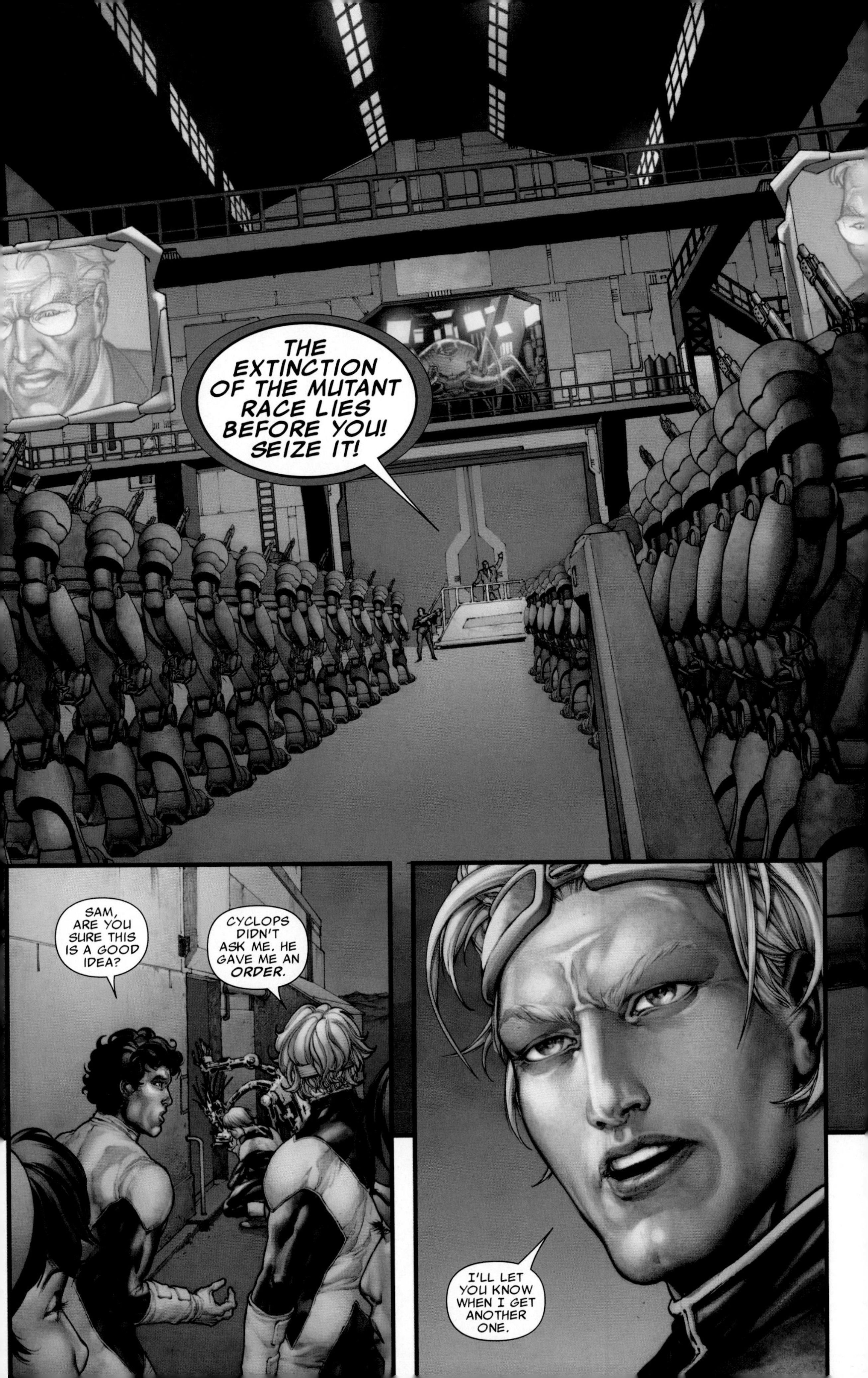
THE EXTINCTION OF THE MUTANT RACE LIES BEFORE YOU! SEIZE IT!
SAM, ARE YOU SURE THIS IS A GOOD IDEA?
CYCLOPS DIDN'T ASK ME. HE GAVE ME AN ORDER.
I'LL LET YOU KNOW WHEN I GET ANOTHER ONE.

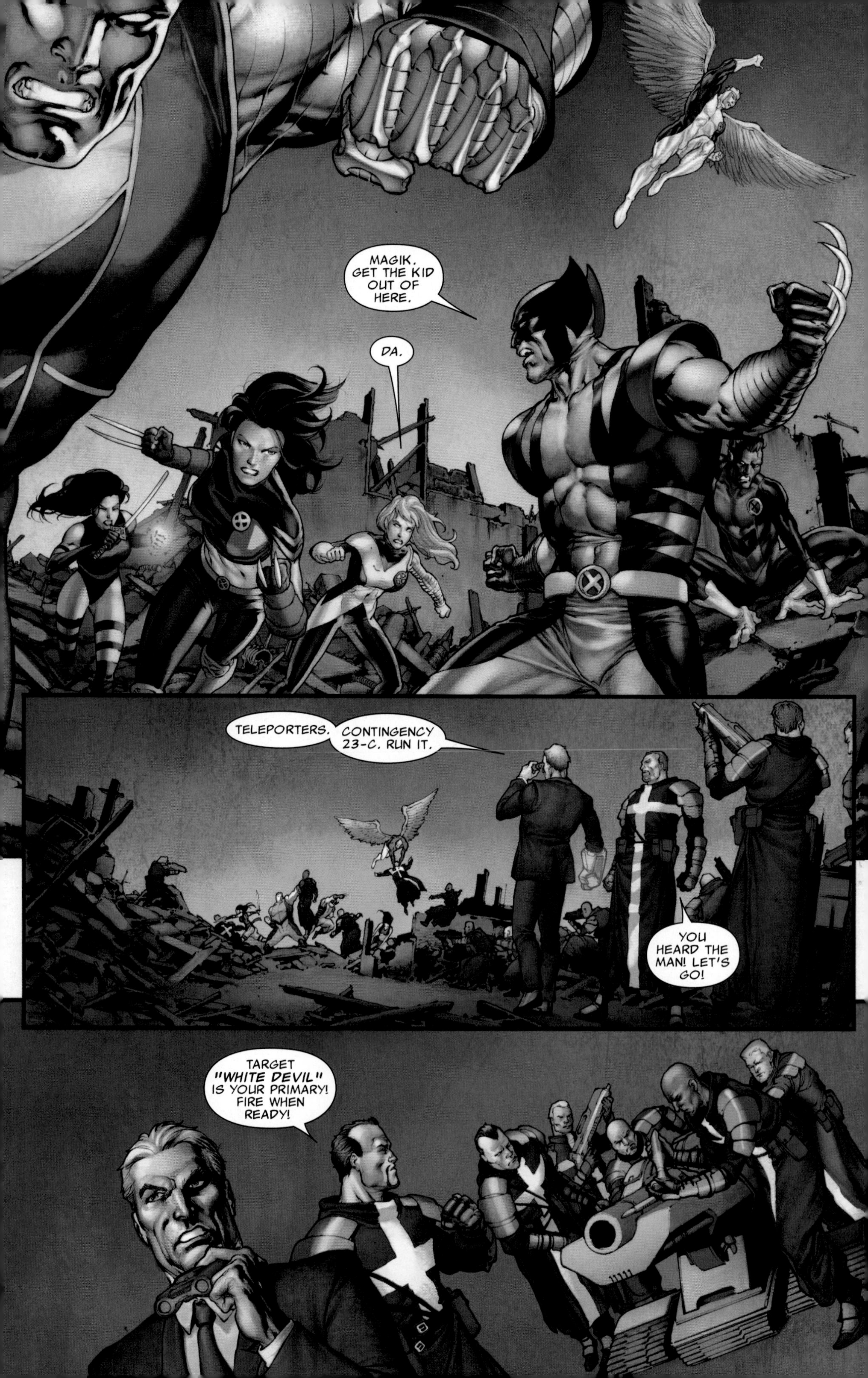
MAGIK. GET THE KID OUT OF HERE.
DA.
TELEPORTERS.
CONTINGENCY 23-C. RUN IT.
YOU HEARD THE MAN! LET'S GO!
TARGET "WHITE DEVIL" IS YOUR PRIMARY! FIRE WHEN READY!

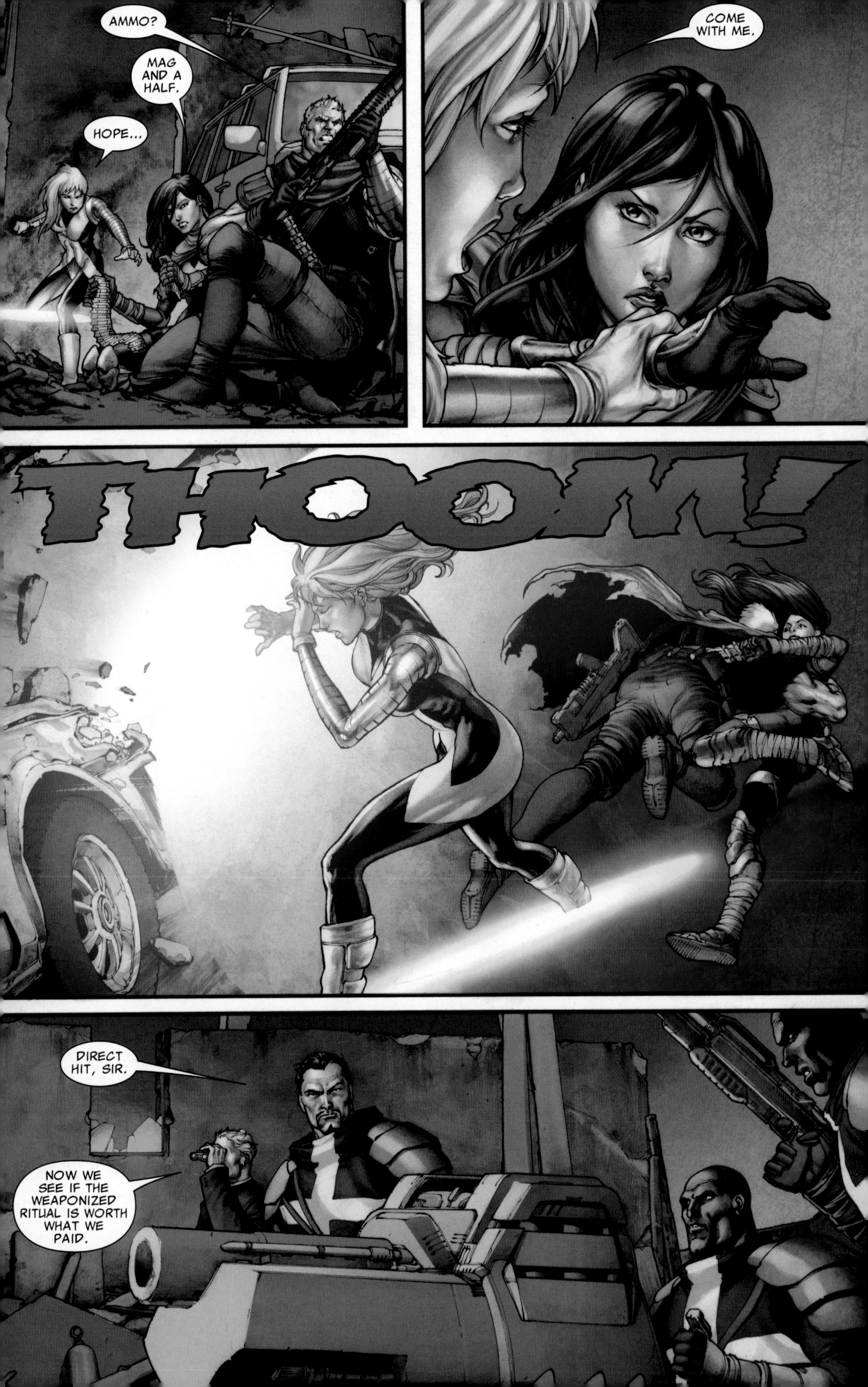
AMMO?
MAG AND A HALF.
HOPE...
COME WITH ME.
THOOM!
DIRECT HIT, SIR.
NOW WE SEE IF THE WEAPONIZED RITUAL IS WORTH WHAT WE PAID.

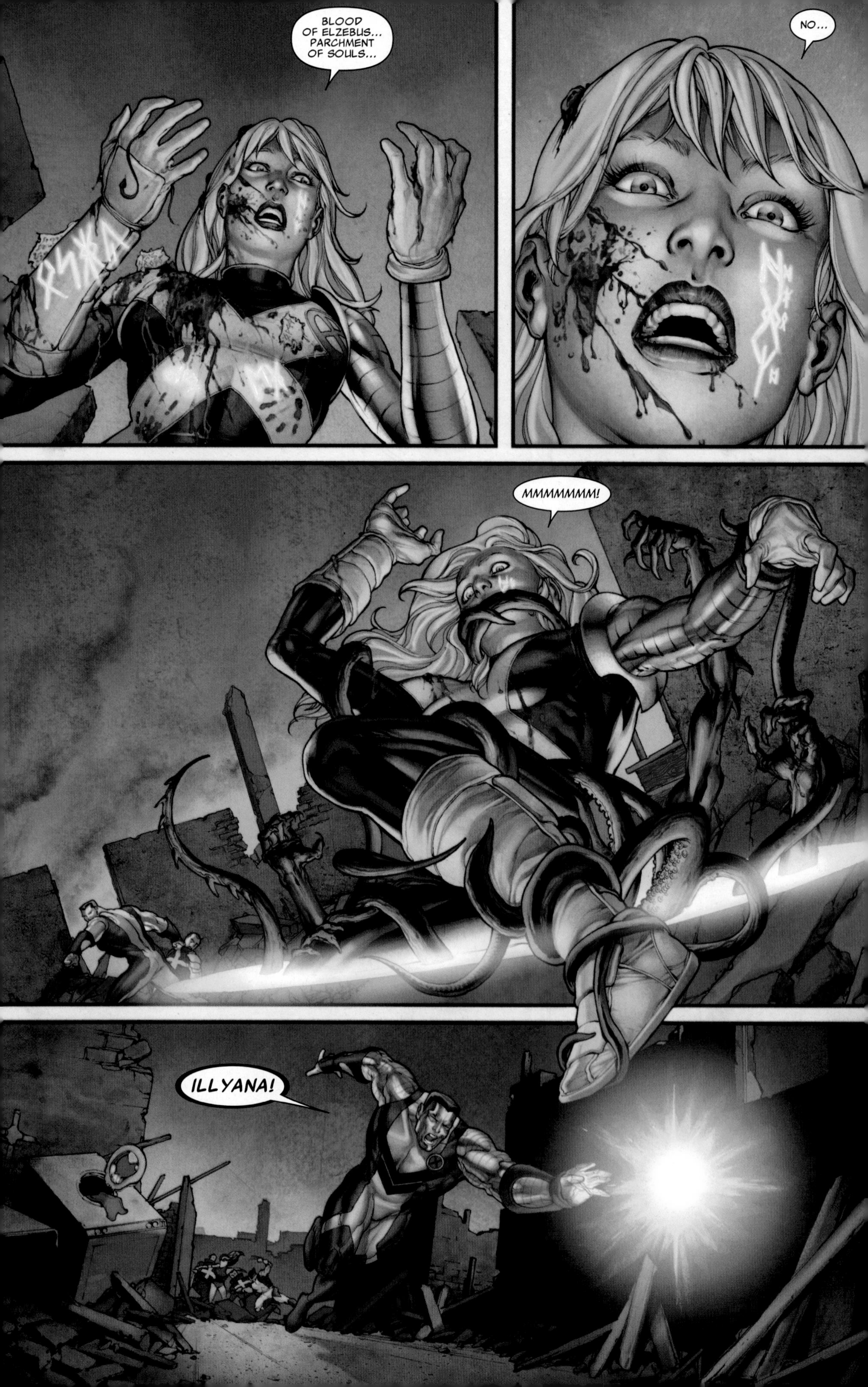
BLOOD OF ELZEBUS... PARCHMENT OF SOULS...
NO...
MMMMMMM!
ILLYANA!

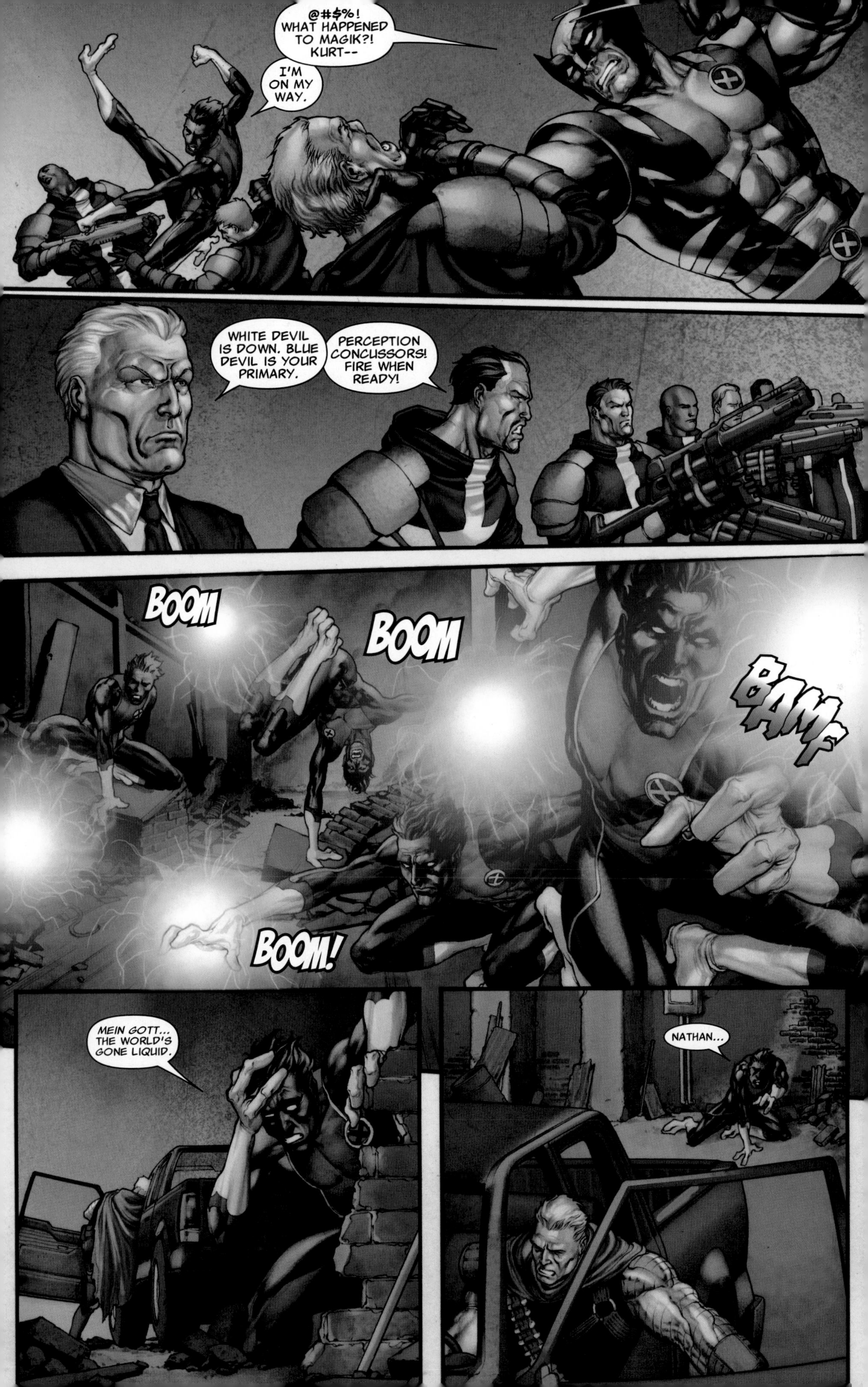
@#$%! WHAT HAPPENED TO MAGIK?! KURT--
I'M ON MY WAY.
WHITE DEVIL IS DOWN. BLUE DEVIL IS YOUR PRIMARY.
PERCEPTION CONCUSSORS! FIRE WHEN READY!
BOOM
BOOM
BAMF
BOOM!
MEIN GOTT... THE WORLD'S GONE LIQUID.
NATHAN...

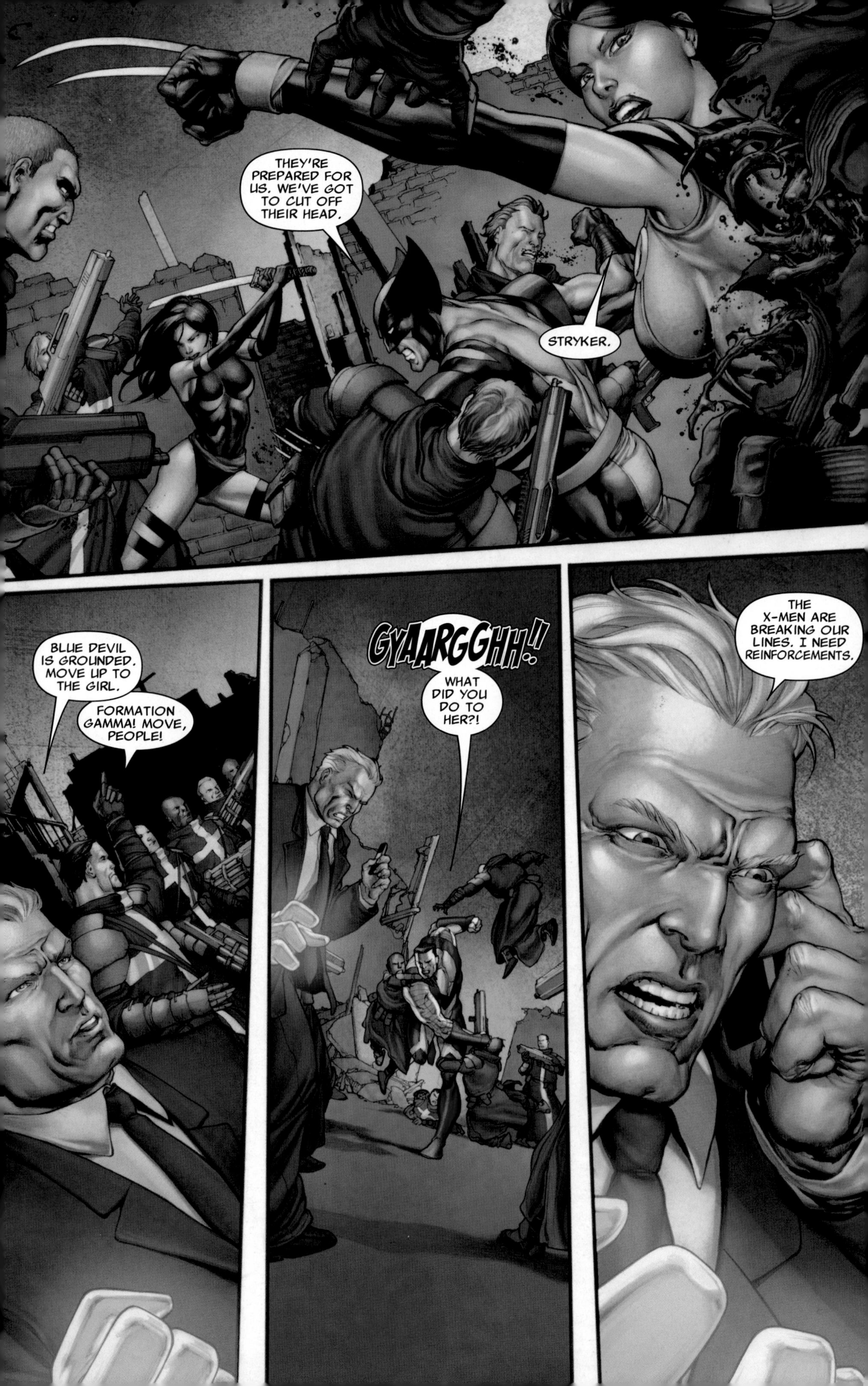
THEY'RE PREPARED FOR US. WE'VE GOT TO CUT OFF THEIR HEAD.
STRYKER.
BLUE DEVIL IS GROUNDED. MOVE UP TO THE GIRL.
FORMATION GAMMA! MOVE, PEOPLE!
GYAARGGHH!!
WHAT DID YOU DO TO HER?!
THE X-MEN ARE BREAKING OUR LINES. I NEED REINFORCEMENTS.

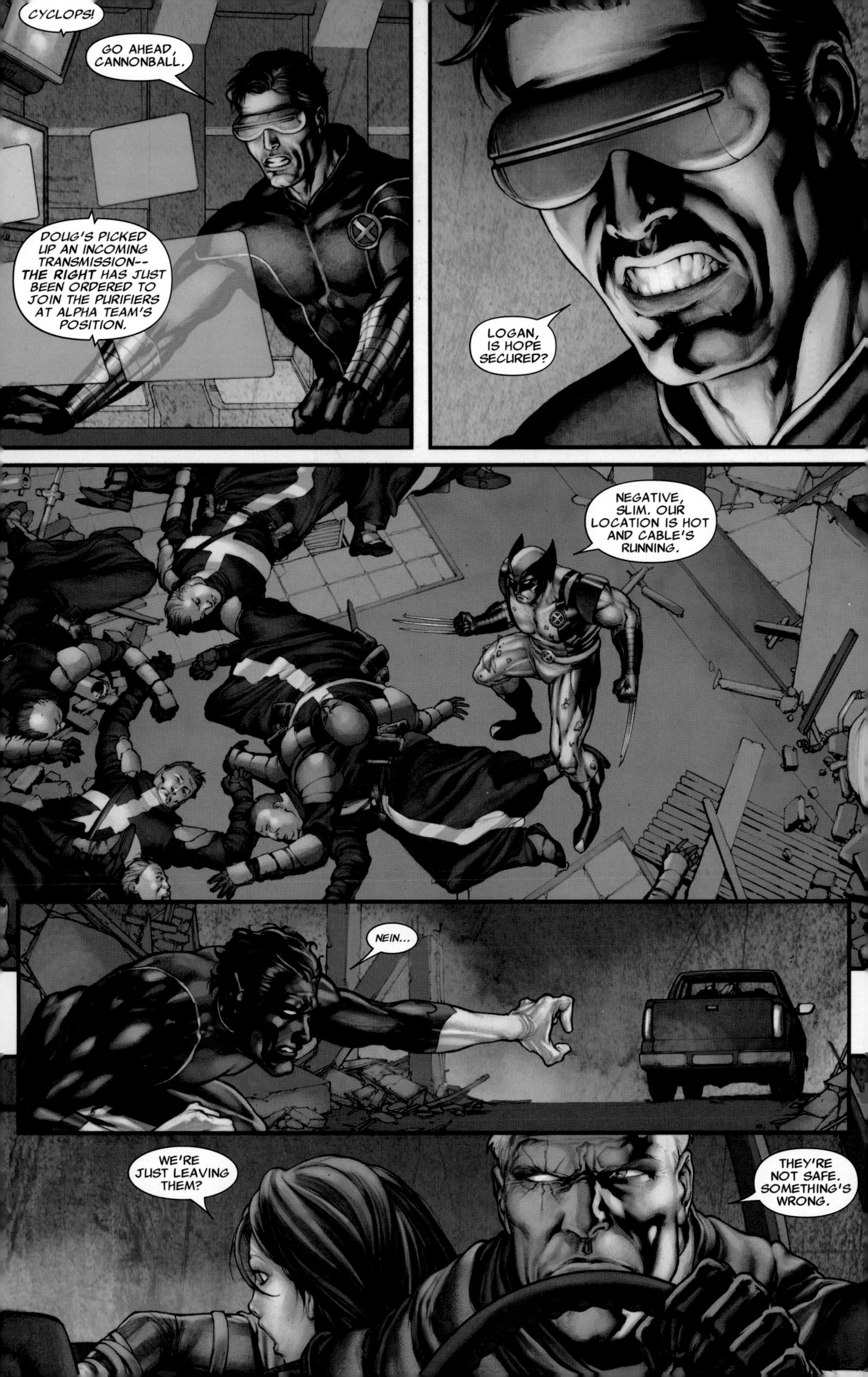
CYCLOPS!
GO AHEAD, CANNONBALL.
DOUG'S PICKED UP AN INCOMING TRANSMISSION-- THE RIGHT HAS JUST BEEN ORDERED TO JOIN THE PURIFIERS AT ALPHA TEAM'S POSITION.
LOGAN, IS HOPE SECURED?
NEGATIVE, SLIM. OUR LOCATION IS HOT AND CABLE'S RUNNING.
NEIN...
WE'RE JUST LEAVING THEM?
THEY'RE NOT SAFE. SOMETHING'S WRONG.

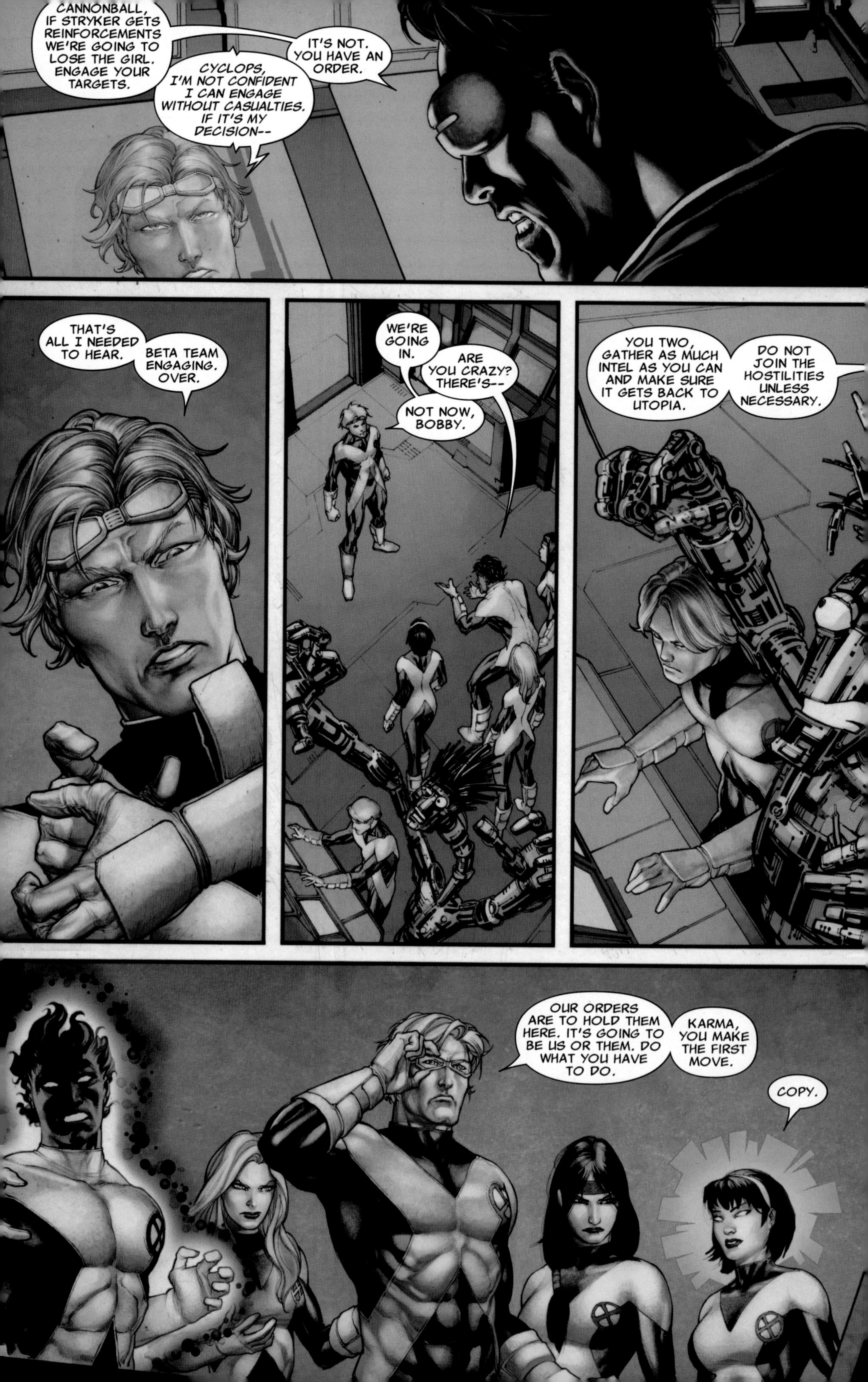
CANNONBALL, IF STRYKER GETS REINFORCEMENTS WE'RE GOING TO LOSE THE GIRL. ENGAGE YOUR TARGETS.
CYCLOPS, I'M NOT CONFIDENT I CAN ENGAGE WITHOUT CASUALTIES. IF IT'S MY DECISION--
IT'S NOT. YOU HAVE AN ORDER.
THAT'S ALL I NEEDED TO HEAR.
BETA TEAM ENGAGING. OVER.
WE'RE GOING IN.
ARE YOU CRAZY? THERE'S--
NOT NOW, BOBBY.
YOU TWO, GATHER AS MUCH INTEL AS YOU CAN AND MAKE SURE IT GETS BACK TO UTOPIA.
DO NOT JOIN THE HOSTILITIES UNLESS NECESSARY.
OUR ORDERS ARE TO HOLD THEM HERE. IT'S GOING TO BE US OR THEM. DO WHAT YOU HAVE TO DO.
KARMA, YOU MAKE THE FIRST MOVE.
COPY.

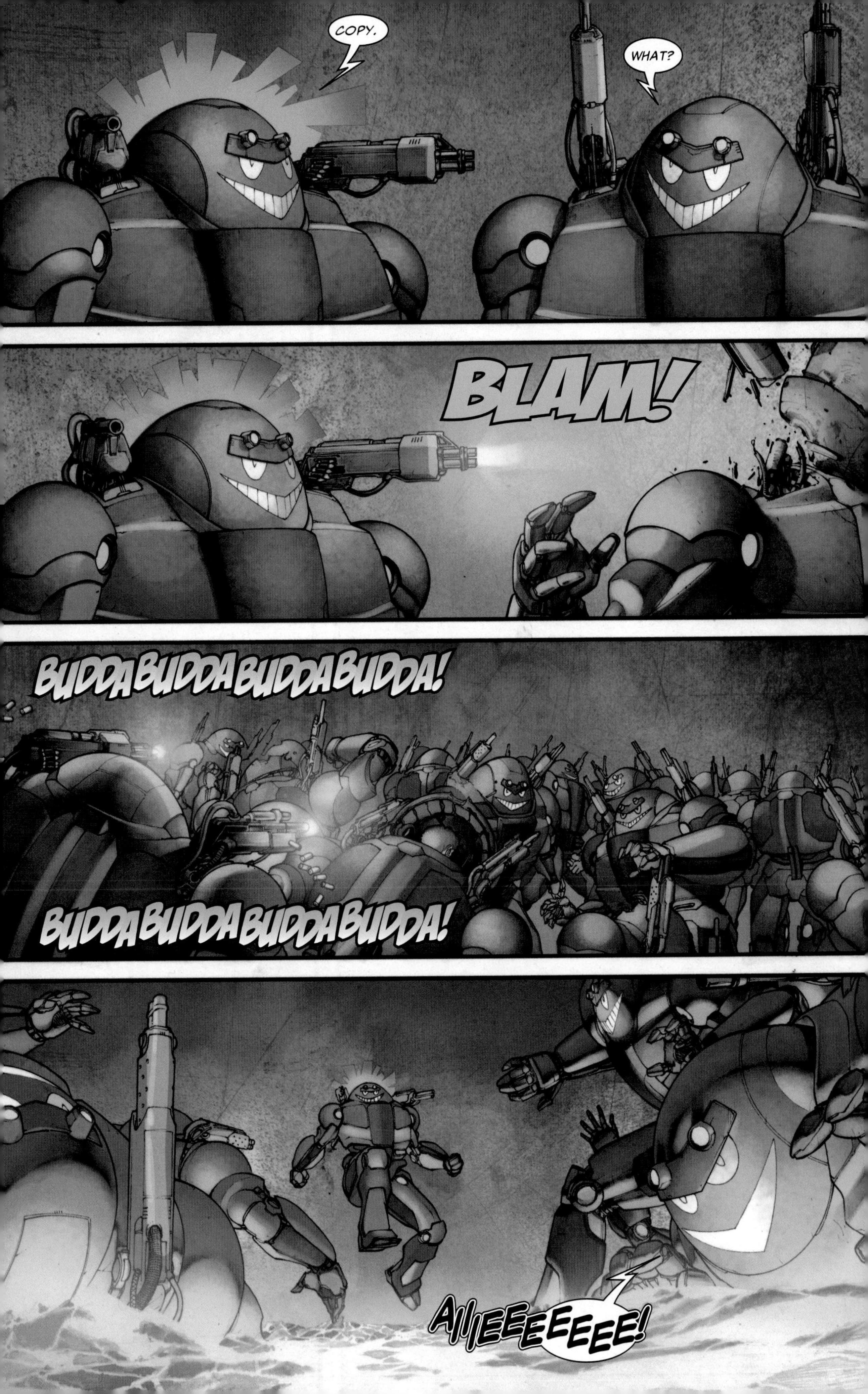
COPY.
WHAT?
BLAM!
BUDDA BUDDA BUDDA BUDDA!
BUDDA BUDDA BUDDA BUDDA!
AIIIEEEEEEEE!

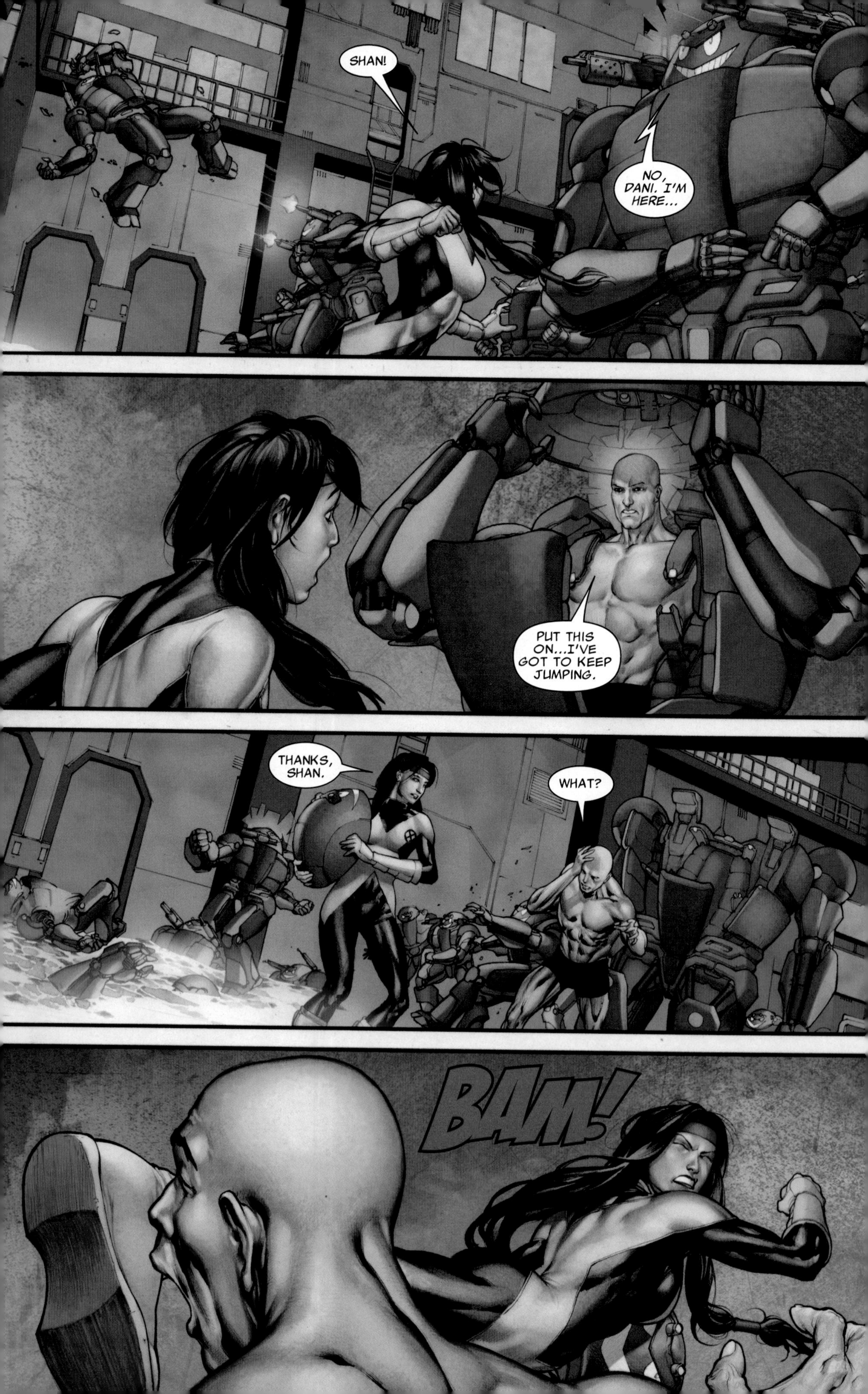
SHAN!
NO, DANI. I'M HERE...
PUT THIS ON...I'VE GOT TO KEEP JUMPING.
THANKS, SHAN.
WHAT?
BAM!

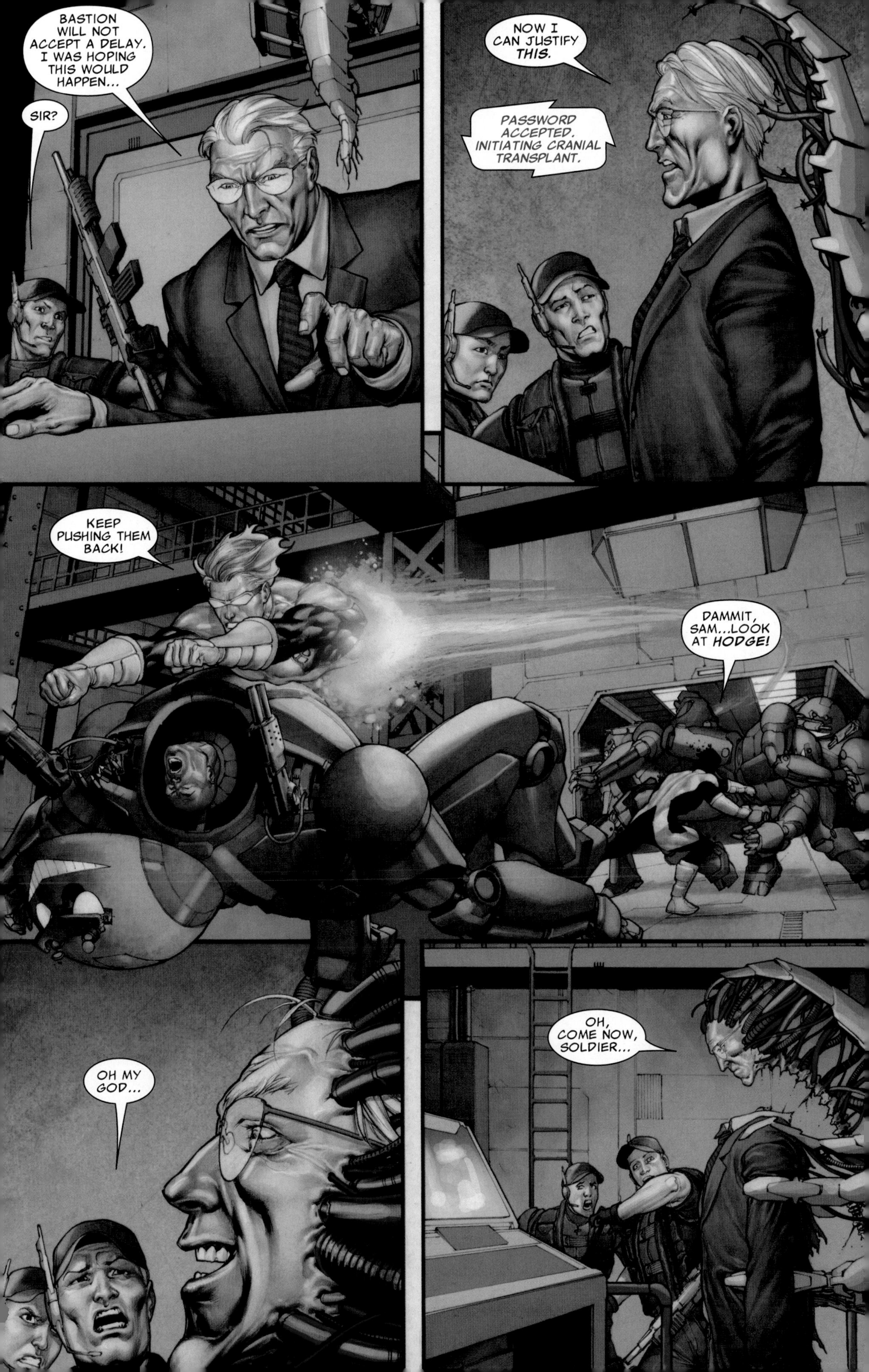
BASTION WILL NOT ACCEPT A DELAY. I WAS HOPING THIS WOULD HAPPEN...
SIR?
NOW I CAN JUSTIFY THIS.
PASSWORD ACCEPTED. INITIATING CRANIAL TRANSPLANT.
KEEP PUSHING THEM BACK!
DAMMIT, SAM...LOOK AT HODGE!
OH MY GOD...
OH, COME NOW, SOLDIER...

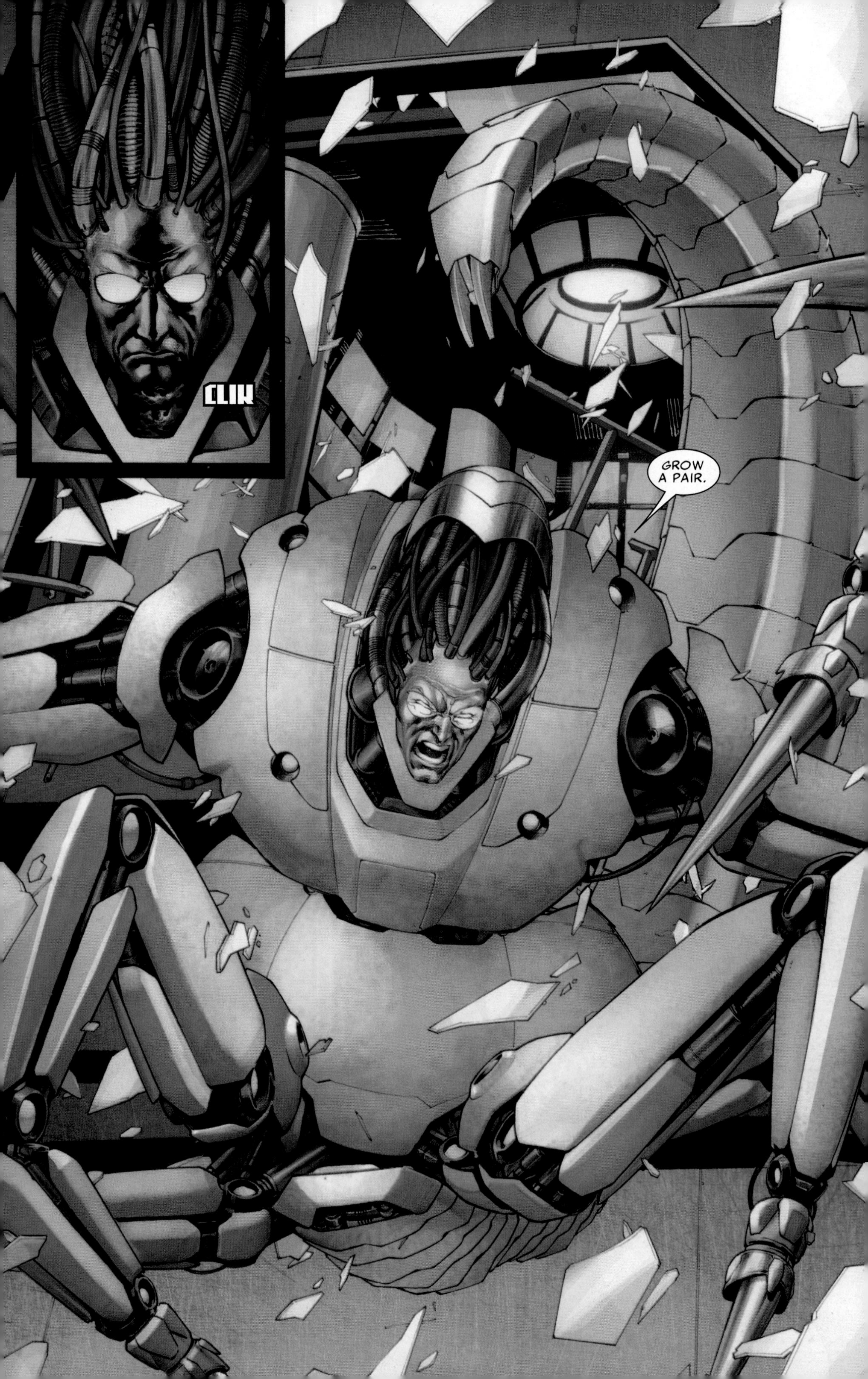
CLIK
GROW A PAIR.

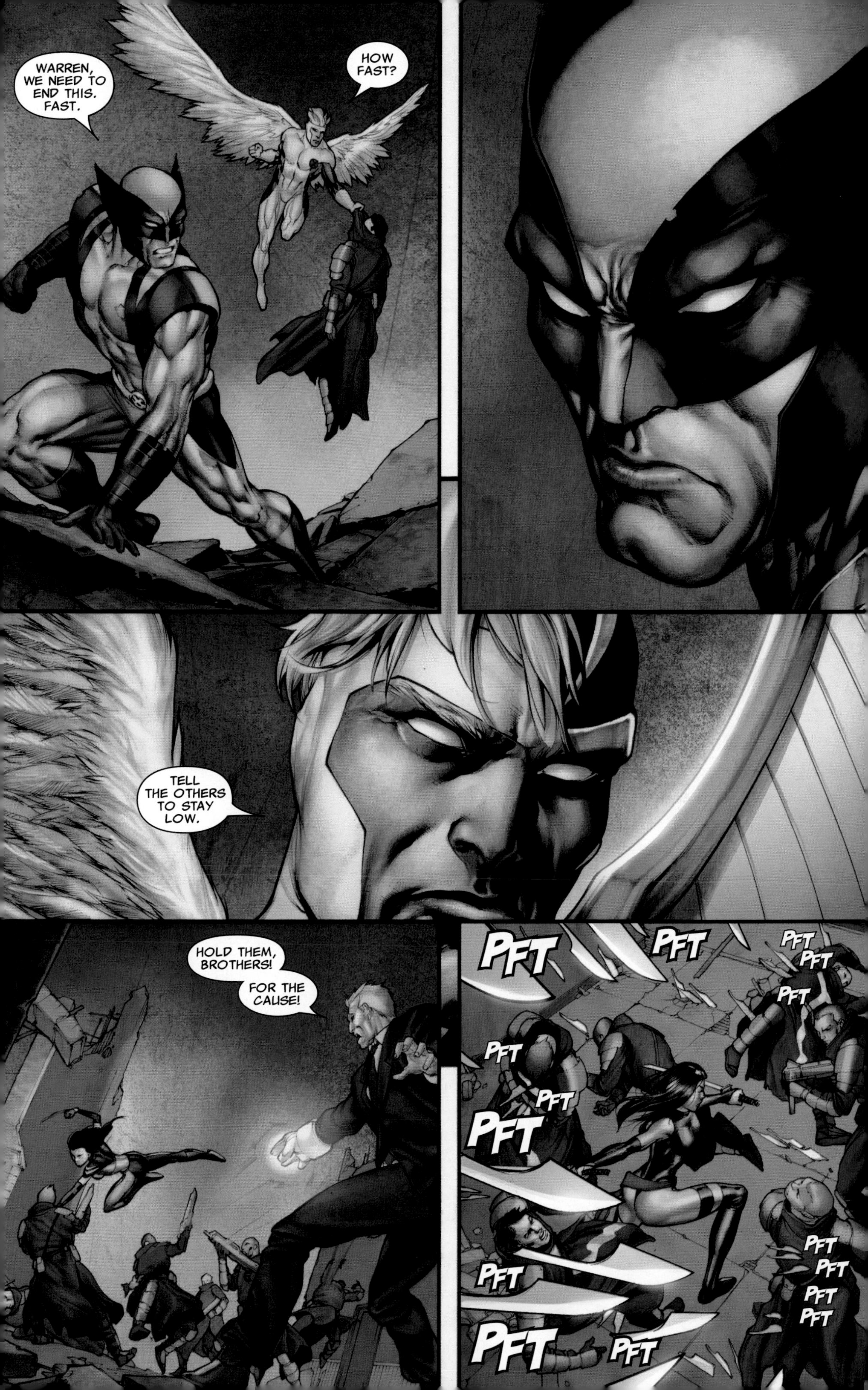
WARREN, WE NEED TO END THIS. FAST.
HOW FAST?
TELL THE OTHERS TO STAY LOW.
HOLD THEM, BROTHERS!
FOR THE CAUSE!
PFT
PFT
PFT
PFT
PFT
PFT
PFT
PFT
PFT
PFT
PFT
PFT
PFT
PFT
PFT

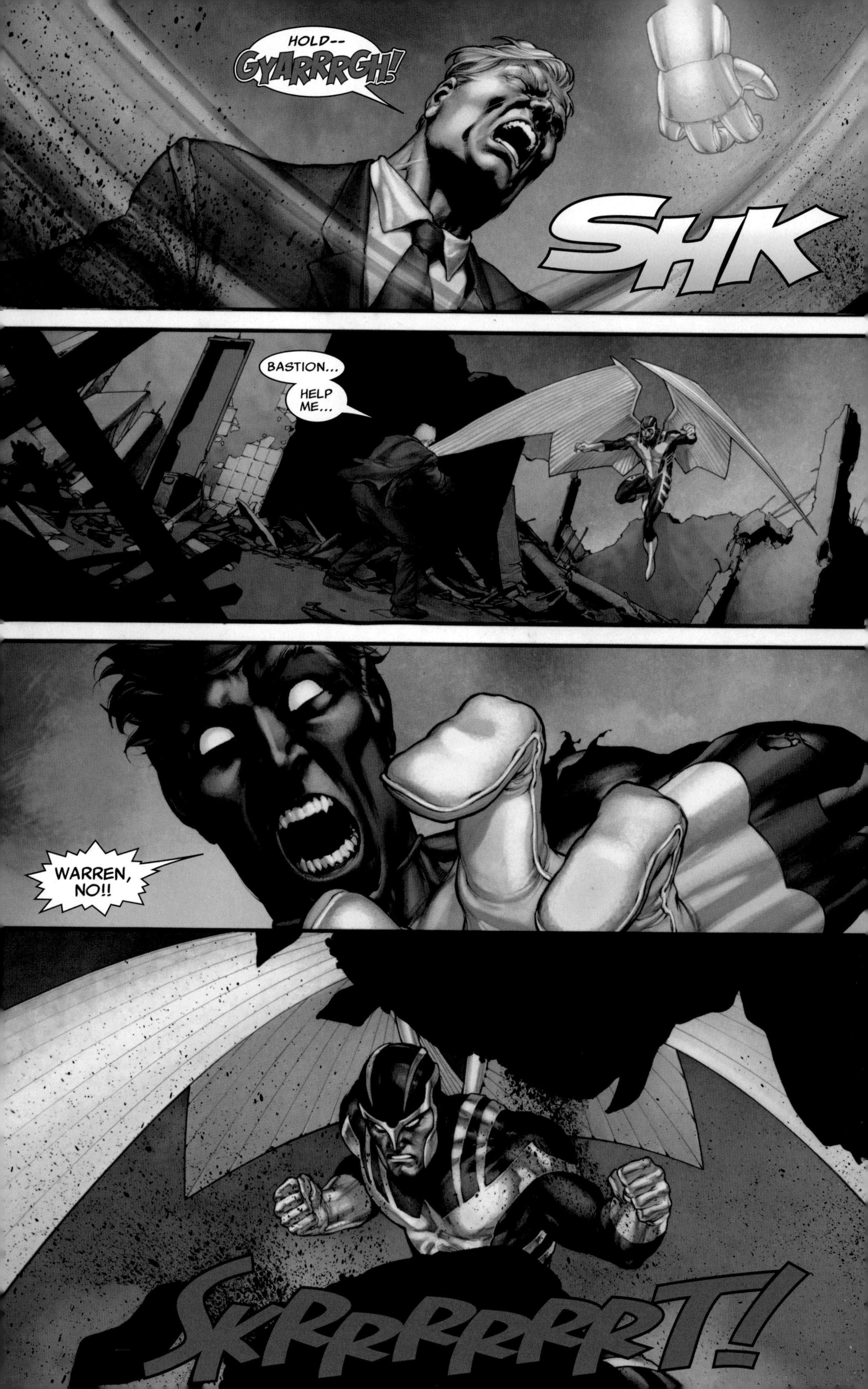
HOLD--
GYARRRGH!
SHK
BASTION... HELP ME...
WARREN, NO!!
SKRRRRRRT!

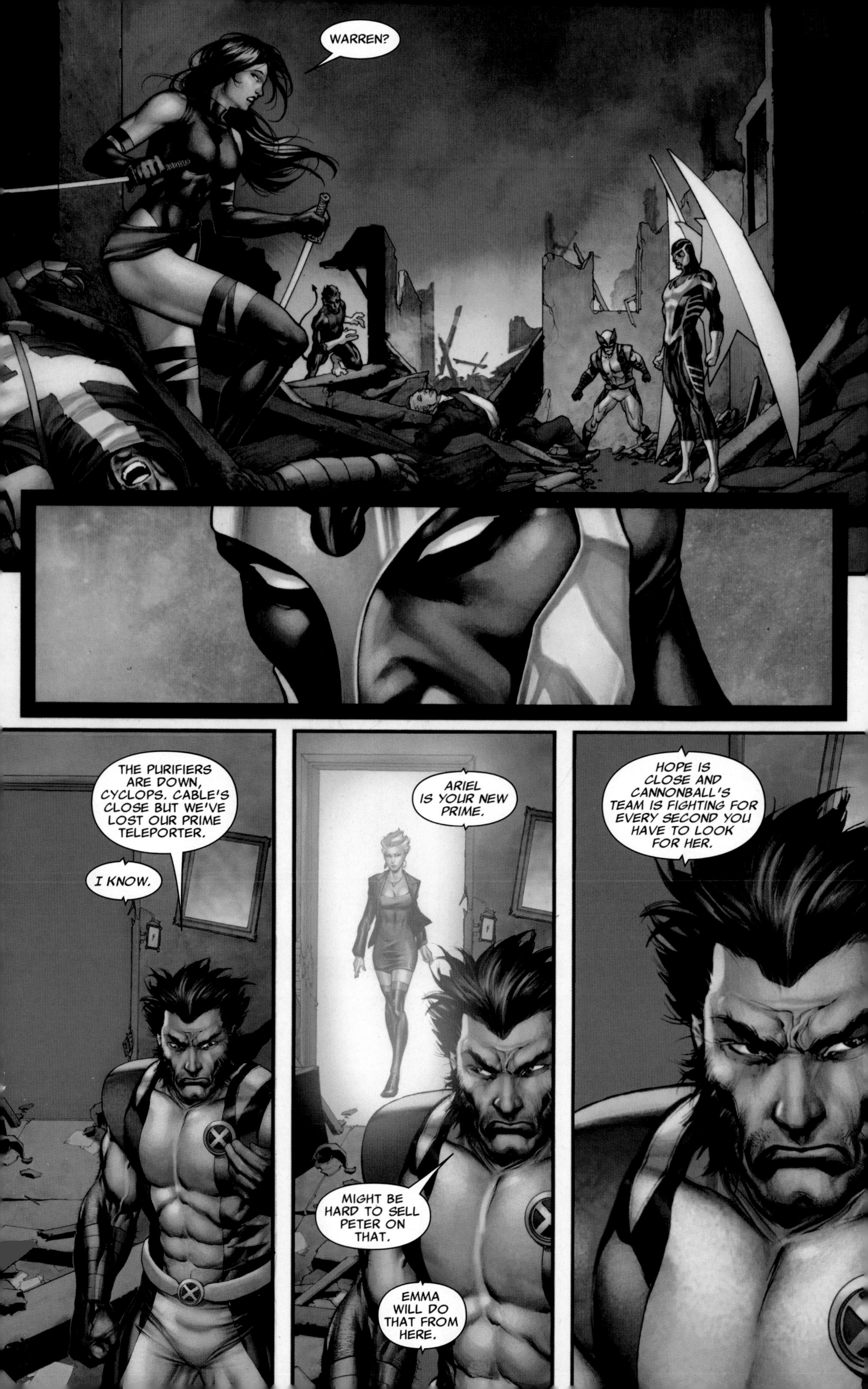
WARREN?
THE PURIFIERS ARE DOWN, CYCLOPS. CABLE'S CLOSE BUT WE'VE LOST OUR PRIME TELEPORTER.
I KNOW.
ARIEL IS YOUR NEW PRIME.
MIGHT BE HARD TO SELL PETER ON THAT.
EMMA WILL DO THAT FROM HERE.
HOPE IS CLOSE AND CANNONBALL'S TEAM IS FIGHTING FOR EVERY SECOND YOU HAVE TO LOOK FOR HER.

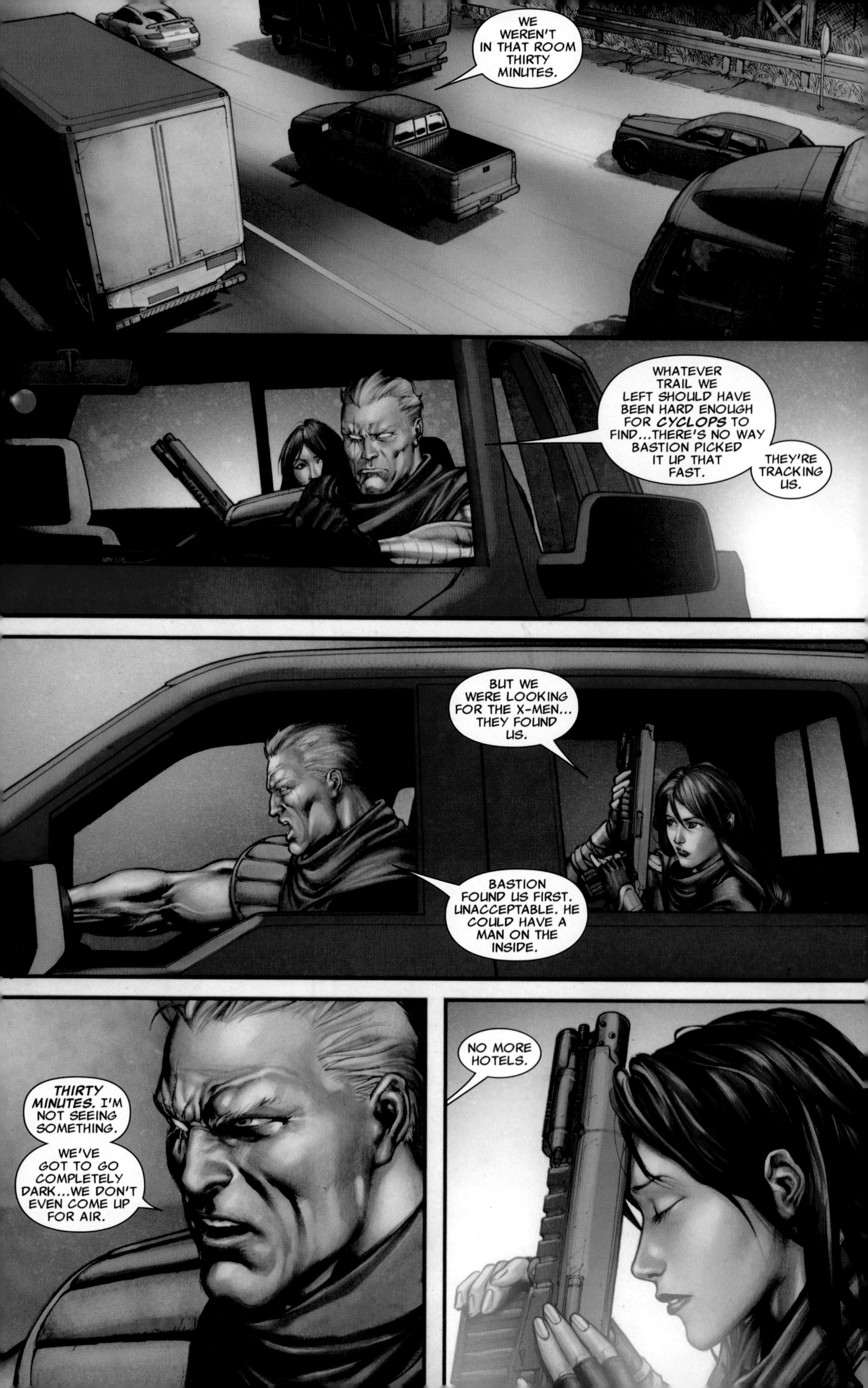
WE WEREN'T IN THAT ROOM THIRTY MINUTES.
WHATEVER TRAIL WE LEFT SHOULD HAVE BEEN HARD ENOUGH FOR CYCLOPS TO FIND...THERE'S NO WAY BASTION PICKED IT UP THAT FAST.
THEY'RE TRACKING US.
BUT WE WERE LOOKING FOR THE X-MEN... THEY FOUND US.
BASTION FOUND US FIRST. UNACCEPTABLE. HE COULD HAVE A MAN ON THE INSIDE.
THIRTY MINUTES. I'M NOT SEEING SOMETHING.
WE'VE GOT TO GO COMPLETELY DARK...WE DON'T EVEN COME UP FOR AIR.
NO MORE HOTELS.

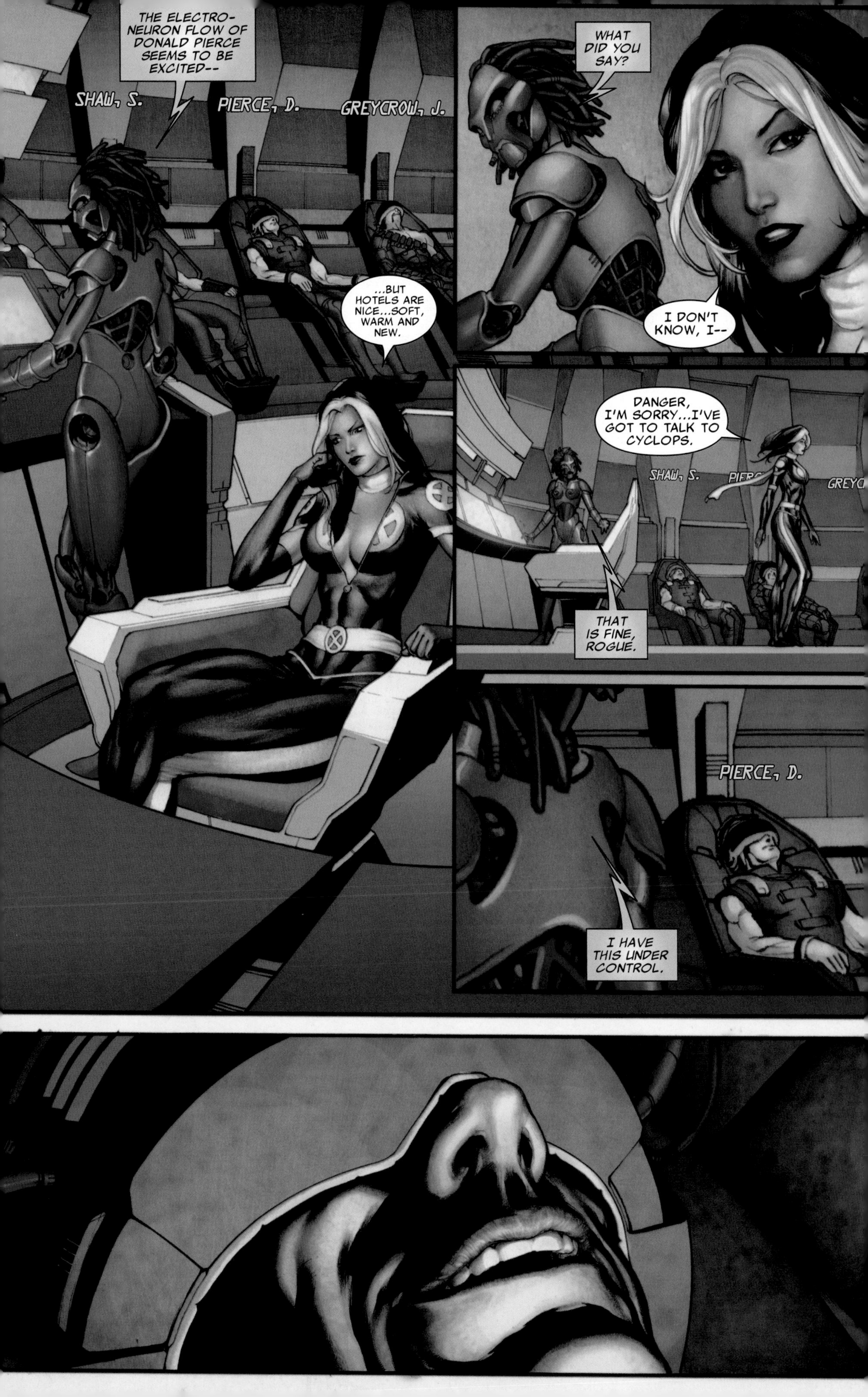
THE ELECTRO-NEURON FLOW OF DONALD PIERCE SEEMS TO BE EXCITED--
SHAW, S.
PIERCE, D.
GREYCROW, J.
...BUT HOTELS ARE NICE...SOFT, WARM AND NEW.
WHAT DID YOU SAY?
I DON'T KNOW, I--
DANGER, I'M SORRY...I'VE GOT TO TALK TO CYCLOPS.
SHAW, S.
THAT IS FINE, ROGUE.
PIERCE, D.
I HAVE THIS UNDER CONTROL.

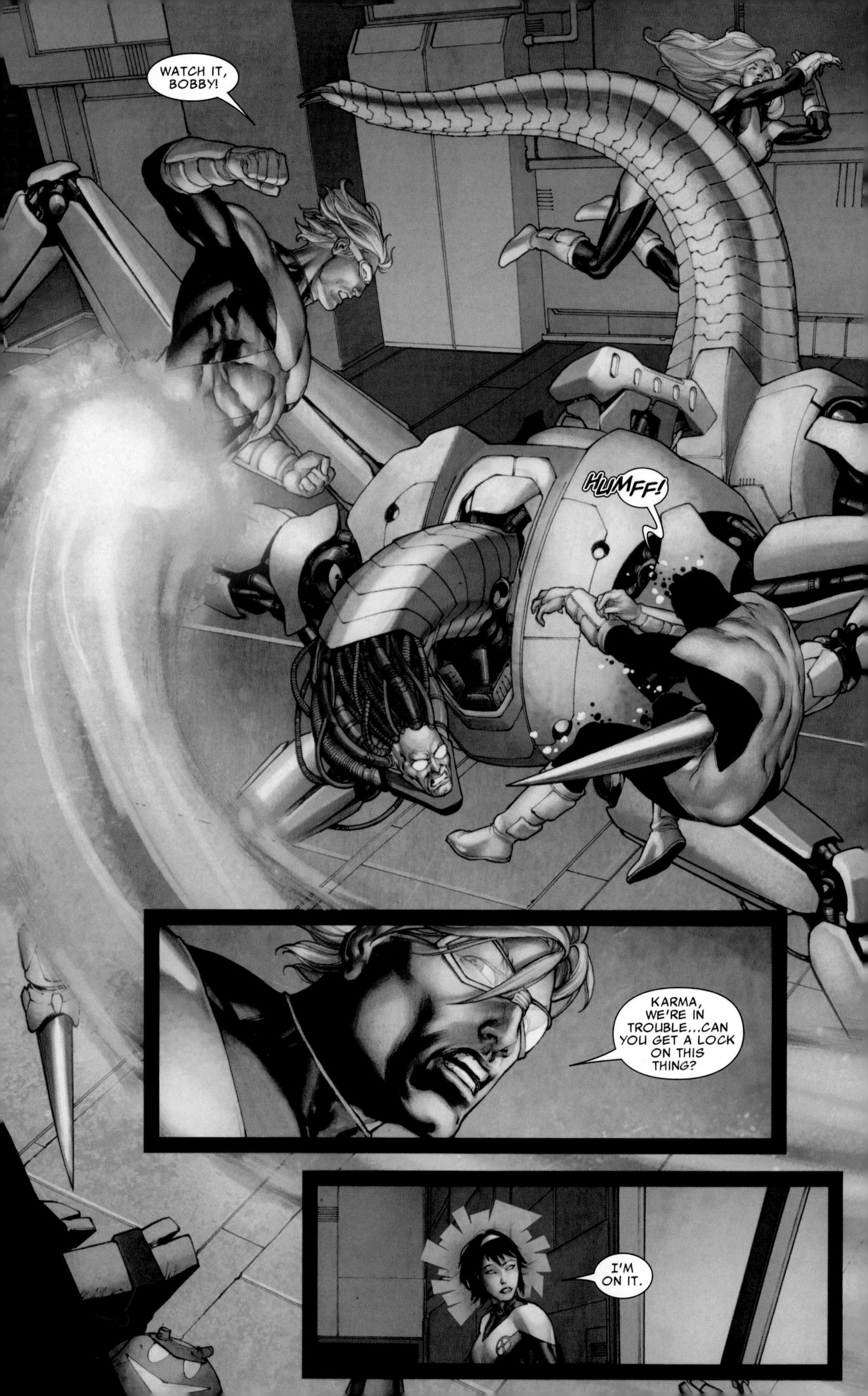
WATCH IT, BOBBY!
HUMFF!
KARMA, WE'RE IN TROUBLE...CAN YOU GET A LOCK ON THIS THING?
I'M ON IT.

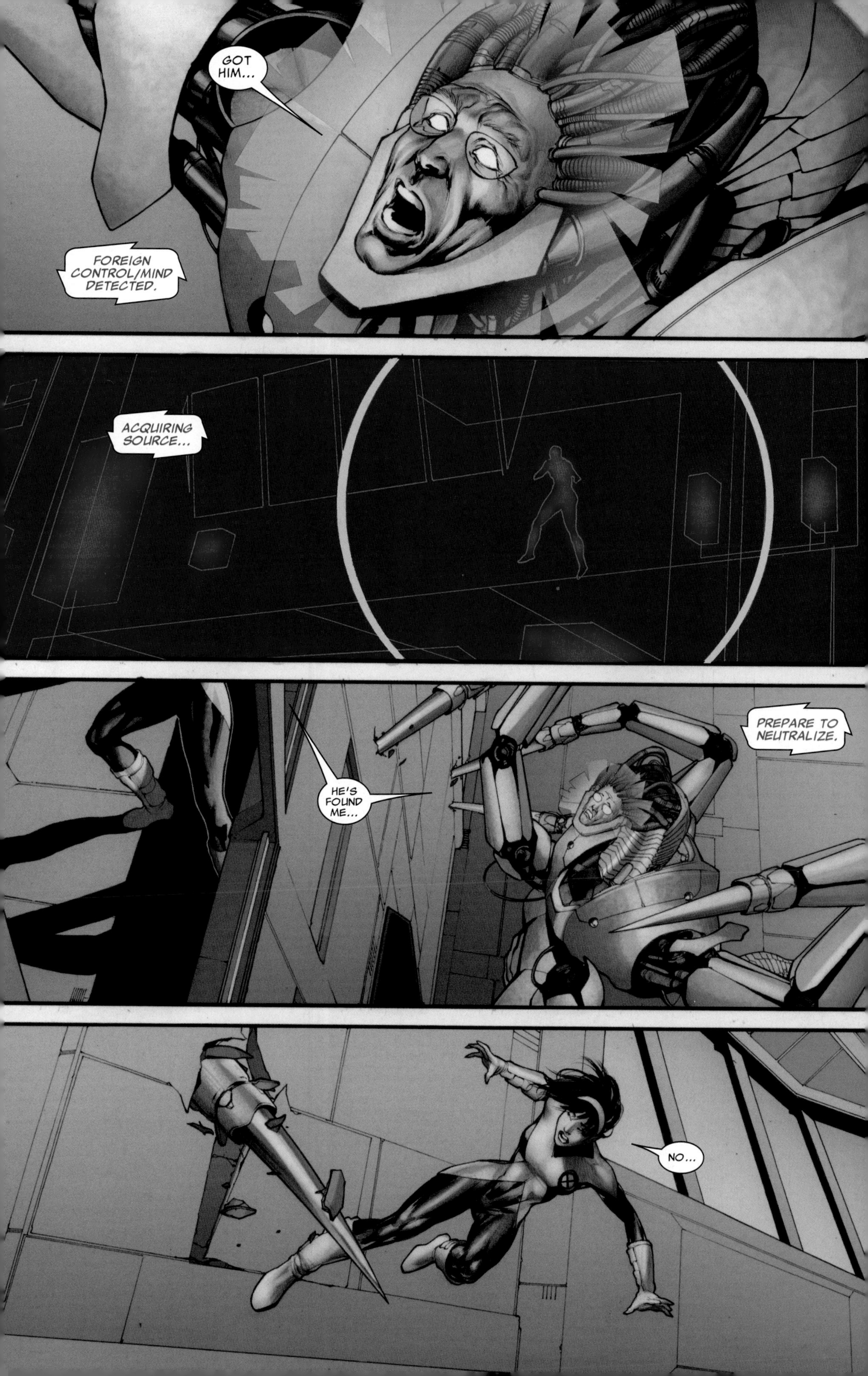
GOT HIM...
FOREIGN CONTROL/MIND DETECTED.
ACQUIRING SOURCE...
HE'S FOUND ME...
PREPARE TO NEUTRALIZE.
NO...

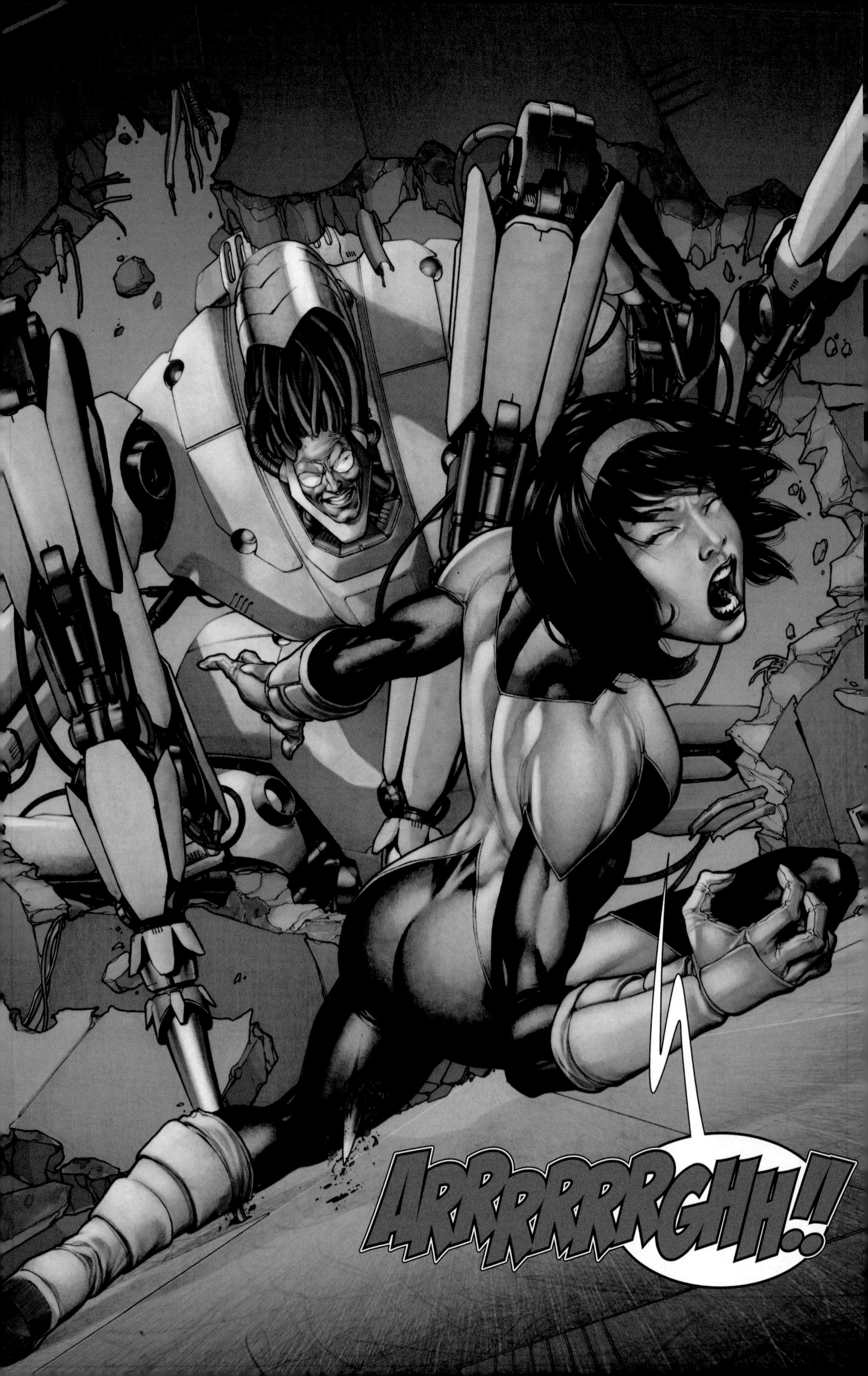
ARRRRRRRGHH!!

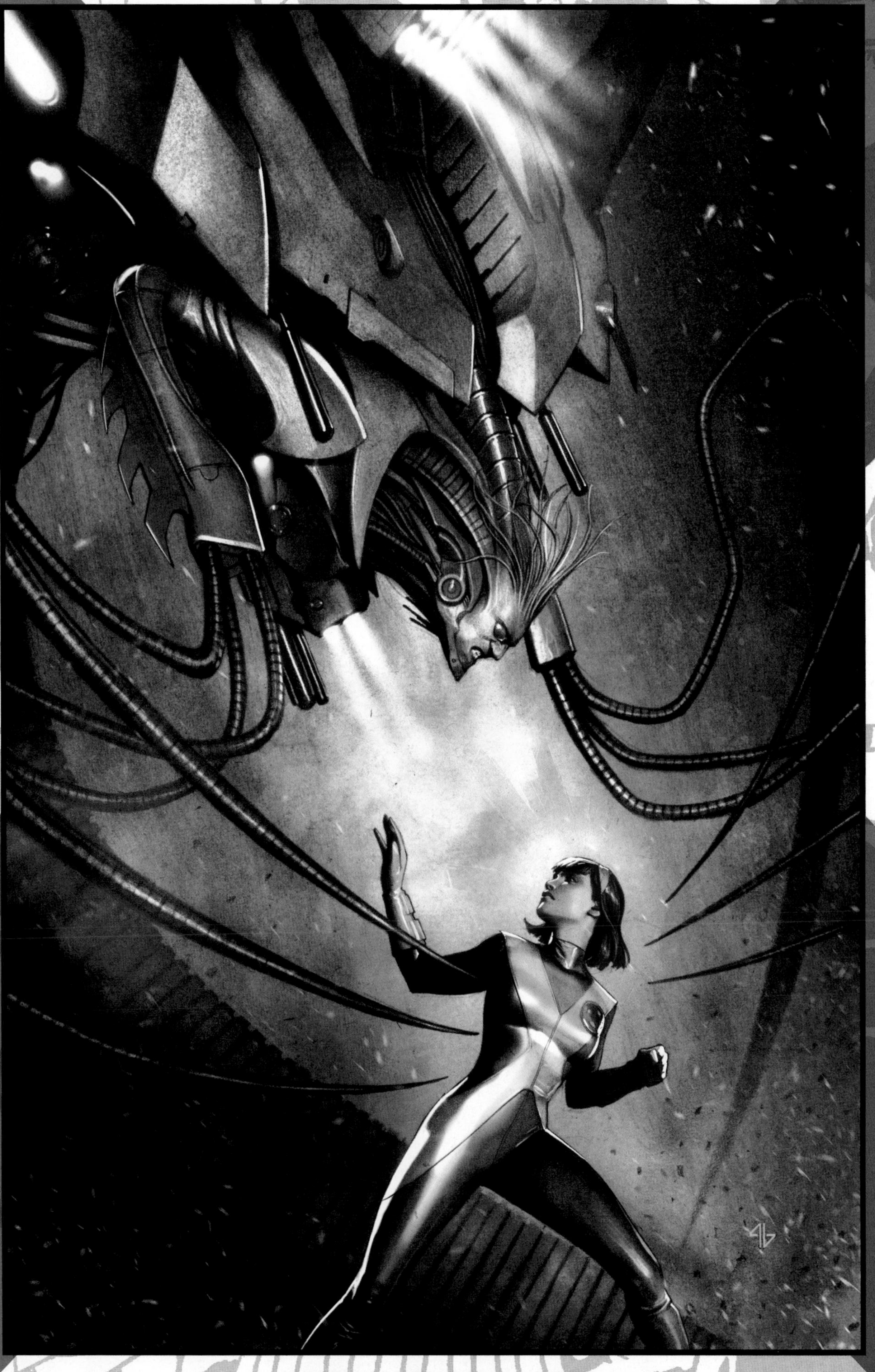

XMEN LEGACY #235

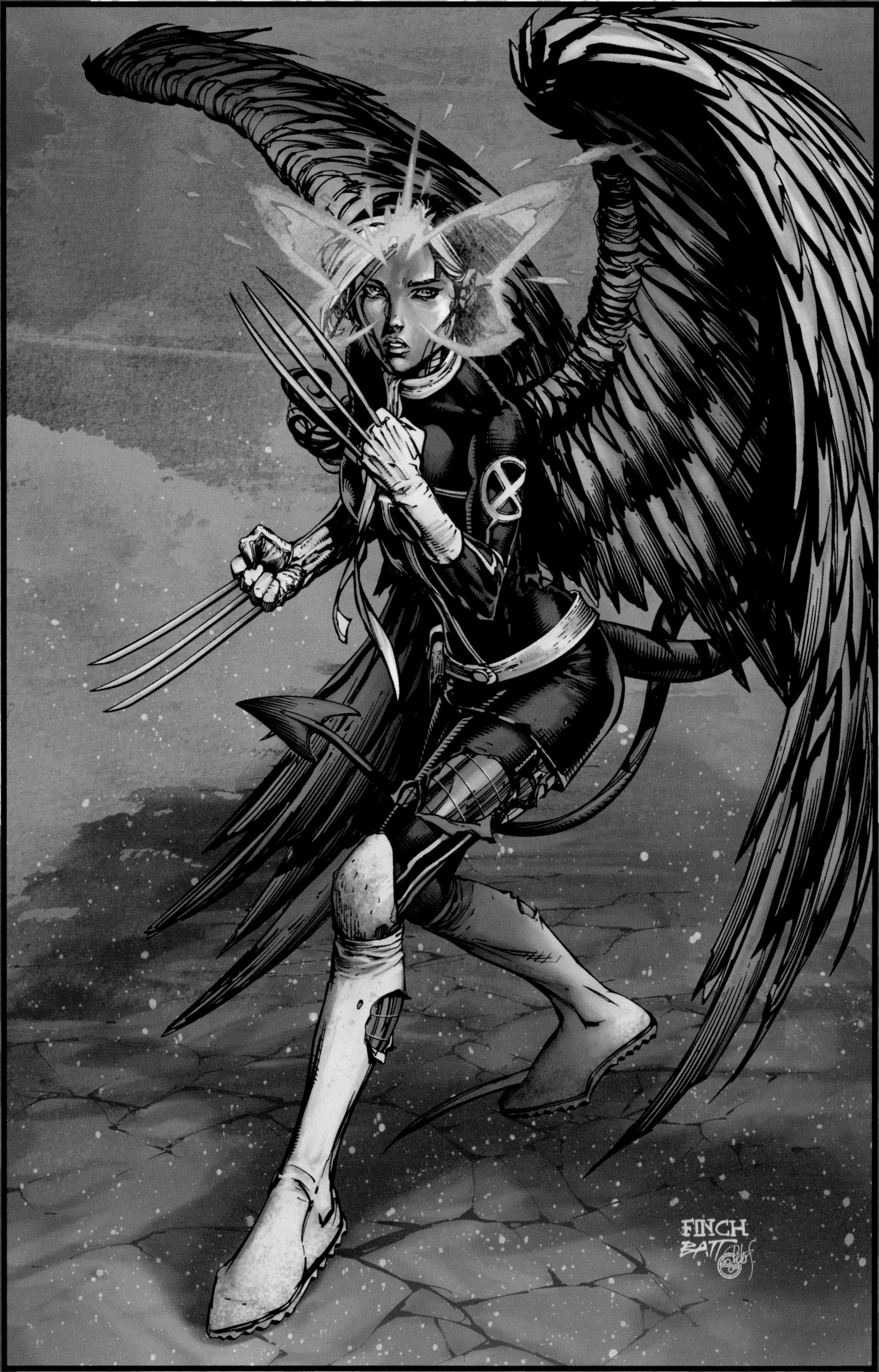
FINCH
BATT

XMEN LEGACY #235
VARIANT

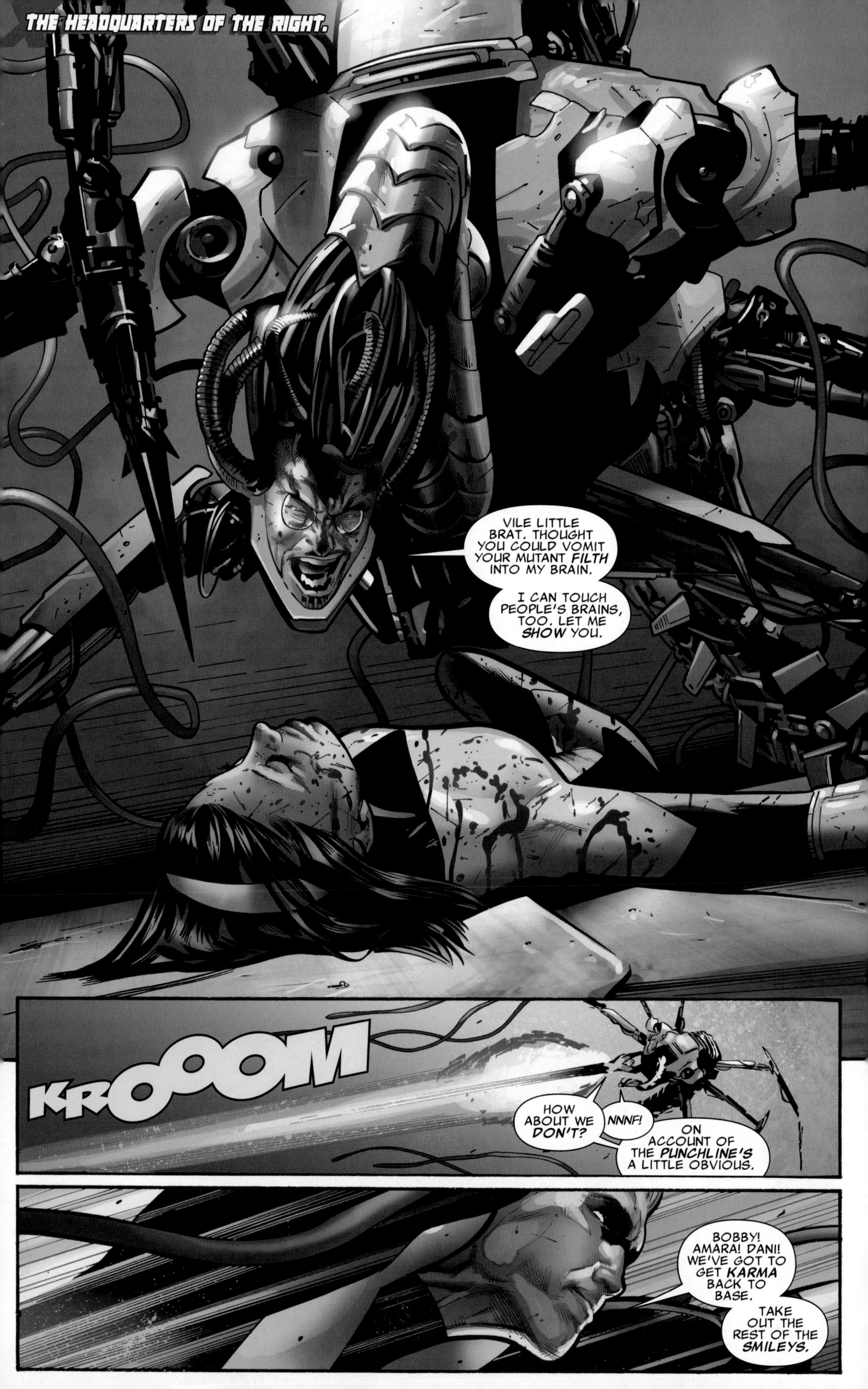
THE HEADQUARTERS OF THE RIGHT.
VILE LITTLE BRAT. THOUGHT YOU COULD VOMIT YOUR MUTANT FILTH INTO MY BRAIN.
I CAN TOUCH PEOPLE'S BRAINS, TOO. LET ME SHOW YOU.
KROOOOM
HOW ABOUT WE DON'T?
NNNF!
ON ACCOUNT OF THE PUNCHLINE'S A LITTLE OBVIOUS.
BOBBY! AMARA! DANI! WE'VE GOT TO GET KARMA BACK TO BASE.
TAKE OUT THE REST OF THE SMILEYS.

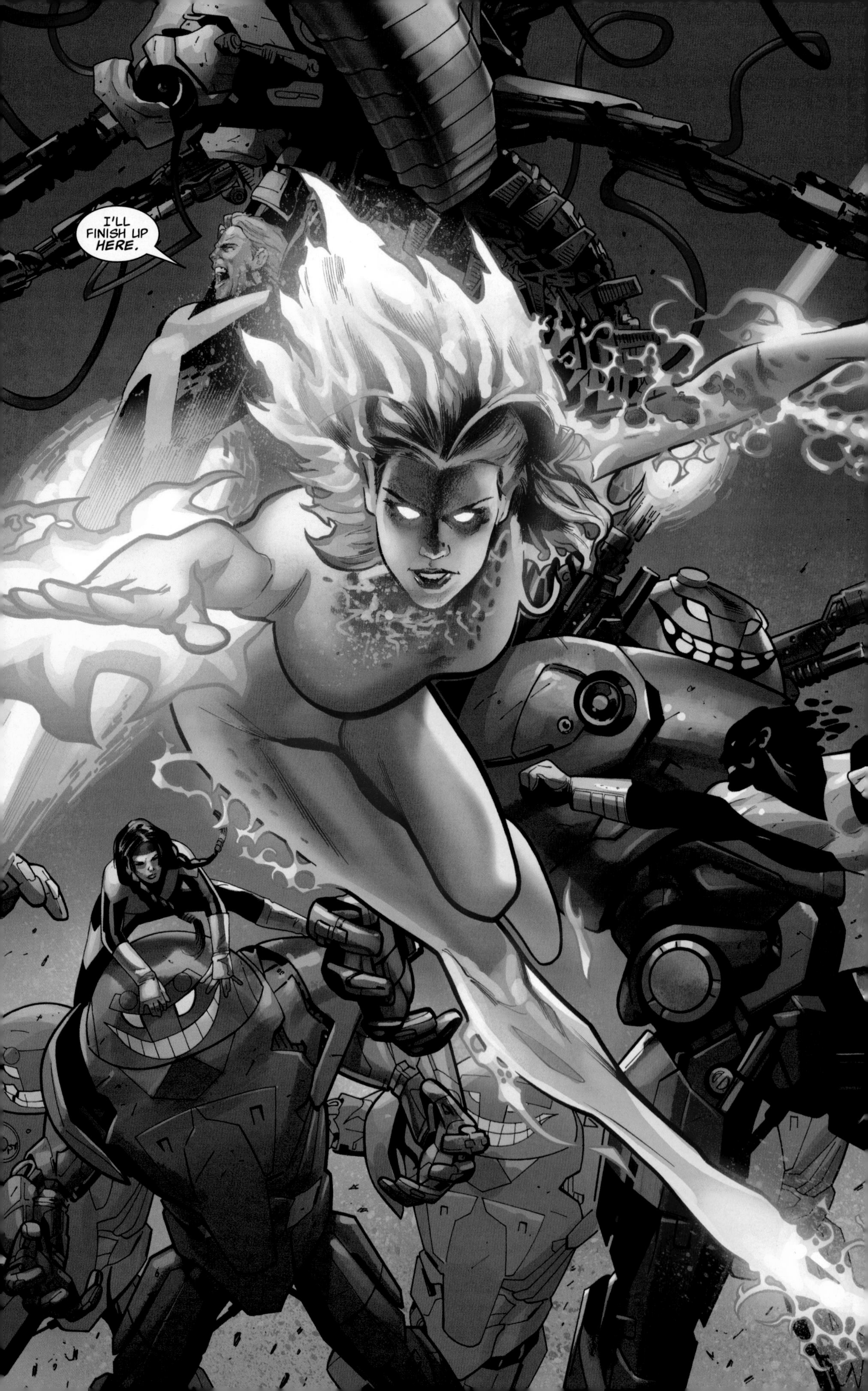
I'LL FINISH UP HERE.

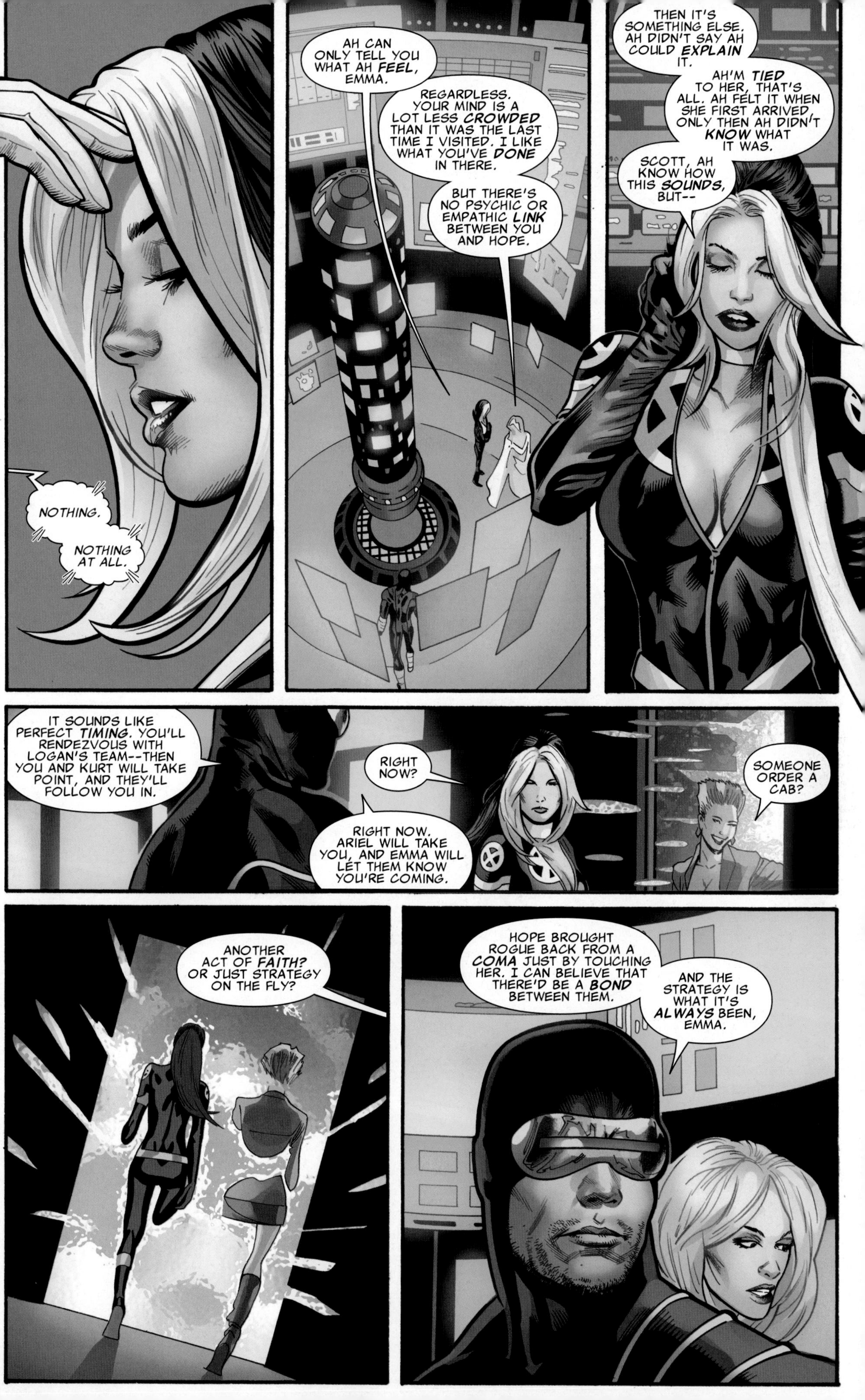
NOTHING.
NOTHING AT ALL.
AH CAN ONLY TELL YOU WHAT AH FEEL, EMMA.
REGARDLESS. YOUR MIND IS A LOT LESS CROWDED THAN IT WAS THE LAST TIME I VISITED. I LIKE WHAT YOU'VE DONE IN THERE.
BUT THERE'S NO PSYCHIC OR EMPATHIC LINK BETWEEN YOU AND HOPE.
THEN IT'S SOMETHING ELSE. AH DIDN'T SAY AH COULD EXPLAIN IT.
AH'M TIED TO HER, THAT'S ALL. AH FELT IT WHEN SHE FIRST ARRIVED, ONLY THEN AH DIDN'T KNOW WHAT IT WAS.
SCOTT, AH KNOW HOW THIS SOUNDS, BUT--
IT SOUNDS LIKE PERFECT TIMING. YOU'LL RENDEZVOUS WITH LOGAN'S TEAM--THEN YOU AND KURT WILL TAKE POINT, AND THEY'LL FOLLOW YOU IN.
RIGHT NOW?
RIGHT NOW. ARIEL WILL TAKE YOU, AND EMMA WILL LET THEM KNOW YOU'RE COMING.
SOMEONE ORDER A CAB?
ANOTHER ACT OF FAITH? OR JUST STRATEGY ON THE FLY?
HOPE BROUGHT ROGUE BACK FROM A COMA JUST BY TOUCHING HER. I CAN BELIEVE THAT THERE'D BE A BOND BETWEEN THEM.
AND THE STRATEGY IS WHAT IT'S ALWAYS BEEN, EMMA.

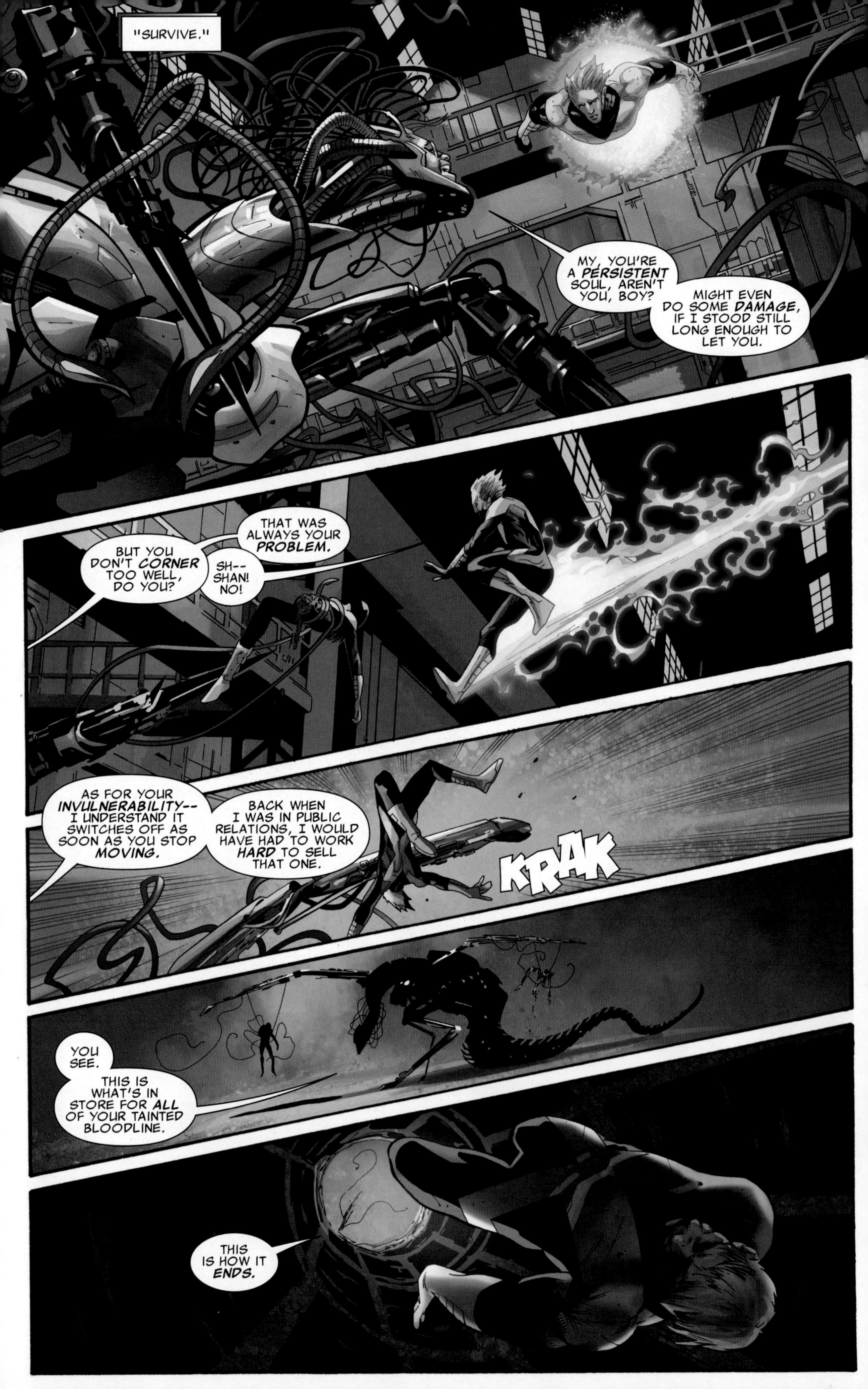
"SURVIVE."
MY, YOU'RE A PERSISTENT SOUL, AREN'T YOU, BOY?
MIGHT EVEN DO SOME DAMAGE, IF I STOOD STILL LONG ENOUGH TO LET YOU.
BUT YOU DON'T CORNER TOO WELL, DO YOU?
THAT WAS ALWAYS YOUR PROBLEM.
SH--SHAN! NO!
AS FOR YOUR INVULNERABILITY-- I UNDERSTAND IT SWITCHES OFF AS SOON AS YOU STOP MOVING.
BACK WHEN I WAS IN PUBLIC RELATIONS, I WOULD HAVE HAD TO WORK HARD TO SELL THAT ONE.
KRAK
YOU SEE.
THIS IS WHAT'S IN STORE FOR ALL OF YOUR TAINTED BLOODLINE.
THIS IS HOW IT ENDS.

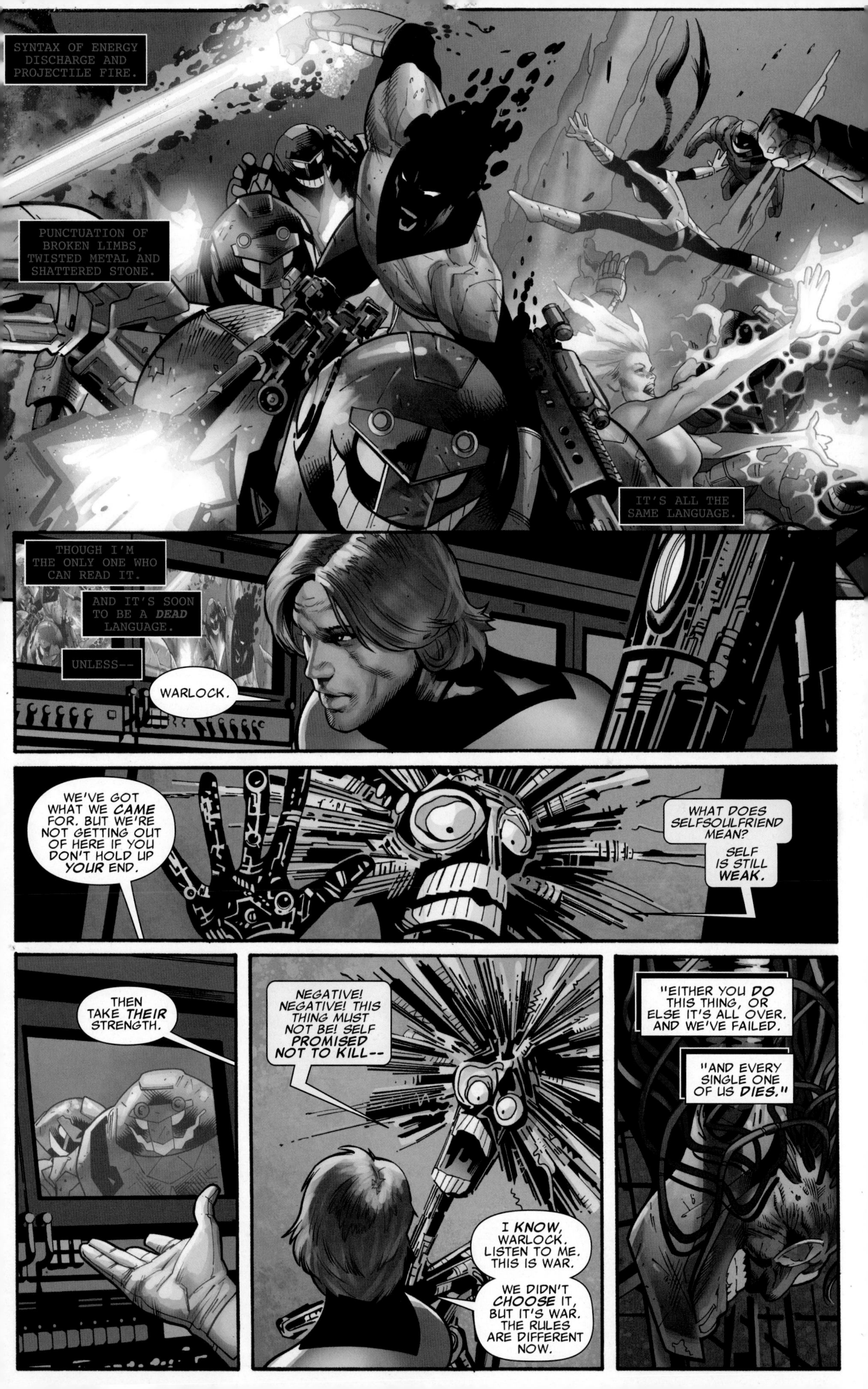
SYNTAX OF ENERGY DISCHARGE AND PROJECTILE FIRE.
PUNCTUATION OF BROKEN LIMBS, TWISTED METAL AND SHATTERED STONE.
IT'S ALL THE SAME LANGUAGE.
THOUGH I'M THE ONLY ONE WHO CAN READ IT.
AND IT'S SOON TO BE A *DEAD* LANGUAGE.
UNLESS--
WARLOCK.
WE'VE GOT WHAT WE *CAME* FOR. BUT WE'RE NOT GETTING OUT OF HERE IF YOU DON'T HOLD UP *YOUR* END.
WHAT DOES SELFSOULFRIEND MEAN?
SELF IS STILL *WEAK.*
THEN TAKE *THEIR* STRENGTH.
NEGATIVE! NEGATIVE! THIS THING MUST NOT BE! SELF *PROMISED NOT TO KILL--*
I *KNOW,* WARLOCK. LISTEN TO ME. THIS IS WAR.
WE DIDN'T *CHOOSE* IT, BUT IT'S WAR. THE RULES ARE DIFFERENT NOW.
"EITHER YOU *DO* THIS THING, OR ELSE IT'S ALL OVER. AND WE'VE FAILED.
"AND EVERY SINGLE ONE OF US *DIES.*"

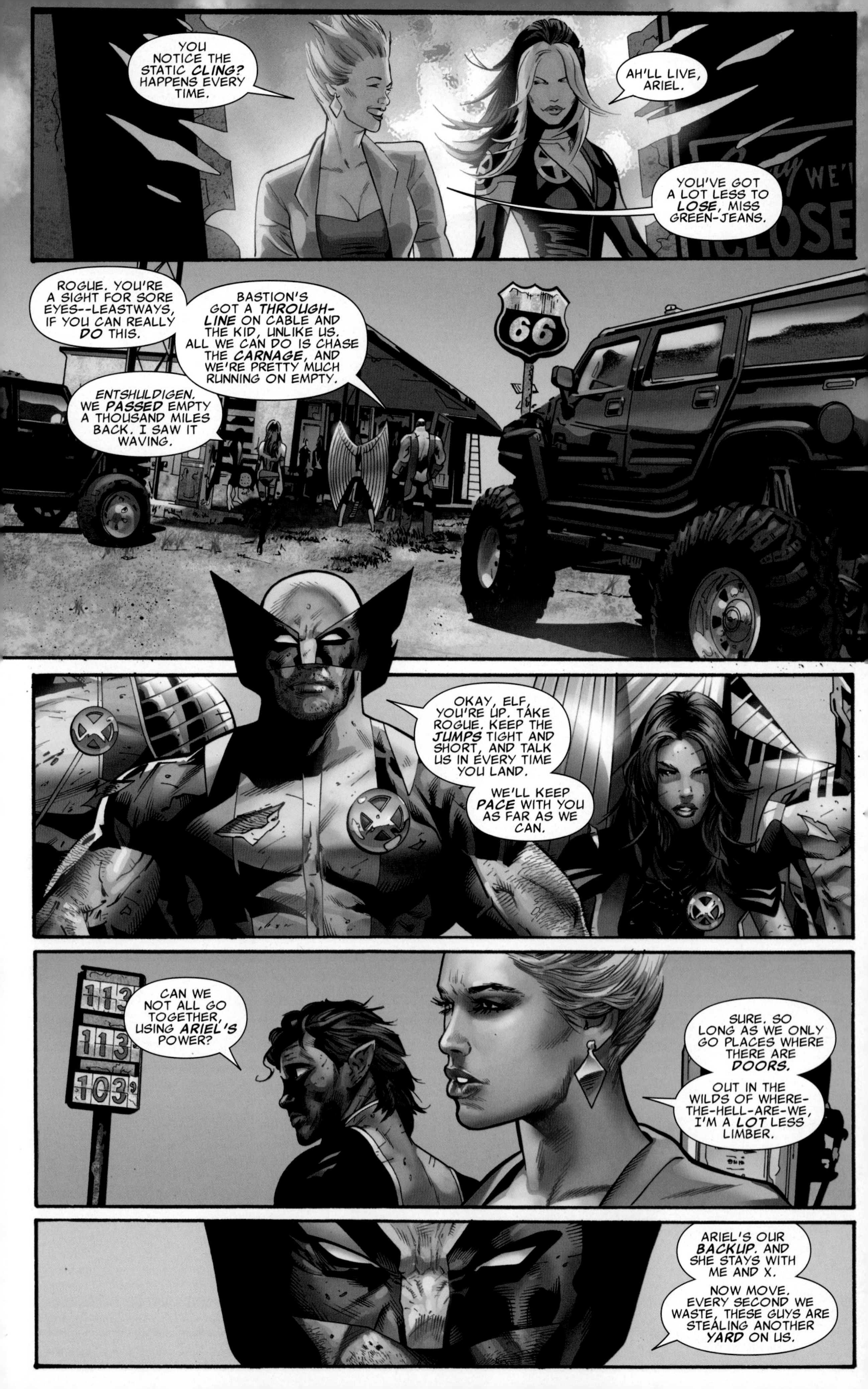
YOU NOTICE THE STATIC CLING? HAPPENS EVERY TIME.
AH'LL LIVE, ARIEL.
YOU'VE GOT A LOT LESS TO LOSE, MISS GREEN-JEANS.
ROGUE. YOU'RE A SIGHT FOR SORE EYES--LEASTWAYS, IF YOU CAN REALLY DO THIS.
BASTION'S GOT A THROUGH-LINE ON CABLE AND THE KID, UNLIKE US. ALL WE CAN DO IS CHASE THE CARNAGE, AND WE'RE PRETTY MUCH RUNNING ON EMPTY.
ENTSHULDIGEN. WE PASSED EMPTY A THOUSAND MILES BACK. I SAW IT WAVING.
66
OKAY, ELF, YOU'RE UP. TAKE ROGUE. KEEP THE JUMPS TIGHT AND SHORT, AND TALK US IN EVERY TIME YOU LAND.
WE'LL KEEP PACE WITH YOU AS FAR AS WE CAN.
CAN WE NOT ALL GO TOGETHER, USING ARIEL'S POWER?
SURE, SO LONG AS WE ONLY GO PLACES WHERE THERE ARE DOORS.
OUT IN THE WILDS OF WHERE-THE-HELL-ARE-WE, I'M A LOT LESS LIMBER.
ARIEL'S OUR BACKUP. AND SHE STAYS WITH ME AND X.
NOW MOVE. EVERY SECOND WE WASTE, THESE GUYS ARE STEALING ANOTHER YARD ON US.

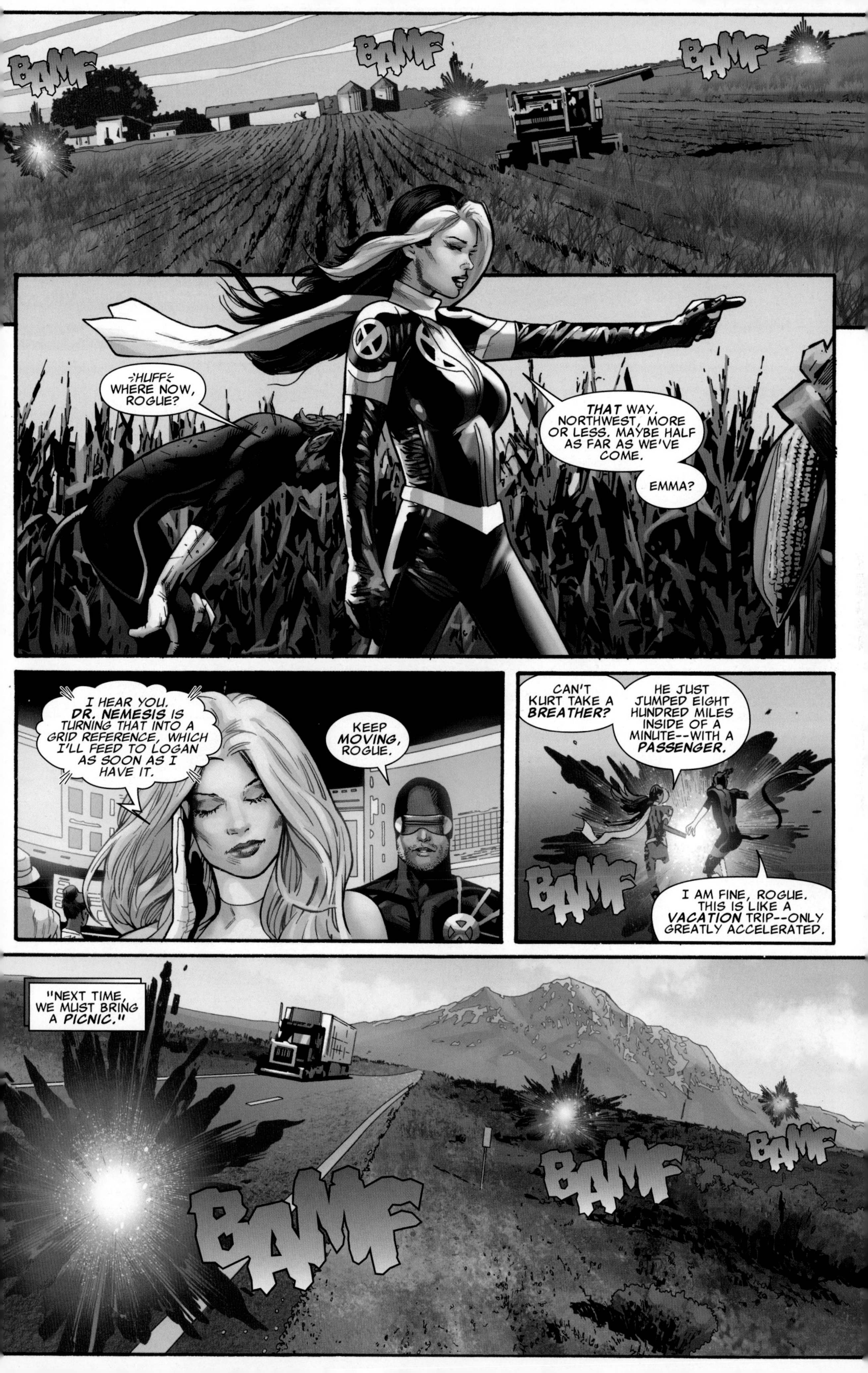
BAMF
BAMF
BAMF
~HUFF~ WHERE NOW, ROGUE?
THAT WAY. NORTHWEST, MORE OR LESS. MAYBE HALF AS FAR AS WE'VE COME.
EMMA?
I HEAR YOU. DR. NEMESIS IS TURNING THAT INTO A GRID REFERENCE, WHICH I'LL FEED TO LOGAN AS SOON AS I HAVE IT.
KEEP MOVING, ROGUE.
CAN'T KURT TAKE A BREATHER?
HE JUST JUMPED EIGHT HUNDRED MILES INSIDE OF A MINUTE--WITH A PASSENGER.
BAMF
I AM FINE, ROGUE. THIS IS LIKE A VACATION TRIP--ONLY GREATLY ACCELERATED.
"NEXT TIME, WE MUST BRING A PICNIC."
BAMF
BAMF
BAMF

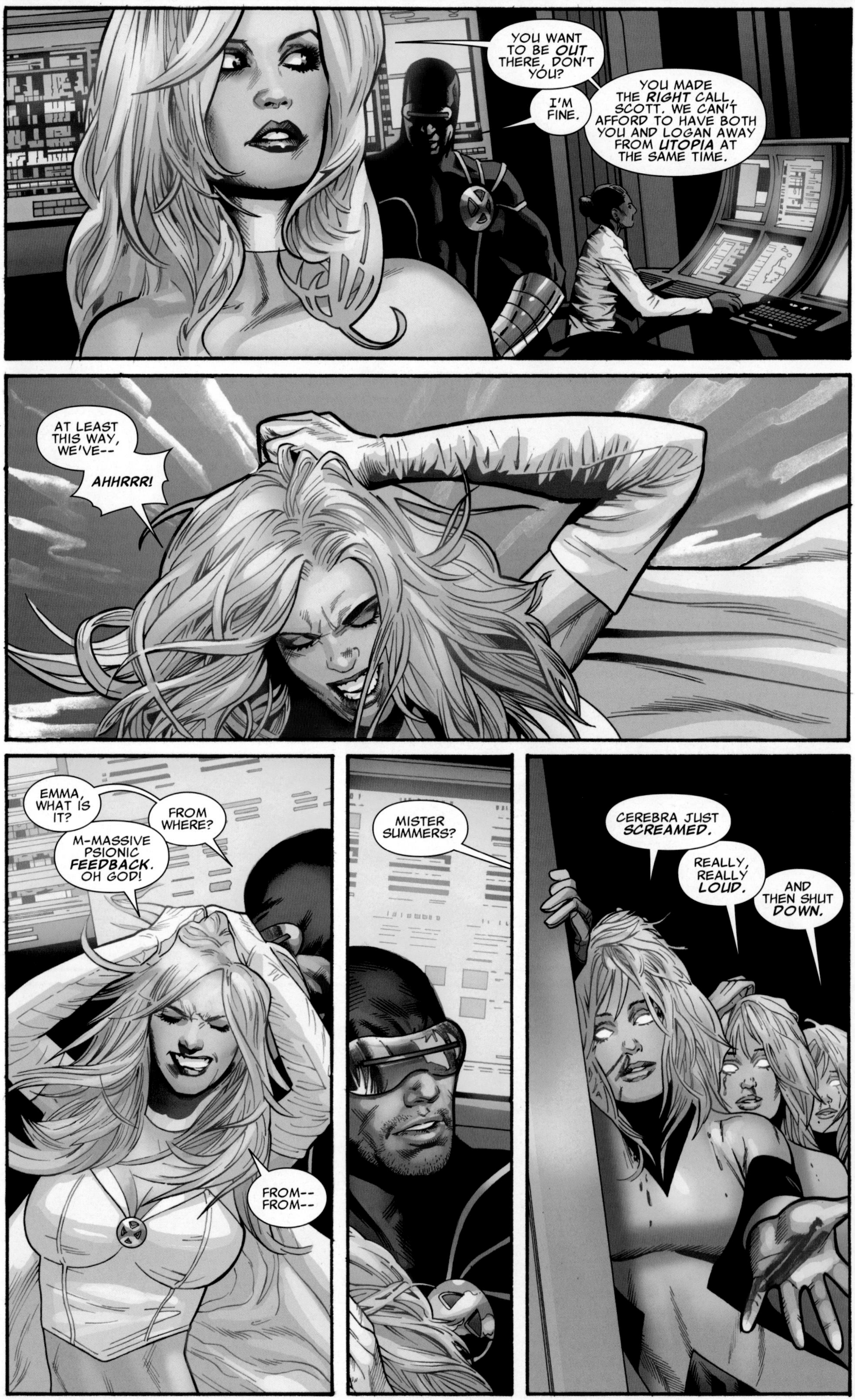
YOU WANT TO BE OUT THERE, DON'T YOU?
I'M FINE.
YOU MADE THE RIGHT CALL, SCOTT. WE CAN'T AFFORD TO HAVE BOTH YOU AND LOGAN AWAY FROM UTOPIA AT THE SAME TIME.
AT LEAST THIS WAY, WE'VE--
AHHRRR!
EMMA, WHAT IS IT?
M-MASSIVE PSIONIC FEEDBACK. OH GOD!
FROM WHERE?
FROM-- FROM--
MISTER SUMMERS?
CEREBRA JUST SCREAMED.
REALLY, REALLY LOUD.
AND THEN SHUT DOWN.

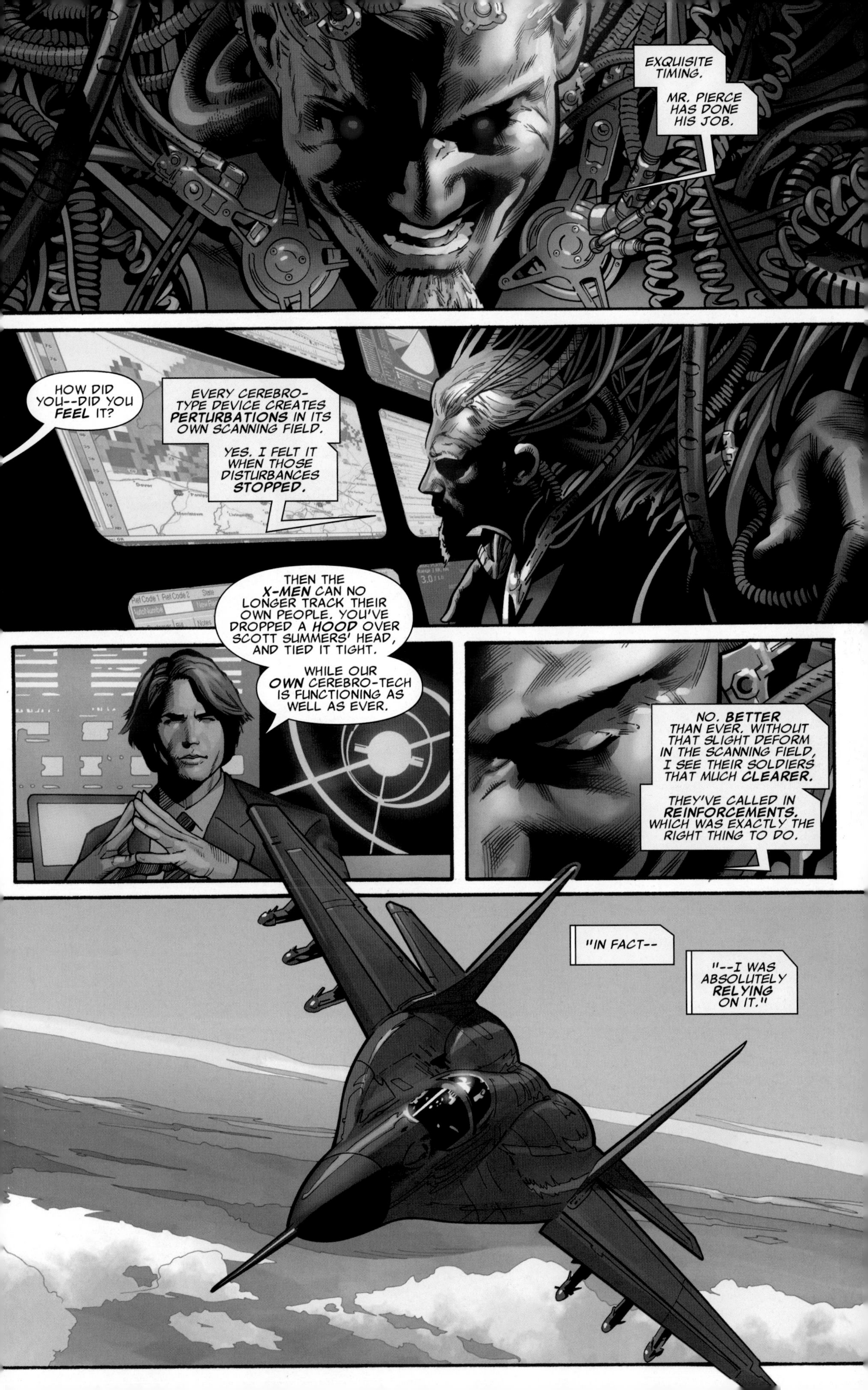
EXQUISITE TIMING.
MR. PIERCE HAS DONE HIS JOB.
HOW DID YOU--DID YOU FEEL IT?
EVERY CEREBRO-TYPE DEVICE CREATES PERTURBATIONS IN ITS OWN SCANNING FIELD.
YES. I FELT IT WHEN THOSE DISTURBANCES STOPPED.
THEN THE X-MEN CAN NO LONGER TRACK THEIR OWN PEOPLE. YOU'VE DROPPED A HOOD OVER SCOTT SUMMERS' HEAD, AND TIED IT TIGHT.
WHILE OUR OWN CEREBRO-TECH IS FUNCTIONING AS WELL AS EVER.
NO. BETTER THAN EVER. WITHOUT THAT SLIGHT DEFORM IN THE SCANNING FIELD, I SEE THEIR SOLDIERS THAT MUCH CLEARER.
THEY'VE CALLED IN REINFORCEMENTS. WHICH WAS EXACTLY THE RIGHT THING TO DO.
"IN FACT--
"--I WAS ABSOLUTELY RELYING ON IT."

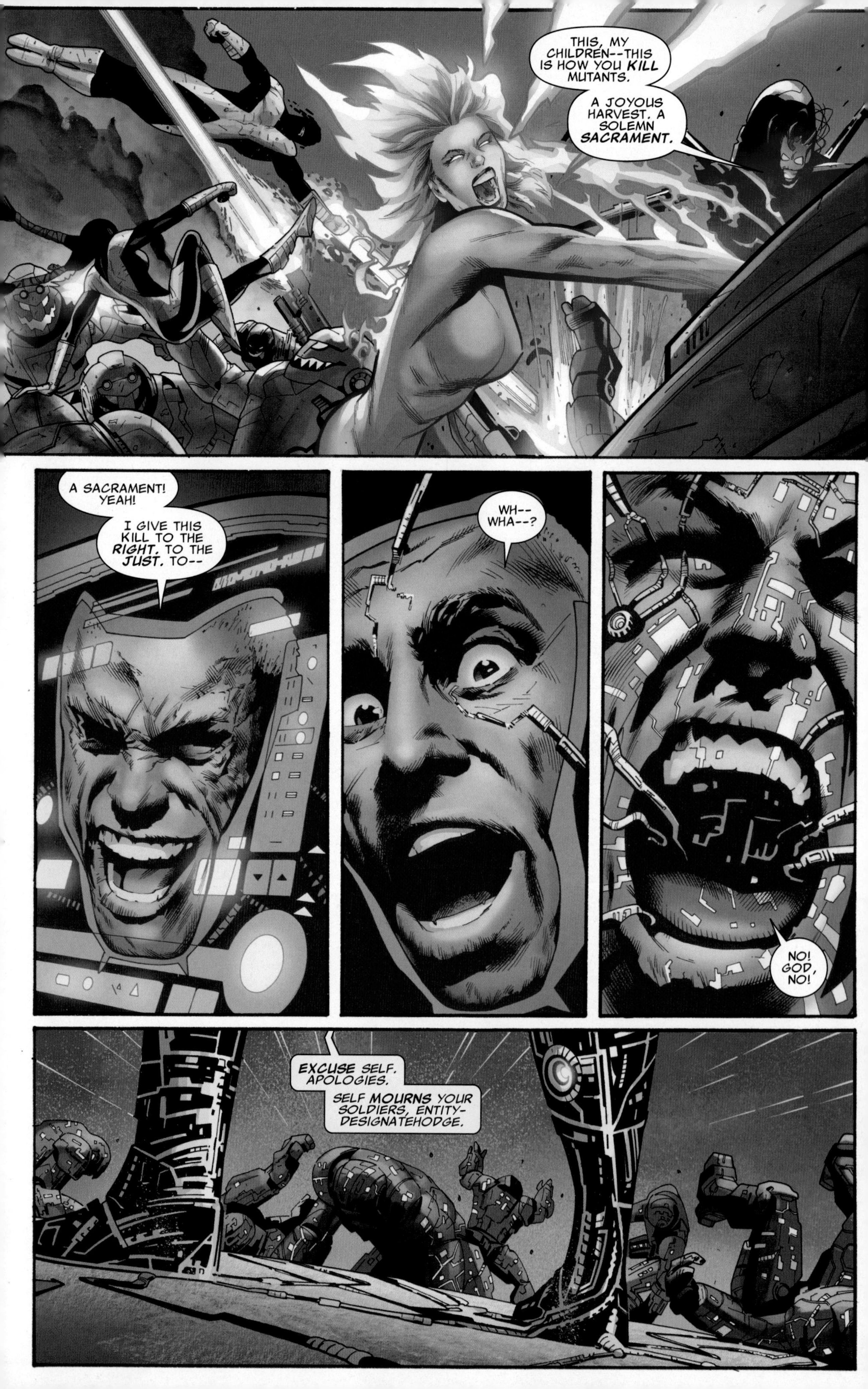
THIS, MY CHILDREN--THIS IS HOW YOU KILL MUTANTS.
A JOYOUS HARVEST. A SOLEMN SACRAMENT.
A SACRAMENT! YEAH!
I GIVE THIS KILL TO THE RIGHT. TO THE JUST. TO--
WH-- WHA--?
NO! GOD, NO!
EXCUSE SELF. APOLOGIES.
SELF MOURNS YOUR SOLDIERS, ENTITY-DESIGNATEHODGE.

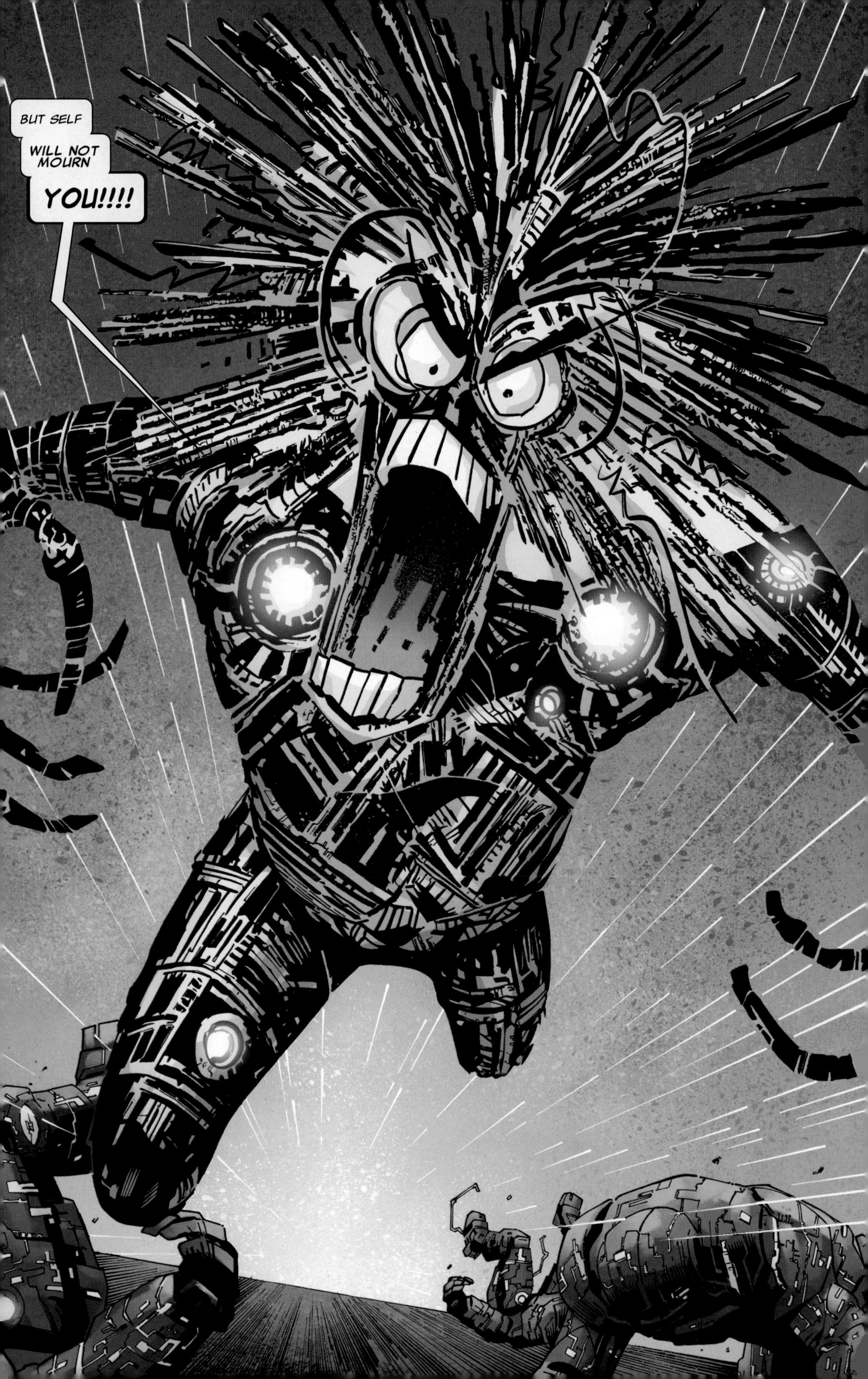
BUT SELF
WILL NOT MOURN
YOU!!!!

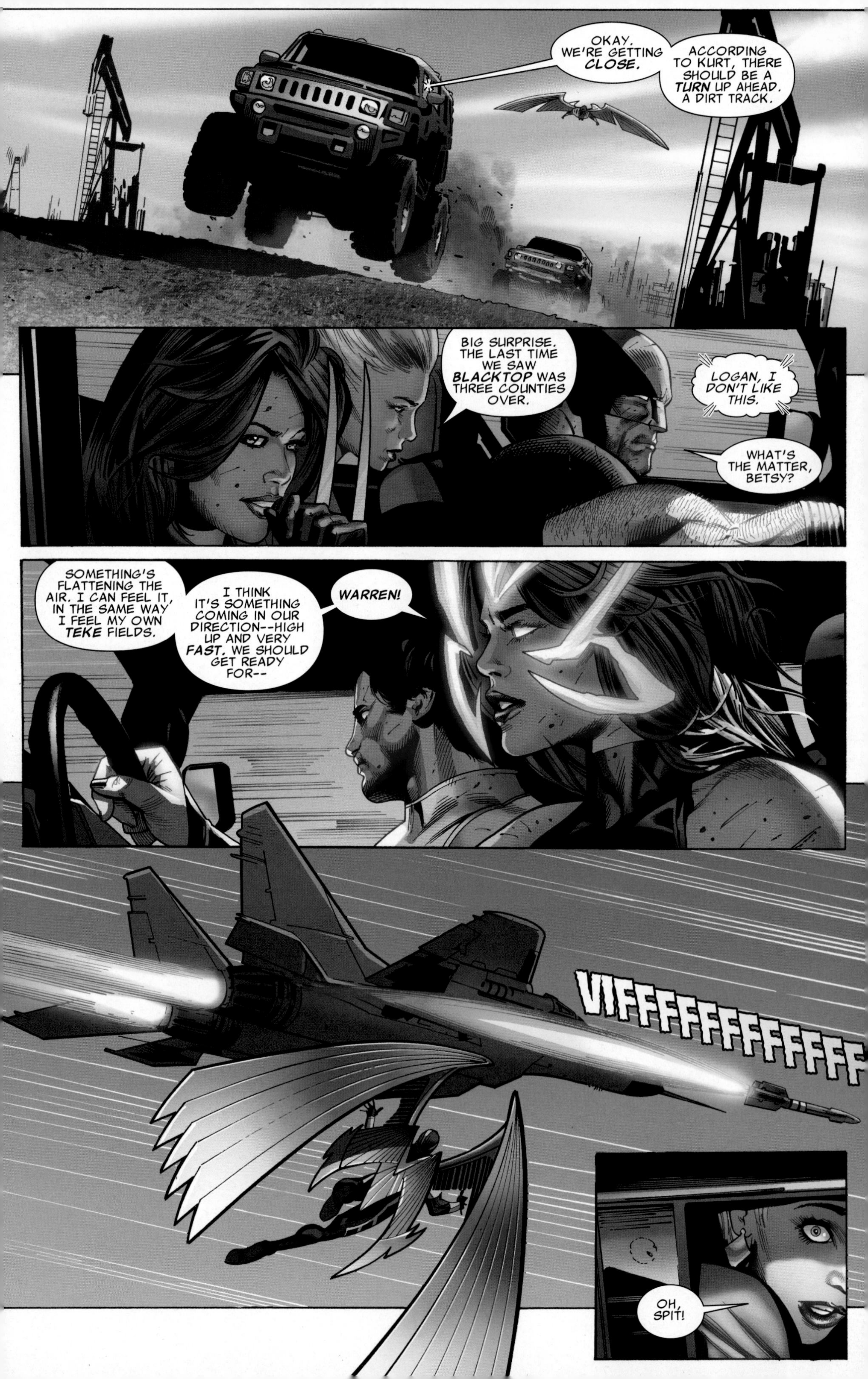
OKAY. WE'RE GETTING CLOSE.
ACCORDING TO KURT, THERE SHOULD BE A TURN UP AHEAD. A DIRT TRACK.
BIG SURPRISE. THE LAST TIME WE SAW BLACKTOP WAS THREE COUNTIES OVER.
LOGAN, I DON'T LIKE THIS.
WHAT'S THE MATTER, BETSY?
SOMETHING'S FLATTENING THE AIR. I CAN FEEL IT, IN THE SAME WAY I FEEL MY OWN TEKE FIELDS.
I THINK IT'S SOMETHING COMING IN OUR DIRECTION--HIGH UP AND VERY FAST. WE SHOULD GET READY FOR--
WARREN!
VIFFFFFFFFFFFF
OH, SPIT!

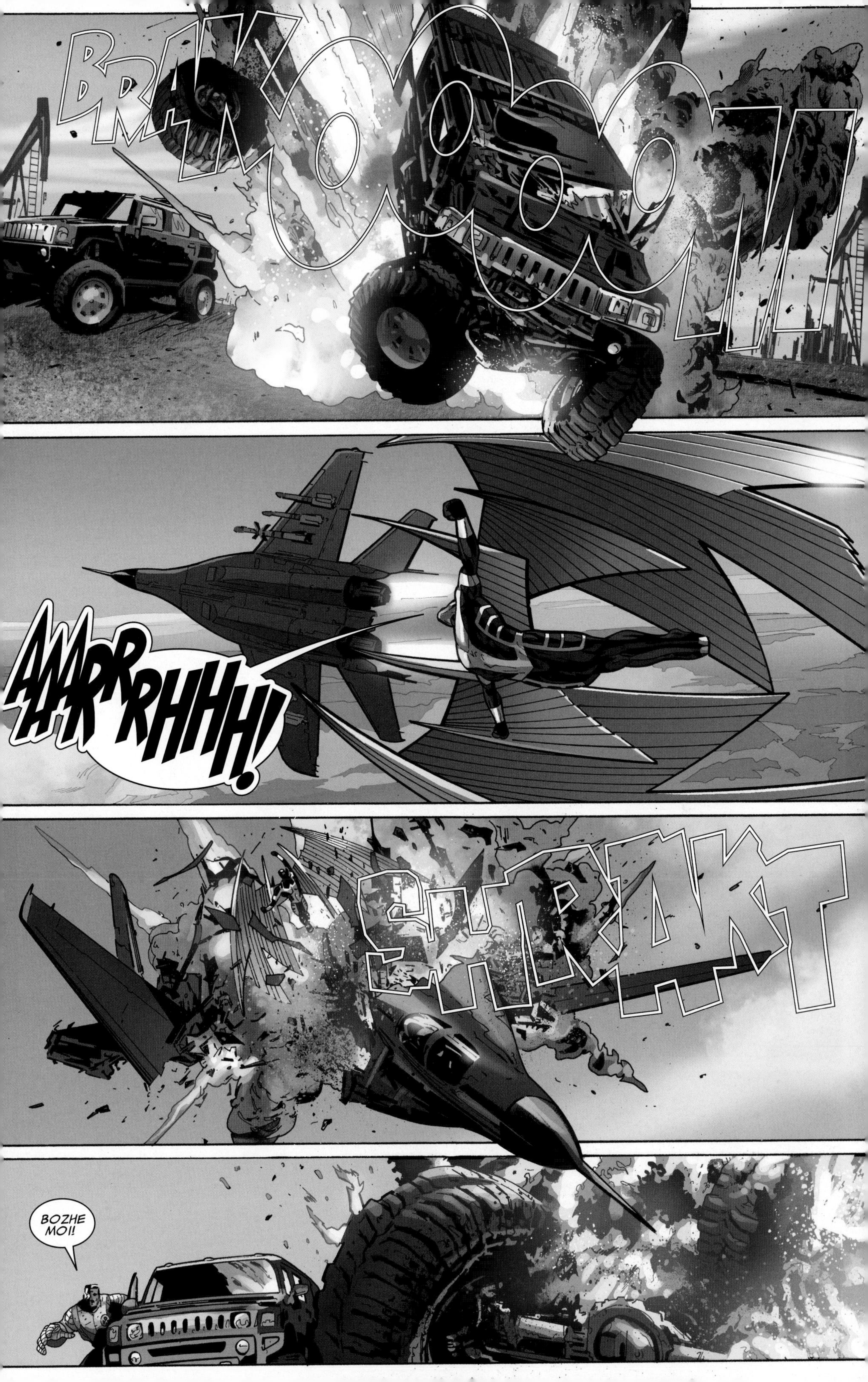
BRAKOOOOOOM!!
AAARRRHHH!
SHRAKT
BOZHE MOI!!

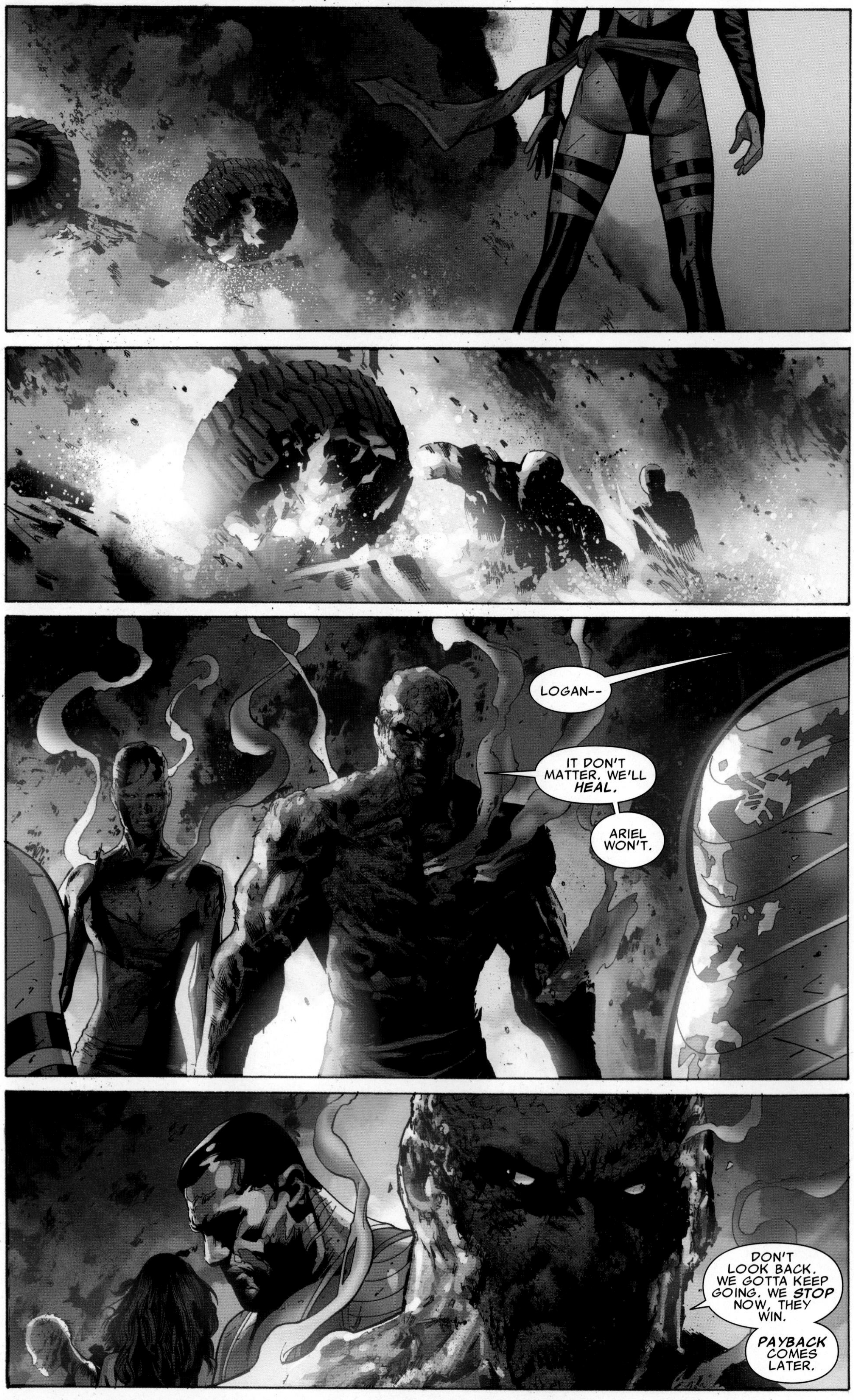
LOGAN--
IT DON'T MATTER. WE'LL HEAL.
ARIEL WON'T.
DON'T LOOK BACK. WE GOTTA KEEP GOING. WE STOP NOW, THEY WIN.
PAYBACK COMES LATER.

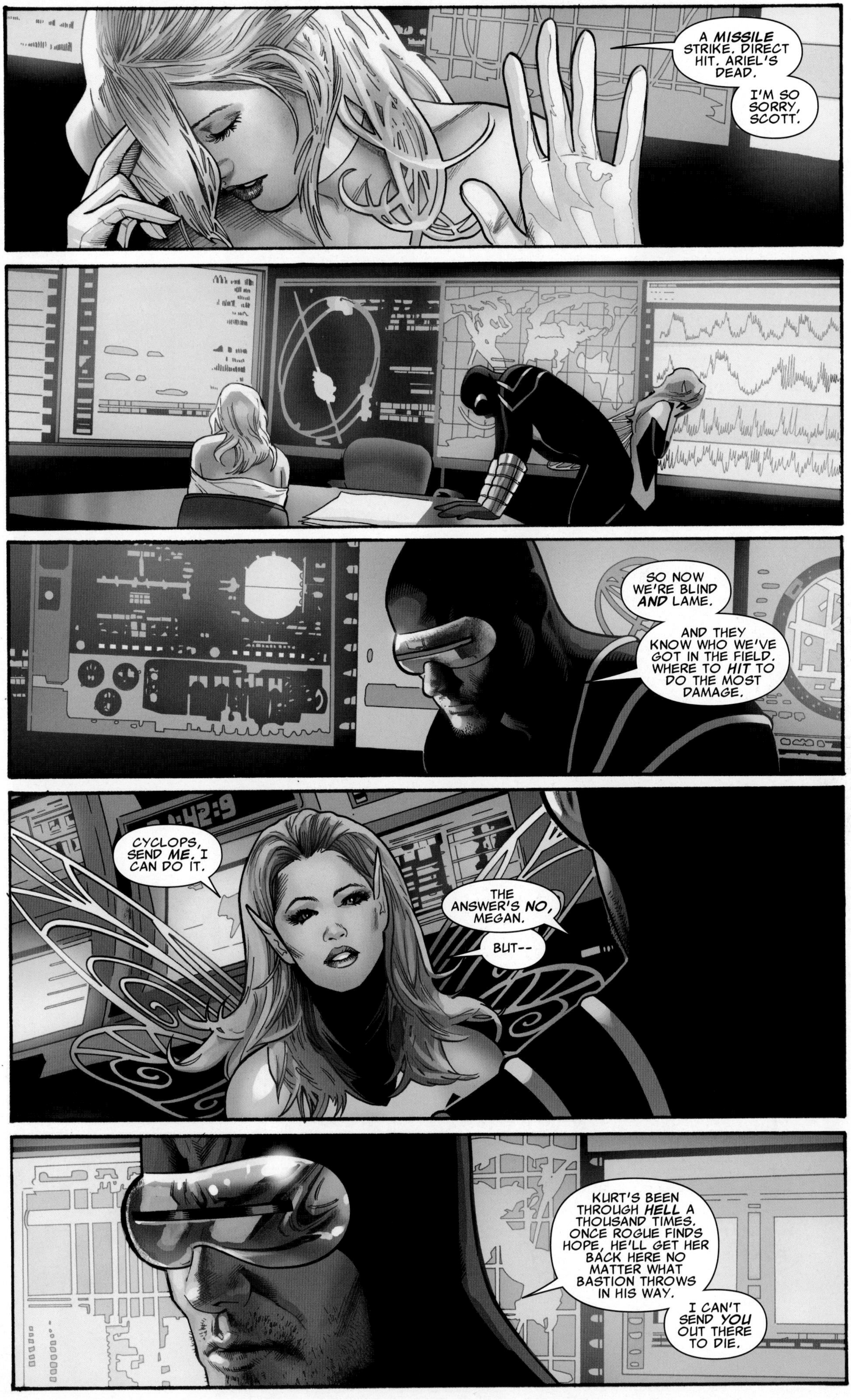
A MISSILE STRIKE. DIRECT HIT. ARIEL'S DEAD.
I'M SO SORRY, SCOTT.
SO NOW WE'RE BLIND AND LAME.
AND THEY KNOW WHO WE'VE GOT IN THE FIELD. WHERE TO HIT TO DO THE MOST DAMAGE.
CYCLOPS, SEND ME. I CAN DO IT.
THE ANSWER'S NO, MEGAN.
BUT--
KURT'S BEEN THROUGH HELL A THOUSAND TIMES. ONCE ROGUE FINDS HOPE, HE'LL GET HER BACK HERE NO MATTER WHAT BASTION THROWS IN HIS WAY.
I CAN'T SEND YOU OUT THERE TO DIE.

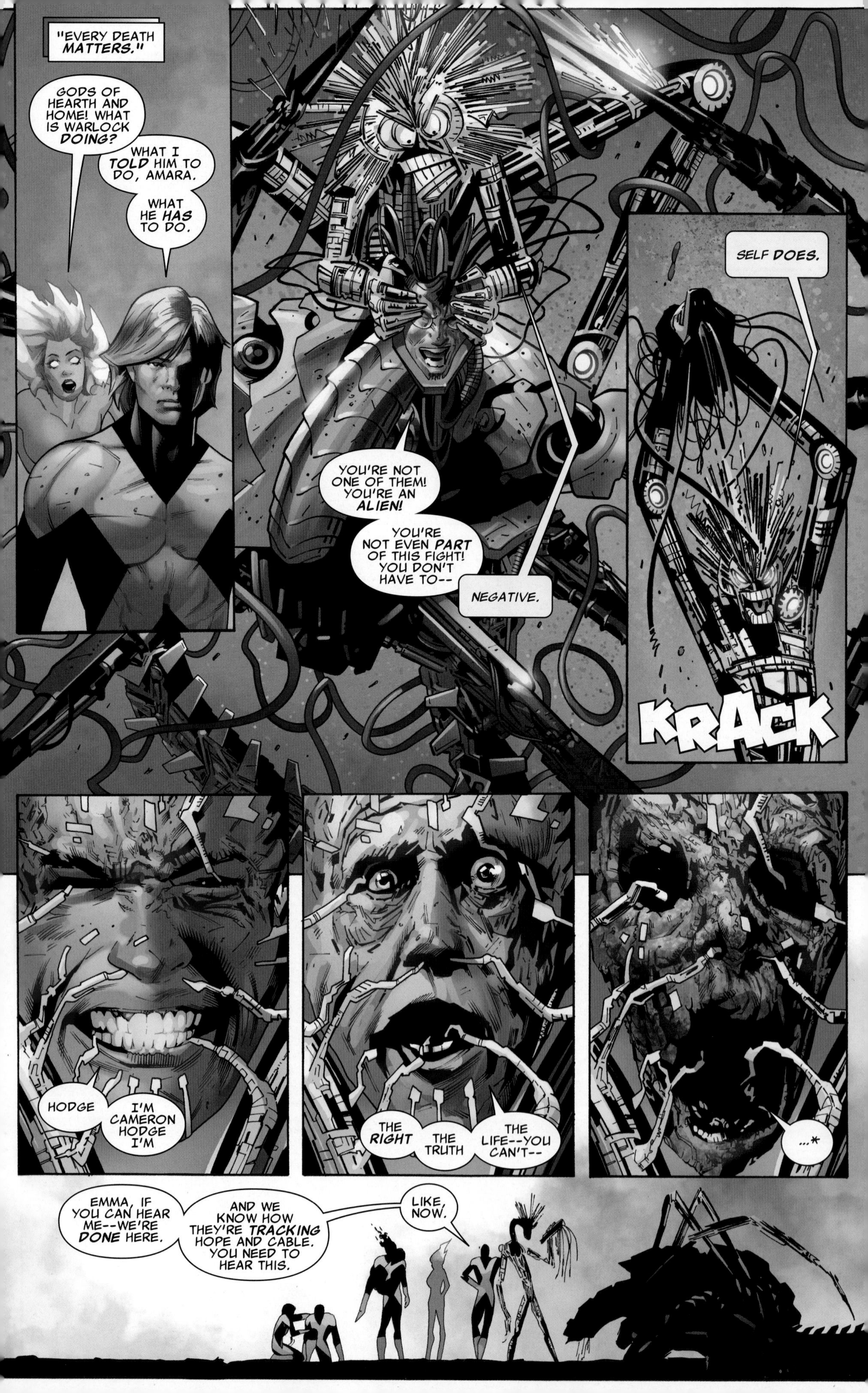
"EVERY DEATH MATTERS."
GODS OF HEARTH AND HOME! WHAT IS WARLOCK DOING?
WHAT I TOLD HIM TO DO, AMARA.
WHAT HE HAS TO DO.
YOU'RE NOT ONE OF THEM! YOU'RE AN ALIEN!
YOU'RE NOT EVEN PART OF THIS FIGHT! YOU DON'T HAVE TO--
NEGATIVE.
SELF DOES.
KRACK
HODGE
I'M CAMERON HODGE I'M
THE RIGHT
THE TRUTH
THE LIFE--YOU CAN'T--
...*
EMMA, IF YOU CAN HEAR ME--WE'RE DONE HERE.
AND WE KNOW HOW THEY'RE TRACKING HOPE AND CABLE. YOU NEED TO HEAR THIS.
LIKE, NOW.

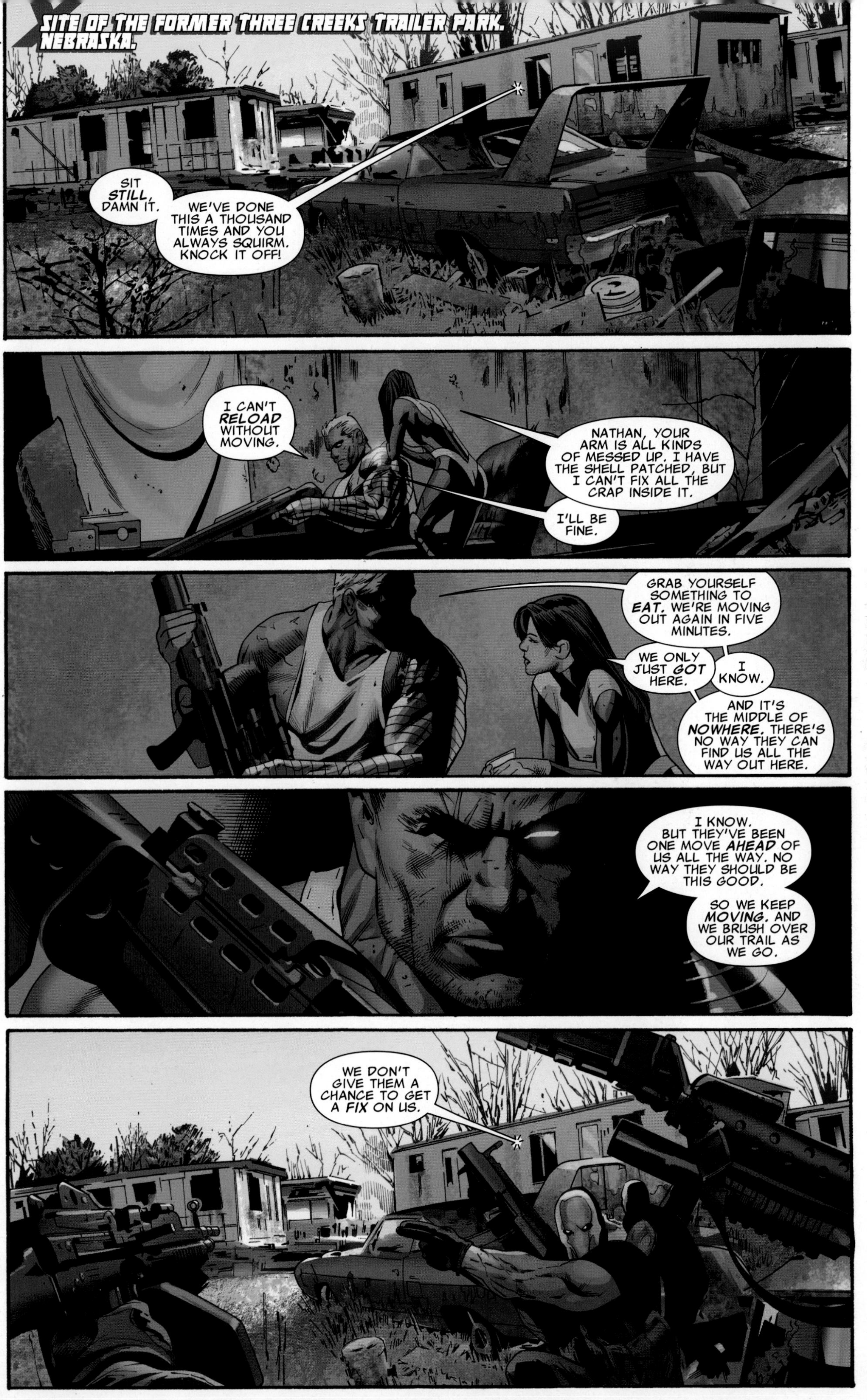
SITE OF THE FORMER THREE CREEKS TRAILER PARK. NEBRASKA.
SIT STILL, DAMN IT.
WE'VE DONE THIS A THOUSAND TIMES AND YOU ALWAYS SQUIRM. KNOCK IT OFF!
I CAN'T RELOAD WITHOUT MOVING.
NATHAN, YOUR ARM IS ALL KINDS OF MESSED UP. I HAVE THE SHELL PATCHED, BUT I CAN'T FIX ALL THE CRAP INSIDE IT.
I'LL BE FINE.
GRAB YOURSELF SOMETHING TO EAT. WE'RE MOVING OUT AGAIN IN FIVE MINUTES.
WE ONLY JUST GOT HERE.
I KNOW.
AND IT'S THE MIDDLE OF NOWHERE. THERE'S NO WAY THEY CAN FIND US ALL THE WAY OUT HERE.
I KNOW. BUT THEY'VE BEEN ONE MOVE AHEAD OF US ALL THE WAY. NO WAY THEY SHOULD BE THIS GOOD.
SO WE KEEP MOVING. AND WE BRUSH OVER OUR TRAIL AS WE GO.
WE DON'T GIVE THEM A CHANCE TO GET A FIX ON US.

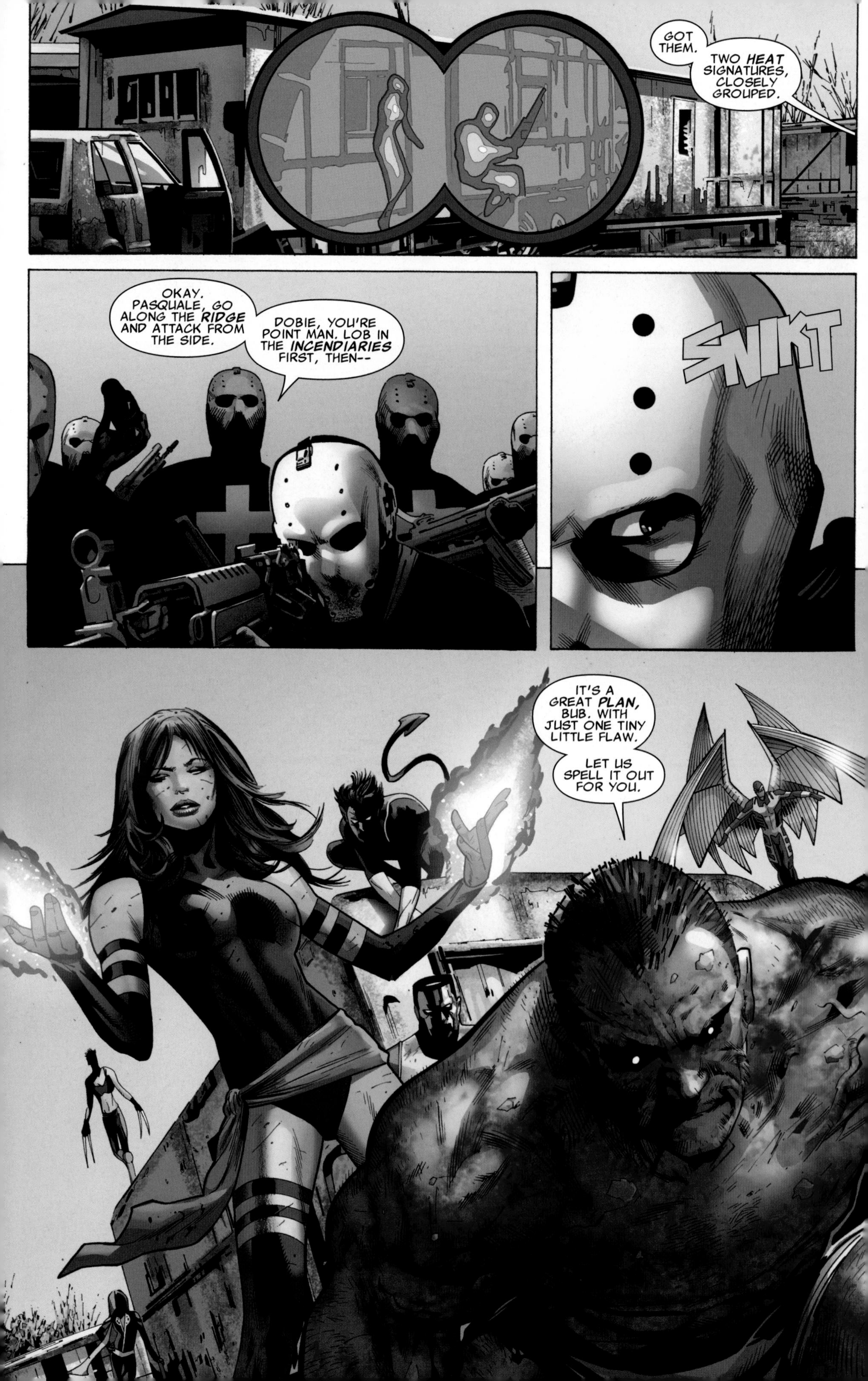
GOT THEM.
TWO HEAT SIGNATURES, CLOSELY GROUPED.
OKAY. PASQUALE, GO ALONG THE RIDGE AND ATTACK FROM THE SIDE.
DOBIE, YOU'RE POINT MAN. LOB IN THE INCENDIARIES FIRST, THEN--
SNIKT
IT'S A GREAT PLAN, BUB. WITH JUST ONE TINY LITTLE FLAW.
LET US SPELL IT OUT FOR YOU.

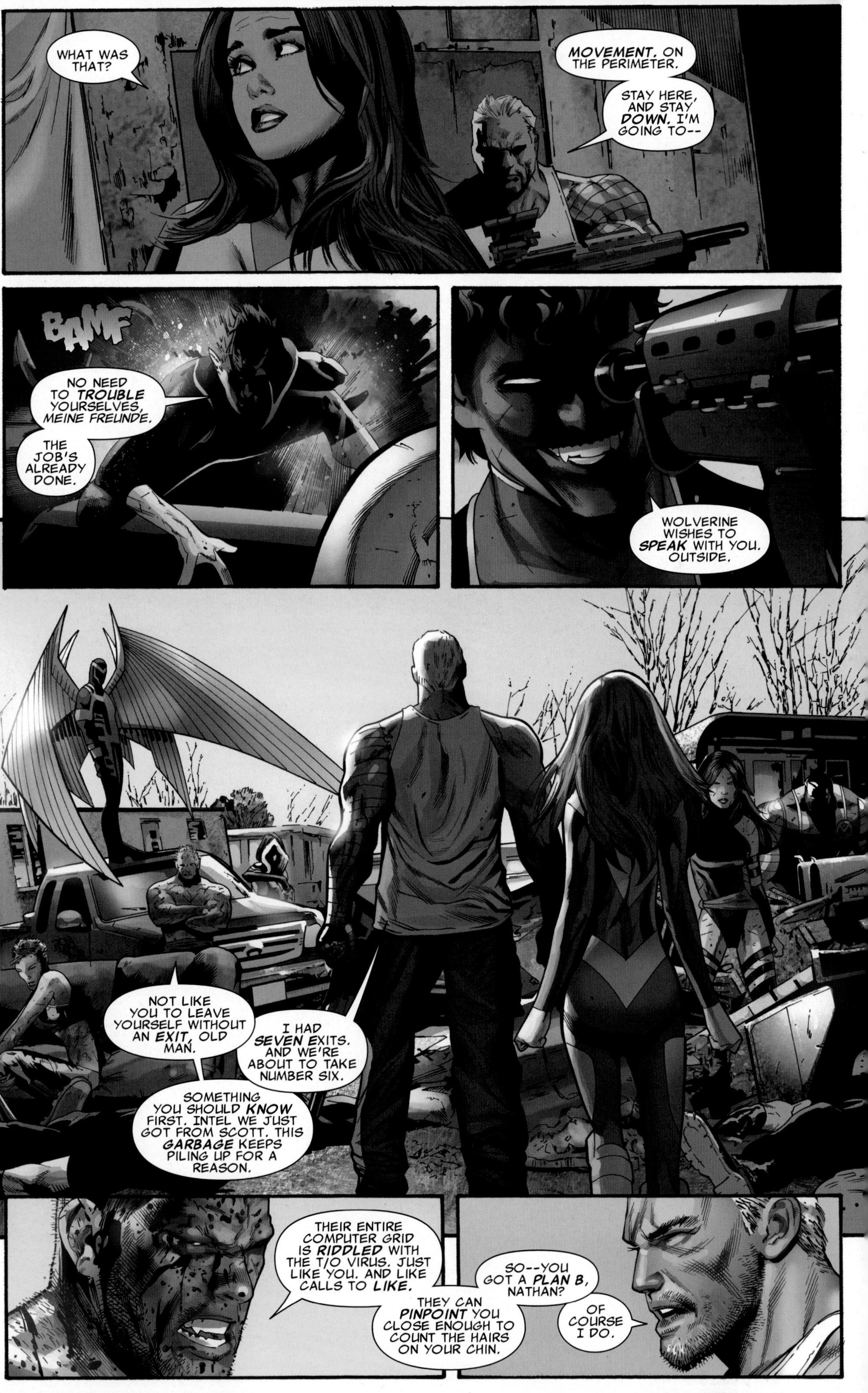
WHAT WAS THAT?
MOVEMENT. ON THE PERIMETER.
STAY HERE, AND STAY DOWN. I'M GOING TO--
BAMF
NO NEED TO TROUBLE YOURSELVES, MEINE FREUNDE.
THE JOB'S ALREADY DONE.
WOLVERINE WISHES TO SPEAK WITH YOU. OUTSIDE.
NOT LIKE YOU TO LEAVE YOURSELF WITHOUT AN EXIT, OLD MAN.
I HAD SEVEN EXITS. AND WE'RE ABOUT TO TAKE NUMBER SIX.
SOMETHING YOU SHOULD KNOW FIRST. INTEL WE JUST GOT FROM SCOTT. THIS GARBAGE KEEPS PILING UP FOR A REASON.
THEIR ENTIRE COMPUTER GRID IS RIDDLED WITH THE T/O VIRUS. JUST LIKE YOU. AND LIKE CALLS TO LIKE.
THEY CAN PINPOINT YOU CLOSE ENOUGH TO COUNT THE HAIRS ON YOUR CHIN.
SO--YOU GOT A PLAN B, NATHAN?
OF COURSE I DO.

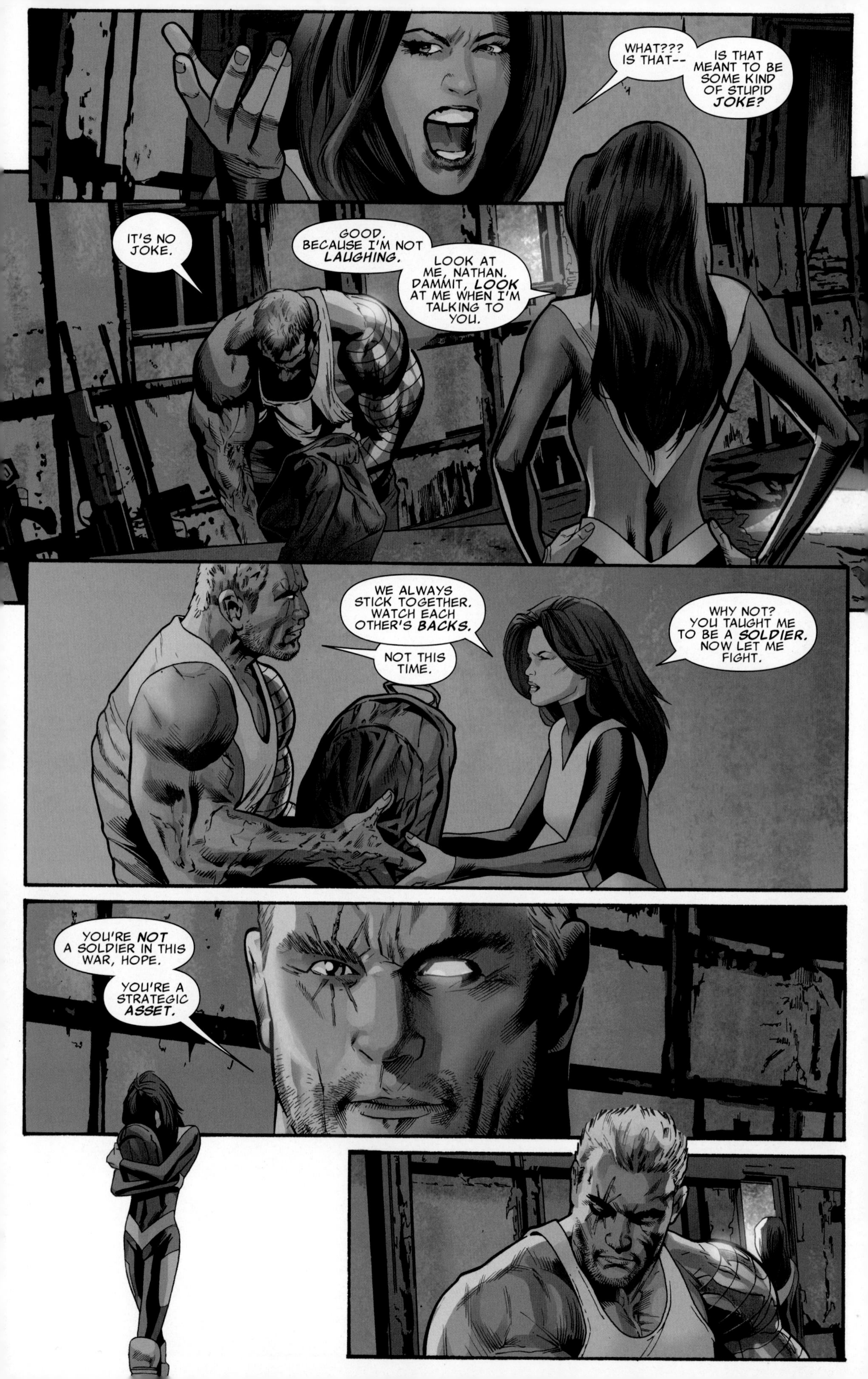
WHAT??? IS THAT--
IS THAT MEANT TO BE SOME KIND OF STUPID JOKE?
IT'S NO JOKE.
GOOD. BECAUSE I'M NOT LAUGHING.
LOOK AT ME, NATHAN. DAMMIT, LOOK AT ME WHEN I'M TALKING TO YOU.
WE ALWAYS STICK TOGETHER. WATCH EACH OTHER'S BACKS.
NOT THIS TIME.
WHY NOT? YOU TAUGHT ME TO BE A SOLDIER. NOW LET ME FIGHT.
YOU'RE NOT A SOLDIER IN THIS WAR, HOPE.
YOU'RE A STRATEGIC ASSET.

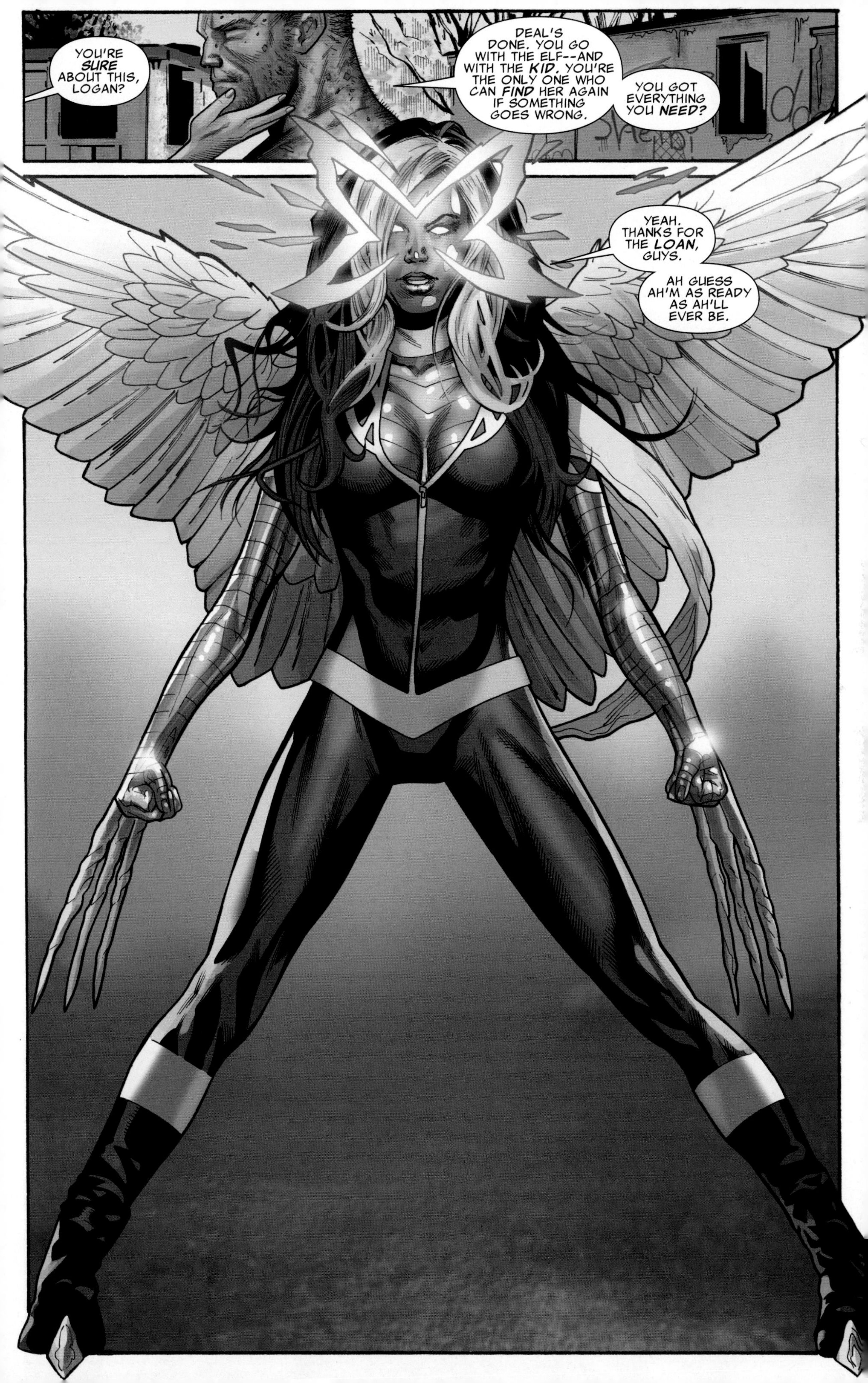
YOU'RE SURE ABOUT THIS, LOGAN?
DEAL'S DONE. YOU GO WITH THE ELF--AND WITH THE KID. YOU'RE THE ONLY ONE WHO CAN FIND HER AGAIN IF SOMETHING GOES WRONG.
YOU GOT EVERYTHING YOU NEED?
YEAH. THANKS FOR THE LOAN, GUYS.
AH GUESS AH'M AS READY AS AH'LL EVER BE.

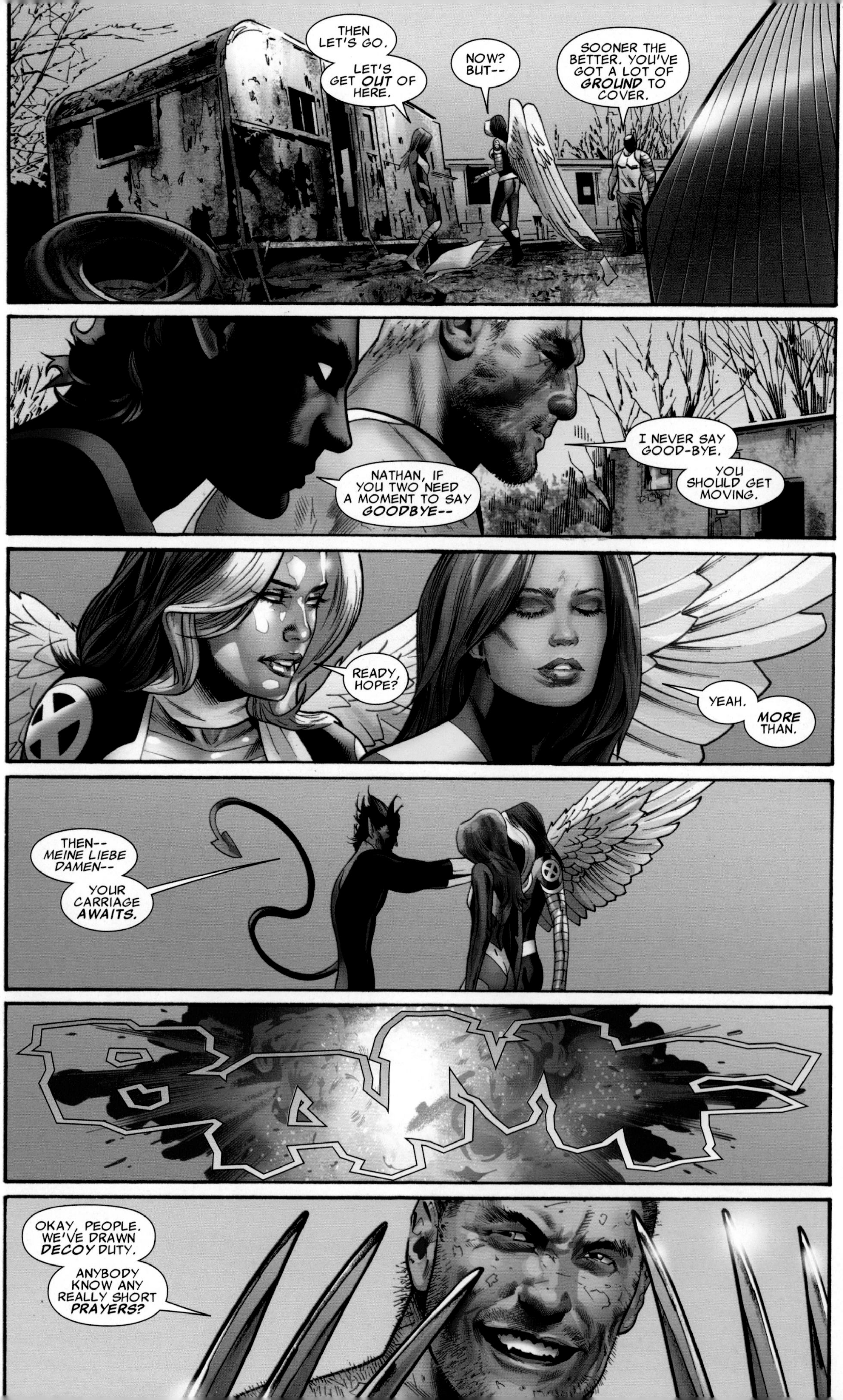

THEN LET'S GO.
LET'S GET OUT OF HERE.
NOW? BUT--
SOONER THE BETTER. YOU'VE GOT A LOT OF GROUND TO COVER.
NATHAN, IF YOU TWO NEED A MOMENT TO SAY GOODBYE--
I NEVER SAY GOOD-BYE.
YOU SHOULD GET MOVING.
READY, HOPE?
YEAH.
MORE THAN.
THEN--
MEINE LIEBE DAMEN--
YOUR CARRIAGE AWAITS.
BAMF
OKAY, PEOPLE. WE'VE DRAWN DECOY DUTY.
ANYBODY KNOW ANY REALLY SHORT PRAYERS?

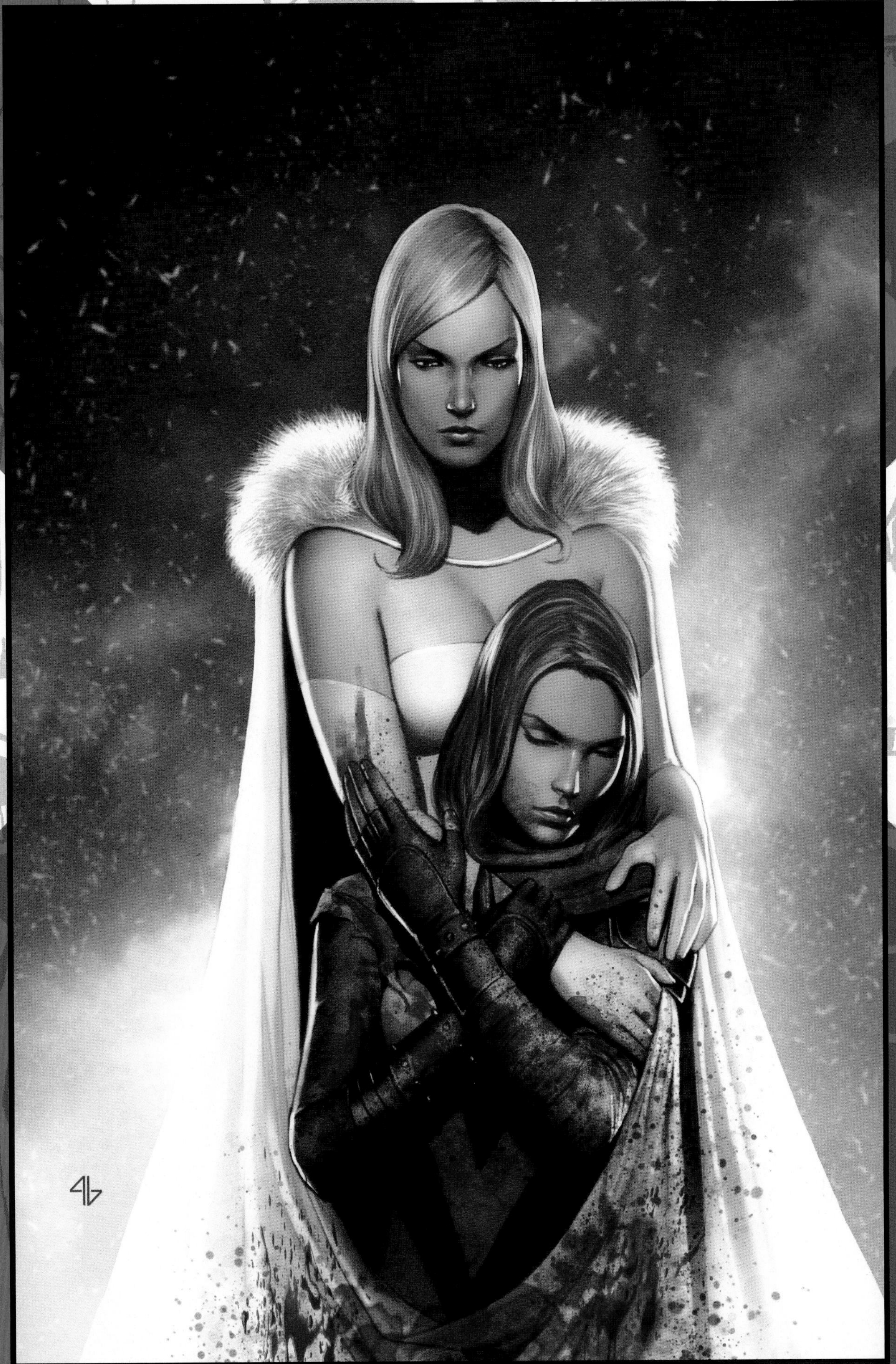

X-FORCE #26

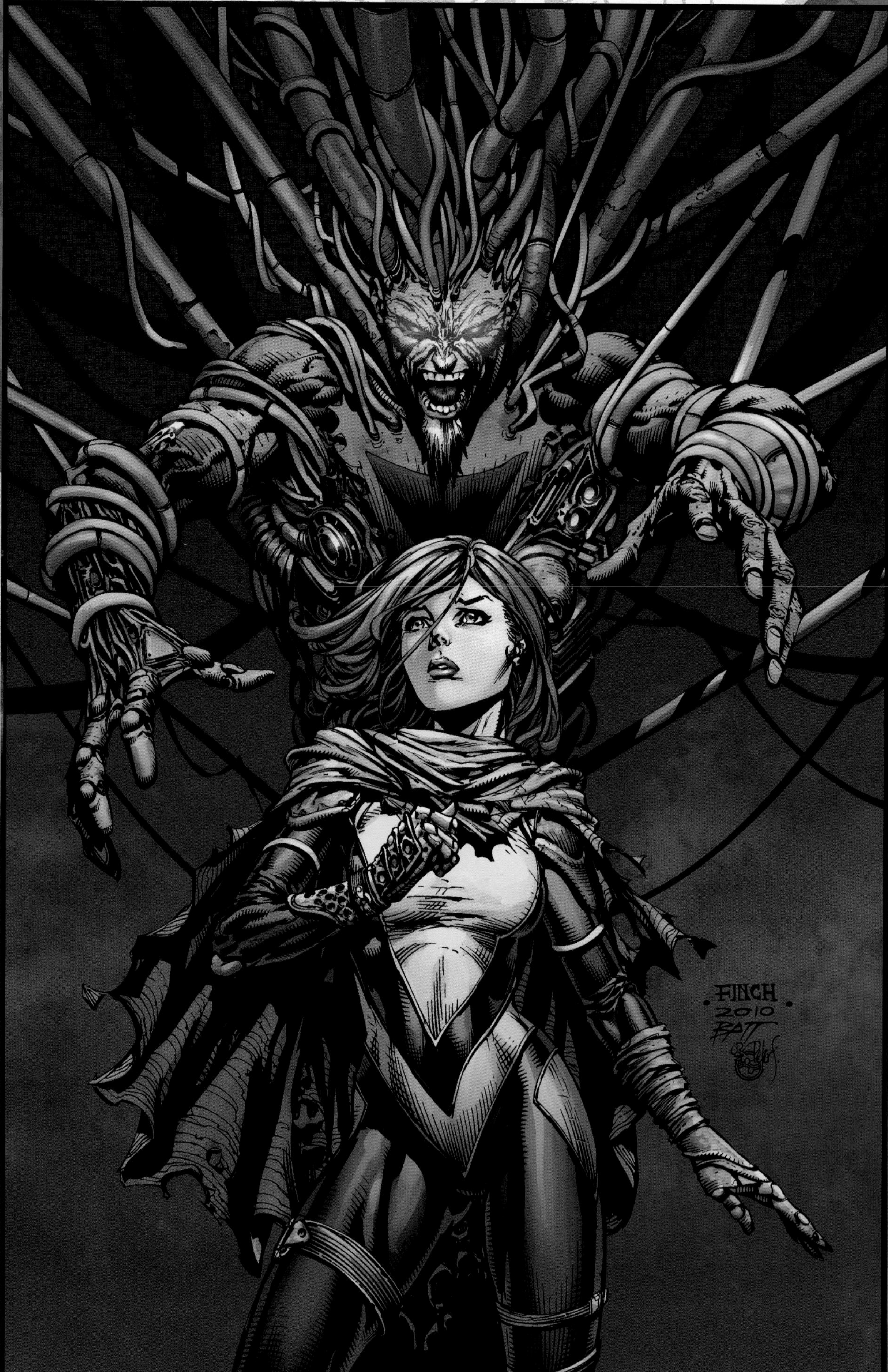
FINCH
2010

X-FORCE #26
VARIANT

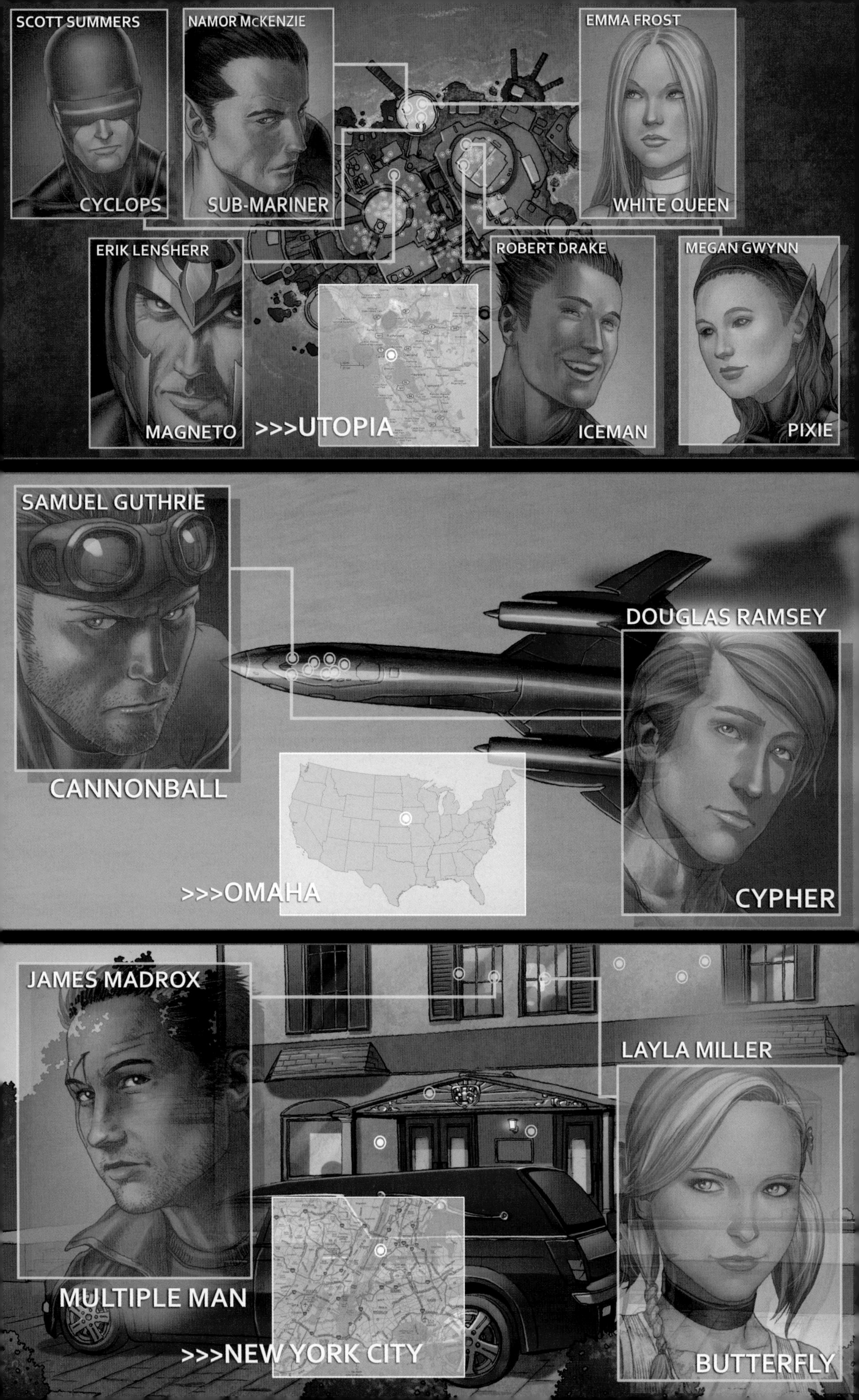
SCOTT SUMMERS
CYCLOPS
NAMOR McKENZIE
SUB-MARINER
EMMA FROST
WHITE QUEEN
ERIK LENSHERR
MAGNETO
>>>UTOPIA
ROBERT DRAKE
ICEMAN
MEGAN GWYNN
PIXIE
SAMUEL GUTHRIE
CANNONBALL
DOUGLAS RAMSEY
CYPHER
>>>OMAHA
JAMES MADROX
MULTIPLE MAN
LAYLA MILLER
BUTTERFLY
>>>NEW YORK CITY

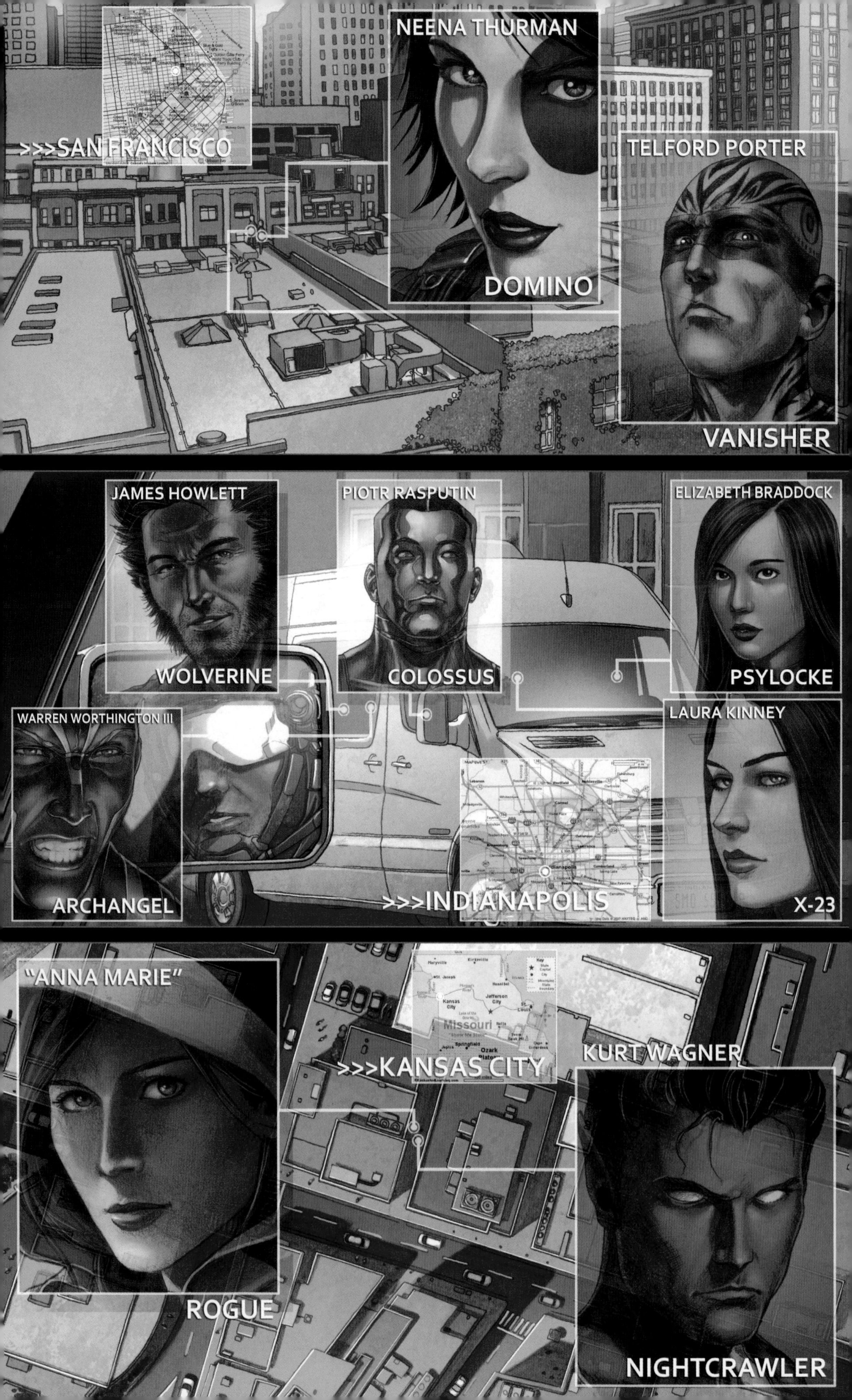

>>>SAN FRANCISCO
NEENA THURMAN
DOMINO
TELFORD PORTER
VANISHER
JAMES HOWLETT
WOLVERINE
PIOTR RASPUTIN
COLOSSUS
ELIZABETH BRADDOCK
PSYLOCKE
WARREN WORTHINGTON III
ARCHANGEL
>>>INDIANAPOLIS
LAURA KINNEY
X-23
"ANNA MARIE"
ROGUE
>>>KANSAS CITY
KURT WAGNER
NIGHTCRAWLER

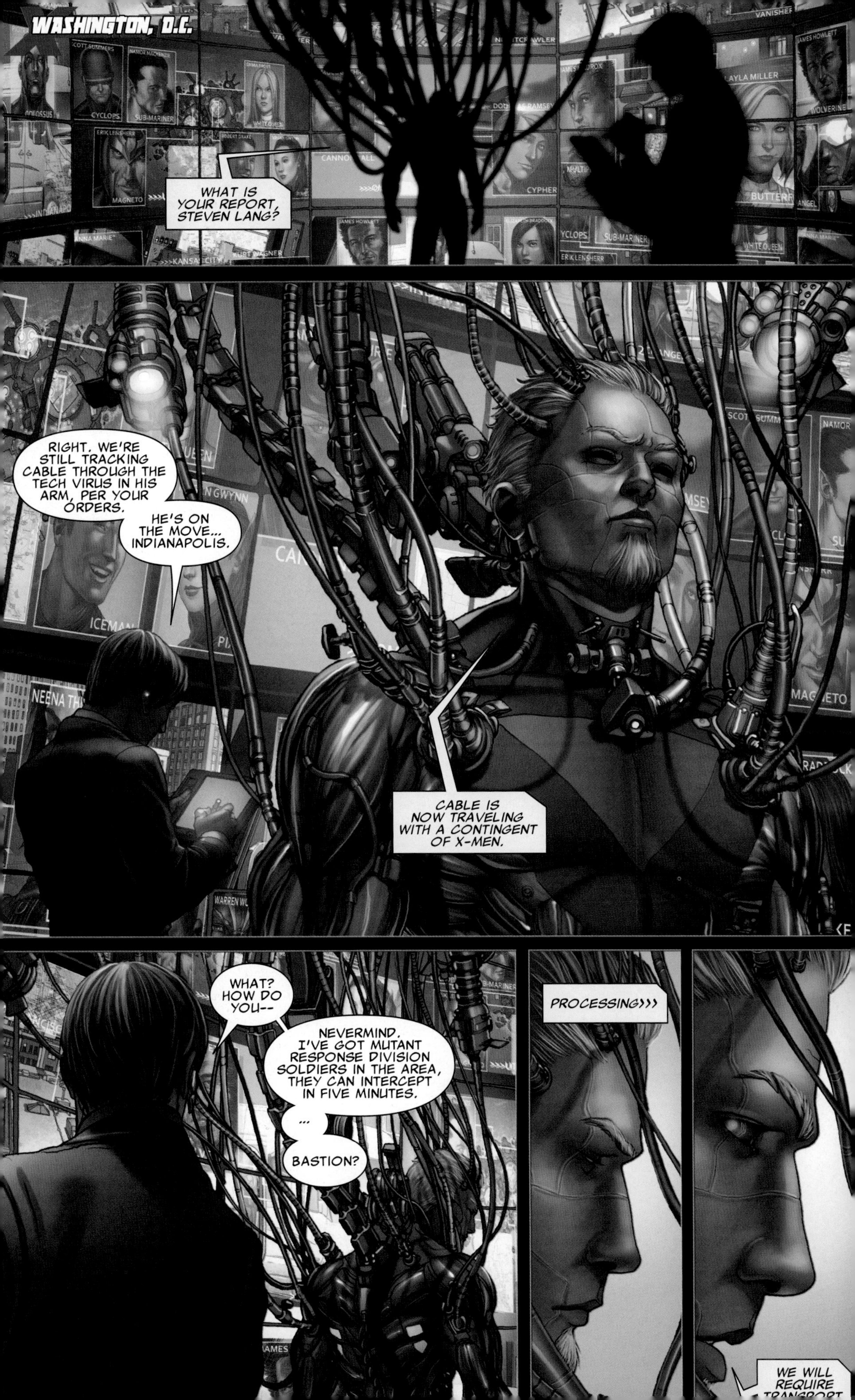
WASHINGTON, D.C.
WHAT IS YOUR REPORT, STEVEN LANG?
RIGHT. WE'RE STILL TRACKING CABLE THROUGH THE TECH VIRUS IN HIS ARM, PER YOUR ORDERS.
HE'S ON THE MOVE... INDIANAPOLIS.
CABLE IS NOW TRAVELING WITH A CONTINGENT OF X-MEN.
WHAT? HOW DO YOU--
NEVERMIND. I'VE GOT MUTANT RESPONSE DIVISION SOLDIERS IN THE AREA, THEY CAN INTERCEPT IN FIVE MINUTES.
...
BASTION?
PROCESSING›››
WE WILL REQUIRE

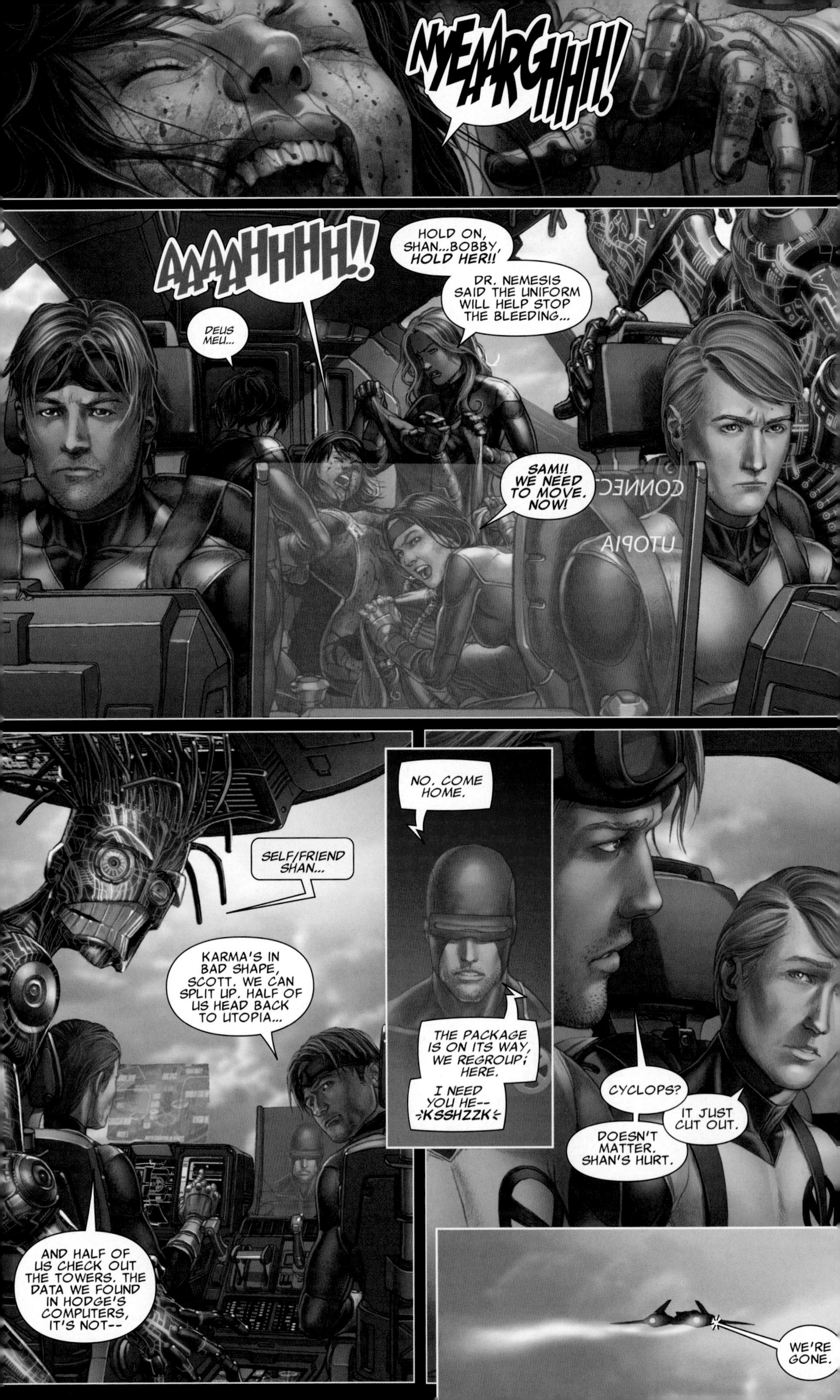

N'YEAARGHHH!
AAAAHHHH!!
DEUS MEU...
HOLD ON, SHAN...BOBBY, HOLD HER!!
DR. NEMESIS SAID THE UNIFORM WILL HELP STOP THE BLEEDING...
SAM!! WE NEED TO MOVE. NOW!
CONNECT
UTOPIA
SELF/FRIEND SHAN...
KARMA'S IN BAD SHAPE, SCOTT. WE CAN SPLIT UP. HALF OF US HEAD BACK TO UTOPIA...
AND HALF OF US CHECK OUT THE TOWERS. THE DATA WE FOUND IN HODGE'S COMPUTERS, IT'S NOT--
NO. COME HOME.
THE PACKAGE IS ON ITS WAY, WE REGROUP; HERE.
I NEED YOU HE-- -KSSHZZK-
CYCLOPS?
IT JUST CUT OUT.
DOESN'T MATTER. SHAN'S HURT.
WE'RE GONE.

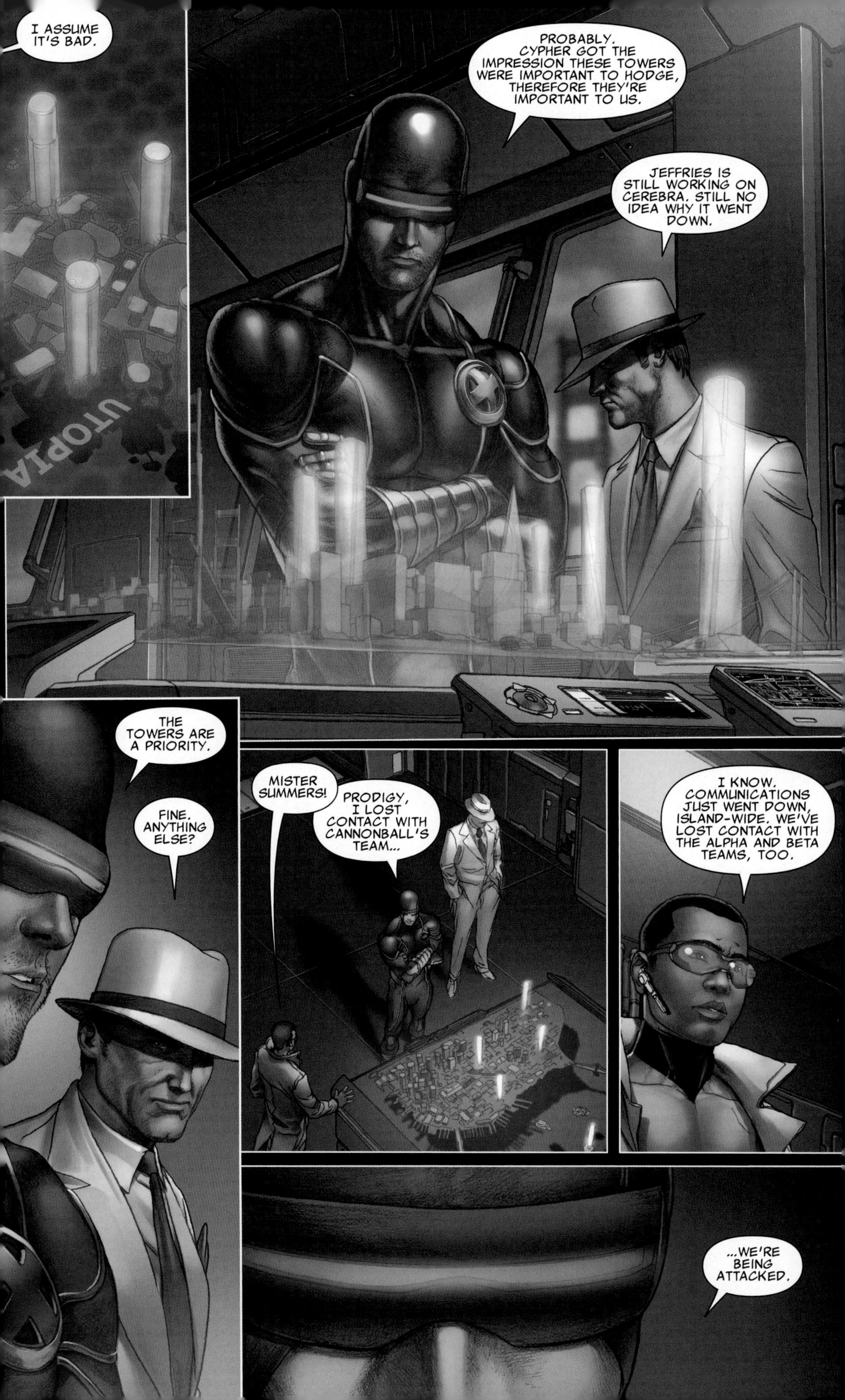
I ASSUME IT'S BAD.
PROBABLY. CYPHER GOT THE IMPRESSION THESE TOWERS WERE IMPORTANT TO HODGE, THEREFORE THEY'RE IMPORTANT TO US.
JEFFRIES IS STILL WORKING ON CEREBRA. STILL NO IDEA WHY IT WENT DOWN.
UTOPIA
THE TOWERS ARE A PRIORITY.
FINE. ANYTHING ELSE?
MISTER SUMMERS!
PRODIGY, I LOST CONTACT WITH CANNONBALL'S TEAM...
I KNOW. COMMUNICATIONS JUST WENT DOWN, ISLAND-WIDE. WE'VE LOST CONTACT WITH THE ALPHA AND BETA TEAMS, TOO.
...WE'RE BEING ATTACKED.

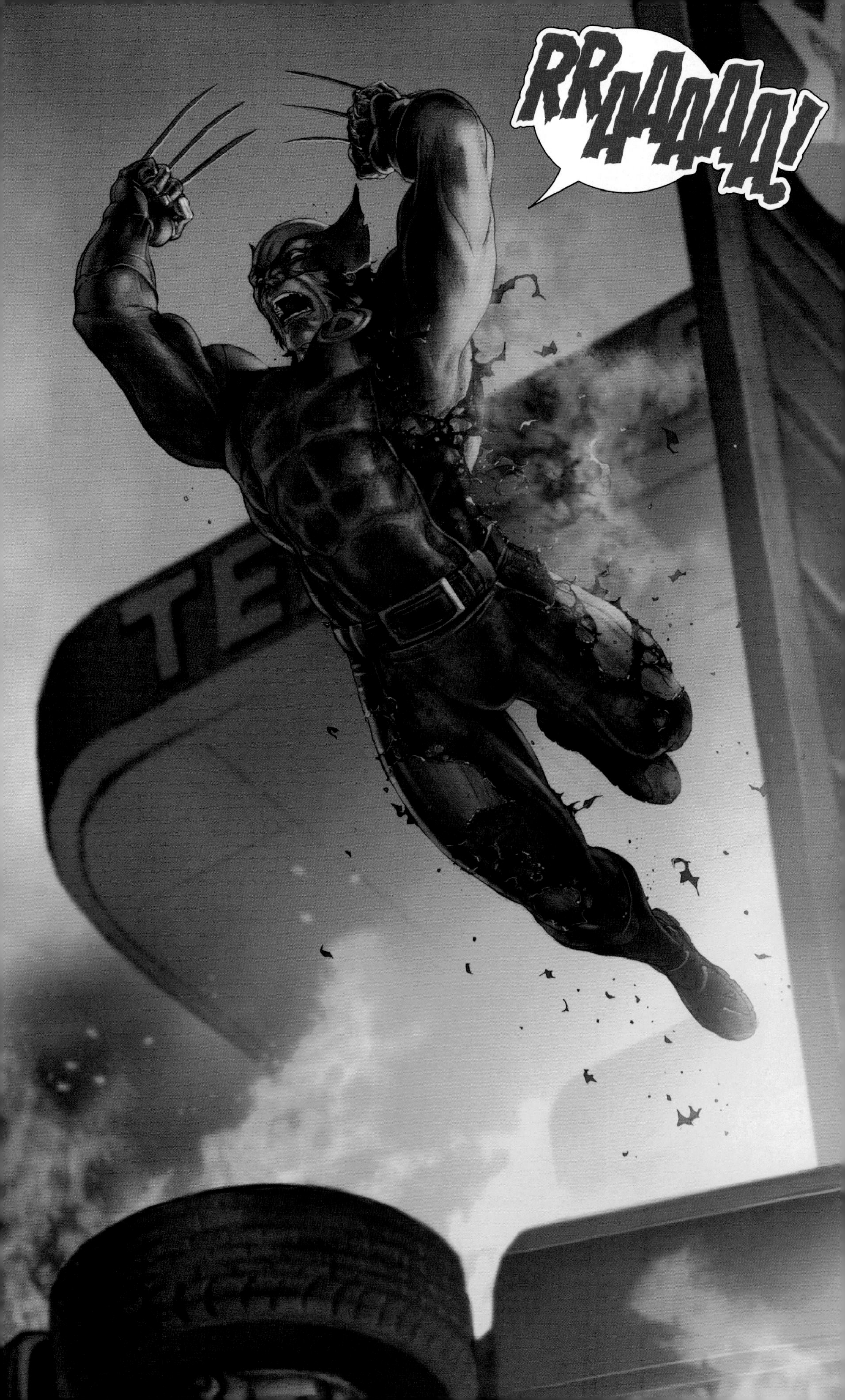
RRAAAAA!

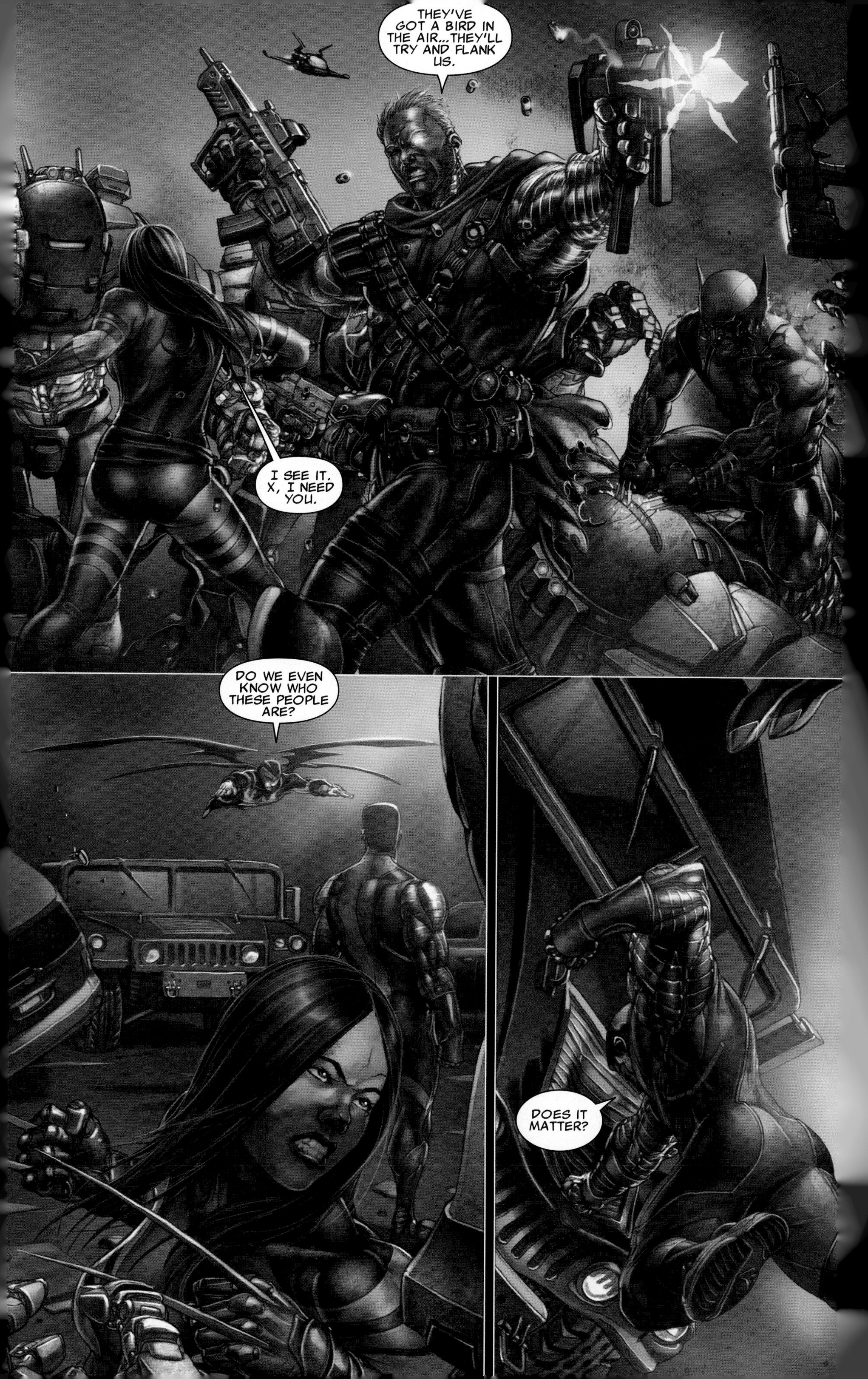
THEY'VE GOT A BIRD IN THE AIR...THEY'LL TRY AND FLANK US.
I SEE IT. X, I NEED YOU.
DO WE EVEN KNOW WHO THESE PEOPLE ARE?
DOES IT MATTER?

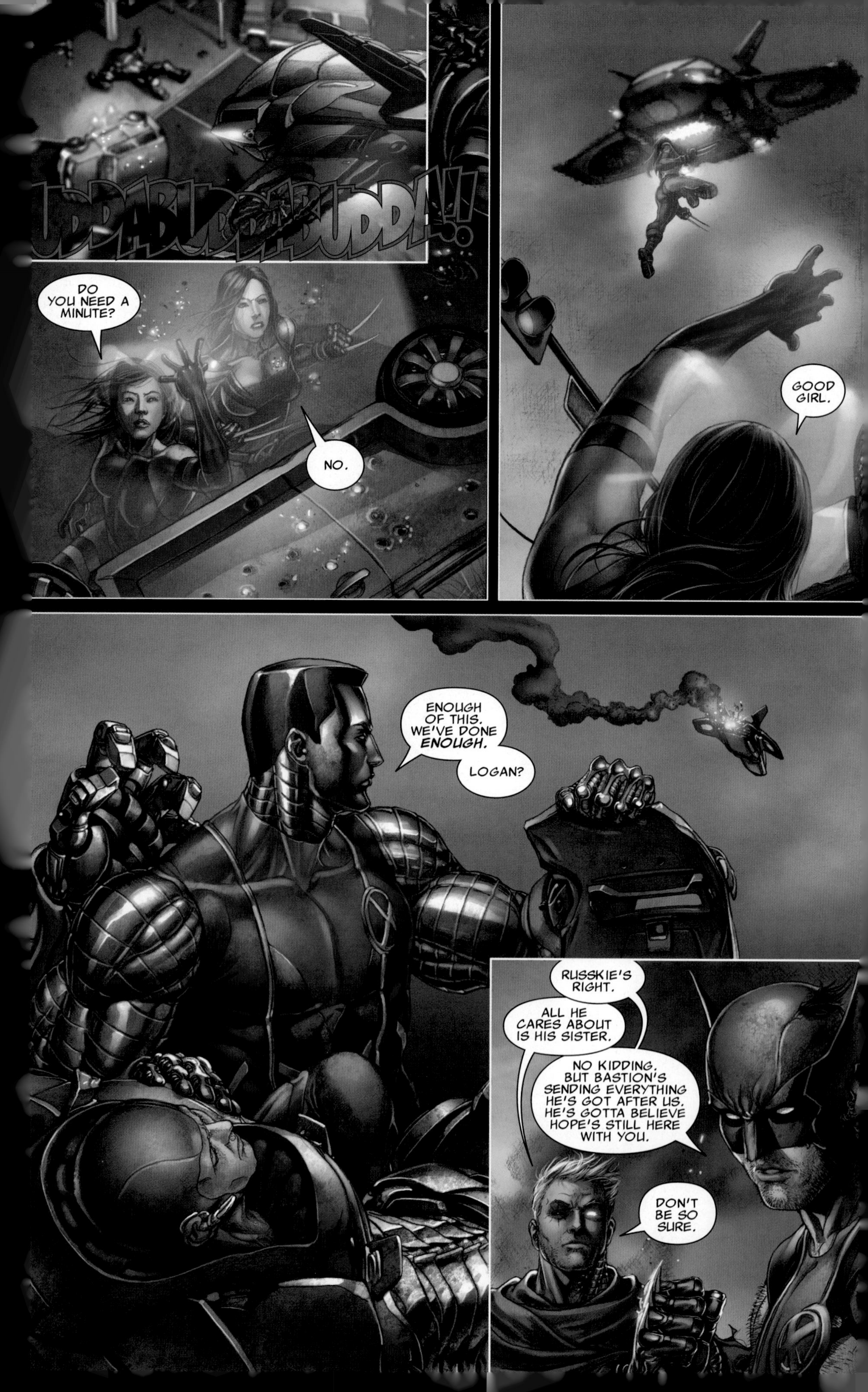
UDDABUDDABUDDA!!
DO YOU NEED A MINUTE?
NO.
GOOD GIRL.
ENOUGH OF THIS. WE'VE DONE ENOUGH.
LOGAN?
RUSSKIE'S RIGHT.
ALL HE CARES ABOUT IS HIS SISTER.
NO KIDDING. BUT BASTION'S SENDING EVERYTHING HE'S GOT AFTER US. HE'S GOTTA BELIEVE HOPE'S STILL HERE WITH YOU.
DON'T BE SO SURE.

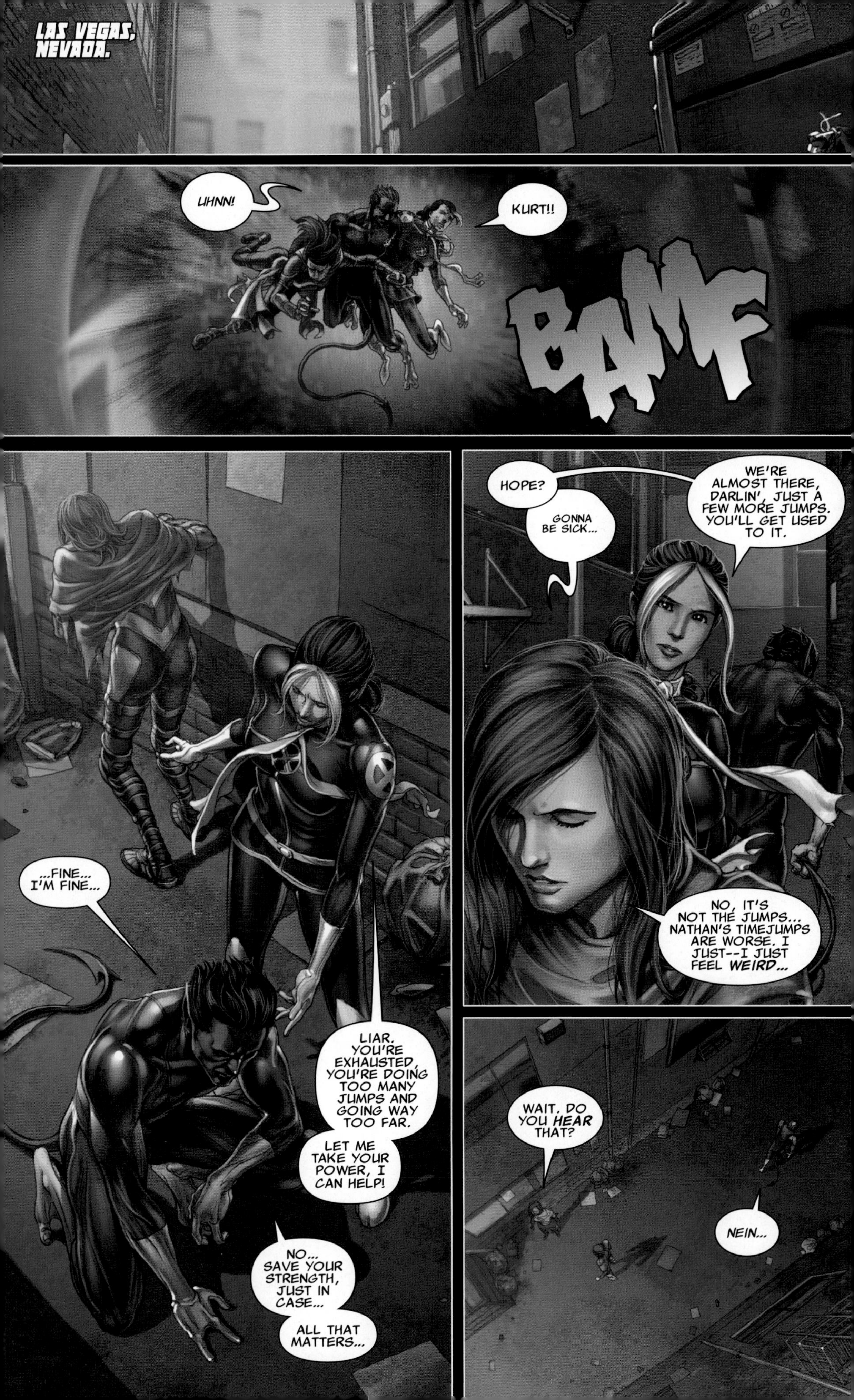
LAS VEGAS, NEVADA.
UHNN!
KURT!!
BAMF
...FINE... I'M FINE...
LIAR. YOU'RE EXHAUSTED, YOU'RE DOING TOO MANY JUMPS AND GOING WAY TOO FAR.
LET ME TAKE YOUR POWER, I CAN HELP!
NO... SAVE YOUR STRENGTH, JUST IN CASE...
ALL THAT MATTERS...
HOPE?
GONNA BE SICK...
WE'RE ALMOST THERE, DARLIN', JUST A FEW MORE JUMPS. YOU'LL GET USED TO IT.
NO, IT'S NOT THE JUMPS... NATHAN'S TIMEJUMPS ARE WORSE. I JUST--I JUST FEEL WEIRD...
WAIT. DO YOU HEAR THAT?
NEIN...

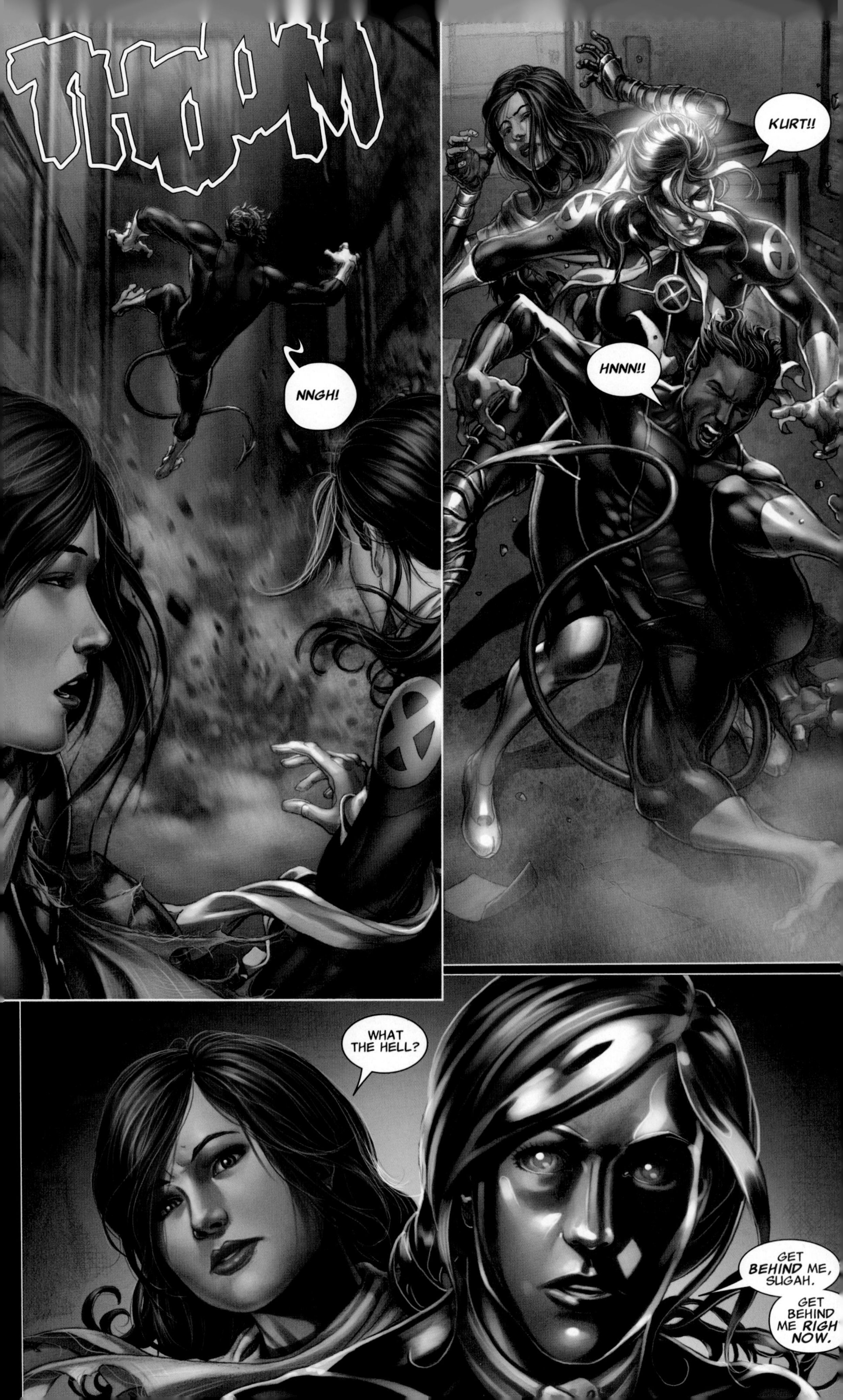
THOOM
NNGH!
KURT!!
HNNN!!
WHAT THE HELL?
GET BEHIND ME, SUGAH.
GET BEHIND ME RIGH NOW.

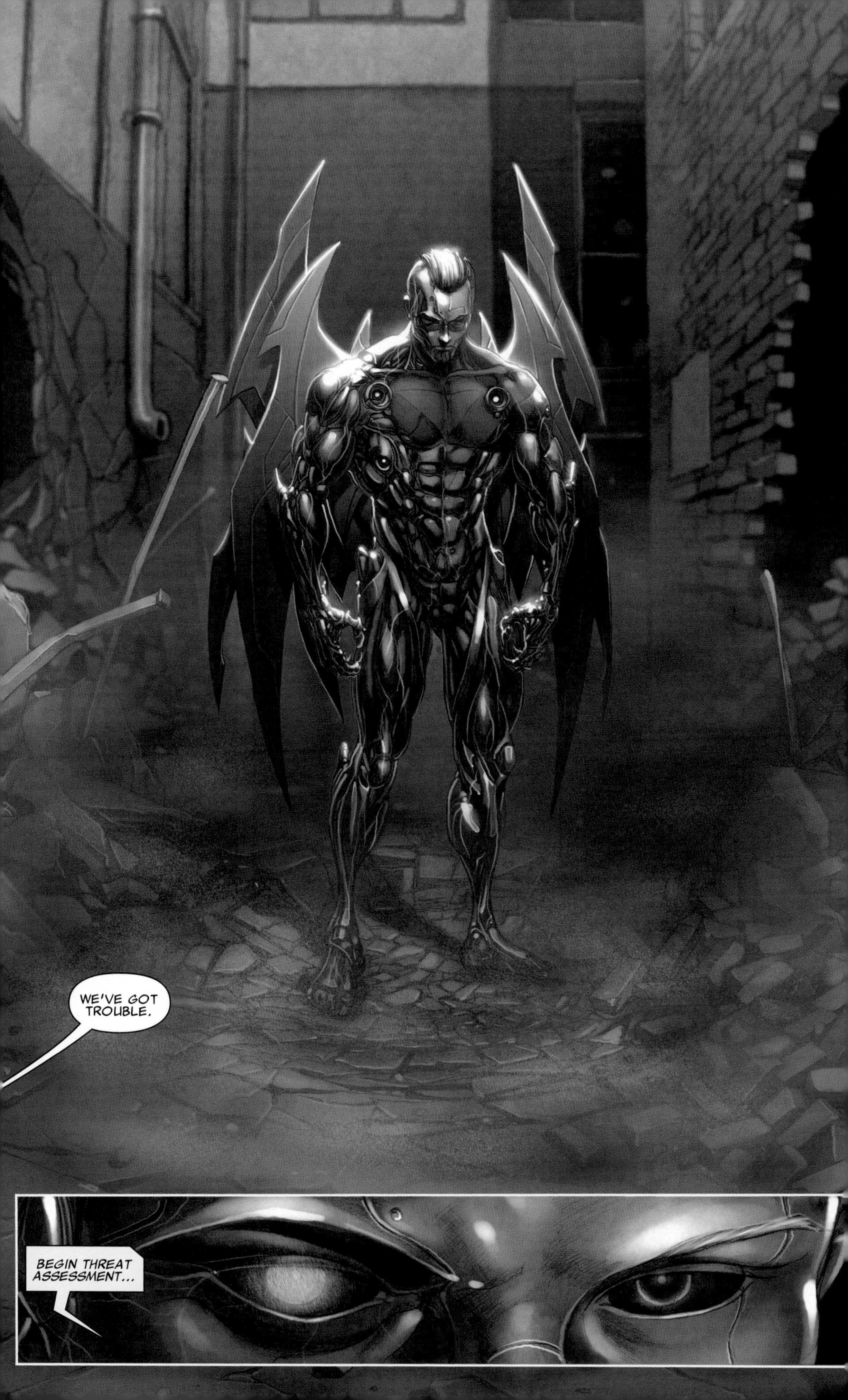
WE'VE GOT TROUBLE.
BEGIN THREAT ASSESSMENT...

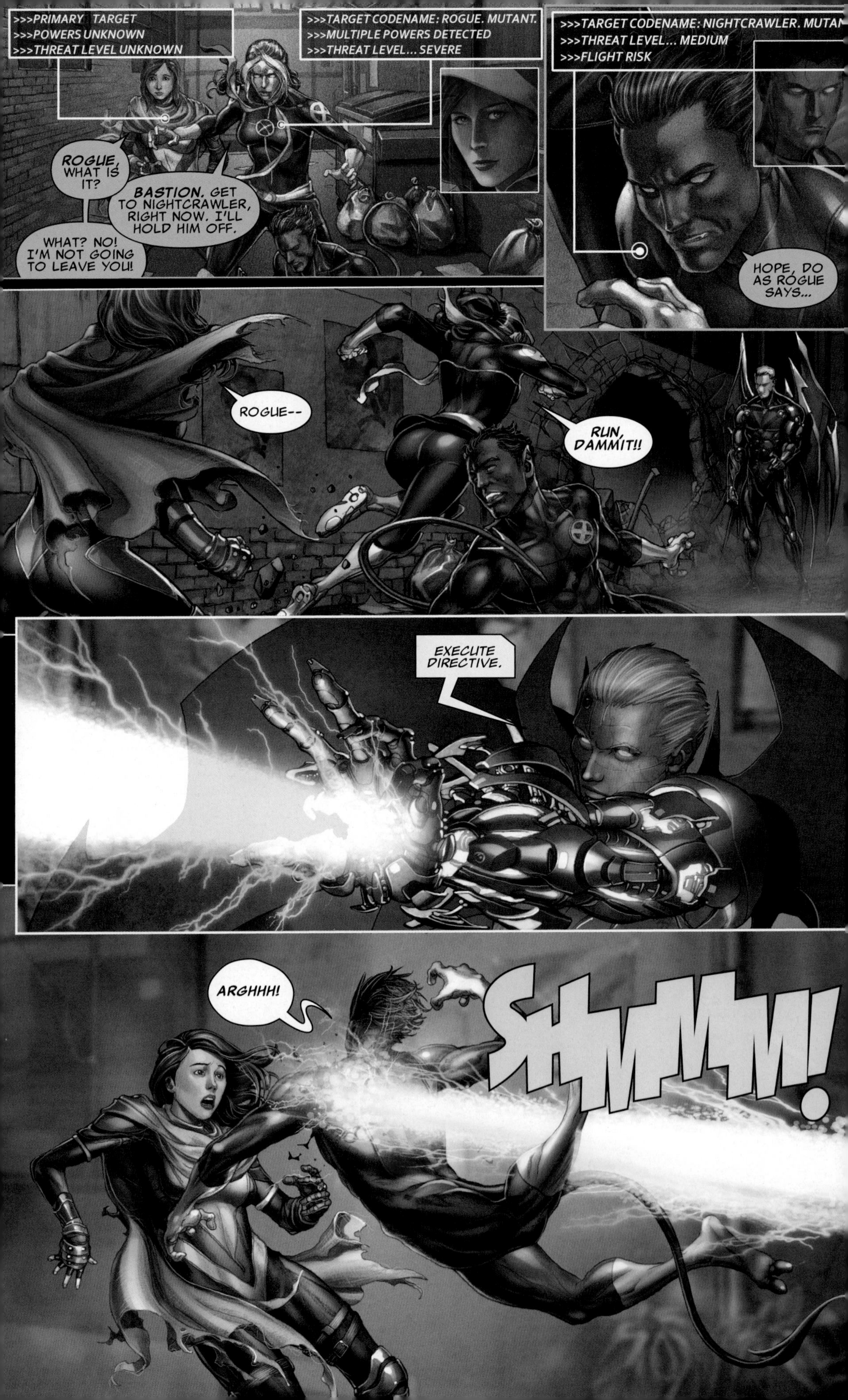
>>>PRIMARY TARGET
>>>POWERS UNKNOWN
>>>THREAT LEVEL UNKNOWN
>>>TARGET CODENAME: ROGUE. MUTANT.
>>>MULTIPLE POWERS DETECTED
>>>THREAT LEVEL... SEVERE
ROGUE, WHAT IS IT?
BASTION. GET TO NIGHTCRAWLER, RIGHT NOW. I'LL HOLD HIM OFF.
WHAT? NO! I'M NOT GOING TO LEAVE YOU!
>>>TARGET CODENAME: NIGHTCRAWLER. MUTAN
>>>THREAT LEVEL... MEDIUM
>>>FLIGHT RISK
HOPE, DO AS ROGUE SAYS...
ROGUE--
RUN, DAMMIT!!
EXECUTE DIRECTIVE.
ARGHHH!
SHMMM!

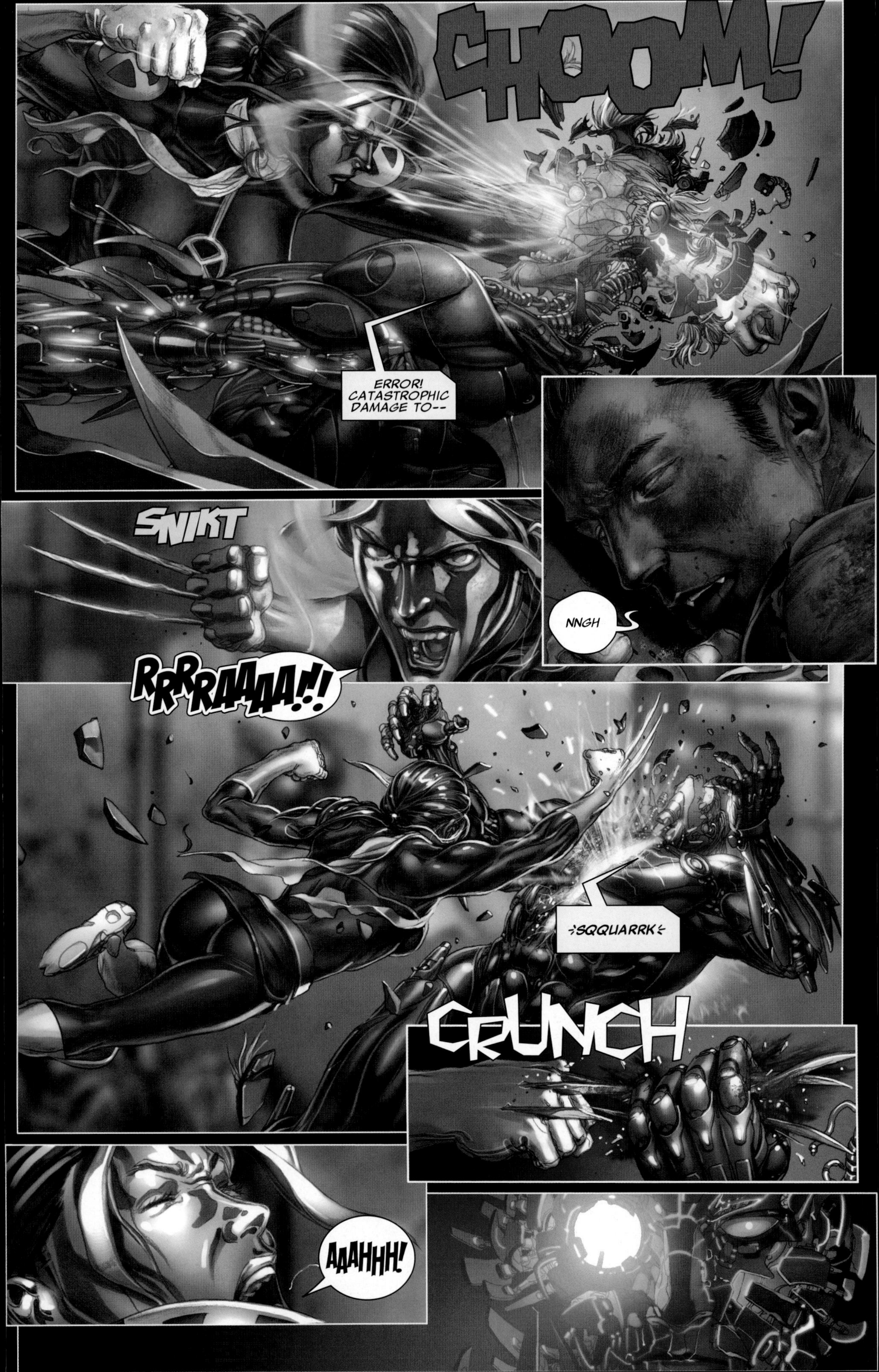
CHOOM!
ERROR! CATASTROPHIC DAMAGE TO--
NNGH
SNIKT
RRRRAAAAA!!!
-SQQUARRK-
CRUNCH
AAAHHH!

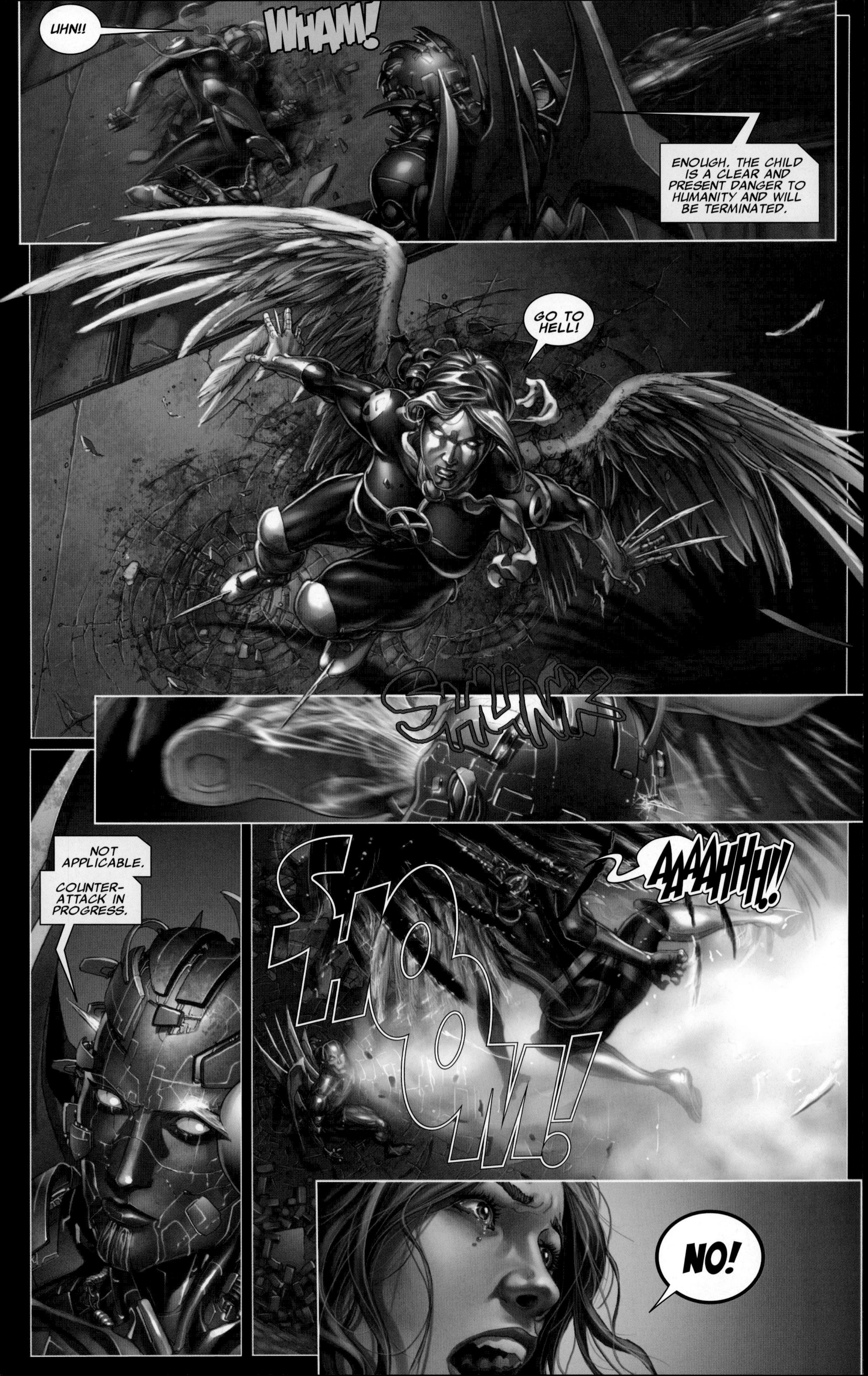
UHN!!
WHAM!
ENOUGH. THE CHILD IS A CLEAR AND PRESENT DANGER TO HUMANITY AND WILL BE TERMINATED.
GO TO HELL!
SHUNK
NOT APPLICABLE.
COUNTER-ATTACK IN PROGRESS.
THOOM!
AAAAHHH!!
NO!

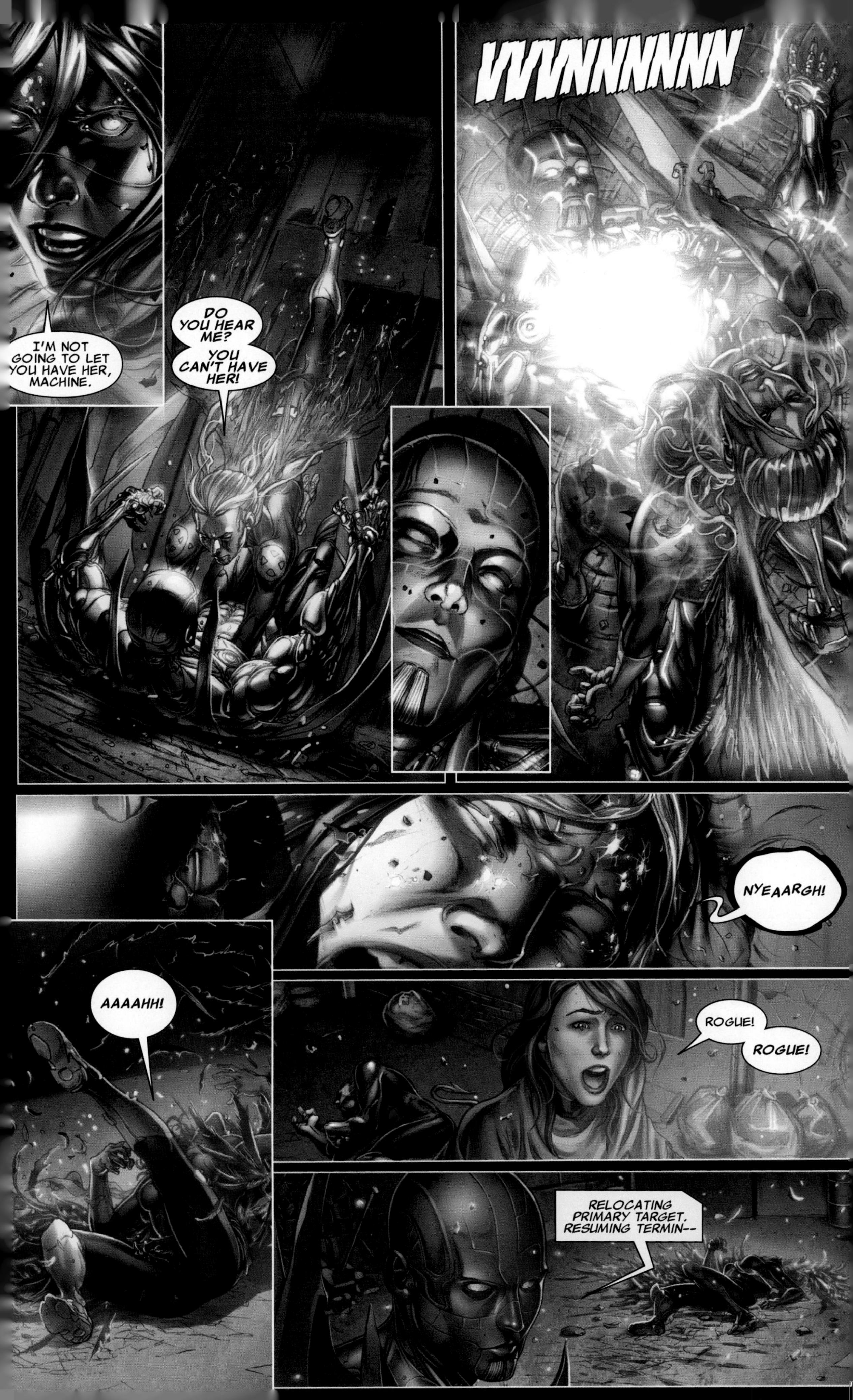
I'M NOT GOING TO LET YOU HAVE HER, MACHINE.
DO YOU HEAR ME? YOU CAN'T HAVE HER!
VVVNNNNNNN
NYEAARGH!
AAAAHH!
ROGUE!
ROGUE!
RELOCATING PRIMARY TARGET. RESUMING TERMIN--

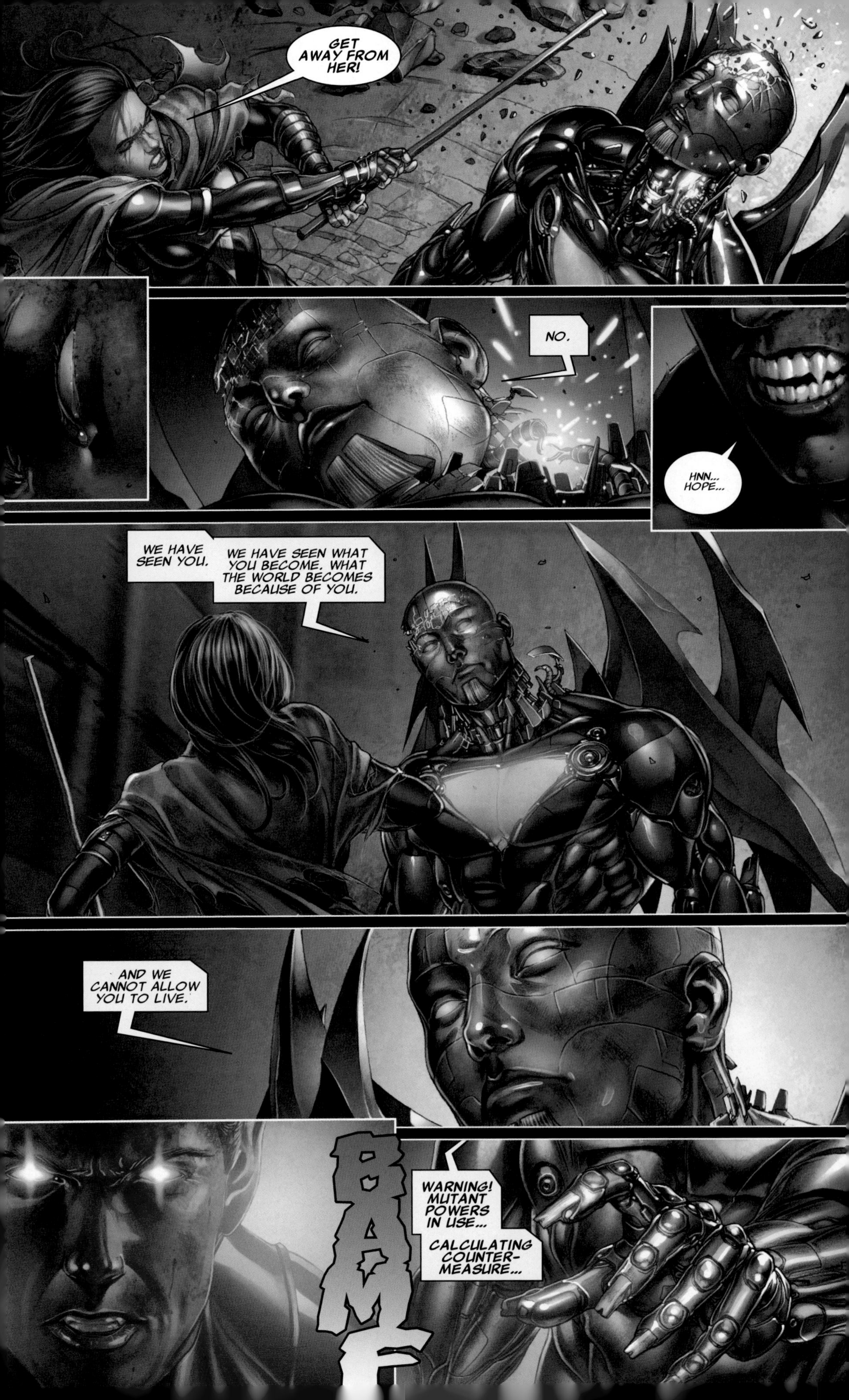
GET AWAY FROM HER!
NO.
HNN... HOPE...
WE HAVE SEEN YOU.
WE HAVE SEEN WHAT YOU BECOME. WHAT THE WORLD BECOMES BECAUSE OF YOU.
AND WE CANNOT ALLOW YOU TO LIVE.
BAMF
WARNING! MUTANT POWERS IN USE...
CALCULATING COUNTER-MEASURE...

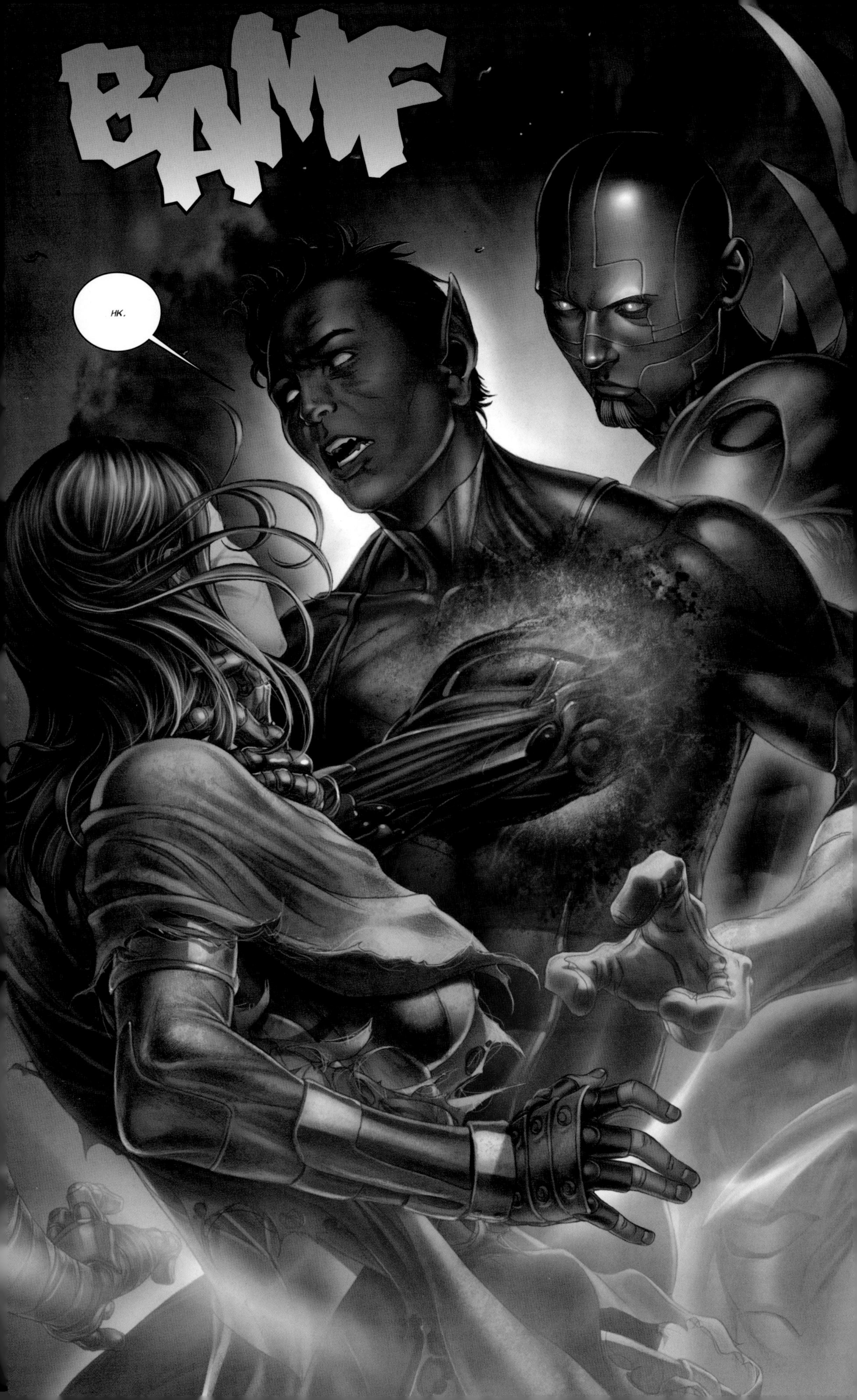
BAMF
HK.

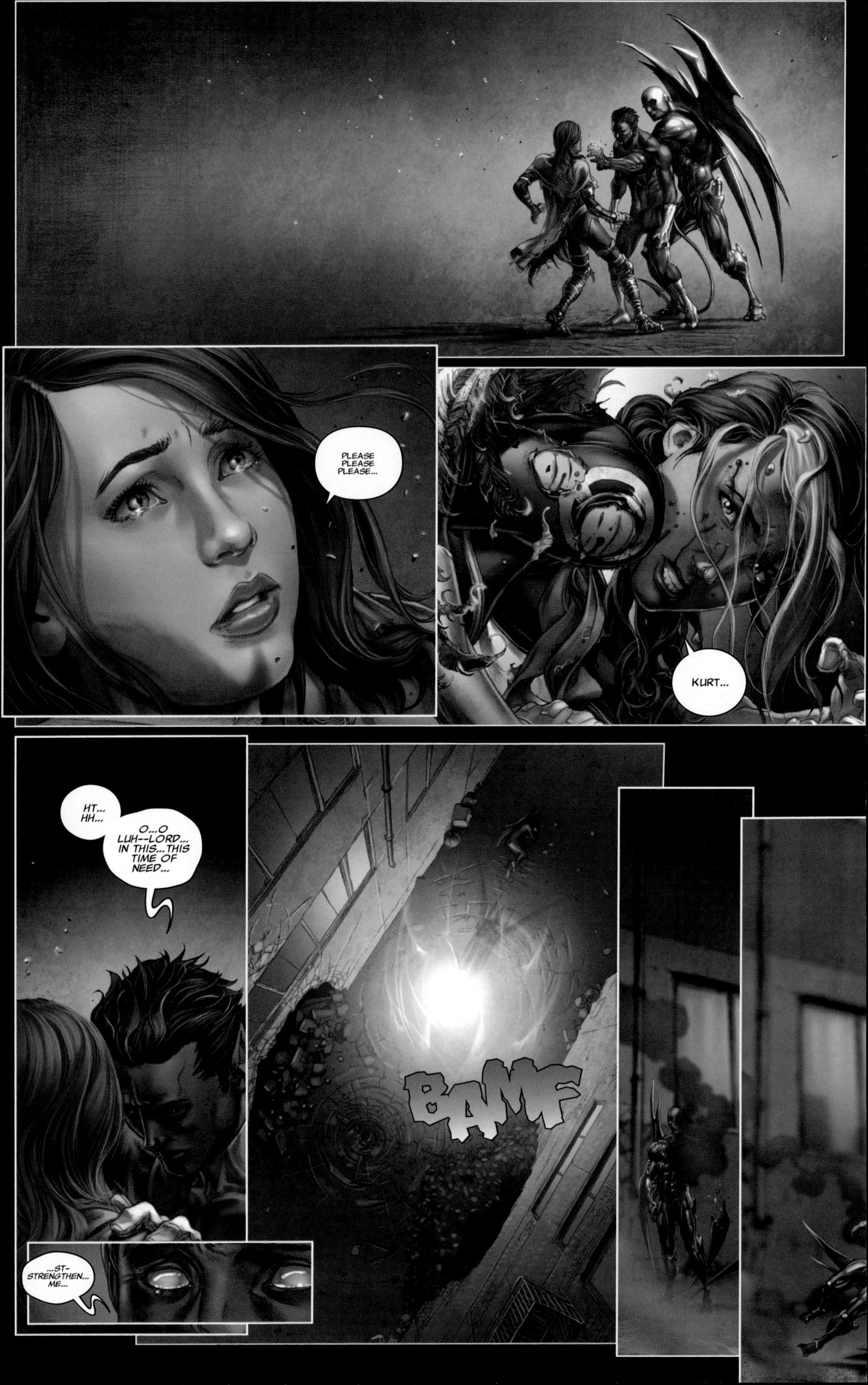
PLEASE PLEASE PLEASE...
KURT...
HT... HH...
O...O LUH--LORD... IN THIS...THIS TIME OF NEED...
...ST-STRENGTHEN... ME...
BAMF

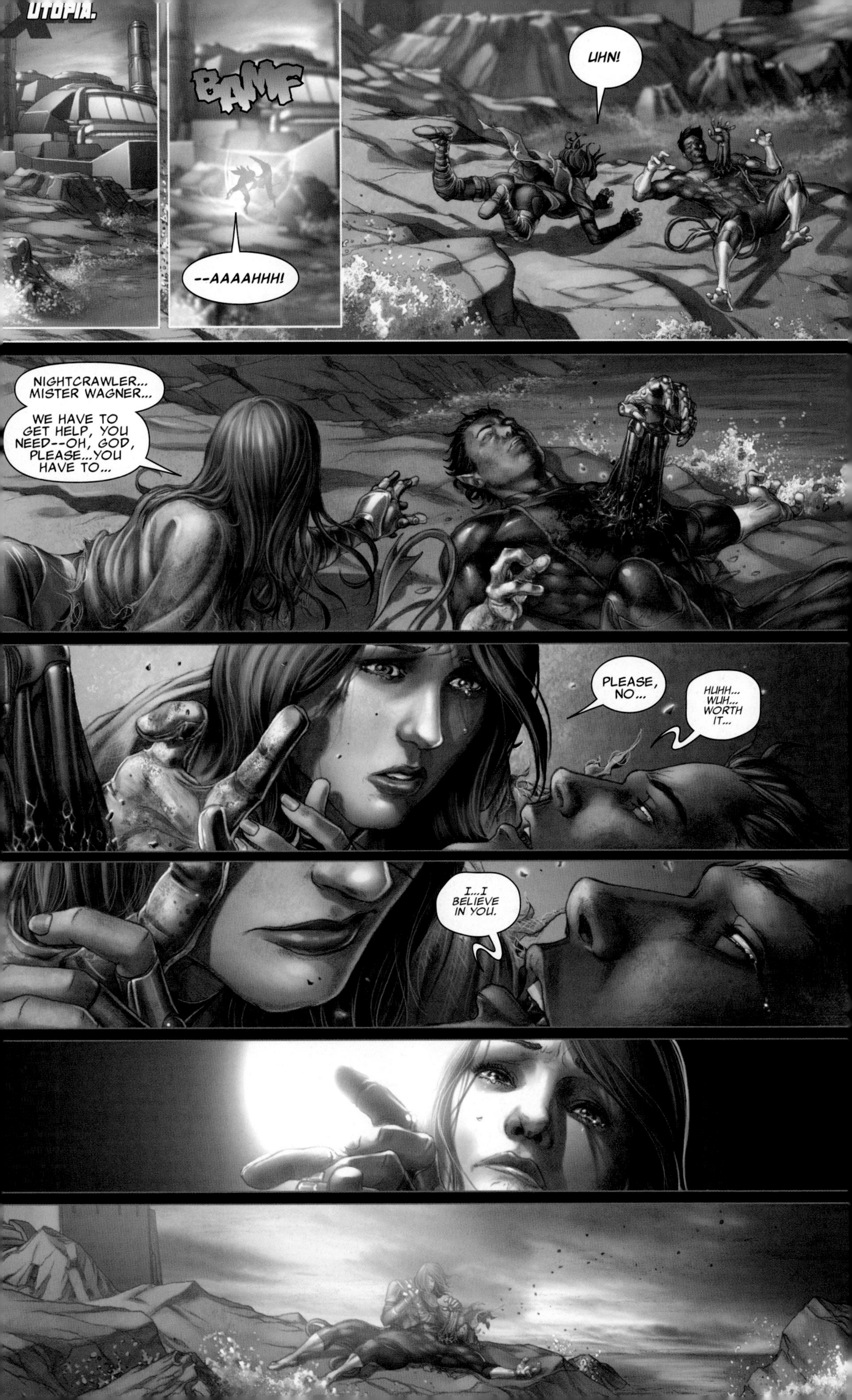
UTOPIA.
BAMF
--AAAAHHH!
UHN!
NIGHTCRAWLER... MISTER WAGNER...
WE HAVE TO GET HELP, YOU NEED--OH, GOD, PLEASE...YOU HAVE TO...
PLEASE, NO...
HUHH... WUH... WORTH IT...
I...I BELIEVE IN YOU.

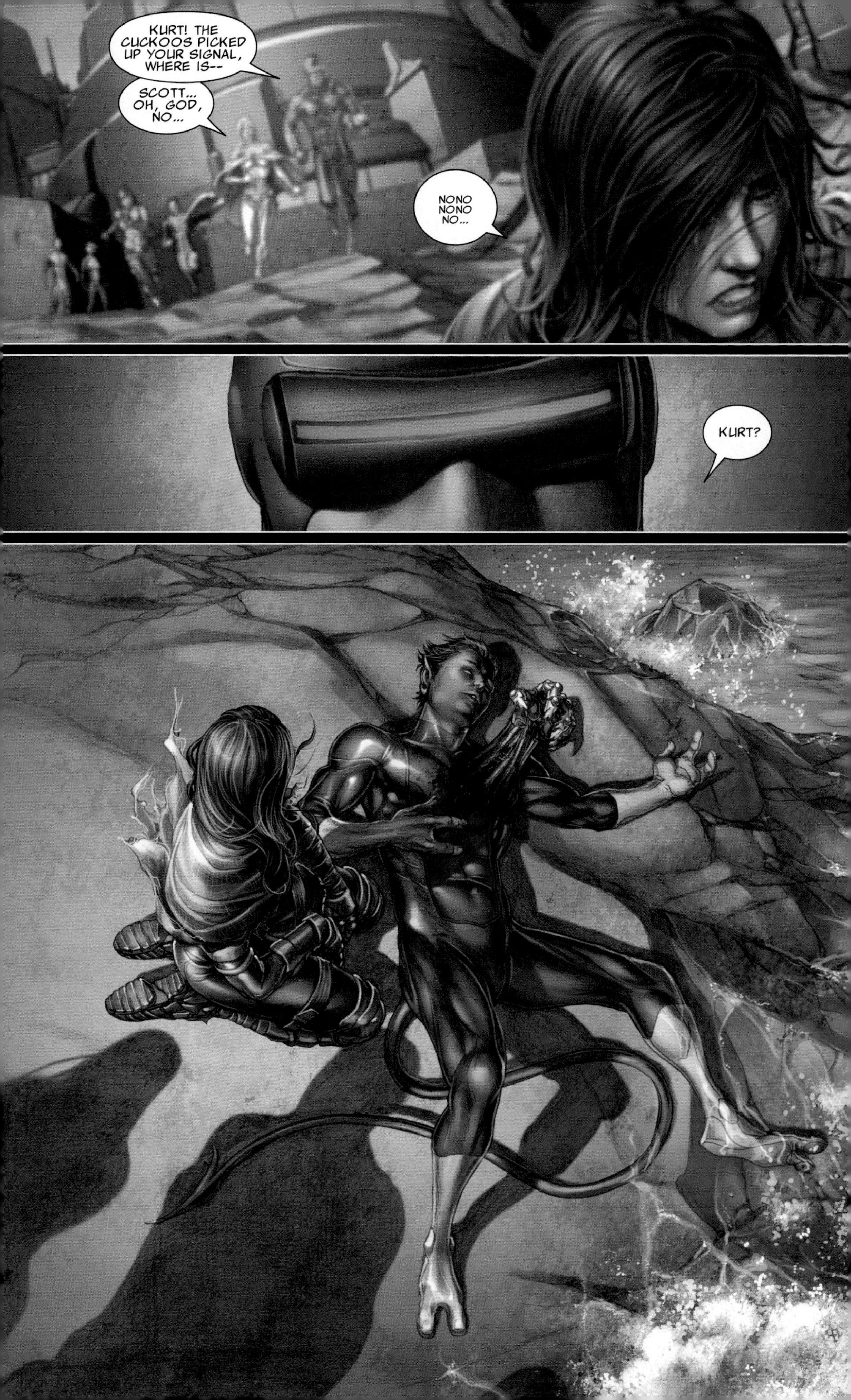
KURT! THE CUCKOOS PICKED UP YOUR SIGNAL, WHERE IS--
SCOTT... OH, GOD, NO...
NONO NONO NO...
KURT?

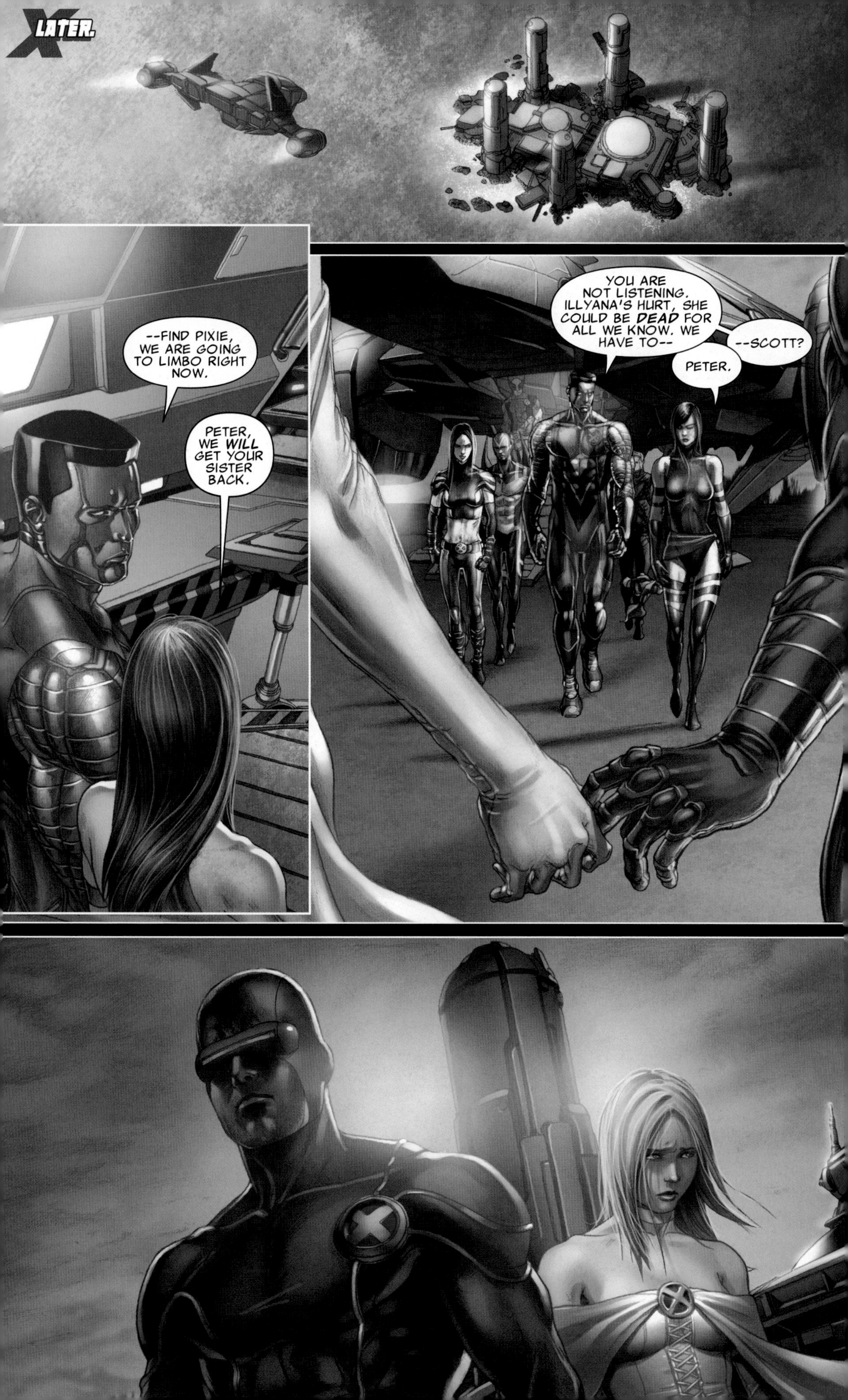
LATER.
--FIND PIXIE, WE ARE GOING TO LIMBO RIGHT NOW.
PETER, WE WILL GET YOUR SISTER BACK.
YOU ARE NOT LISTENING. ILLYANA'S HURT, SHE COULD BE DEAD FOR ALL WE KNOW. WE HAVE TO--
--SCOTT?
PETER.

WHO?

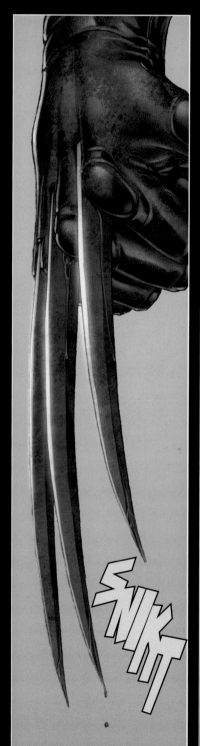

SNIKT

ELF.

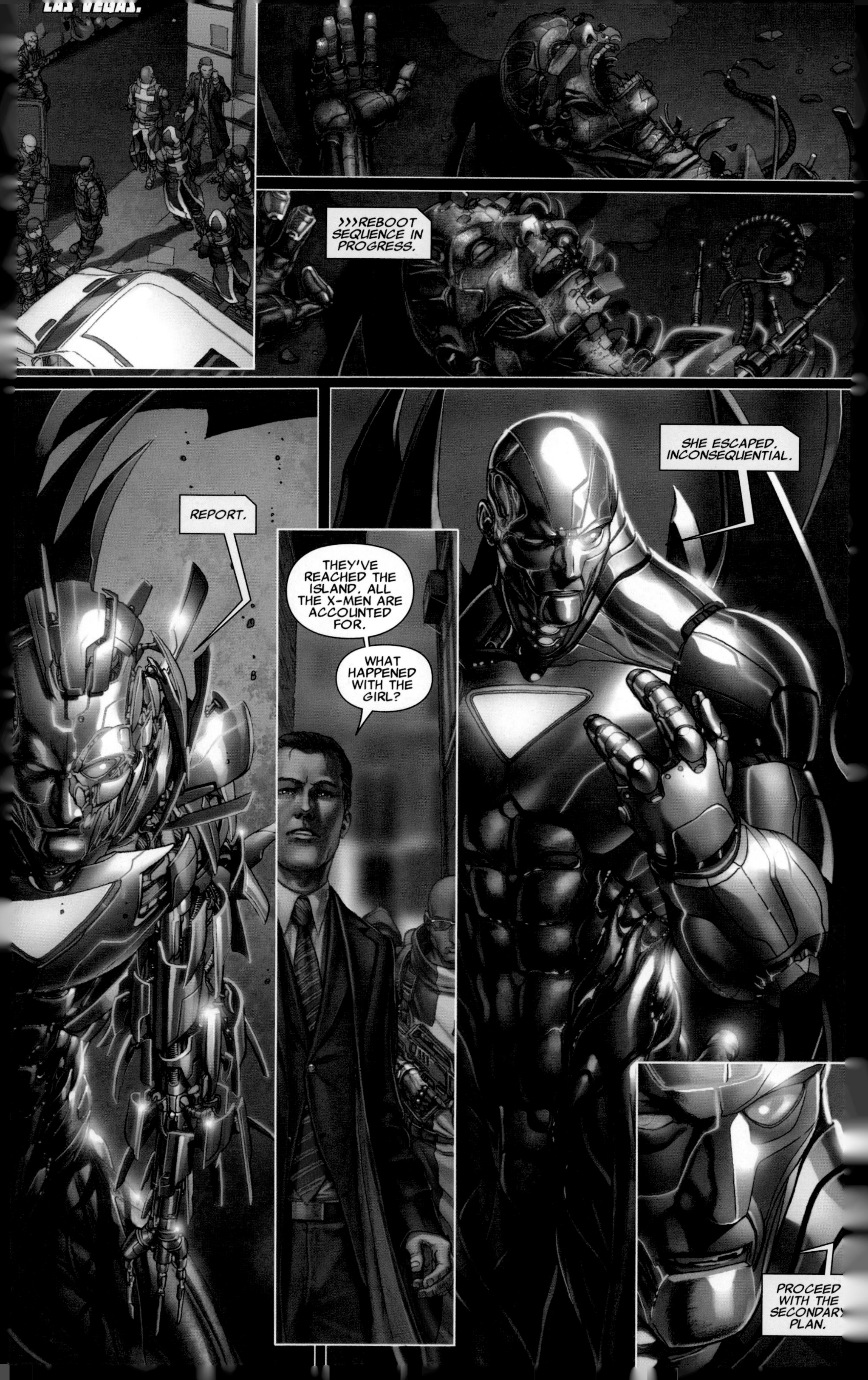
LAS VEGAS.
>>>REBOOT SEQUENCE IN PROGRESS.
REPORT.
THEY'VE REACHED THE ISLAND. ALL THE X-MEN ARE ACCOUNTED FOR.
WHAT HAPPENED WITH THE GIRL?
SHE ESCAPED. INCONSEQUENTIAL.
PROCEED WITH THE SECONDARY PLAN.

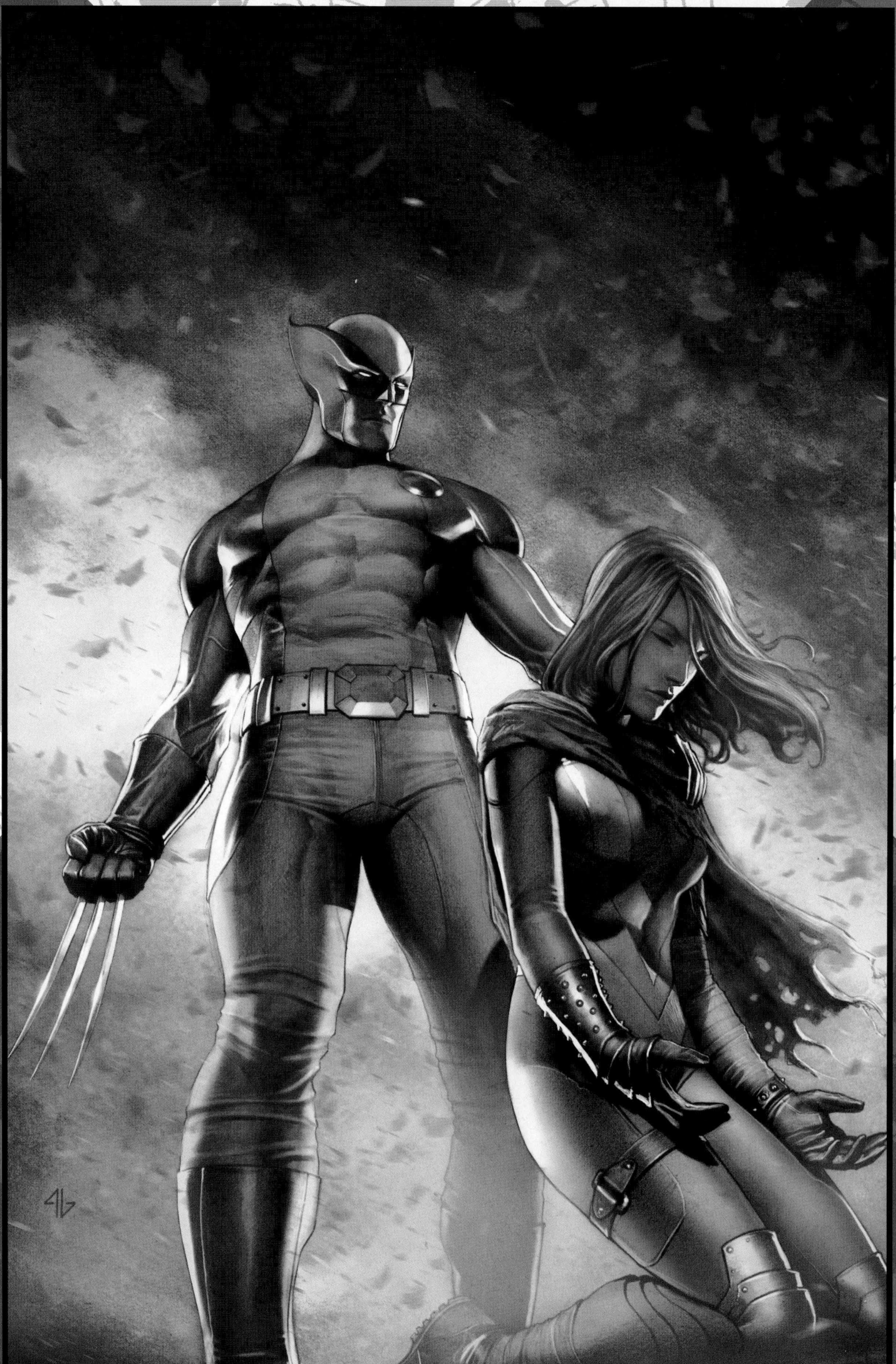

UNCANNY X-MEN #524

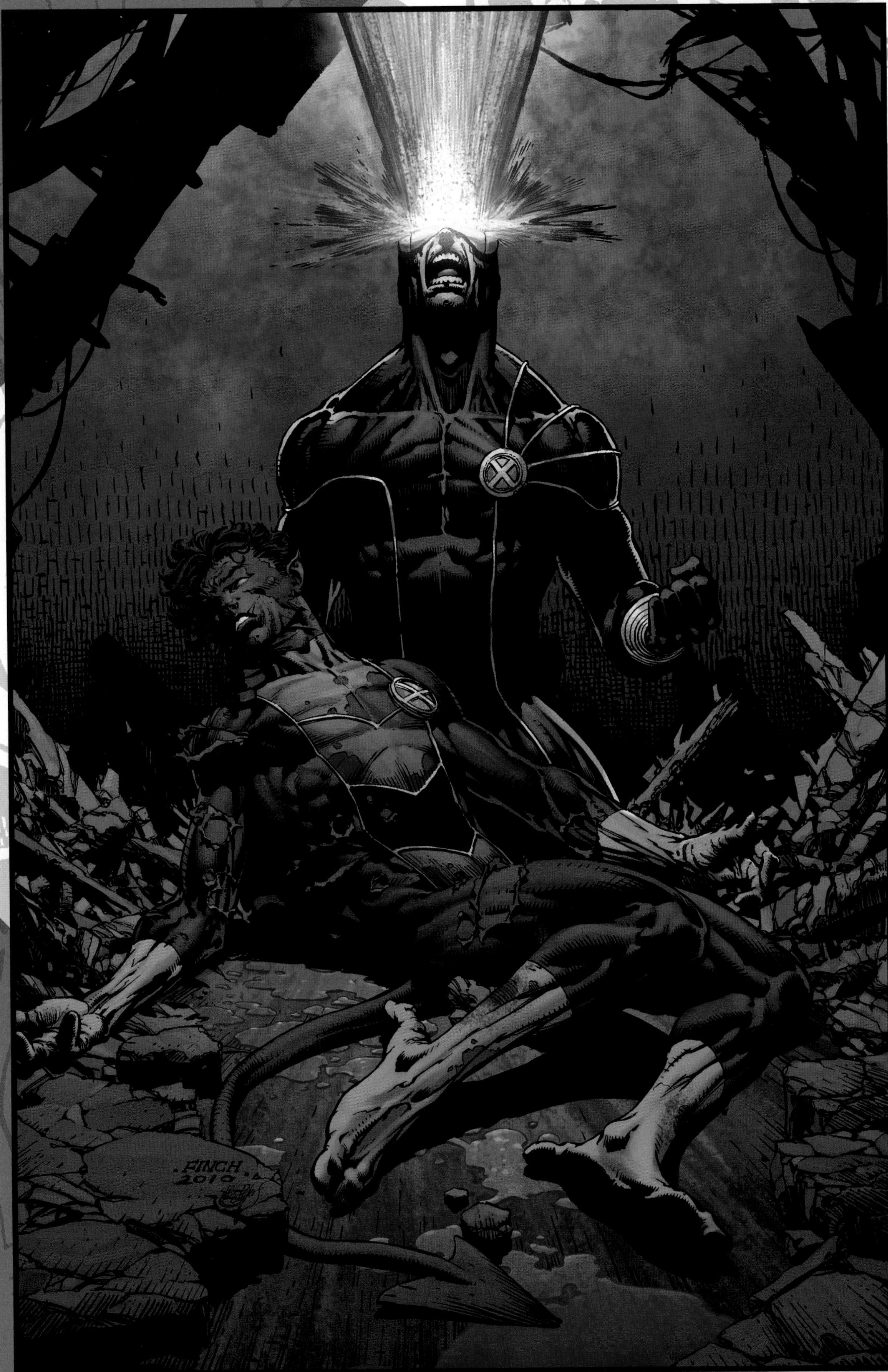
FINCH 2010

UNCANNY X-MEN #524
VARIANT

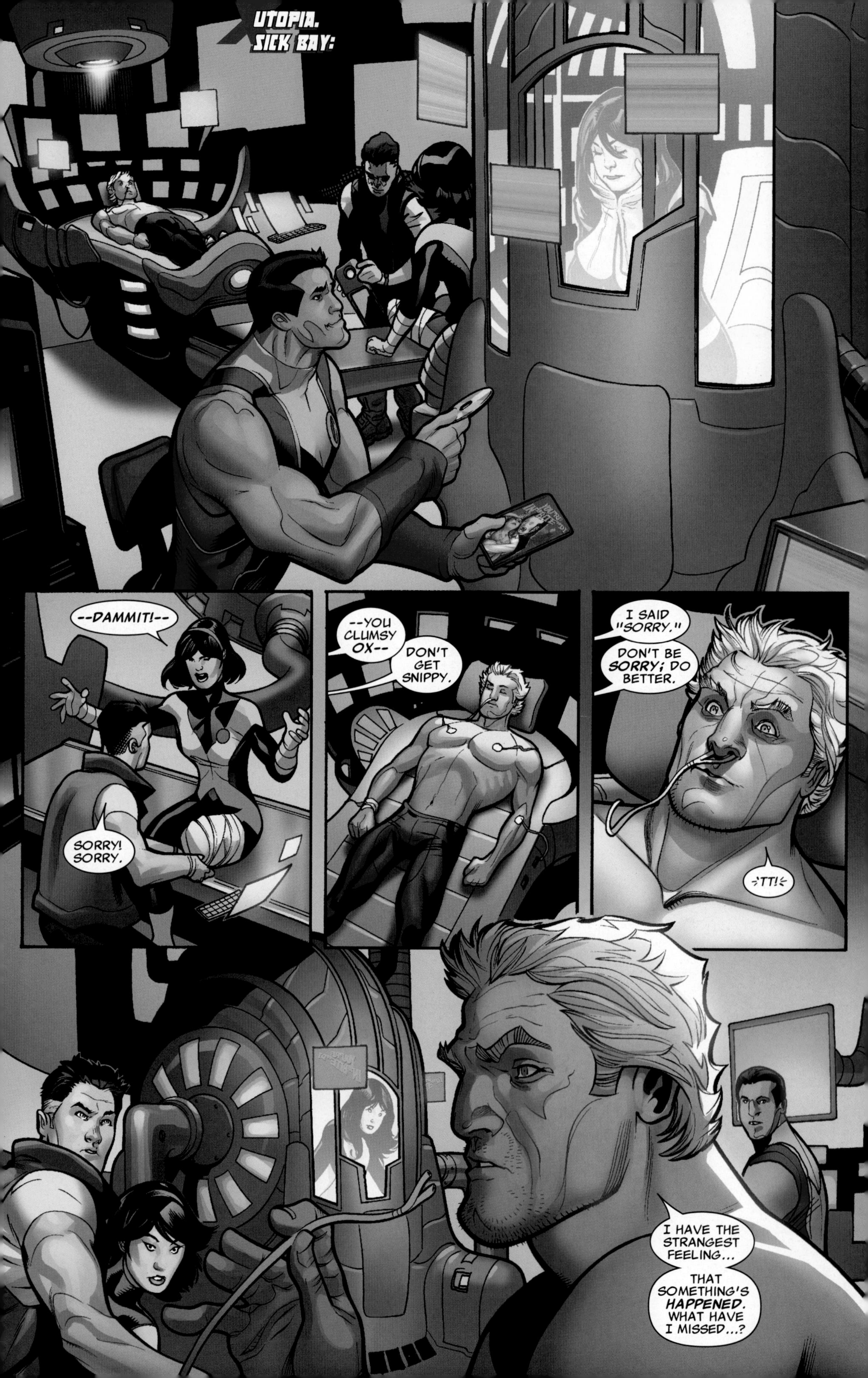
UTOPIA. SICK BAY:
--DAMMIT!--
SORRY! SORRY.
--YOU CLUMSY OX--
DON'T GET SNIPPY.
I SAID "SORRY."
DON'T BE SORRY; DO BETTER.
TT!
I HAVE THE STRANGEST FEELING...
THAT SOMETHING'S HAPPENED. WHAT HAVE I MISSED...?

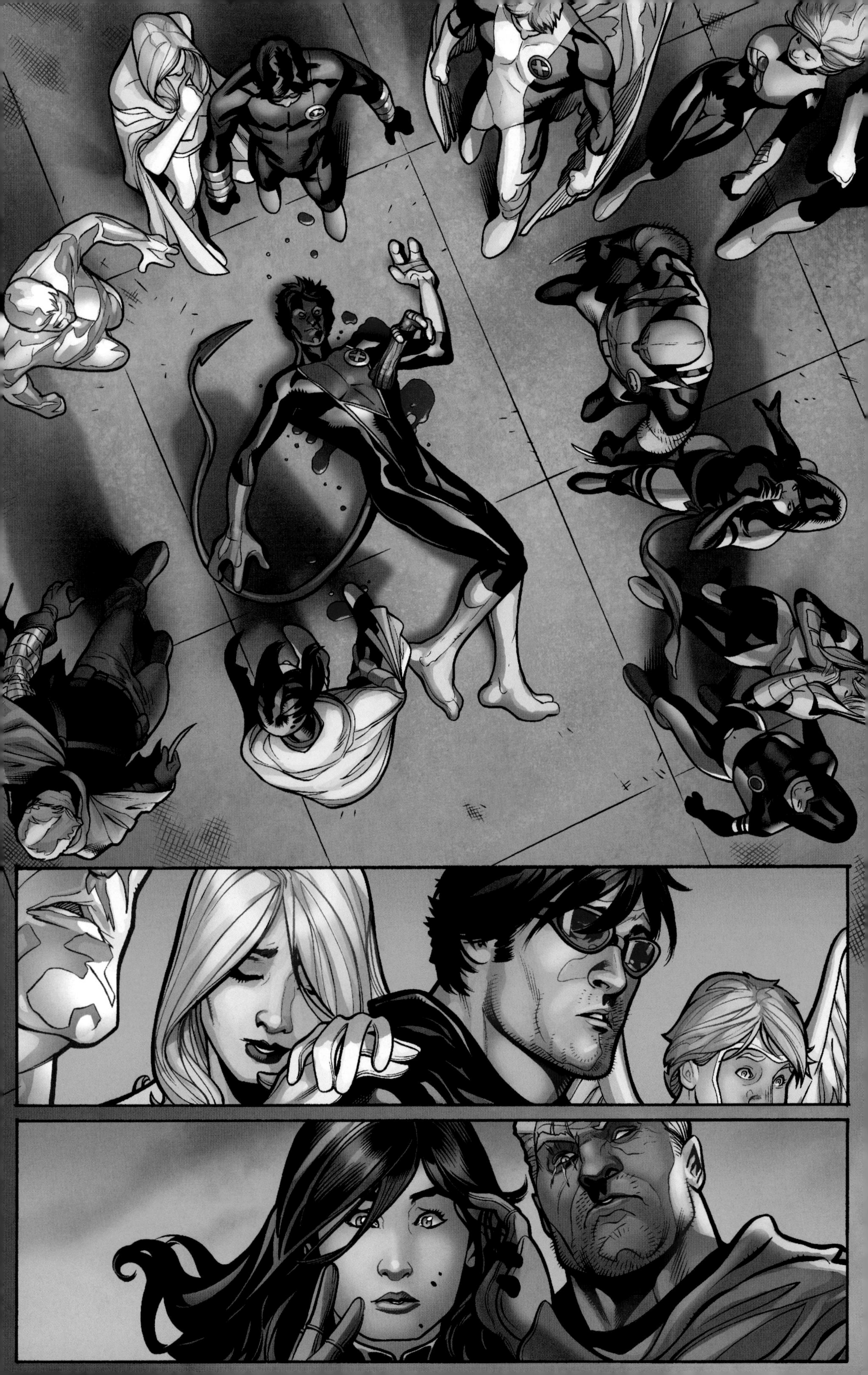

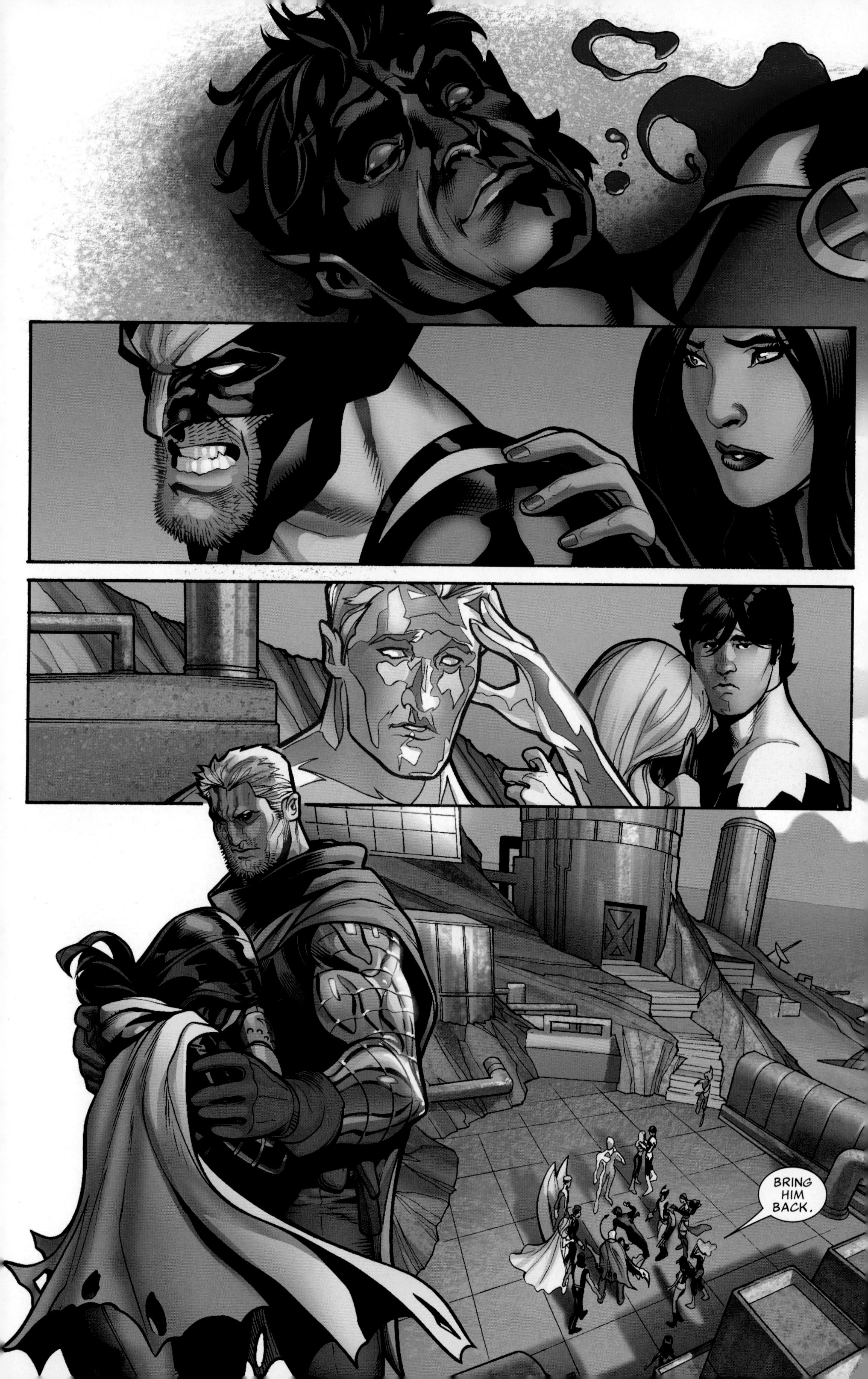
BRING HIM BACK.

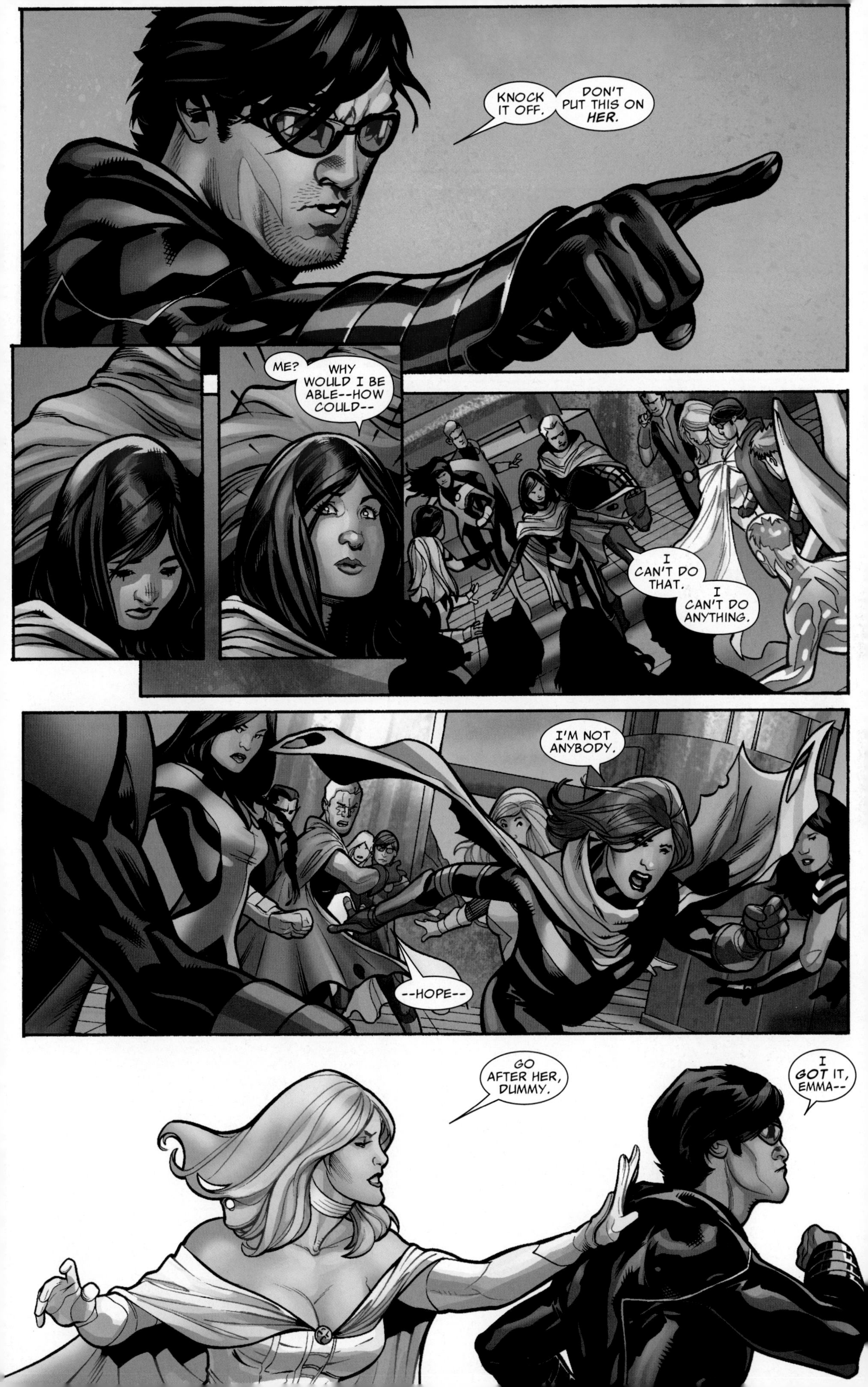
KNOCK IT OFF.
DON'T PUT THIS ON HER.
ME?
WHY WOULD I BE ABLE--HOW COULD--
I CAN'T DO THAT.
I CAN'T DO ANYTHING.
I'M NOT ANYBODY.
--HOPE--
GO AFTER HER, DUMMY.
I GOT IT, EMMA--

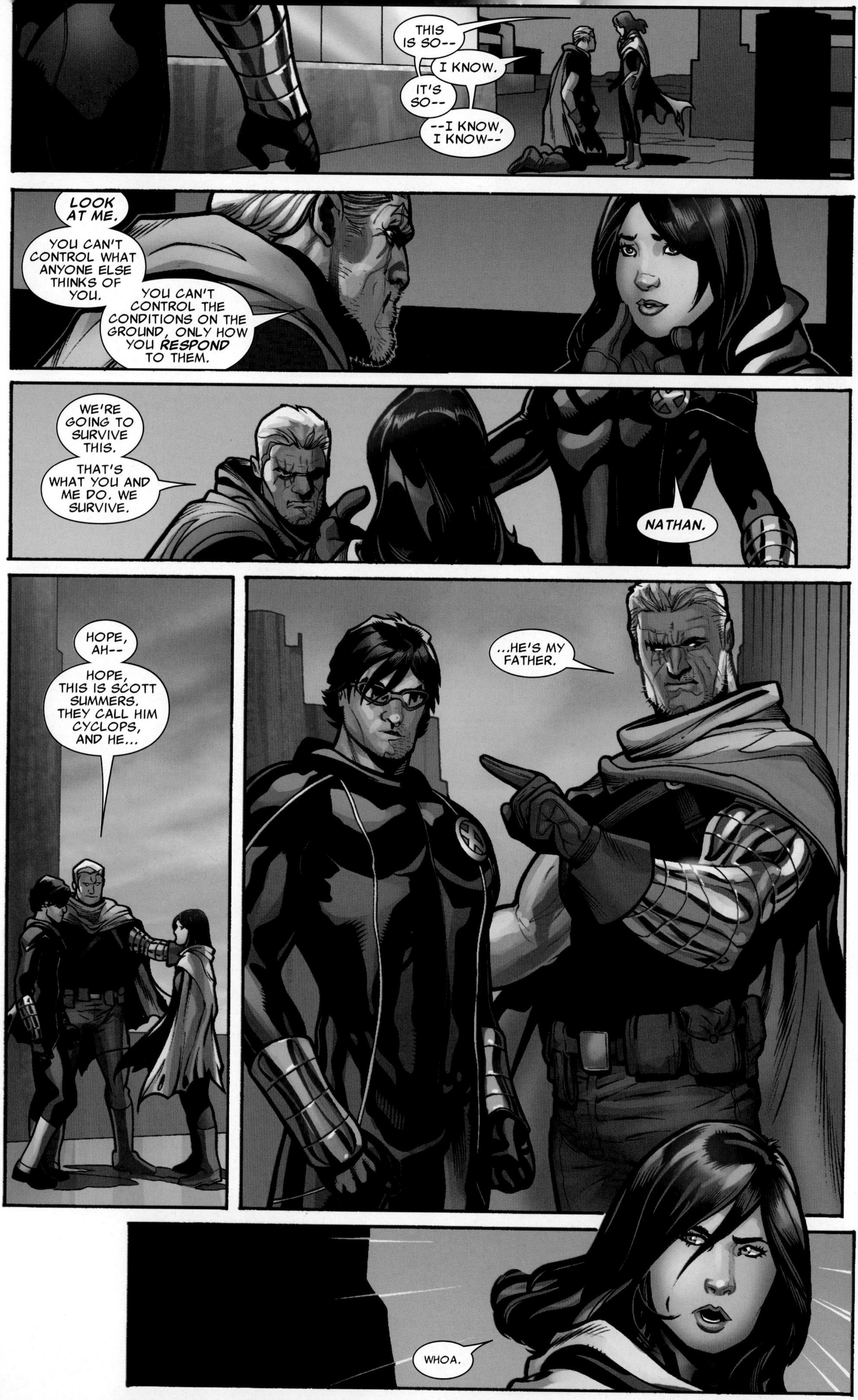
THIS IS SO--
I KNOW.
IT'S SO--
--I KNOW, I KNOW--
LOOK AT ME.
YOU CAN'T CONTROL WHAT ANYONE ELSE THINKS OF YOU.
YOU CAN'T CONTROL THE CONDITIONS ON THE GROUND, ONLY HOW YOU RESPOND TO THEM.
WE'RE GOING TO SURVIVE THIS.
THAT'S WHAT YOU AND ME DO. WE SURVIVE.
NATHAN.
HOPE, AH--
HOPE, THIS IS SCOTT SUMMERS. THEY CALL HIM CYCLOPS, AND HE...
...HE'S MY FATHER.
WHOA.

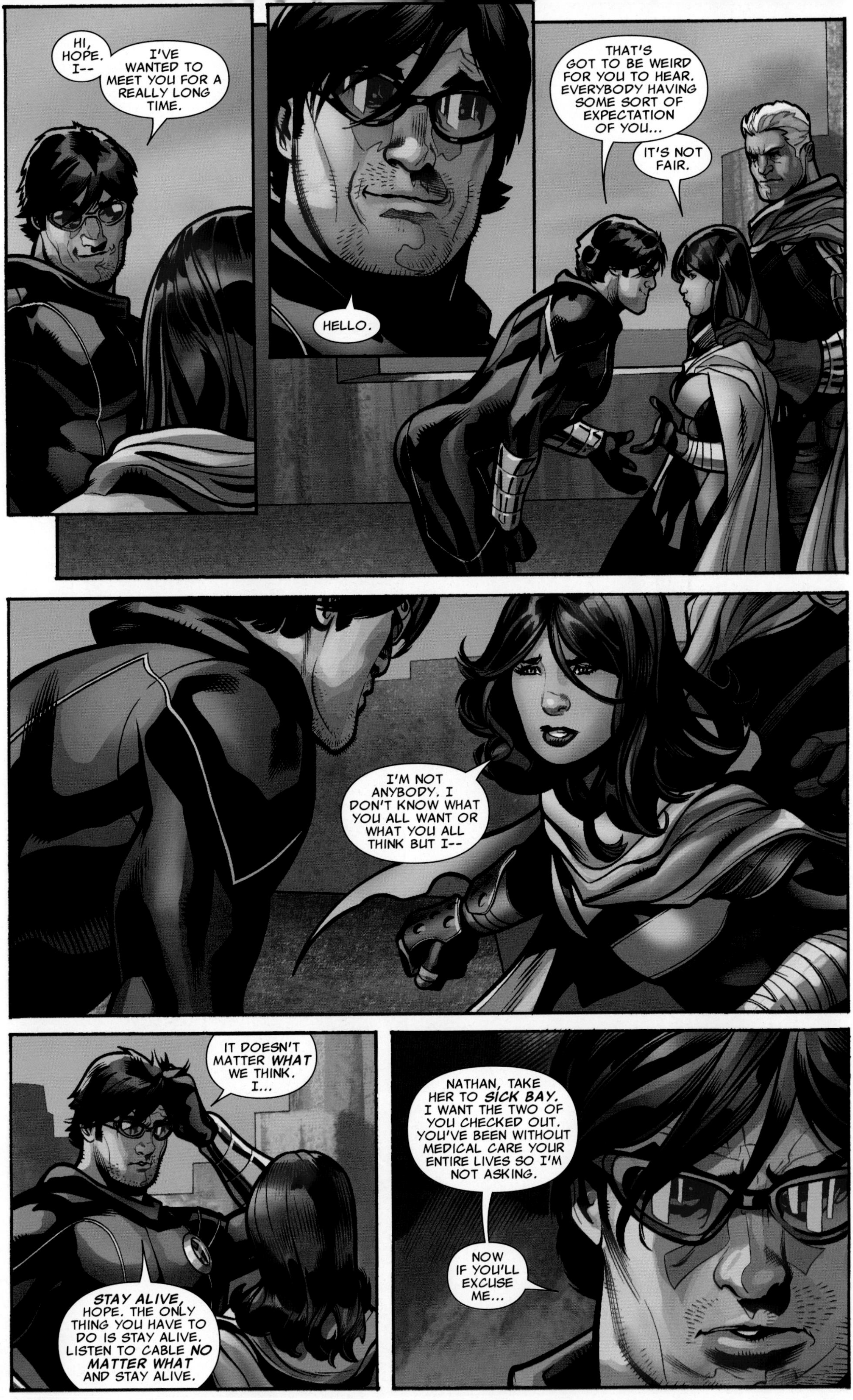

HI, HOPE. I--
I'VE WANTED TO MEET YOU FOR A REALLY LONG TIME.
HELLO.
THAT'S GOT TO BE WEIRD FOR YOU TO HEAR. EVERYBODY HAVING SOME SORT OF EXPECTATION OF YOU...
IT'S NOT FAIR.
I'M NOT ANYBODY. I DON'T KNOW WHAT YOU ALL WANT OR WHAT YOU ALL THINK BUT I--
IT DOESN'T MATTER WHAT WE THINK. I...
STAY ALIVE, HOPE. THE ONLY THING YOU HAVE TO DO IS STAY ALIVE. LISTEN TO CABLE NO MATTER WHAT AND STAY ALIVE.
NATHAN, TAKE HER TO SICK BAY. I WANT THE TWO OF YOU CHECKED OUT. YOU'VE BEEN WITHOUT MEDICAL CARE YOUR ENTIRE LIVES SO I'M NOT ASKING.
NOW IF YOU'LL EXCUSE ME...

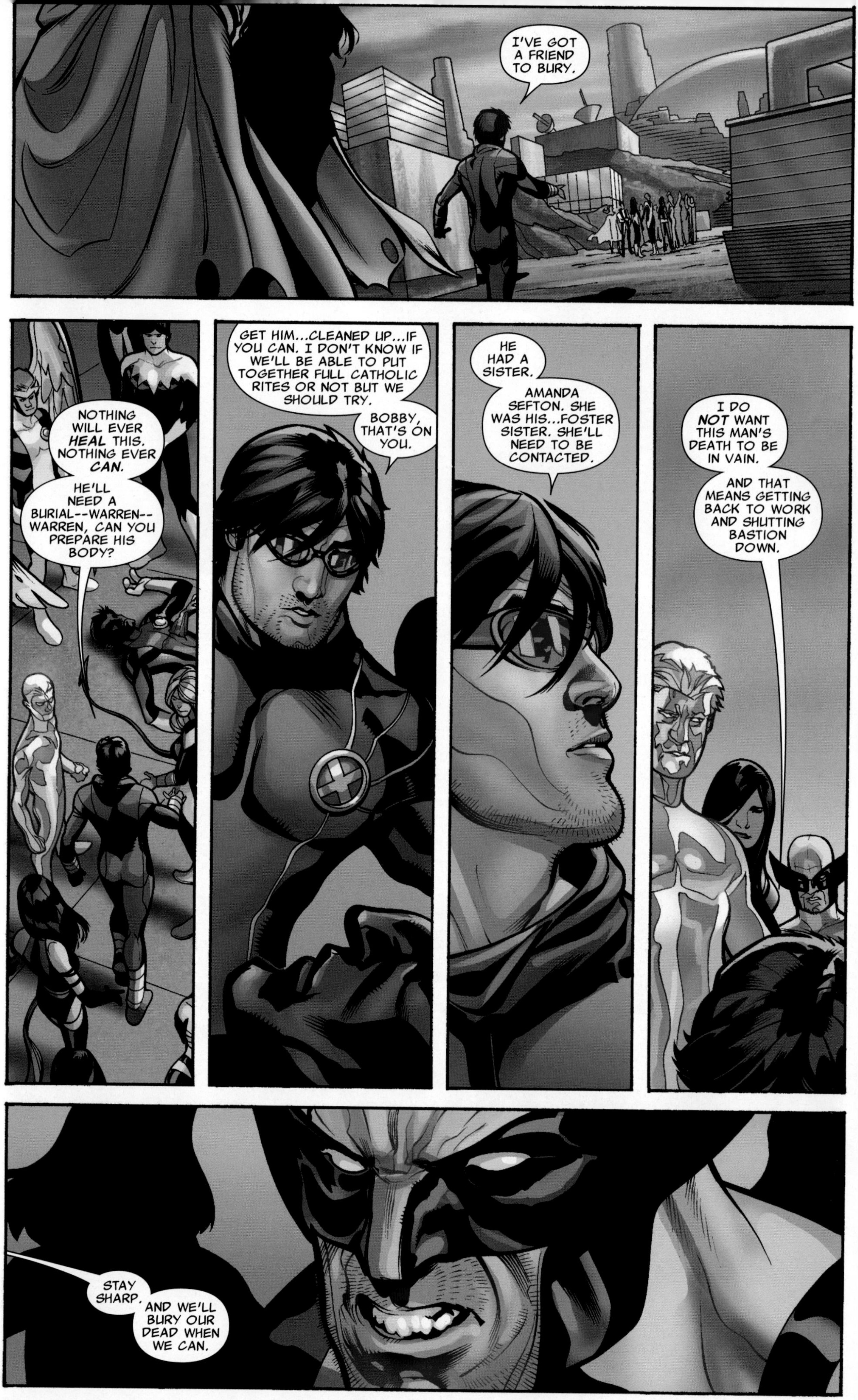
I'VE GOT A FRIEND TO BURY.
NOTHING WILL EVER HEAL THIS. NOTHING EVER CAN.
HE'LL NEED A BURIAL--WARREN--WARREN, CAN YOU PREPARE HIS BODY?
GET HIM...CLEANED UP...IF YOU CAN. I DON'T KNOW IF WE'LL BE ABLE TO PUT TOGETHER FULL CATHOLIC RITES OR NOT BUT WE SHOULD TRY.
BOBBY, THAT'S ON YOU.
HE HAD A SISTER.
AMANDA SEFTON. SHE WAS HIS...FOSTER SISTER. SHE'LL NEED TO BE CONTACTED.
I DO NOT WANT THIS MAN'S DEATH TO BE IN VAIN.
AND THAT MEANS GETTING BACK TO WORK AND SHUTTING BASTION DOWN.
STAY SHARP.
AND WE'LL BURY OUR DEAD WHEN WE CAN.

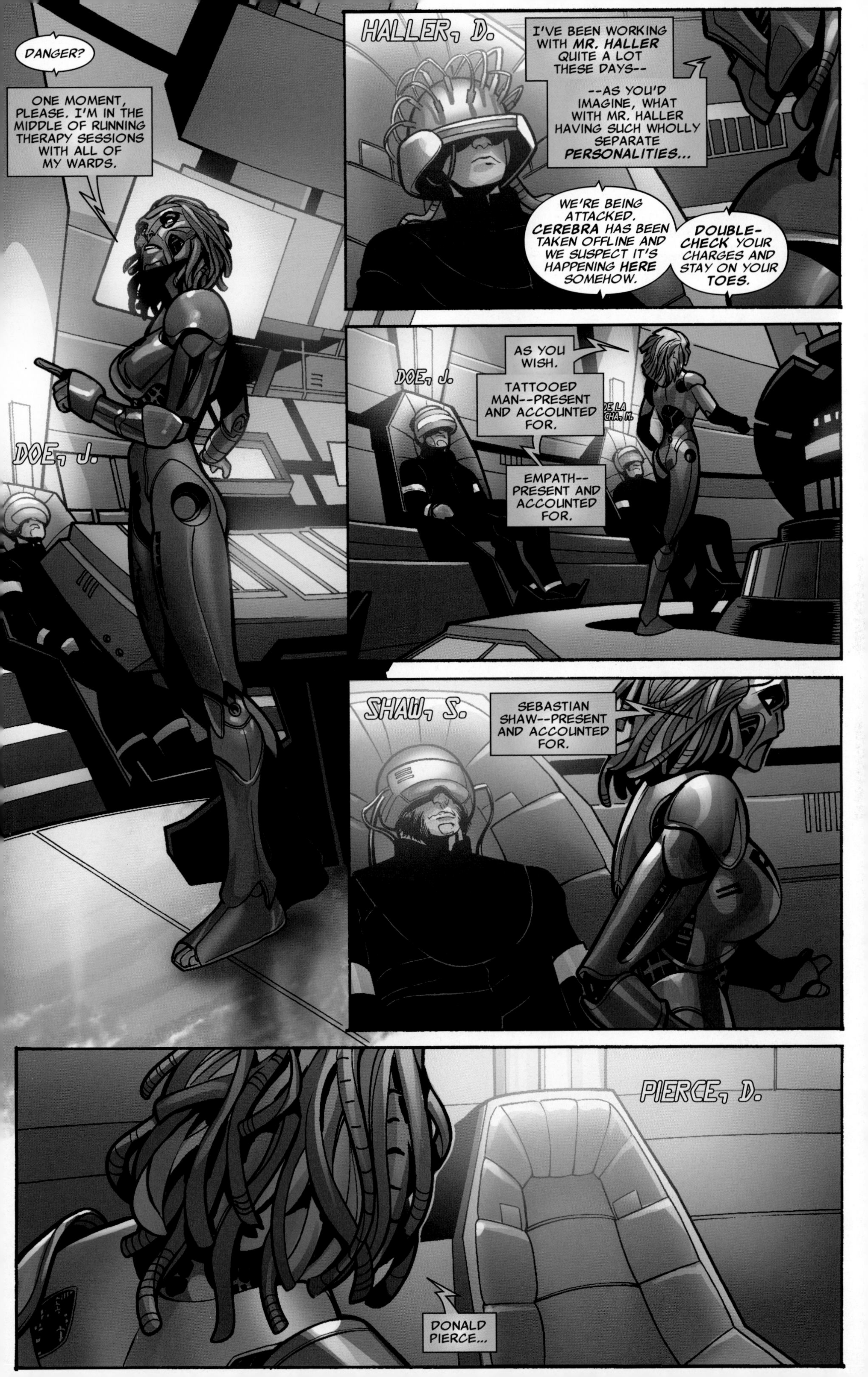
DANGER?
ONE MOMENT, PLEASE. I'M IN THE MIDDLE OF RUNNING THERAPY SESSIONS WITH ALL OF MY WARDS.
DOE, J.
HALLER, D.
I'VE BEEN WORKING WITH MR. HALLER QUITE A LOT THESE DAYS--
--AS YOU'D IMAGINE, WHAT WITH MR. HALLER HAVING SUCH WHOLLY SEPARATE PERSONALITIES...
WE'RE BEING ATTACKED. CEREBRA HAS BEEN TAKEN OFFLINE AND WE SUSPECT IT'S HAPPENING HERE SOMEHOW.
DOUBLE-CHECK YOUR CHARGES AND STAY ON YOUR TOES.
DOE, J.
AS YOU WISH.
TATTOOED MAN--PRESENT AND ACCOUNTED FOR.
EMPATH--PRESENT AND ACCOUNTED FOR.
SHAW, S.
SEBASTIAN SHAW--PRESENT AND ACCOUNTED FOR.
PIERCE, D.
DONALD PIERCE...

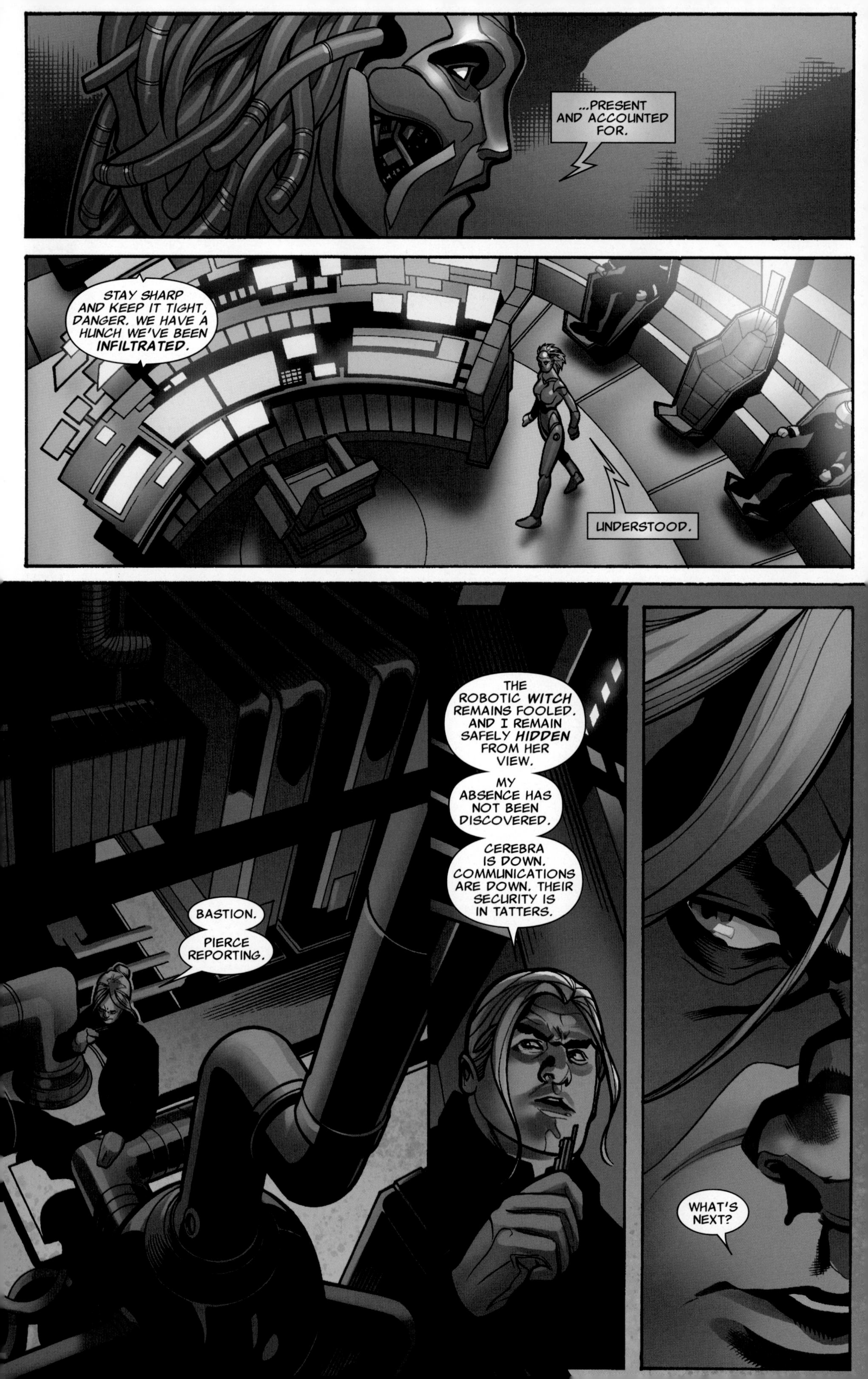
...PRESENT AND ACCOUNTED FOR.
STAY SHARP AND KEEP IT TIGHT, DANGER. WE HAVE A HUNCH WE'VE BEEN INFILTRATED.
UNDERSTOOD.
BASTION.
PIERCE REPORTING.
THE ROBOTIC WITCH REMAINS FOOLED. AND I REMAIN SAFELY HIDDEN FROM HER VIEW.
MY ABSENCE HAS NOT BEEN DISCOVERED.
CEREBRA IS DOWN. COMMUNICATIONS ARE DOWN. THEIR SECURITY IS IN TATTERS.
WHAT'S NEXT?

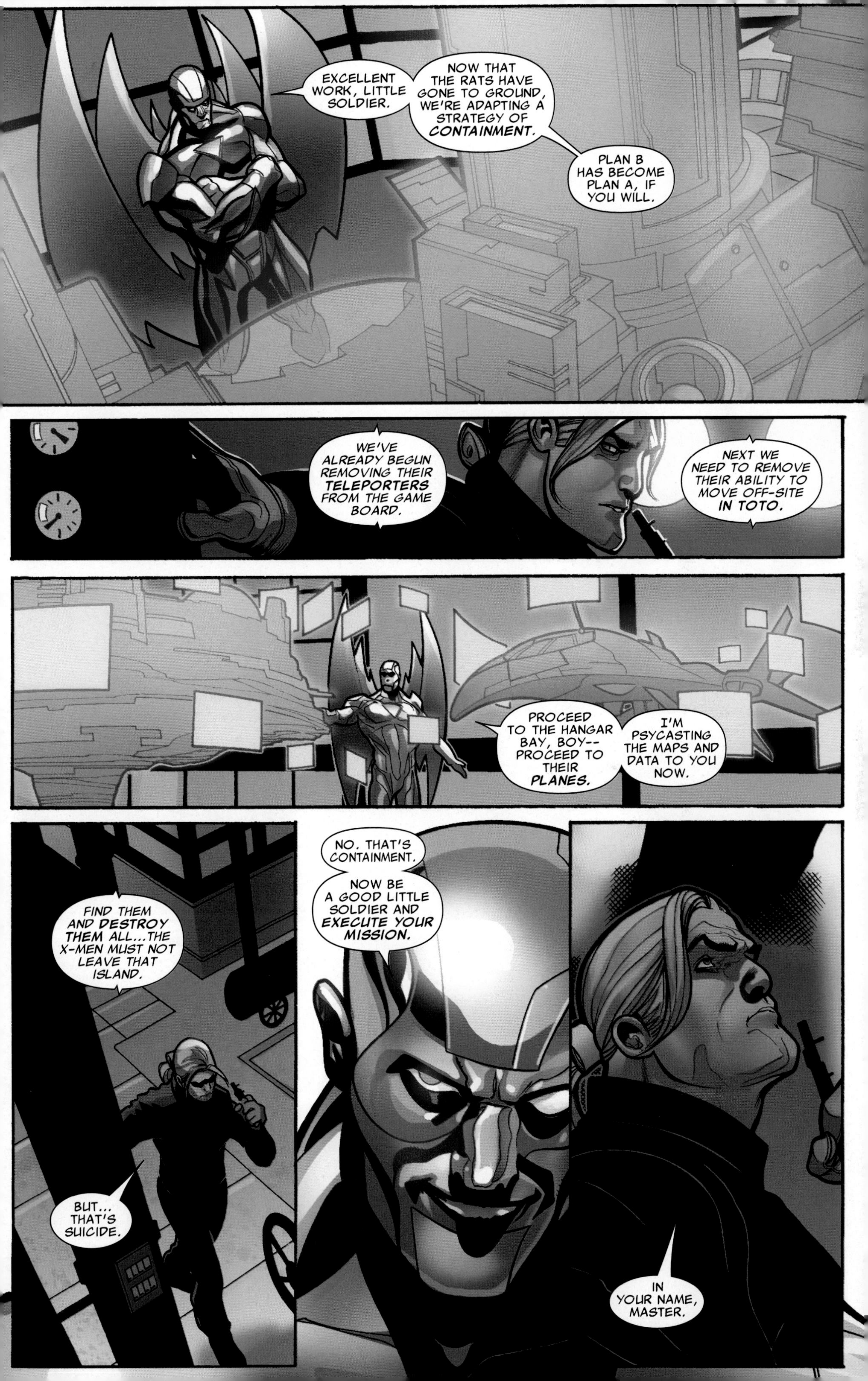
EXCELLENT WORK, LITTLE SOLDIER.
NOW THAT THE RATS HAVE GONE TO GROUND, WE'RE ADAPTING A STRATEGY OF CONTAINMENT.
PLAN B HAS BECOME PLAN A, IF YOU WILL.
WE'VE ALREADY BEGUN REMOVING THEIR TELEPORTERS FROM THE GAME BOARD.
NEXT WE NEED TO REMOVE THEIR ABILITY TO MOVE OFF-SITE IN TOTO.
PROCEED TO THE HANGAR BAY, BOY-- PROCEED TO THEIR PLANES.
I'M PSYCASTING THE MAPS AND DATA TO YOU NOW.
FIND THEM AND DESTROY THEM ALL...THE X-MEN MUST NOT LEAVE THAT ISLAND.
BUT... THAT'S SUICIDE.
NO. THAT'S CONTAINMENT.
NOW BE A GOOD LITTLE SOLDIER AND EXECUTE YOUR MISSION.
IN YOUR NAME, MASTER.

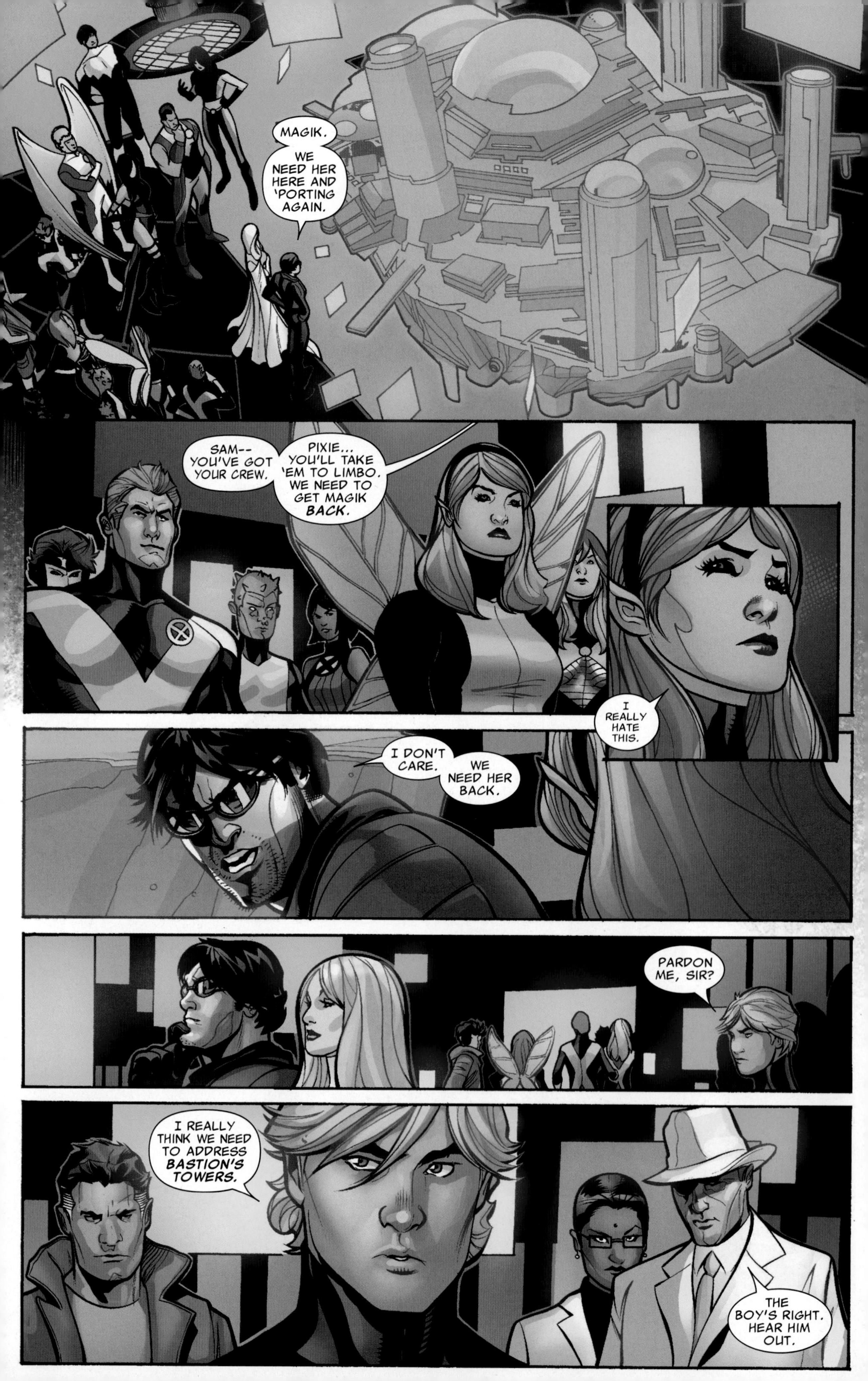
MAGIK.
WE NEED HER HERE AND 'PORTING AGAIN.
SAM-- YOU'VE GOT YOUR CREW.
PIXIE... YOU'LL TAKE 'EM TO LIMBO. WE NEED TO GET MAGIK BACK.
I REALLY HATE THIS.
I DON'T CARE.
WE NEED HER BACK.
PARDON ME, SIR?
I REALLY THINK WE NEED TO ADDRESS BASTION'S TOWERS.
THE BOY'S RIGHT. HEAR HIM OUT.

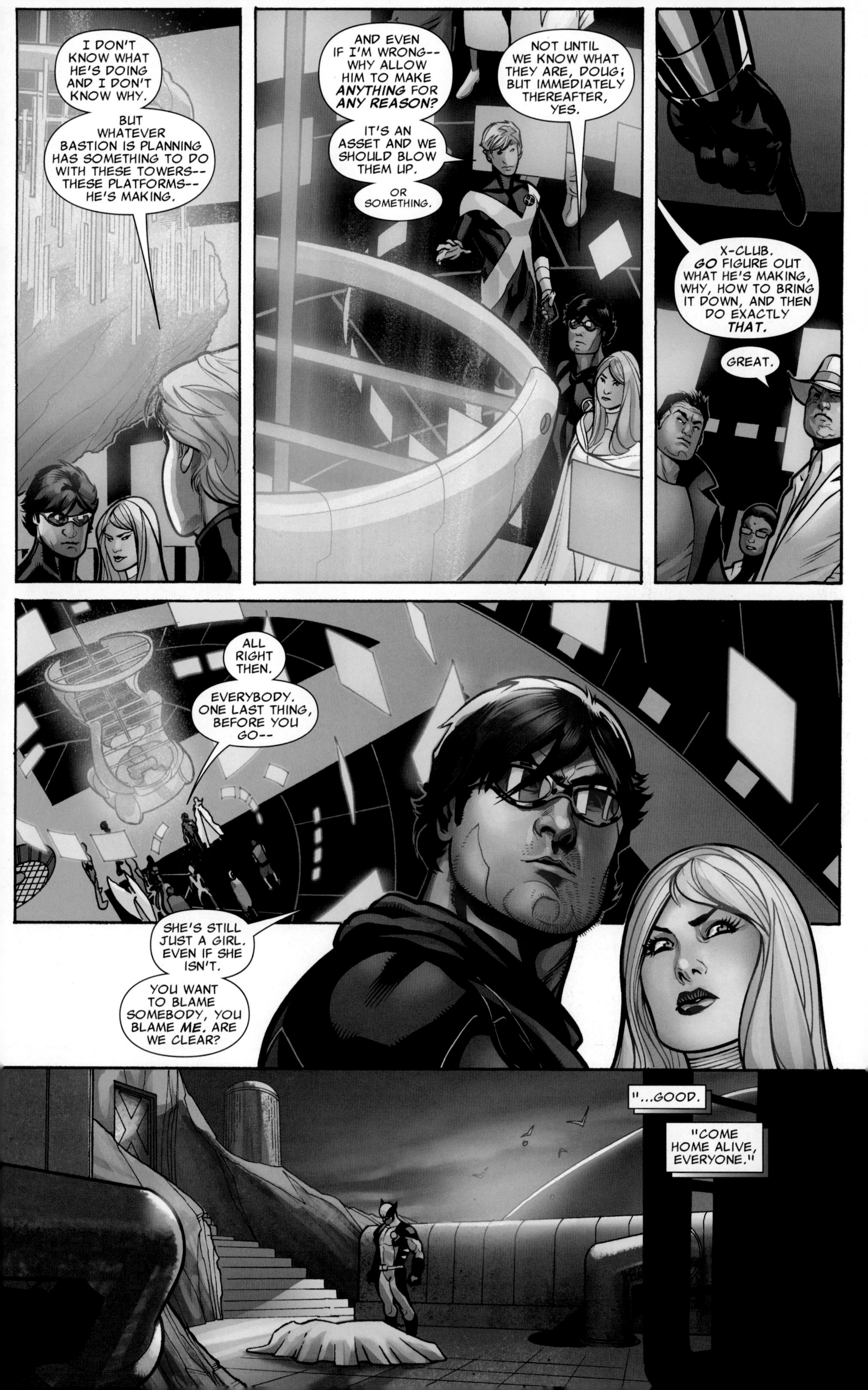
I DON'T KNOW WHAT HE'S DOING AND I DON'T KNOW WHY.
BUT WHATEVER BASTION IS PLANNING HAS SOMETHING TO DO WITH THESE TOWERS-- THESE PLATFORMS-- HE'S MAKING.
AND EVEN IF I'M WRONG-- WHY ALLOW HIM TO MAKE ANYTHING FOR ANY REASON?
IT'S AN ASSET AND WE SHOULD BLOW THEM UP.
OR SOMETHING.
NOT UNTIL WE KNOW WHAT THEY ARE, DOUG; BUT IMMEDIATELY THEREAFTER, YES.
X-CLUB. GO FIGURE OUT WHAT HE'S MAKING, WHY, HOW TO BRING IT DOWN, AND THEN DO EXACTLY THAT.
GREAT.
ALL RIGHT THEN.
EVERYBODY. ONE LAST THING, BEFORE YOU GO--
SHE'S STILL JUST A GIRL. EVEN IF SHE ISN'T.
YOU WANT TO BLAME SOMEBODY, YOU BLAME ME. ARE WE CLEAR?
"...GOOD.
"COME HOME ALIVE, EVERYONE."

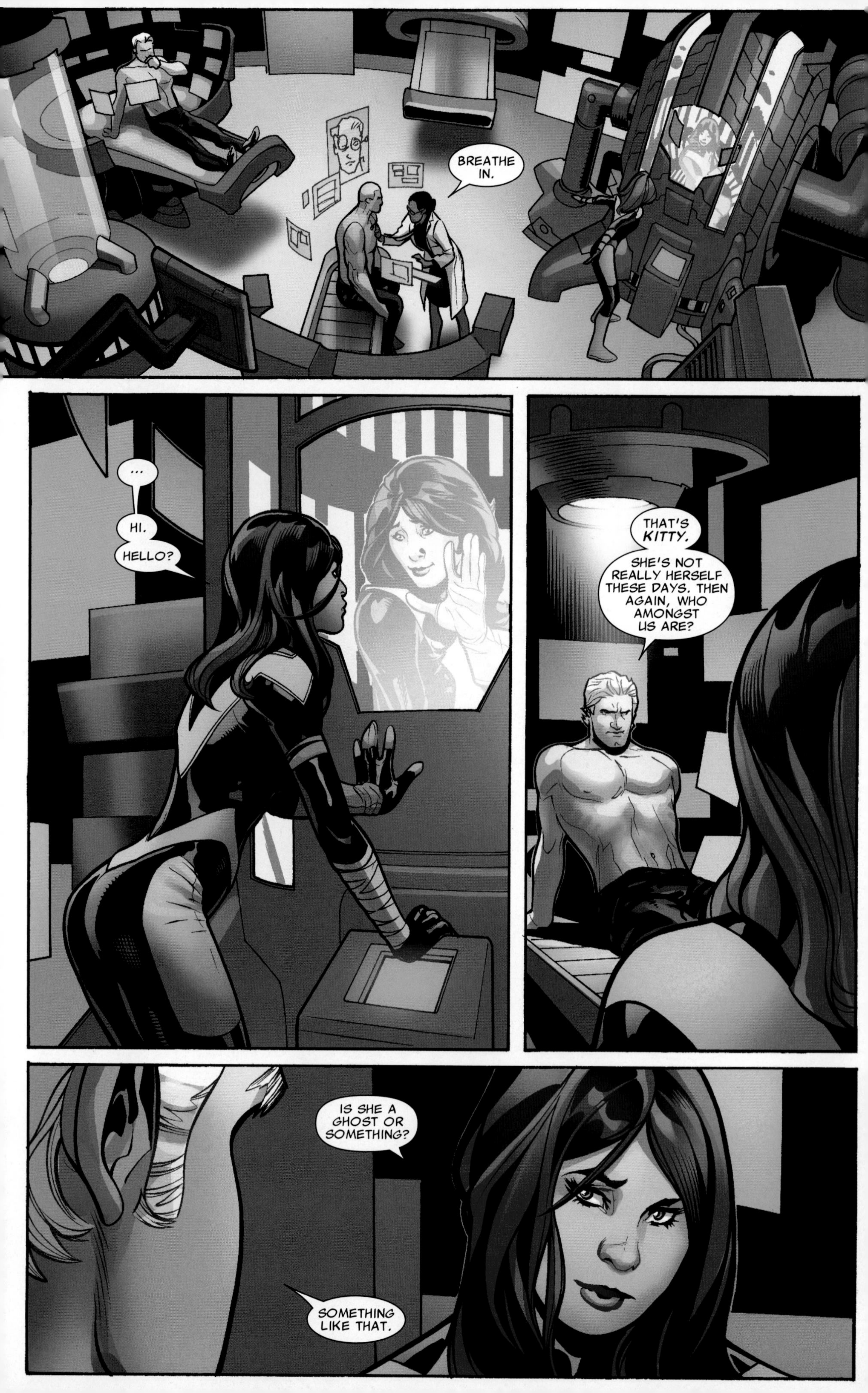
BREATHE IN.
...
HI.
HELLO?
THAT'S *KITTY.*
SHE'S NOT REALLY HERSELF THESE DAYS. THEN AGAIN, WHO AMONGST US ARE?
IS SHE A GHOST OR SOMETHING?
SOMETHING LIKE THAT.

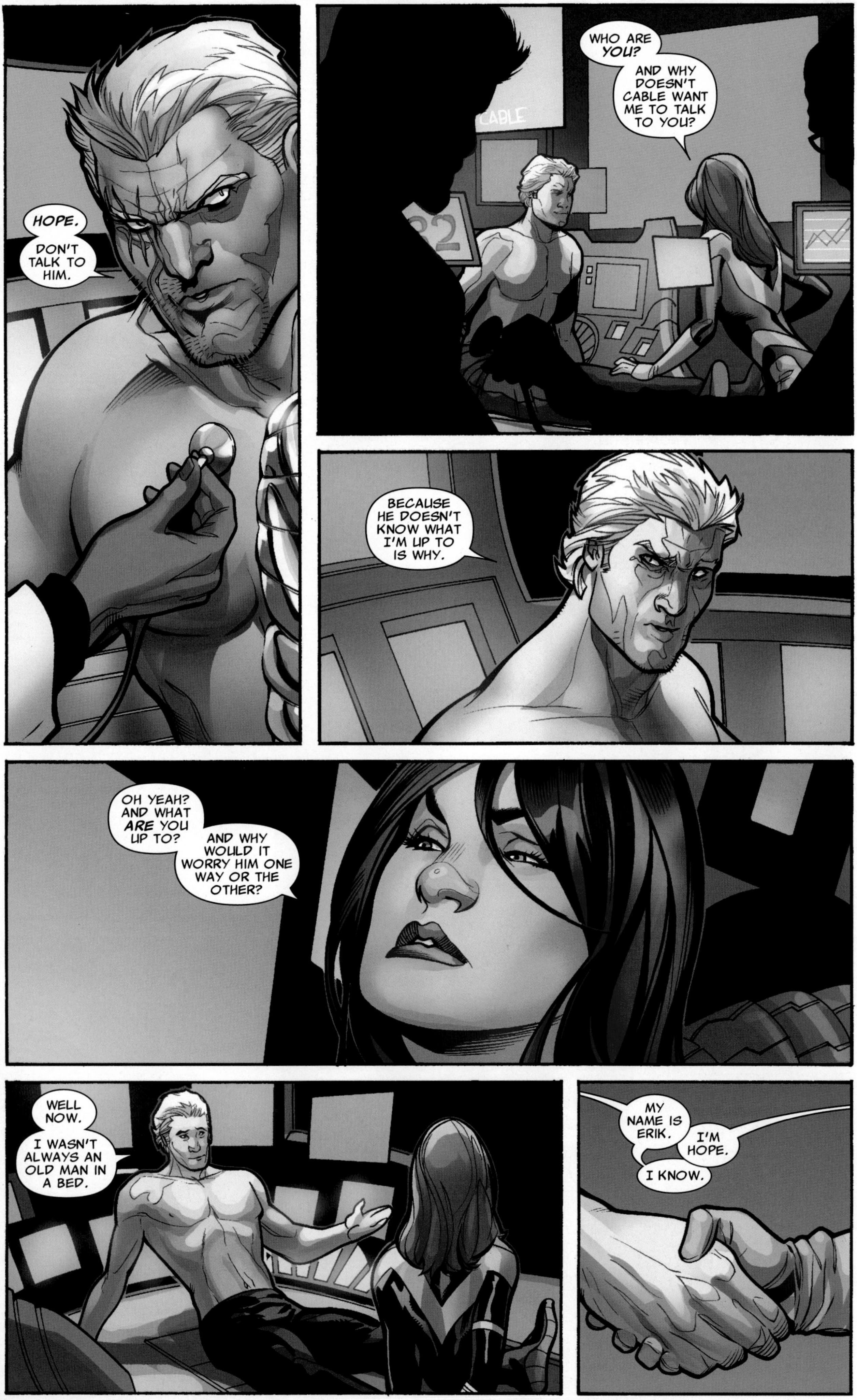
HOPE.
DON'T TALK TO HIM.
WHO ARE YOU?
AND WHY DOESN'T CABLE WANT ME TO TALK TO YOU?
BECAUSE HE DOESN'T KNOW WHAT I'M UP TO IS WHY.
OH YEAH? AND WHAT ARE YOU UP TO?
AND WHY WOULD IT WORRY HIM ONE WAY OR THE OTHER?
WELL NOW.
I WASN'T ALWAYS AN OLD MAN IN A BED.
MY NAME IS ERIK.
I'M HOPE.
I KNOW.

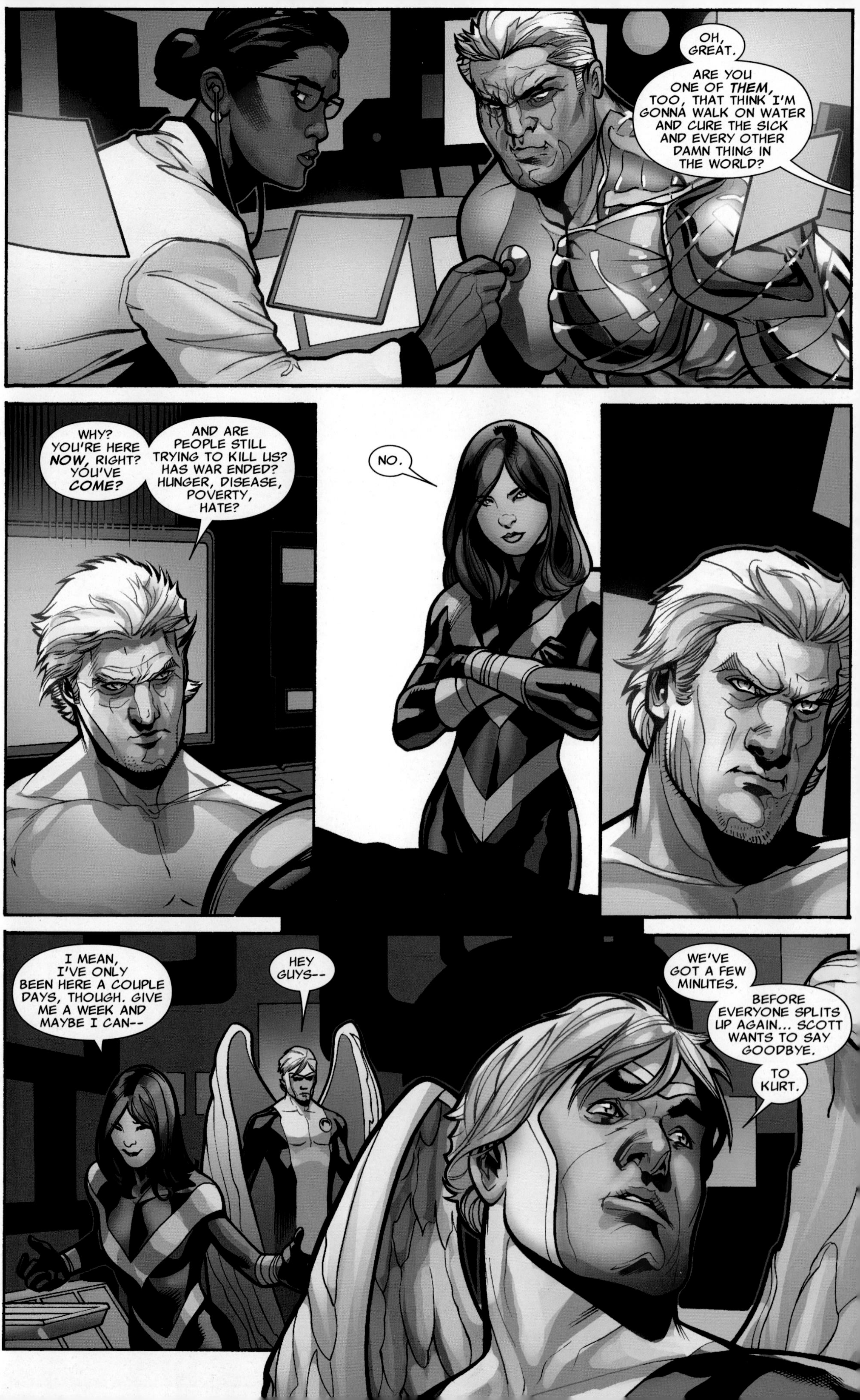
OH, GREAT.
ARE YOU ONE OF THEM, TOO, THAT THINK I'M GONNA WALK ON WATER AND CURE THE SICK AND EVERY OTHER DAMN THING IN THE WORLD?
WHY? YOU'RE HERE NOW, RIGHT? YOU'VE COME?
AND ARE PEOPLE STILL TRYING TO KILL US? HAS WAR ENDED? HUNGER, DISEASE, POVERTY, HATE?
NO.
I MEAN, I'VE ONLY BEEN HERE A COUPLE DAYS, THOUGH. GIVE ME A WEEK AND MAYBE I CAN--
HEY GUYS--
WE'VE GOT A FEW MINUTES.
BEFORE EVERYONE SPLITS UP AGAIN... SCOTT WANTS TO SAY GOODBYE.
TO KURT.

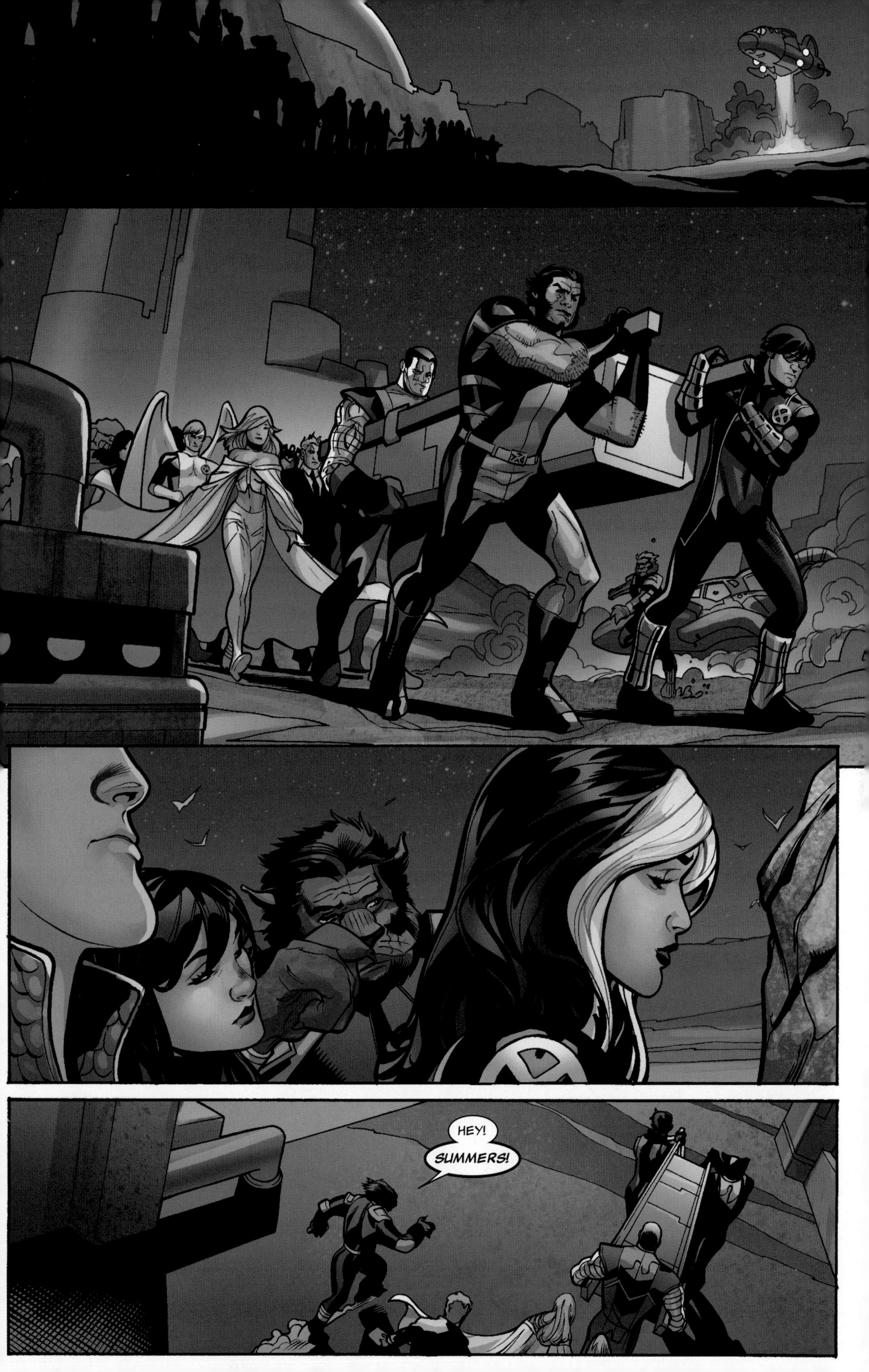
HEY!
SUMMERS!

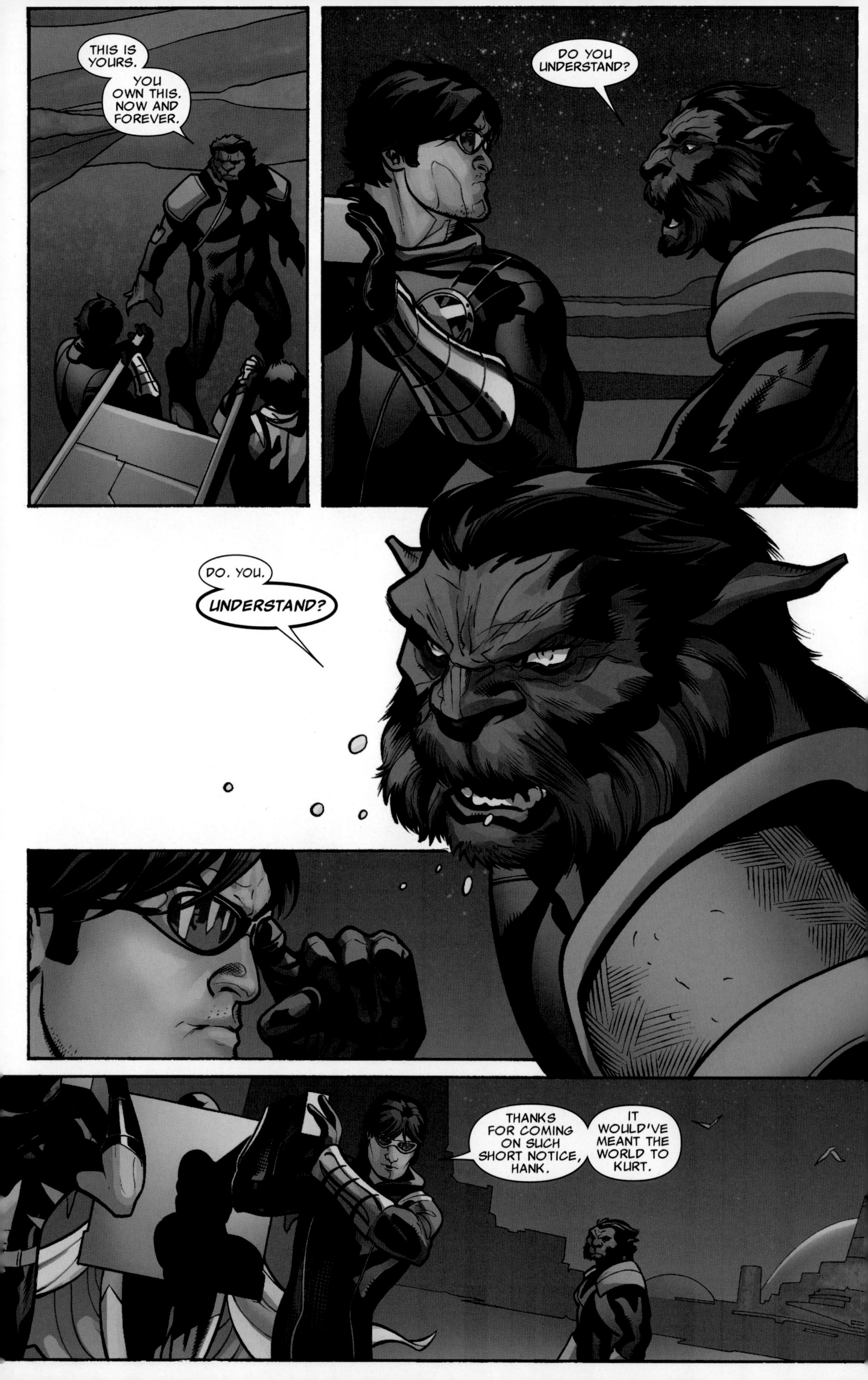
THIS IS YOURS.
YOU OWN THIS. NOW AND FOREVER.
DO YOU UNDERSTAND?
DO. YOU.
UNDERSTAND?
THANKS FOR COMING ON SUCH SHORT NOTICE, HANK.
IT WOULD'VE MEANT THE WORLD TO KURT.

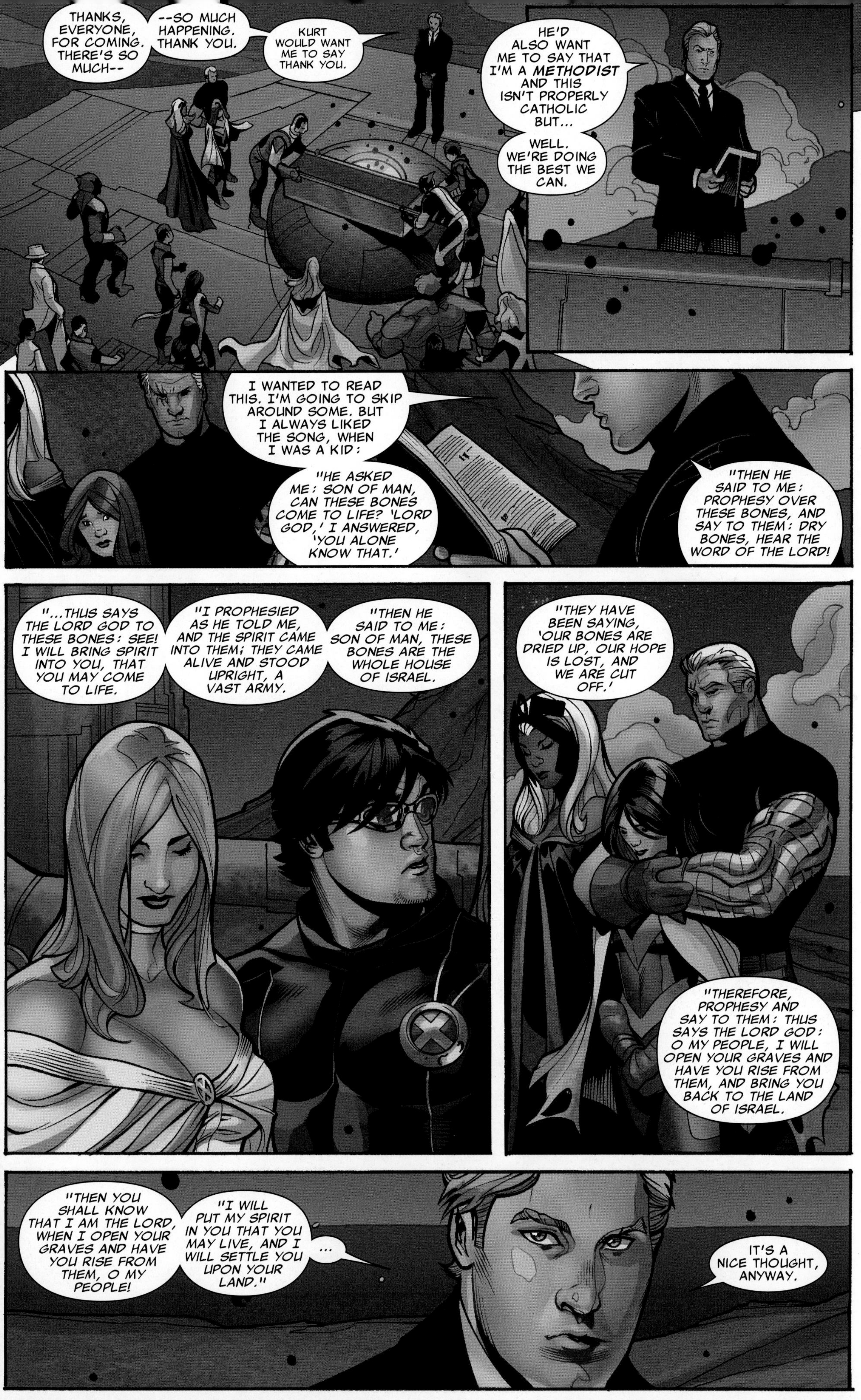
THANKS, EVERYONE, FOR COMING. THERE'S SO MUCH--
--SO MUCH HAPPENING. THANK YOU.
KURT WOULD WANT ME TO SAY THANK YOU.
HE'D ALSO WANT ME TO SAY THAT I'M A METHODIST AND THIS ISN'T PROPERLY CATHOLIC BUT...
WELL. WE'RE DOING THE BEST WE CAN.
I WANTED TO READ THIS. I'M GOING TO SKIP AROUND SOME. BUT I ALWAYS LIKED THE SONG, WHEN I WAS A KID:
"HE ASKED ME: SON OF MAN, CAN THESE BONES COME TO LIFE? 'LORD GOD,' I ANSWERED, 'YOU ALONE KNOW THAT.'
"THEN HE SAID TO ME: PROPHESY OVER THESE BONES, AND SAY TO THEM: DRY BONES, HEAR THE WORD OF THE LORD!
"...THUS SAYS THE LORD GOD TO THESE BONES: SEE! I WILL BRING SPIRIT INTO YOU, THAT YOU MAY COME TO LIFE.
"I PROPHESIED AS HE TOLD ME, AND THE SPIRIT CAME INTO THEM; THEY CAME ALIVE AND STOOD UPRIGHT, A VAST ARMY.
"THEN HE SAID TO ME: SON OF MAN, THESE BONES ARE THE WHOLE HOUSE OF ISRAEL.
"THEY HAVE BEEN SAYING, 'OUR BONES ARE DRIED UP, OUR HOPE IS LOST, AND WE ARE CUT OFF.'
"THEREFORE, PROPHESY AND SAY TO THEM: THUS SAYS THE LORD GOD: O MY PEOPLE, I WILL OPEN YOUR GRAVES AND HAVE YOU RISE FROM THEM, AND BRING YOU BACK TO THE LAND OF ISRAEL.
"THEN YOU SHALL KNOW THAT I AM THE LORD, WHEN I OPEN YOUR GRAVES AND HAVE YOU RISE FROM THEM, O MY PEOPLE!
"I WILL PUT MY SPIRIT IN YOU THAT YOU MAY LIVE, AND I WILL SETTLE YOU UPON YOUR LAND."
...
IT'S A NICE THOUGHT, ANYWAY.

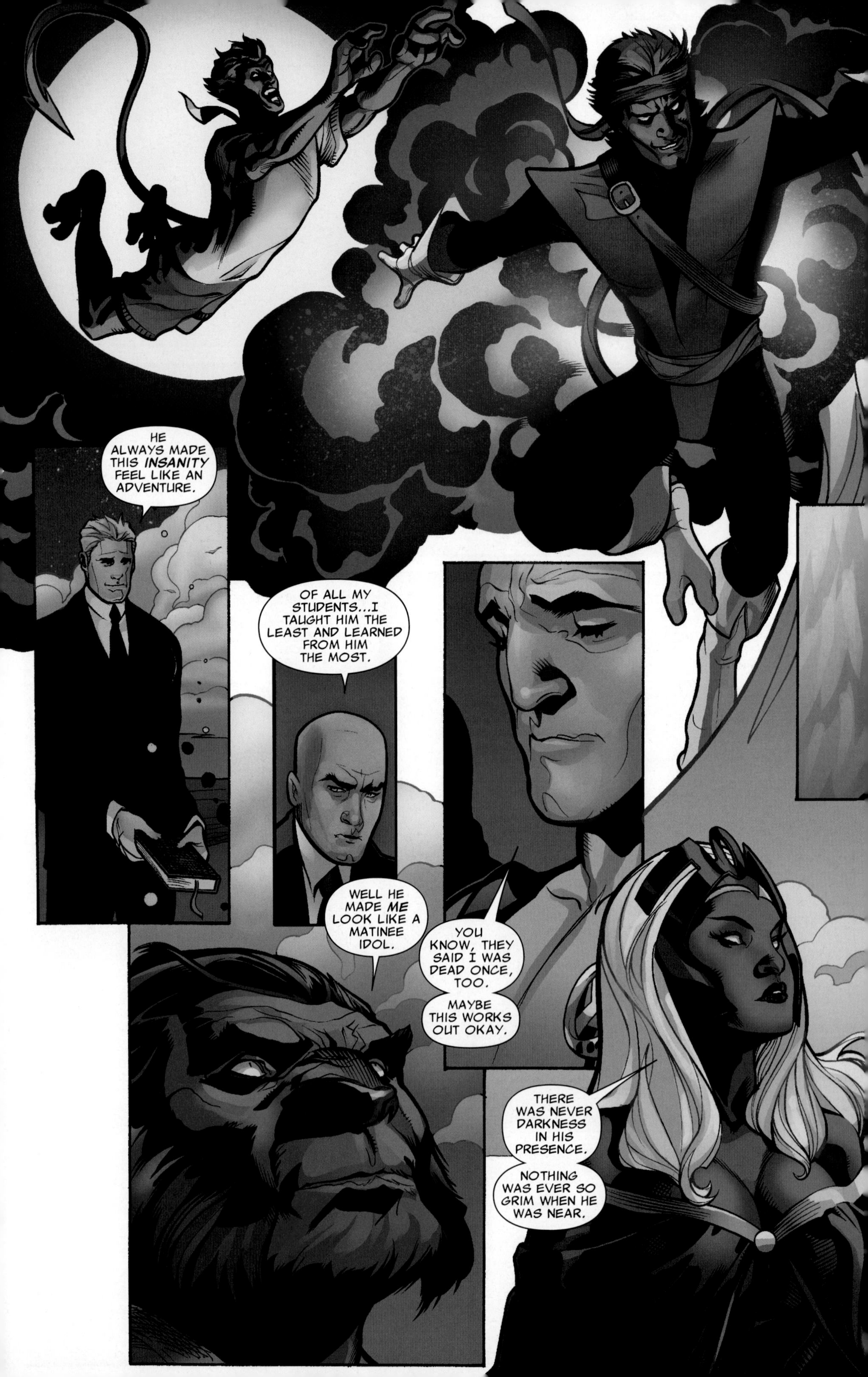
HE ALWAYS MADE THIS INSANITY FEEL LIKE AN ADVENTURE.
OF ALL MY STUDENTS...I TAUGHT HIM THE LEAST AND LEARNED FROM HIM THE MOST.
WELL HE MADE ME LOOK LIKE A MATINEE IDOL.
YOU KNOW, THEY SAID I WAS DEAD ONCE, TOO.
MAYBE THIS WORKS OUT OKAY.
THERE WAS NEVER DARKNESS IN HIS PRESENCE.
NOTHING WAS EVER SO GRIM WHEN HE WAS NEAR.

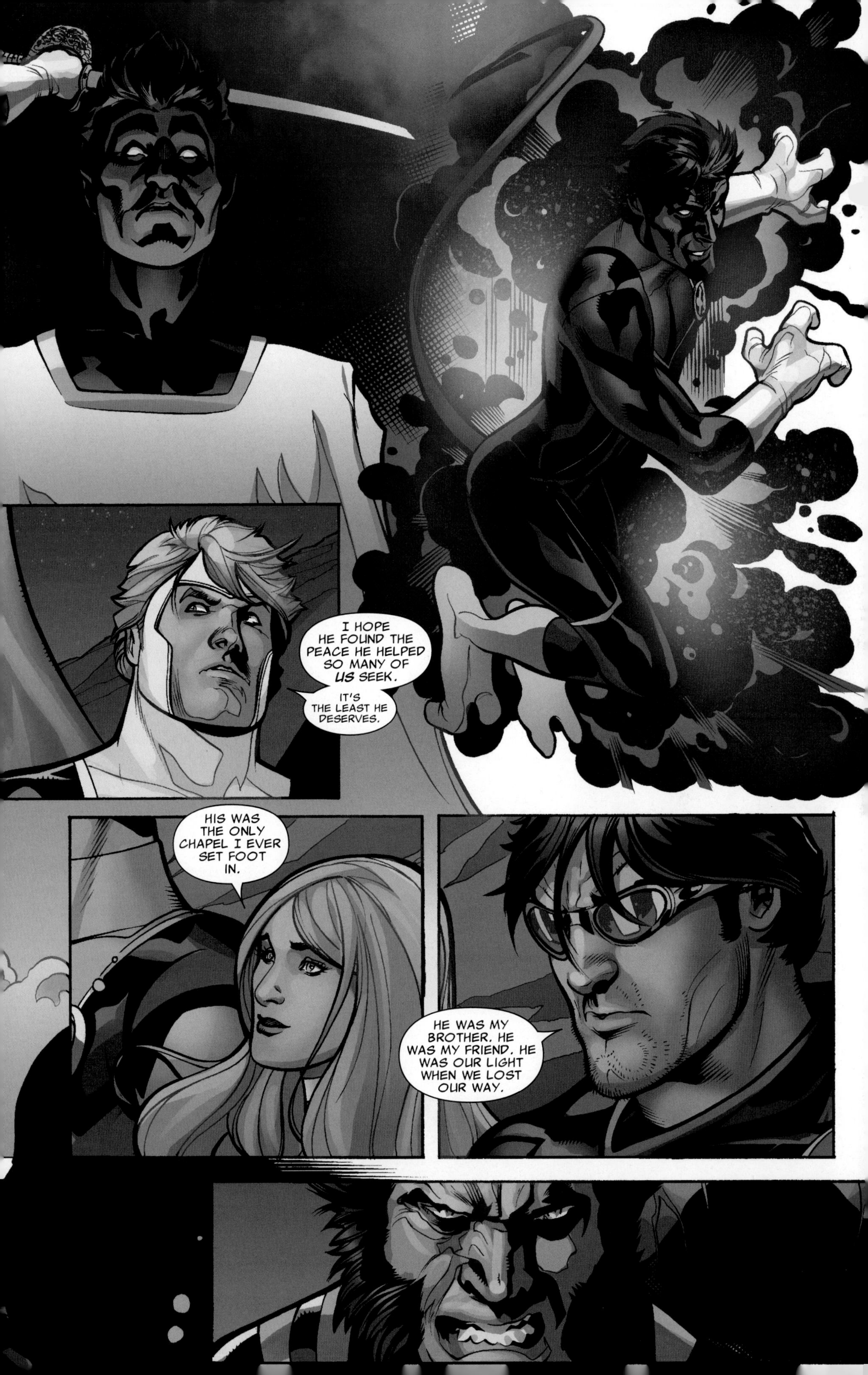
I HOPE HE FOUND THE PEACE HE HELPED SO MANY OF US SEEK.
IT'S THE LEAST HE DESERVES.
HIS WAS THE ONLY CHAPEL I EVER SET FOOT IN.
HE WAS MY BROTHER. HE WAS MY FRIEND. HE WAS OUR LIGHT WHEN WE LOST OUR WAY.

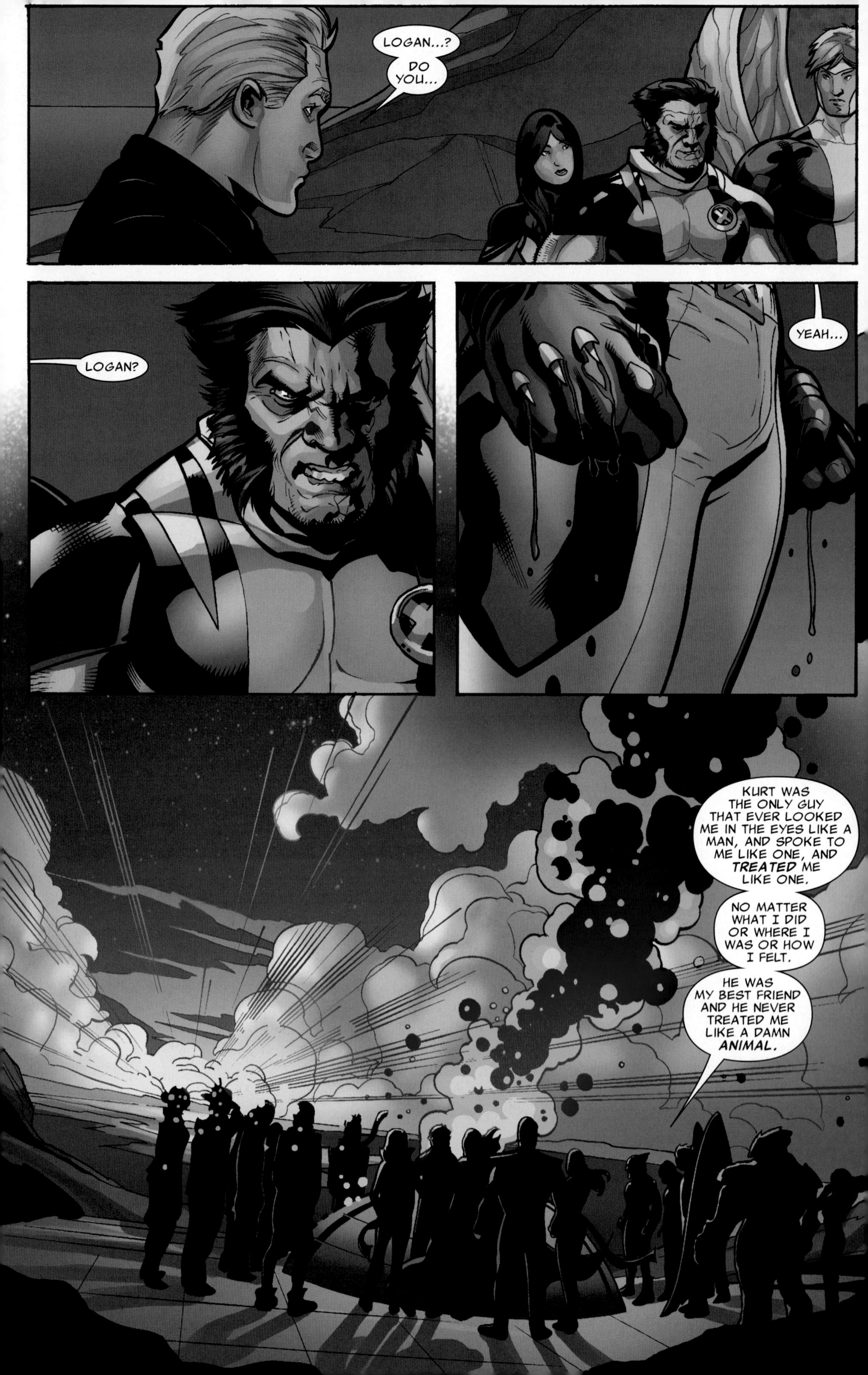
LOGAN...?
DO YOU...
LOGAN?
YEAH...
KURT WAS THE ONLY GUY THAT EVER LOOKED ME IN THE EYES LIKE A MAN, AND SPOKE TO ME LIKE ONE, AND TREATED ME LIKE ONE.
NO MATTER WHAT I DID OR WHERE I WAS OR HOW I FELT.
HE WAS MY BEST FRIEND AND HE NEVER TREATED ME LIKE A DAMN ANIMAL.

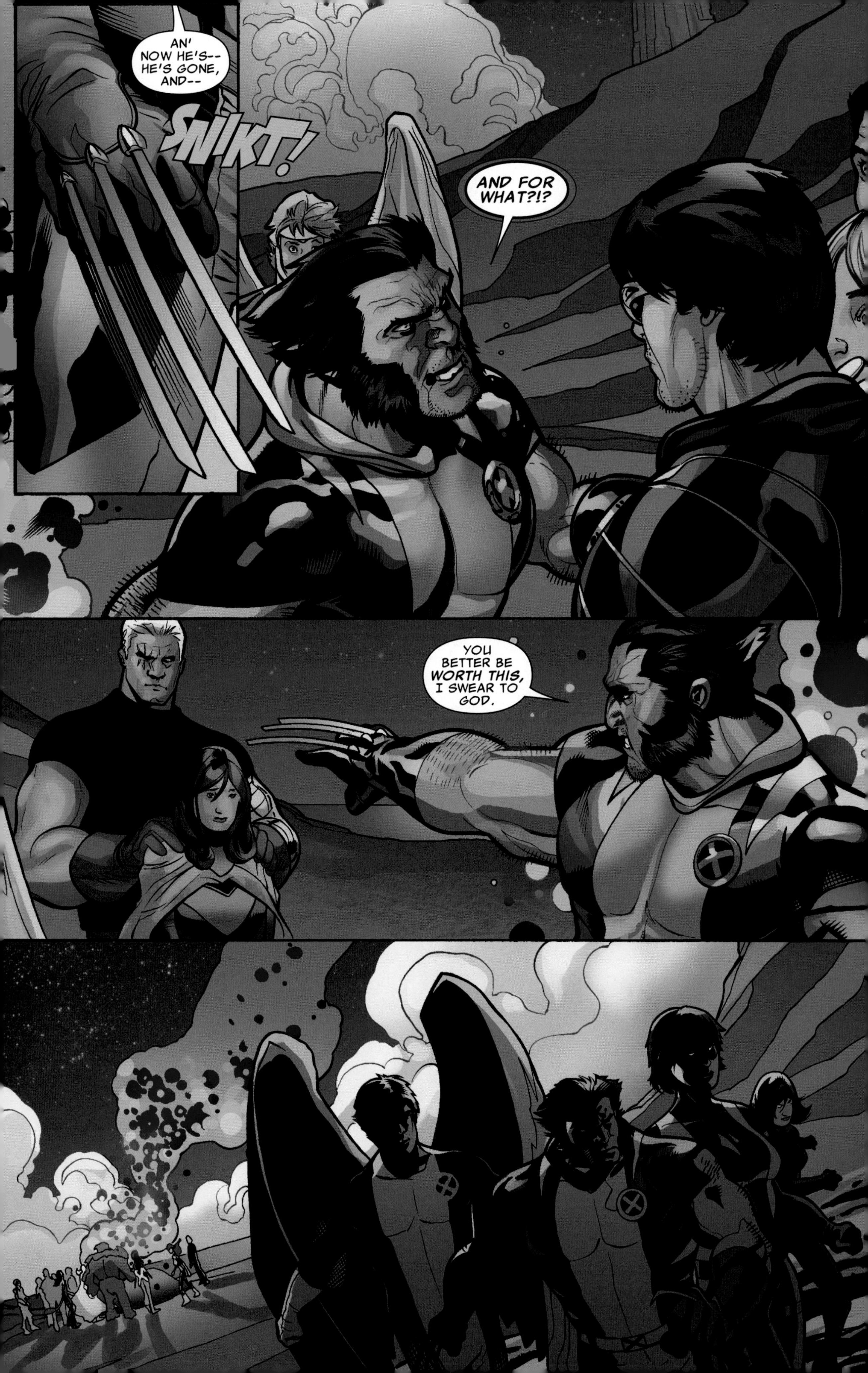
AN' NOW HE'S-- HE'S GONE, AND--
SNIKT!
AND FOR WHAT?!?
YOU BETTER BE WORTH THIS, I SWEAR TO GOD.

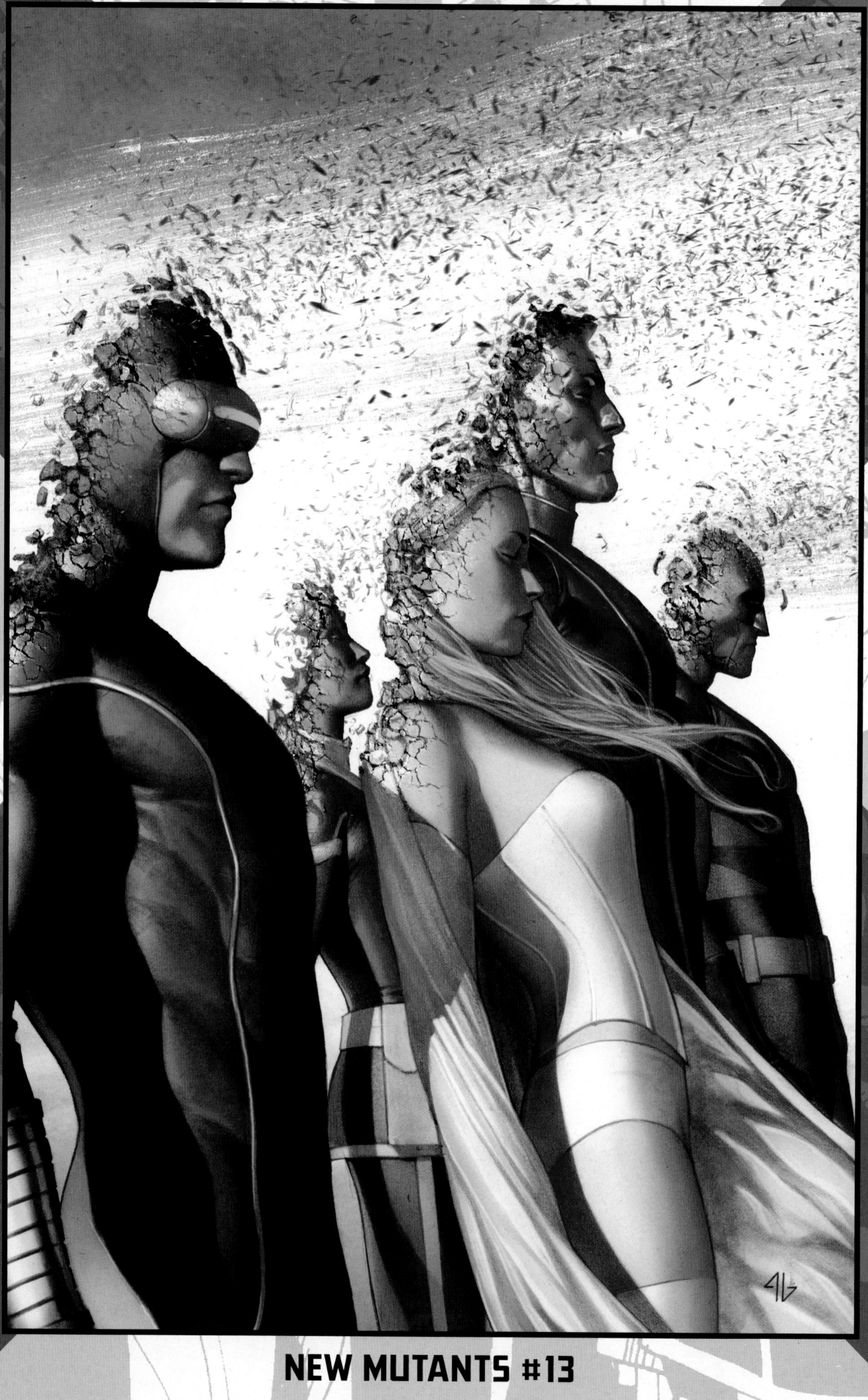

NEW MUTANTS #13

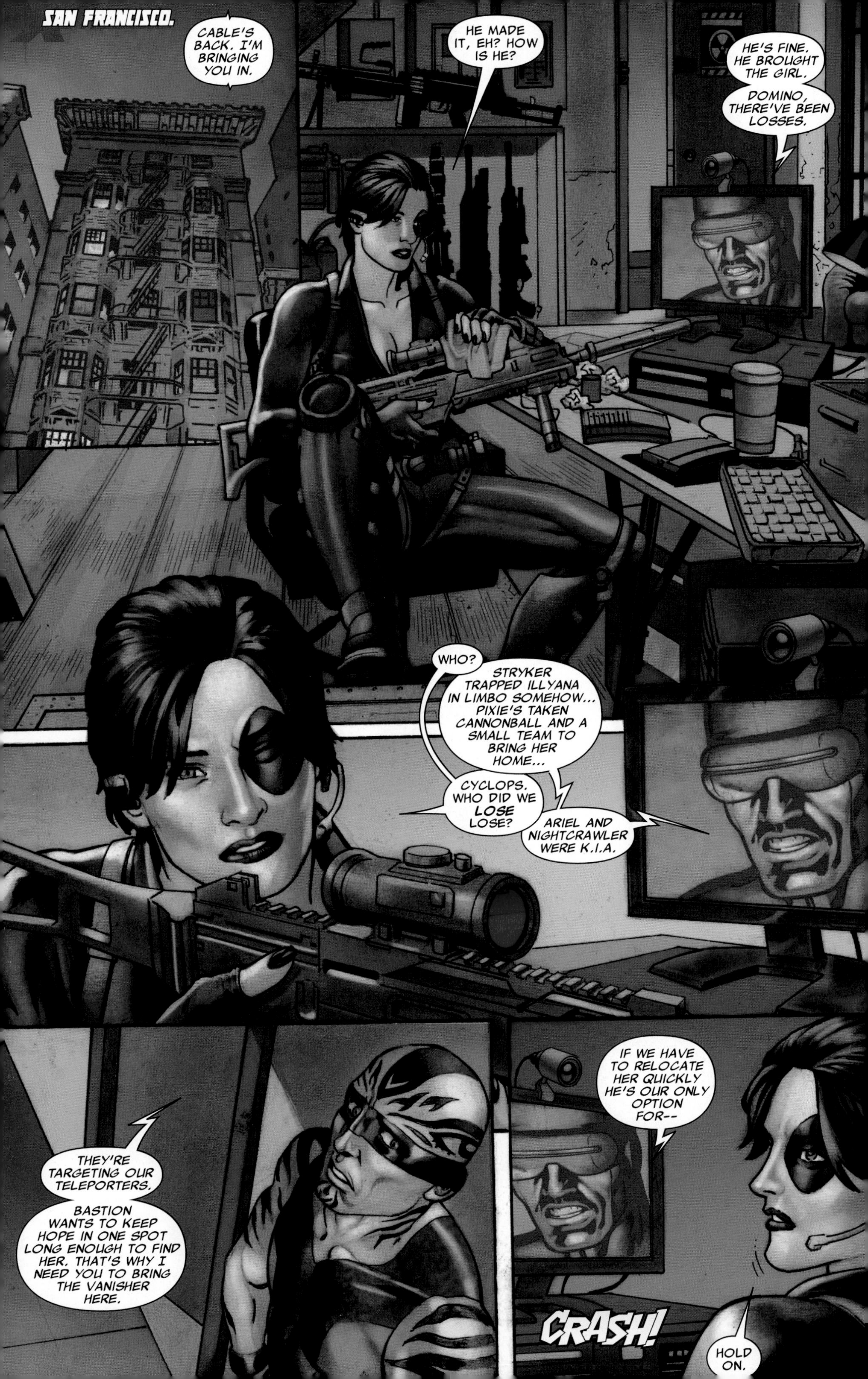
SAN FRANCISCO.
CABLE'S BACK. I'M BRINGING YOU IN.
HE MADE IT, EH? HOW IS HE?
HE'S FINE. HE BROUGHT THE GIRL.
DOMINO, THERE'VE BEEN LOSSES.
WHO?
STRYKER TRAPPED ILLYANA IN LIMBO SOMEHOW... PIXIE'S TAKEN CANNONBALL AND A SMALL TEAM TO BRING HER HOME...
CYCLOPS. WHO DID WE LOSE LOSE?
ARIEL AND NIGHTCRAWLER WERE K.I.A.
THEY'RE TARGETING OUR TELEPORTERS.
BASTION WANTS TO KEEP HOPE IN ONE SPOT LONG ENOUGH TO FIND HER. THAT'S WHY I NEED YOU TO BRING THE VANISHER HERE.
IF WE HAVE TO RELOCATE HER QUICKLY HE'S OUR ONLY OPTION FOR--
CRASH!
HOLD ON.

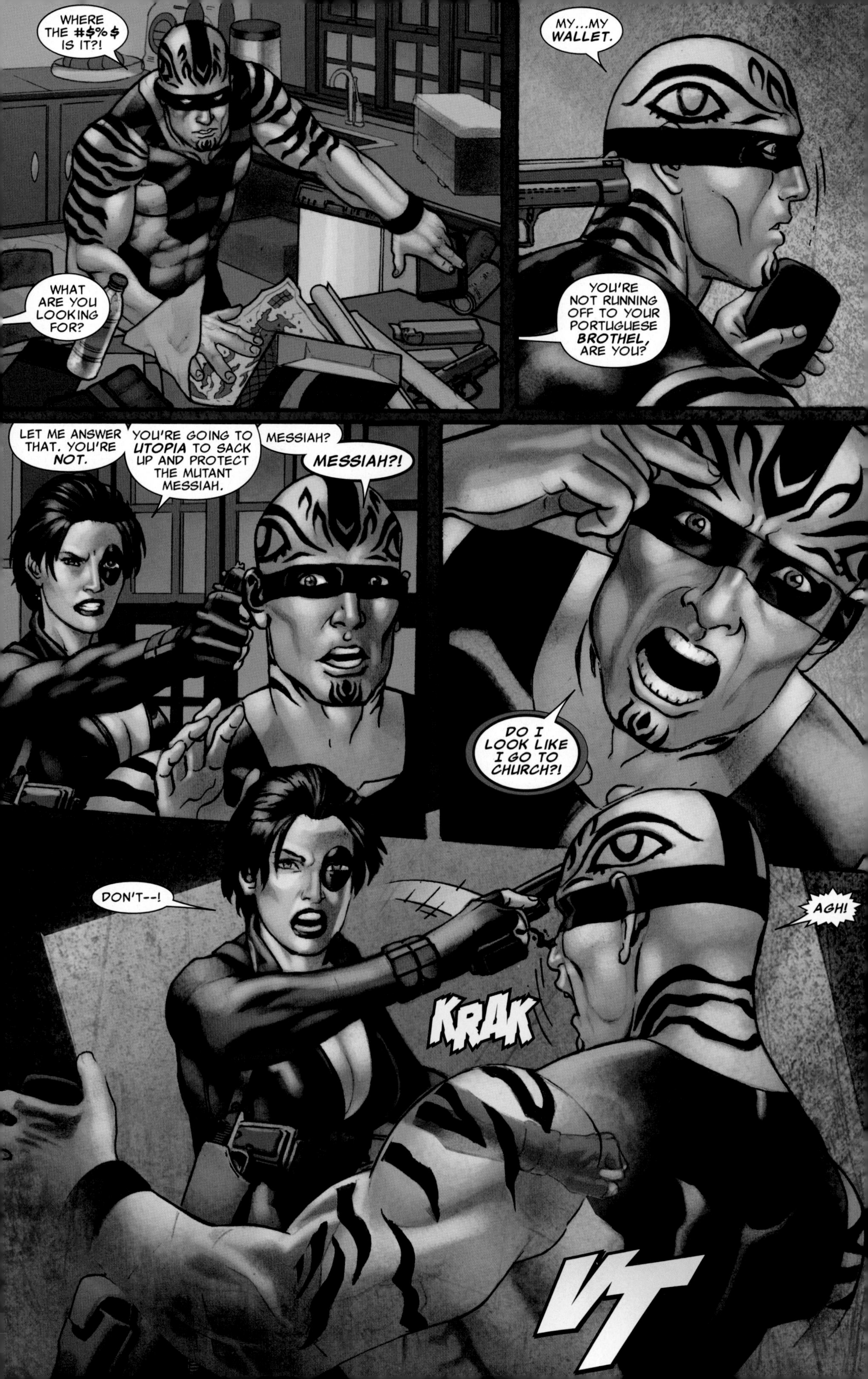
WHERE THE #$%$ IS IT?!
WHAT ARE YOU LOOKING FOR?
MY...MY WALLET.
YOU'RE NOT RUNNING OFF TO YOUR PORTUGUESE BROTHEL, ARE YOU?
LET ME ANSWER THAT. YOU'RE NOT.
YOU'RE GOING TO UTOPIA TO SACK UP AND PROTECT THE MUTANT MESSIAH.
MESSIAH?
MESSIAH?!
DO I LOOK LIKE I GO TO CHURCH?!
DON'T--!
AGH!
KRAK
VT

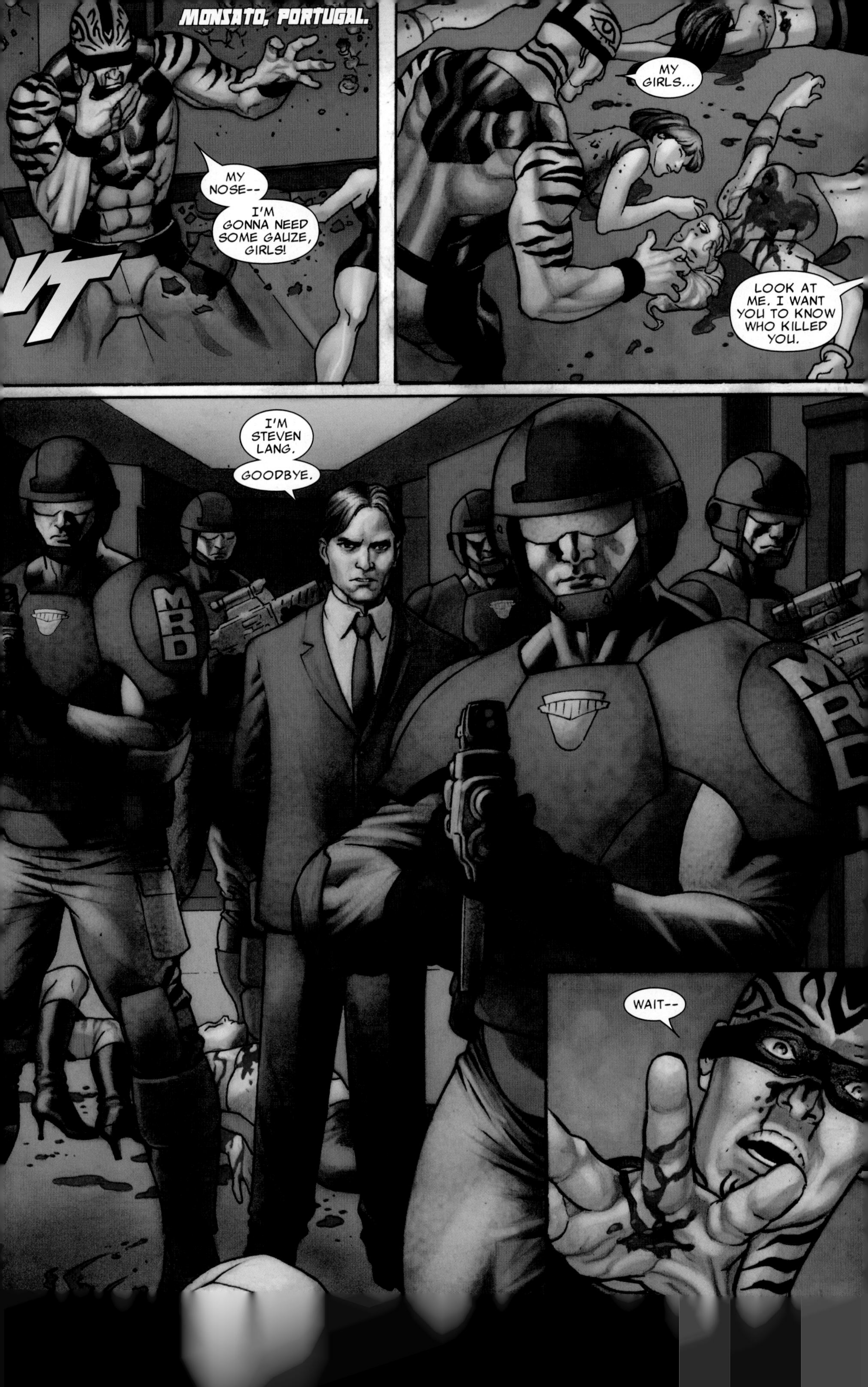
MONSATO, PORTUGAL.
MY NOSE--
I'M GONNA NEED SOME GAUZE, GIRLS!
MY GIRLS...
LOOK AT ME. I WANT YOU TO KNOW WHO KILLED YOU.
I'M STEVEN LANG.
GOODBYE.
M R D
WAIT--

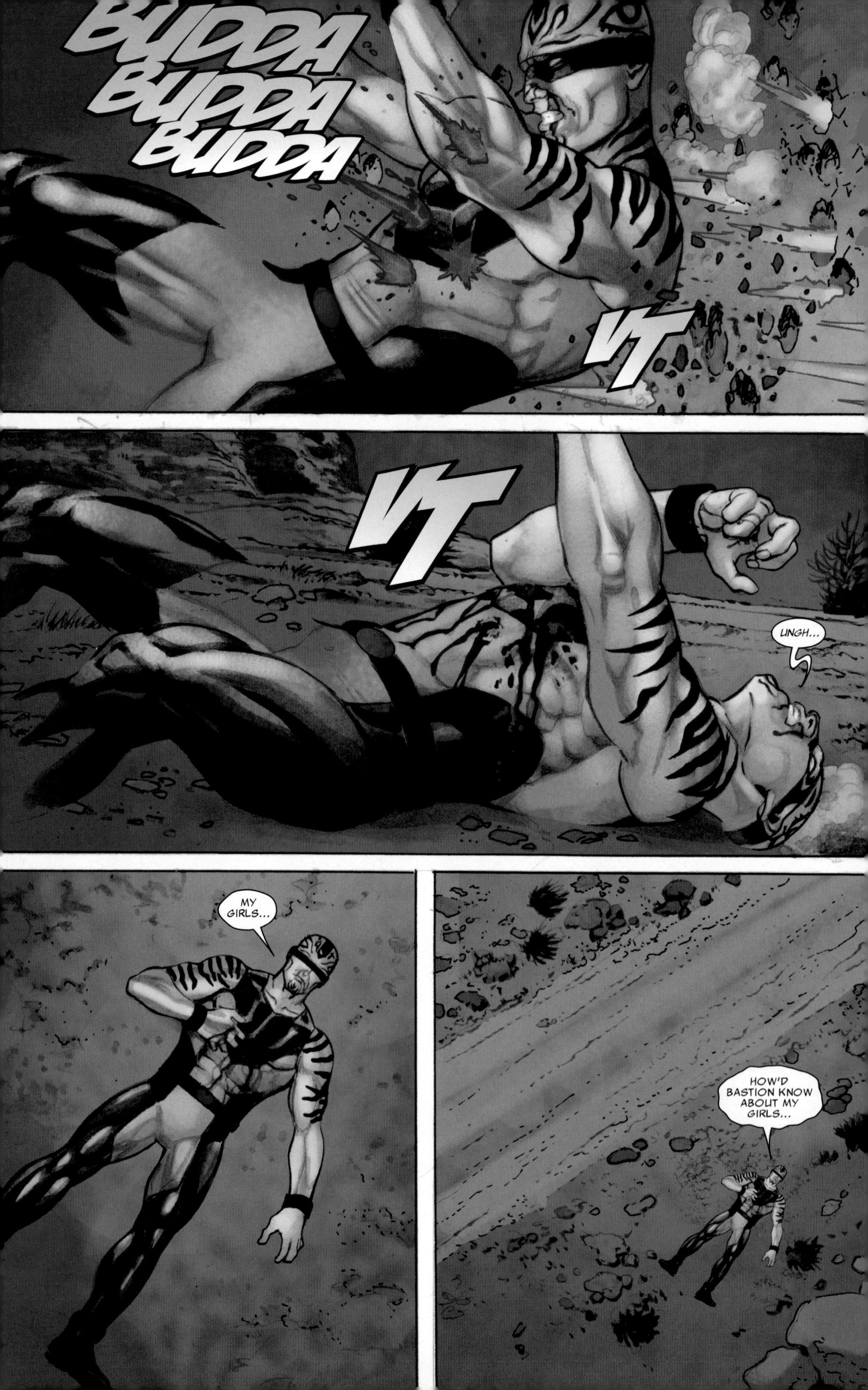
BUDDA BUDDA BUDDA
VT
VT
UNGH...
MY GIRLS...
HOW'D BASTION KNOW ABOUT MY GIRLS...

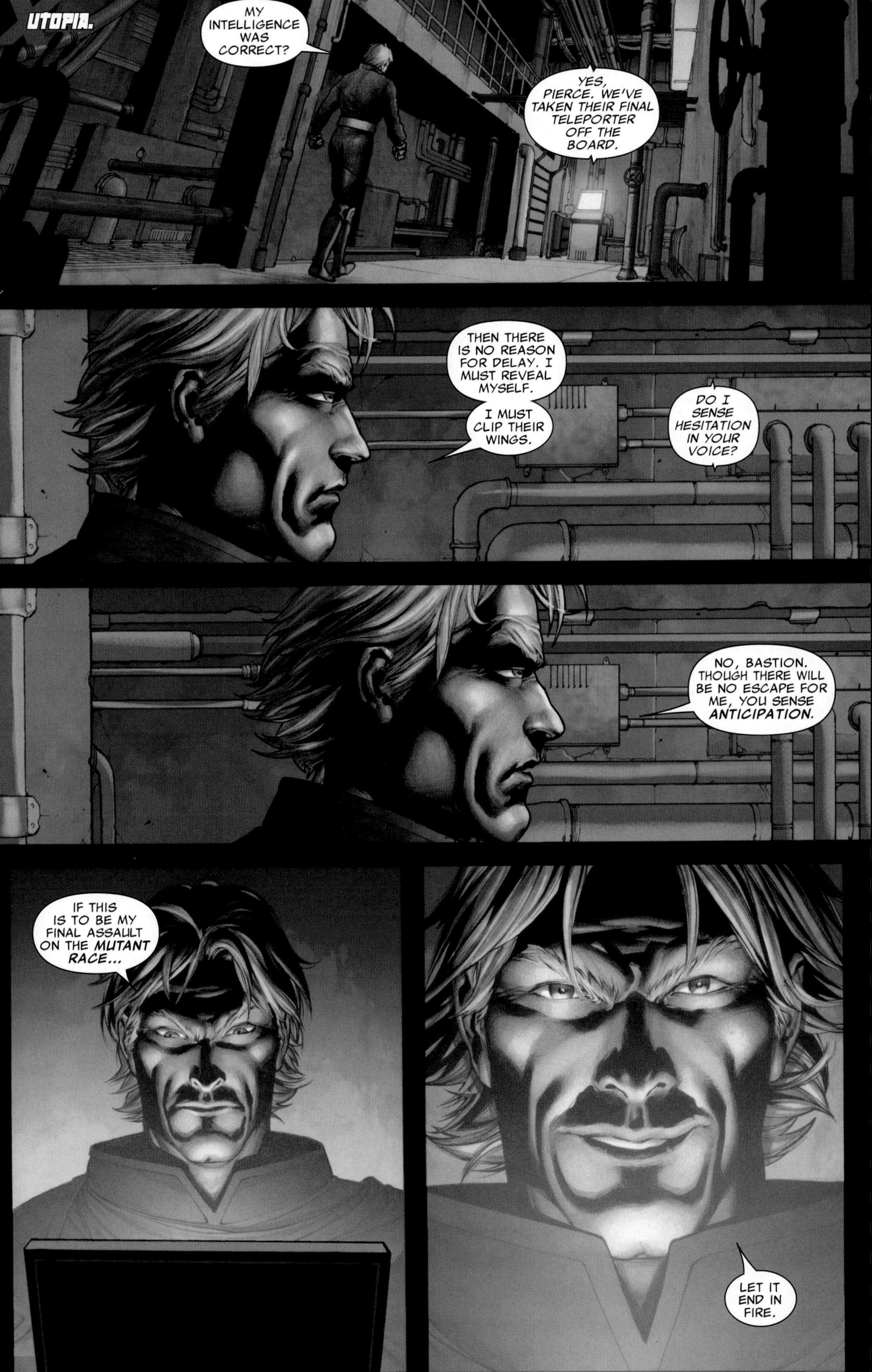
UTOPIA.
MY INTELLIGENCE WAS CORRECT?
YES, PIERCE. WE'VE TAKEN THEIR FINAL TELEPORTER OFF THE BOARD.
THEN THERE IS NO REASON FOR DELAY. I MUST REVEAL MYSELF.
I MUST CLIP THEIR WINGS.
DO I SENSE HESITATION IN YOUR VOICE?
NO, BASTION. THOUGH THERE WILL BE NO ESCAPE FOR ME, YOU SENSE ANTICIPATION.
IF THIS IS TO BE MY FINAL ASSAULT ON THE MUTANT RACE...
LET IT END IN FIRE.

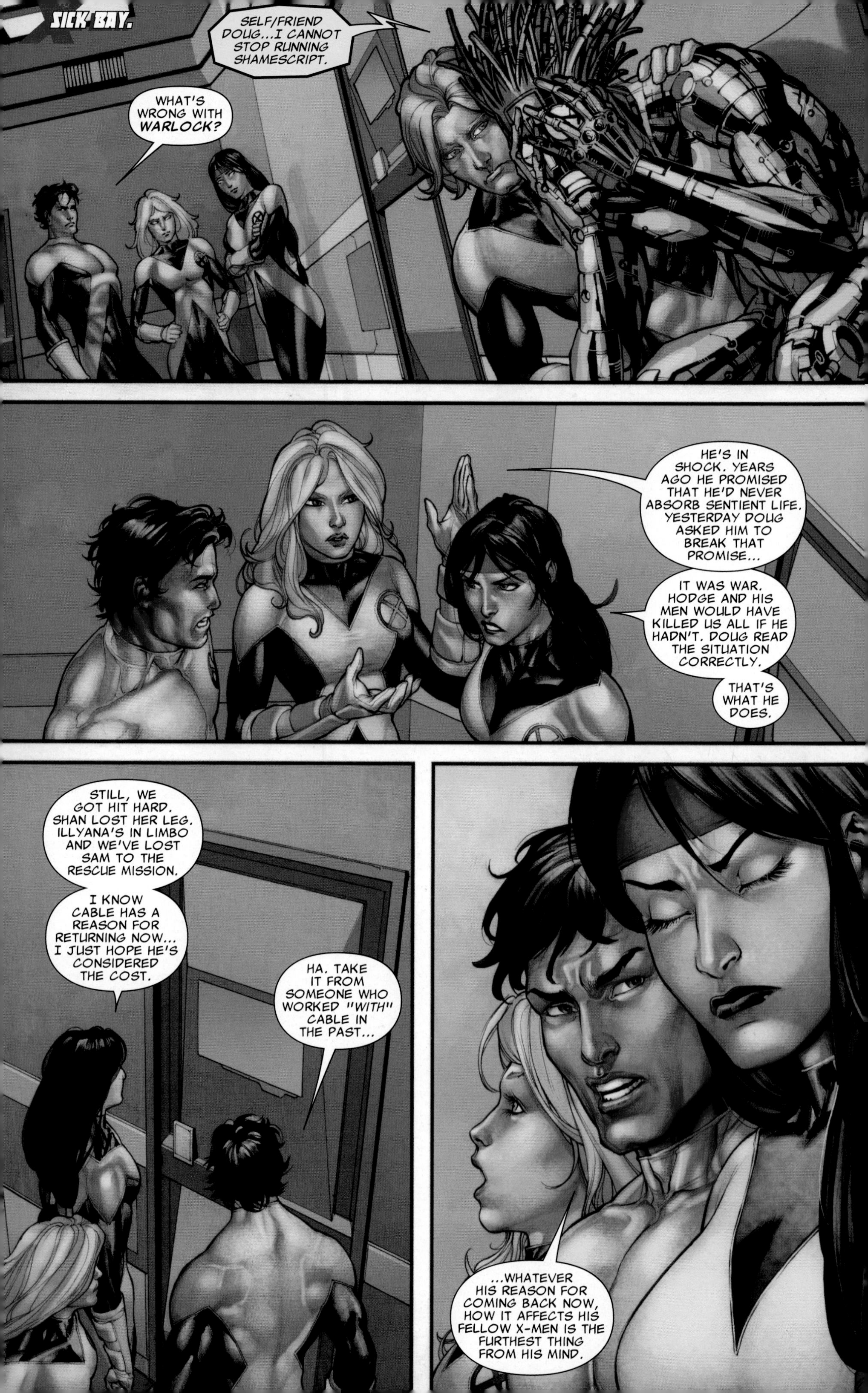
SICK BAY.
SELF/FRIEND DOUG...I CANNOT STOP RUNNING SHAMESCRIPT.
WHAT'S WRONG WITH WARLOCK?
HE'S IN SHOCK. YEARS AGO HE PROMISED THAT HE'D NEVER ABSORB SENTIENT LIFE. YESTERDAY DOUG ASKED HIM TO BREAK THAT PROMISE...
IT WAS WAR. HODGE AND HIS MEN WOULD HAVE KILLED US ALL IF HE HADN'T. DOUG READ THE SITUATION CORRECTLY.
THAT'S WHAT HE DOES.
STILL, WE GOT HIT HARD. SHAN LOST HER LEG. ILLYANA'S IN LIMBO AND WE'VE LOST SAM TO THE RESCUE MISSION.
I KNOW CABLE HAS A REASON FOR RETURNING NOW... I JUST HOPE HE'S CONSIDERED THE COST.
HA. TAKE IT FROM SOMEONE WHO WORKED "WITH" CABLE IN THE PAST...
...WHATEVER HIS REASON FOR COMING BACK NOW, HOW IT AFFECTS HIS FELLOW X-MEN IS THE FURTHEST THING FROM HIS MIND.

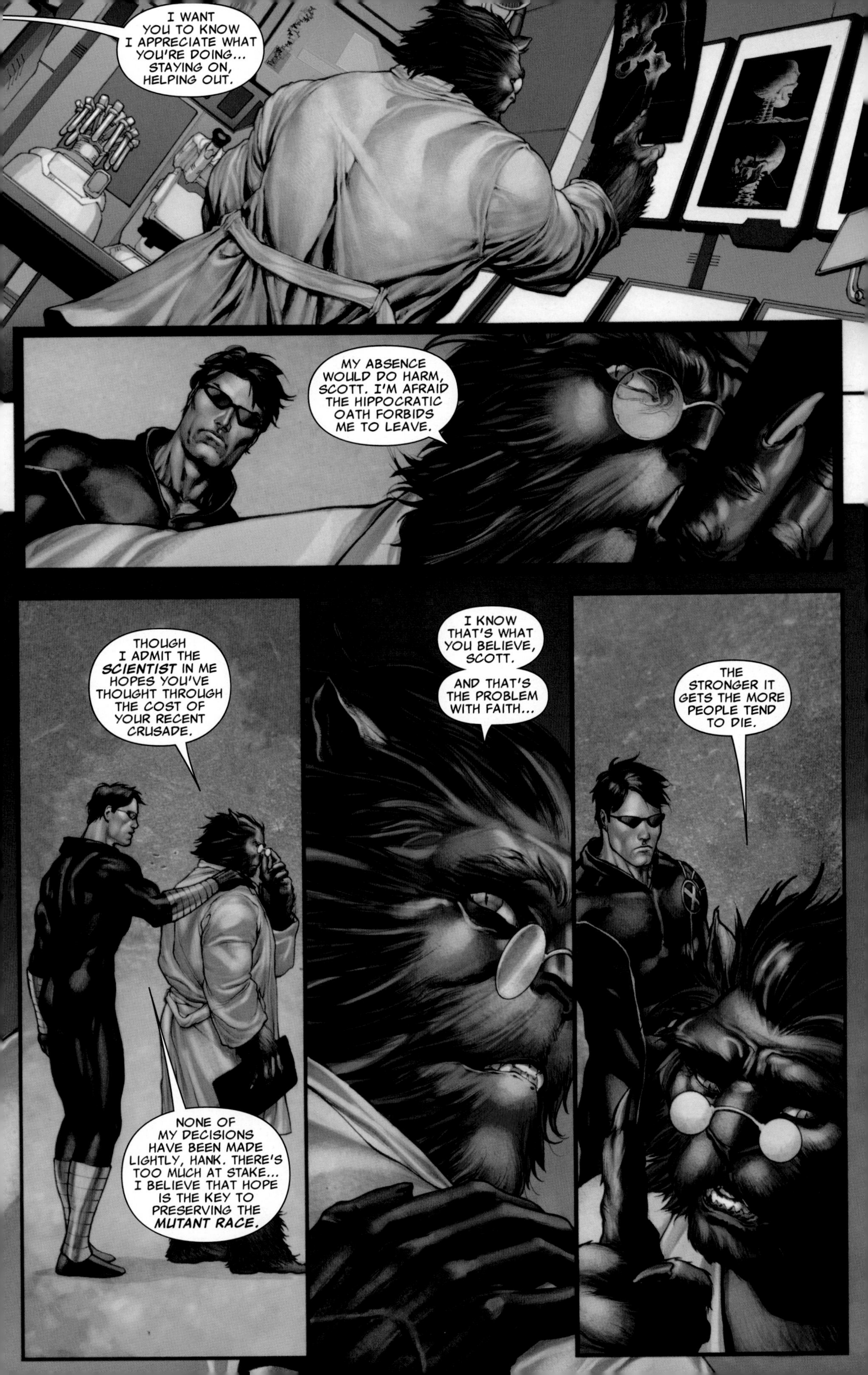
I WANT YOU TO KNOW I APPRECIATE WHAT YOU'RE DOING... STAYING ON, HELPING OUT.
MY ABSENCE WOULD DO HARM, SCOTT. I'M AFRAID THE HIPPOCRATIC OATH FORBIDS ME TO LEAVE.
THOUGH I ADMIT THE SCIENTIST IN ME HOPES YOU'VE THOUGHT THROUGH THE COST OF YOUR RECENT CRUSADE.
NONE OF MY DECISIONS HAVE BEEN MADE LIGHTLY, HANK. THERE'S TOO MUCH AT STAKE... I BELIEVE THAT HOPE IS THE KEY TO PRESERVING THE MUTANT RACE.
I KNOW THAT'S WHAT YOU BELIEVE, SCOTT.
AND THAT'S THE PROBLEM WITH FAITH...
THE STRONGER IT GETS THE MORE PEOPLE TEND TO DIE.

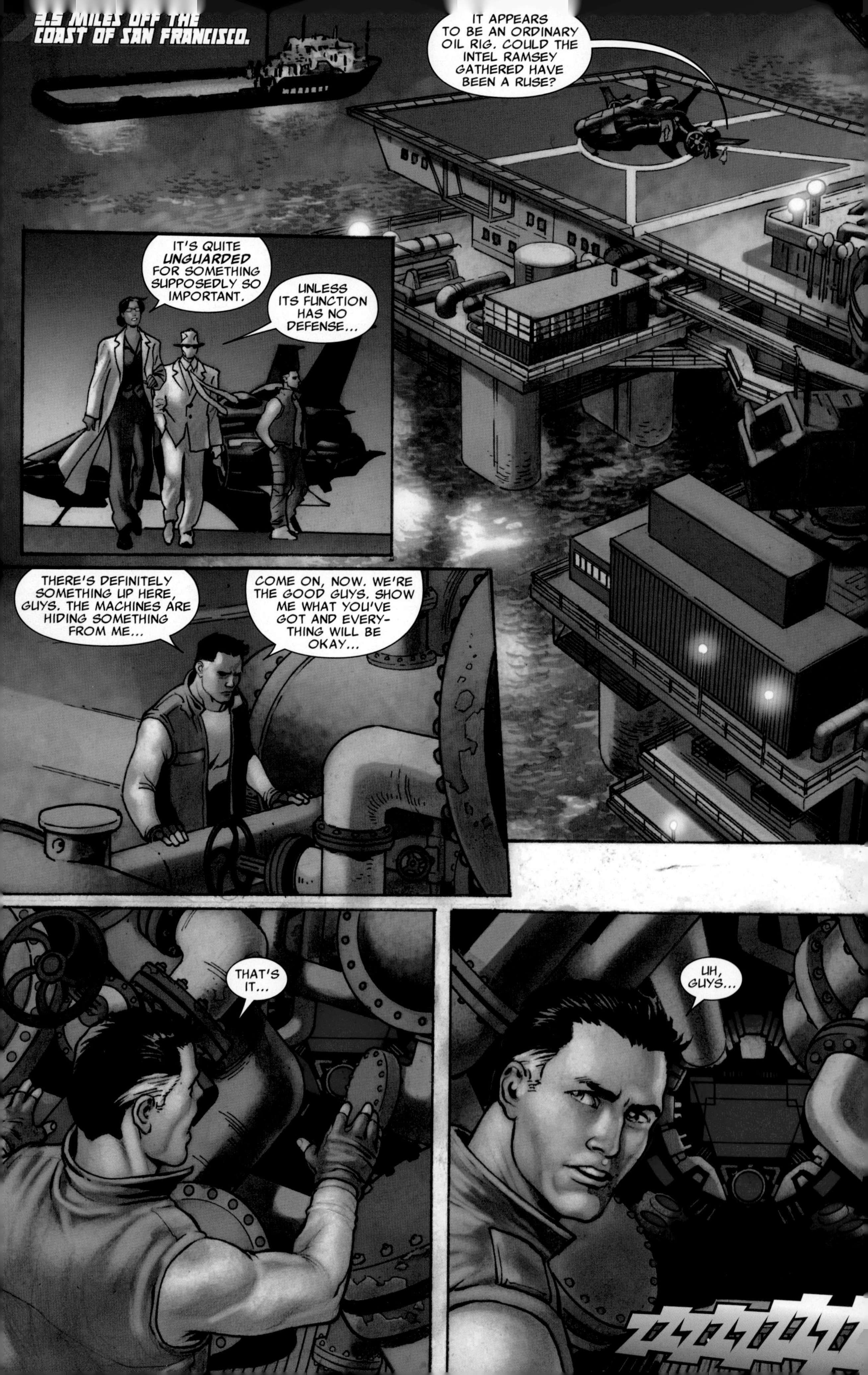
3.5 MILES OFF THE COAST OF SAN FRANCISCO.
IT APPEARS TO BE AN ORDINARY OIL RIG. COULD THE INTEL RAMSEY GATHERED HAVE BEEN A RUSE?
IT'S QUITE UNGUARDED FOR SOMETHING SUPPOSEDLY SO IMPORTANT.
UNLESS ITS FUNCTION HAS NO DEFENSE...
THERE'S DEFINITELY SOMETHING UP HERE, GUYS. THE MACHINES ARE HIDING SOMETHING FROM ME...
COME ON, NOW. WE'RE THE GOOD GUYS. SHOW ME WHAT YOU'VE GOT AND EVERYTHING WILL BE OKAY...
THAT'S IT...
UH, GUYS...

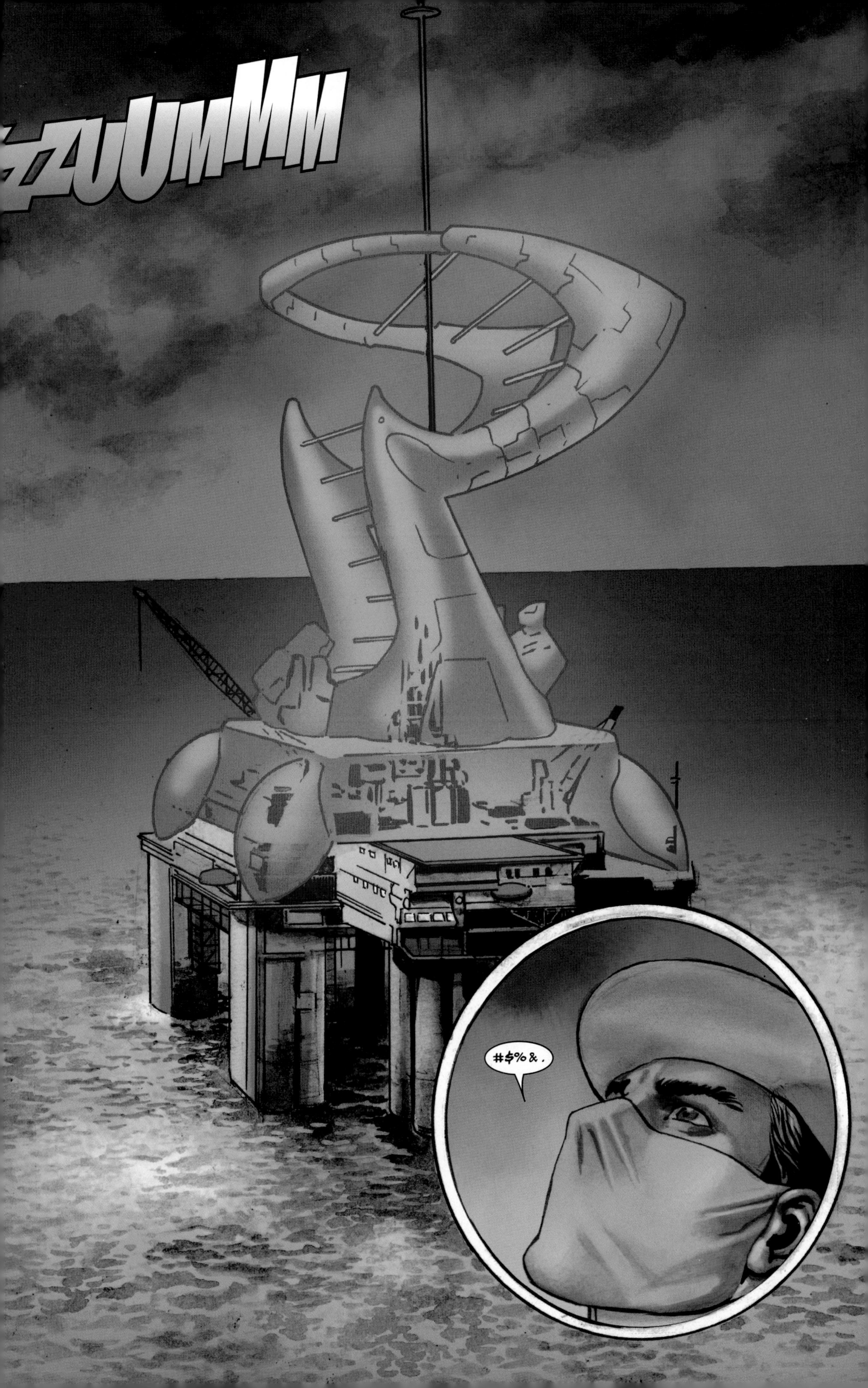
ZZUUMMMM
#$%&.

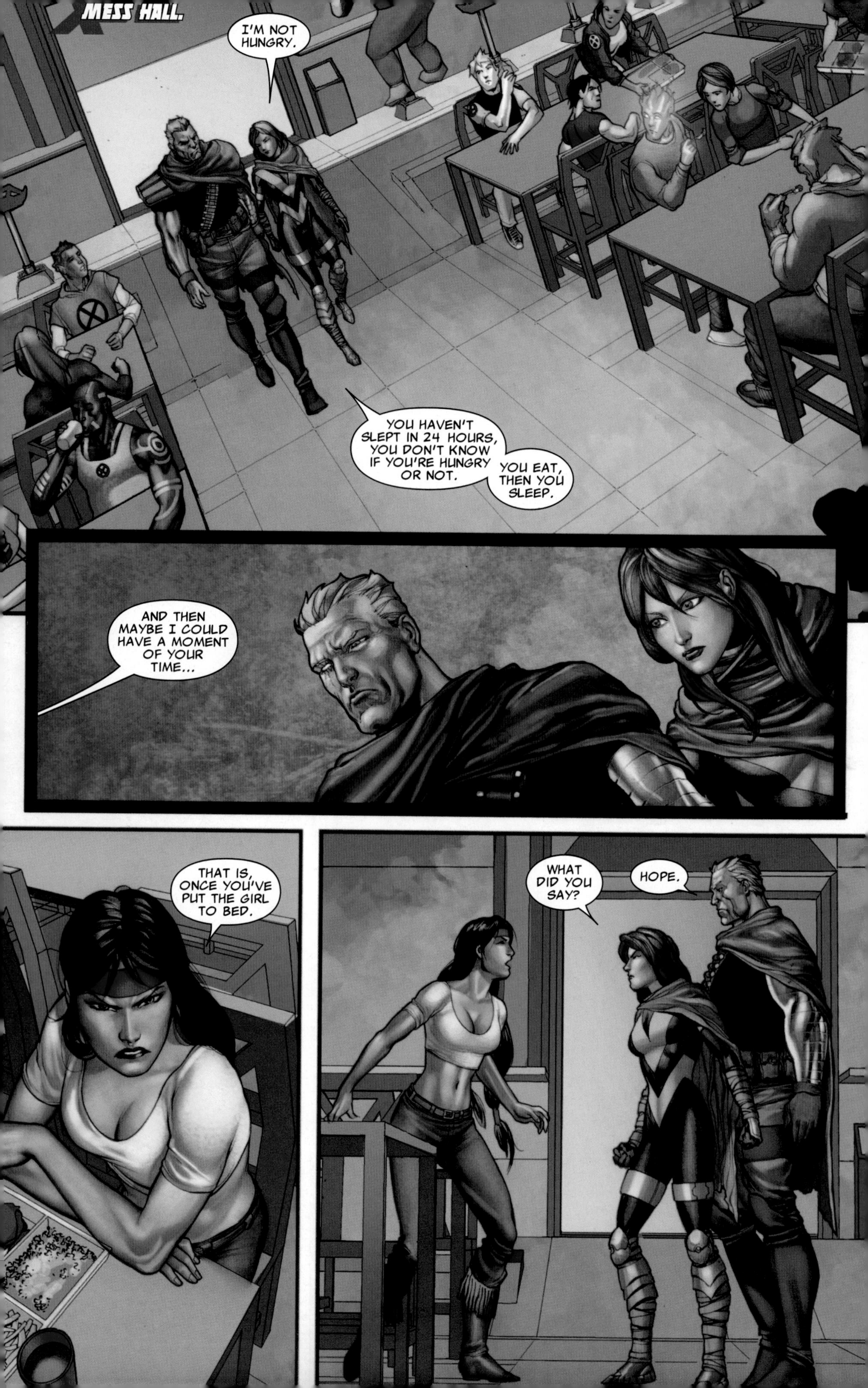
MESS HALL.
I'M NOT HUNGRY.
YOU HAVEN'T SLEPT IN 24 HOURS, YOU DON'T KNOW IF YOU'RE HUNGRY OR NOT.
YOU EAT, THEN YOU SLEEP.
AND THEN MAYBE I COULD HAVE A MOMENT OF YOUR TIME...
THAT IS, ONCE YOU'VE PUT THE GIRL TO BED.
WHAT DID YOU SAY?
HOPE.

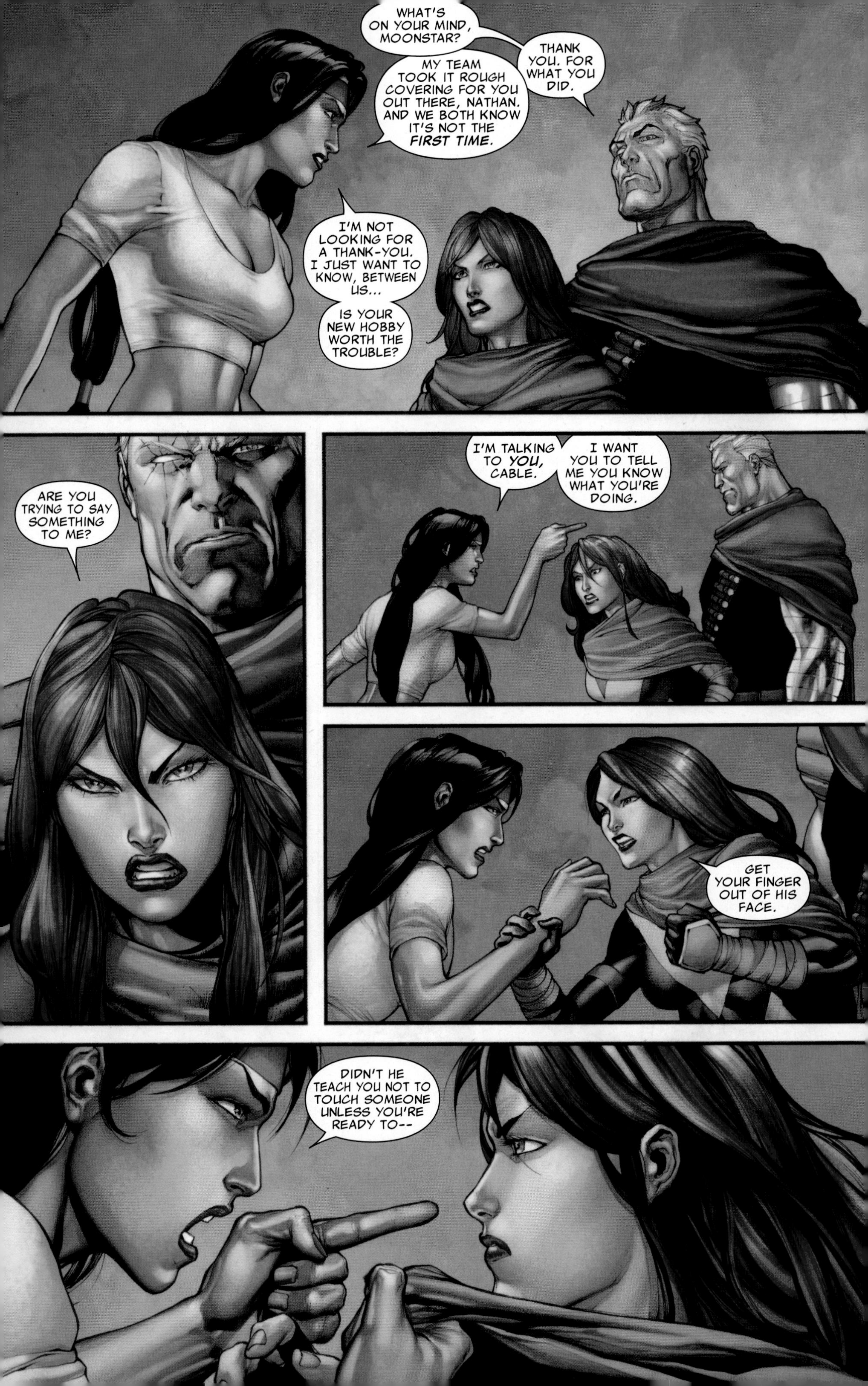
WHAT'S ON YOUR MIND, MOONSTAR?
THANK YOU. FOR WHAT YOU DID.
MY TEAM TOOK IT ROUGH COVERING FOR YOU OUT THERE, NATHAN. AND WE BOTH KNOW IT'S NOT THE FIRST TIME.
I'M NOT LOOKING FOR A THANK-YOU. I JUST WANT TO KNOW, BETWEEN US...
IS YOUR NEW HOBBY WORTH THE TROUBLE?
ARE YOU TRYING TO SAY SOMETHING TO ME?
I'M TALKING TO YOU, CABLE.
I WANT YOU TO TELL ME YOU KNOW WHAT YOU'RE DOING.
GET YOUR FINGER OUT OF HIS FACE.
DIDN'T HE TEACH YOU NOT TO TOUCH SOMEONE UNLESS YOU'RE READY TO--

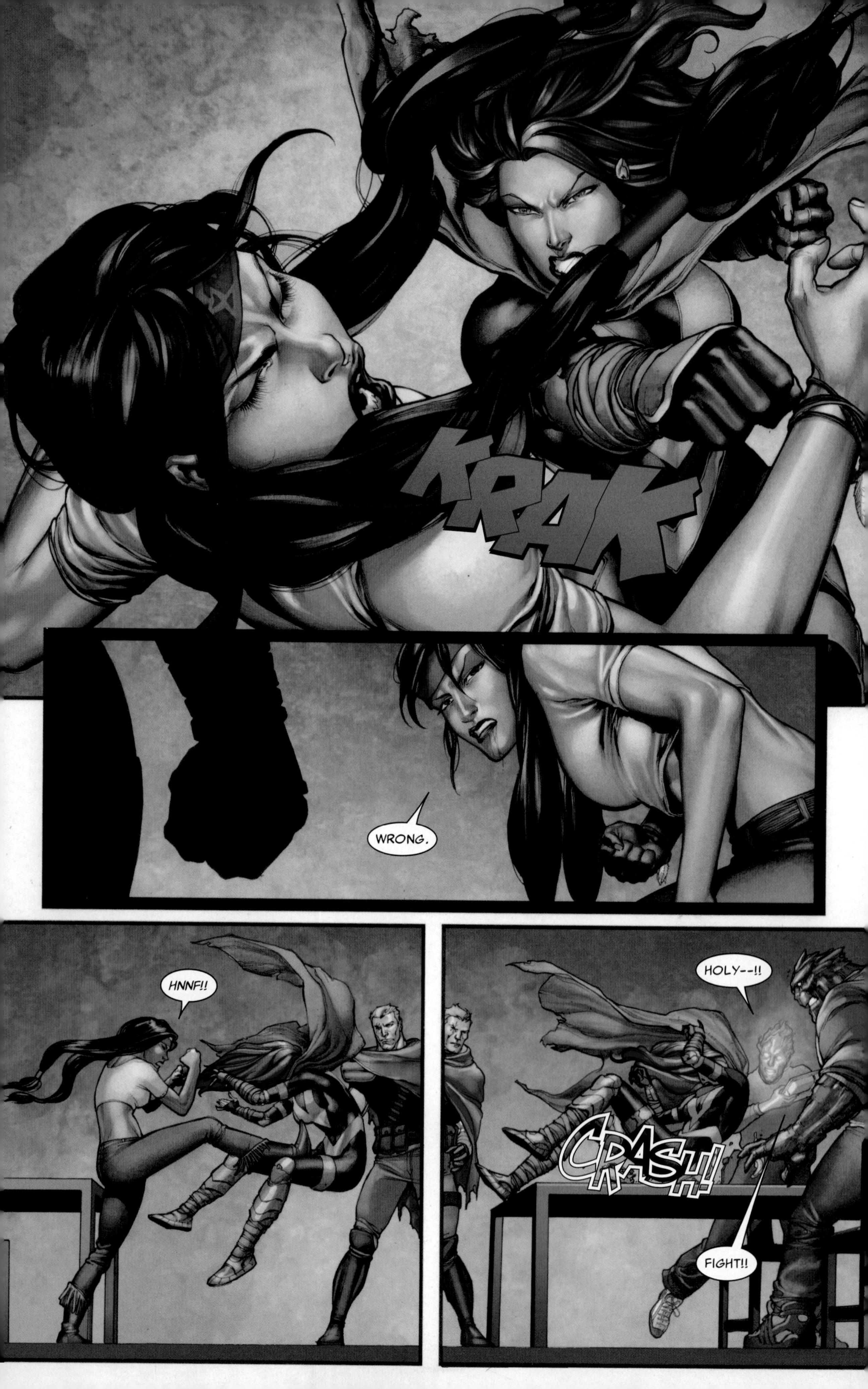
KRAK
WRONG.
HNNF!!
HOLY--!!
CRASH!!
FIGHT!!

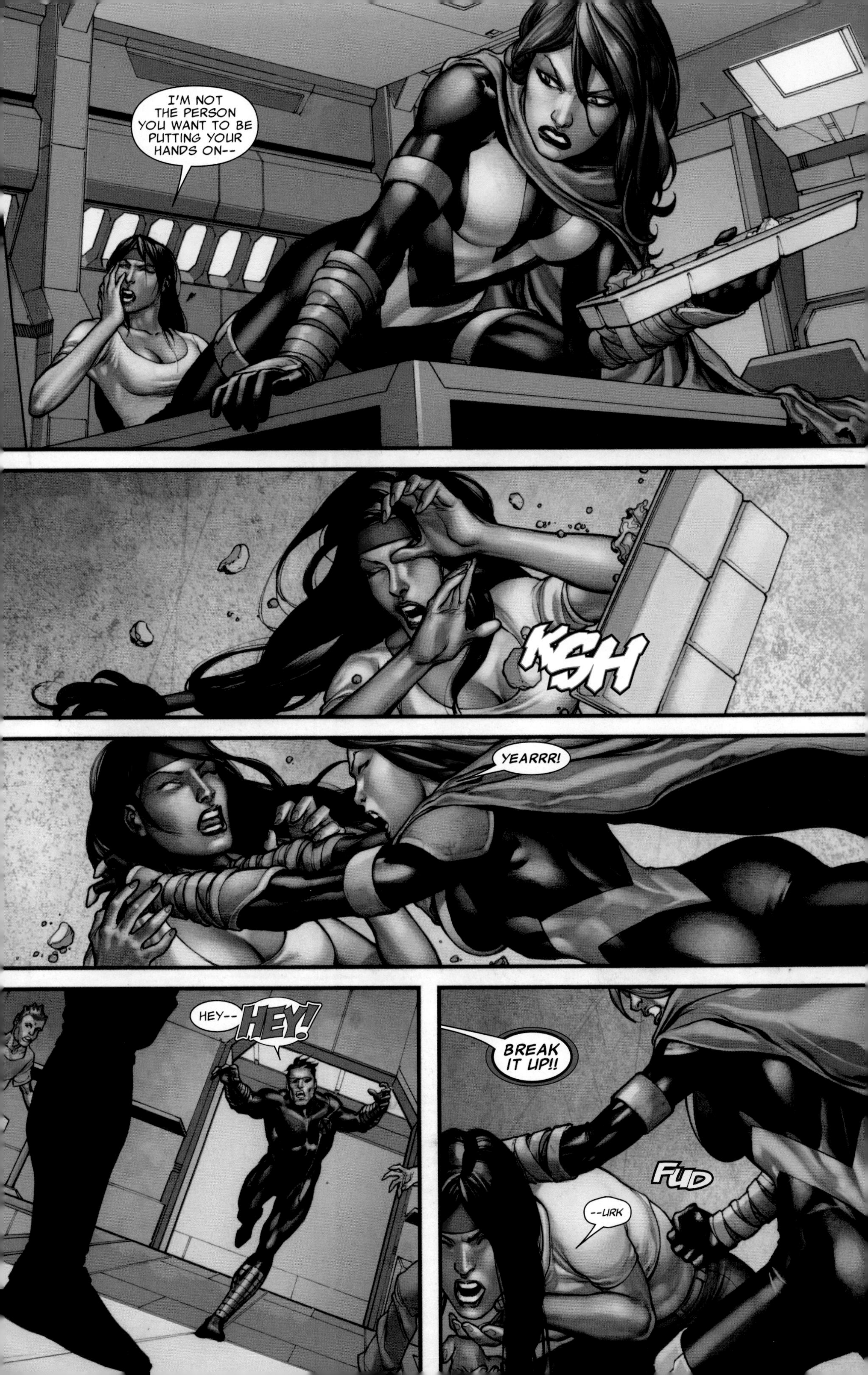
I'M NOT THE PERSON YOU WANT TO BE PUTTING YOUR HANDS ON--
KSH
YEARRR!
HEY--
HEY!
BREAK IT UP!!
FUD
--URK

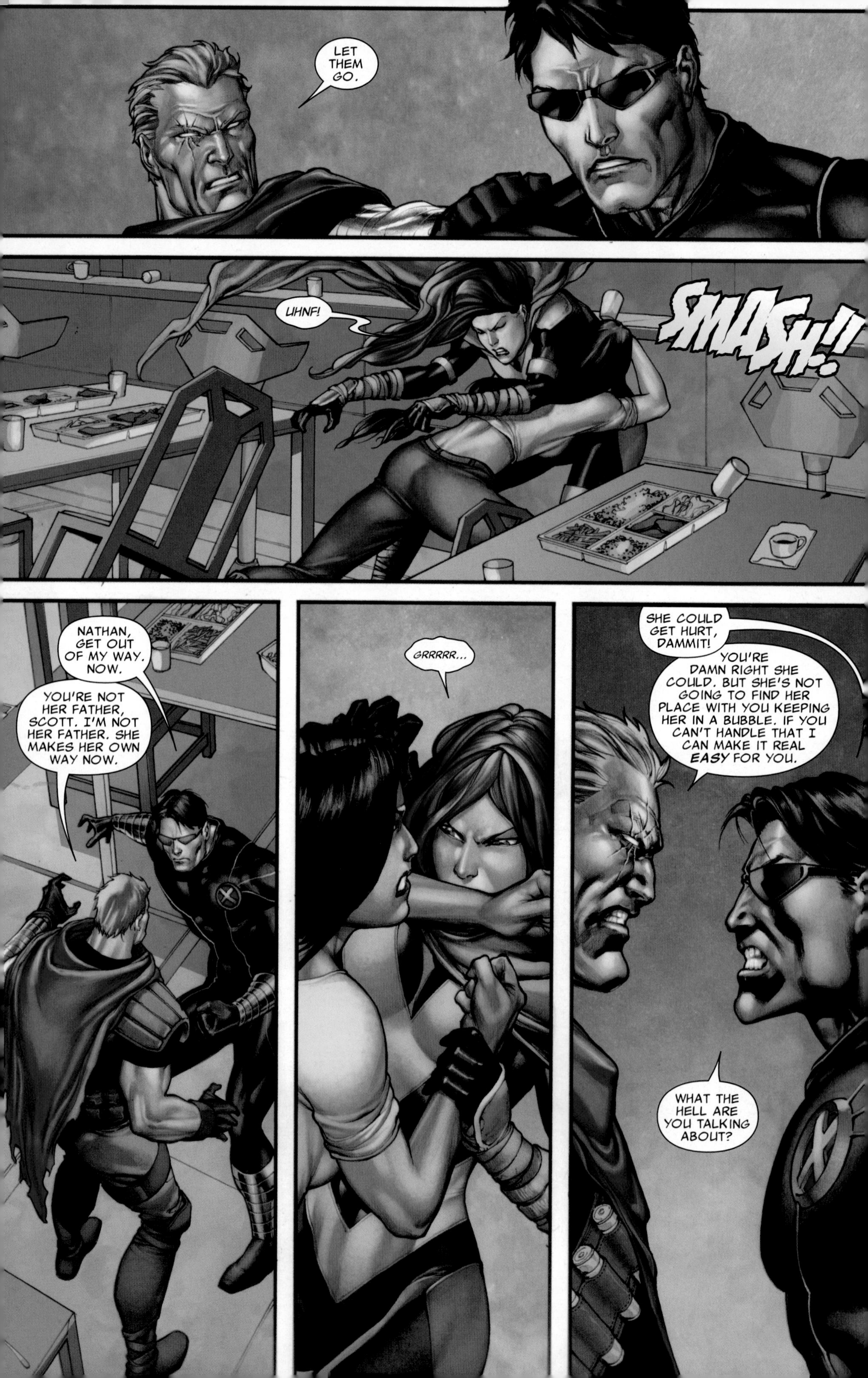
LET THEM GO.
UHNF!
SMASH!!
NATHAN, GET OUT OF MY WAY. NOW.
YOU'RE NOT HER FATHER, SCOTT. I'M NOT HER FATHER. SHE MAKES HER OWN WAY NOW.
GRRRRR...
SHE COULD GET HURT, DAMMIT!
YOU'RE DAMN RIGHT SHE COULD. BUT SHE'S NOT GOING TO FIND HER PLACE WITH YOU KEEPING HER IN A BUBBLE. IF YOU CAN'T HANDLE THAT I CAN MAKE IT REAL EASY FOR YOU.
WHAT THE HELL ARE YOU TALKING ABOUT?

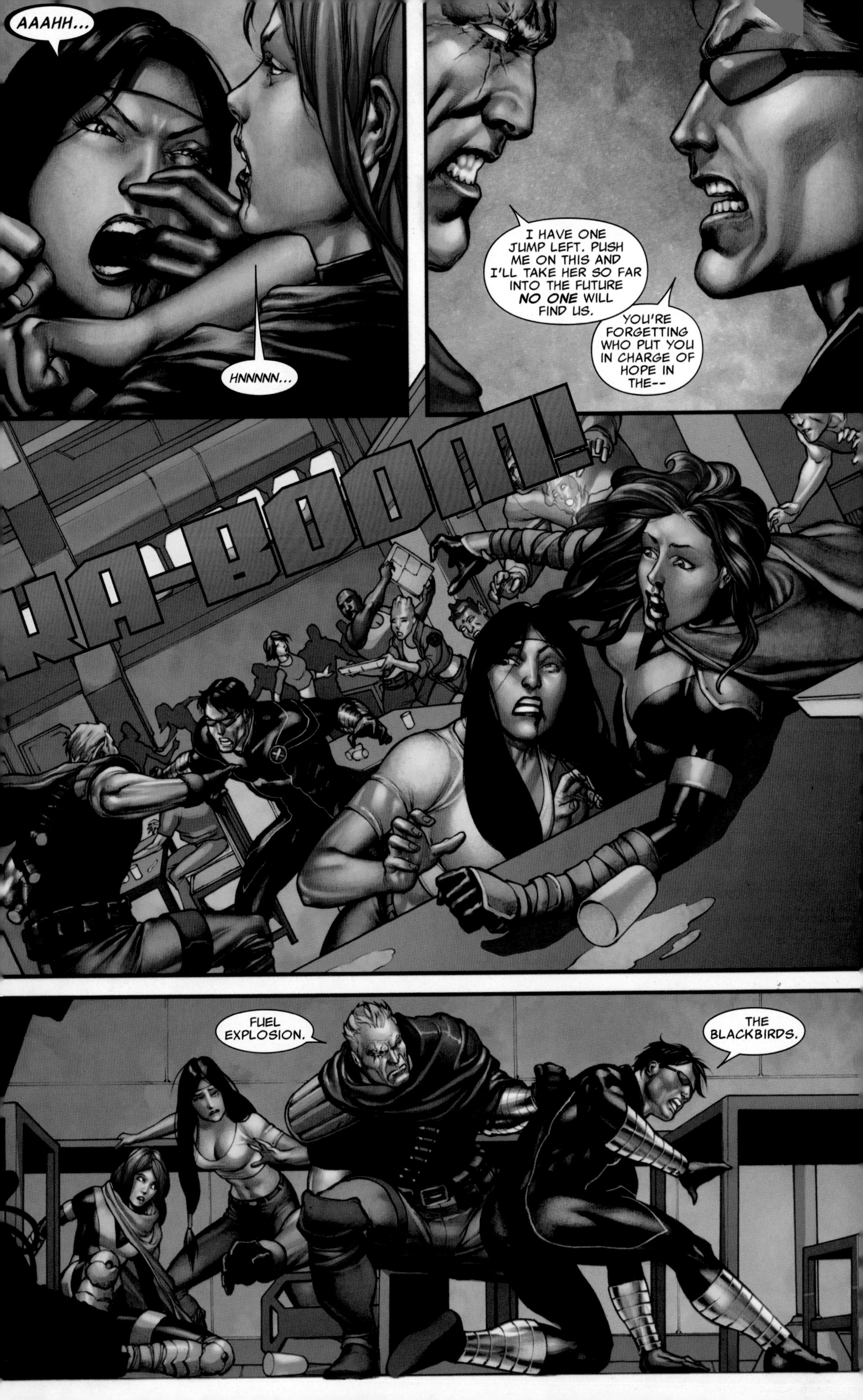
AAAHH...
HNNNNN...
I HAVE ONE JUMP LEFT. PUSH ME ON THIS AND I'LL TAKE HER SO FAR INTO THE FUTURE NO ONE WILL FIND US.
YOU'RE FORGETTING WHO PUT YOU IN CHARGE OF HOPE IN THE--
KA-BOOM!
FUEL EXPLOSION.
THE BLACKBIRDS.

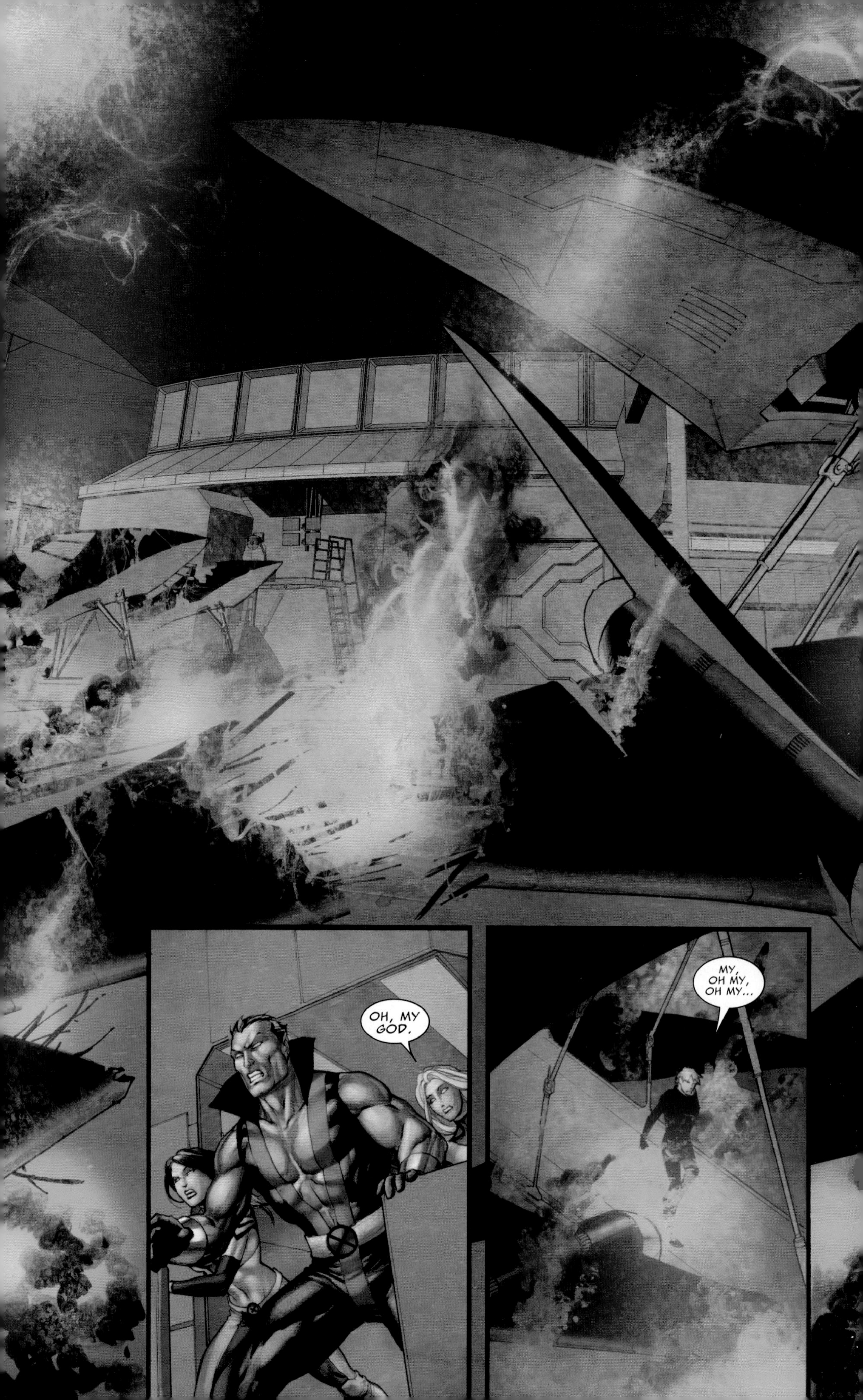
OH, MY GOD.
MY, OH MY, OH MY...

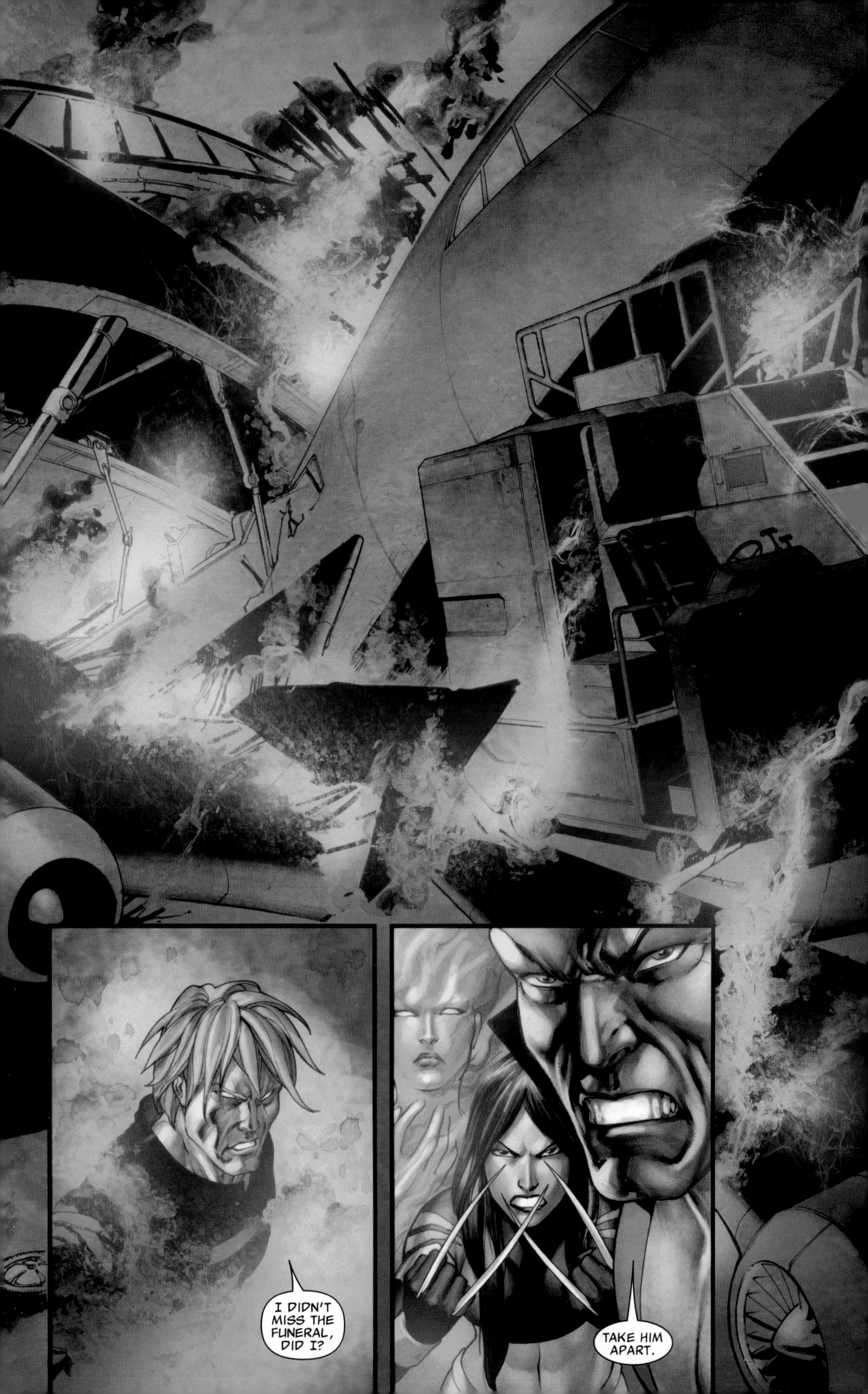
I DIDN'T MISS THE FUNERAL, DID I?
TAKE HIM APART.

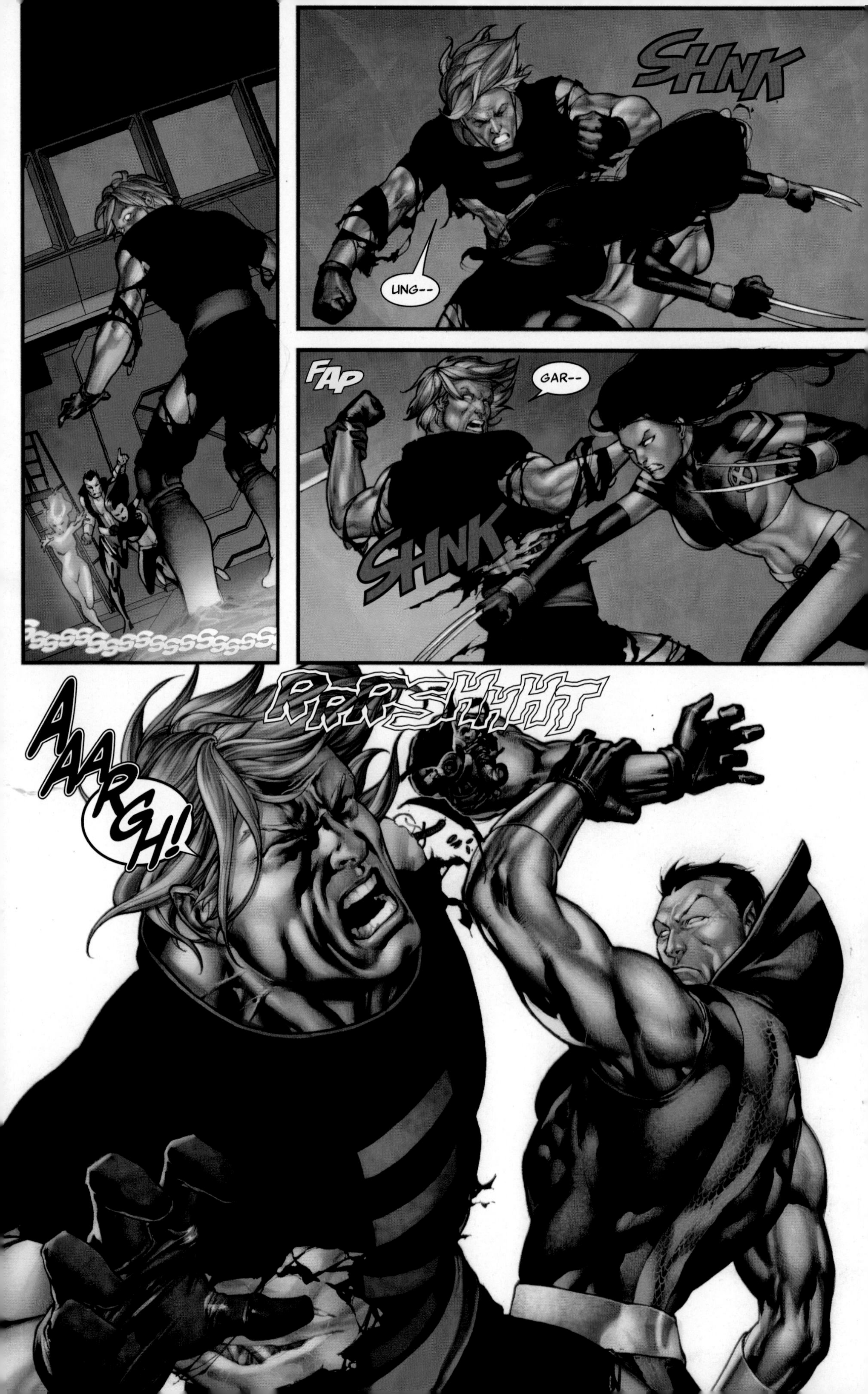
SSSSSSSSSSSSSS
SHNK
UNG--
FAP
GAR--
SHNK
RRRSHHHT
AAARGH!

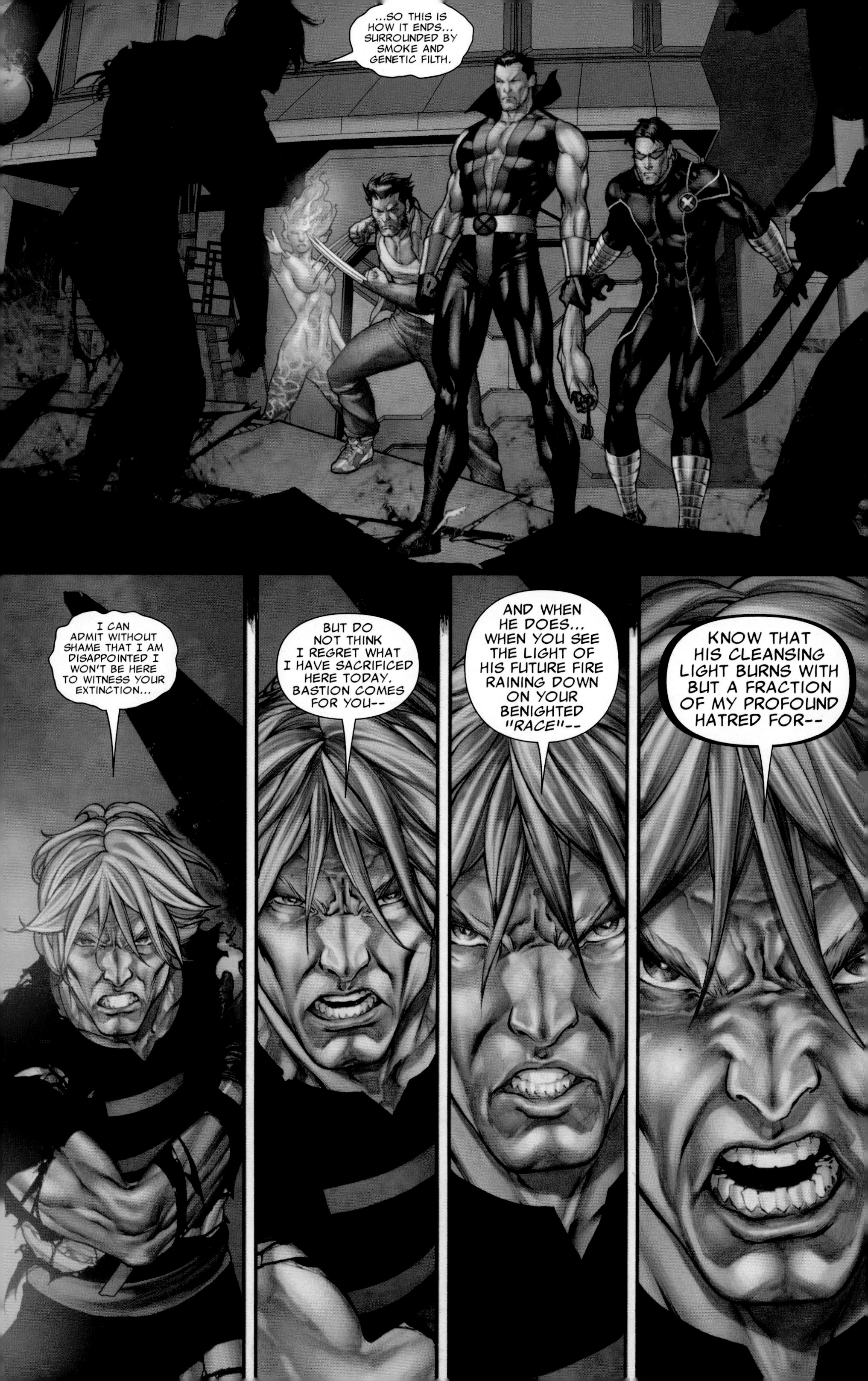
...SO THIS IS HOW IT ENDS... SURROUNDED BY SMOKE AND GENETIC FILTH.
I CAN ADMIT WITHOUT SHAME THAT I AM DISAPPOINTED I WON'T BE HERE TO WITNESS YOUR EXTINCTION...
BUT DO NOT THINK I REGRET WHAT I HAVE SACRIFICED HERE TODAY. BASTION COMES FOR YOU--
AND WHEN HE DOES... WHEN YOU SEE THE LIGHT OF HIS FUTURE FIRE RAINING DOWN ON YOUR BENIGHTED "RACE"--
KNOW THAT HIS CLEANSING LIGHT BURNS WITH BUT A FRACTION OF MY PROFOUND HATRED FOR--

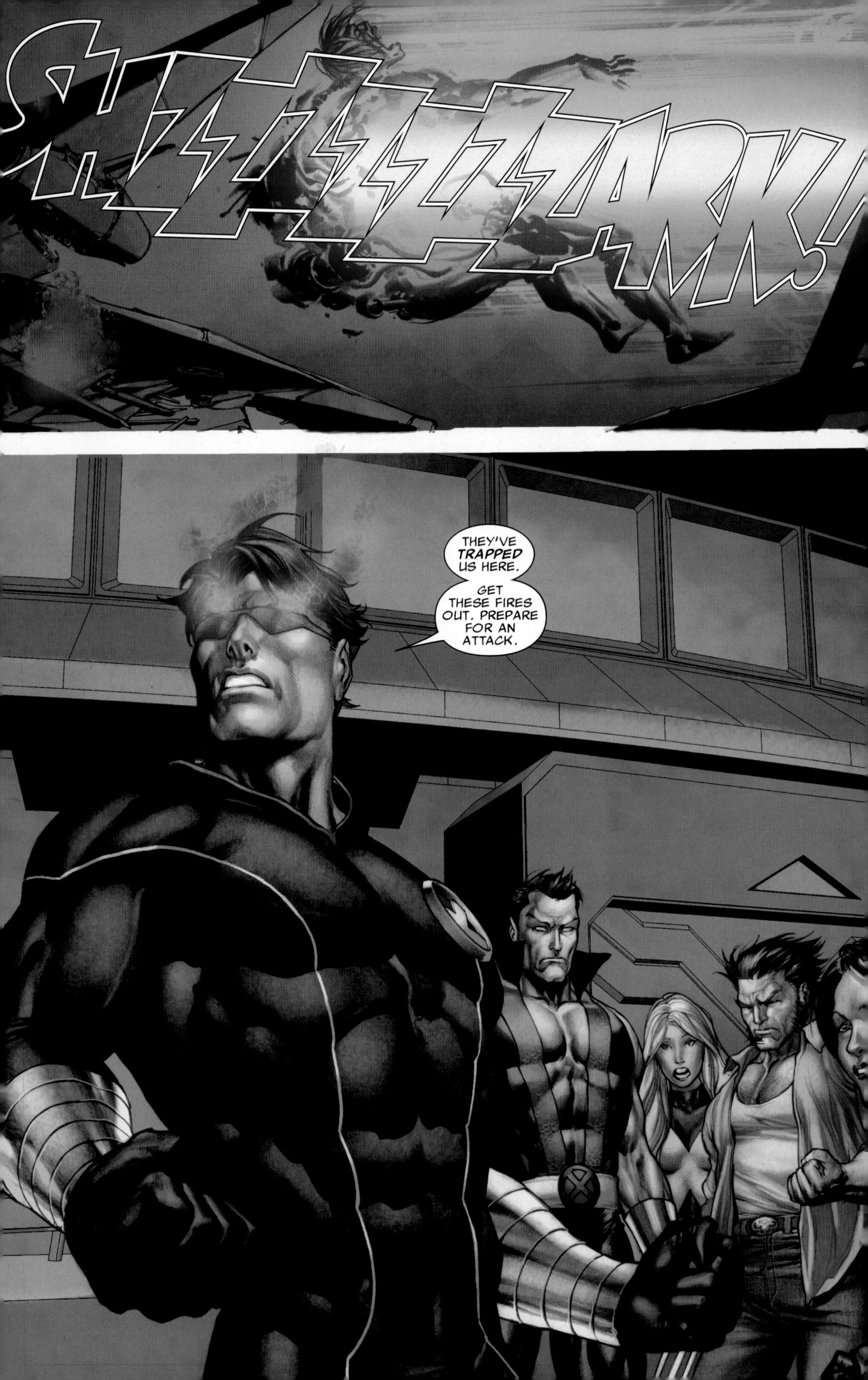
SHZZZZZARK!
THEY'VE TRAPPED US HERE.
GET THESE FIRES OUT. PREPARE FOR AN ATTACK.

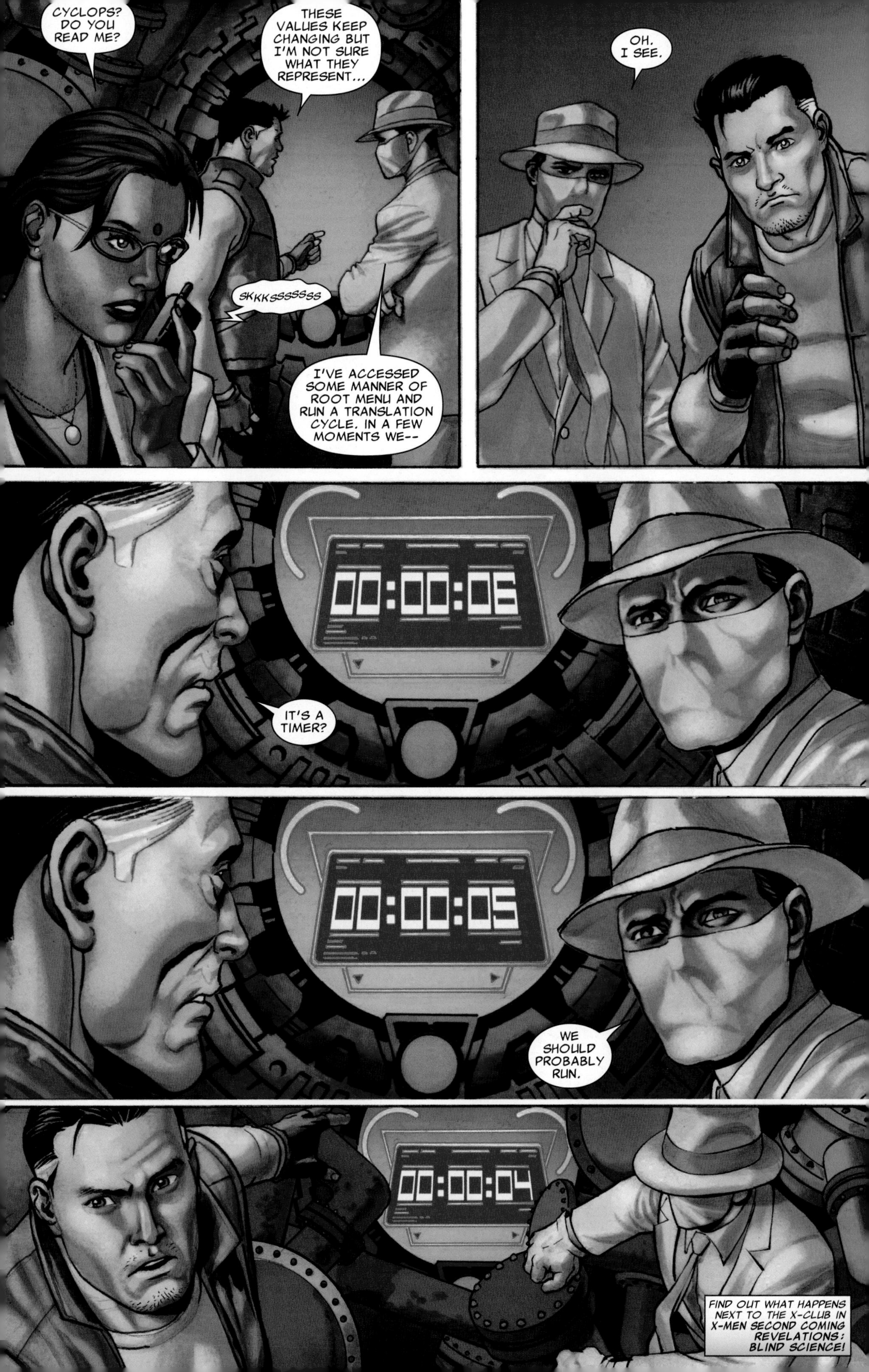
CYCLOPS? DO YOU READ ME?
THESE VALUES KEEP CHANGING BUT I'M NOT SURE WHAT THEY REPRESENT...
SKKKSSSSSSS
I'VE ACCESSED SOME MANNER OF ROOT MENU AND RUN A TRANSLATION CYCLE. IN A FEW MOMENTS WE--
OH. I SEE.
00:00:06
IT'S A TIMER?
00:00:05
WE SHOULD PROBABLY RUN.
00:00:04
FIND OUT WHAT HAPPENS NEXT TO THE X-CLUB IN X-MEN SECOND COMING REVELATIONS: BLIND SCIENCE!

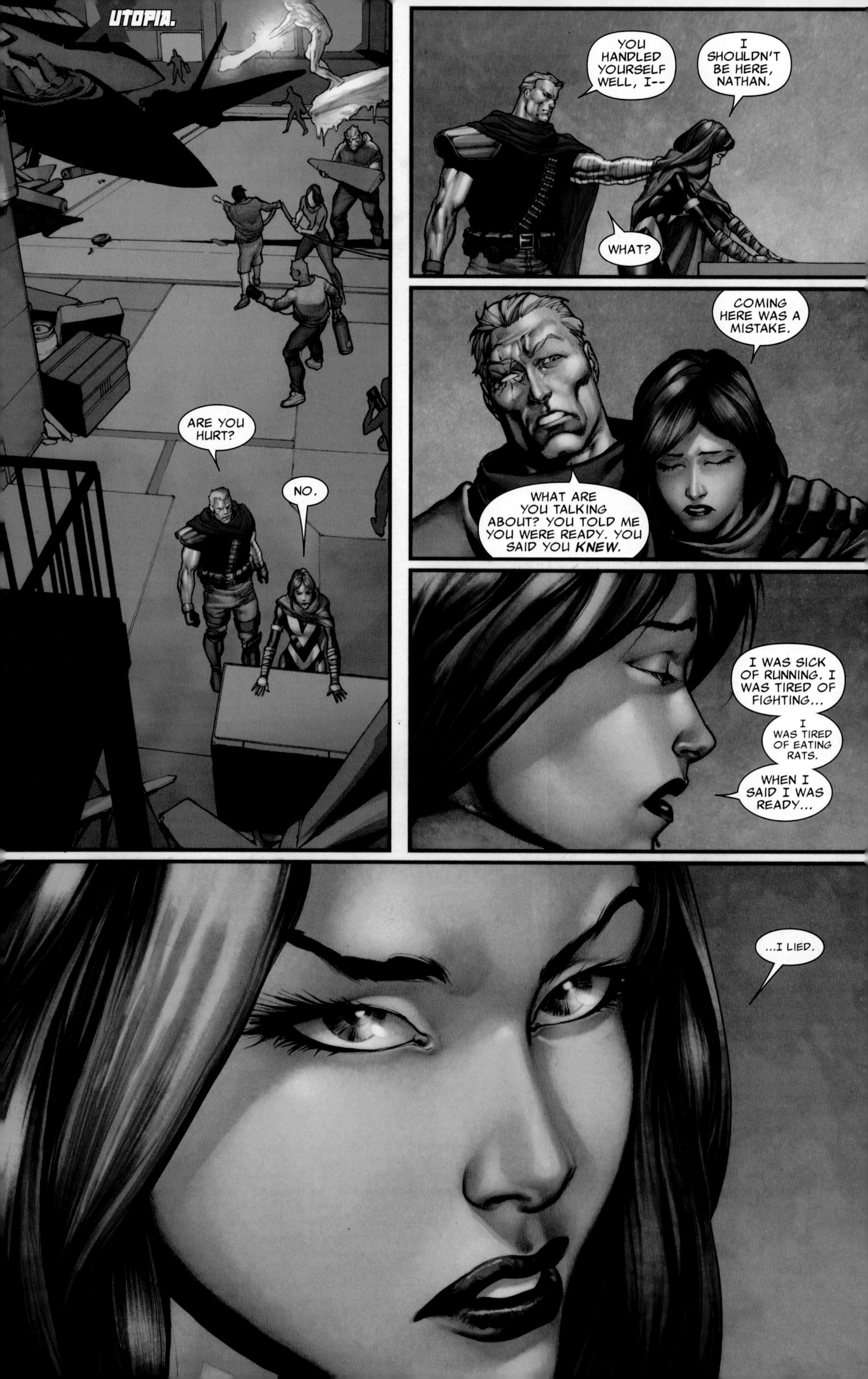
UTOPIA.
ARE YOU HURT?
NO.
YOU HANDLED YOURSELF WELL, I--
I SHOULDN'T BE HERE, NATHAN.
WHAT?
COMING HERE WAS A MISTAKE.
WHAT ARE YOU TALKING ABOUT? YOU TOLD ME YOU WERE READY. YOU SAID YOU KNEW.
I WAS SICK OF RUNNING. I WAS TIRED OF FIGHTING...
I WAS TIRED OF EATING RATS.
WHEN I SAID I WAS READY...
...I LIED.

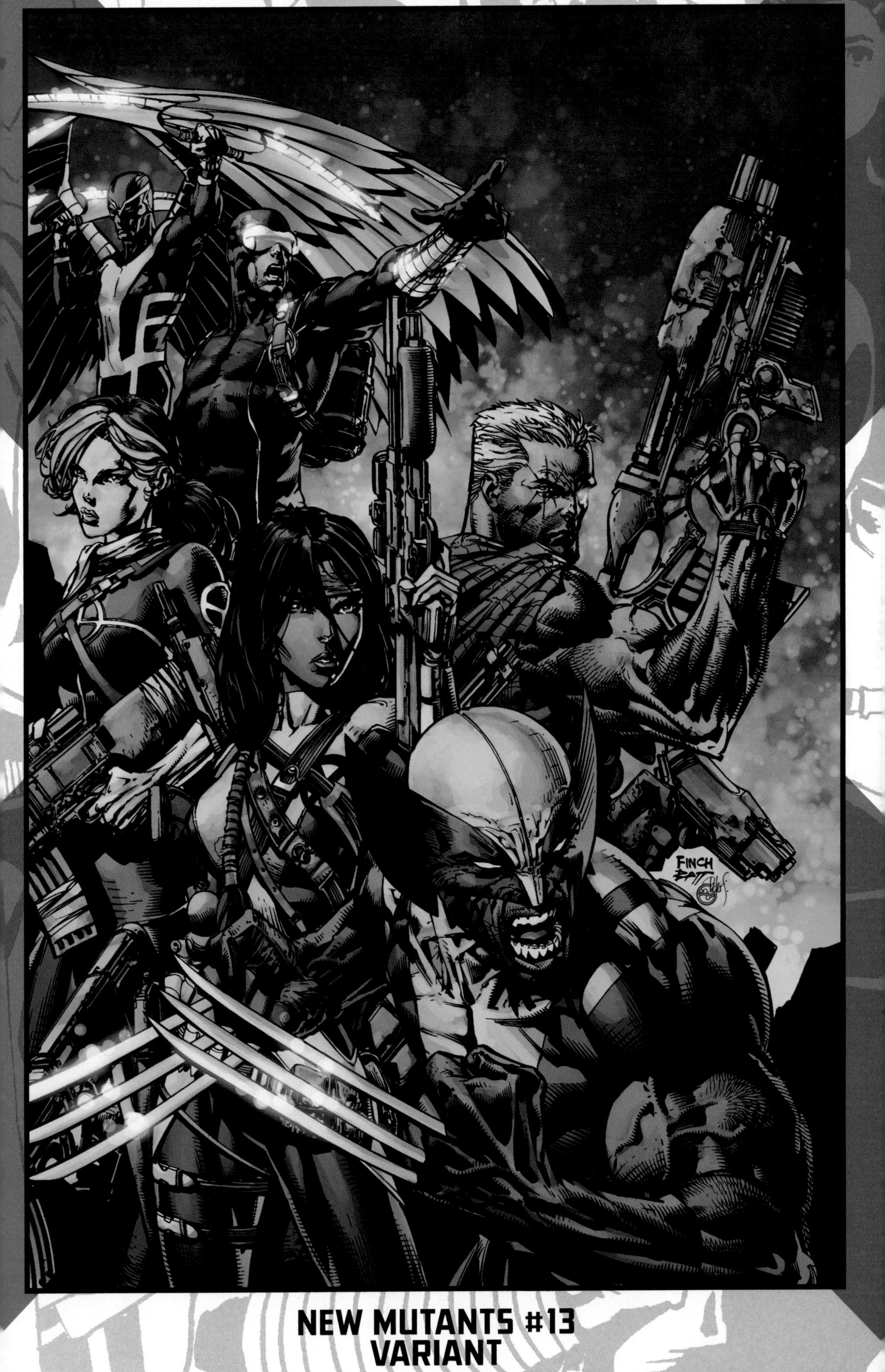
FINCH
BATT

NEW MUTANTS #13
VARIANT

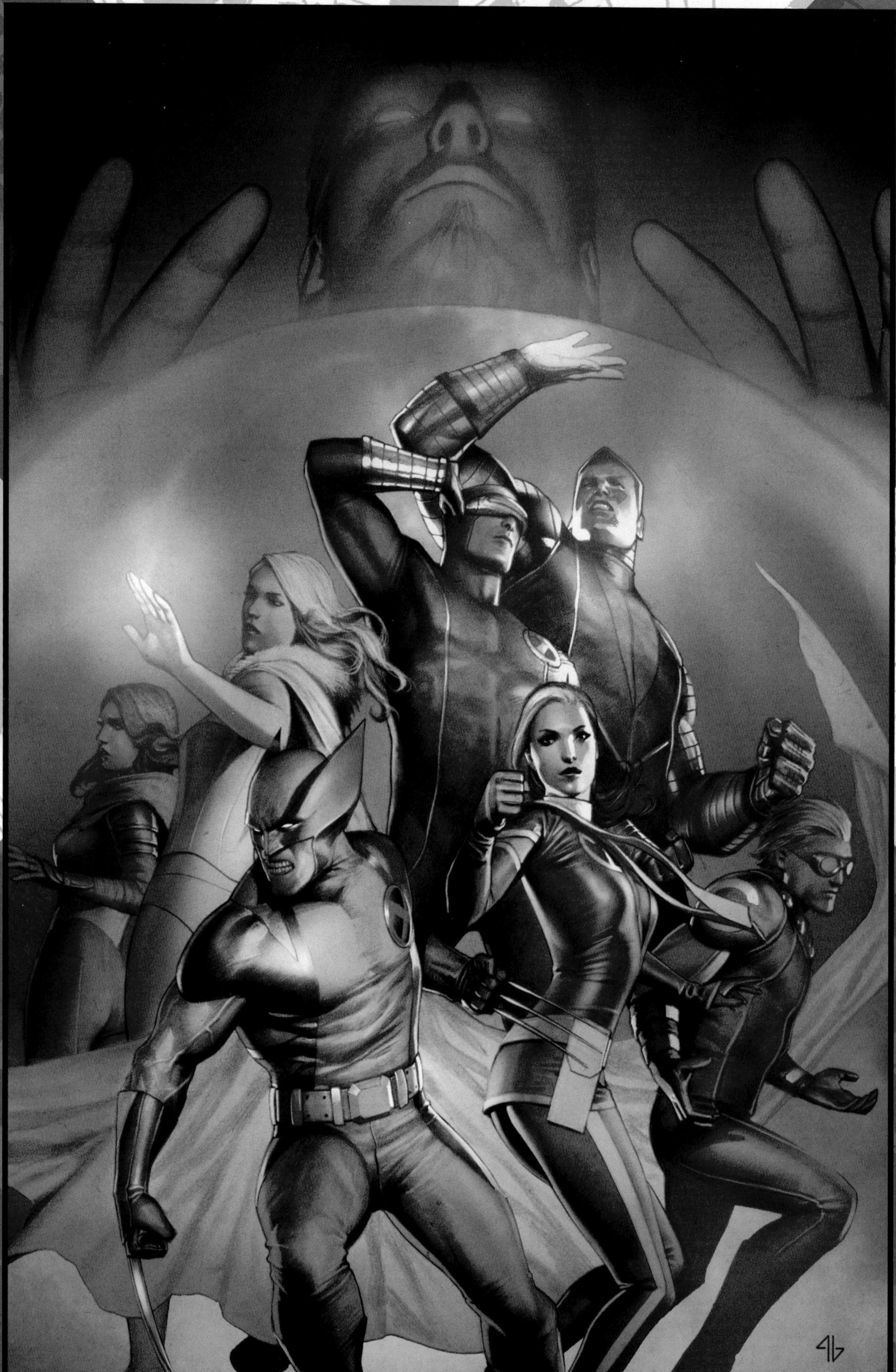

X-MEN LEGACY #236

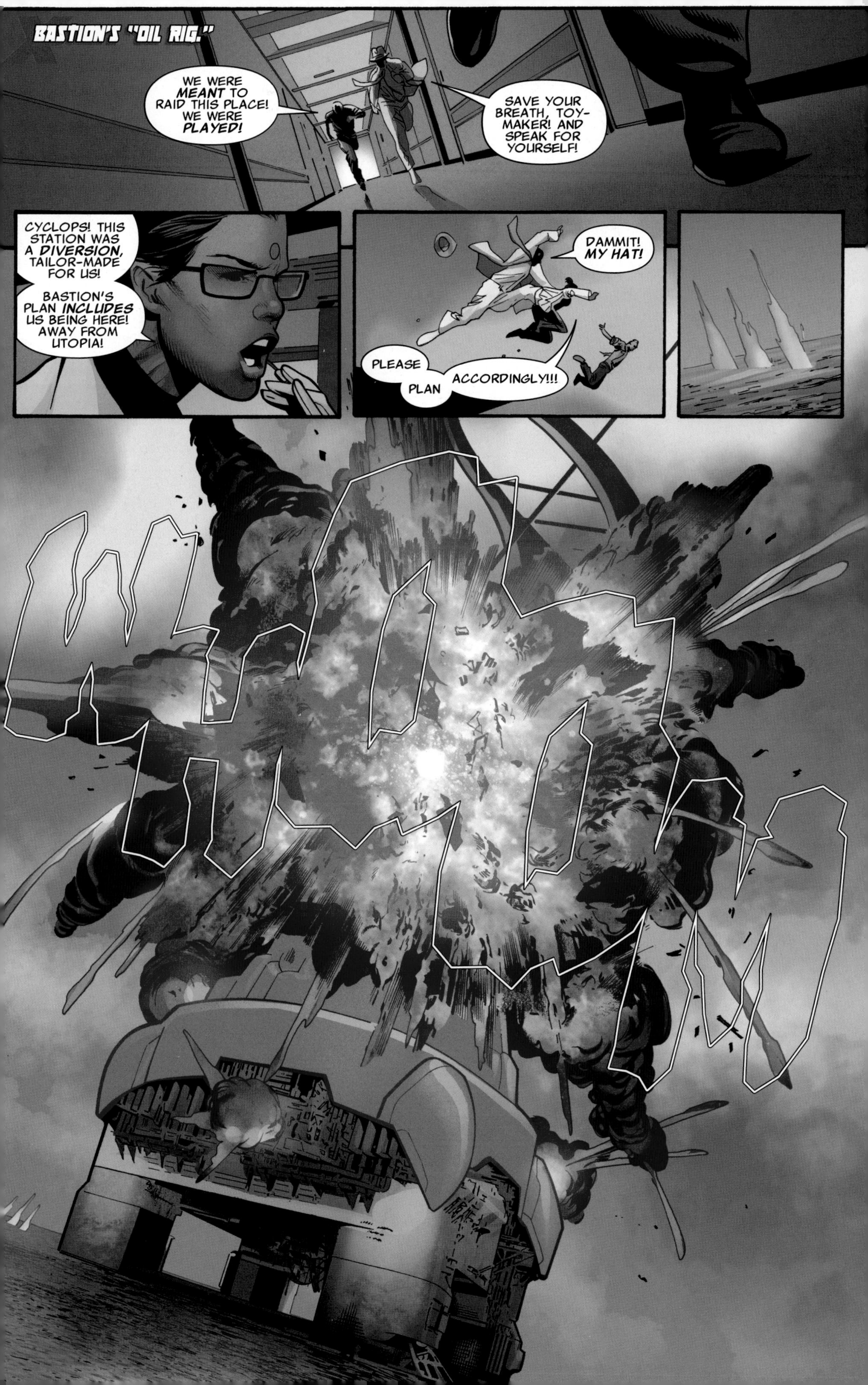
BASTION'S "OIL RIG."
WE WERE MEANT TO RAID THIS PLACE! WE WERE PLAYED!
SAVE YOUR BREATH, TOY-MAKER! AND SPEAK FOR YOURSELF!
CYCLOPS! THIS STATION WAS A DIVERSION, TAILOR-MADE FOR US!
BASTION'S PLAN INCLUDES US BEING HERE! AWAY FROM UTOPIA!
DAMMIT! MY HAT!
PLEASE PLAN ACCORDINGLY!!!
WHOOM

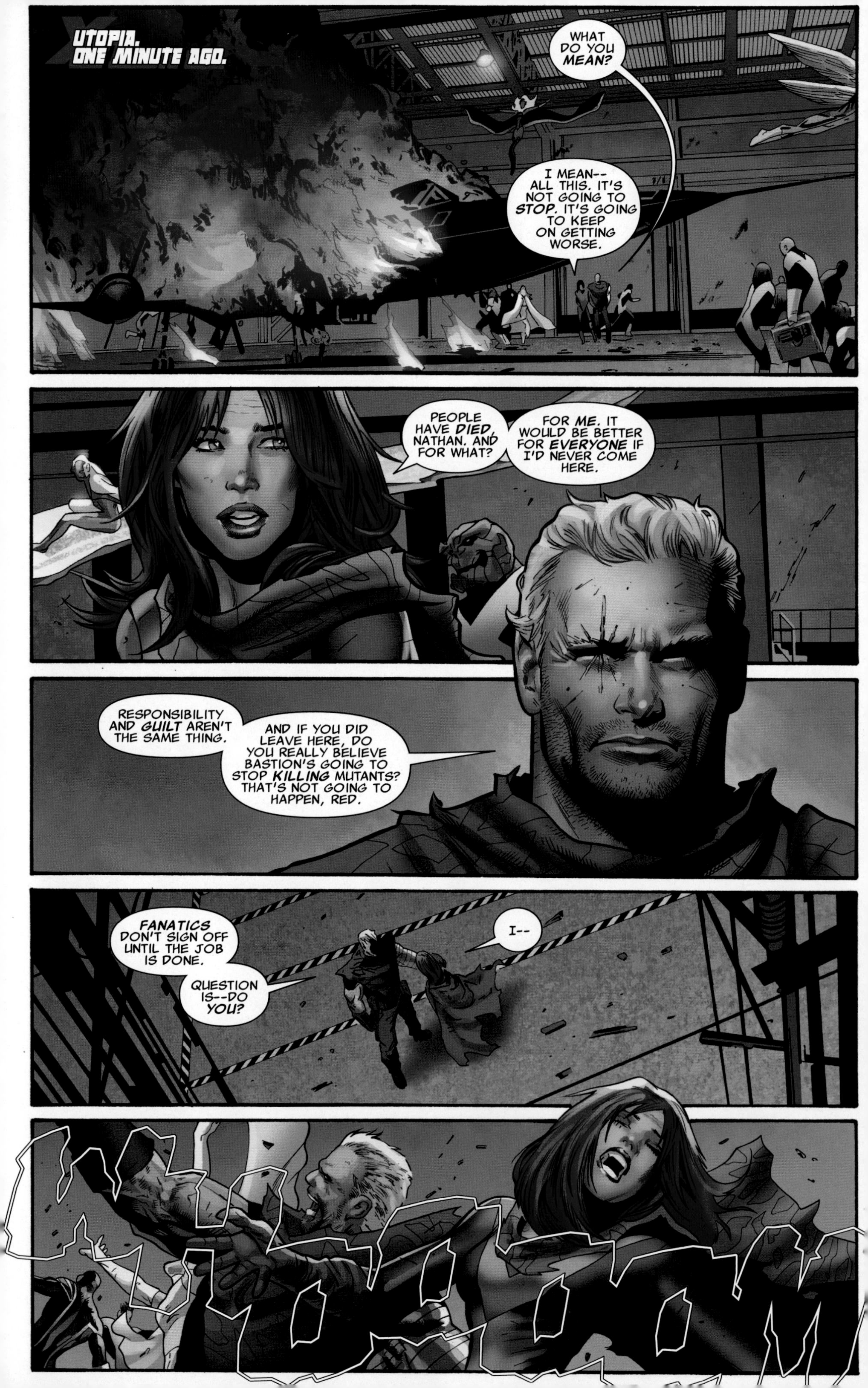

UTOPIA. ONE MINUTE AGO.
WHAT DO YOU MEAN?
I MEAN-- ALL THIS. IT'S NOT GOING TO STOP. IT'S GOING TO KEEP ON GETTING WORSE.
PEOPLE HAVE DIED, NATHAN. AND FOR WHAT?
FOR ME. IT WOULD BE BETTER FOR EVERYONE IF I'D NEVER COME HERE.
RESPONSIBILITY AND GUILT AREN'T THE SAME THING.
AND IF YOU DID LEAVE HERE, DO YOU REALLY BELIEVE BASTION'S GOING TO STOP KILLING MUTANTS? THAT'S NOT GOING TO HAPPEN, RED.
FANATICS DON'T SIGN OFF UNTIL THE JOB IS DONE.
QUESTION IS--DO YOU?
I--

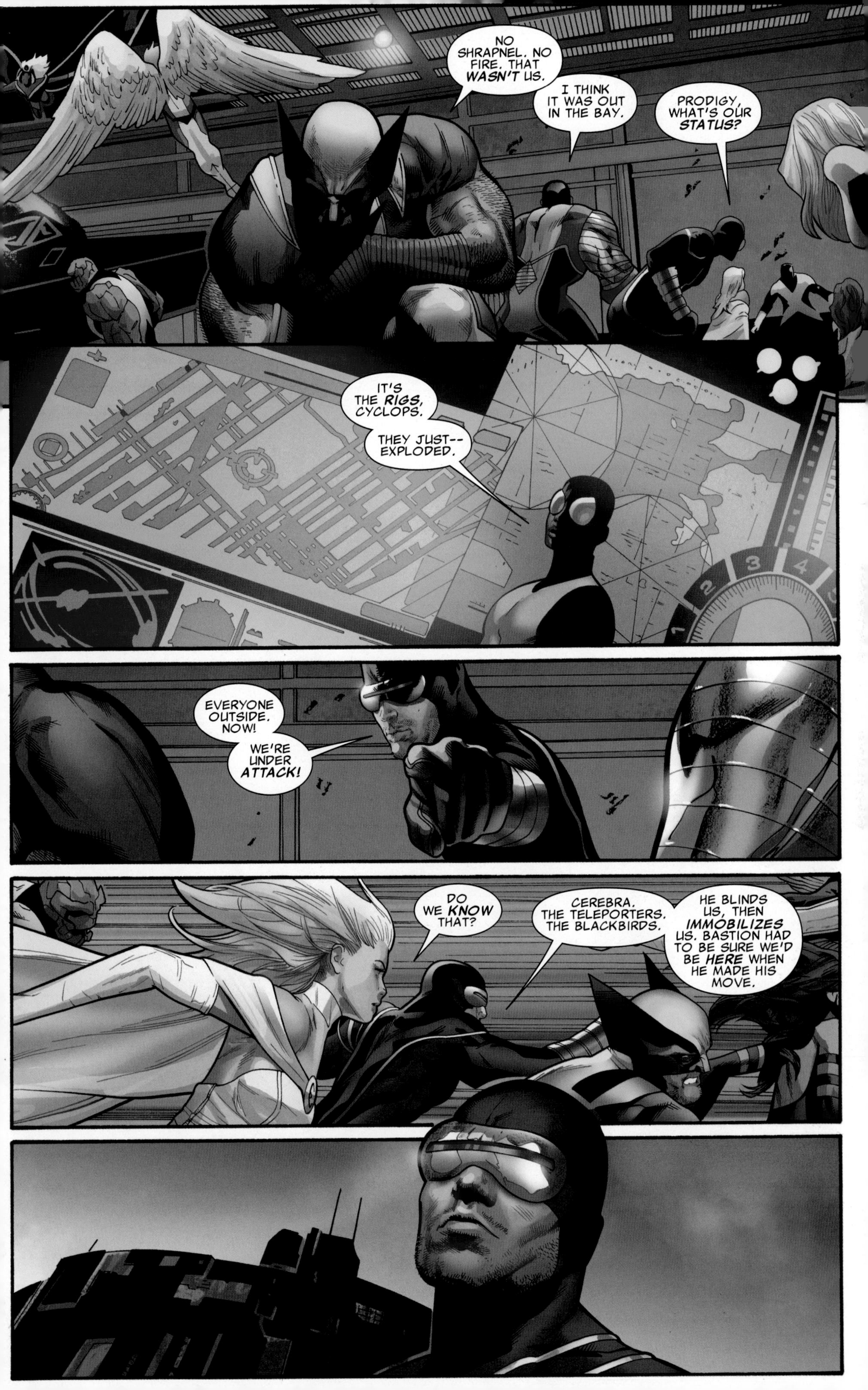

NO SHRAPNEL. NO FIRE. THAT WASN'T US.
I THINK IT WAS OUT IN THE BAY.
PRODIGY, WHAT'S OUR STATUS?
IT'S THE RIGS, CYCLOPS.
THEY JUST-- EXPLODED.
EVERYONE OUTSIDE. NOW!
WE'RE UNDER ATTACK!
DO WE KNOW THAT?
CEREBRA. THE TELEPORTERS. THE BLACKBIRDS.
HE BLINDS US, THEN IMMOBILIZES US. BASTION HAD TO BE SURE WE'D BE HERE WHEN HE MADE HIS MOVE.

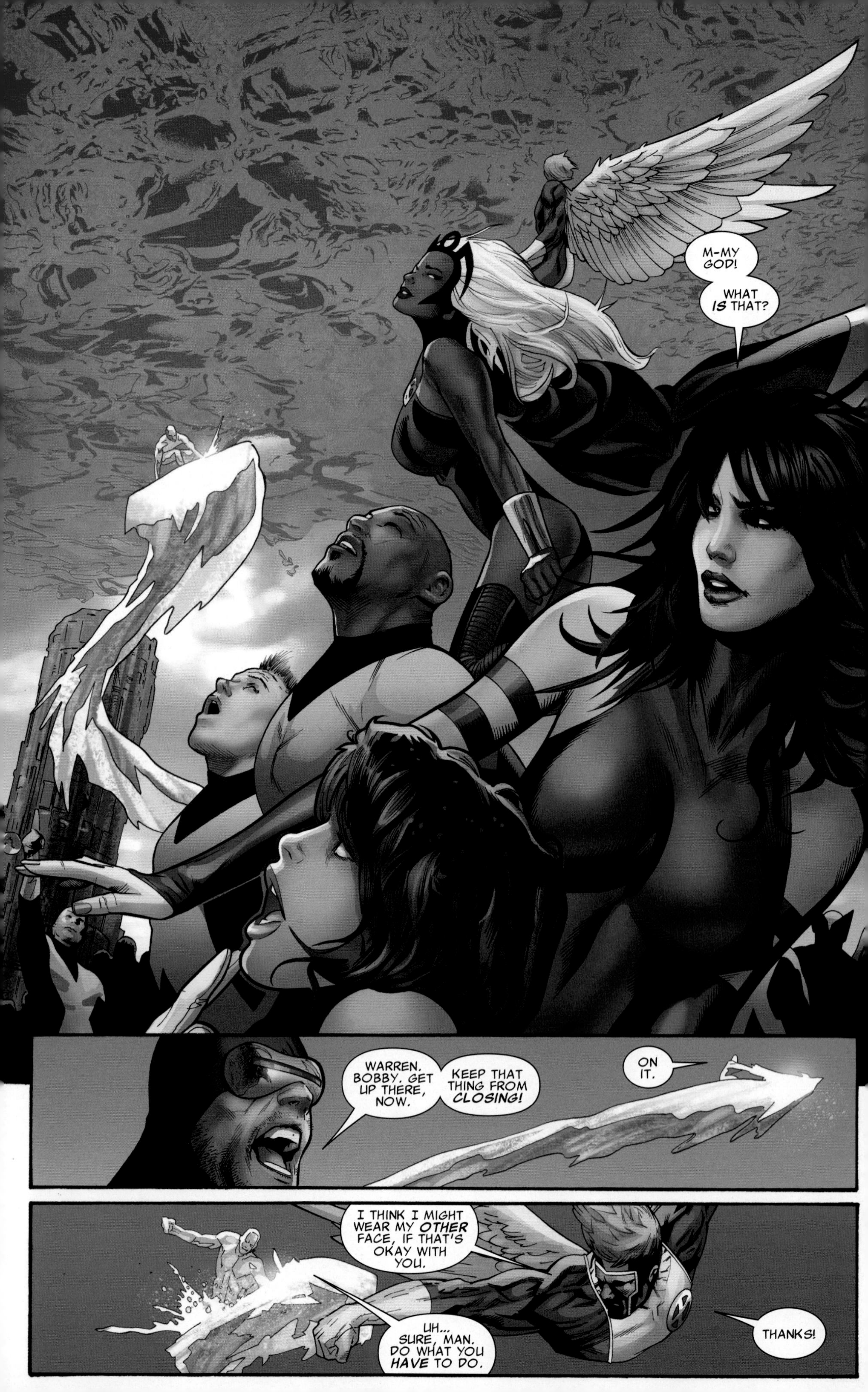
M-MY GOD!
WHAT IS THAT?
WARREN. BOBBY. GET UP THERE, NOW.
KEEP THAT THING FROM CLOSING!
ON IT.
I THINK I MIGHT WEAR MY OTHER FACE, IF THAT'S OKAY WITH YOU.
UH... SURE, MAN. DO WHAT YOU HAVE TO DO.
THANKS!

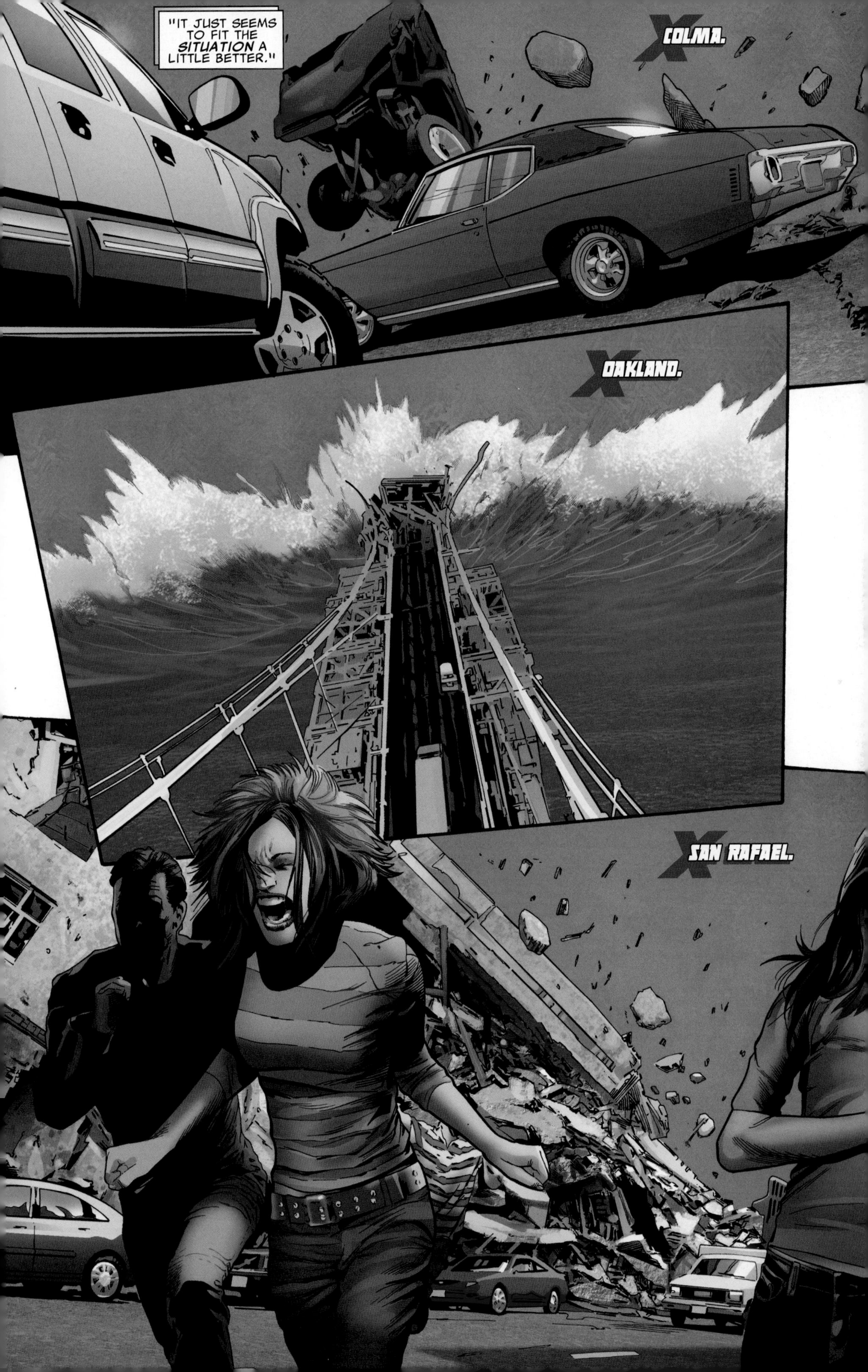
"IT JUST SEEMS TO FIT THE SITUATION A LITTLE BETTER."
COLMA.
OAKLAND.
SAN RAFAEL.

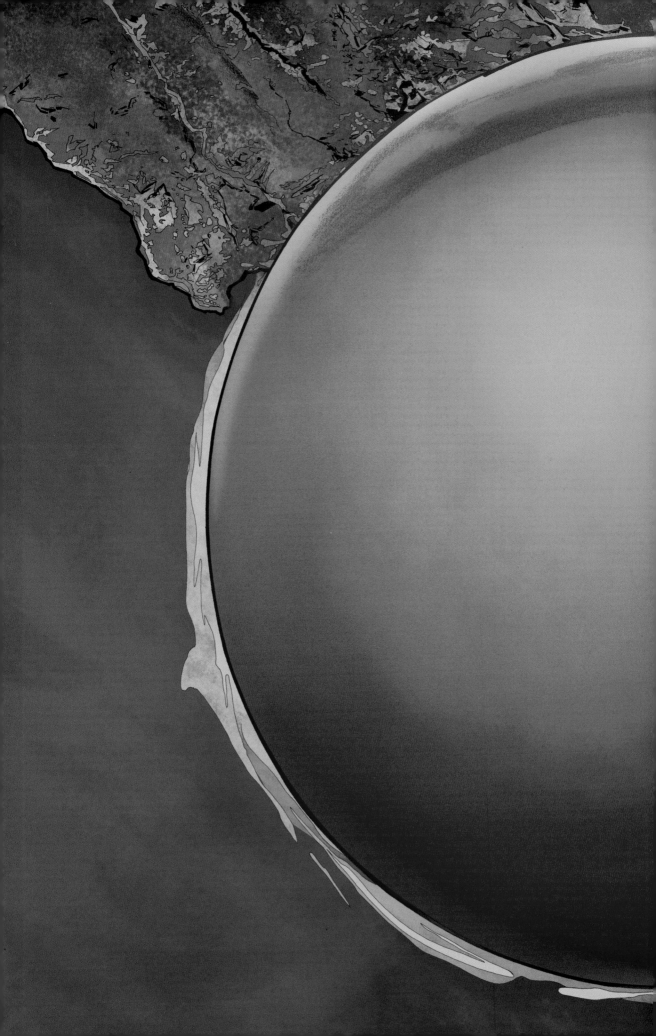

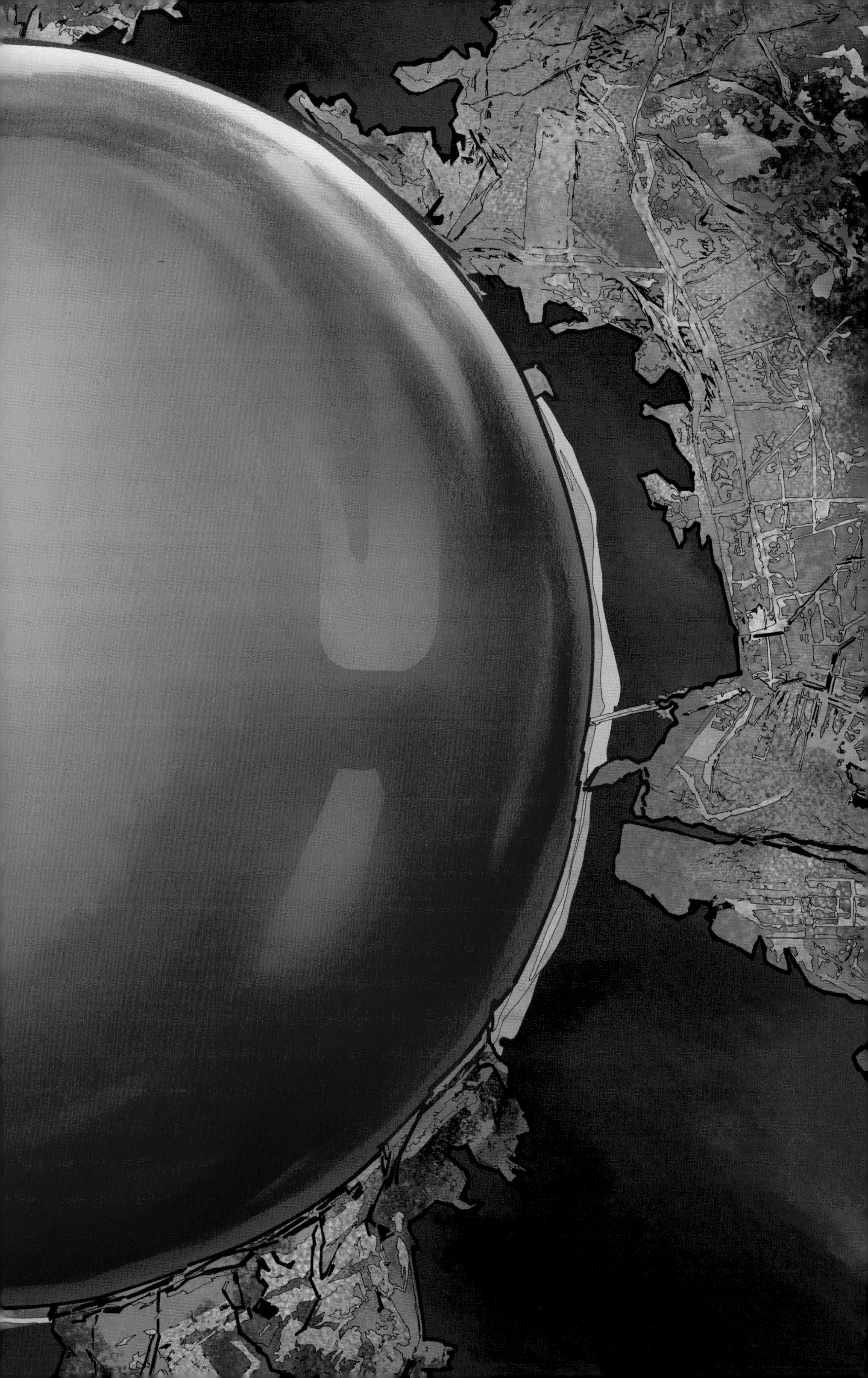

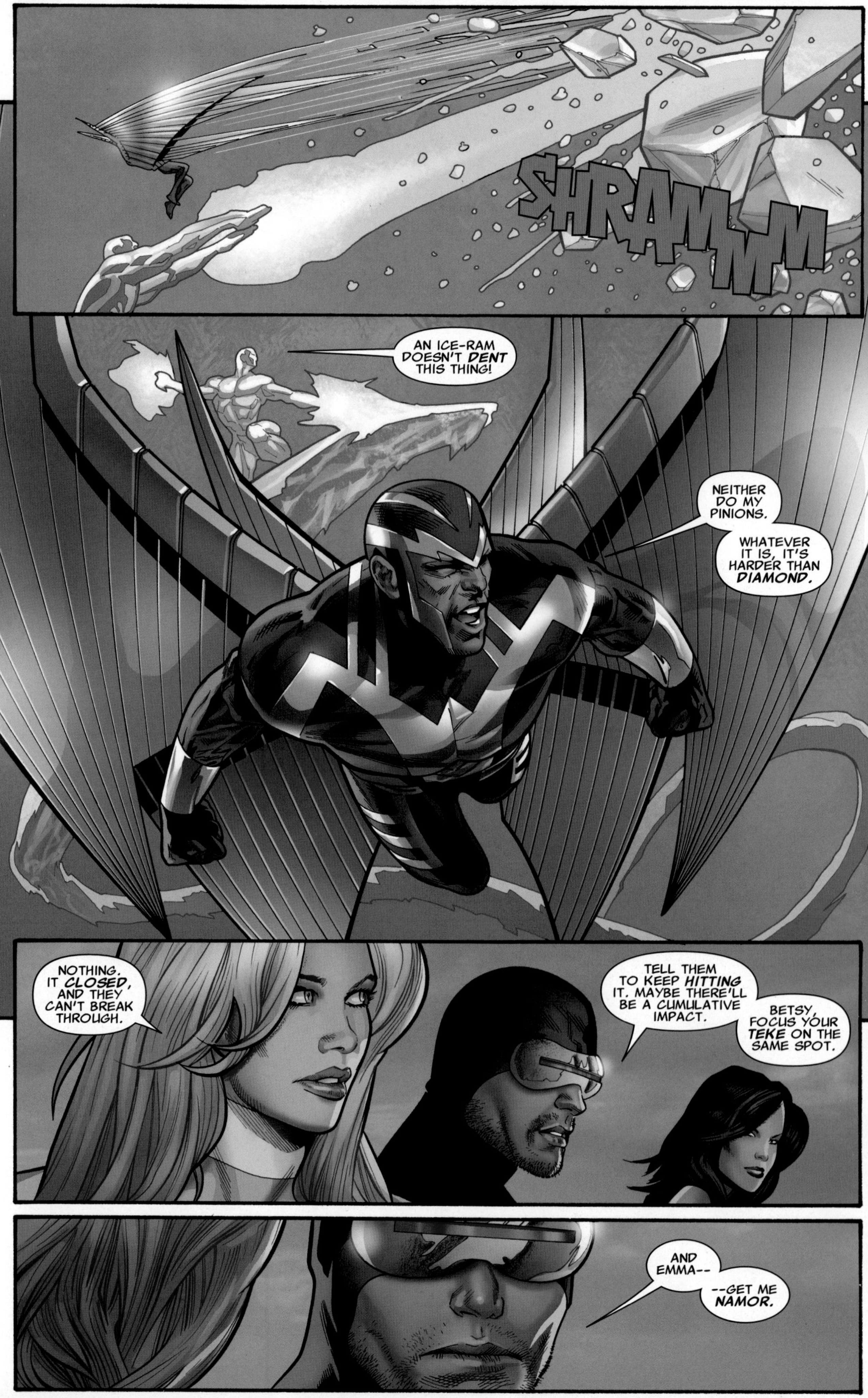
SHRAMMMM
AN ICE-RAM DOESN'T DENT THIS THING!
NEITHER DO MY PINIONS.
WHATEVER IT IS, IT'S HARDER THAN DIAMOND.
NOTHING. IT CLOSED, AND THEY CAN'T BREAK THROUGH.
TELL THEM TO KEEP HITTING IT. MAYBE THERE'LL BE A CUMULATIVE IMPACT.
BETSY, FOCUS YOUR TEKE ON THE SAME SPOT.
AND EMMA--
--GET ME NAMOR.

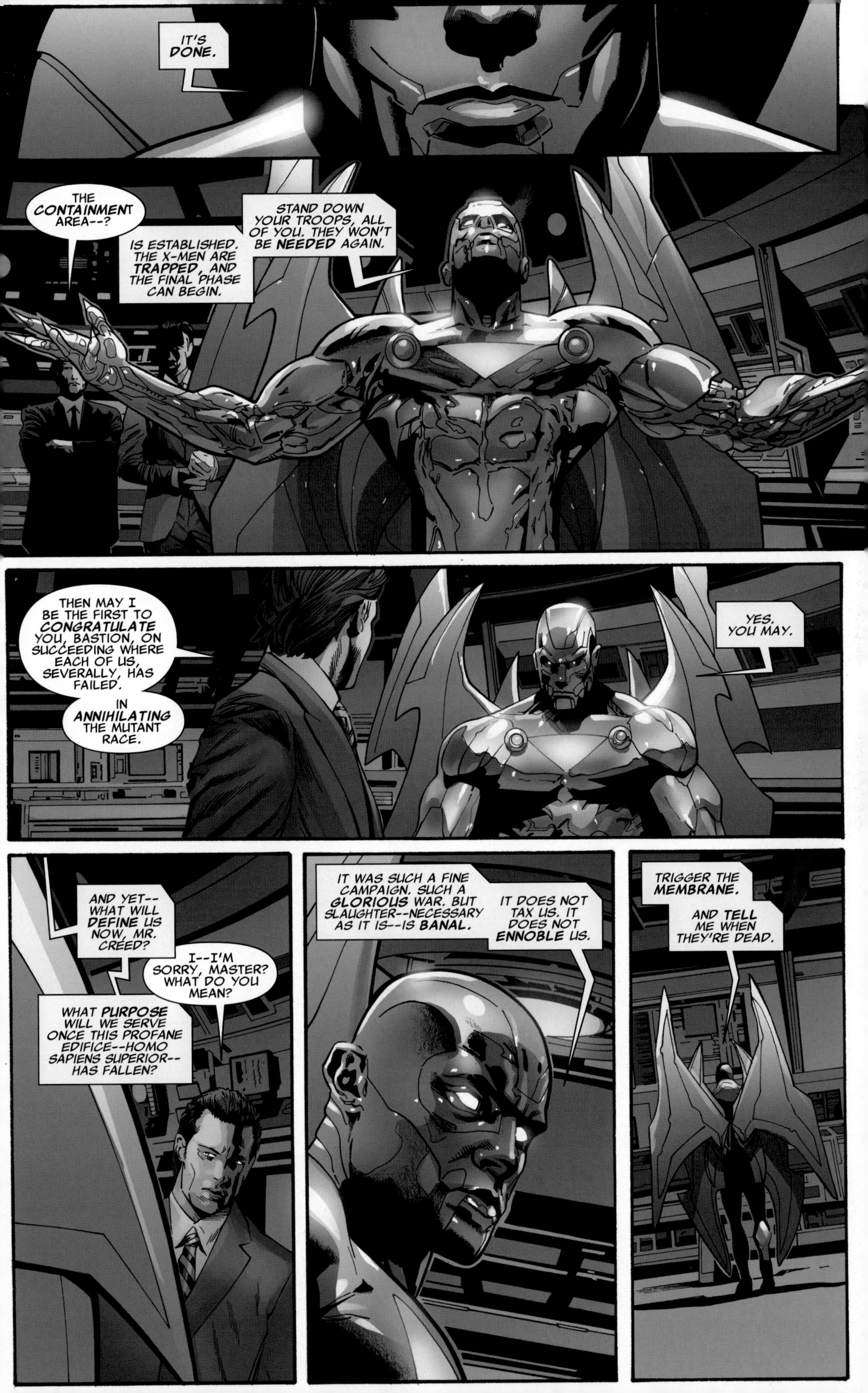
IT'S DONE.
THE CONTAINMENT AREA--?
IS ESTABLISHED. THE X-MEN ARE TRAPPED, AND THE FINAL PHASE CAN BEGIN.
STAND DOWN YOUR TROOPS, ALL OF YOU. THEY WON'T BE NEEDED AGAIN.
THEN MAY I BE THE FIRST TO CONGRATULATE YOU, BASTION, ON SUCCEEDING WHERE EACH OF US, SEVERALLY, HAS FAILED.
IN ANNIHILATING THE MUTANT RACE.
YES. YOU MAY.
AND YET-- WHAT WILL DEFINE US NOW, MR. CREED?
I--I'M SORRY, MASTER? WHAT DO YOU MEAN?
WHAT PURPOSE WILL WE SERVE ONCE THIS PROFANE EDIFICE--HOMO SAPIENS SUPERIOR--HAS FALLEN?
IT WAS SUCH A FINE CAMPAIGN. SUCH A GLORIOUS WAR. BUT SLAUGHTER--NECESSARY AS IT IS--IS BANAL.
IT DOES NOT TAX US. IT DOES NOT ENNOBLE US.
TRIGGER THE MEMBRANE.
AND TELL ME WHEN THEY'RE DEAD.

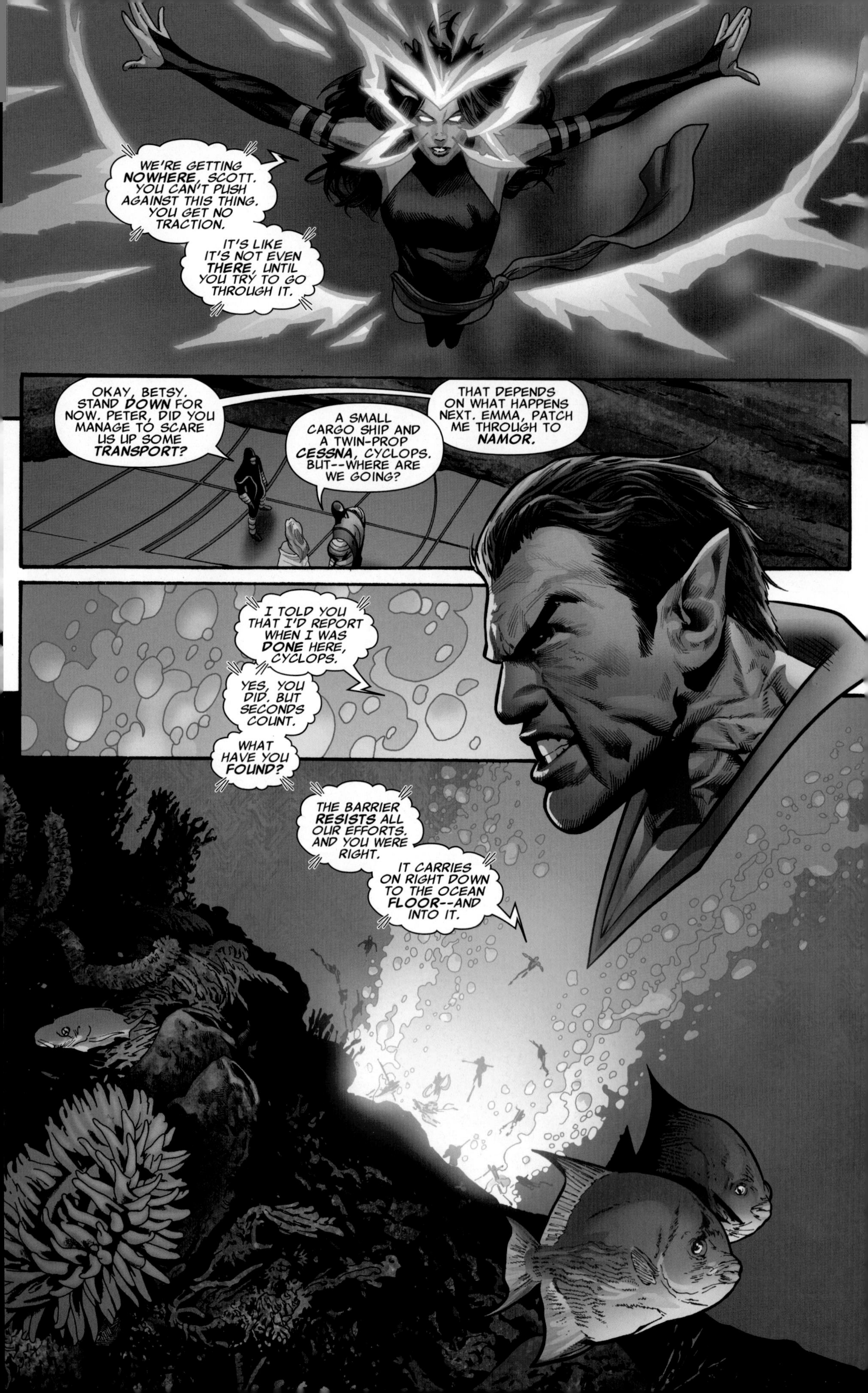
WE'RE GETTING NOWHERE, SCOTT. YOU CAN'T PUSH AGAINST THIS THING. YOU GET NO TRACTION.
IT'S LIKE IT'S NOT EVEN THERE, UNTIL YOU TRY TO GO THROUGH IT.
OKAY, BETSY. STAND DOWN FOR NOW. PETER, DID YOU MANAGE TO SCARE US UP SOME TRANSPORT?
A SMALL CARGO SHIP AND A TWIN-PROP CESSNA, CYCLOPS. BUT--WHERE ARE WE GOING?
THAT DEPENDS ON WHAT HAPPENS NEXT. EMMA, PATCH ME THROUGH TO NAMOR.
I TOLD YOU THAT I'D REPORT WHEN I WAS DONE HERE, CYCLOPS.
YES, YOU DID. BUT SECONDS COUNT.
WHAT HAVE YOU FOUND?
THE BARRIER RESISTS ALL OUR EFFORTS. AND YOU WERE RIGHT.
IT CARRIES ON RIGHT DOWN TO THE OCEAN FLOOR--AND INTO IT.

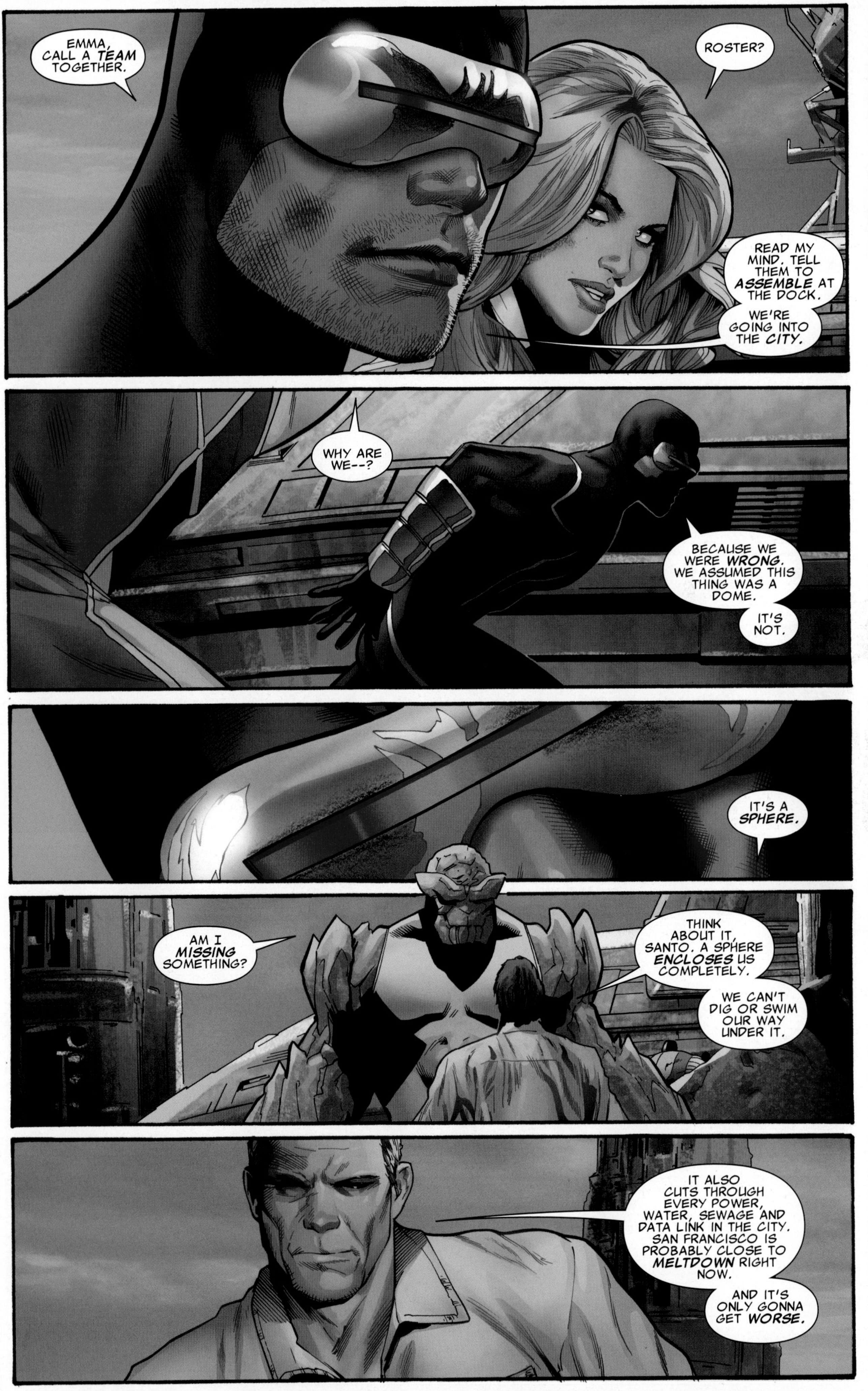
EMMA, CALL A TEAM TOGETHER.
ROSTER?
READ MY MIND. TELL THEM TO ASSEMBLE AT THE DOCK.
WE'RE GOING INTO THE CITY.
WHY ARE WE--?
BECAUSE WE WERE WRONG. WE ASSUMED THIS THING WAS A DOME.
IT'S NOT.
IT'S A SPHERE.
AM I MISSING SOMETHING?
THINK ABOUT IT, SANTO. A SPHERE ENCLOSES US COMPLETELY.
WE CAN'T DIG OR SWIM OUR WAY UNDER IT.
IT ALSO CUTS THROUGH EVERY POWER, WATER, SEWAGE AND DATA LINK IN THE CITY. SAN FRANCISCO IS PROBABLY CLOSE TO MELTDOWN RIGHT NOW.
AND IT'S ONLY GONNA GET WORSE.

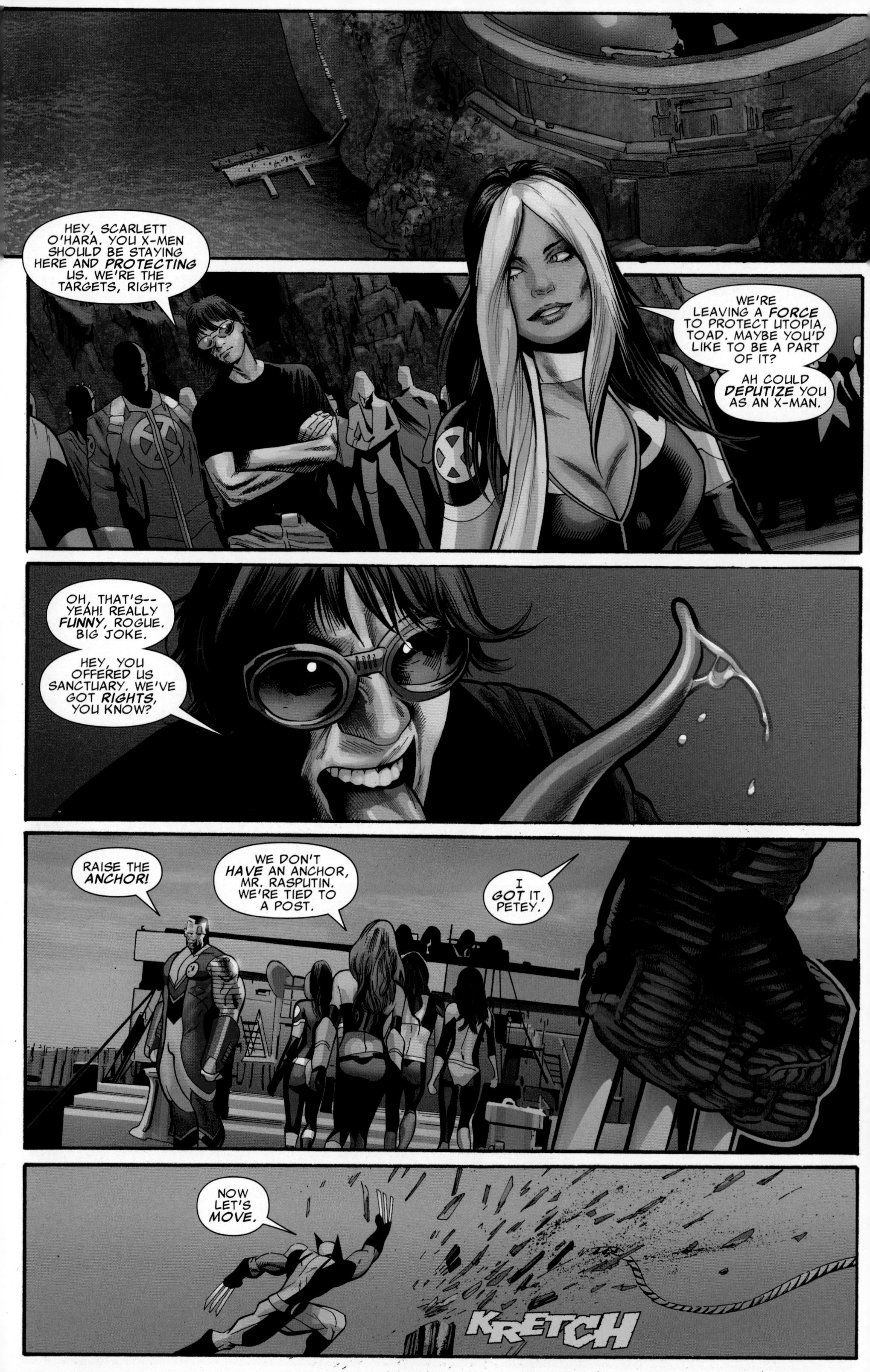
HEY, SCARLETT O'HARA. YOU X-MEN SHOULD BE STAYING HERE AND PROTECTING US. WE'RE THE TARGETS, RIGHT?
WE'RE LEAVING A FORCE TO PROTECT UTOPIA, TOAD. MAYBE YOU'D LIKE TO BE A PART OF IT?
AH COULD DEPUTIZE YOU AS AN X-MAN.
OH, THAT'S-- YEAH! REALLY FUNNY, ROGUE. BIG JOKE.
HEY, YOU OFFERED US SANCTUARY. WE'VE GOT RIGHTS, YOU KNOW?
RAISE THE ANCHOR!
WE DON'T HAVE AN ANCHOR, MR. RASPUTIN. WE'RE TIED TO A POST.
I GOT IT, PETEY.
NOW LET'S MOVE.
KRETCH

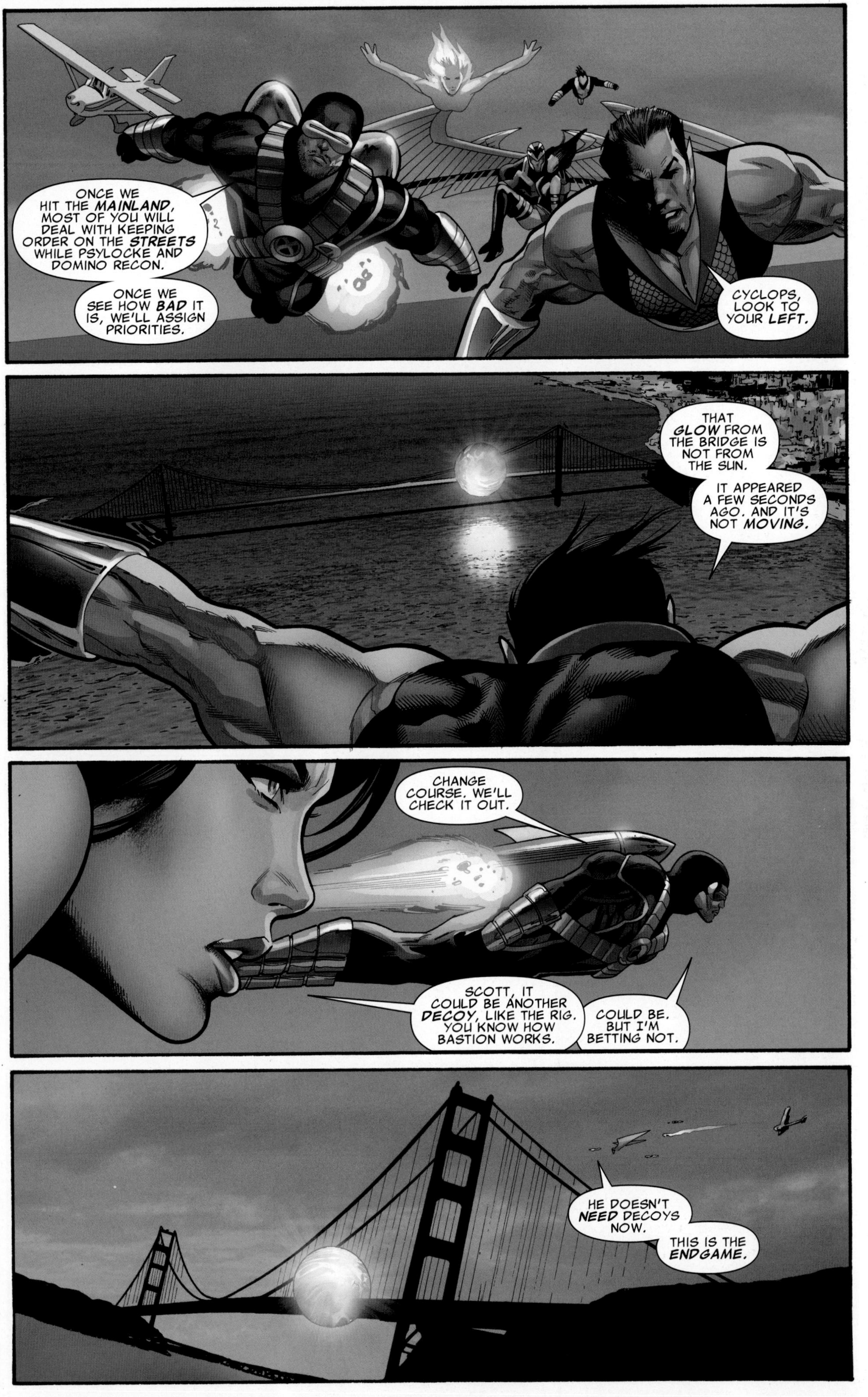
ONCE WE HIT THE MAINLAND, MOST OF YOU WILL DEAL WITH KEEPING ORDER ON THE STREETS WHILE PSYLOCKE AND DOMINO RECON.
ONCE WE SEE HOW BAD IT IS, WE'LL ASSIGN PRIORITIES.
CYCLOPS, LOOK TO YOUR LEFT.
THAT GLOW FROM THE BRIDGE IS NOT FROM THE SUN.
IT APPEARED A FEW SECONDS AGO. AND IT'S NOT MOVING.
CHANGE COURSE. WE'LL CHECK IT OUT.
SCOTT, IT COULD BE ANOTHER DECOY, LIKE THE RIG. YOU KNOW HOW BASTION WORKS.
COULD BE. BUT I'M BETTING NOT.
HE DOESN'T NEED DECOYS NOW.
THIS IS THE ENDGAME.

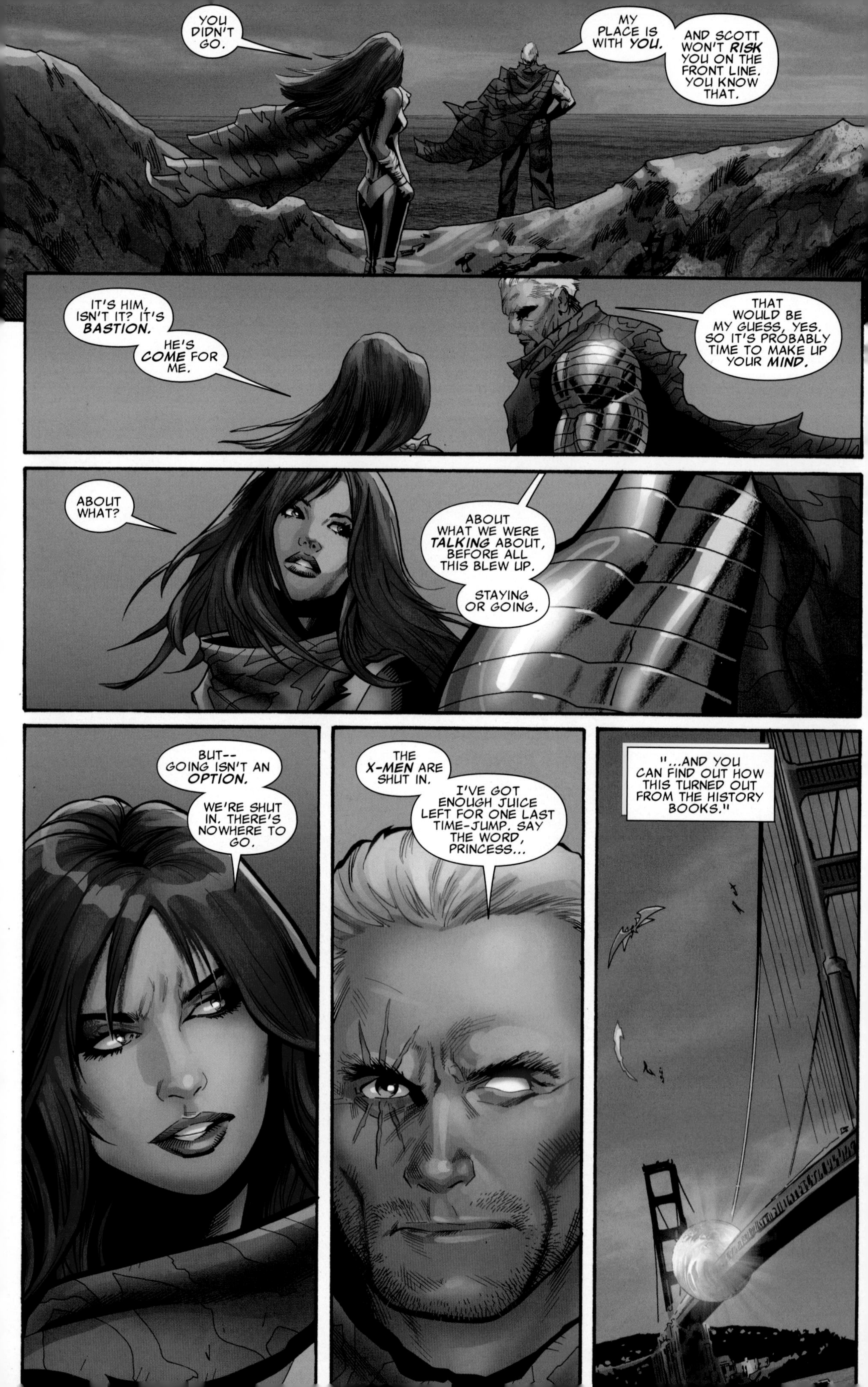
YOU DIDN'T GO.
MY PLACE IS WITH YOU.
AND SCOTT WON'T RISK YOU ON THE FRONT LINE. YOU KNOW THAT.
IT'S HIM, ISN'T IT? IT'S BASTION.
HE'S COME FOR ME.
THAT WOULD BE MY GUESS, YES. SO IT'S PROBABLY TIME TO MAKE UP YOUR MIND.
ABOUT WHAT?
ABOUT WHAT WE WERE TALKING ABOUT, BEFORE ALL THIS BLEW UP.
STAYING OR GOING.
BUT-- GOING ISN'T AN OPTION.
WE'RE SHUT IN. THERE'S NOWHERE TO GO.
THE X-MEN ARE SHUT IN.
I'VE GOT ENOUGH JUICE LEFT FOR ONE LAST TIME-JUMP. SAY THE WORD, PRINCESS...
"...AND YOU CAN FIND OUT HOW THIS TURNED OUT FROM THE HISTORY BOOKS."

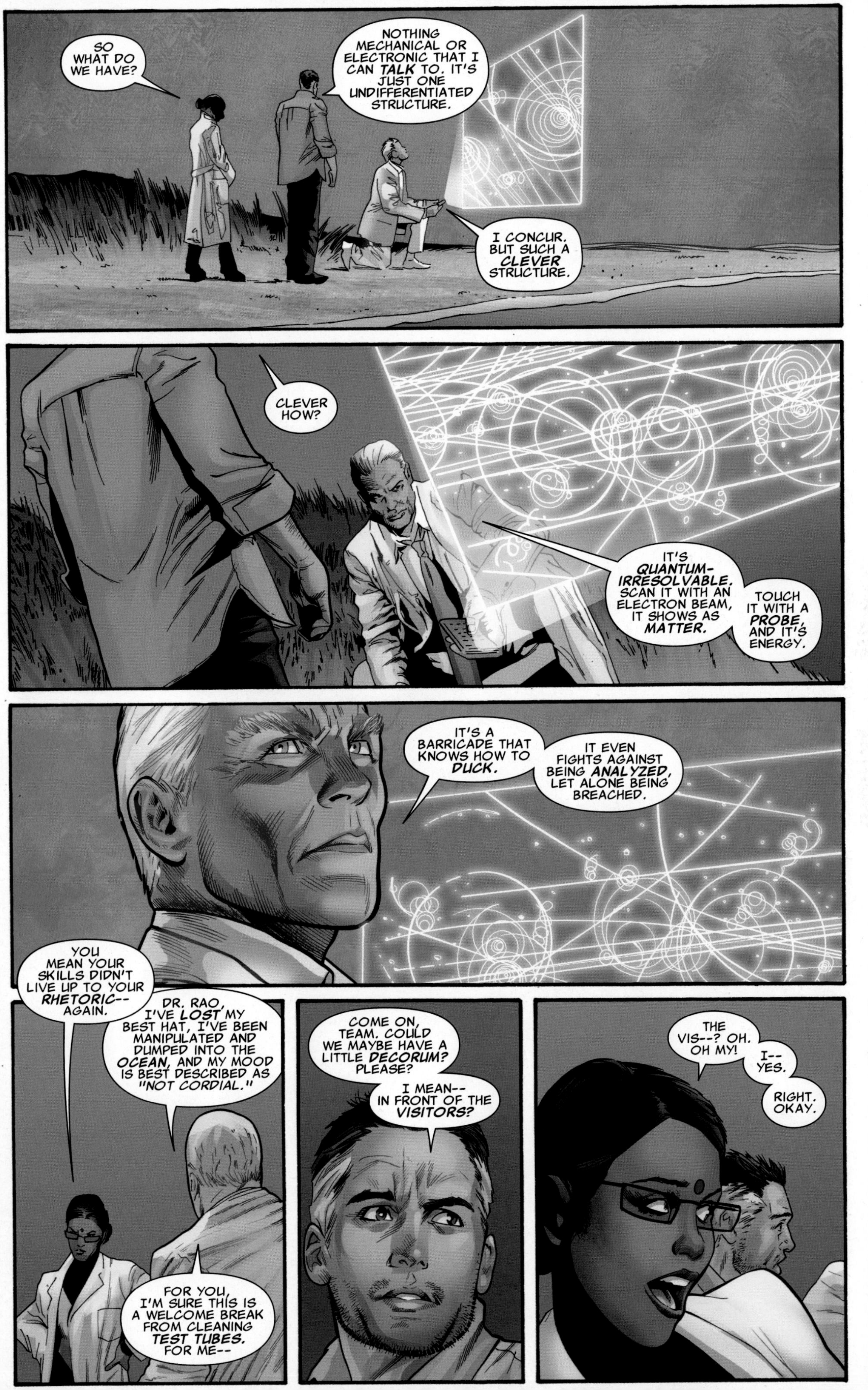
SO WHAT DO WE HAVE?
NOTHING MECHANICAL OR ELECTRONIC THAT I CAN TALK TO. IT'S JUST ONE UNDIFFERENTIATED STRUCTURE.
I CONCUR. BUT SUCH A CLEVER STRUCTURE.
CLEVER HOW?
IT'S QUANTUM-IRRESOLVABLE. SCAN IT WITH AN ELECTRON BEAM, IT SHOWS AS MATTER.
TOUCH IT WITH A PROBE, AND IT'S ENERGY.
IT'S A BARRICADE THAT KNOWS HOW TO DUCK.
IT EVEN FIGHTS AGAINST BEING ANALYZED, LET ALONE BEING BREACHED.
YOU MEAN YOUR SKILLS DIDN'T LIVE UP TO YOUR RHETORIC-- AGAIN.
DR. RAO, I'VE LOST MY BEST HAT, I'VE BEEN MANIPULATED AND DUMPED INTO THE OCEAN, AND MY MOOD IS BEST DESCRIBED AS "NOT CORDIAL."
FOR YOU, I'M SURE THIS IS A WELCOME BREAK FROM CLEANING TEST TUBES. FOR ME--
COME ON, TEAM. COULD WE MAYBE HAVE A LITTLE DECORUM? PLEASE?
I MEAN-- IN FRONT OF THE VISITORS?
THE VIS--? OH. OH MY!
I-- YES.
RIGHT. OKAY.

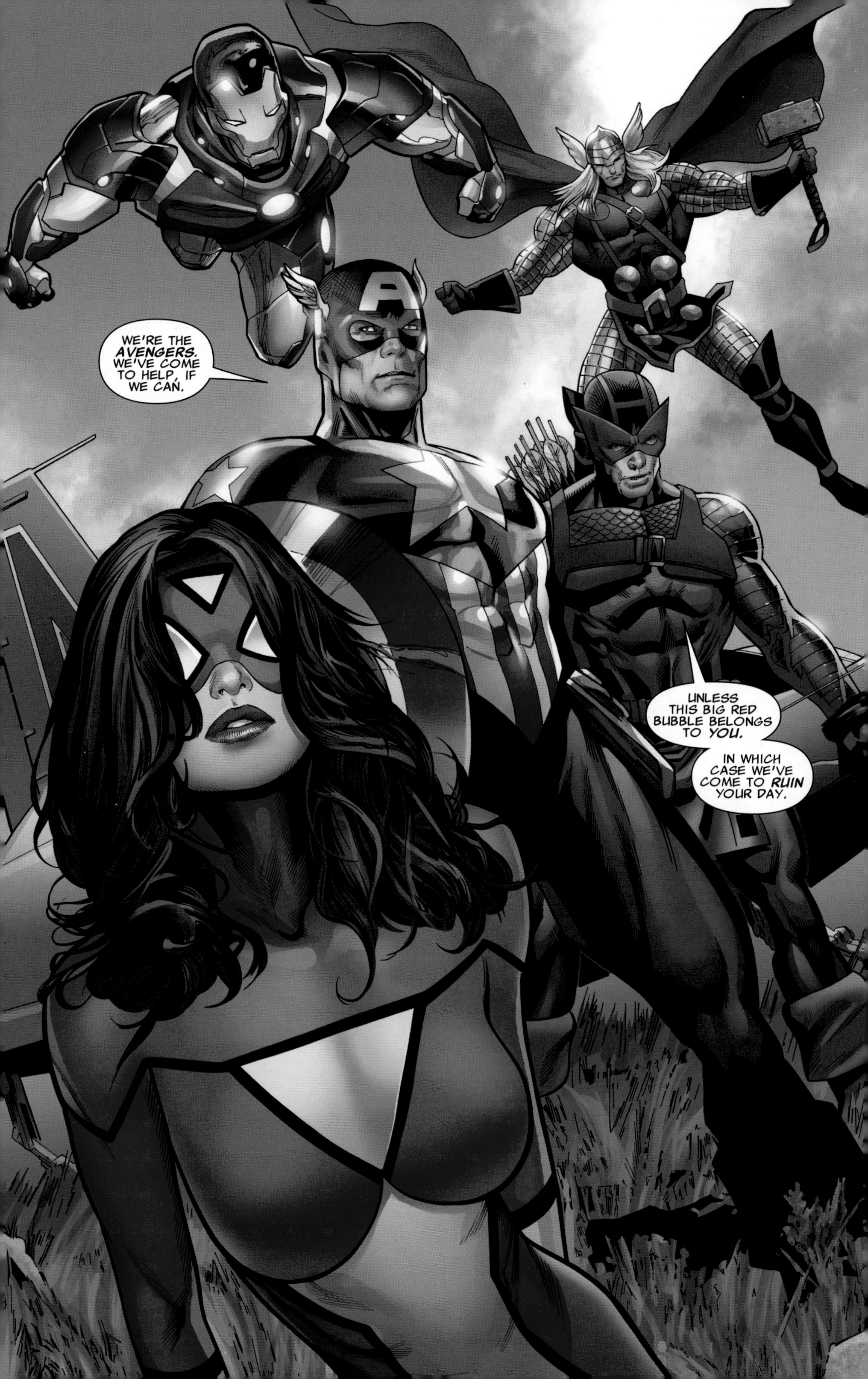
WE'RE THE AVENGERS. WE'VE COME TO HELP, IF WE CAN.
UNLESS THIS BIG RED BUBBLE BELONGS TO YOU.
IN WHICH CASE WE'VE COME TO RUIN YOUR DAY.

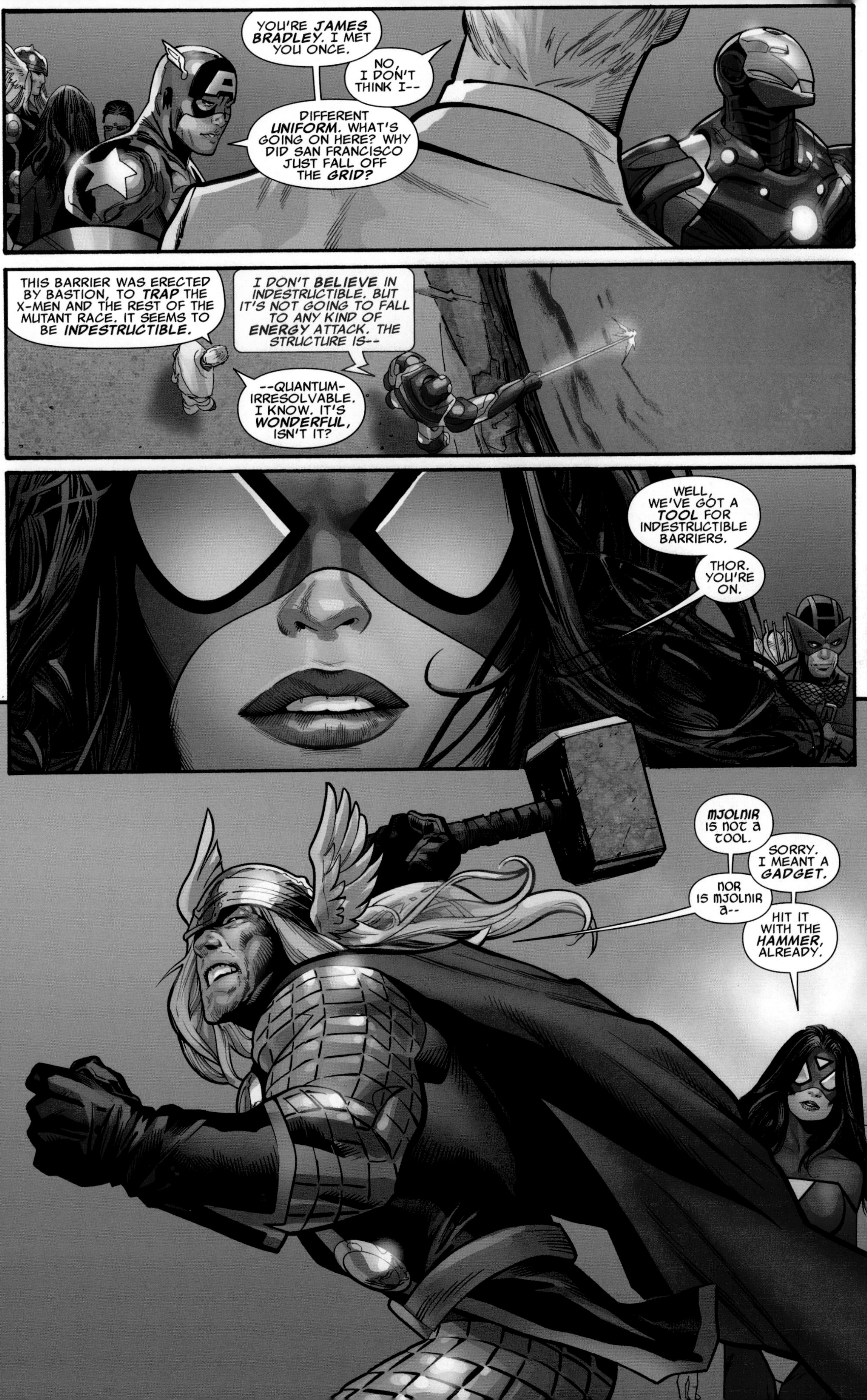
YOU'RE JAMES BRADLEY. I MET YOU ONCE.
NO, I DON'T THINK I--
DIFFERENT UNIFORM. WHAT'S GOING ON HERE? WHY DID SAN FRANCISCO JUST FALL OFF THE GRID?
THIS BARRIER WAS ERECTED BY BASTION, TO TRAP THE X-MEN AND THE REST OF THE MUTANT RACE. IT SEEMS TO BE INDESTRUCTIBLE.
I DON'T BELIEVE IN INDESTRUCTIBLE. BUT IT'S NOT GOING TO FALL TO ANY KIND OF ENERGY ATTACK. THE STRUCTURE IS--
--QUANTUM-IRRESOLVABLE. I KNOW. IT'S WONDERFUL, ISN'T IT?
WELL, WE'VE GOT A TOOL FOR INDESTRUCTIBLE BARRIERS.
THOR. YOU'RE ON.
MJOLNIR IS NOT A TOOL.
SORRY. I MEANT A GADGET.
NOR IS MJOLNIR A--
HIT IT WITH THE HAMMER, ALREADY.

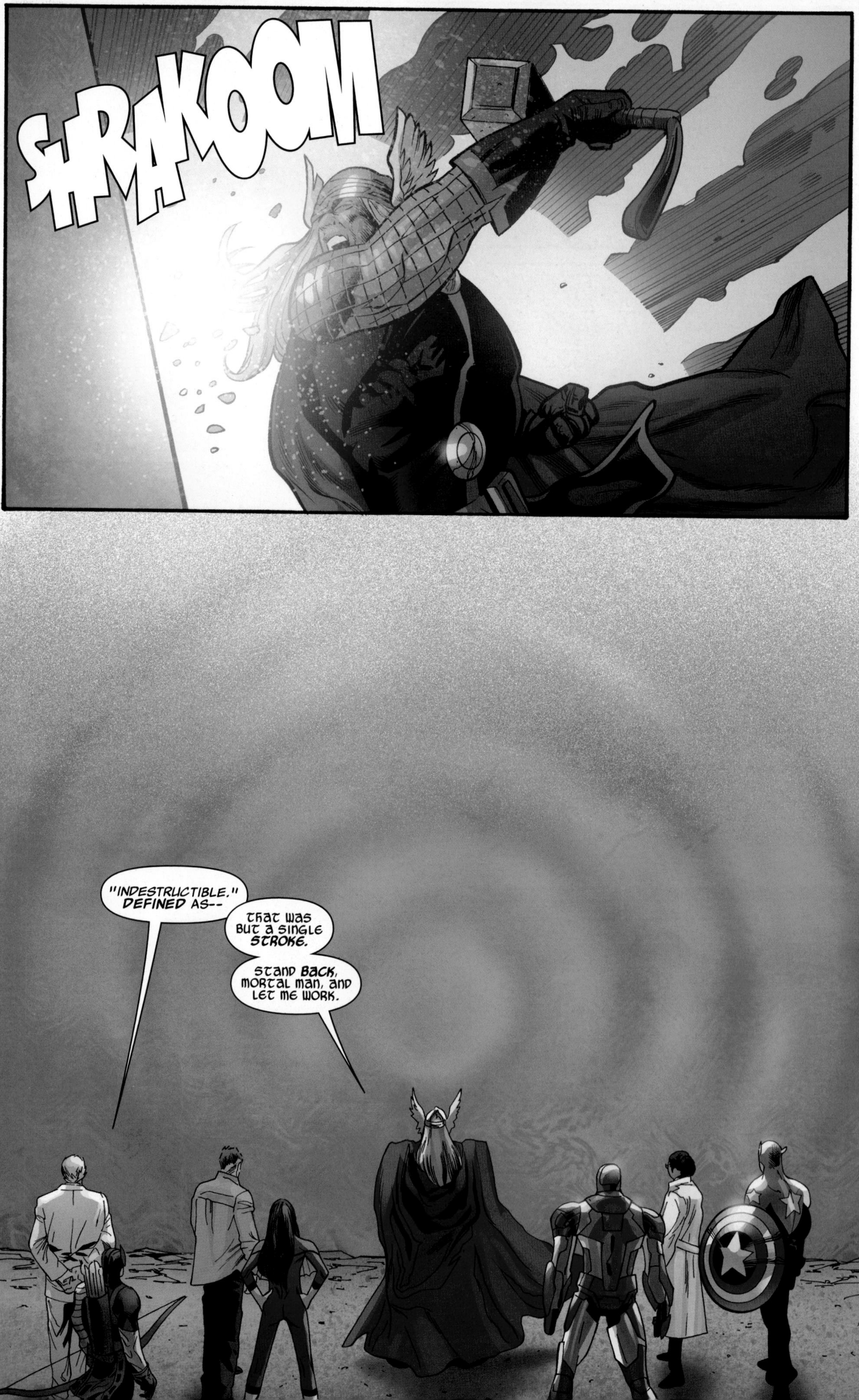
SHRAKOOM
"INDESTRUCTIBLE." DEFINED AS--
THAT WAS BUT A SINGLE STROKE.
STAND BACK, MORTAL MAN, AND LET ME WORK.

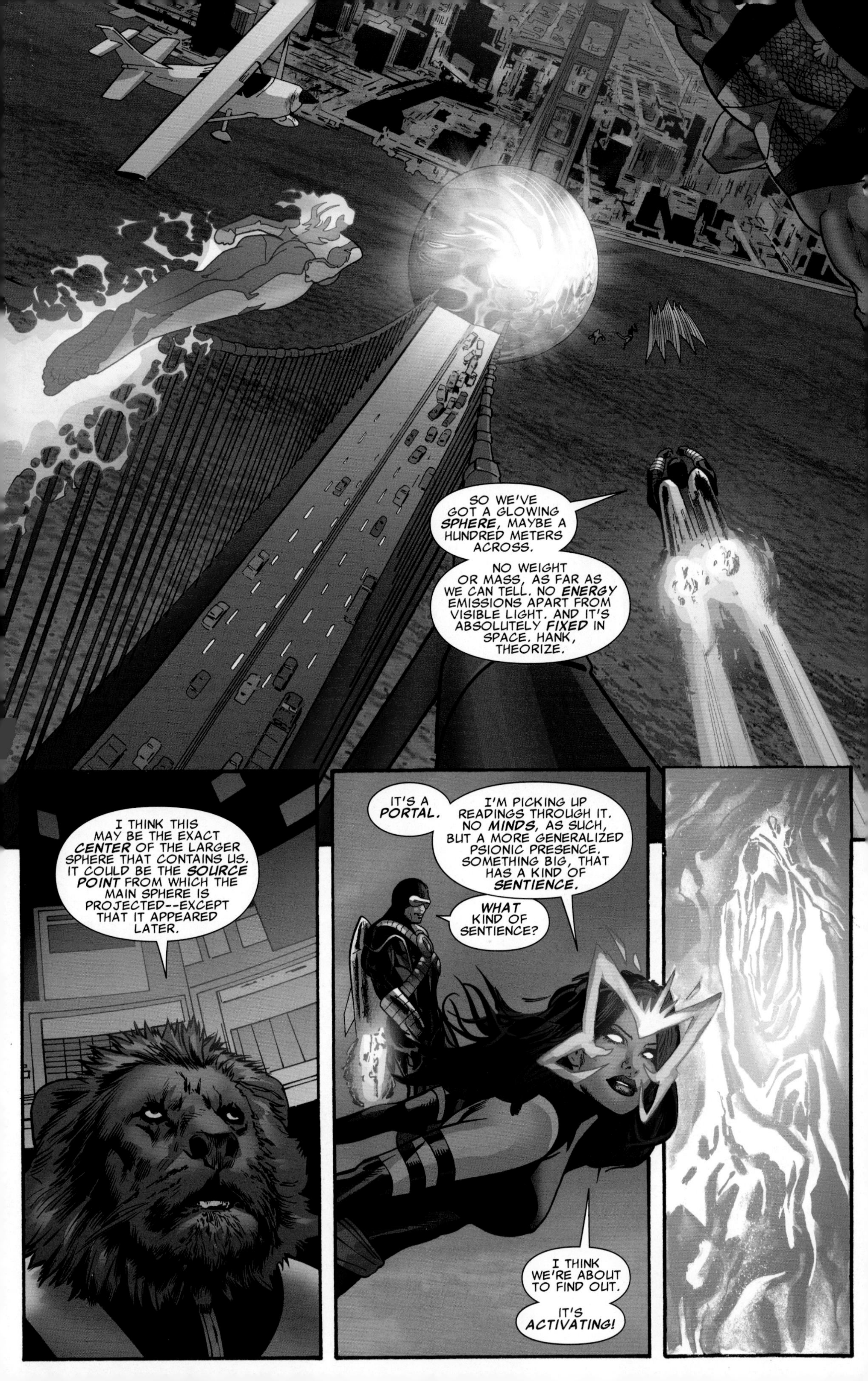
SO WE'VE GOT A GLOWING SPHERE, MAYBE A HUNDRED METERS ACROSS.
NO WEIGHT OR MASS, AS FAR AS WE CAN TELL. NO ENERGY EMISSIONS APART FROM VISIBLE LIGHT. AND IT'S ABSOLUTELY FIXED IN SPACE. HANK, THEORIZE.
I THINK THIS MAY BE THE EXACT CENTER OF THE LARGER SPHERE THAT CONTAINS US. IT COULD BE THE SOURCE POINT FROM WHICH THE MAIN SPHERE IS PROJECTED--EXCEPT THAT IT APPEARED LATER.
IT'S A PORTAL.
I'M PICKING UP READINGS THROUGH IT. NO MINDS, AS SUCH, BUT A MORE GENERALIZED PSIONIC PRESENCE. SOMETHING BIG, THAT HAS A KIND OF SENTIENCE.
WHAT KIND OF SENTIENCE?
I THINK WE'RE ABOUT TO FIND OUT.
IT'S ACTIVATING!

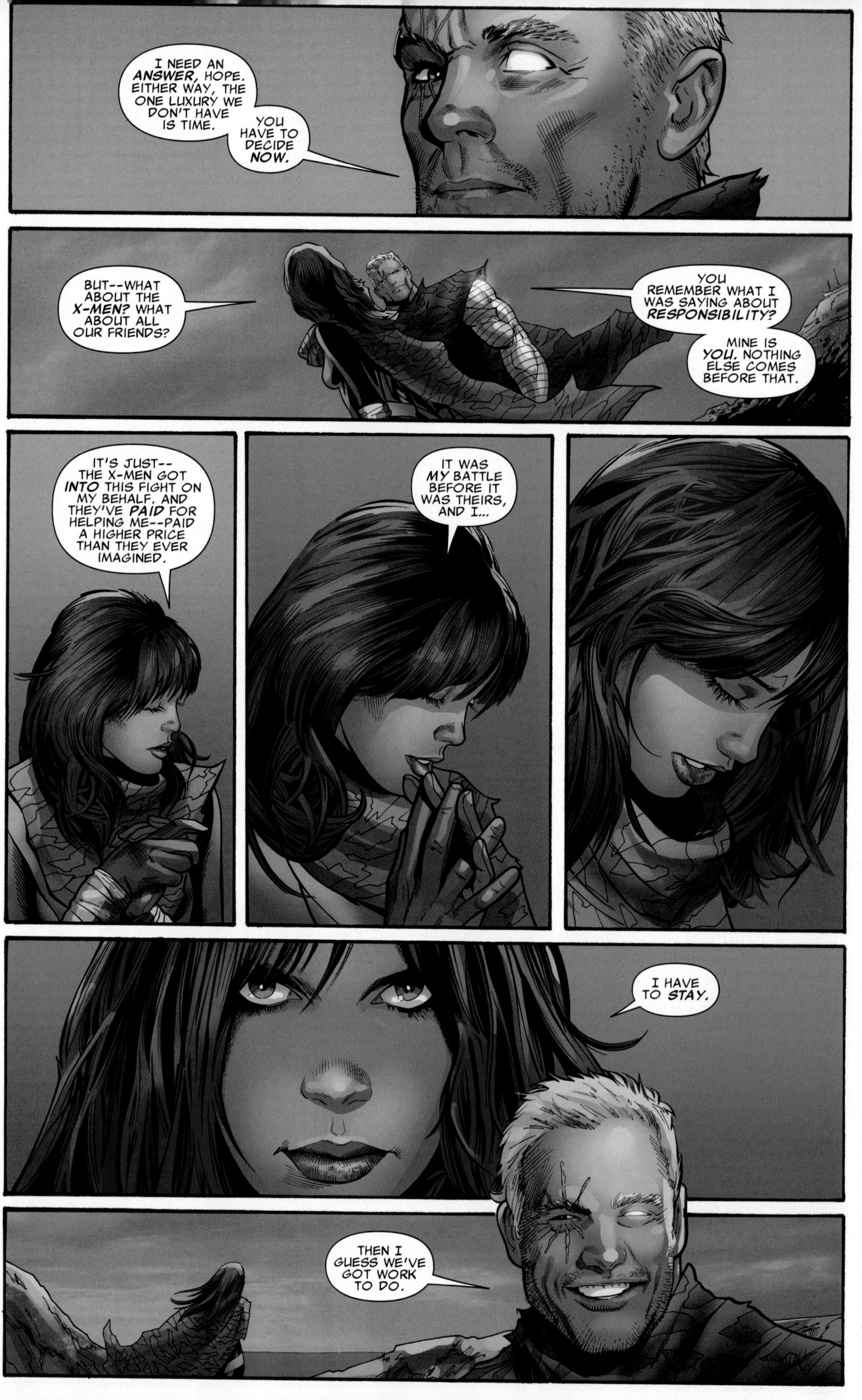
I NEED AN ANSWER, HOPE. EITHER WAY, THE ONE LUXURY WE DON'T HAVE IS TIME.
YOU HAVE TO DECIDE NOW.
BUT--WHAT ABOUT THE X-MEN? WHAT ABOUT ALL OUR FRIENDS?
YOU REMEMBER WHAT I WAS SAYING ABOUT RESPONSIBILITY?
MINE IS YOU. NOTHING ELSE COMES BEFORE THAT.
IT'S JUST-- THE X-MEN GOT INTO THIS FIGHT ON MY BEHALF. AND THEY'VE PAID FOR HELPING ME--PAID A HIGHER PRICE THAN THEY EVER IMAGINED.
IT WAS MY BATTLE BEFORE IT WAS THEIRS, AND I...
I HAVE TO STAY.
THEN I GUESS WE'VE GOT WORK TO DO.

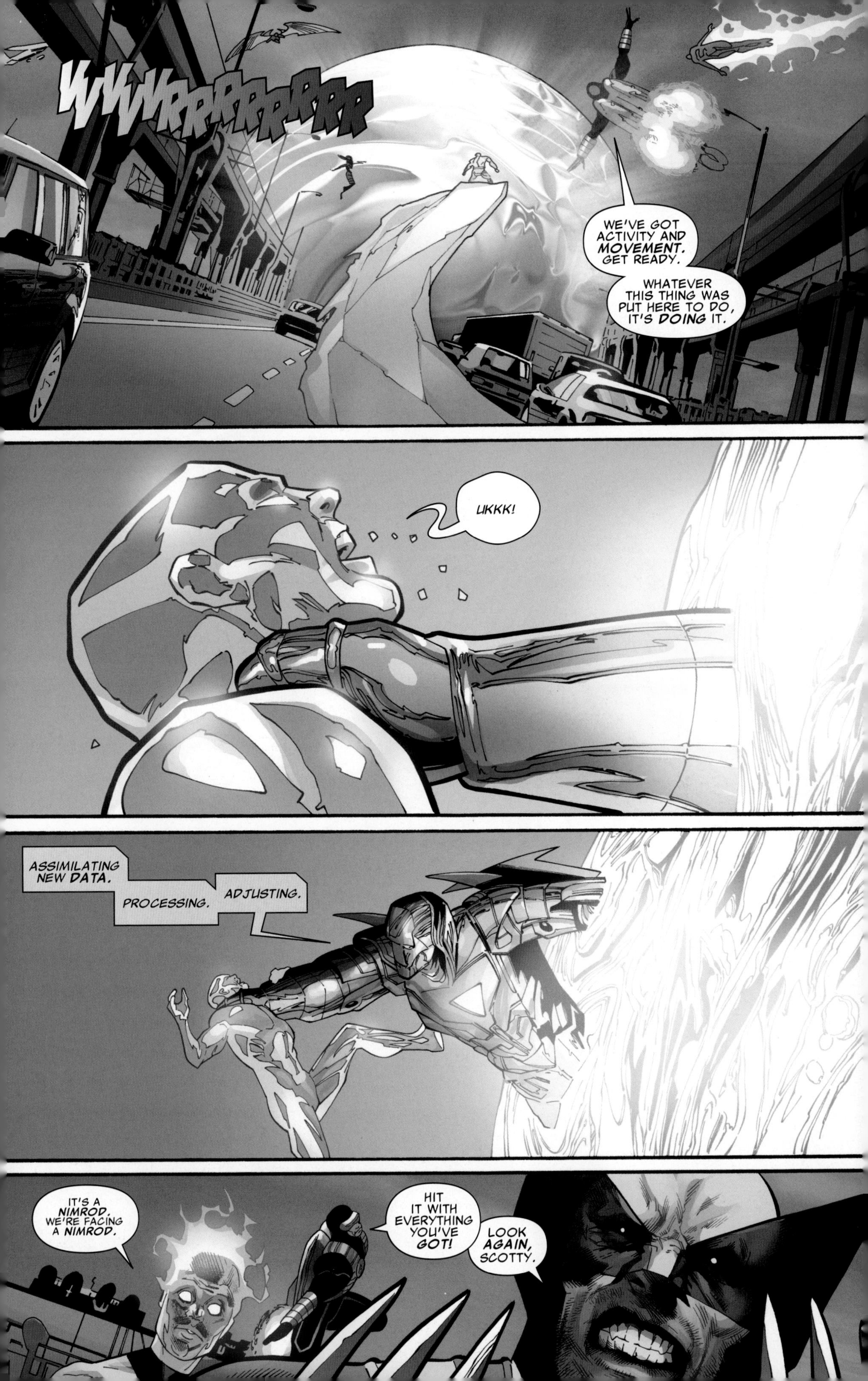
WWWRRRRRRRRRR
WE'VE GOT ACTIVITY AND MOVEMENT. GET READY.
WHATEVER THIS THING WAS PUT HERE TO DO, IT'S DOING IT.
UKKK!
ASSIMILATING NEW DATA.
PROCESSING.
ADJUSTING.
IT'S A NIMROD. WE'RE FACING A NIMROD.
HIT IT WITH EVERYTHING YOU'VE GOT!
LOOK AGAIN, SCOTTY.

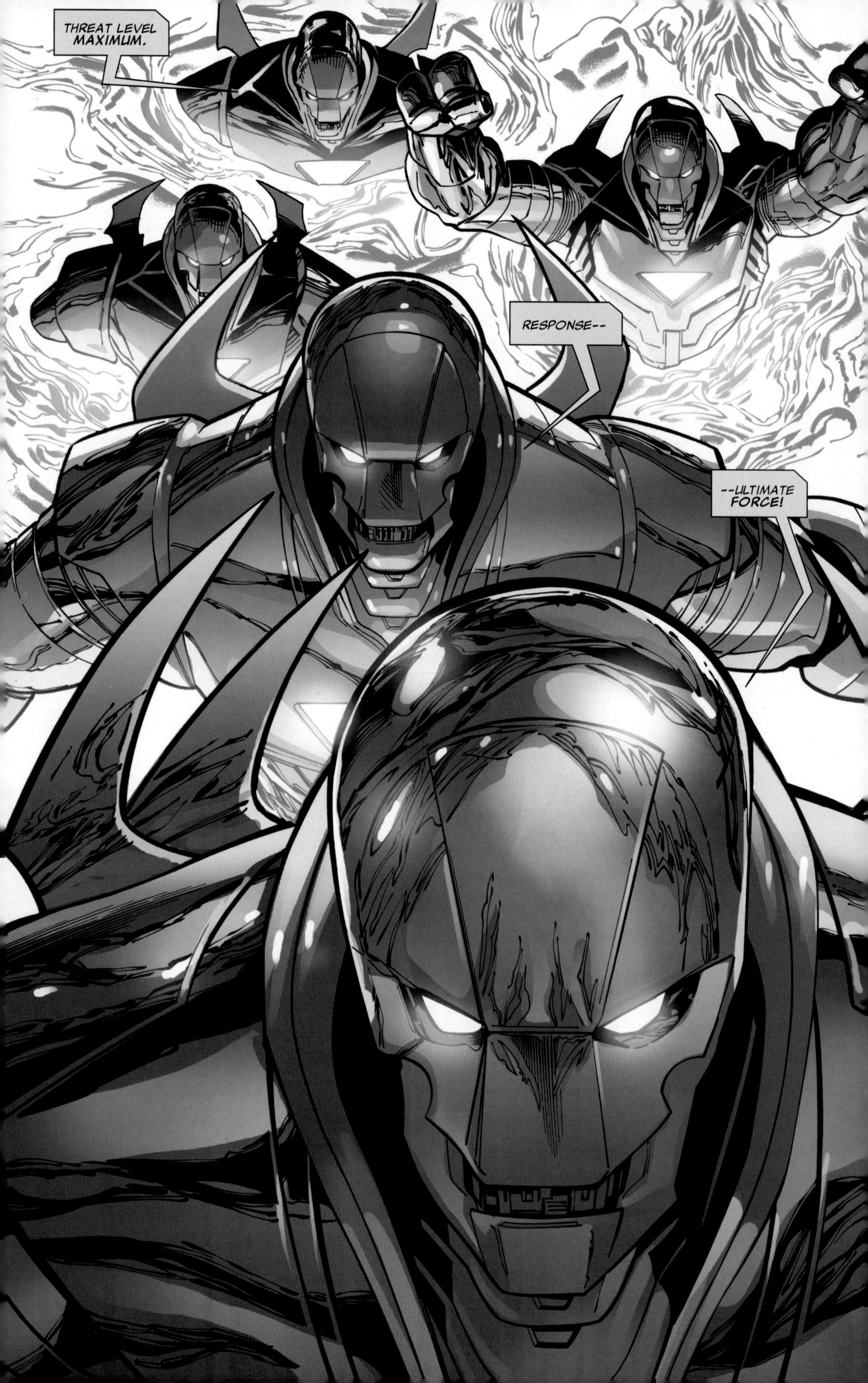
THREAT LEVEL MAXIMUM.
RESPONSE--
--ULTIMATE FORCE!

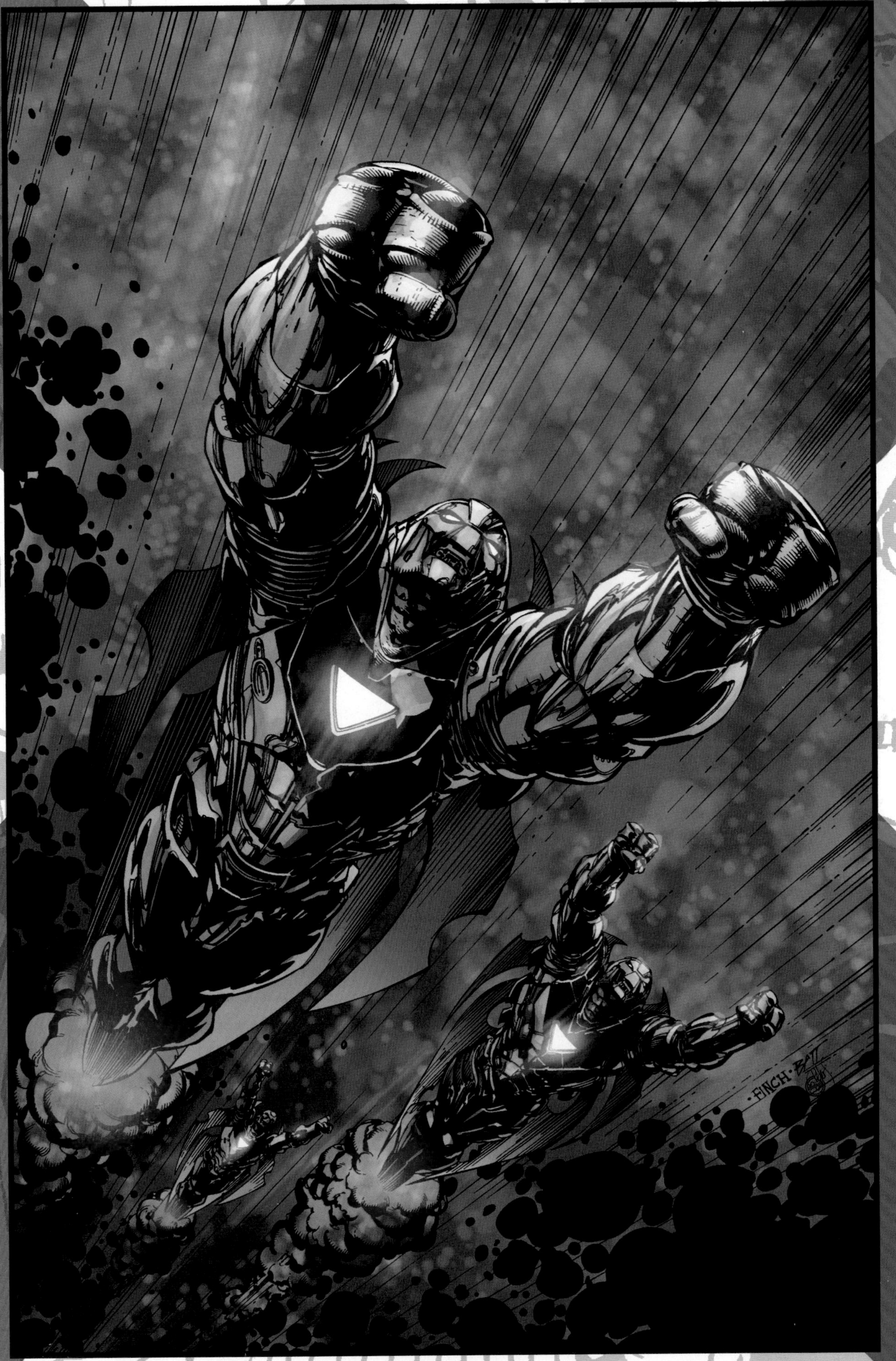
FINCH·BATT

X-MEN LEGACY #236
VARIANT

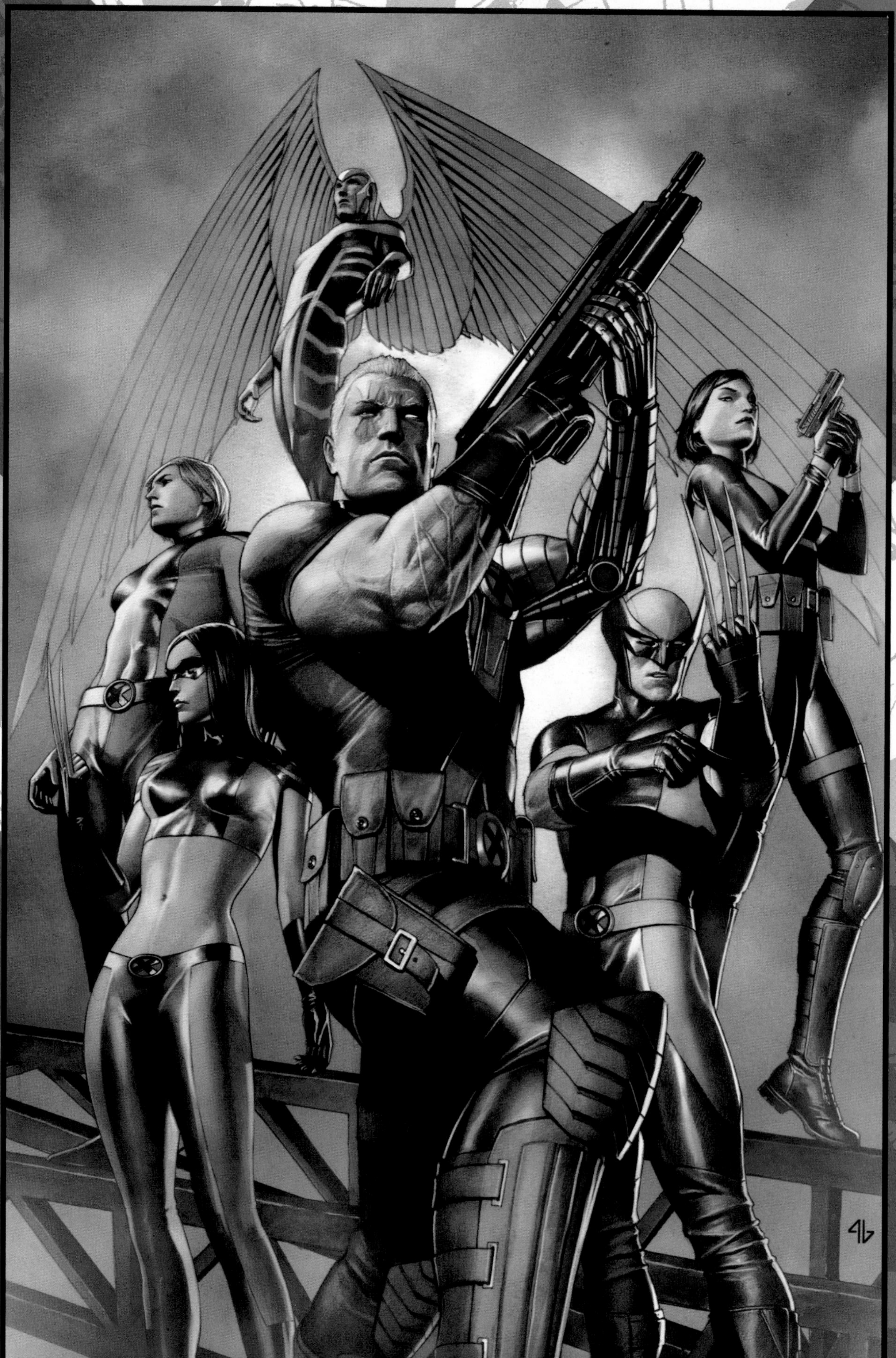
AG

X-FORCE #27

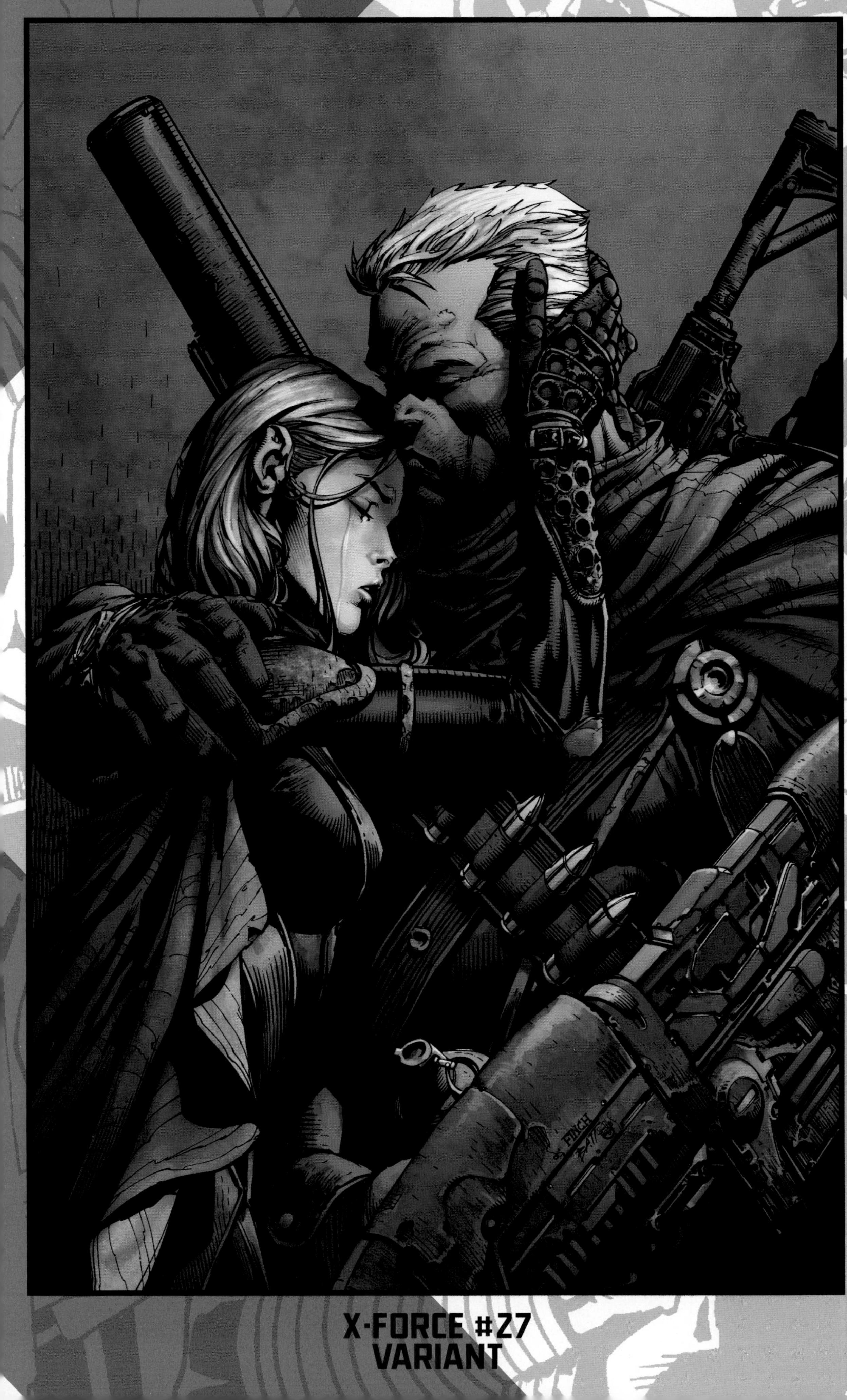
FINCH

X-FORCE #27
VARIANT

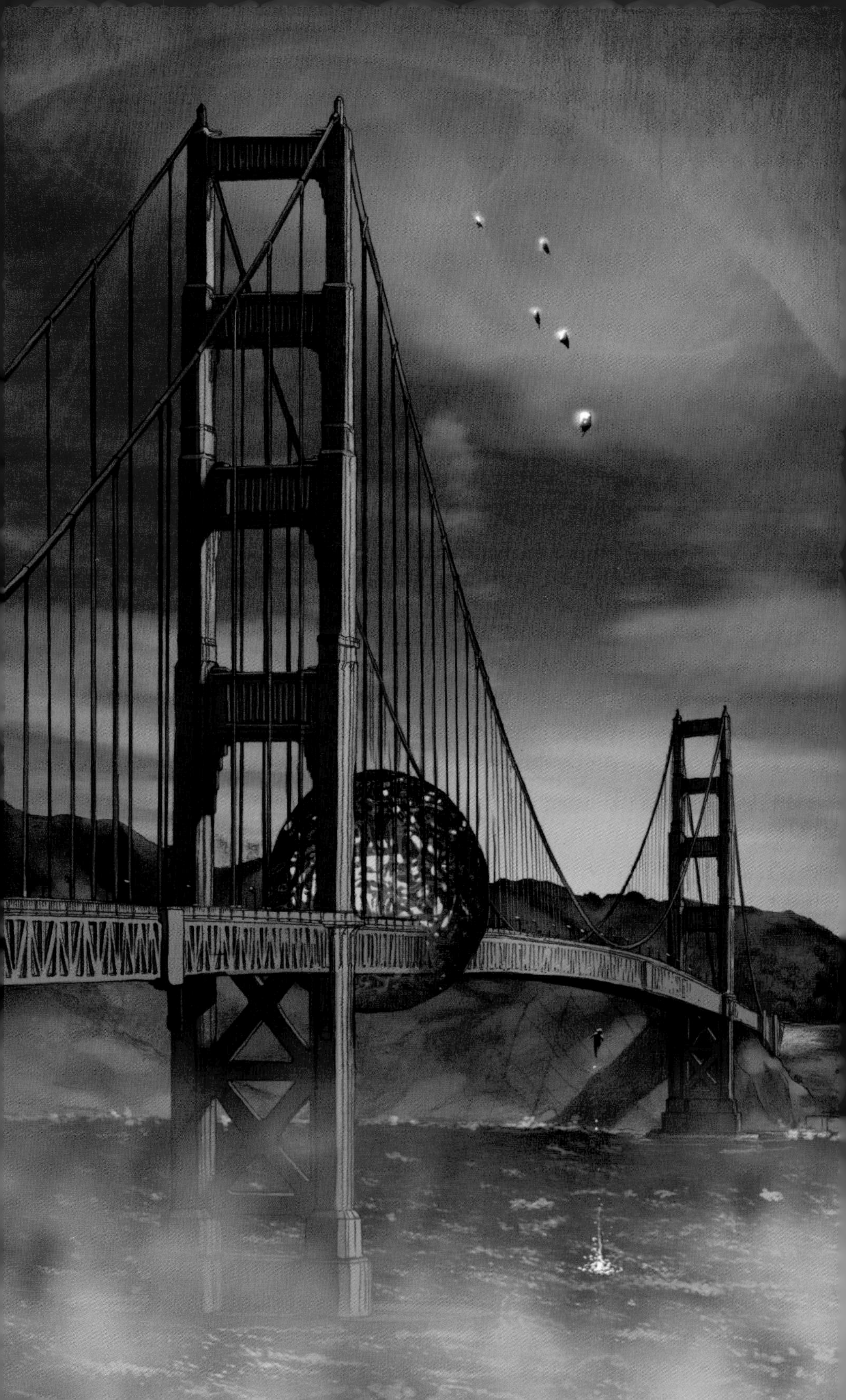

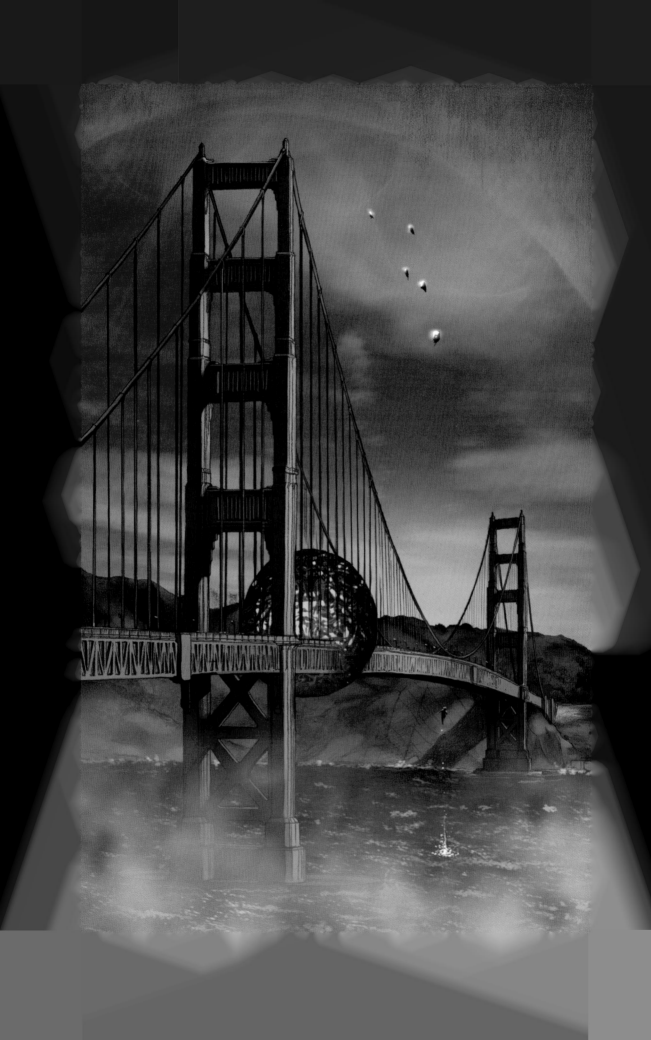

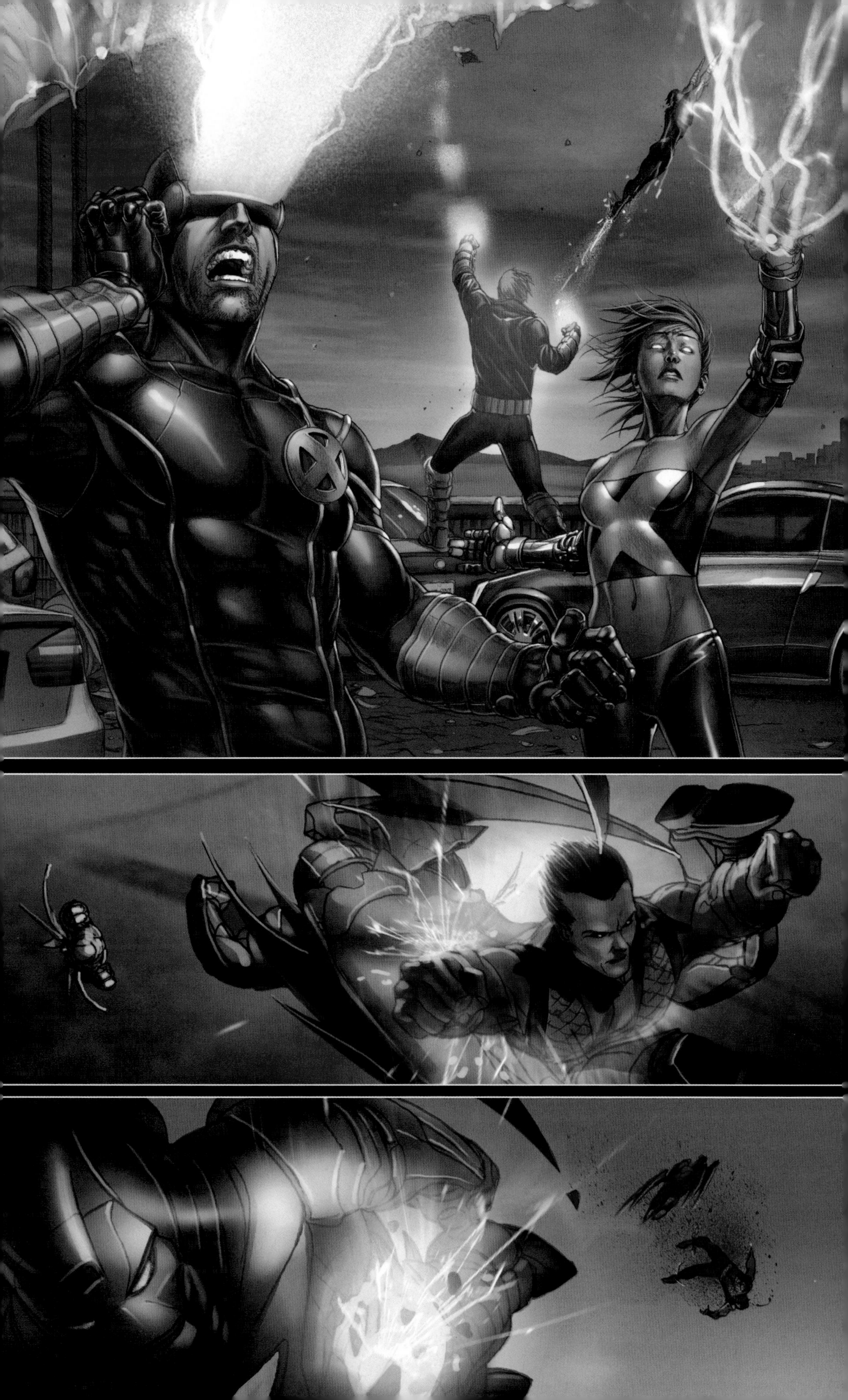

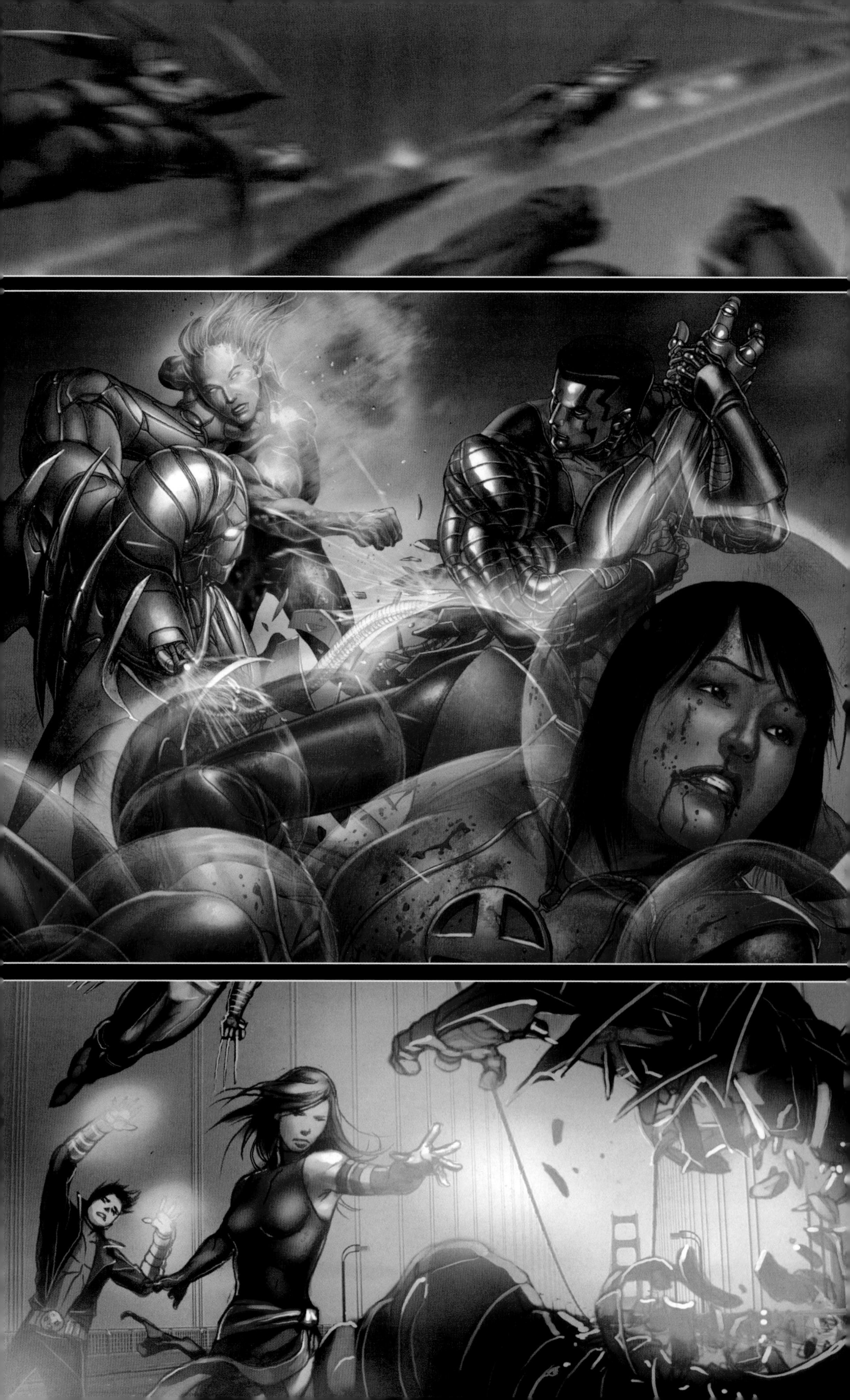

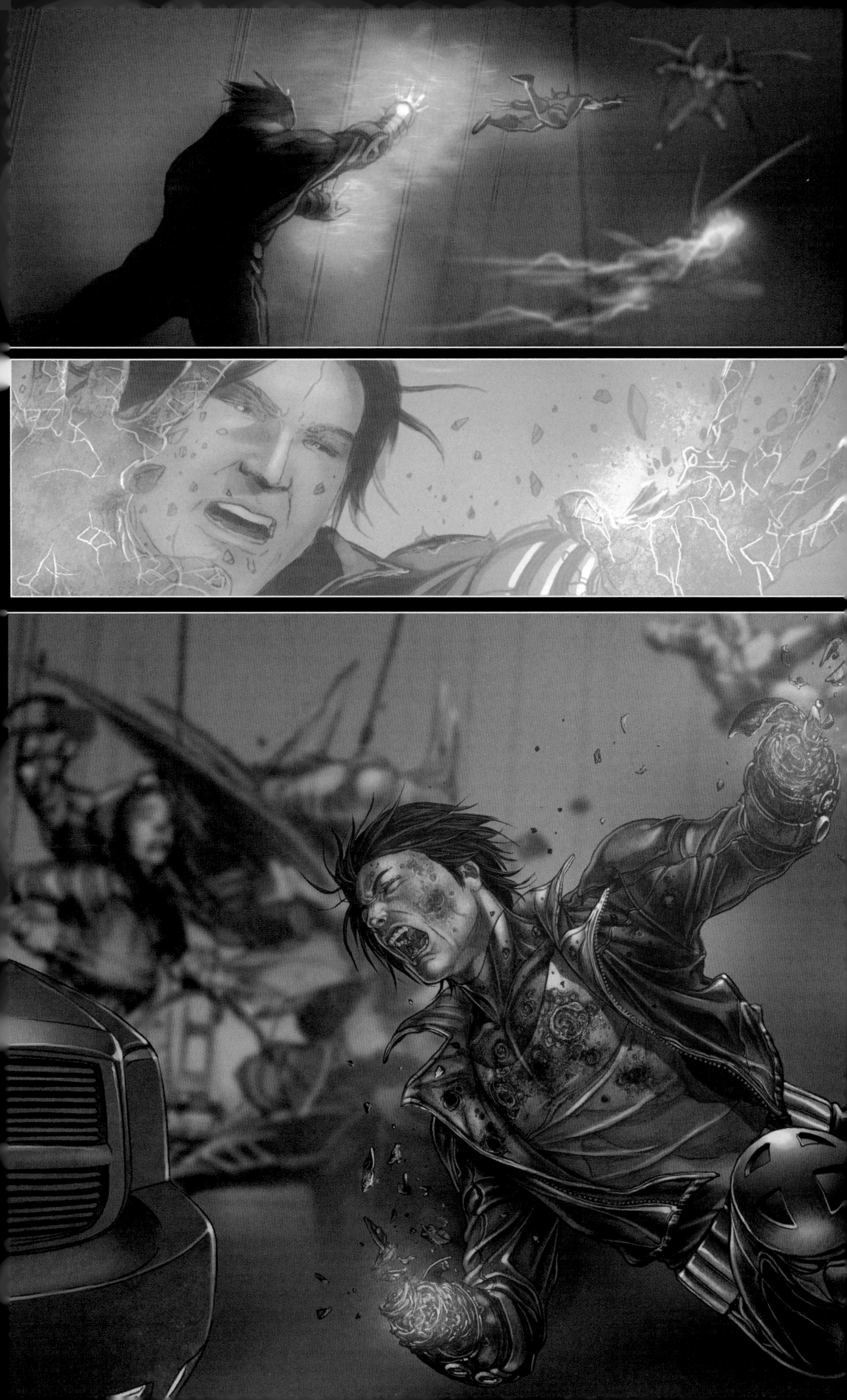

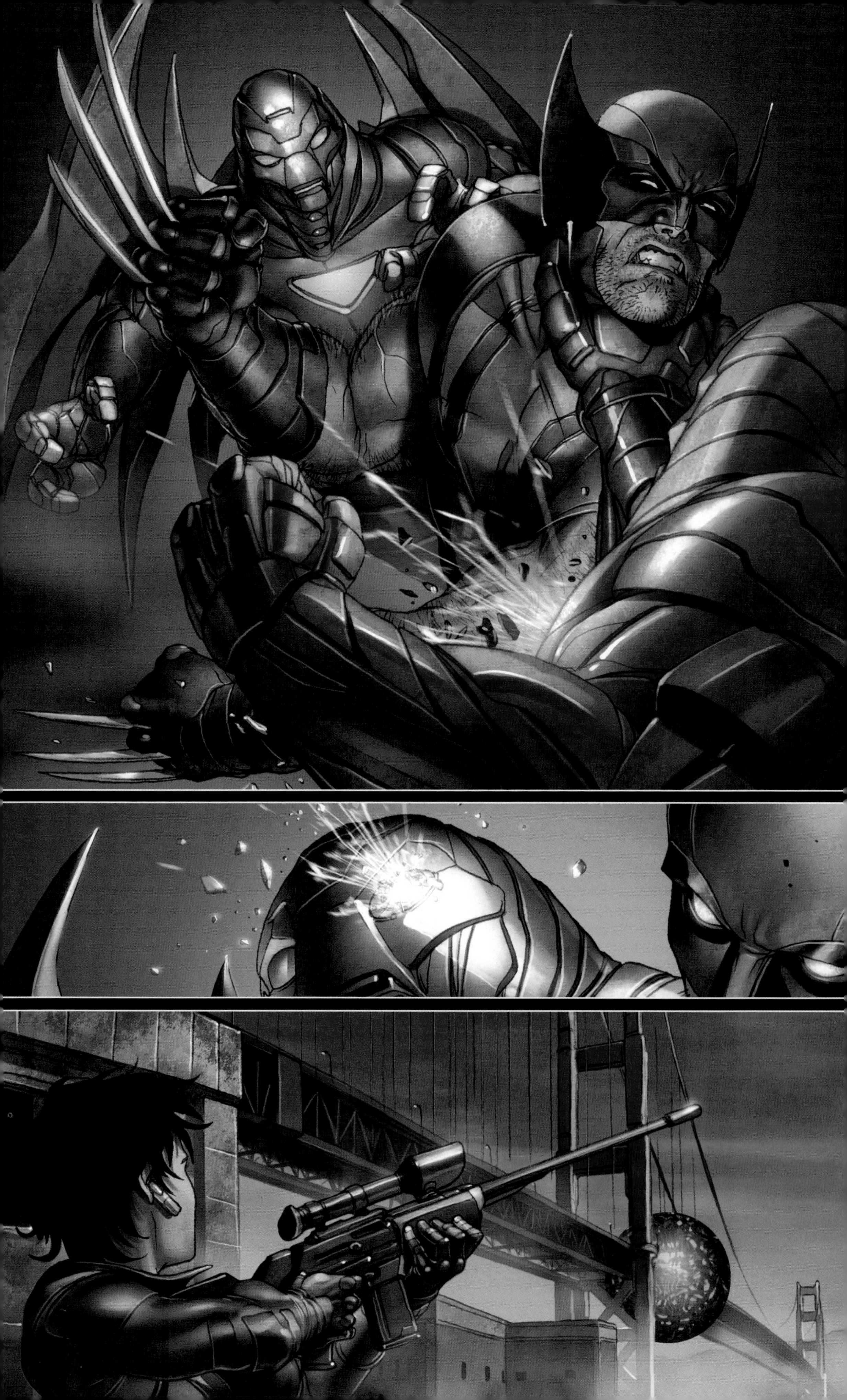

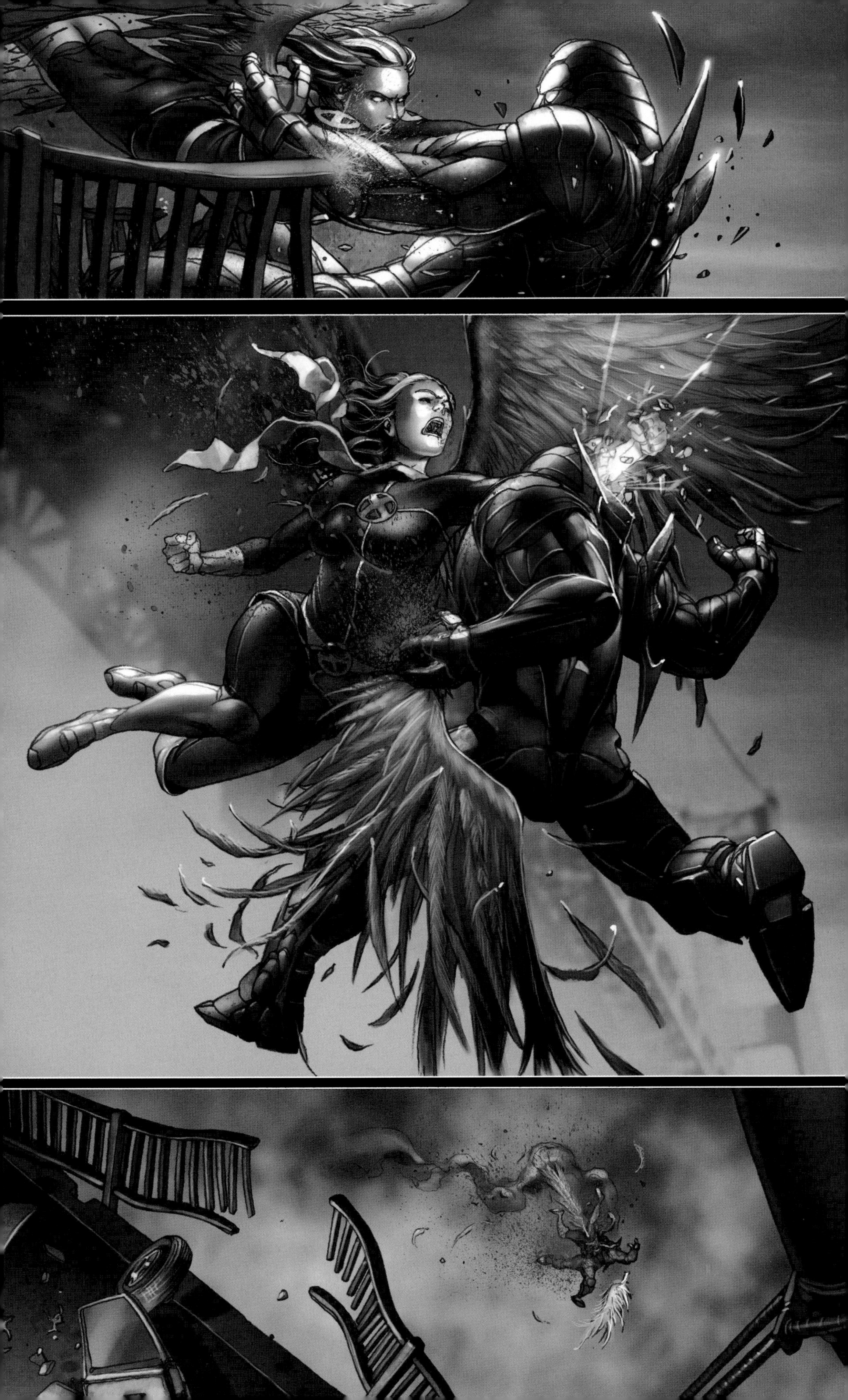

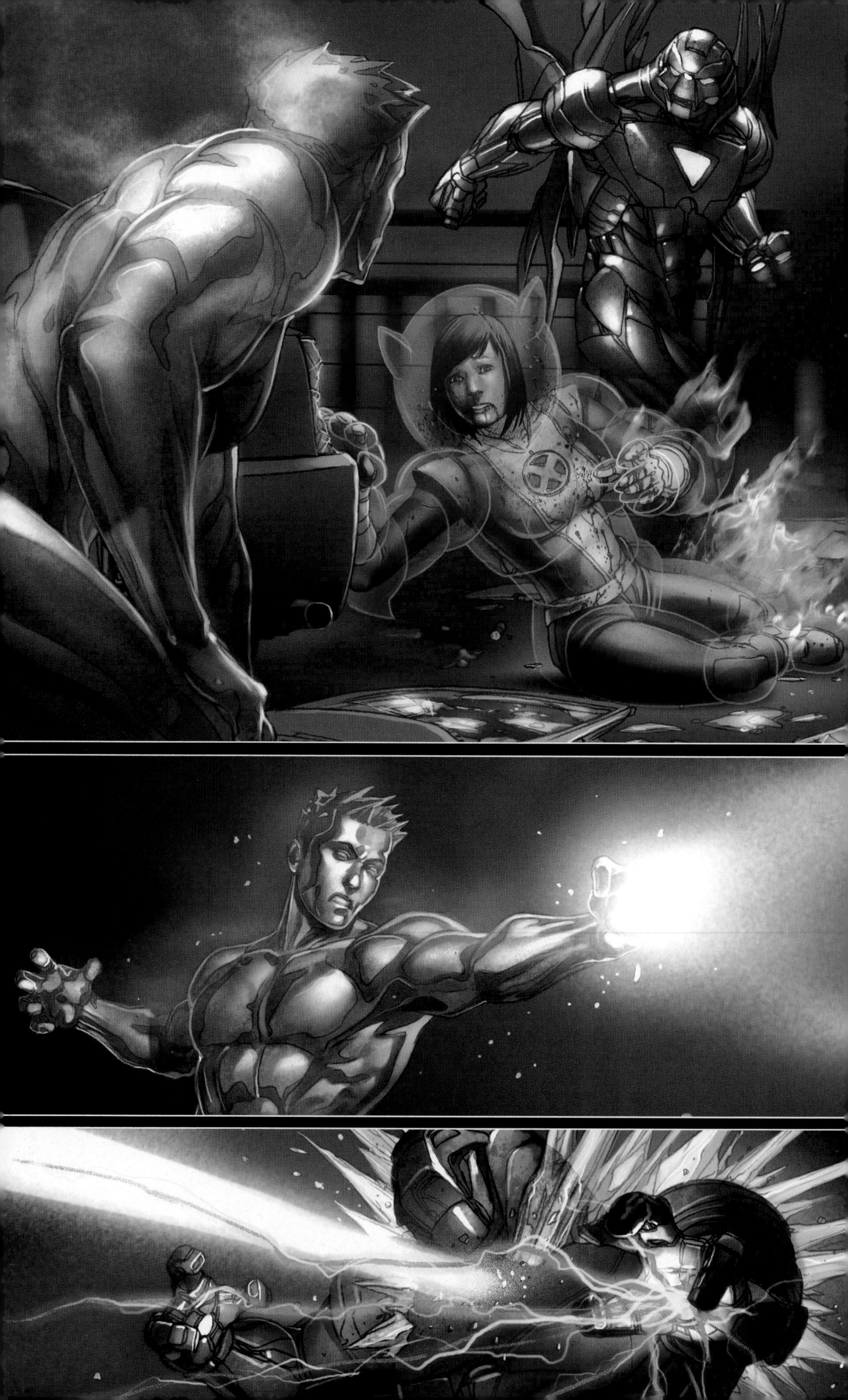

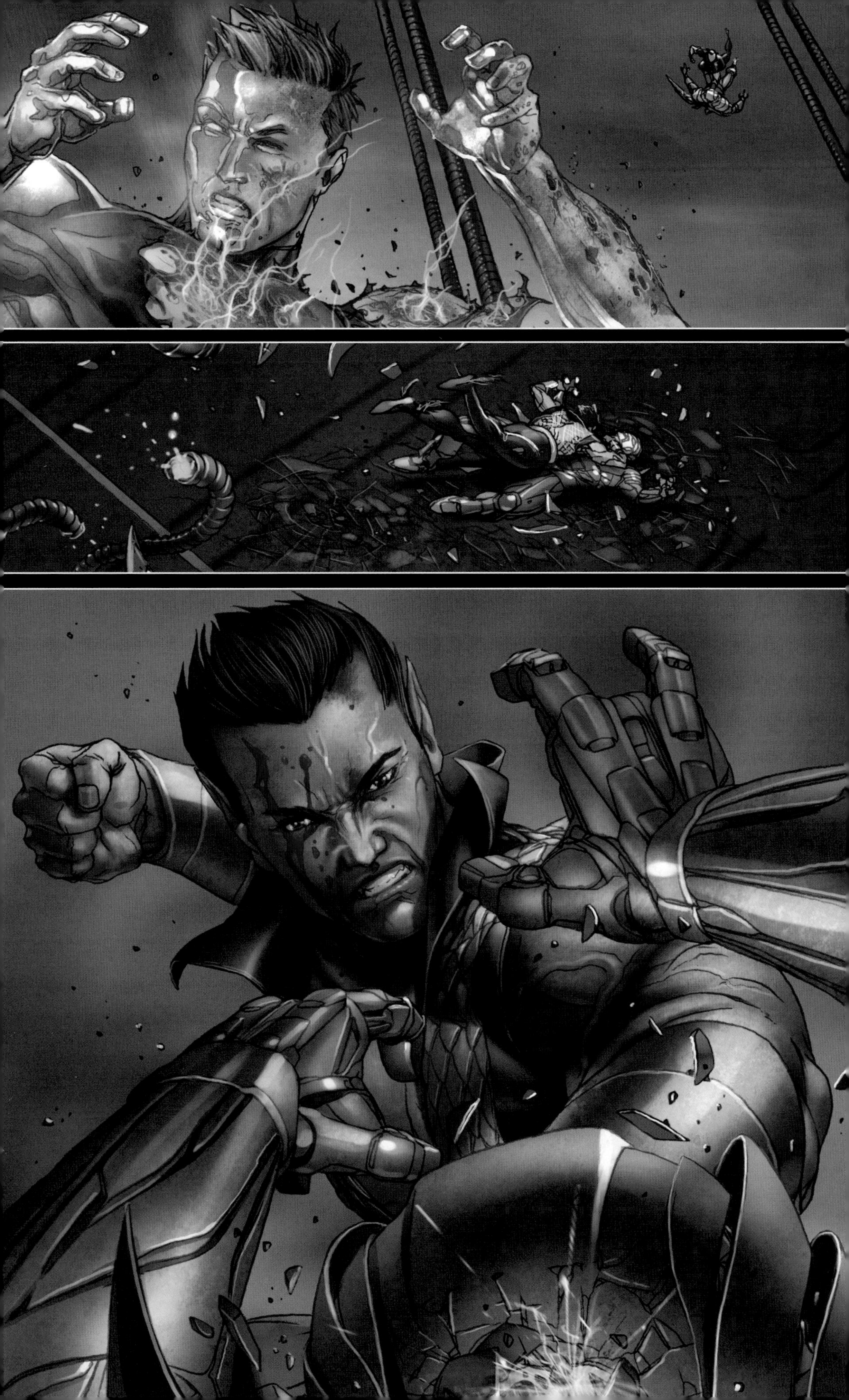

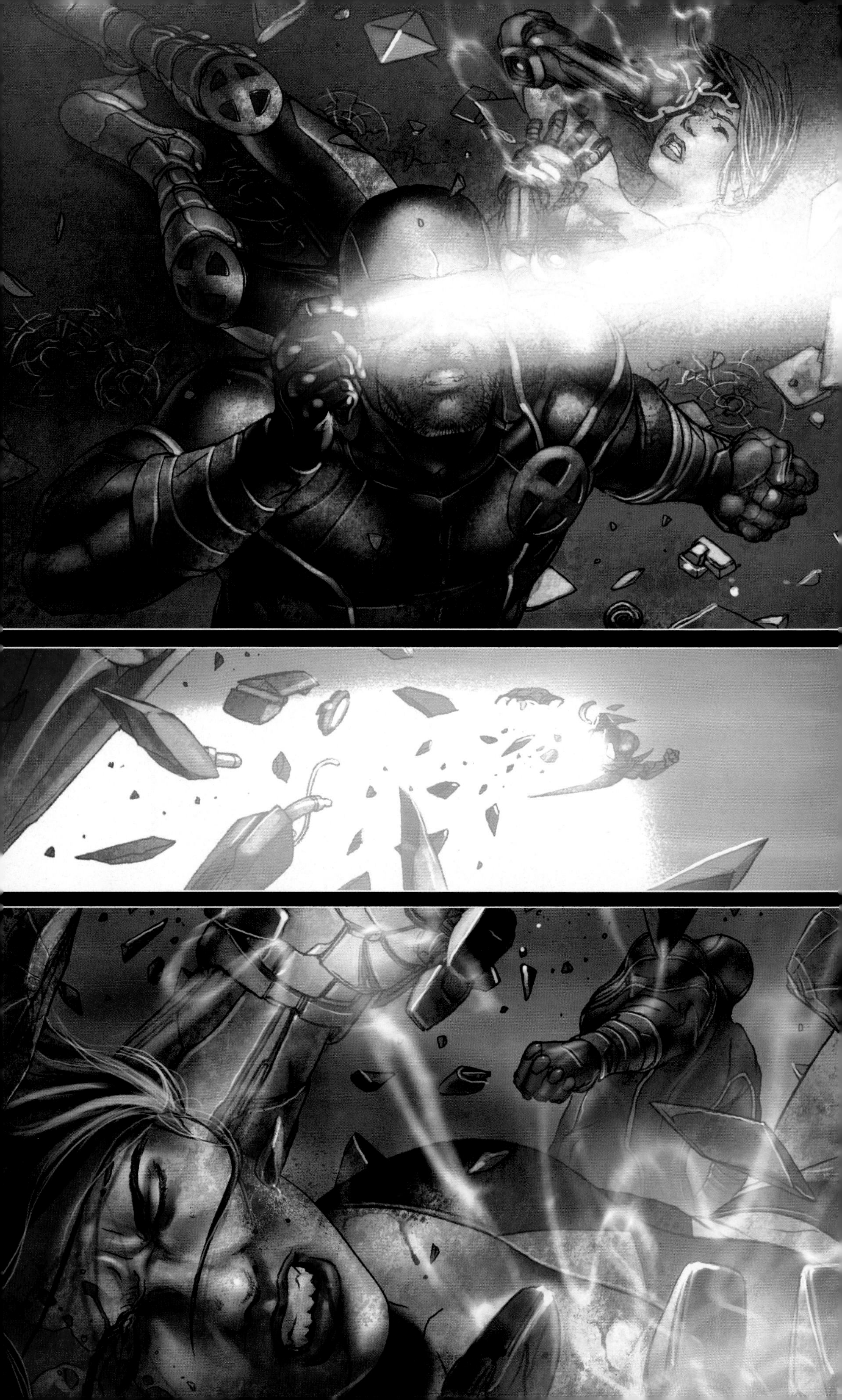

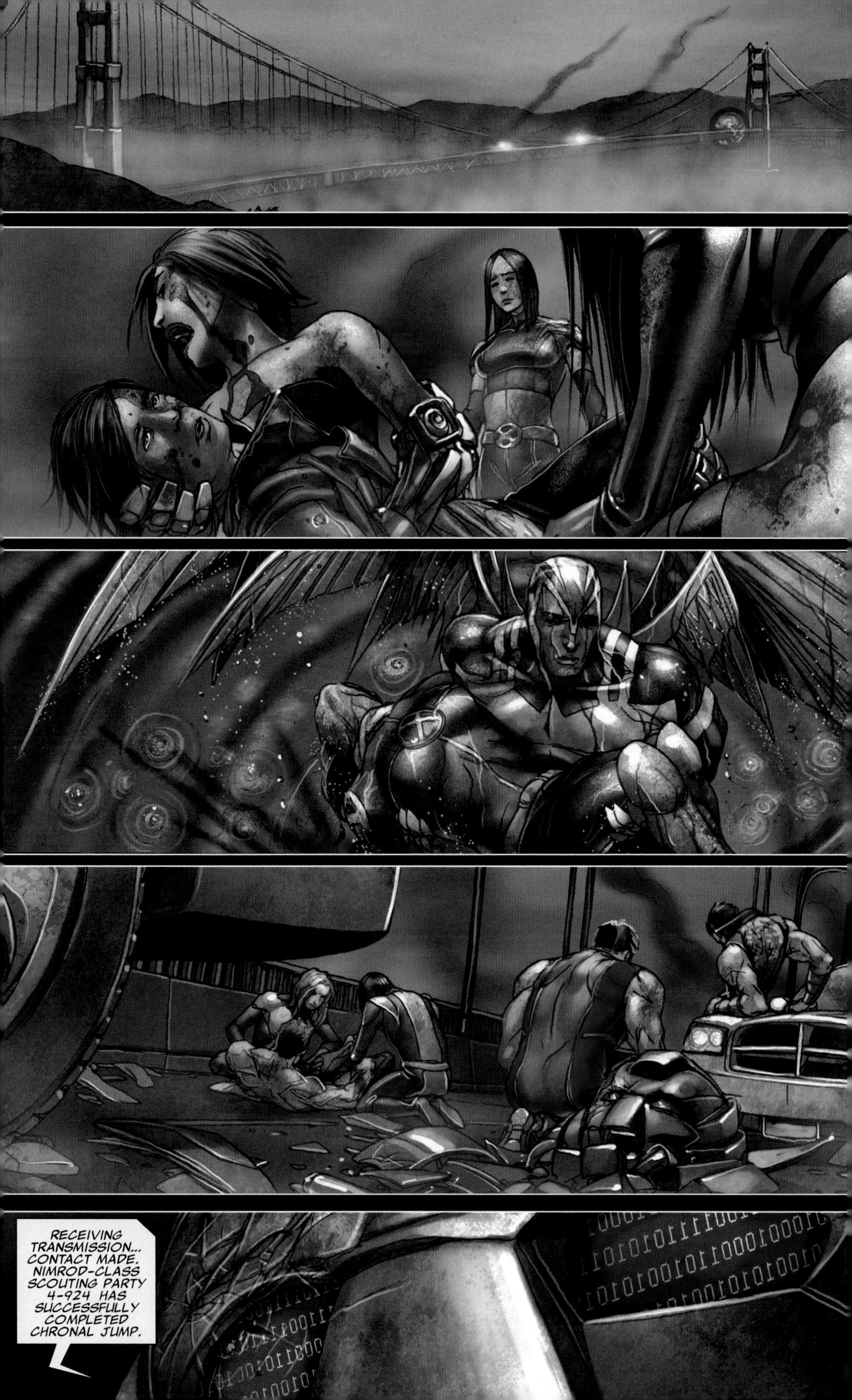
RECEIVING TRANSMISSION... CONTACT MADE. NIMROD-CLASS SCOUTING PARTY 4-924 HAS SUCCESSFULLY COMPLETED CHRONAL JUMP.

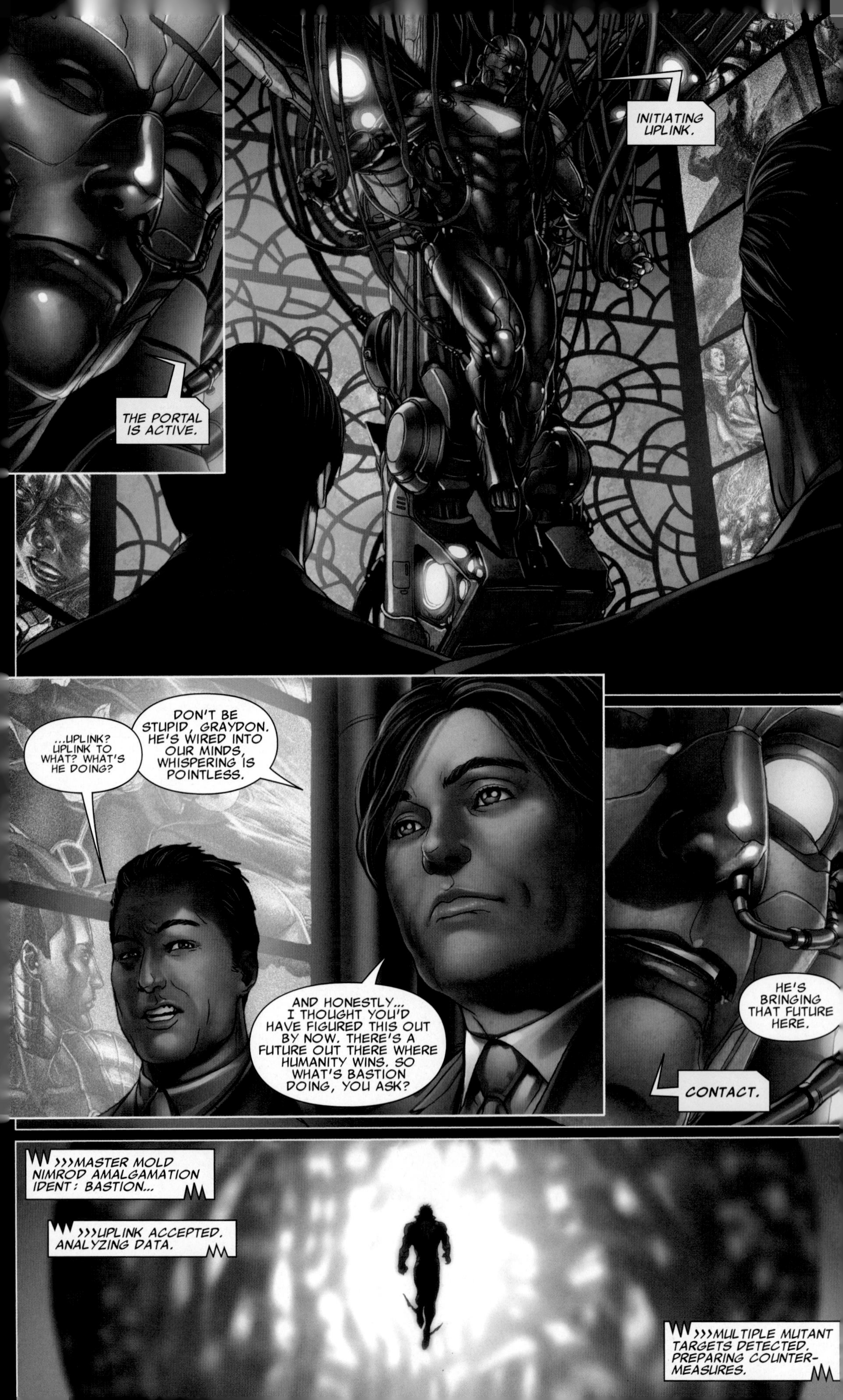
INITIATING UPLINK.
THE PORTAL IS ACTIVE.
...UPLINK? UPLINK TO WHAT? WHAT'S HE DOING?
DON'T BE STUPID, GRAYDON. HE'S WIRED INTO OUR MINDS, WHISPERING IS POINTLESS.
AND HONESTLY... I THOUGHT YOU'D HAVE FIGURED THIS OUT BY NOW. THERE'S A FUTURE OUT THERE WHERE HUMANITY WINS. SO WHAT'S BASTION DOING, YOU ASK?
HE'S BRINGING THAT FUTURE HERE.
CONTACT.
>>>MASTER MOLD NIMROD AMALGAMATION IDENT: BASTION...
>>>UPLINK ACCEPTED. ANALYZING DATA.
>>>MULTIPLE MUTANT TARGETS DETECTED. PREPARING COUNTER-MEASURES.

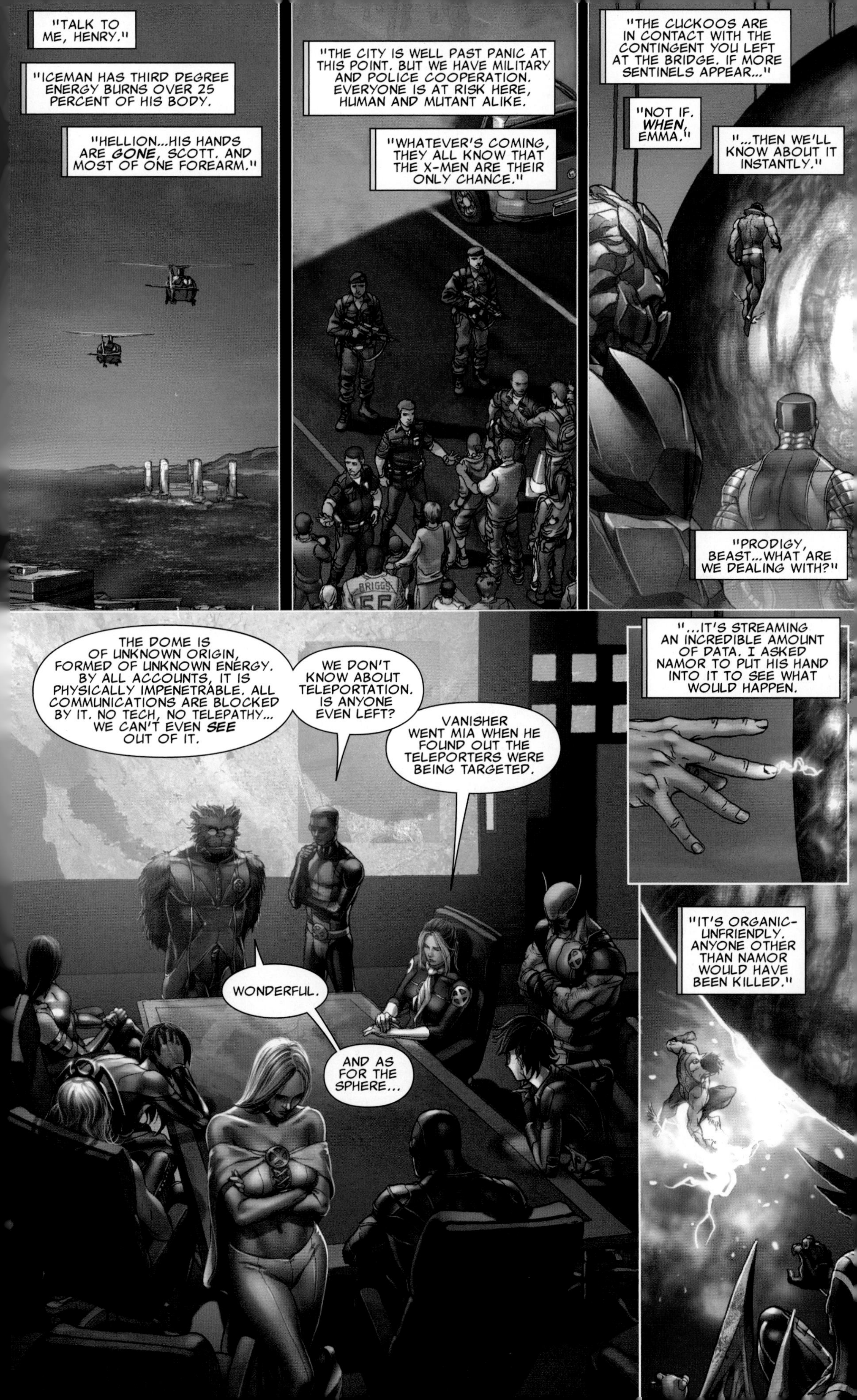
"TALK TO ME, HENRY."
"ICEMAN HAS THIRD DEGREE ENERGY BURNS OVER 25 PERCENT OF HIS BODY.
"HELLION...HIS HANDS ARE GONE, SCOTT. AND MOST OF ONE FOREARM."
"THE CITY IS WELL PAST PANIC AT THIS POINT. BUT WE HAVE MILITARY AND POLICE COOPERATION. EVERYONE IS AT RISK HERE, HUMAN AND MUTANT ALIKE.
"WHATEVER'S COMING, THEY ALL KNOW THAT THE X-MEN ARE THEIR ONLY CHANCE."
BRIGGS 55
"THE CUCKOOS ARE IN CONTACT WITH THE CONTINGENT YOU LEFT AT THE BRIDGE. IF MORE SENTINELS APPEAR..."
"NOT IF. WHEN, EMMA."
"...THEN WE'LL KNOW ABOUT IT INSTANTLY."
"PRODIGY, BEAST...WHAT ARE WE DEALING WITH?"
THE DOME IS OF UNKNOWN ORIGIN, FORMED OF UNKNOWN ENERGY. BY ALL ACCOUNTS, IT IS PHYSICALLY IMPENETRABLE. ALL COMMUNICATIONS ARE BLOCKED BY IT. NO TECH, NO TELEPATHY... WE CAN'T EVEN SEE OUT OF IT.
WE DON'T KNOW ABOUT TELEPORTATION. IS ANYONE EVEN LEFT?
VANISHER WENT MIA WHEN HE FOUND OUT THE TELEPORTERS WERE BEING TARGETED.
WONDERFUL.
AND AS FOR THE SPHERE...
"...IT'S STREAMING AN INCREDIBLE AMOUNT OF DATA. I ASKED NAMOR TO PUT HIS HAND INTO IT TO SEE WHAT WOULD HAPPEN.
"IT'S ORGANIC-UNFRIENDLY. ANYONE OTHER THAN NAMOR WOULD HAVE BEEN KILLED."

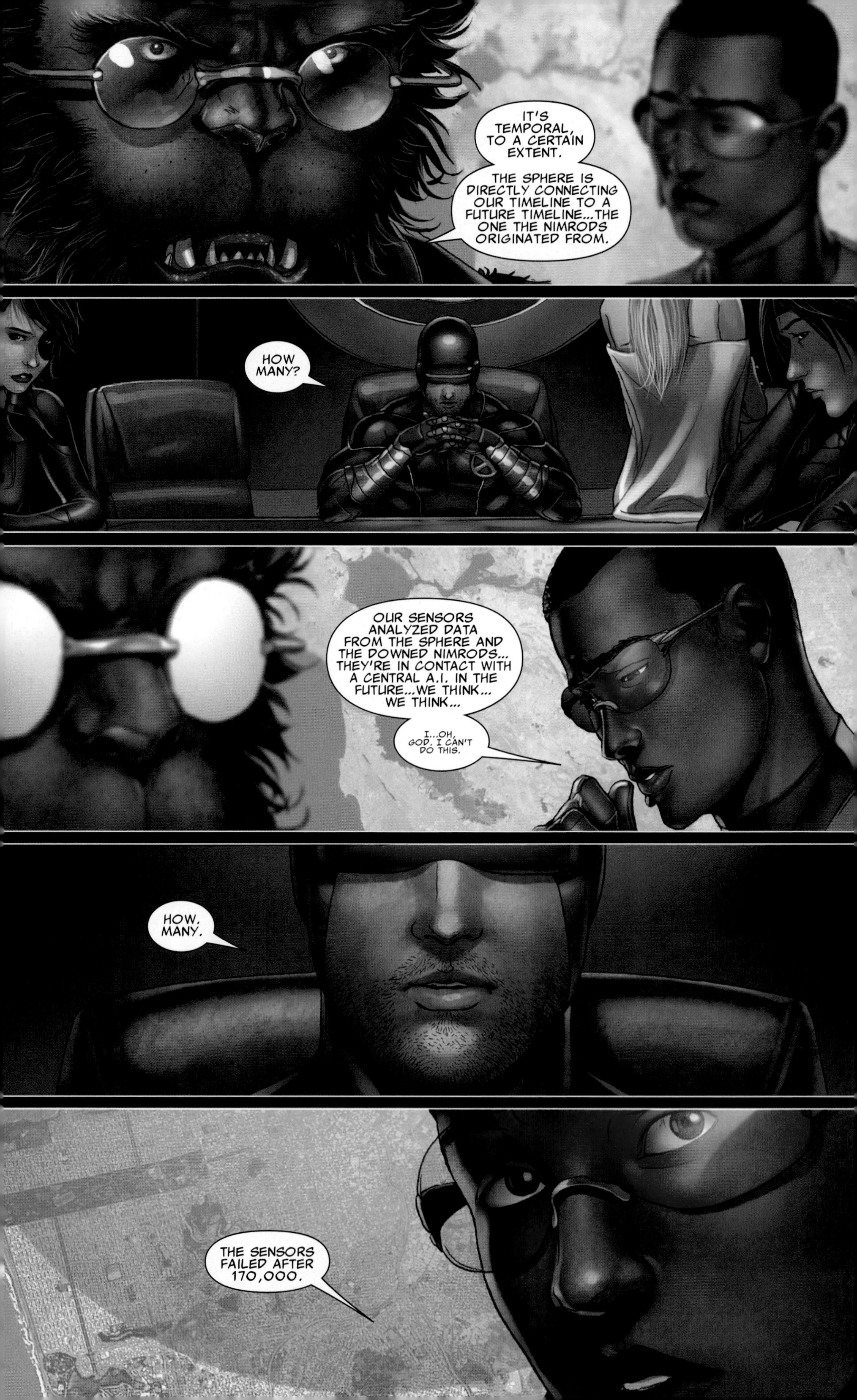
IT'S TEMPORAL, TO A CERTAIN EXTENT.
THE SPHERE IS DIRECTLY CONNECTING OUR TIMELINE TO A FUTURE TIMELINE...THE ONE THE NIMRODS ORIGINATED FROM.
HOW MANY?
OUR SENSORS ANALYZED DATA FROM THE SPHERE AND THE DOWNED NIMRODS... THEY'RE IN CONTACT WITH A CENTRAL A.I. IN THE FUTURE...WE THINK... WE THINK...
I...OH, GOD. I CAN'T DO THIS.
HOW. MANY.
THE SENSORS FAILED AFTER 170,000.

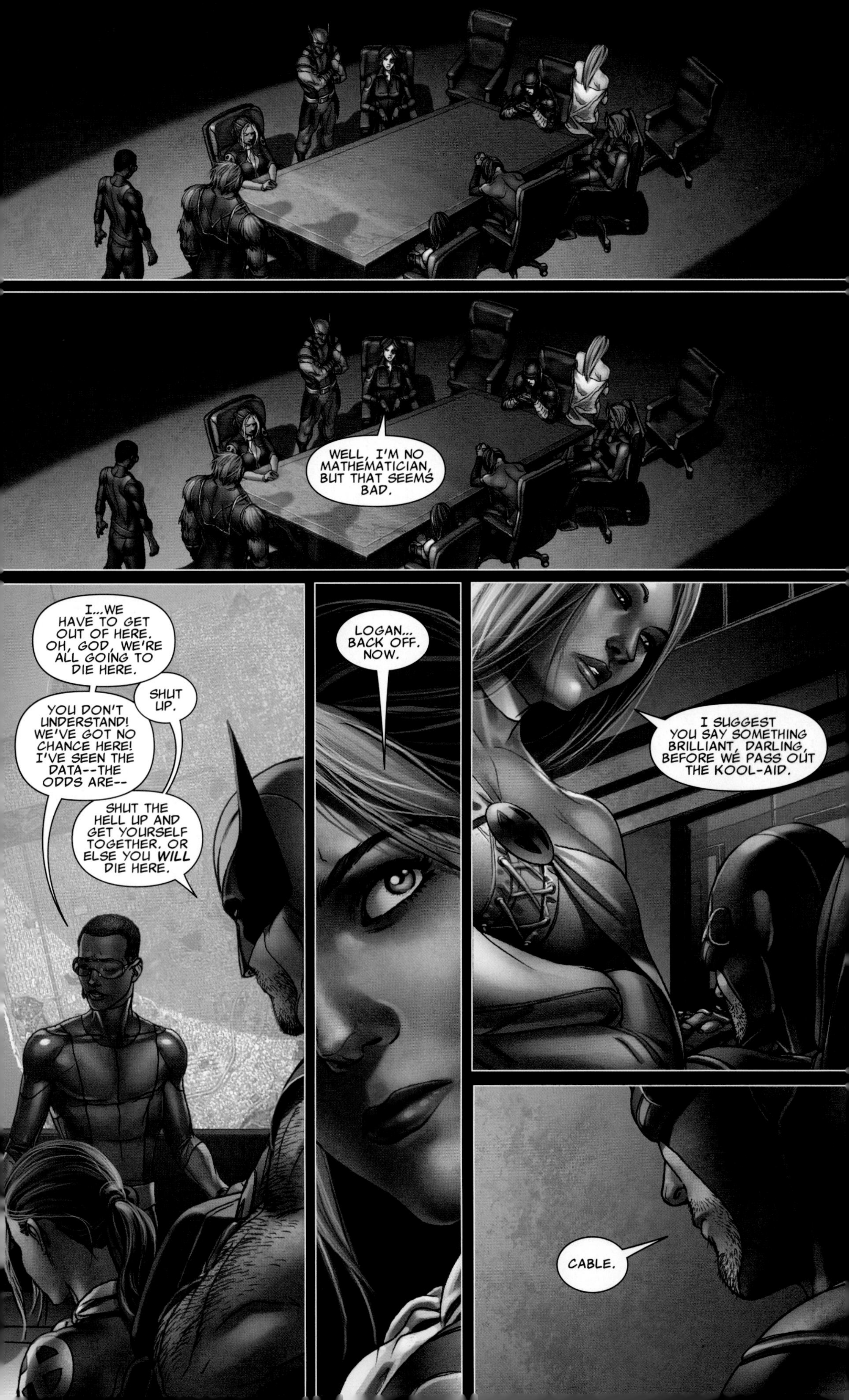
WELL, I'M NO MATHEMATICIAN, BUT THAT SEEMS BAD.
I...WE HAVE TO GET OUT OF HERE. OH, GOD, WE'RE ALL GOING TO DIE HERE.
SHUT UP.
YOU DON'T UNDERSTAND! WE'VE GOT NO CHANCE HERE! I'VE SEEN THE DATA--THE ODDS ARE--
SHUT THE HELL UP AND GET YOURSELF TOGETHER. OR ELSE YOU WILL DIE HERE.
LOGAN... BACK OFF. NOW.
I SUGGEST YOU SAY SOMETHING BRILLIANT, DARLING, BEFORE WE PASS OUT THE KOOL-AID.
CABLE.

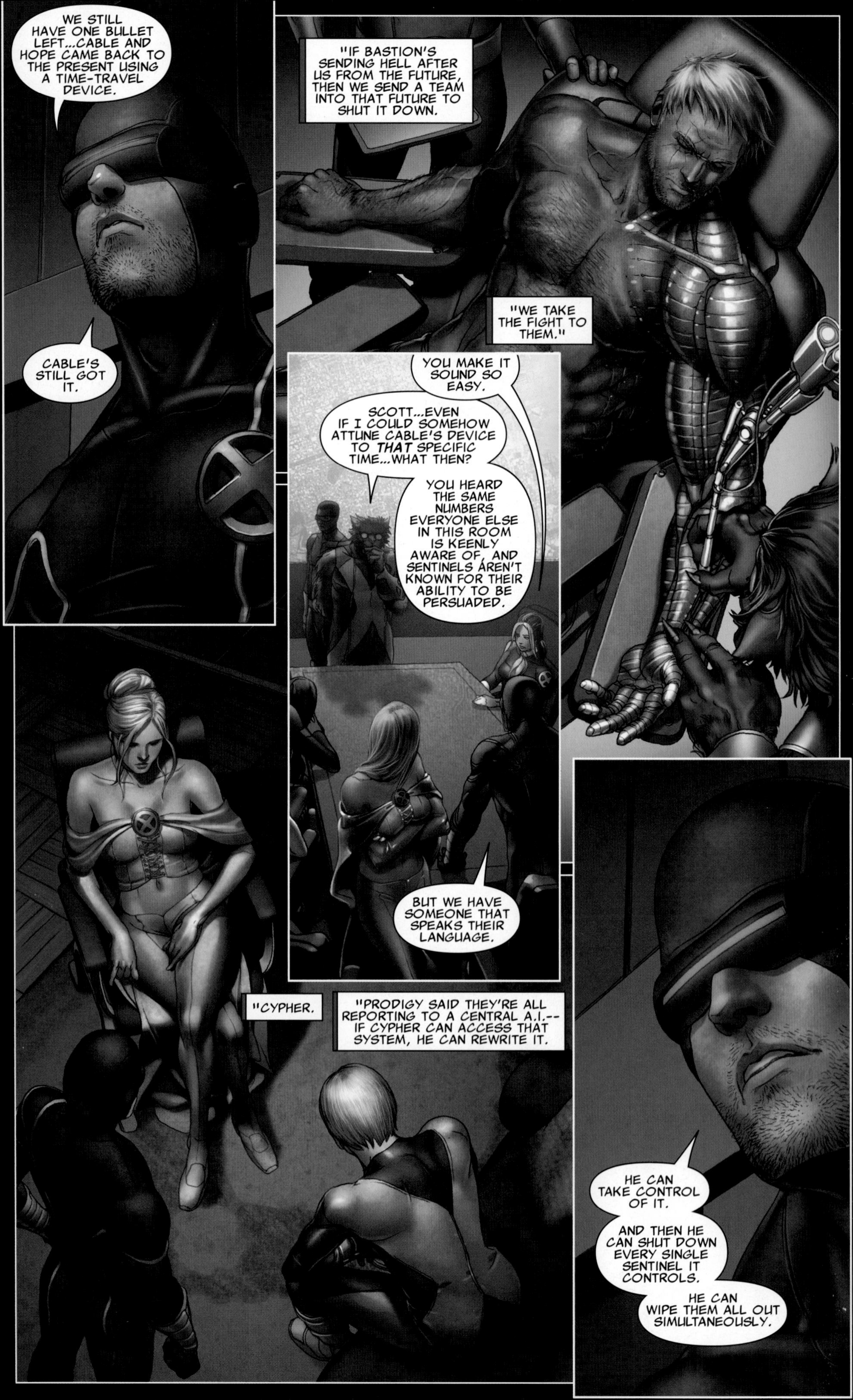
WE STILL HAVE ONE BULLET LEFT...CABLE AND HOPE CAME BACK TO THE PRESENT USING A TIME-TRAVEL DEVICE.
CABLE'S STILL GOT IT.
"IF BASTION'S SENDING HELL AFTER US FROM THE FUTURE, THEN WE SEND A TEAM INTO THAT FUTURE TO SHUT IT DOWN.
"WE TAKE THE FIGHT TO THEM."
YOU MAKE IT SOUND SO EASY.
SCOTT...EVEN IF I COULD SOMEHOW ATTUNE CABLE'S DEVICE TO *THAT* SPECIFIC TIME...WHAT THEN?
YOU HEARD THE SAME NUMBERS EVERYONE ELSE IN THIS ROOM IS KEENLY AWARE OF, AND SENTINELS AREN'T KNOWN FOR THEIR ABILITY TO BE PERSUADED.
BUT WE HAVE SOMEONE THAT SPEAKS THEIR LANGUAGE.
"CYPHER.
"PRODIGY SAID THEY'RE ALL REPORTING TO A CENTRAL A.I.--IF CYPHER CAN ACCESS THAT SYSTEM, HE CAN REWRITE IT.
HE CAN TAKE CONTROL OF IT.
AND THEN HE CAN SHUT DOWN EVERY SINGLE SENTINEL IT CONTROLS.
HE CAN WIPE THEM ALL OUT SIMULTANEOUSLY.

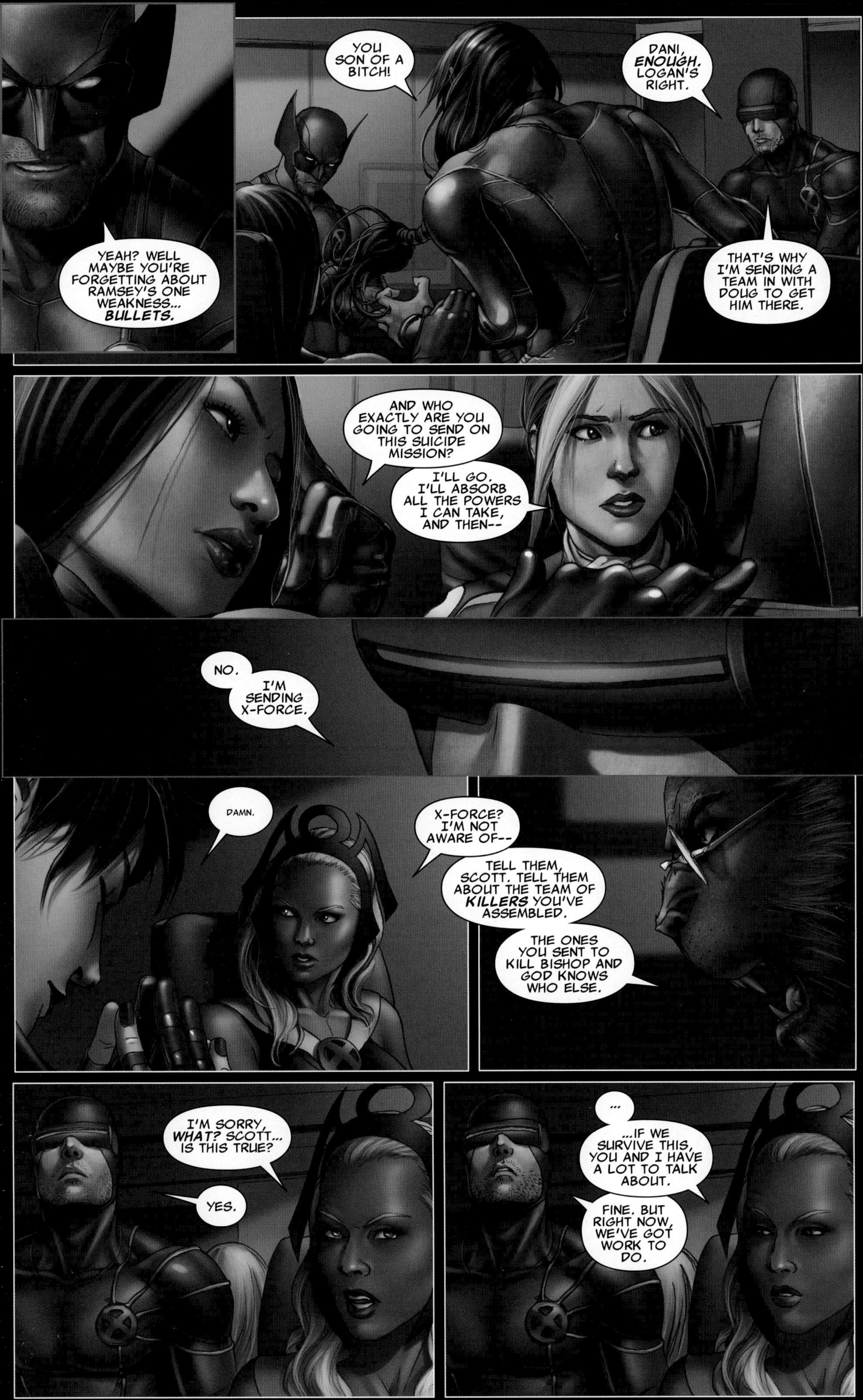
YEAH? WELL MAYBE YOU'RE FORGETTING ABOUT RAMSEY'S ONE WEAKNESS... BULLETS.
YOU SON OF A BITCH!
DANI, ENOUGH. LOGAN'S RIGHT.
THAT'S WHY I'M SENDING A TEAM IN WITH DOUG TO GET HIM THERE.
AND WHO EXACTLY ARE YOU GOING TO SEND ON THIS SUICIDE MISSION?
I'LL GO. I'LL ABSORB ALL THE POWERS I CAN TAKE, AND THEN--
NO.
I'M SENDING X-FORCE.
DAMN.
X-FORCE? I'M NOT AWARE OF--
TELL THEM, SCOTT. TELL THEM ABOUT THE TEAM OF KILLERS YOU'VE ASSEMBLED.
THE ONES YOU SENT TO KILL BISHOP AND GOD KNOWS WHO ELSE.
I'M SORRY, WHAT? SCOTT... IS THIS TRUE?
YES.
...
...IF WE SURVIVE THIS, YOU AND I HAVE A LOT TO TALK ABOUT.
FINE. BUT RIGHT NOW, WE'VE GOT WORK TO DO.

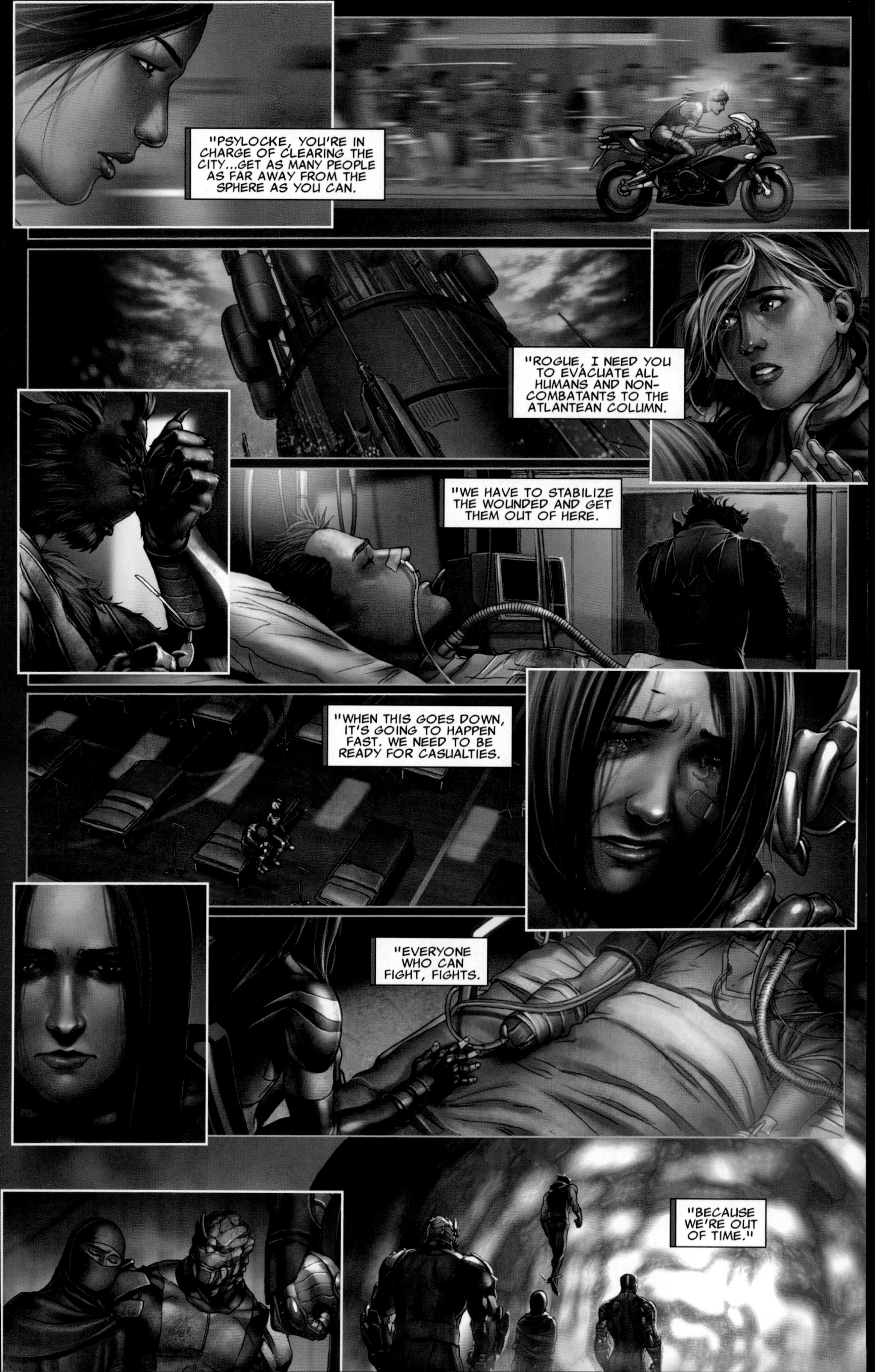
"PSYLOCKE, YOU'RE IN CHARGE OF CLEARING THE CITY...GET AS MANY PEOPLE AS FAR AWAY FROM THE SPHERE AS YOU CAN.
"ROGUE, I NEED YOU TO EVACUATE ALL HUMANS AND NON-COMBATANTS TO THE ATLANTEAN COLUMN.
"WE HAVE TO STABILIZE THE WOUNDED AND GET THEM OUT OF HERE.
"WHEN THIS GOES DOWN, IT'S GOING TO HAPPEN FAST. WE NEED TO BE READY FOR CASUALTIES.
"EVERYONE WHO CAN FIGHT, FIGHTS.
"BECAUSE WE'RE OUT OF TIME."

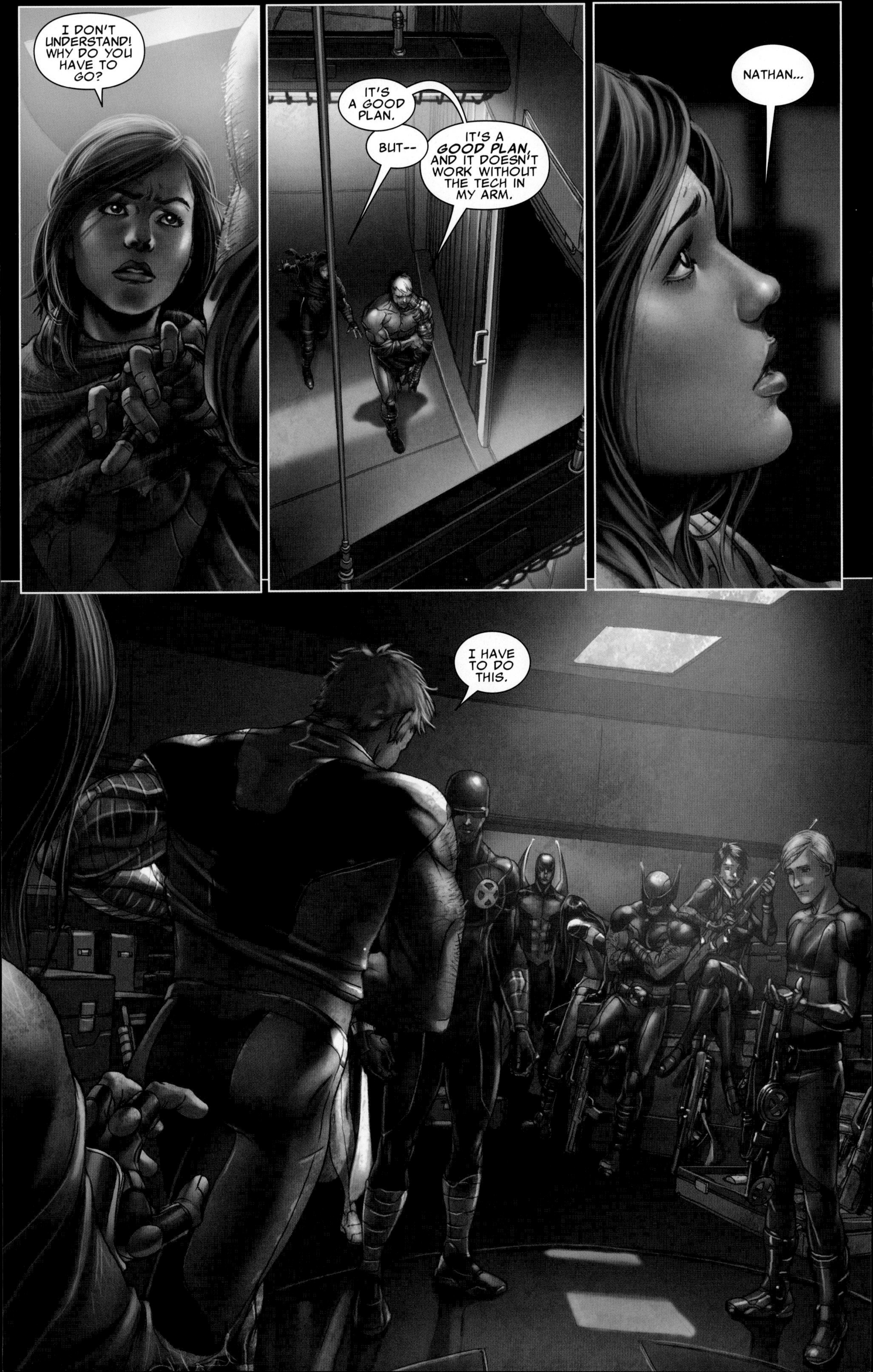
I DON'T UNDERSTAND! WHY DO YOU HAVE TO GO?
IT'S A GOOD PLAN.
BUT--
IT'S A GOOD PLAN, AND IT DOESN'T WORK WITHOUT THE TECH IN MY ARM.
NATHAN...
I HAVE TO DO THIS.

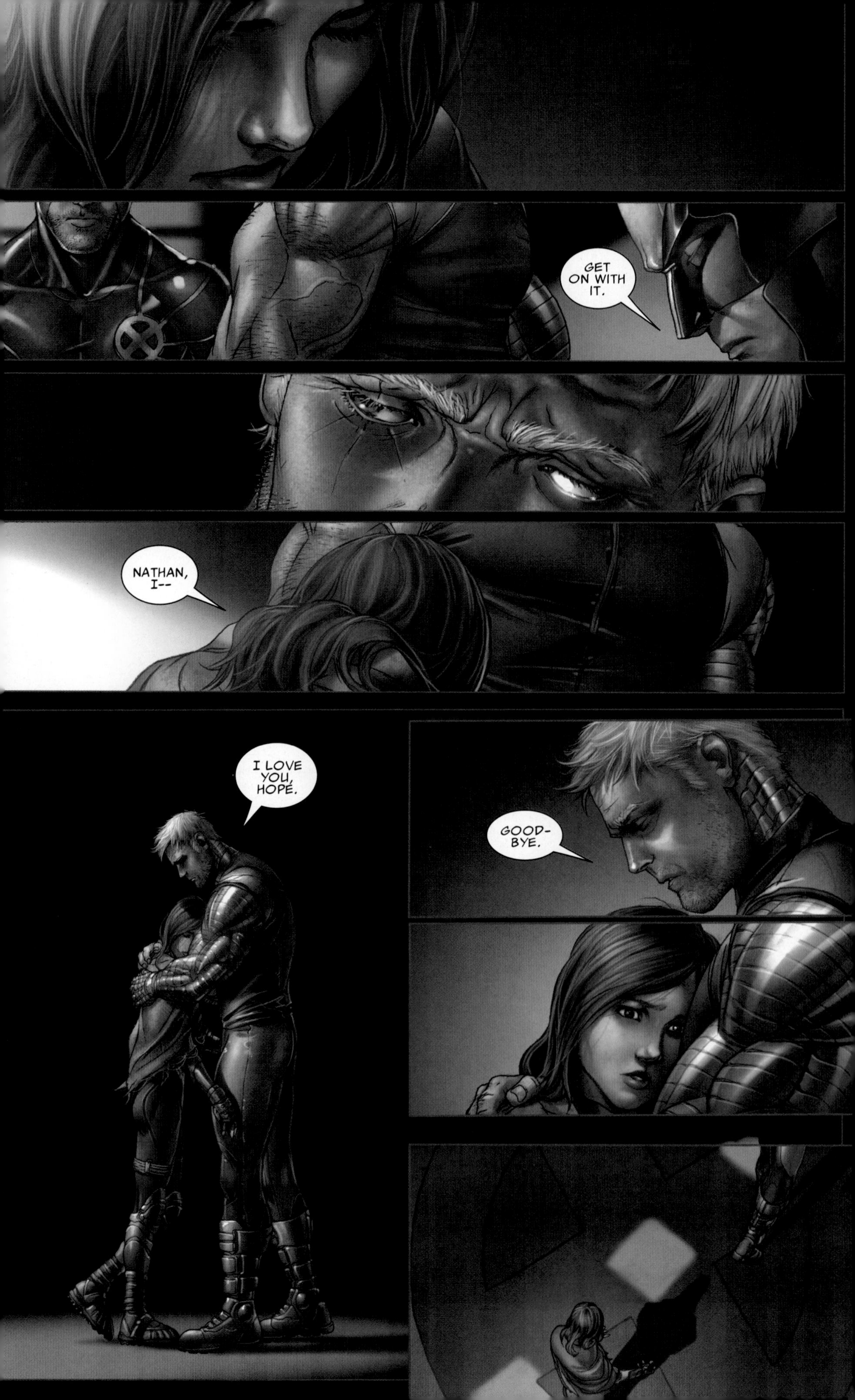
GET ON WITH IT.
NATHAN, I--
I LOVE YOU, HOPE.
GOOD-BYE.

CYCLOPS...

...IT'S HAPPENING.

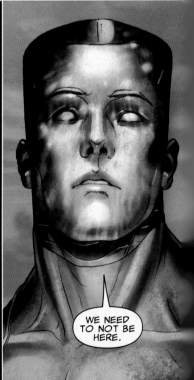

WE NEED TO NOT BE HERE.

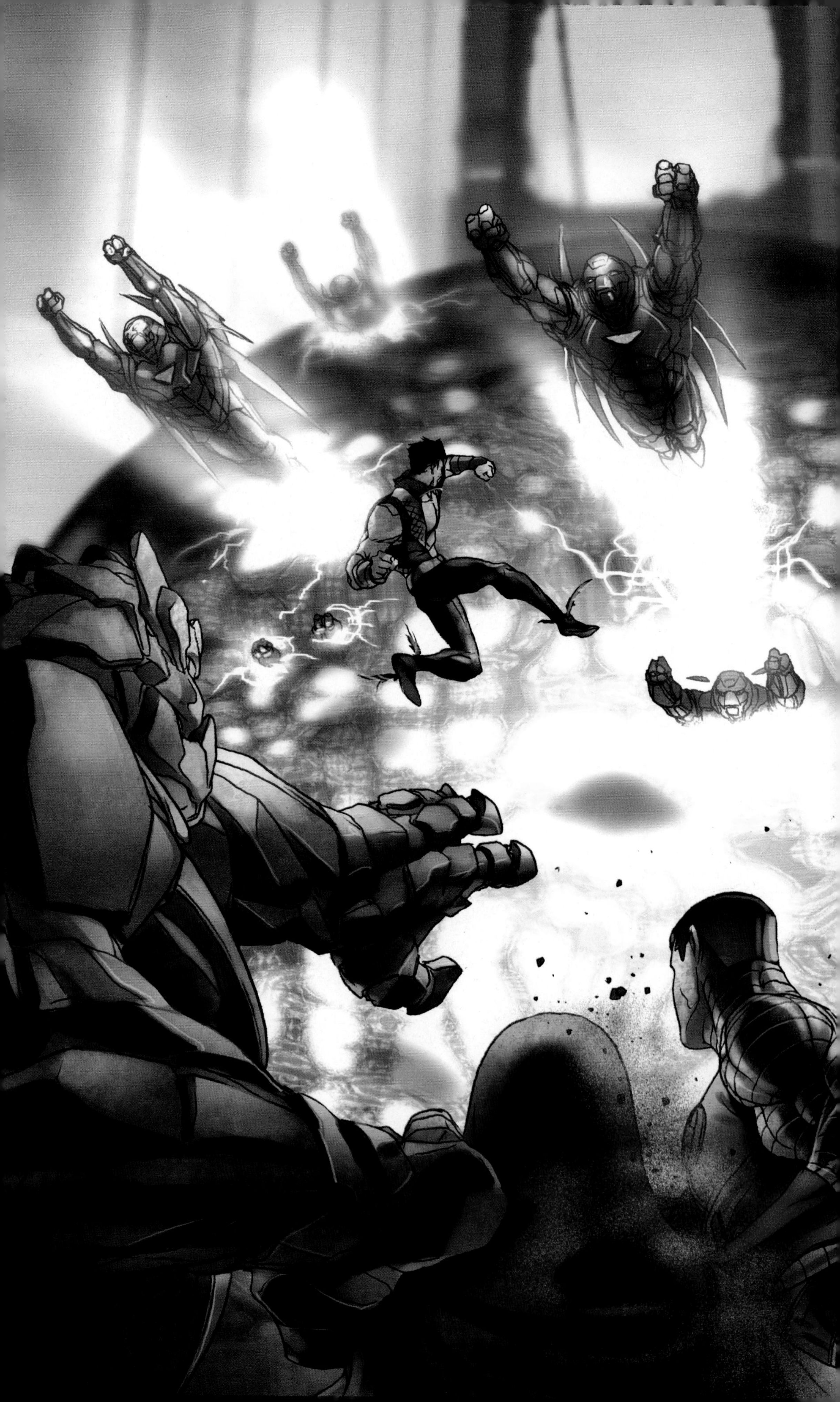

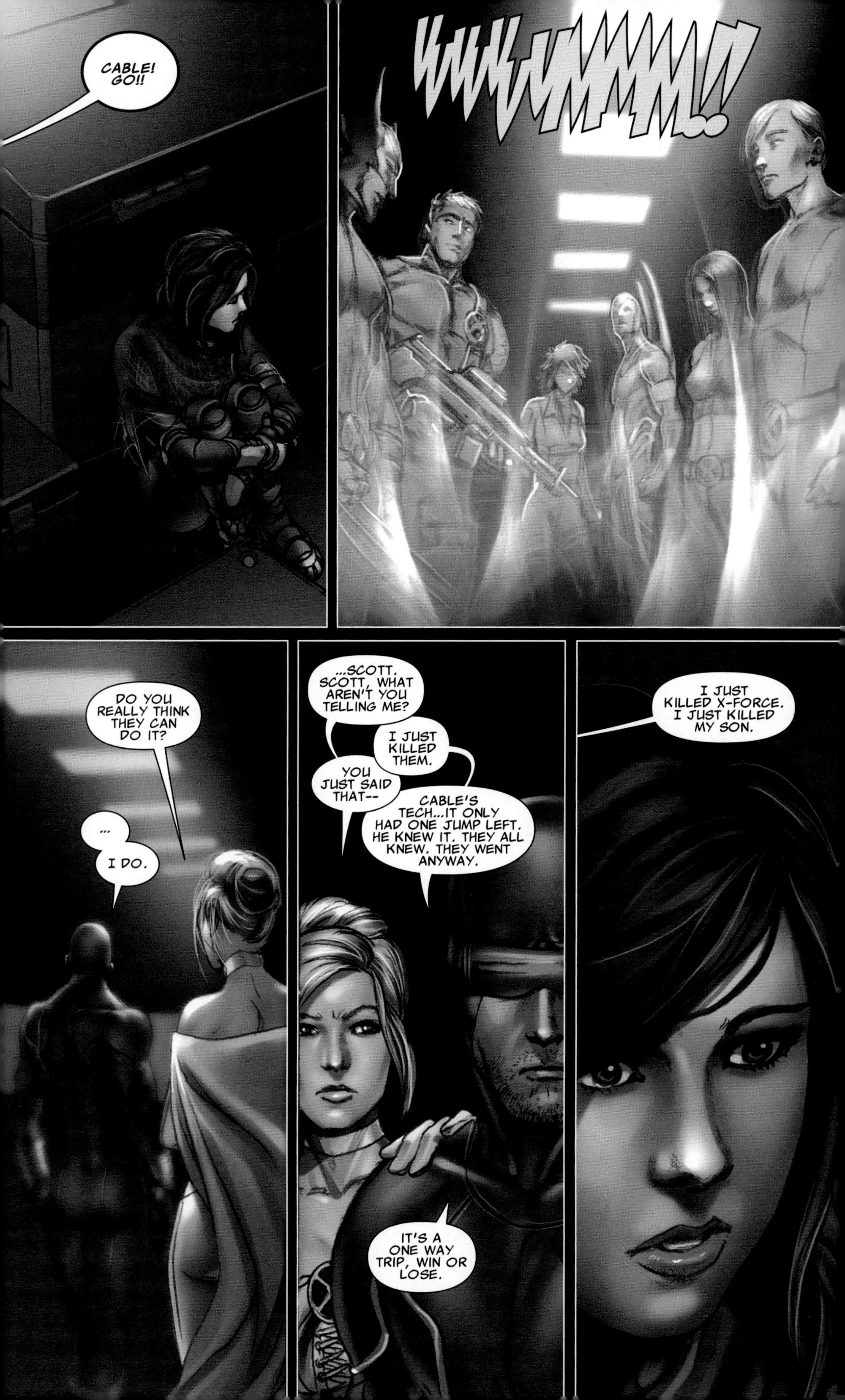
CABLE! GO!!
VVVVK-VMMM!!
DO YOU REALLY THINK THEY CAN DO IT?
...
I DO.
...SCOTT. SCOTT, WHAT AREN'T YOU TELLING ME?
I JUST KILLED THEM.
YOU JUST SAID THAT--
CABLE'S TECH...IT ONLY HAD ONE JUMP LEFT. HE KNEW IT. THEY ALL KNEW. THEY WENT ANYWAY.
IT'S A ONE WAY TRIP, WIN OR LOSE.
I JUST KILLED X-FORCE. I JUST KILLED MY SON.

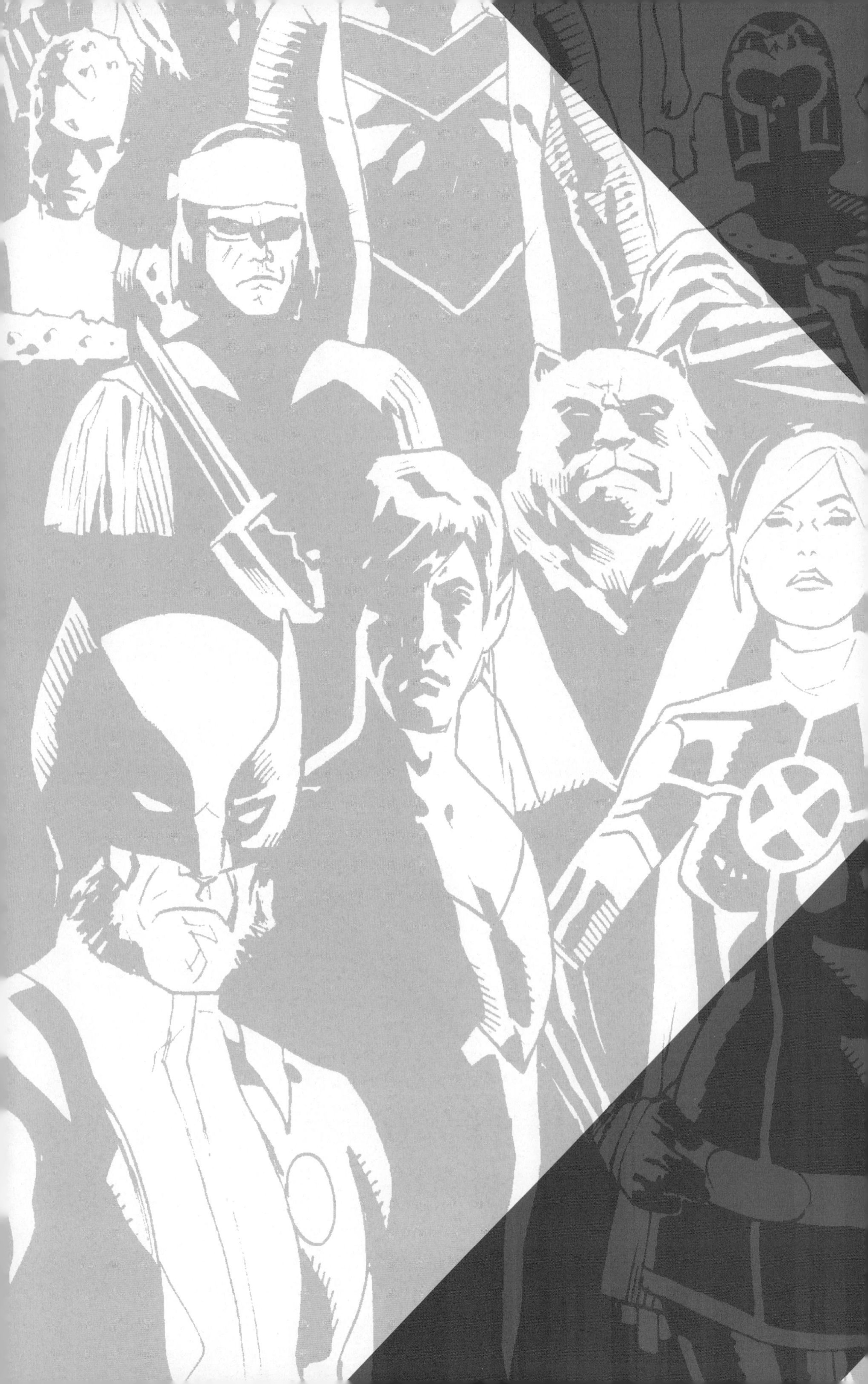

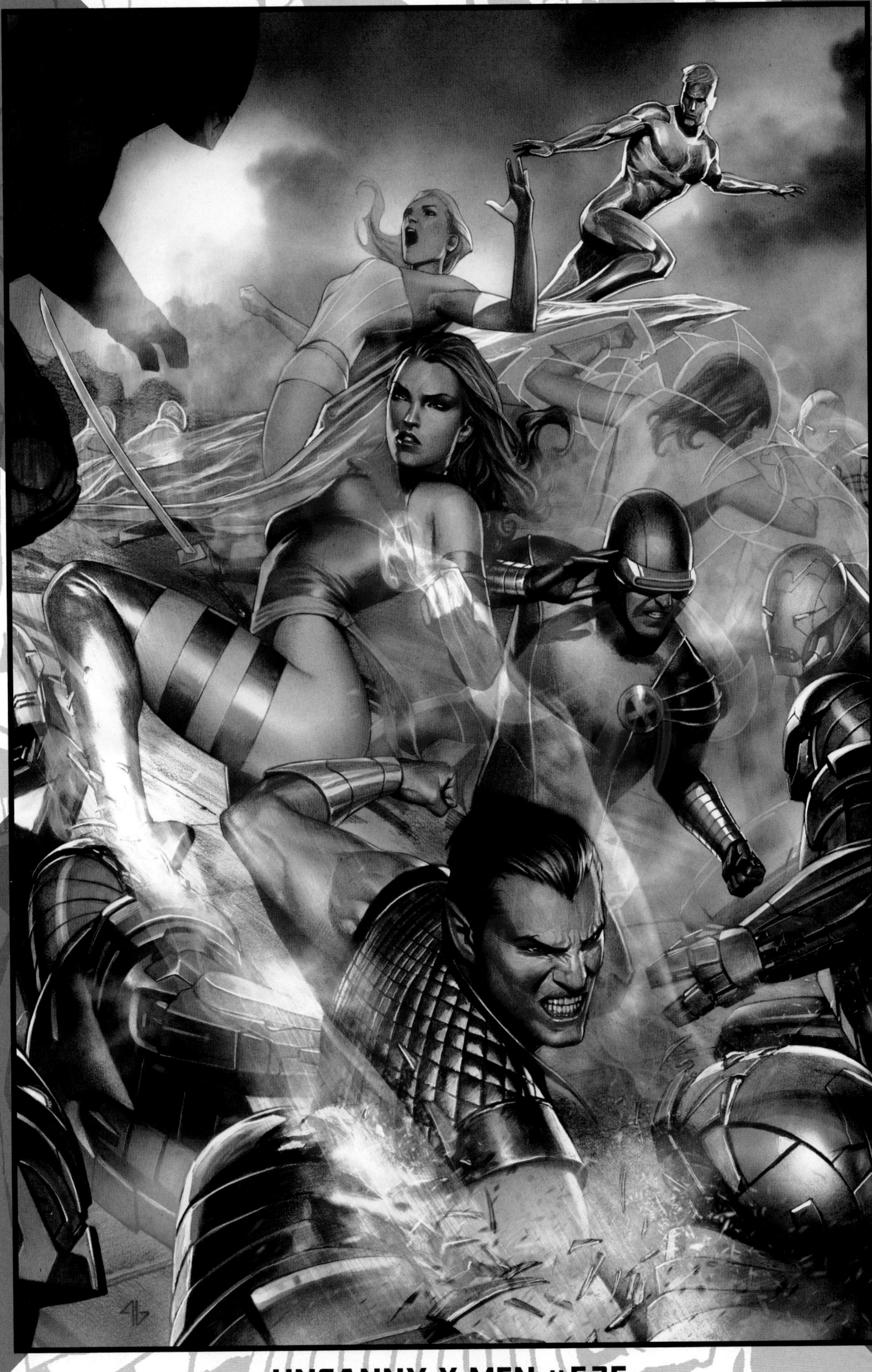

UNCANNY X-MEN #525

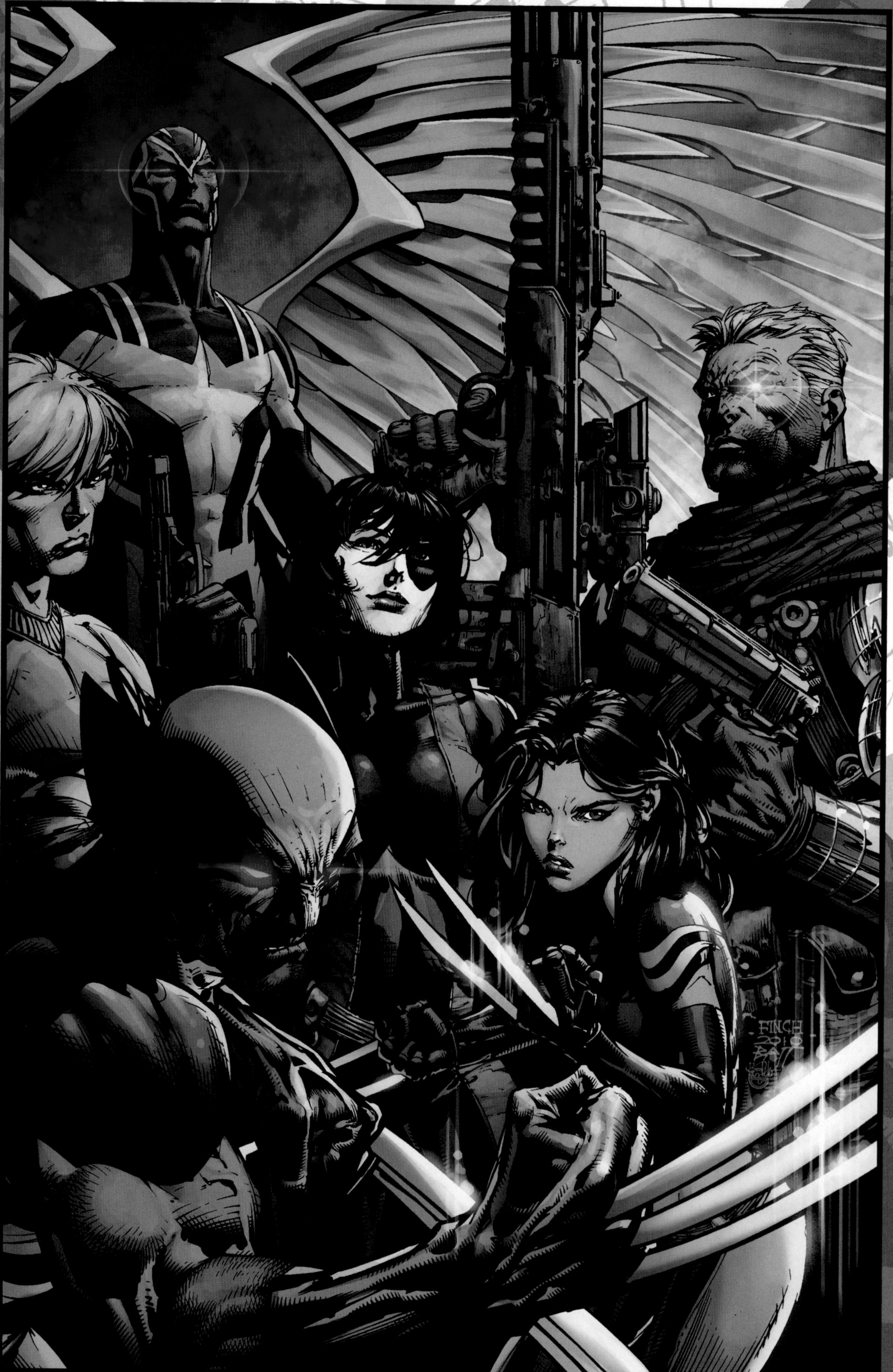
FINCH
2010

UNCANNY X-MEN #525
VARIANT

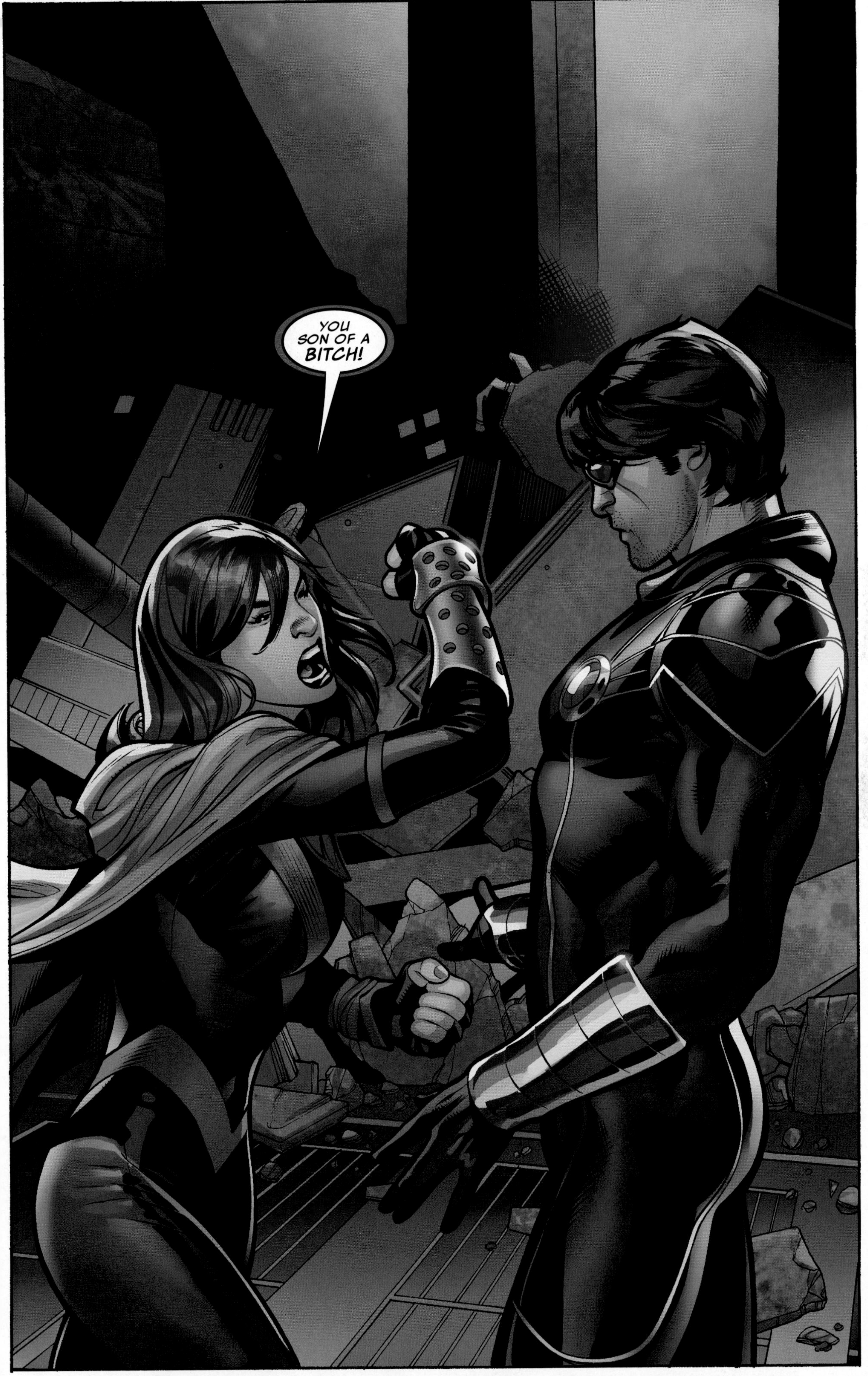
YOU SON OF A BITCH!

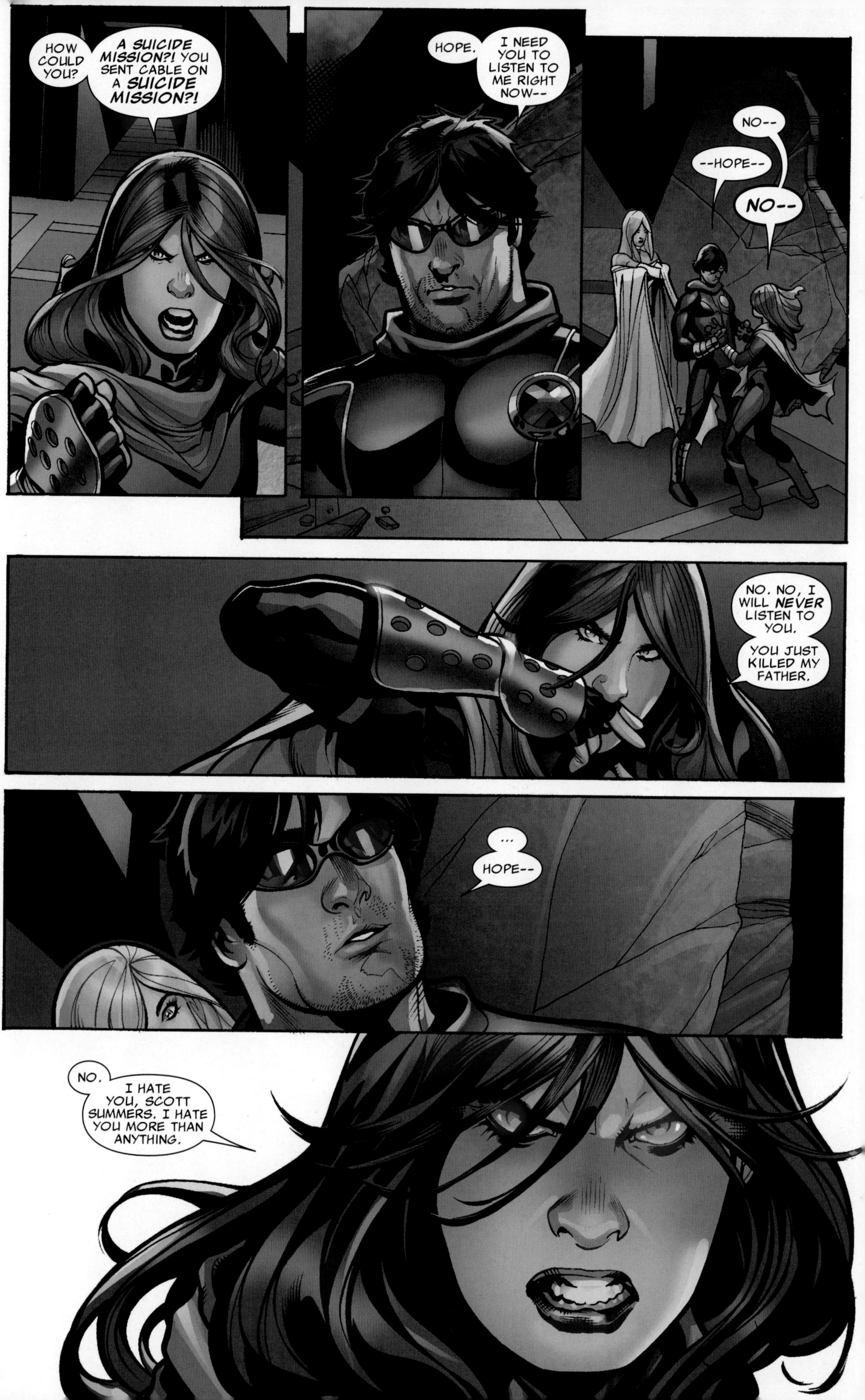
HOW COULD YOU?
A SUICIDE MISSION?! YOU SENT CABLE ON A SUICIDE MISSION?!
HOPE.
I NEED YOU TO LISTEN TO ME RIGHT NOW--
NO--
--HOPE--
NO--
NO. NO, I WILL NEVER LISTEN TO YOU.
YOU JUST KILLED MY FATHER.
...
HOPE--
NO.
I HATE YOU, SCOTT SUMMERS. I HATE YOU MORE THAN ANYTHING.

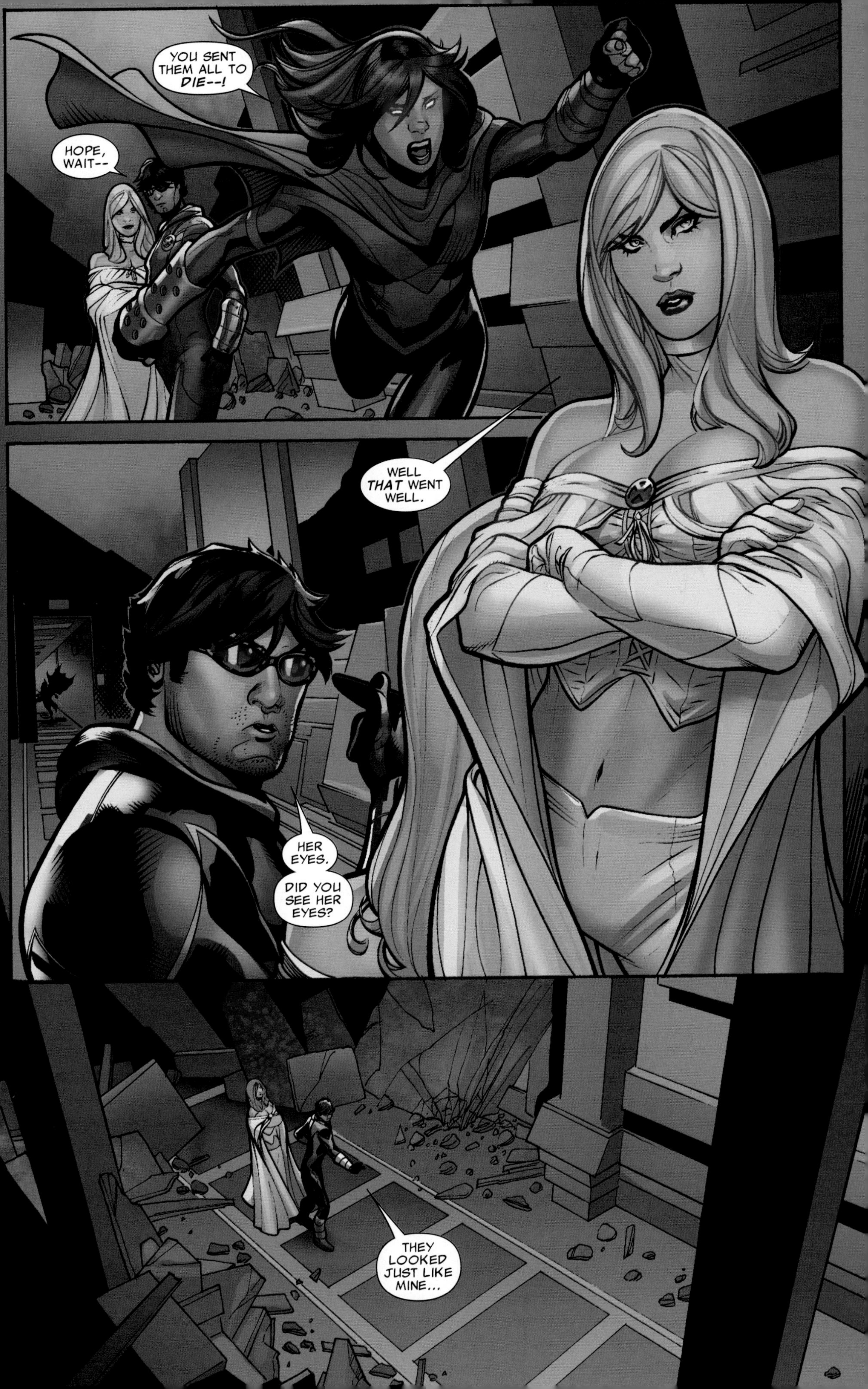
YOU SENT THEM ALL TO DIE--!
HOPE, WAIT--
WELL THAT WENT WELL.
HER EYES.
DID YOU SEE HER EYES?
THEY LOOKED JUST LIKE MINE...

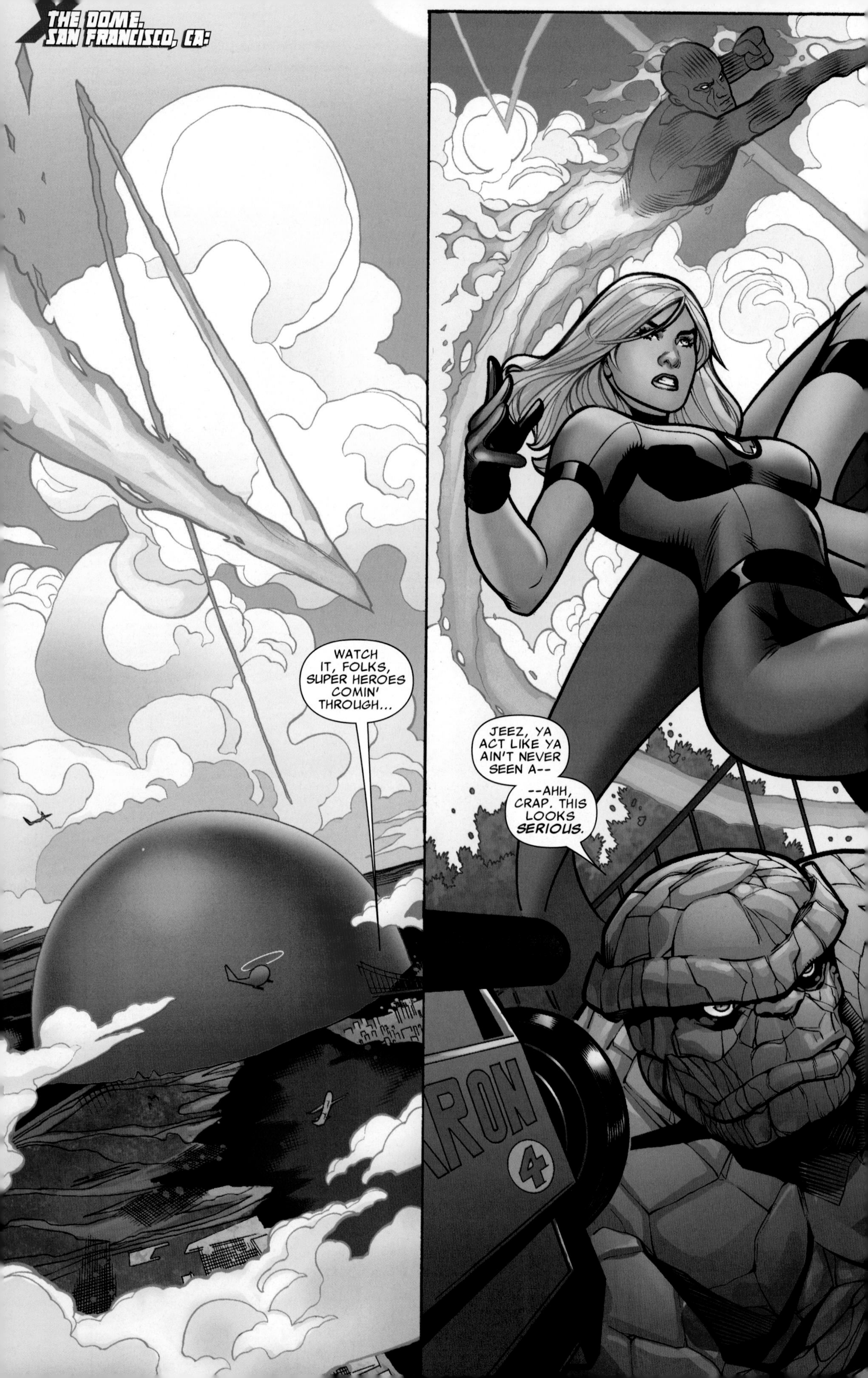
THE DOME. SAN FRANCISCO, CA:
WATCH IT, FOLKS, SUPER HEROES COMIN' THROUGH...
JEEZ, YA ACT LIKE YA AIN'T NEVER SEEN A--
--AHH, CRAP. THIS LOOKS SERIOUS.
RON
4

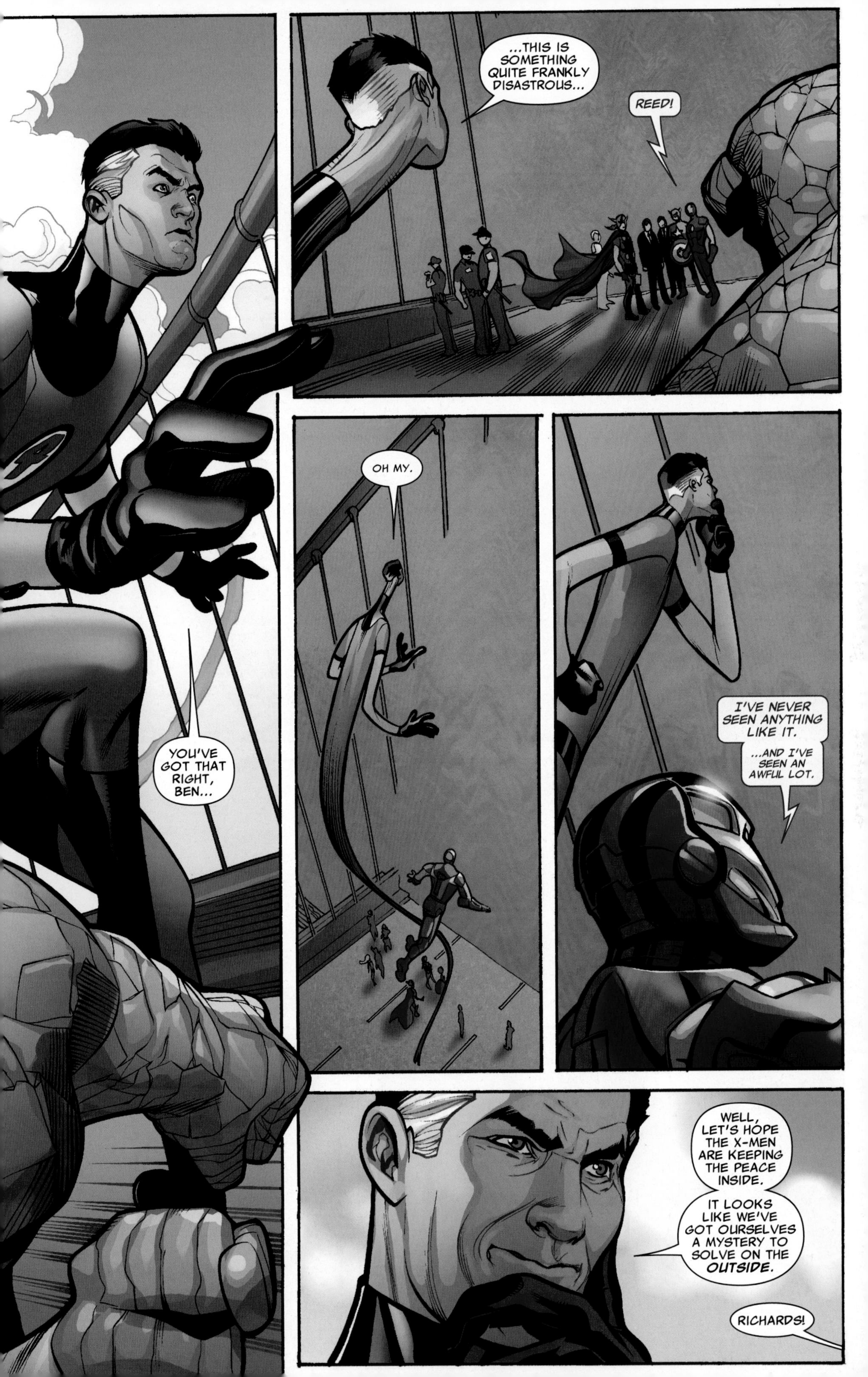
YOU'VE GOT THAT RIGHT, BEN...
...THIS IS SOMETHING QUITE FRANKLY DISASTROUS...
REED!
OH MY.
I'VE NEVER SEEN ANYTHING LIKE IT.
...AND I'VE SEEN AN AWFUL LOT.
WELL, LET'S HOPE THE X-MEN ARE KEEPING THE PEACE INSIDE.
IT LOOKS LIKE WE'VE GOT OURSELVES A MYSTERY TO SOLVE ON THE OUTSIDE.
RICHARDS!

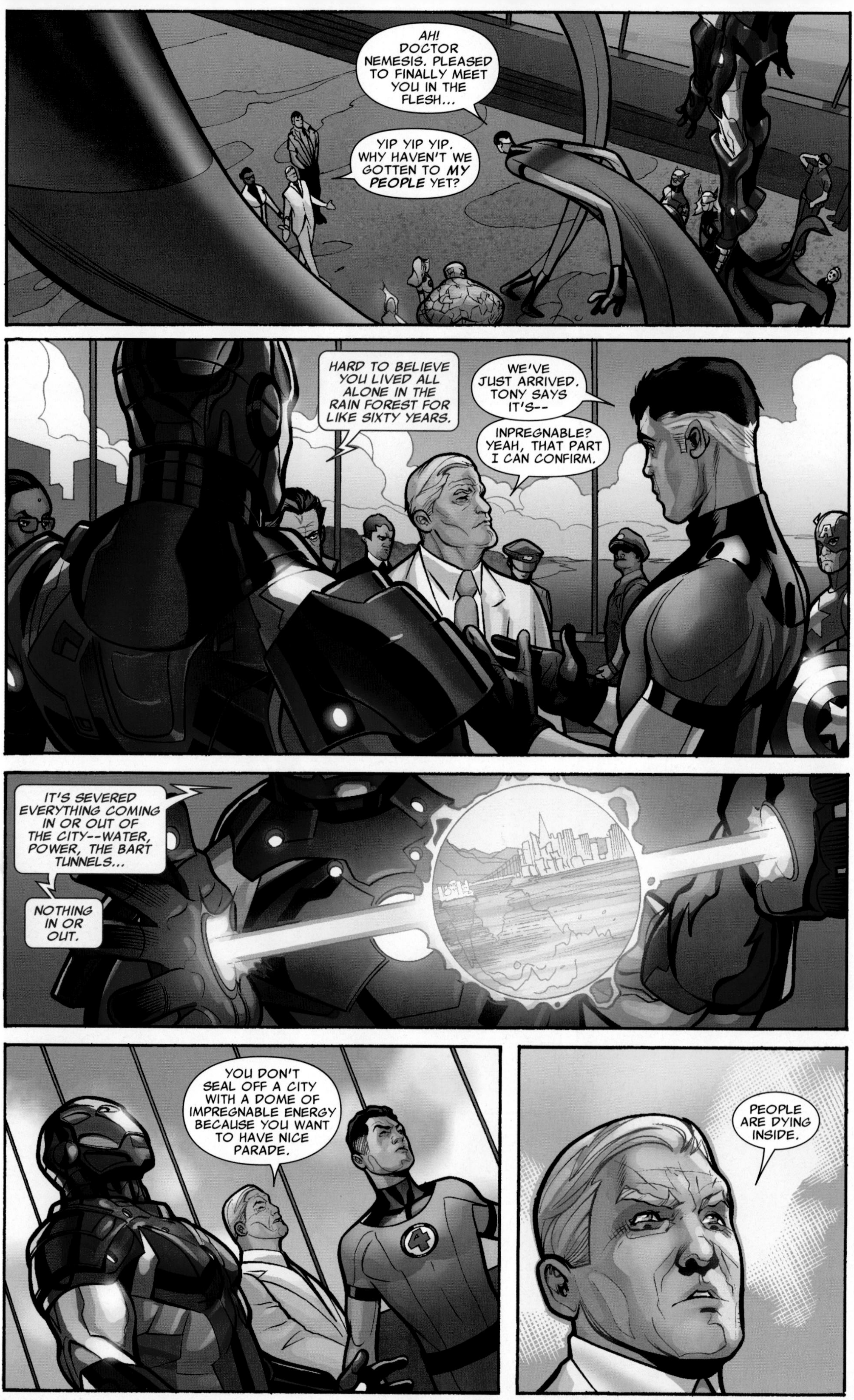

AH! DOCTOR NEMESIS. PLEASED TO FINALLY MEET YOU IN THE FLESH...
YIP YIP YIP. WHY HAVEN'T WE GOTTEN TO MY PEOPLE YET?
HARD TO BELIEVE YOU LIVED ALL ALONE IN THE RAIN FOREST FOR LIKE SIXTY YEARS.
WE'VE JUST ARRIVED. TONY SAYS IT'S--
INPREGNABLE? YEAH, THAT PART I CAN CONFIRM.
IT'S SEVERED EVERYTHING COMING IN OR OUT OF THE CITY--WATER, POWER, THE BART TUNNELS...
NOTHING IN OR OUT.
YOU DON'T SEAL OFF A CITY WITH A DOME OF IMPREGNABLE ENERGY BECAUSE YOU WANT TO HAVE NICE PARADE.
PEOPLE ARE DYING INSIDE.

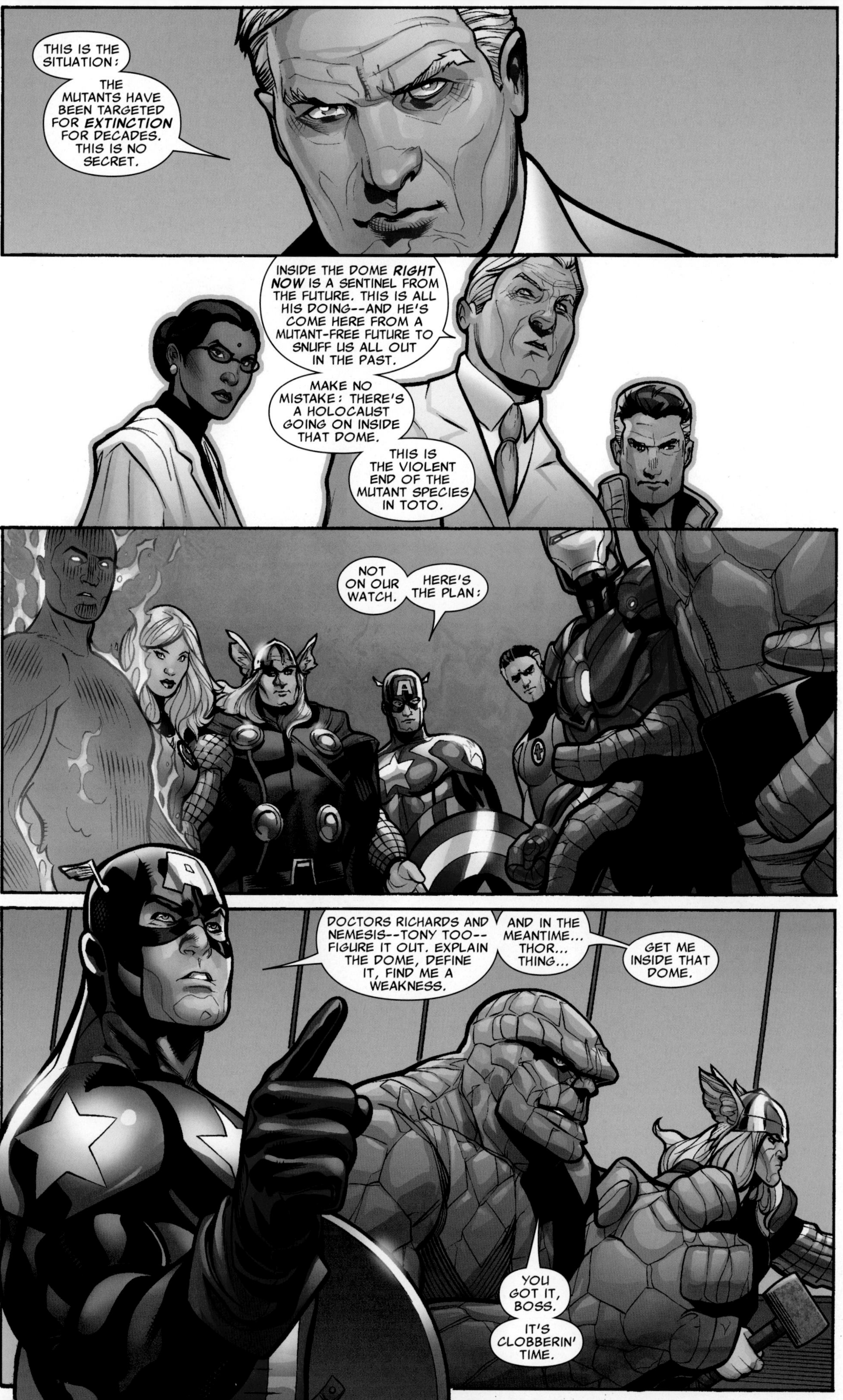
THIS IS THE SITUATION:
THE MUTANTS HAVE BEEN TARGETED FOR **EXTINCTION** FOR DECADES. THIS IS NO SECRET.
INSIDE THE DOME **RIGHT NOW** IS A SENTINEL FROM THE FUTURE. THIS IS ALL HIS DOING--AND HE'S COME HERE FROM A MUTANT-FREE FUTURE TO SNUFF US ALL OUT IN THE PAST.
MAKE NO MISTAKE: THERE'S A HOLOCAUST GOING ON INSIDE THAT DOME.
THIS IS THE VIOLENT END OF THE MUTANT SPECIES IN TOTO.
NOT ON OUR WATCH.
HERE'S THE PLAN:
DOCTORS RICHARDS AND NEMESIS--TONY TOO--FIGURE IT OUT. EXPLAIN THE DOME, DEFINE IT, FIND ME A WEAKNESS.
AND IN THE MEANTIME... THOR... THING...
GET ME INSIDE THAT DOME.
YOU GOT IT, BOSS.
IT'S CLOBBERIN' TIME.

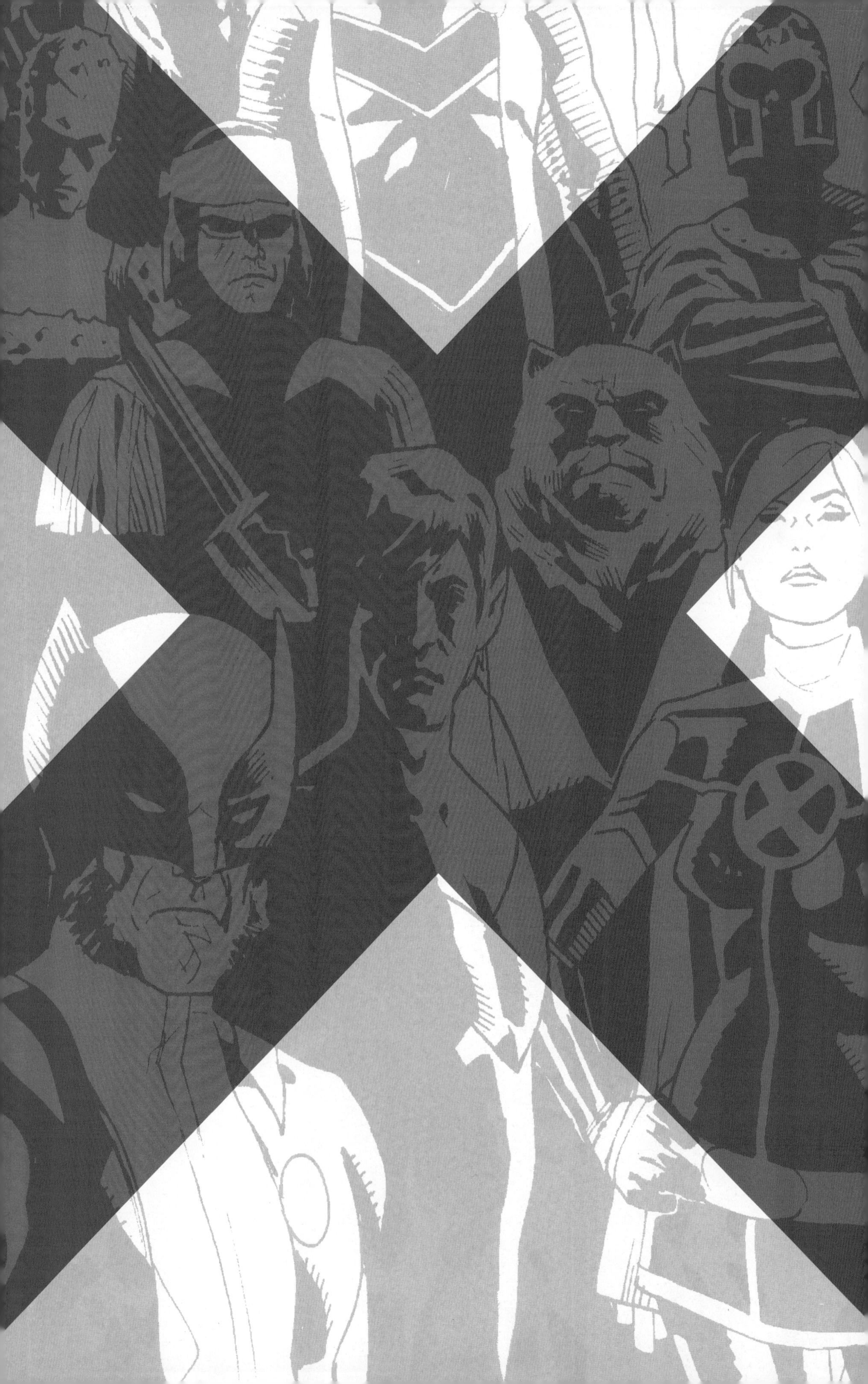

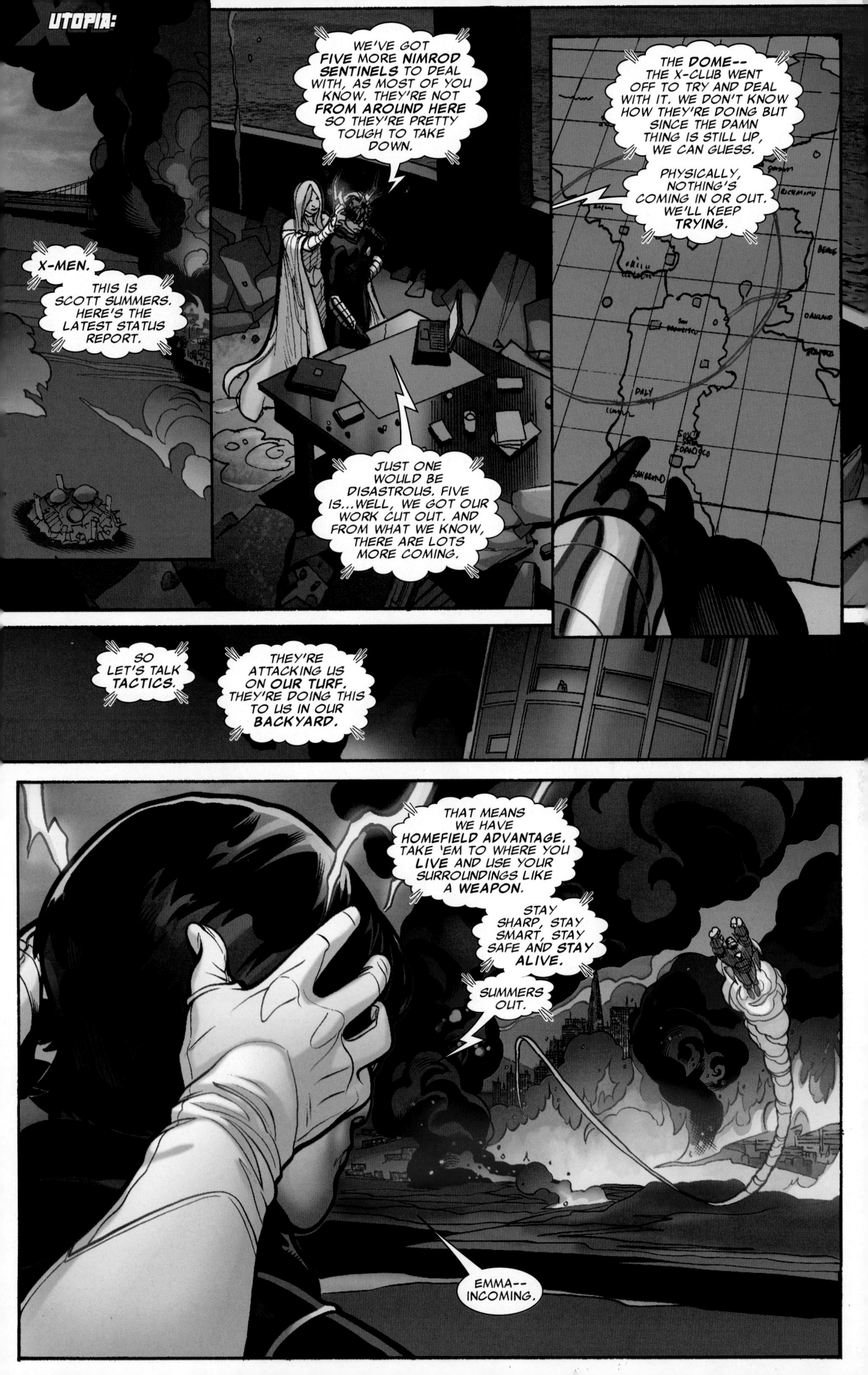
UTOPIA:
X-MEN.
THIS IS SCOTT SUMMERS. HERE'S THE LATEST STATUS REPORT.
WE'VE GOT FIVE MORE NIMROD SENTINELS TO DEAL WITH, AS MOST OF YOU KNOW. THEY'RE NOT FROM AROUND HERE SO THEY'RE PRETTY TOUGH TO TAKE DOWN.
JUST ONE WOULD BE DISASTROUS. FIVE IS...WELL, WE GOT OUR WORK CUT OUT. AND FROM WHAT WE KNOW, THERE ARE LOTS MORE COMING.
THE DOME-- THE X-CLUB WENT OFF TO TRY AND DEAL WITH IT. WE DON'T KNOW HOW THEY'RE DOING BUT SINCE THE DAMN THING IS STILL UP, WE CAN GUESS.
PHYSICALLY, NOTHING'S COMING IN OR OUT. WE'LL KEEP TRYING.
SO LET'S TALK TACTICS.
THEY'RE ATTACKING US ON OUR TURF. THEY'RE DOING THIS TO US IN OUR BACKYARD.
THAT MEANS WE HAVE HOMEFIELD ADVANTAGE. TAKE 'EM TO WHERE YOU LIVE AND USE YOUR SURROUNDINGS LIKE A WEAPON.
STAY SHARP, STAY SMART, STAY SAFE AND STAY ALIVE.
SUMMERS OUT.
EMMA-- INCOMING.

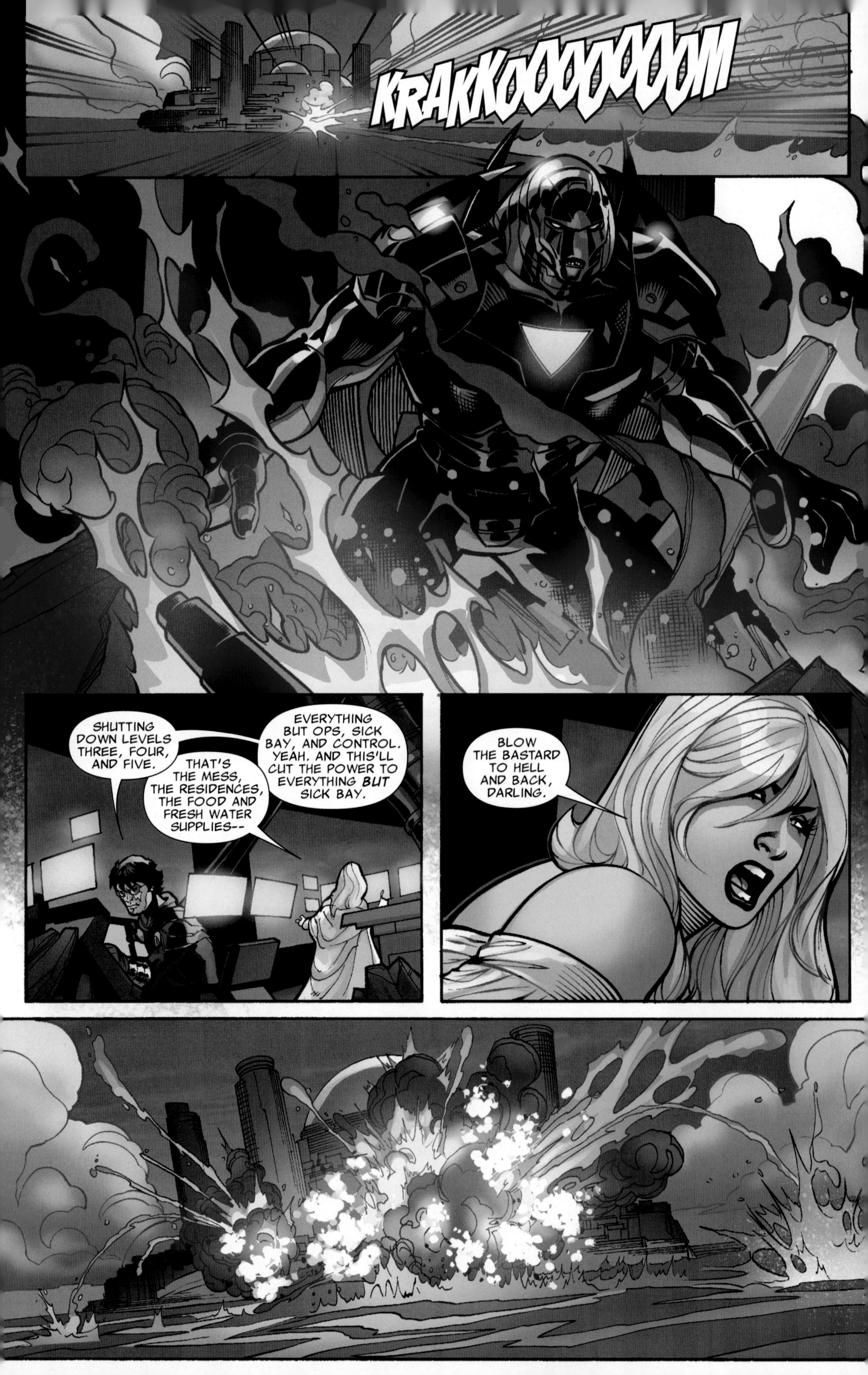
KRAKKOOOOOOOOM
SHUTTING DOWN LEVELS THREE, FOUR, AND FIVE.
THAT'S THE MESS, THE RESIDENCES, THE FOOD AND FRESH WATER SUPPLIES--
EVERYTHING BUT OPS, SICK BAY, AND CONTROL. YEAH. AND THIS'LL CUT THE POWER TO EVERYTHING **BUT** SICK BAY.
BLOW THE BASTARD TO HELL AND BACK, DARLING.

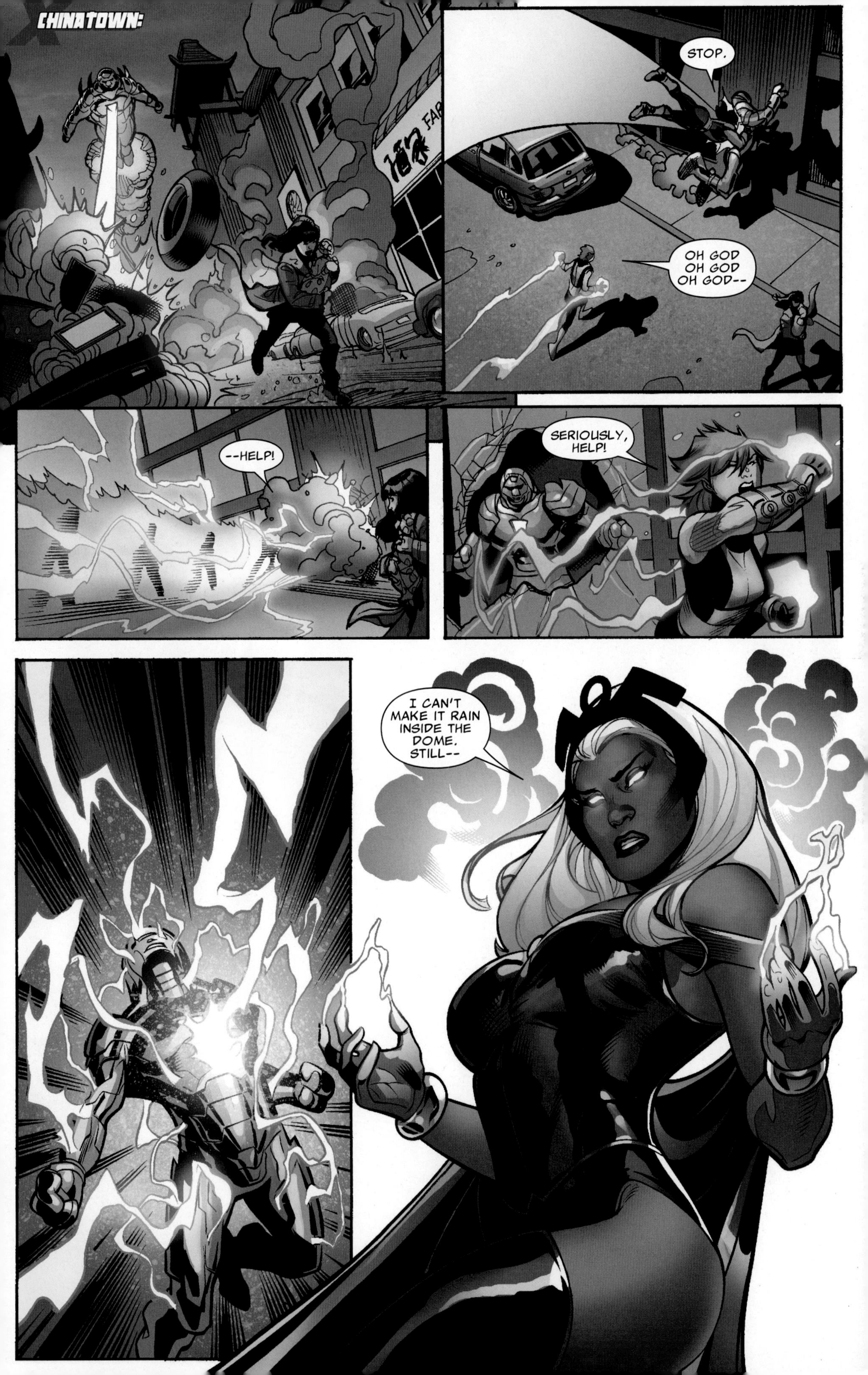
CHINATOWN:
STOP.
OH GOD
OH GOD
OH GOD--
--HELP!
SERIOUSLY, HELP!
I CAN'T MAKE IT RAIN INSIDE THE DOME. STILL--

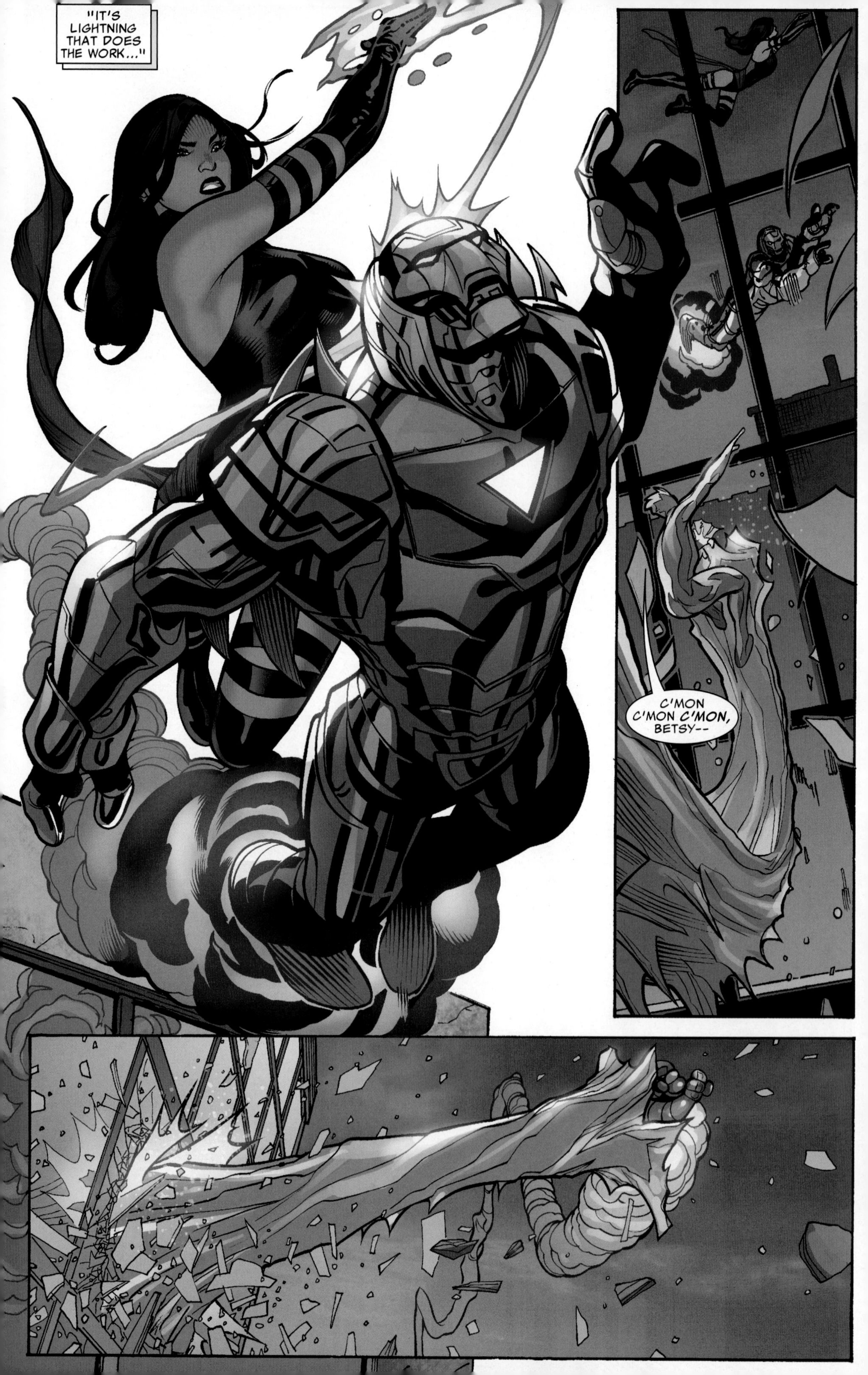
"IT'S LIGHTNING THAT DOES THE WORK..."
C'MON C'MON C'MON, BETSY--

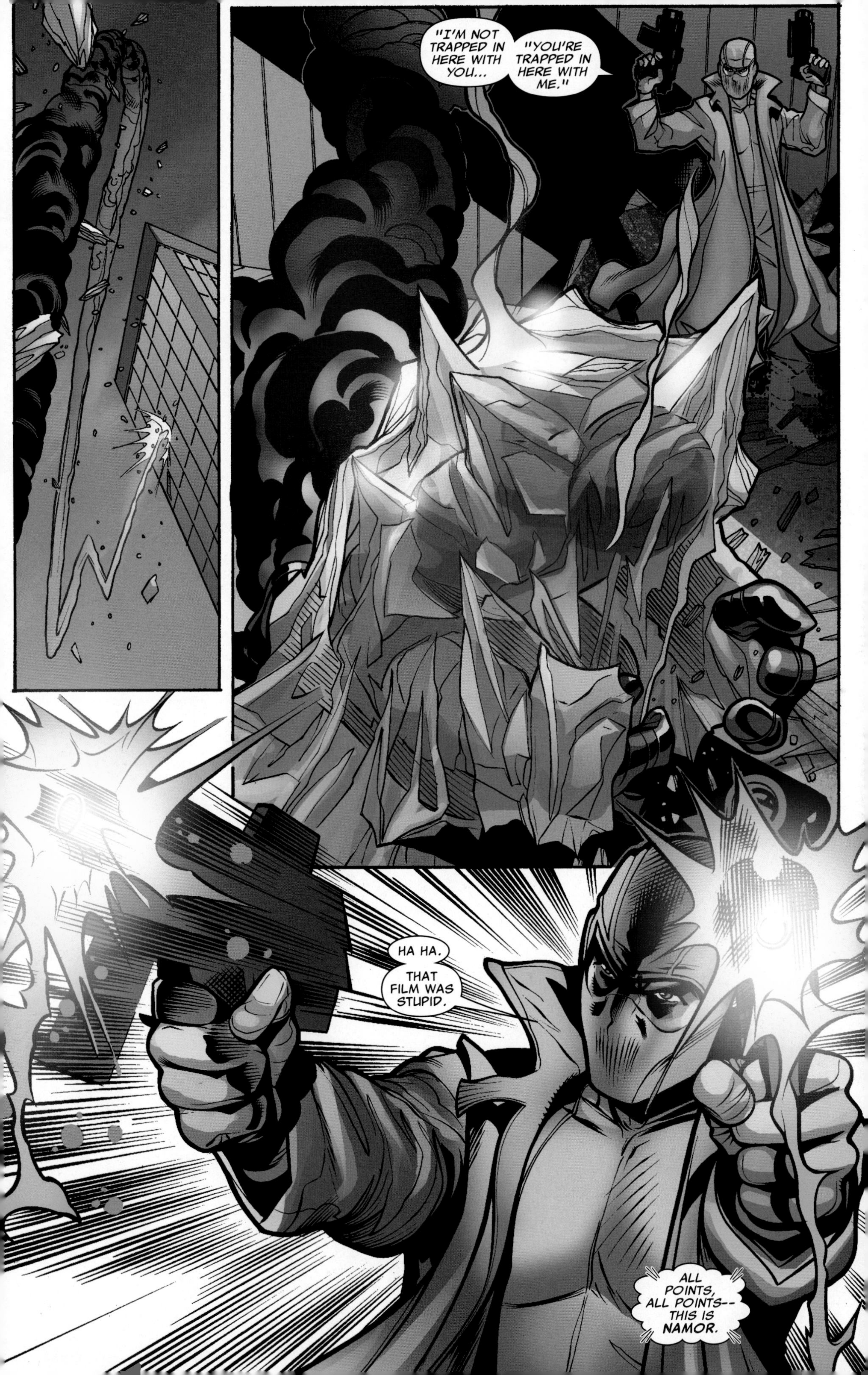
"I'M NOT TRAPPED IN HERE WITH YOU...
"YOU'RE TRAPPED IN HERE WITH ME."
HA HA.
THAT FILM WAS STUPID.
ALL POINTS, ALL POINTS-- THIS IS NAMOR.

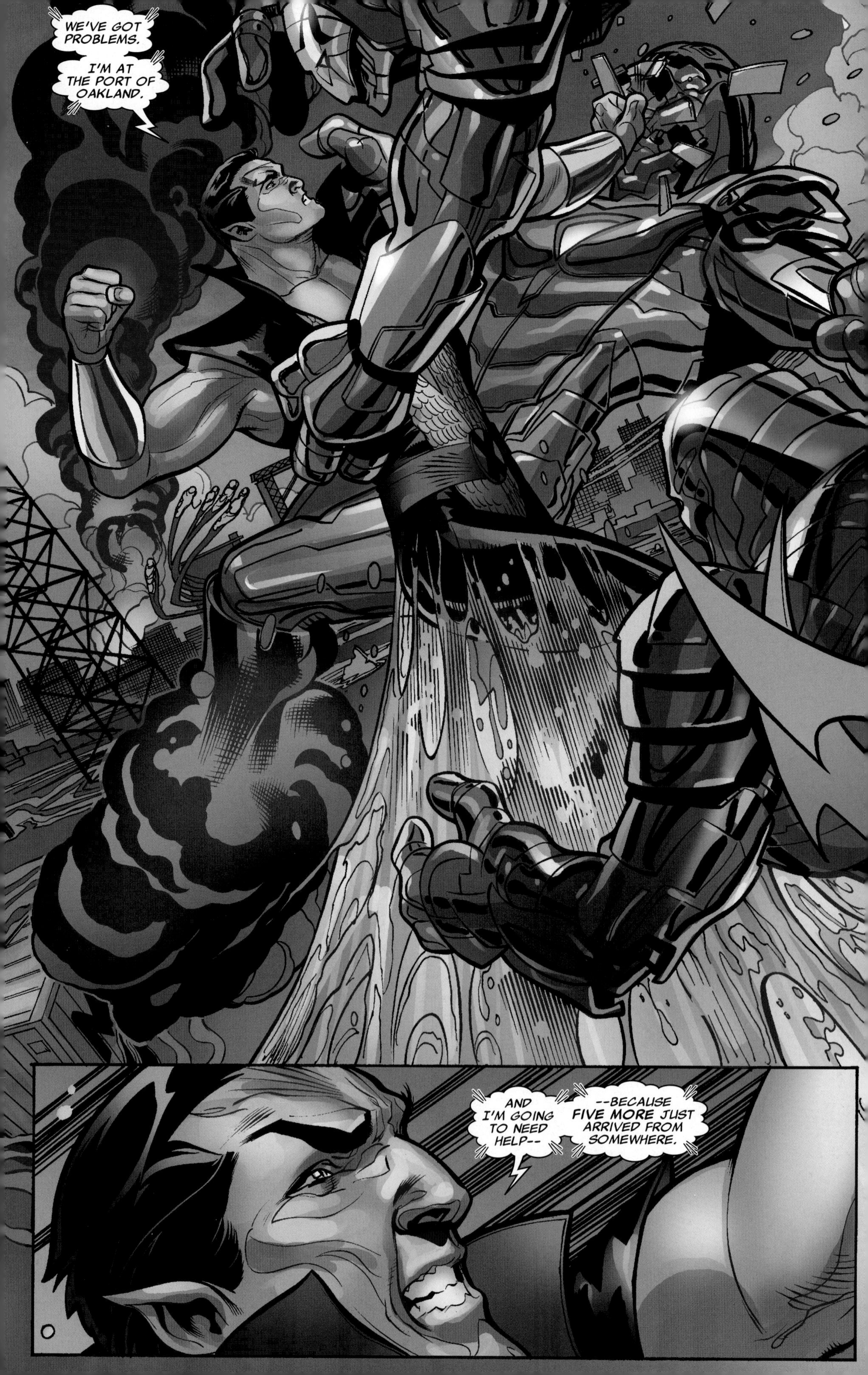
WE'VE GOT PROBLEMS.
I'M AT THE PORT OF OAKLAND.
AND I'M GOING TO NEED HELP--
--BECAUSE FIVE MORE JUST ARRIVED FROM SOMEWHERE.

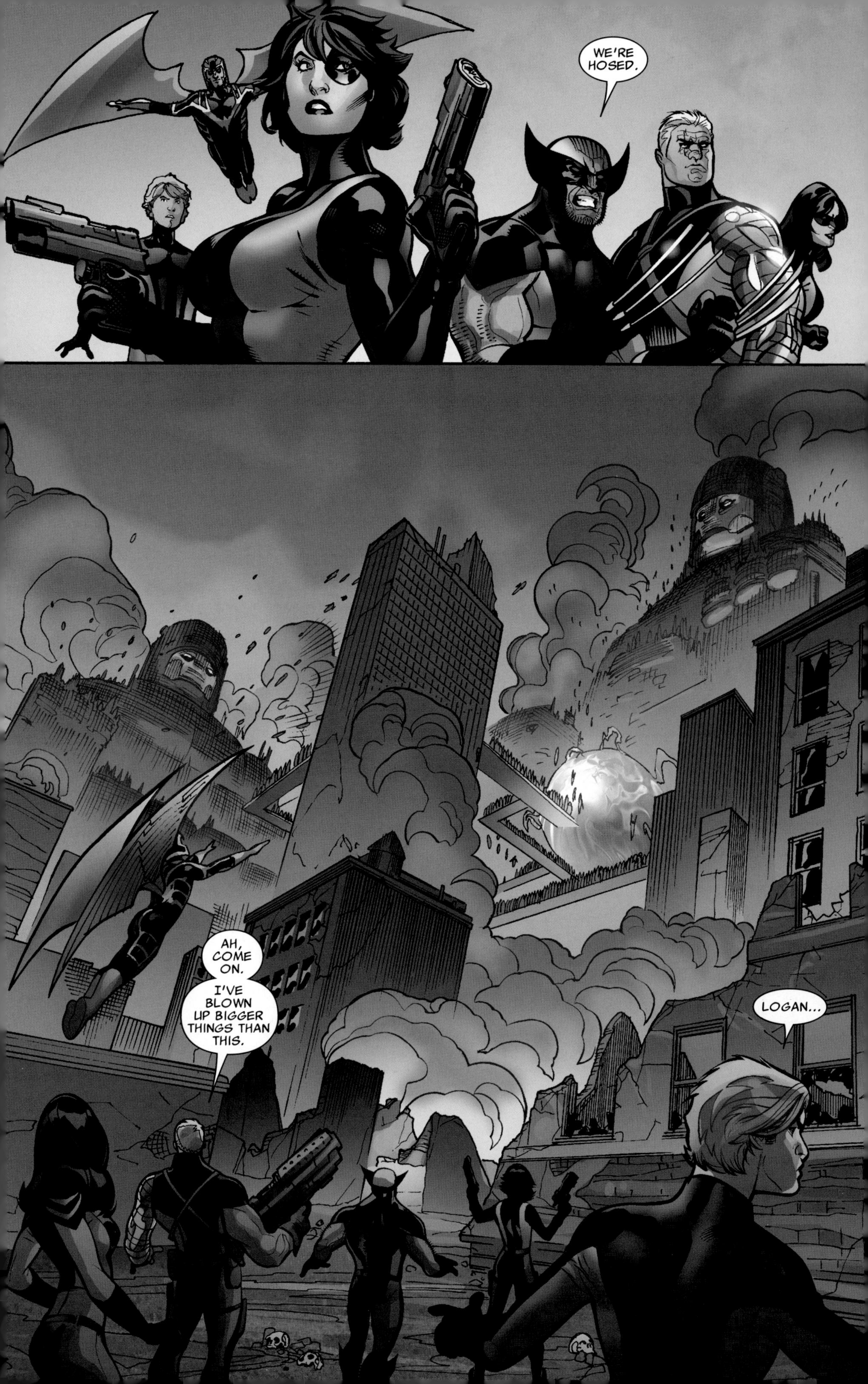
WE'RE HOSED.
AH, COME ON.
I'VE BLOWN UP BIGGER THINGS THAN THIS.
LOGAN...

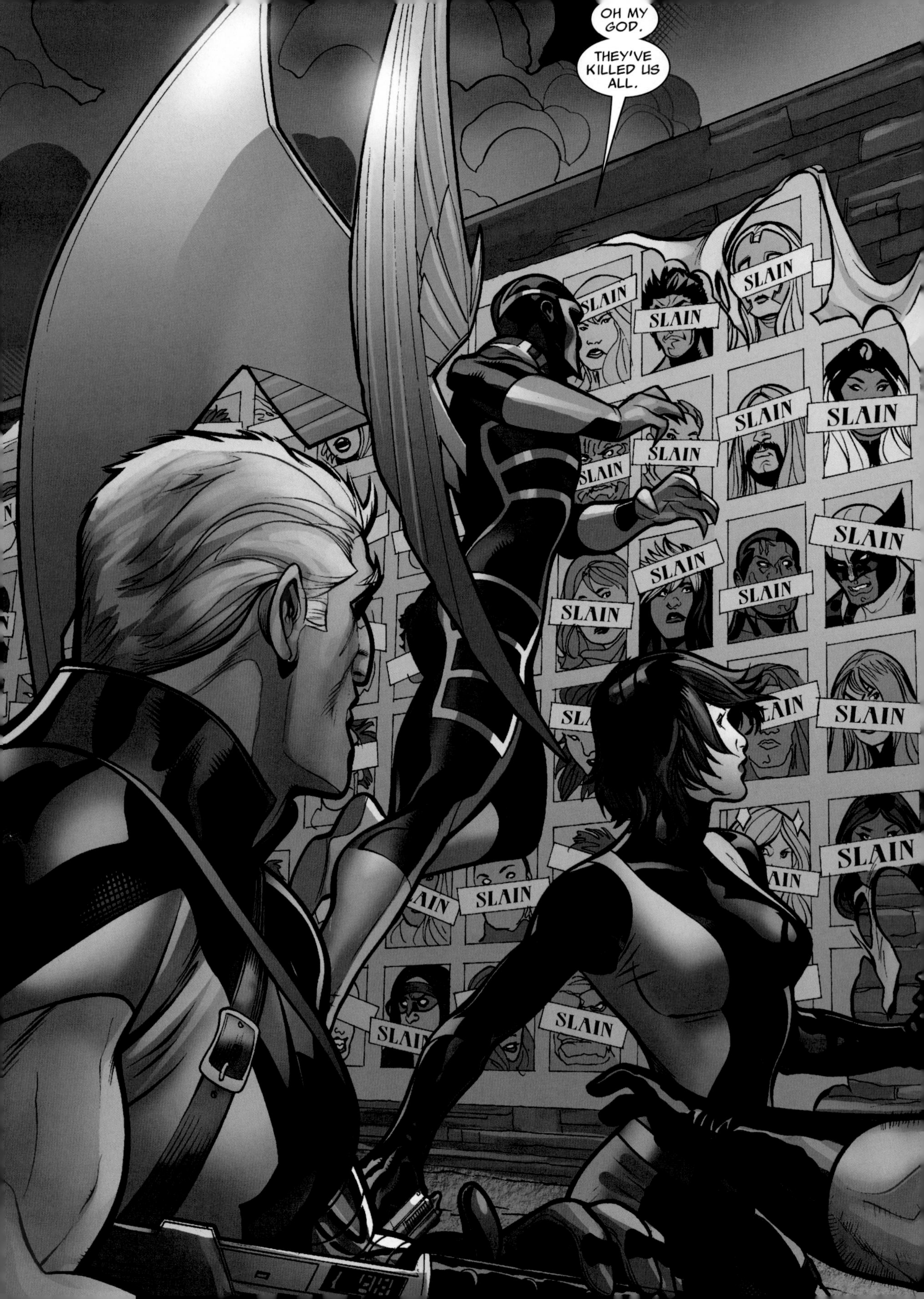
OH MY GOD.
THEY'VE KILLED US ALL.
SLAIN

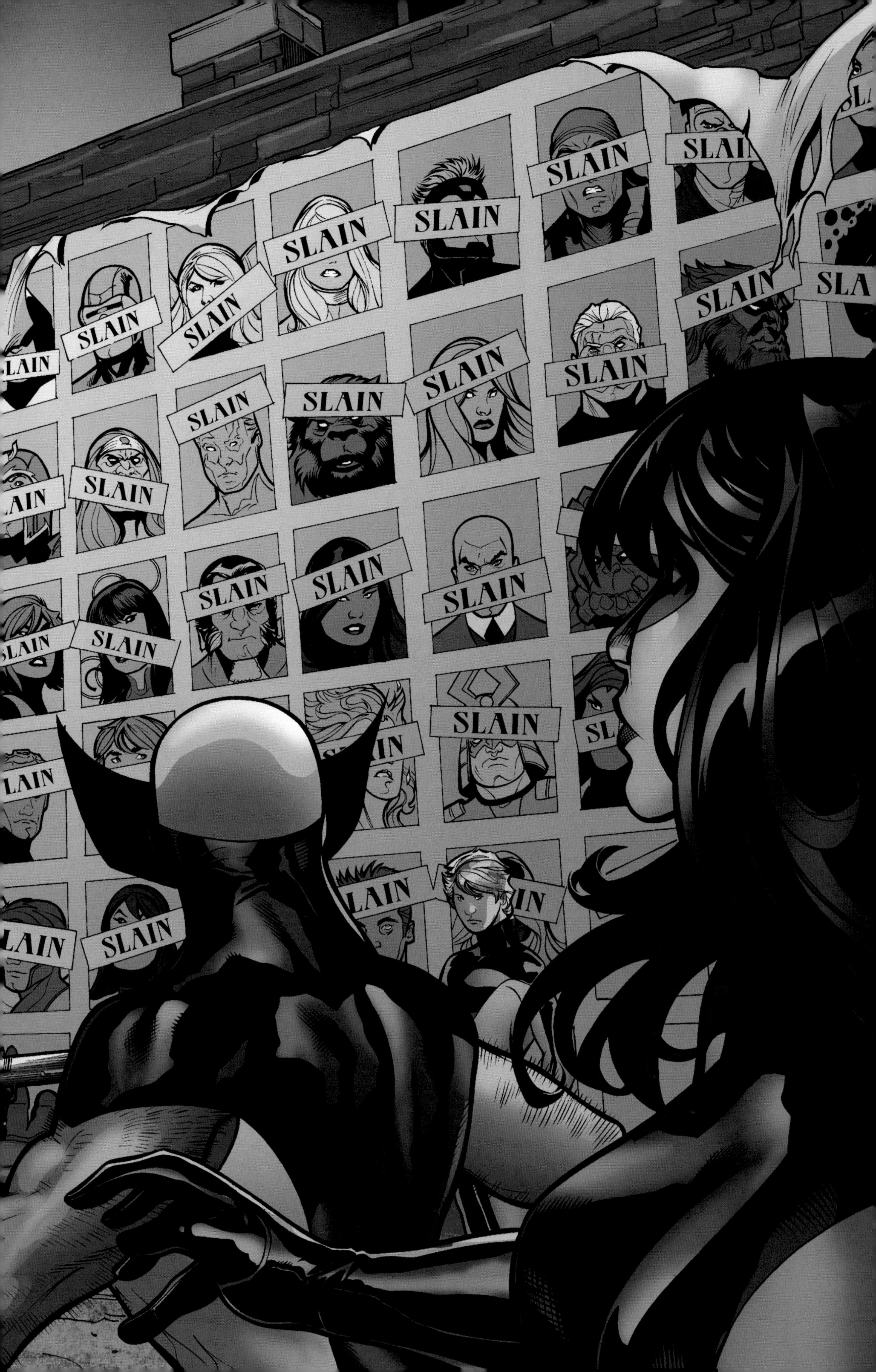
SLAIN
SLAIN
SLAIN
SLAIN
SLAIN
SLAIN
SLAIN
SLAIN
SLAIN
SLAIN
SLAIN
SLAIN
SLAIN
SLAIN
SLAIN
SLAIN
SLAIN

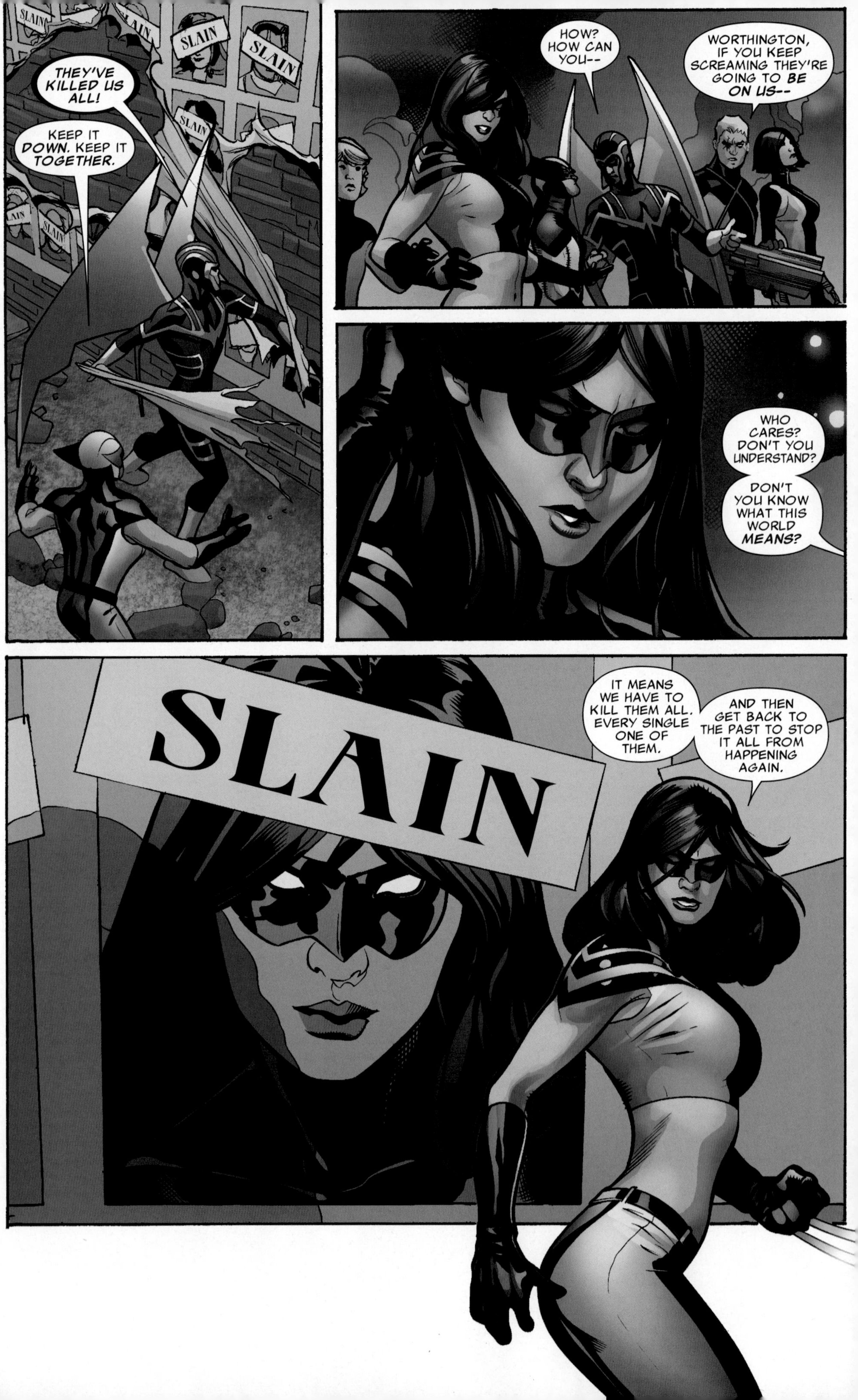
SLAIN
SLAIN
SLAIN
SLAIN
THEY'VE KILLED US ALL!
KEEP IT DOWN. KEEP IT TOGETHER.
SLAIN
SLAIN
HOW? HOW CAN YOU--
WORTHINGTON, IF YOU KEEP SCREAMING THEY'RE GOING TO BE ON US--
WHO CARES? DON'T YOU UNDERSTAND?
DON'T YOU KNOW WHAT THIS WORLD MEANS?
SLAIN
IT MEANS WE HAVE TO KILL THEM ALL. EVERY SINGLE ONE OF THEM.
AND THEN GET BACK TO THE PAST TO STOP IT ALL FROM HAPPENING AGAIN.

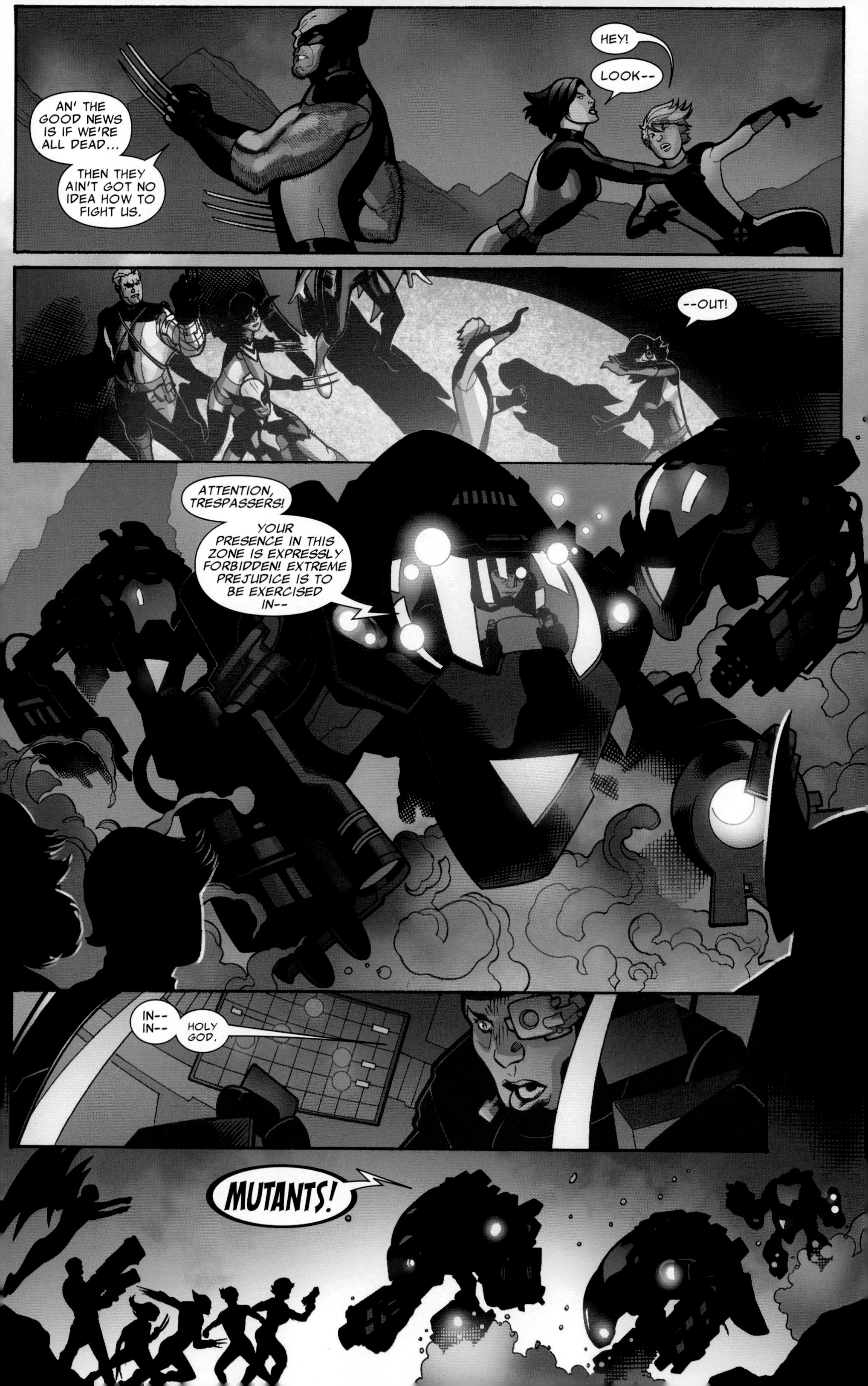

AN' THE GOOD NEWS IS IF WE'RE ALL DEAD...
THEN THEY AIN'T GOT NO IDEA HOW TO FIGHT US.
HEY!
LOOK--
--OUT!
ATTENTION, TRESPASSERS!
YOUR PRESENCE IN THIS ZONE IS EXPRESSLY FORBIDDEN! EXTREME PREJUDICE IS TO BE EXERCISED IN--
IN-- IN--
HOLY GOD.
MUTANTS!

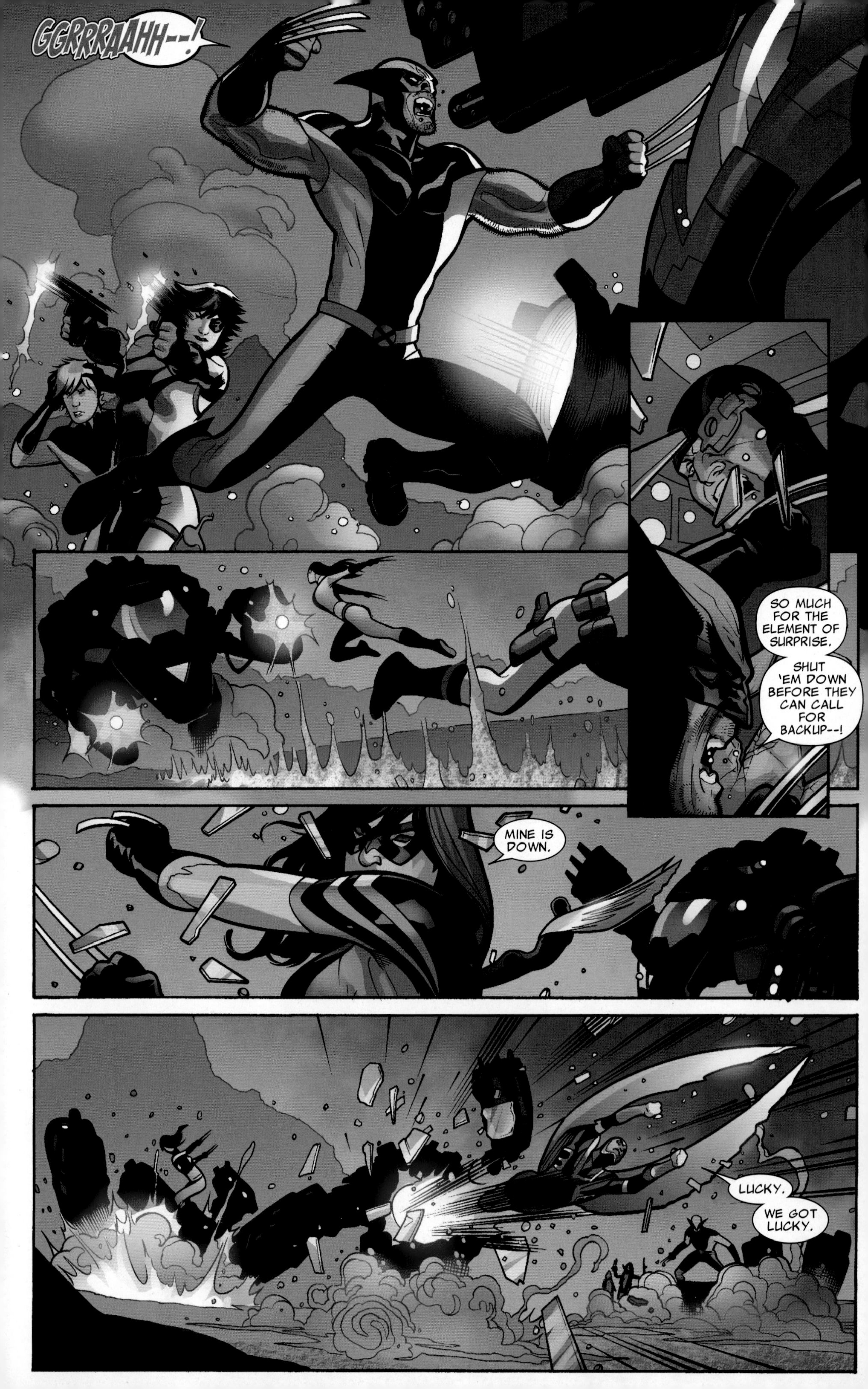
GGRRRAAHH--!
SO MUCH FOR THE ELEMENT OF SURPRISE.
SHUT 'EM DOWN BEFORE THEY CAN CALL FOR BACKUP--!
MINE IS DOWN.
LUCKY.
WE GOT LUCKY.

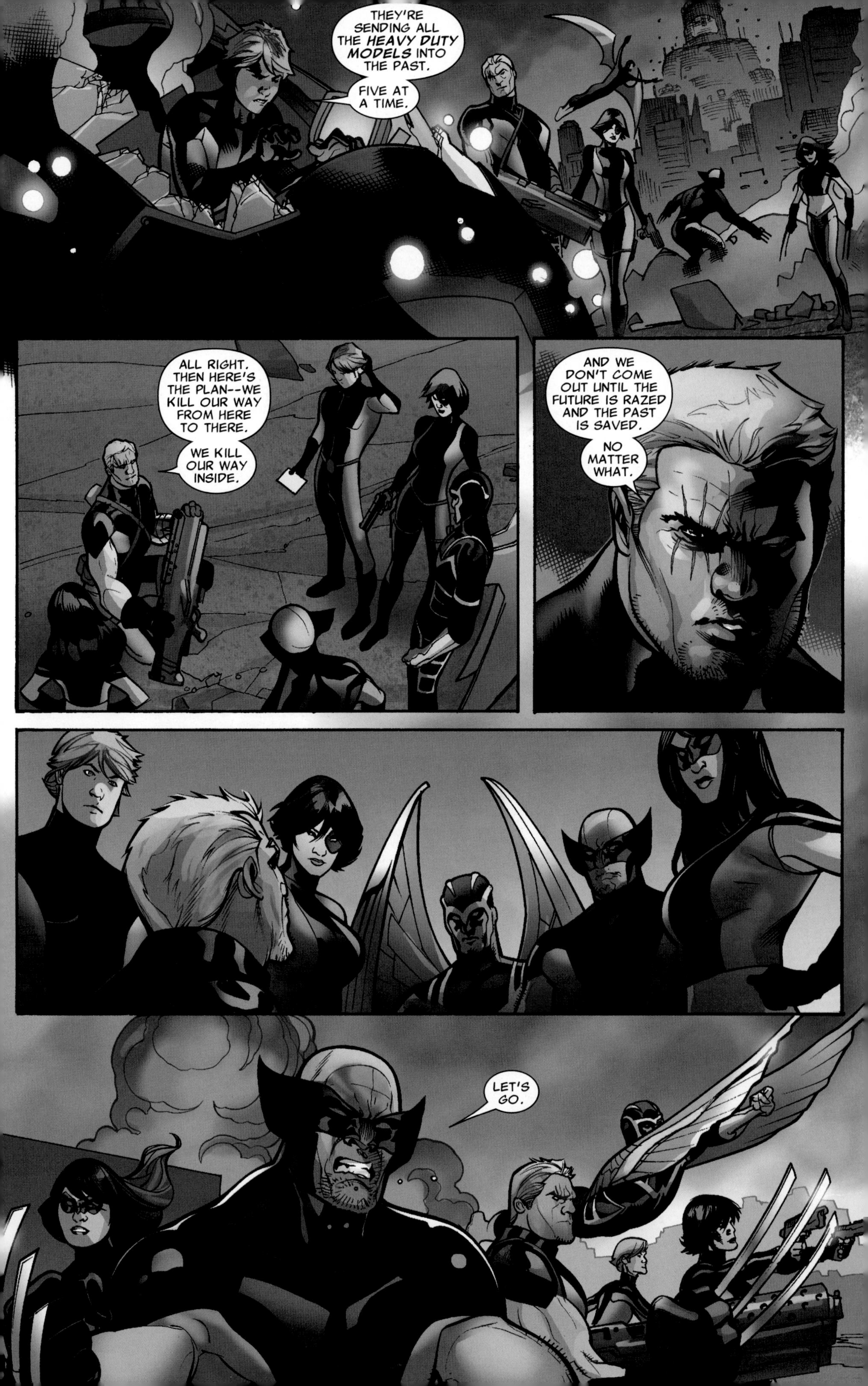
THEY'RE SENDING ALL THE HEAVY DUTY MODELS INTO THE PAST.
FIVE AT A TIME.
ALL RIGHT. THEN HERE'S THE PLAN--WE KILL OUR WAY FROM HERE TO THERE.
WE KILL OUR WAY INSIDE.
AND WE DON'T COME OUT UNTIL THE FUTURE IS RAZED AND THE PAST IS SAVED.
NO MATTER WHAT.
LET'S GO.

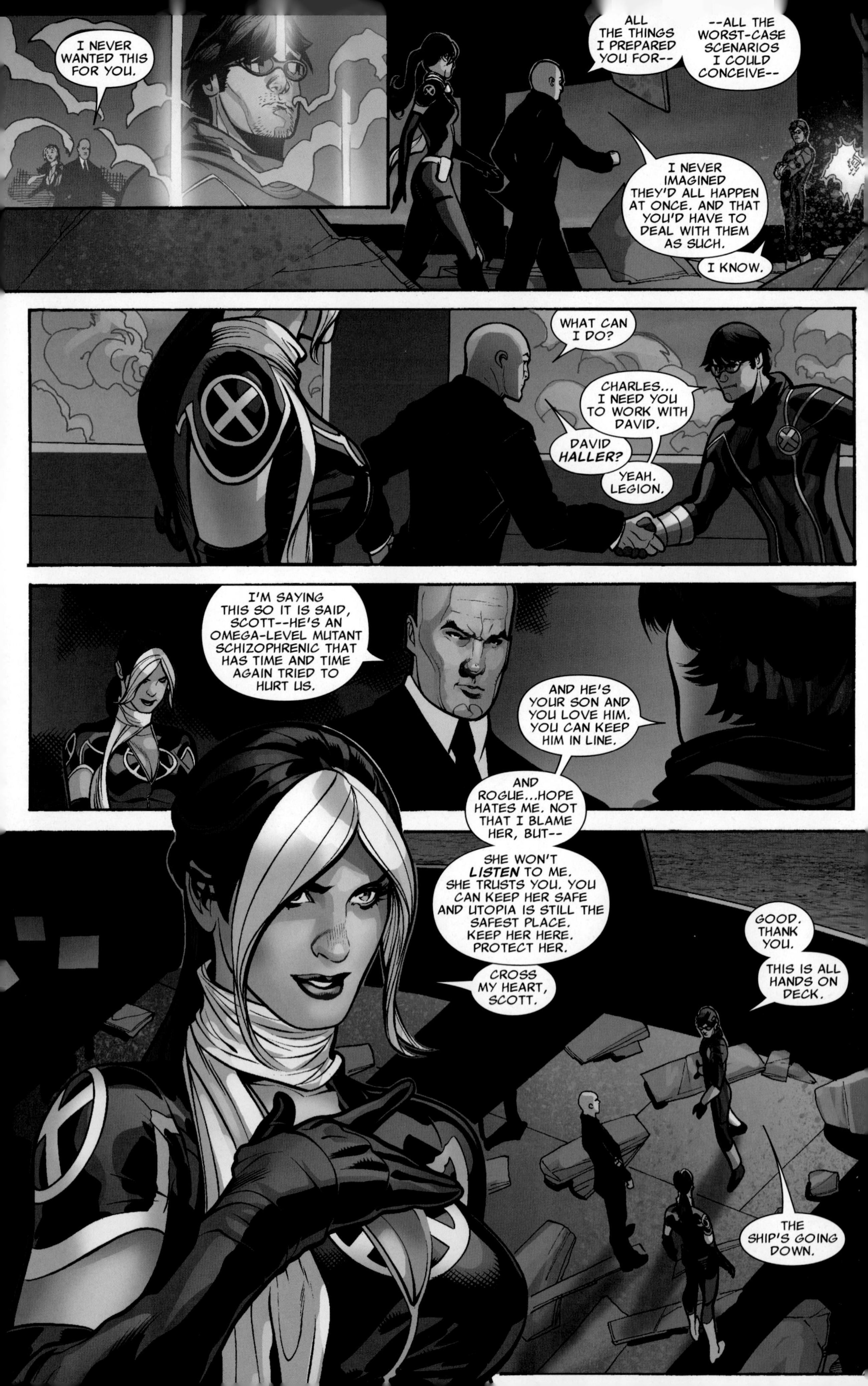

I NEVER WANTED THIS FOR YOU.
ALL THE THINGS I PREPARED YOU FOR--
--ALL THE WORST-CASE SCENARIOS I COULD CONCEIVE--
I NEVER IMAGINED THEY'D ALL HAPPEN AT ONCE. AND THAT YOU'D HAVE TO DEAL WITH THEM AS SUCH.
I KNOW.
WHAT CAN I DO?
CHARLES... I NEED YOU TO WORK WITH DAVID.
DAVID HALLER?
YEAH. LEGION.
I'M SAYING THIS SO IT IS SAID, SCOTT--HE'S AN OMEGA-LEVEL MUTANT SCHIZOPHRENIC THAT HAS TIME AND TIME AGAIN TRIED TO HURT US.
AND HE'S YOUR SON AND YOU LOVE HIM. YOU CAN KEEP HIM IN LINE.
AND ROGUE...HOPE HATES ME. NOT THAT I BLAME HER, BUT--
SHE WON'T LISTEN TO ME. SHE TRUSTS YOU. YOU CAN KEEP HER SAFE AND UTOPIA IS STILL THE SAFEST PLACE. KEEP HER HERE. PROTECT HER.
CROSS MY HEART, SCOTT.
GOOD. THANK YOU.
THIS IS ALL HANDS ON DECK.
THE SHIP'S GOING DOWN.

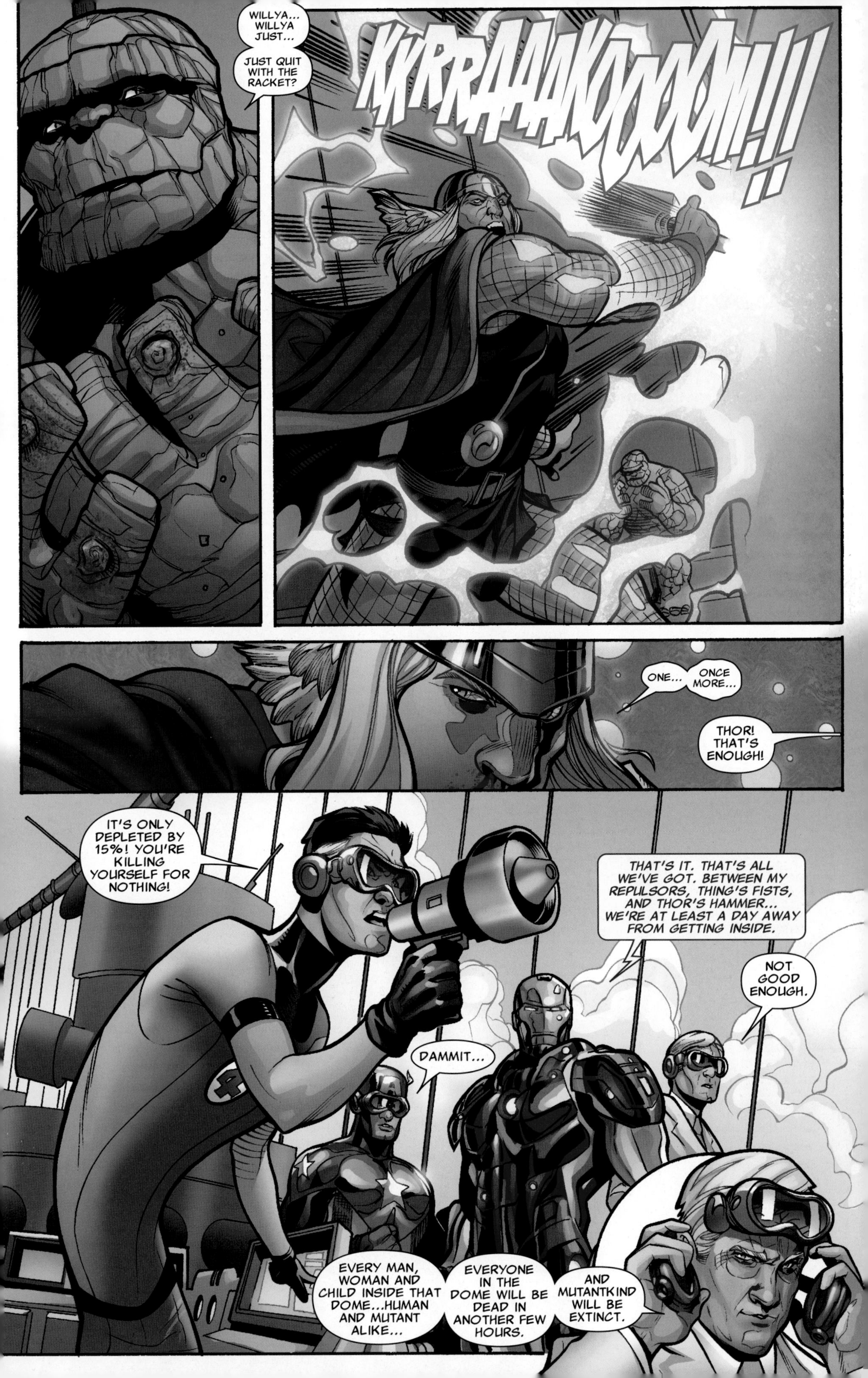
WILLYA... WILLYA JUST...
JUST QUIT WITH THE RACKET?
KKRRAAAKOOOOOM!!
ONE...
ONCE MORE...
THOR! THAT'S ENOUGH!
IT'S ONLY DEPLETED BY 15%! YOU'RE KILLING YOURSELF FOR NOTHING!
THAT'S IT. THAT'S ALL WE'VE GOT. BETWEEN MY REPULSORS, THING'S FISTS, AND THOR'S HAMMER... WE'RE AT LEAST A DAY AWAY FROM GETTING INSIDE.
NOT GOOD ENOUGH.
DAMMIT...
EVERY MAN, WOMAN AND CHILD INSIDE THAT DOME...HUMAN AND MUTANT ALIKE...
EVERYONE IN THE DOME WILL BE DEAD IN ANOTHER FEW HOURS.
AND MUTANTKIND WILL BE EXTINCT.

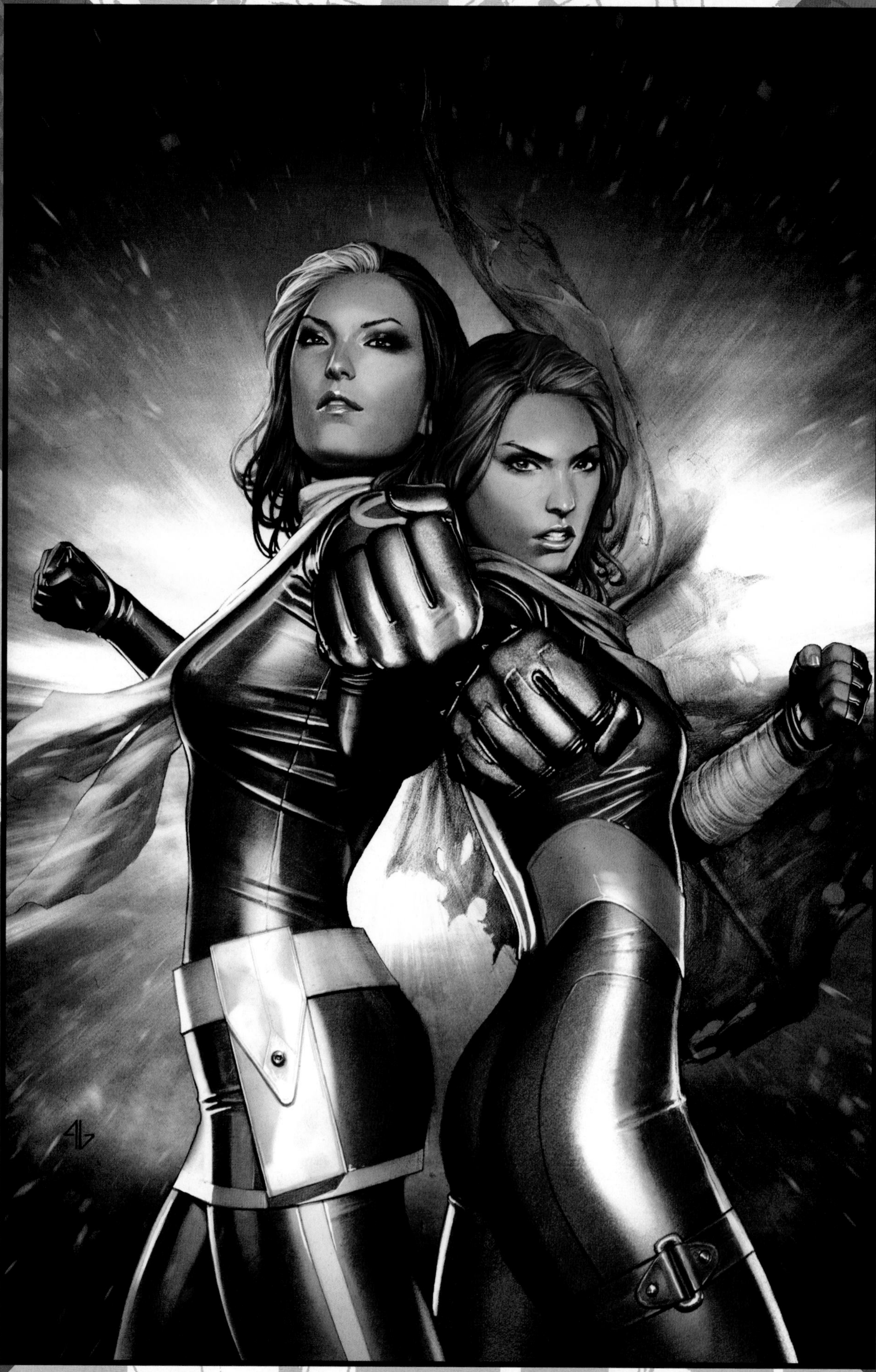

NEW MUTANTS #14

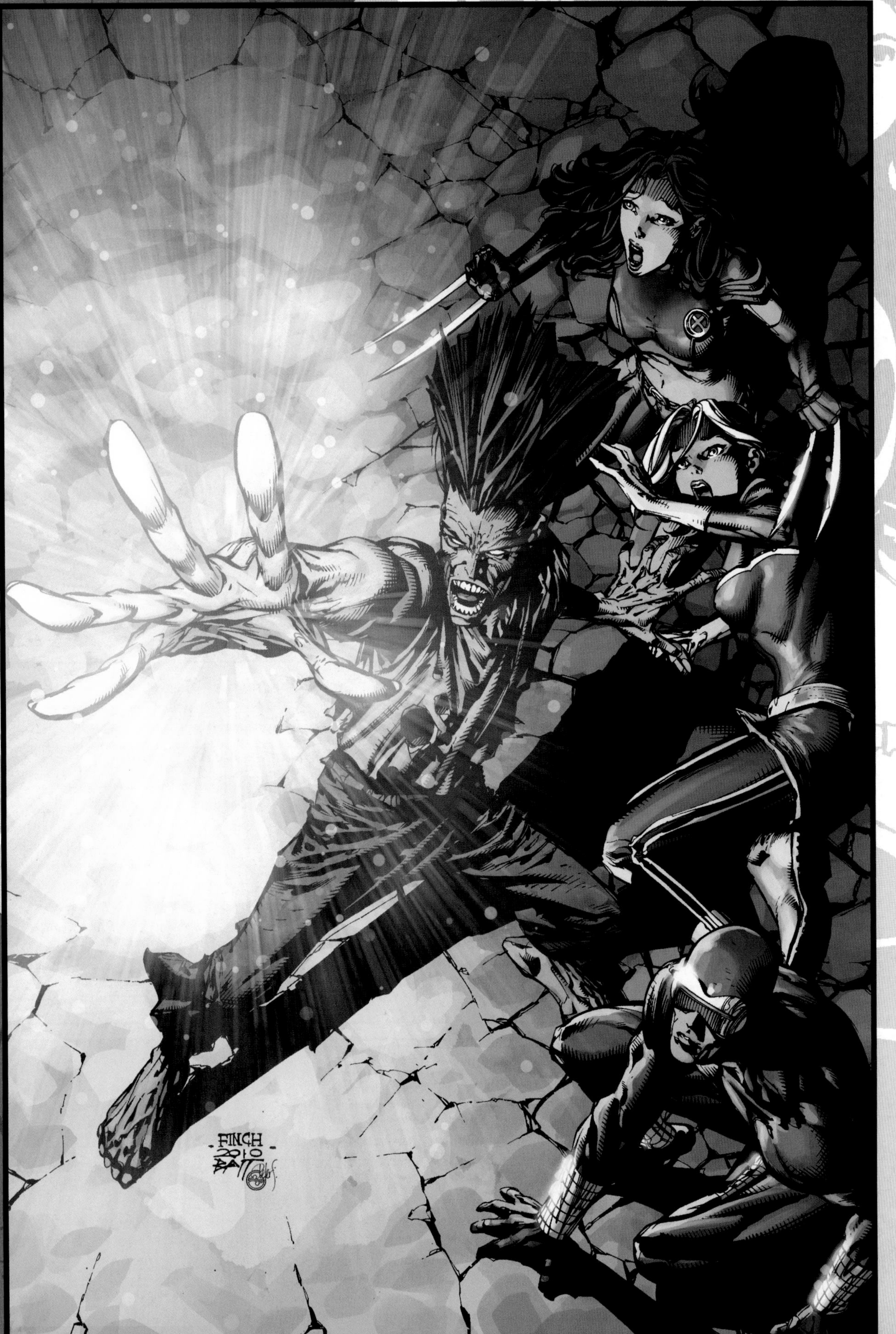
FINCH
2010

NEW MUTANTS #14
VARIANT

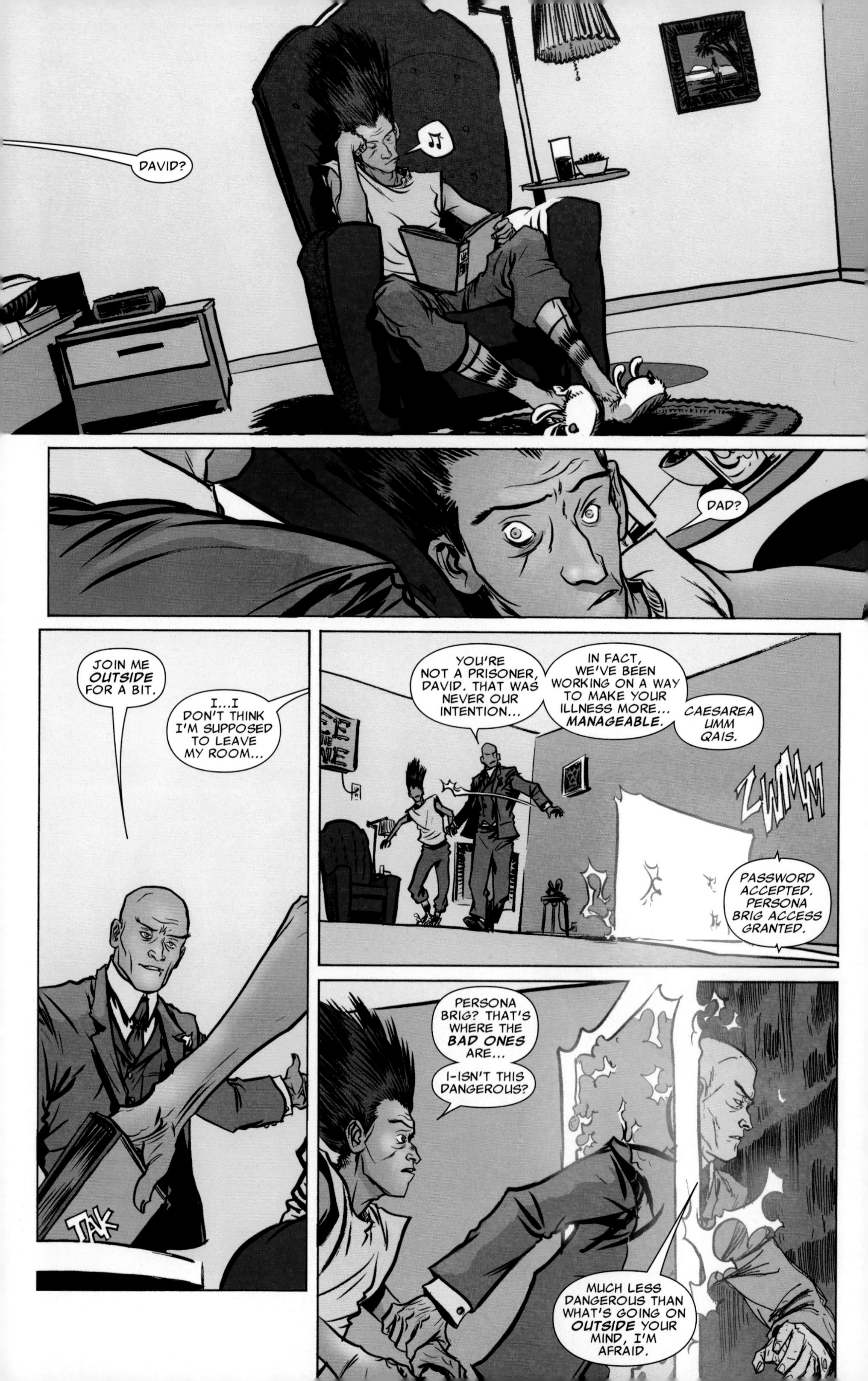
DAVID?
♫
DAD?
JOIN ME OUTSIDE FOR A BIT.
I...I DON'T THINK I'M SUPPOSED TO LEAVE MY ROOM...
TAK
YOU'RE NOT A PRISONER, DAVID. THAT WAS NEVER OUR INTENTION...
IN FACT, WE'VE BEEN WORKING ON A WAY TO MAKE YOUR ILLNESS MORE... MANAGEABLE.
CAESAREA UMM QAIS.
ZWMM
PASSWORD ACCEPTED. PERSONA BRIG ACCESS GRANTED.
PERSONA BRIG? THAT'S WHERE THE BAD ONES ARE...
I-ISN'T THIS DANGEROUS?
MUCH LESS DANGEROUS THAN WHAT'S GOING ON OUTSIDE YOUR MIND, I'M AFRAID.

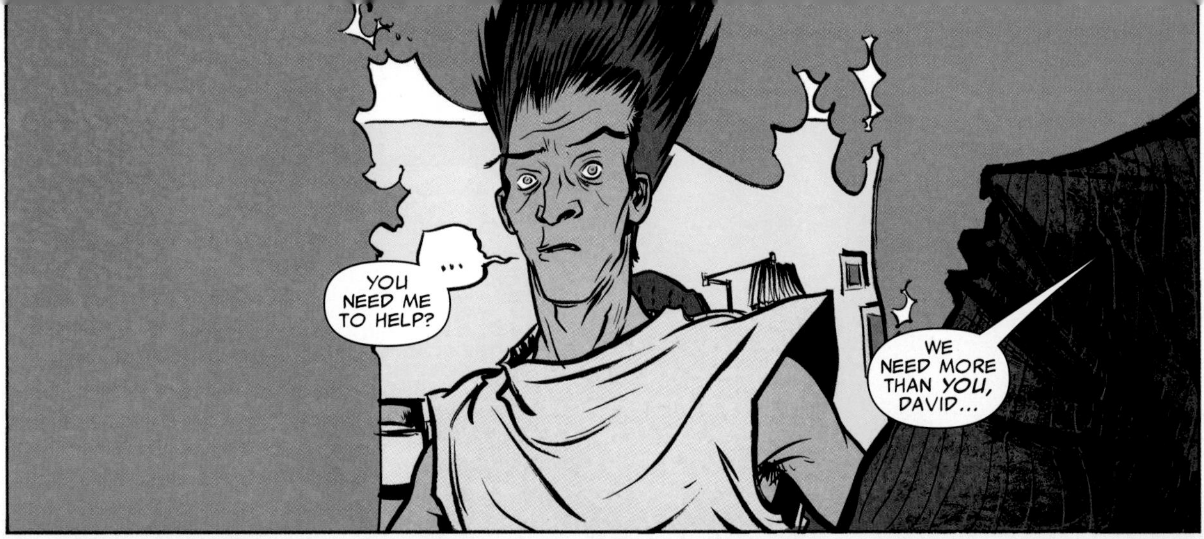
...
YOU NEED ME TO HELP?
WE NEED MORE THAN YOU, DAVID...

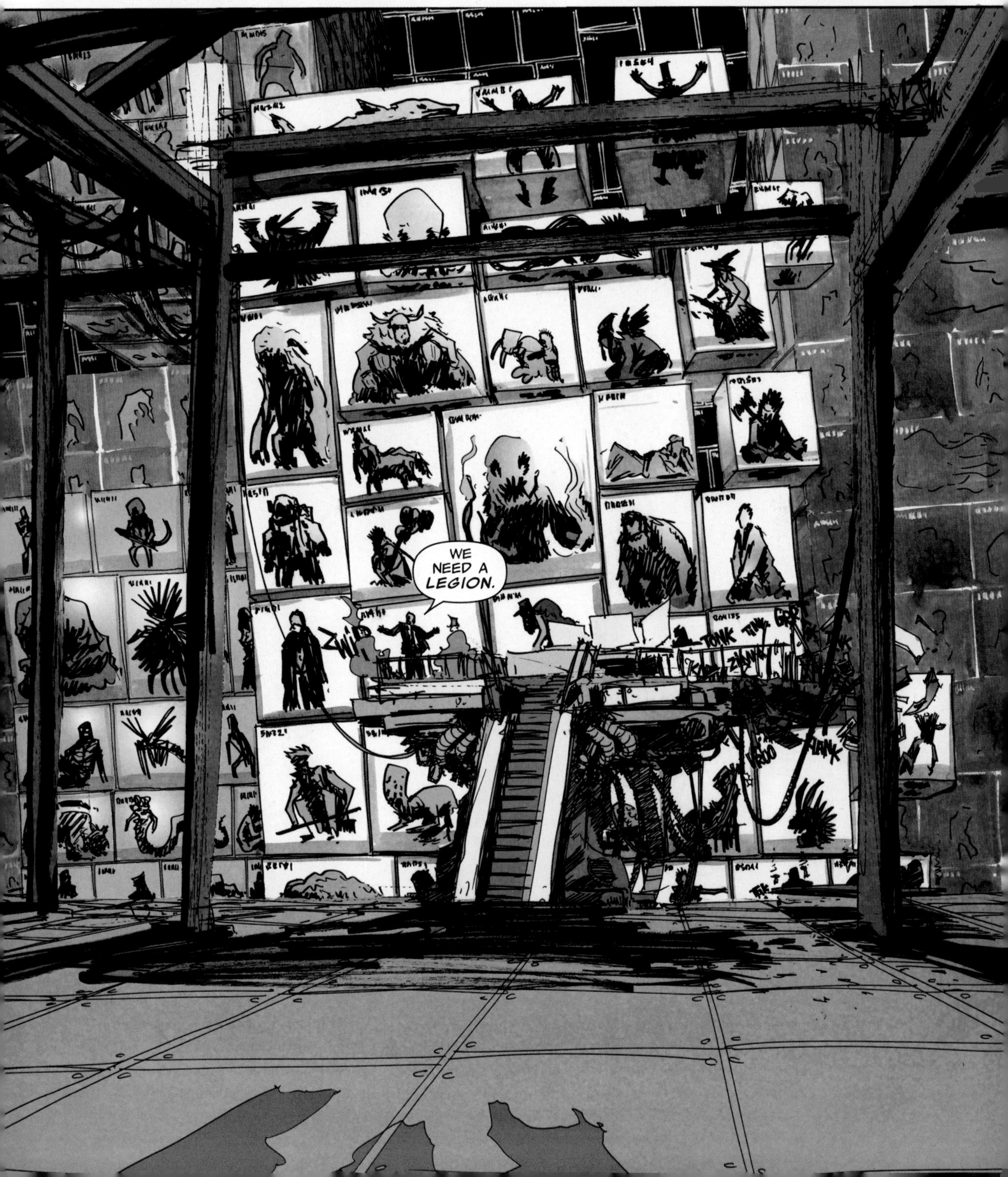
WE NEED A LEGION.

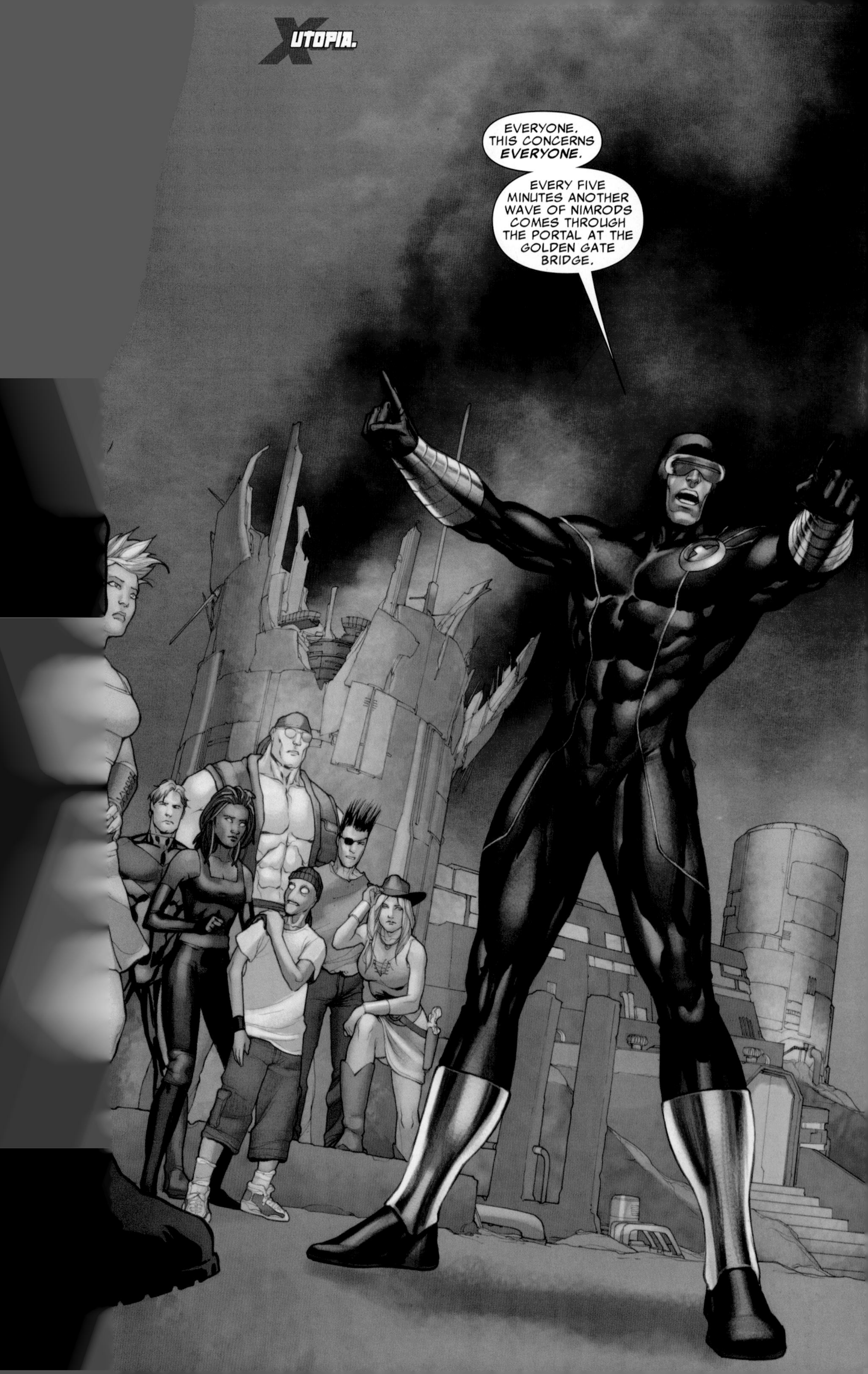
X UTOPIA.
EVERYONE. THIS CONCERNS EVERYONE.
EVERY FIVE MINUTES ANOTHER WAVE OF NIMRODS COMES THROUGH THE PORTAL AT THE GOLDEN GATE BRIDGE.

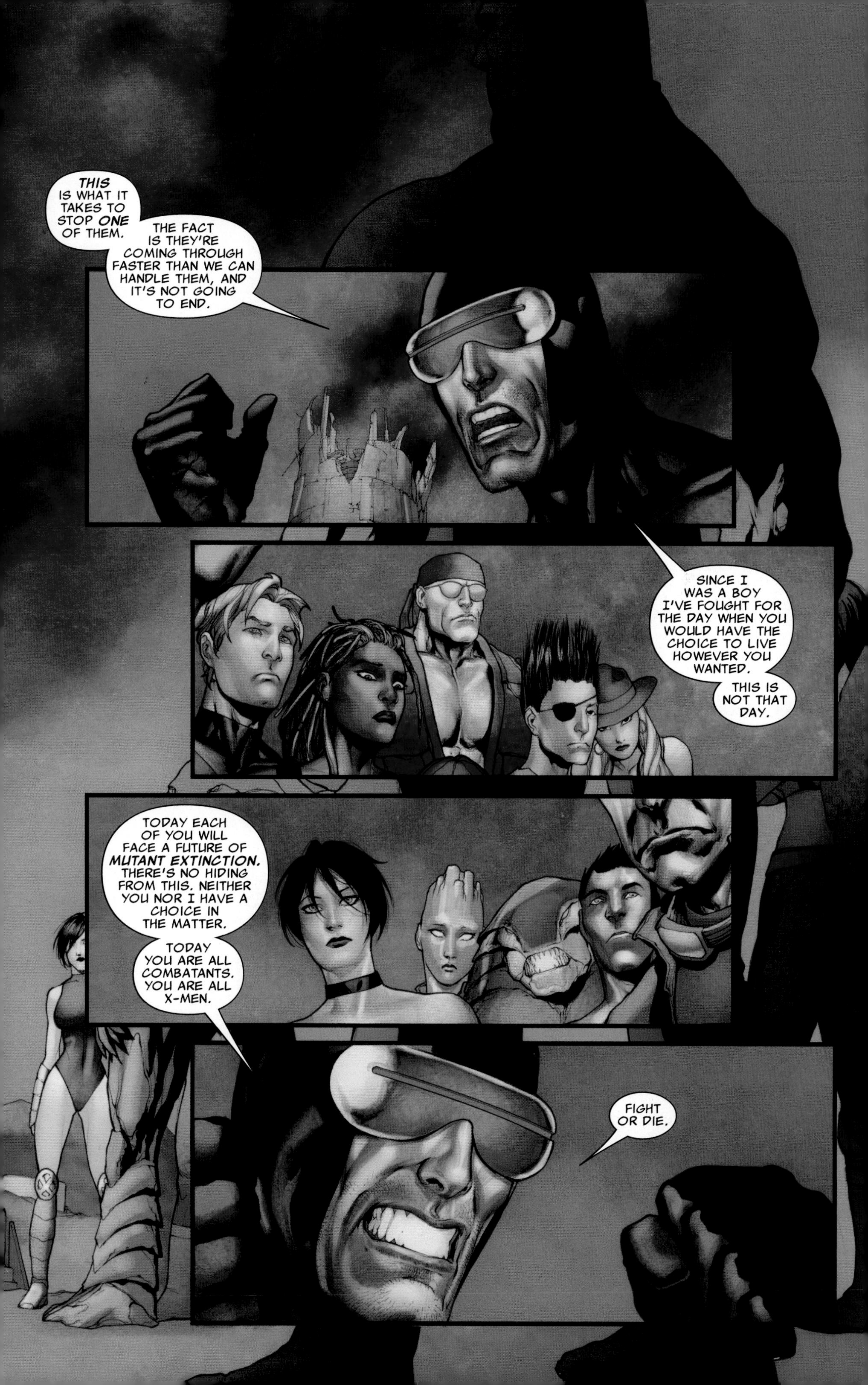
THIS IS WHAT IT TAKES TO STOP ONE OF THEM.
THE FACT IS THEY'RE COMING THROUGH FASTER THAN WE CAN HANDLE THEM, AND IT'S NOT GOING TO END.
SINCE I WAS A BOY I'VE FOUGHT FOR THE DAY WHEN YOU WOULD HAVE THE CHOICE TO LIVE HOWEVER YOU WANTED.
THIS IS NOT THAT DAY.
TODAY EACH OF YOU WILL FACE A FUTURE OF MUTANT EXTINCTION. THERE'S NO HIDING FROM THIS. NEITHER YOU NOR I HAVE A CHOICE IN THE MATTER.
TODAY YOU ARE ALL COMBATANTS. YOU ARE ALL X-MEN.
FIGHT OR DIE.

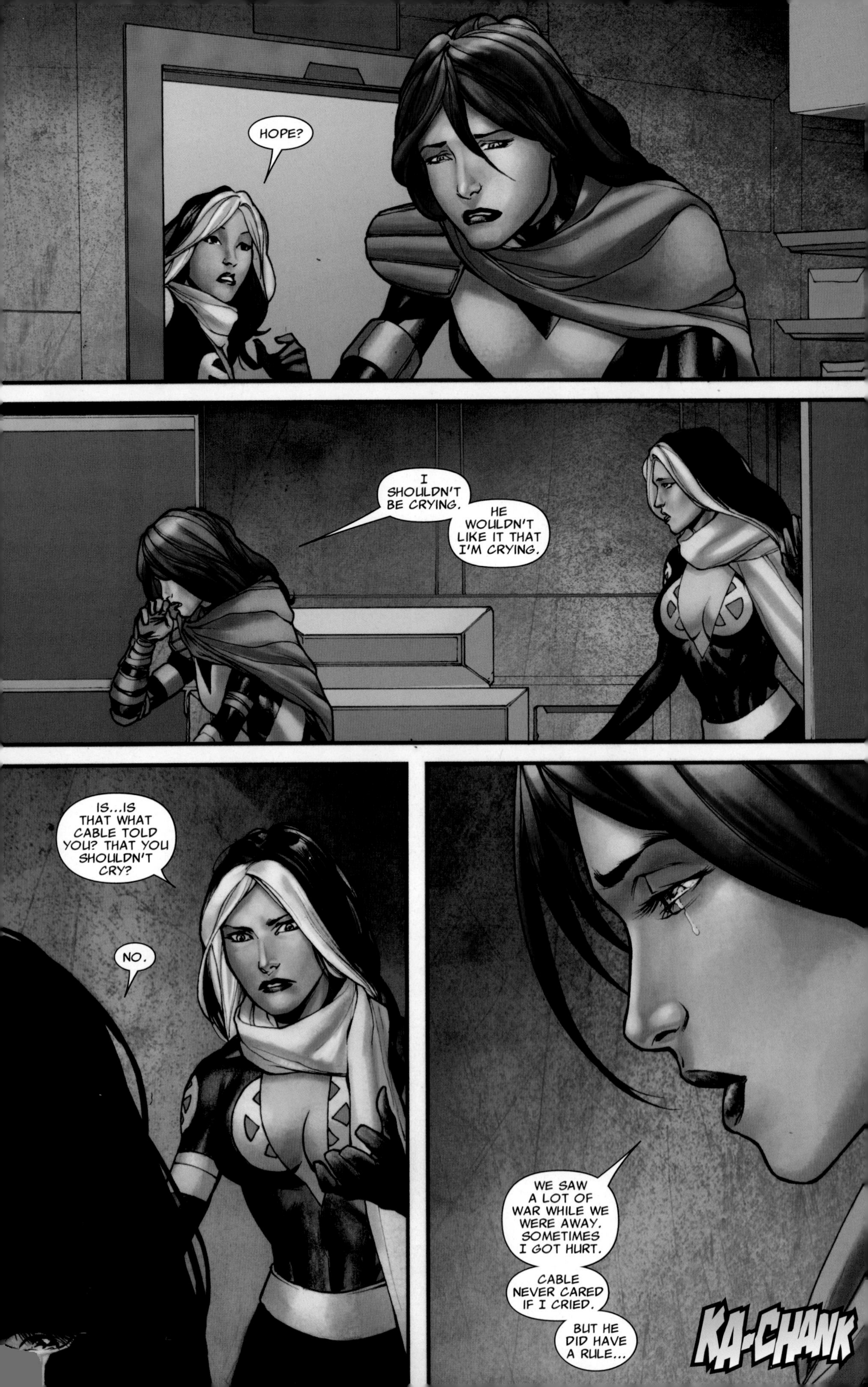
HOPE?
I SHOULDN'T BE CRYING.
HE WOULDN'T LIKE IT THAT I'M CRYING.
IS...IS THAT WHAT CABLE TOLD YOU? THAT YOU SHOULDN'T CRY?
NO.
WE SAW A LOT OF WAR WHILE WE WERE AWAY. SOMETIMES I GOT HURT.
CABLE NEVER CARED IF I CRIED.
BUT HE DID HAVE A RULE...
KA-CHANK

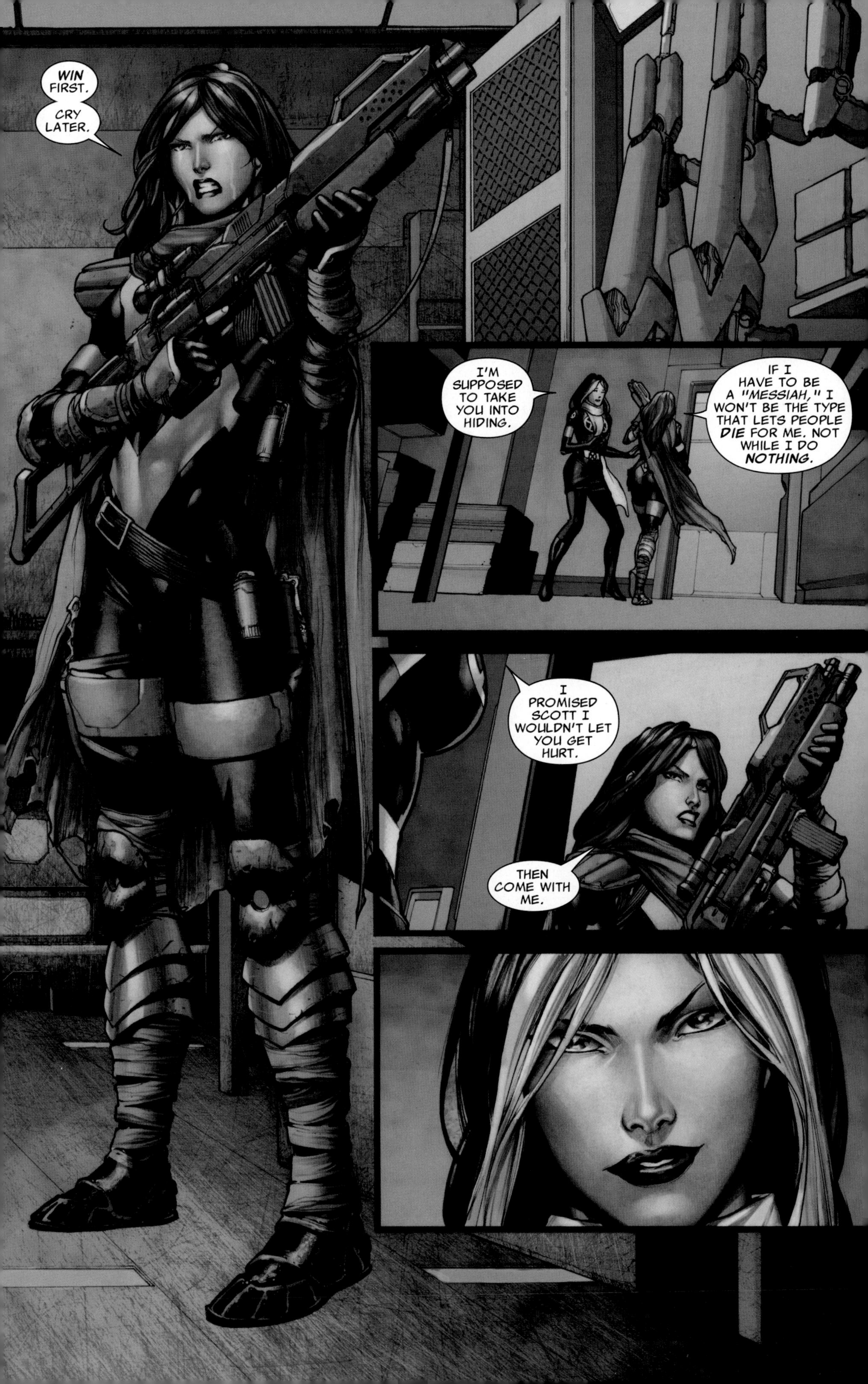
WIN FIRST.
CRY LATER.
I'M SUPPOSED TO TAKE YOU INTO HIDING.
IF I HAVE TO BE A "MESSIAH," I WON'T BE THE TYPE THAT LETS PEOPLE DIE FOR ME. NOT WHILE I DO NOTHING.
I PROMISED SCOTT I WOULDN'T LET YOU GET HURT.
THEN COME WITH ME.

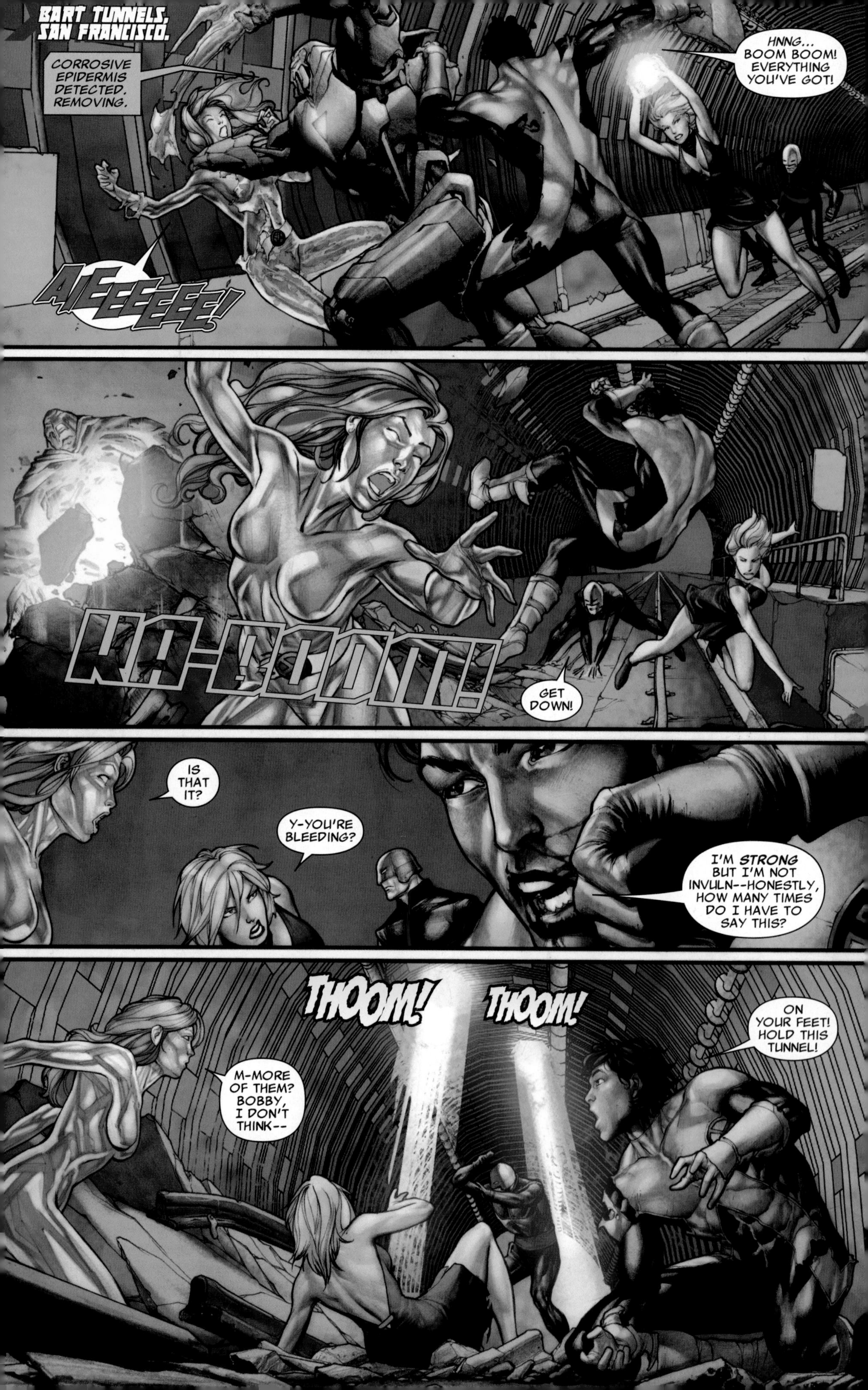
BART TUNNELS, SAN FRANCISCO.
CORROSIVE EPIDERMIS DETECTED. REMOVING.
HNNG... BOOM BOOM! EVERYTHING YOU'VE GOT!
AIEEEEEE!
KA-BOOM!
GET DOWN!
IS THAT IT?
Y-YOU'RE BLEEDING?
I'M STRONG BUT I'M NOT INVULN--HONESTLY, HOW MANY TIMES DO I HAVE TO SAY THIS?
THOOM! THOOM!
M-MORE OF THEM? BOBBY, I DON'T THINK--
ON YOUR FEET! HOLD THIS TUNNEL!

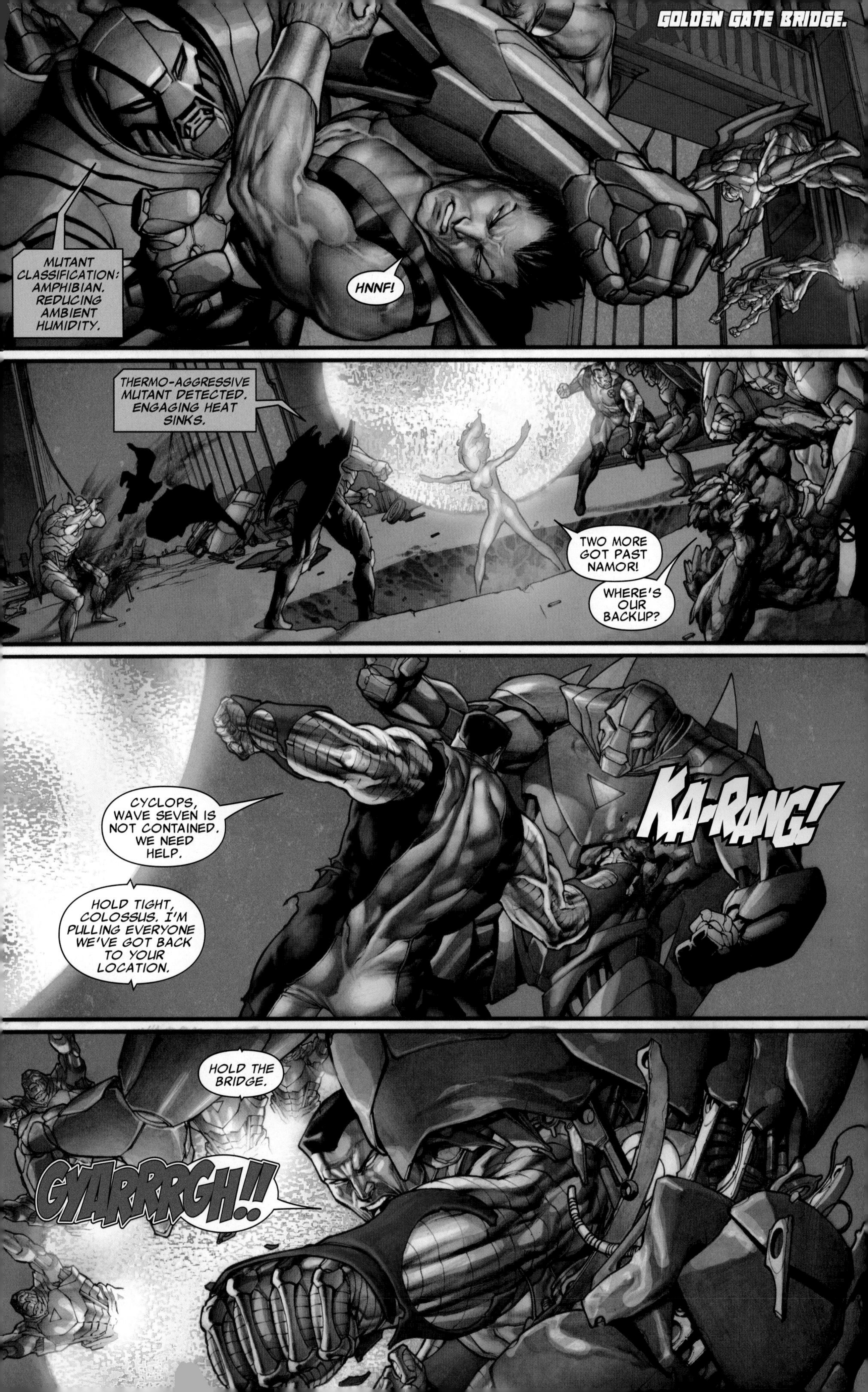
GOLDEN GATE BRIDGE.
MUTANT CLASSIFICATION: AMPHIBIAN. REDUCING AMBIENT HUMIDITY.
HNNF!
THERMO-AGGRESSIVE MUTANT DETECTED. ENGAGING HEAT SINKS.
TWO MORE GOT PAST NAMOR!
WHERE'S OUR BACKUP?
CYCLOPS, WAVE SEVEN IS NOT CONTAINED. WE NEED HELP.
KA-RANG!
HOLD TIGHT, COLOSSUS. I'M PULLING EVERYONE WE'VE GOT BACK TO YOUR LOCATION.
HOLD THE BRIDGE.
GYARRRGH!!

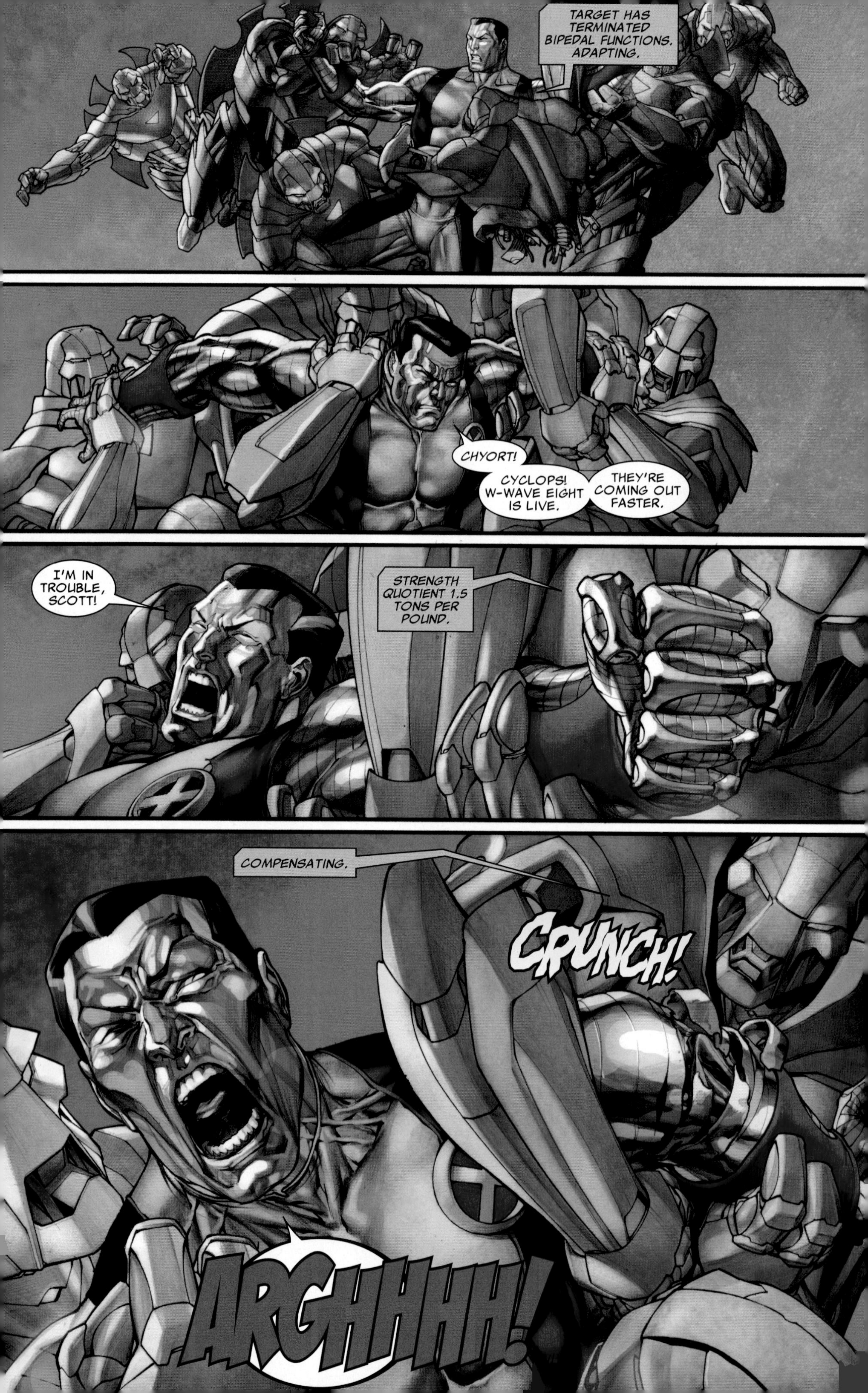
TARGET HAS TERMINATED BIPEDAL FUNCTIONS. ADAPTING.
CHYORT!
CYCLOPS! W-WAVE EIGHT IS LIVE.
THEY'RE COMING OUT FASTER.
I'M IN TROUBLE, SCOTT!
STRENGTH QUOTIENT 1.5 TONS PER POUND.
COMPENSATING.
CRUNCH!
ARGHHHH!

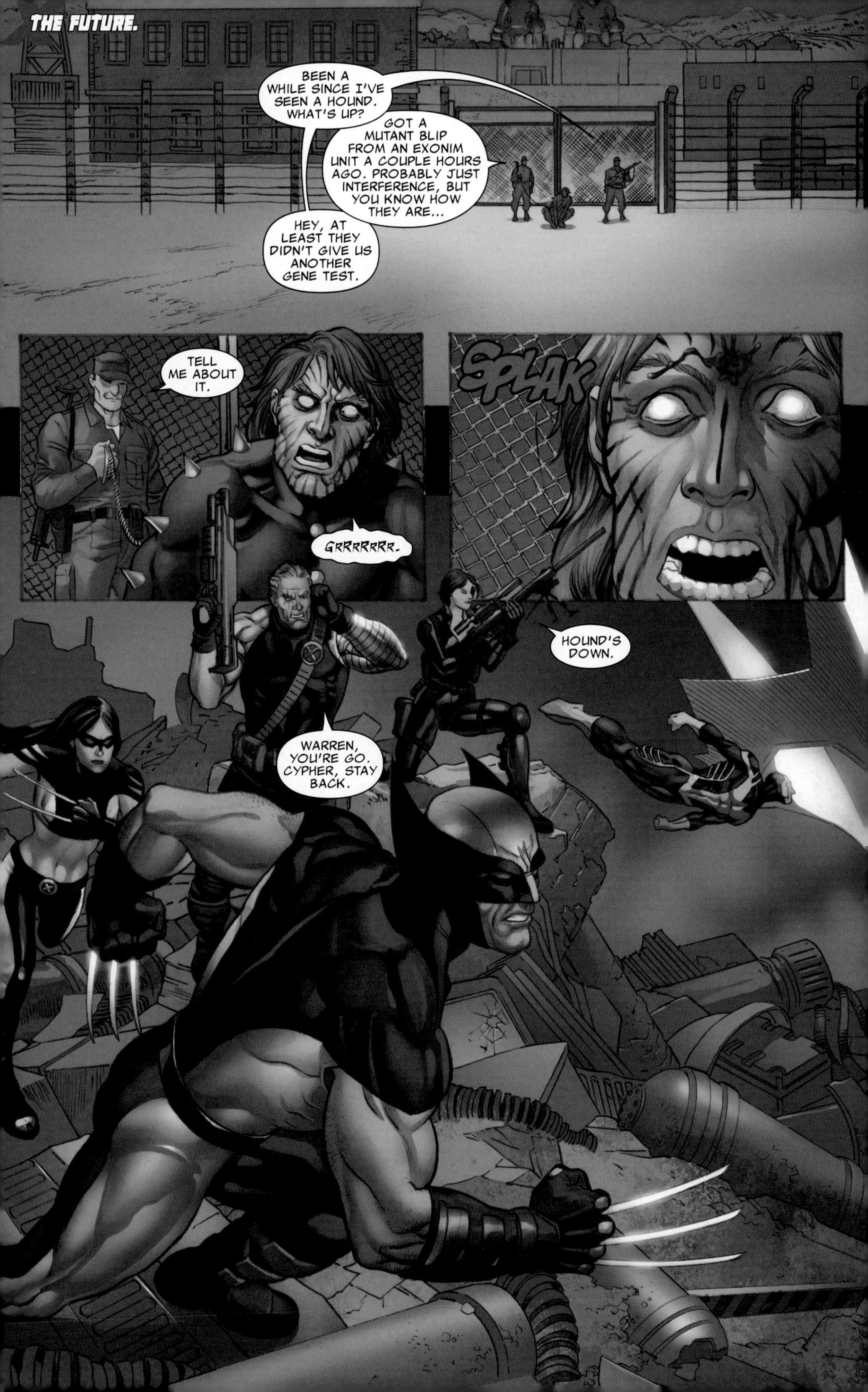
THE FUTURE.
BEEN A WHILE SINCE I'VE SEEN A HOUND. WHAT'S UP?
GOT A MUTANT BLIP FROM AN EXONIM UNIT A COUPLE HOURS AGO. PROBABLY JUST INTERFERENCE, BUT YOU KNOW HOW THEY ARE...
HEY, AT LEAST THEY DIDN'T GIVE US ANOTHER GENE TEST.
TELL ME ABOUT IT.
GRRRRRRR.
SPLAK
HOUND'S DOWN.
WARREN, YOU'RE GO. CYPHER, STAY BACK.

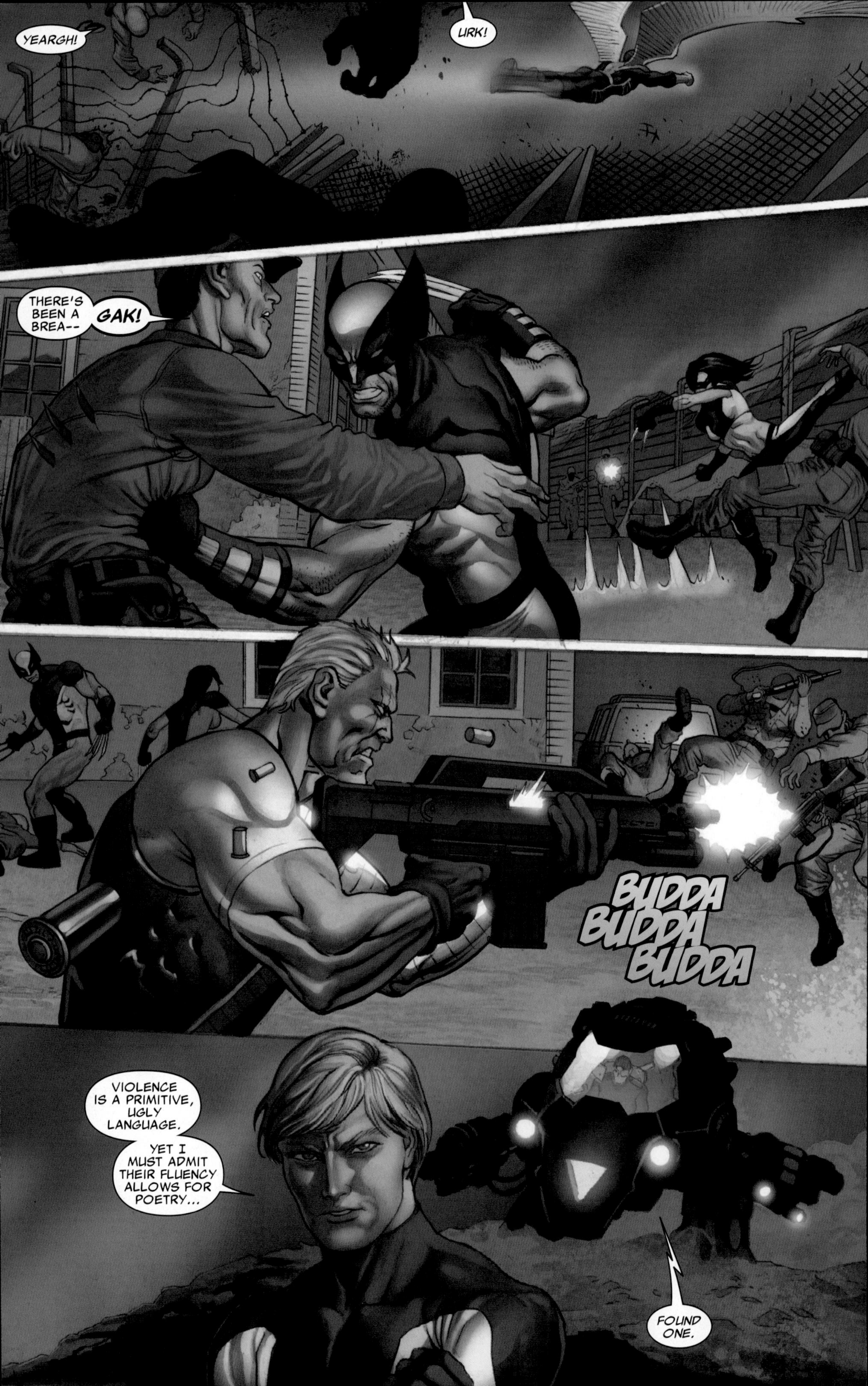
YEARGH!
URK!
THERE'S BEEN A BREA--
GAK!
BUDDA BUDDA BUDDA
VIOLENCE IS A PRIMITIVE, UGLY LANGUAGE.
YET I MUST ADMIT THEIR FLUENCY ALLOWS FOR POETRY...
FOUND ONE.

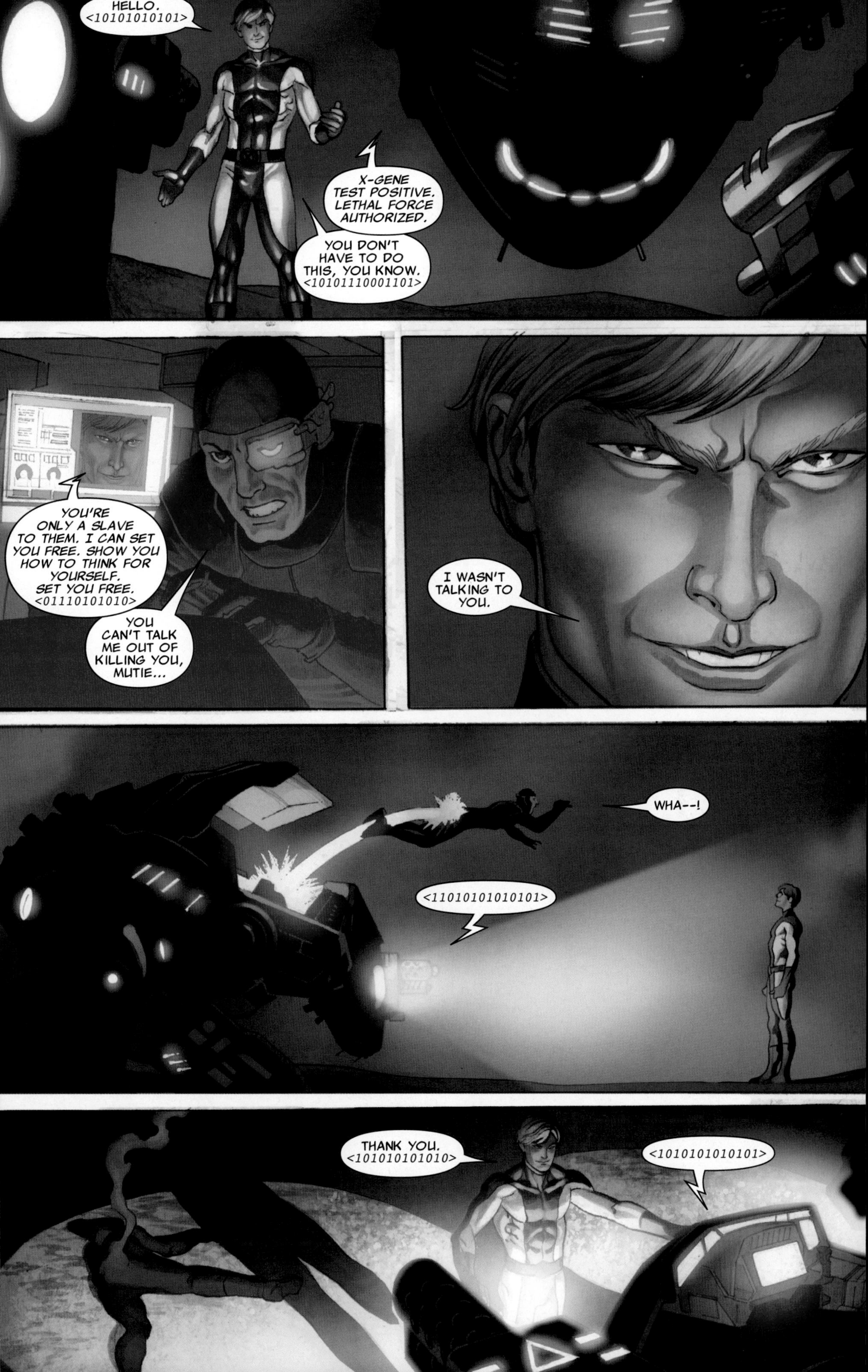
HELLO. <10101010101>
X-GENE TEST POSITIVE. LETHAL FORCE AUTHORIZED.
YOU DON'T HAVE TO DO THIS, YOU KNOW. <10101110001101>
YOU'RE ONLY A SLAVE TO THEM. I CAN SET YOU FREE. SHOW YOU HOW TO THINK FOR YOURSELF. SET YOU FREE. <01110101010>
YOU CAN'T TALK ME OUT OF KILLING YOU, MUTIE...
I WASN'T TALKING TO YOU.
WHA--!
<11010101010101>
THANK YOU. <101010101010>
<1010101010101>

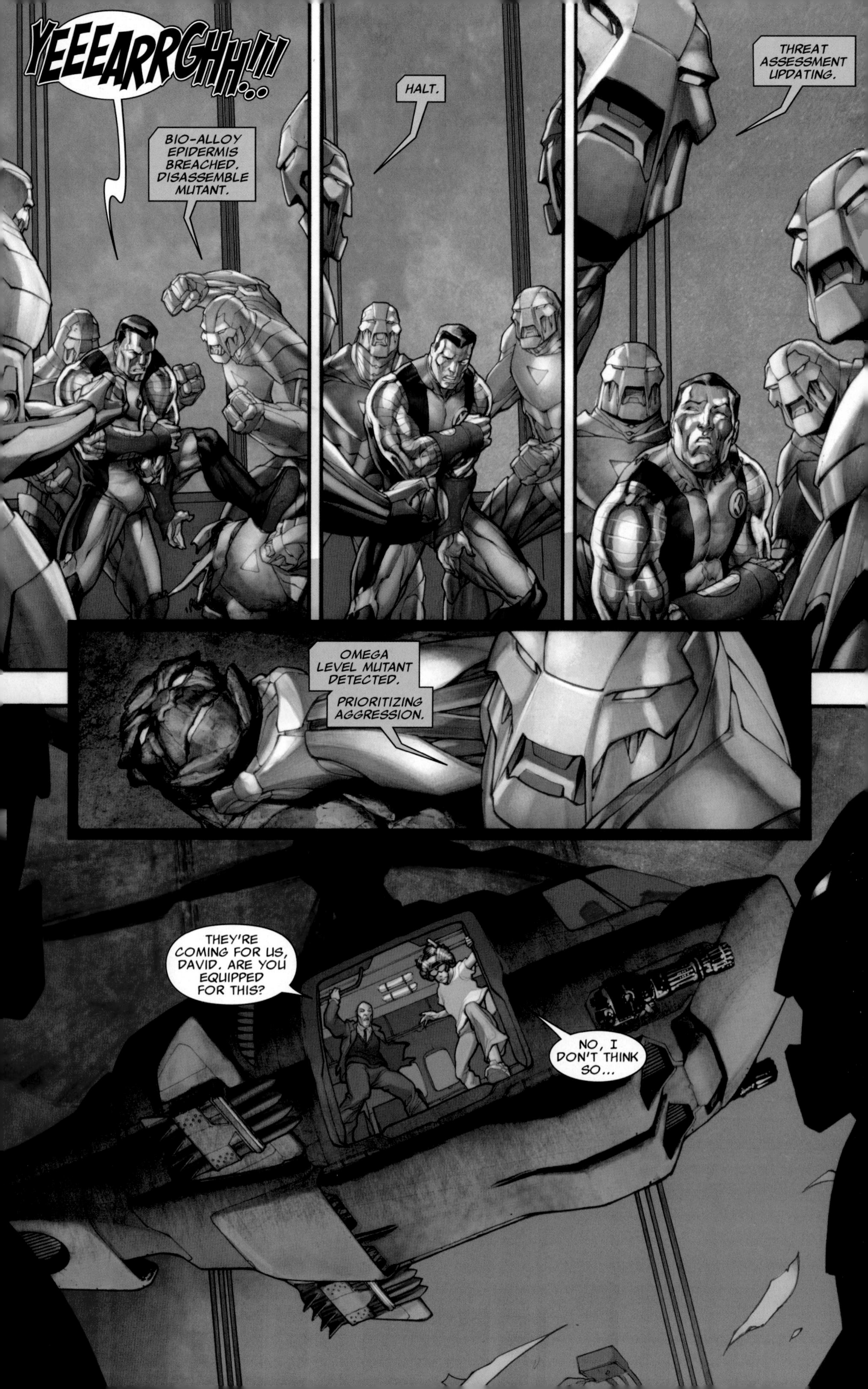
YEEEARRGHH!!!..
BIO-ALLOY EPIDERMIS BREACHED. DISASSEMBLE MUTANT.
HALT.
THREAT ASSESSMENT UPDATING.
OMEGA LEVEL MUTANT DETECTED.
PRIORITIZING AGGRESSION.
THEY'RE COMING FOR US, DAVID. ARE YOU EQUIPPED FOR THIS?
NO, I DON'T THINK SO...

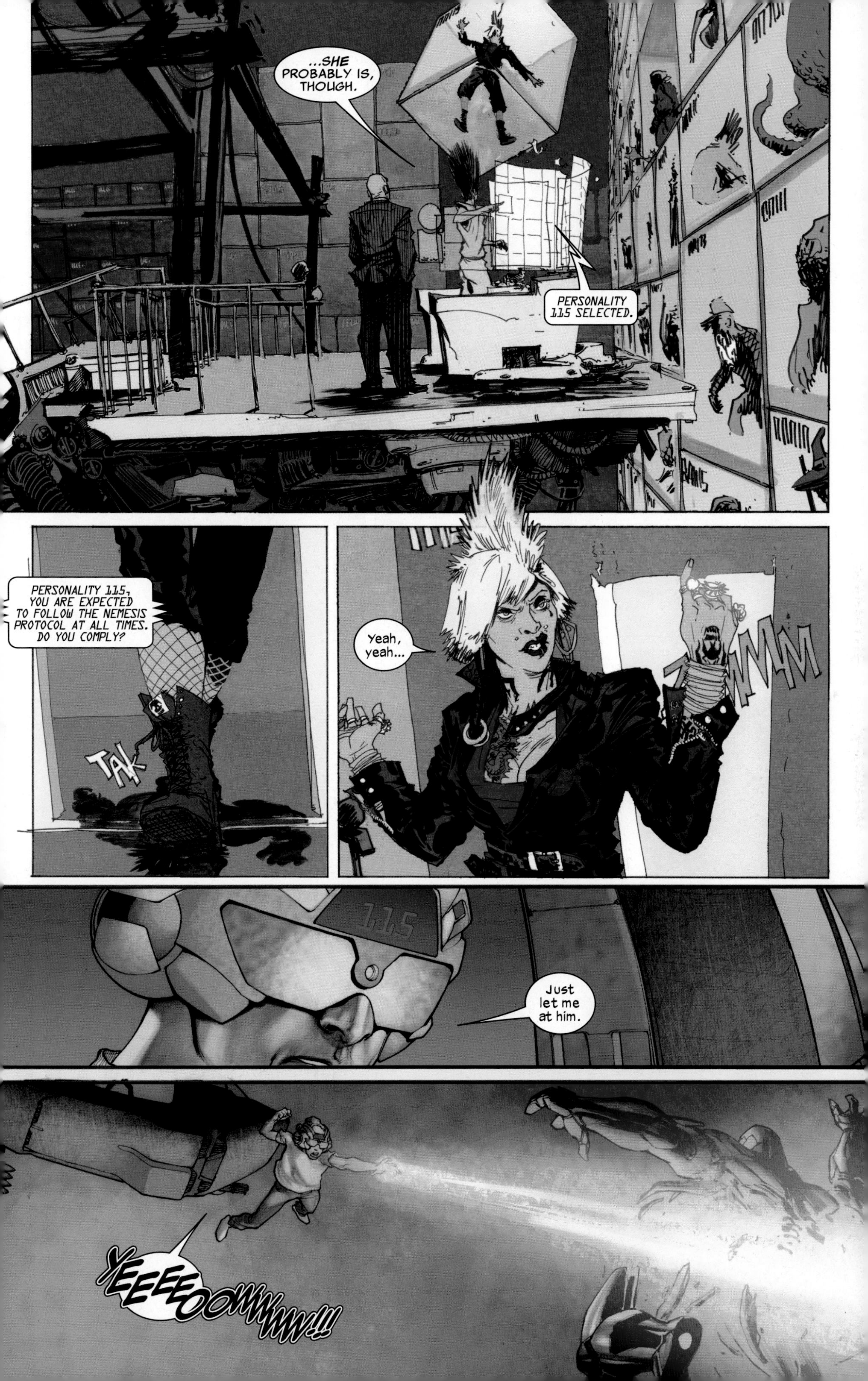
...SHE PROBABLY IS, THOUGH.
PERSONALITY 115 SELECTED.
PERSONALITY 115, YOU ARE EXPECTED TO FOLLOW THE NEMESIS PROTOCOL AT ALL TIMES. DO YOU COMPLY?
TAK
Yeah, yeah...
Just let me at him.
YEEEEOOWWWW!!!

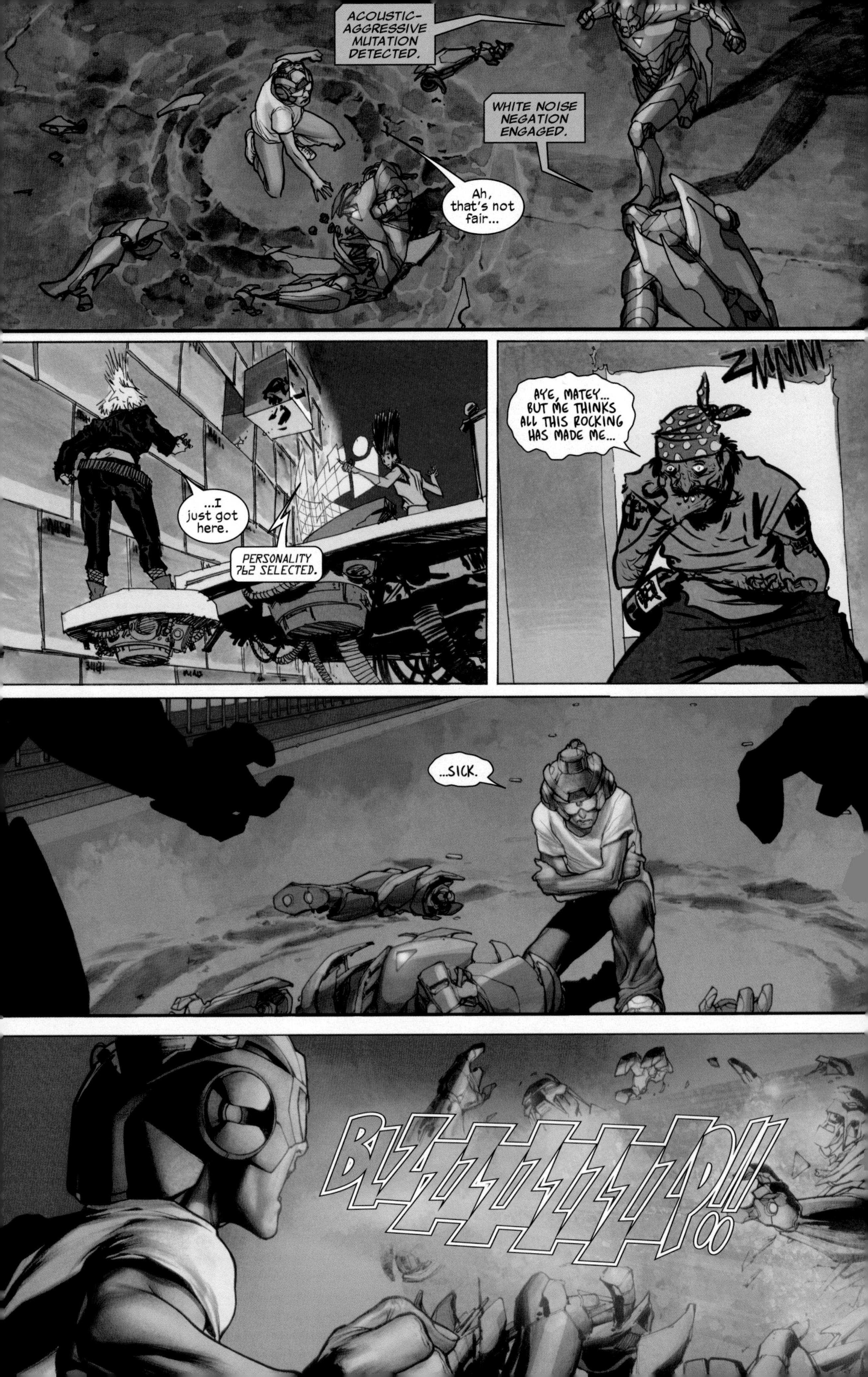
ACOUSTIC-AGGRESSIVE MUTATION DETECTED.
WHITE NOISE NEGATION ENGAGED.
Ah, that's not fair...
...I just got here.
PERSONALITY 762 SELECTED.
ZMMM
AYE, MATEY... BUT ME THINKS ALL THIS ROCKING HAS MADE ME...
...SICK.

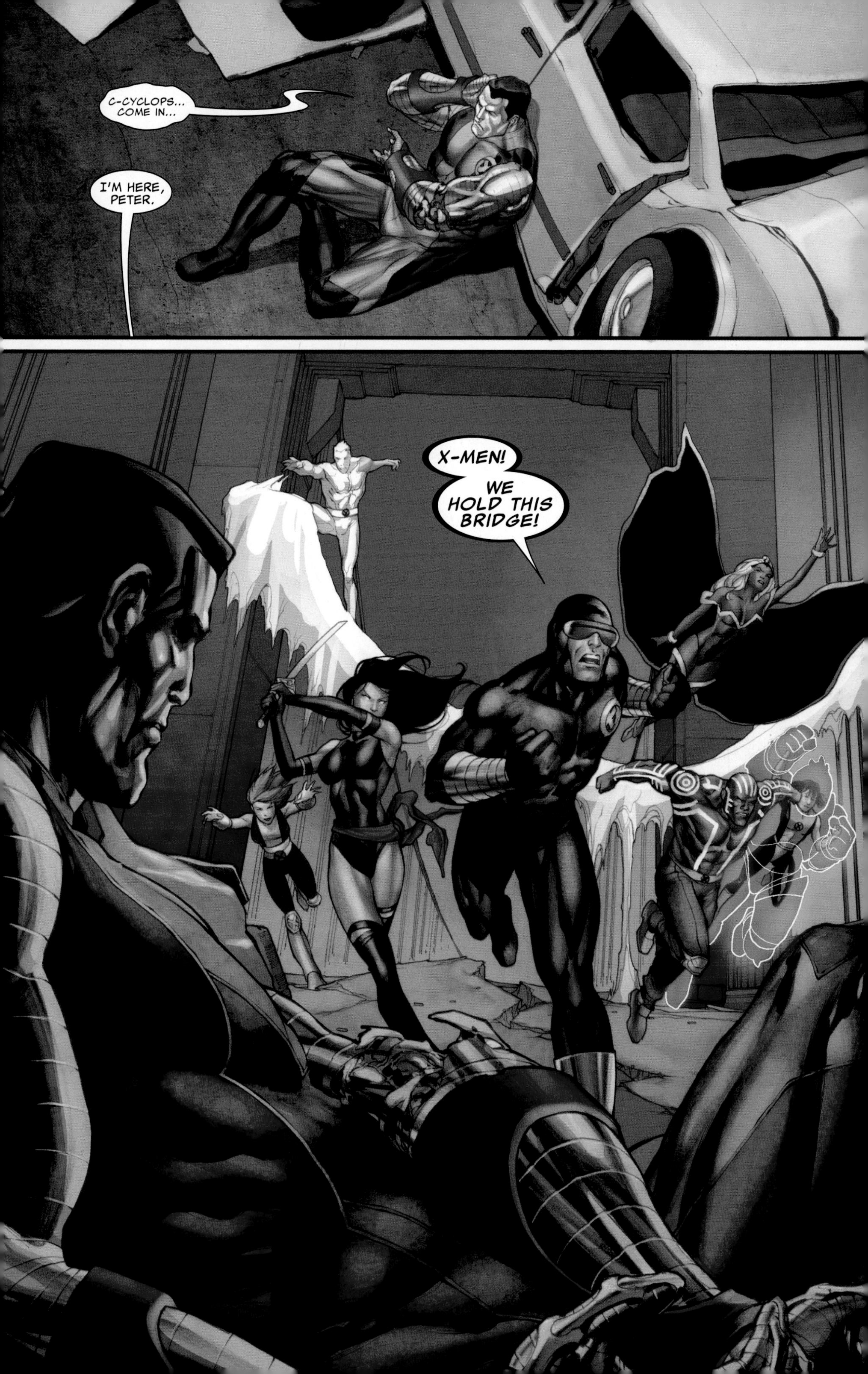
C-CYCLOPS... COME IN...
I'M HERE, PETER.
X-MEN!
WE HOLD THIS BRIDGE!

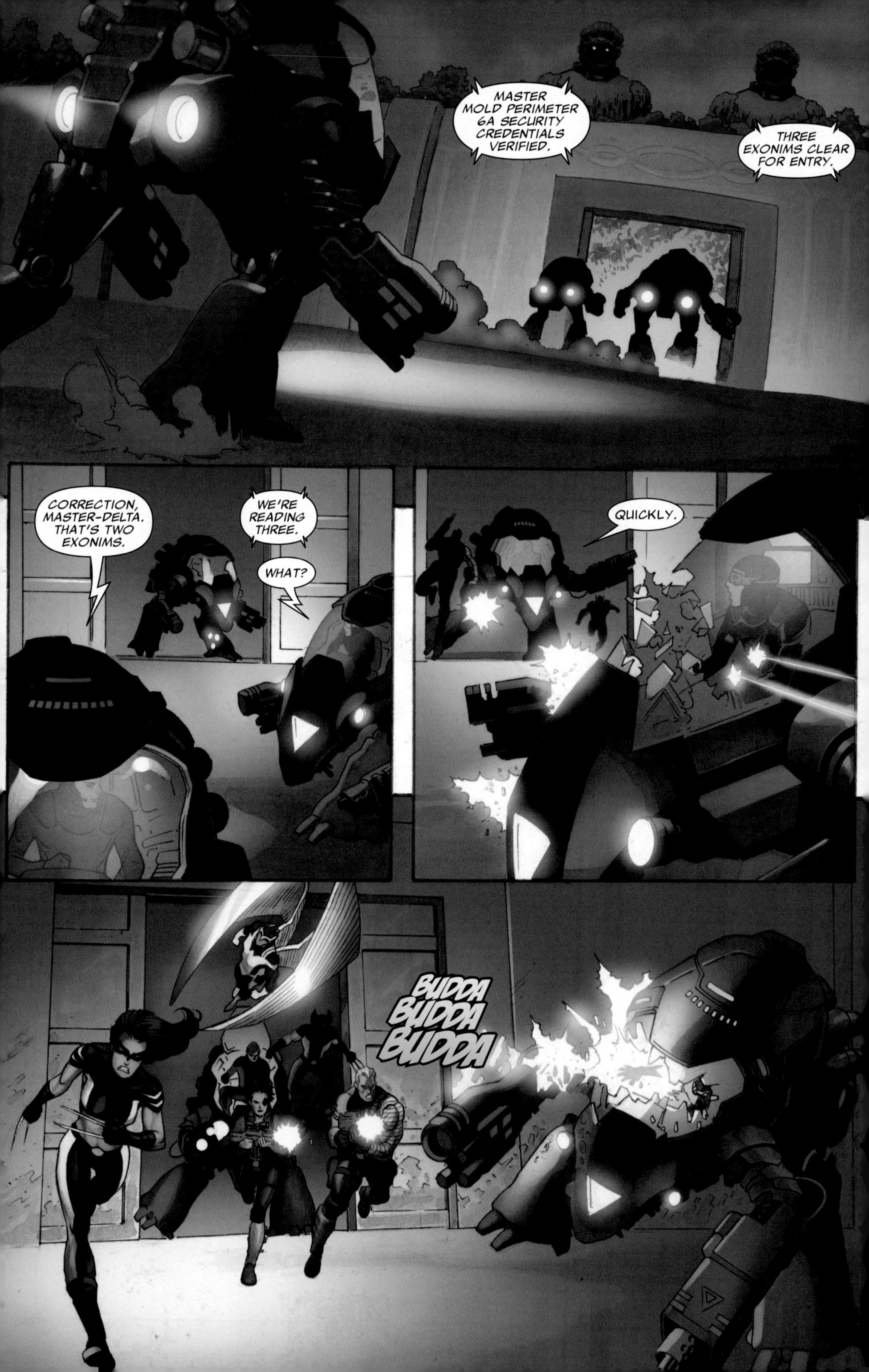

MASTER MOLD PERIMETER 6A SECURITY CREDENTIALS VERIFIED.
THREE EXONIMS CLEAR FOR ENTRY.
CORRECTION, MASTER-DELTA. THAT'S TWO EXONIMS.
WE'RE READING THREE.
WHAT?
QUICKLY.
BUDDA BUDDA BUDDA

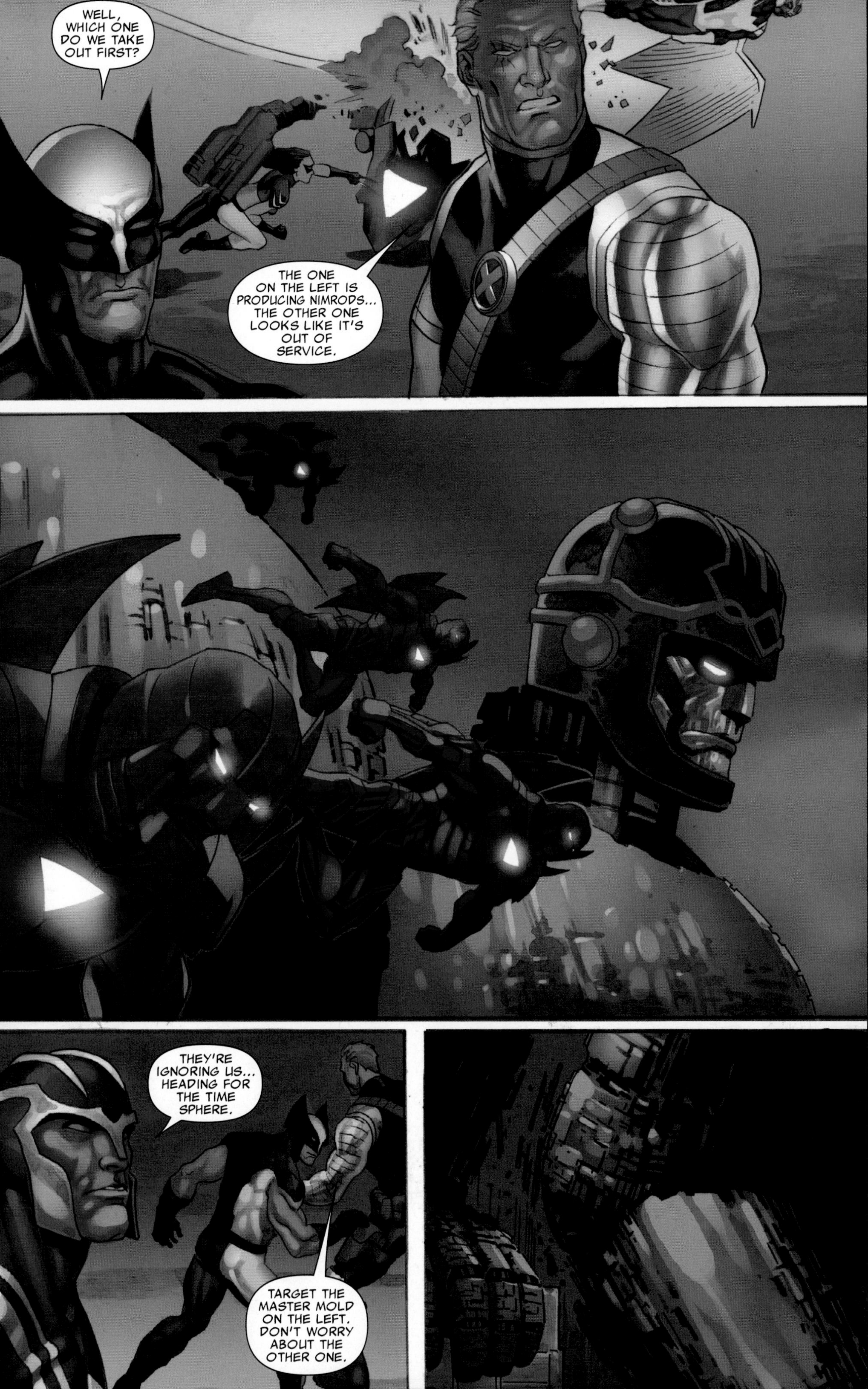
WELL, WHICH ONE DO WE TAKE OUT FIRST?
THE ONE ON THE LEFT IS PRODUCING NIMRODS... THE OTHER ONE LOOKS LIKE IT'S OUT OF SERVICE.
THEY'RE IGNORING US... HEADING FOR THE TIME SPHERE.
TARGET THE MASTER MOLD ON THE LEFT. DON'T WORRY ABOUT THE OTHER ONE.

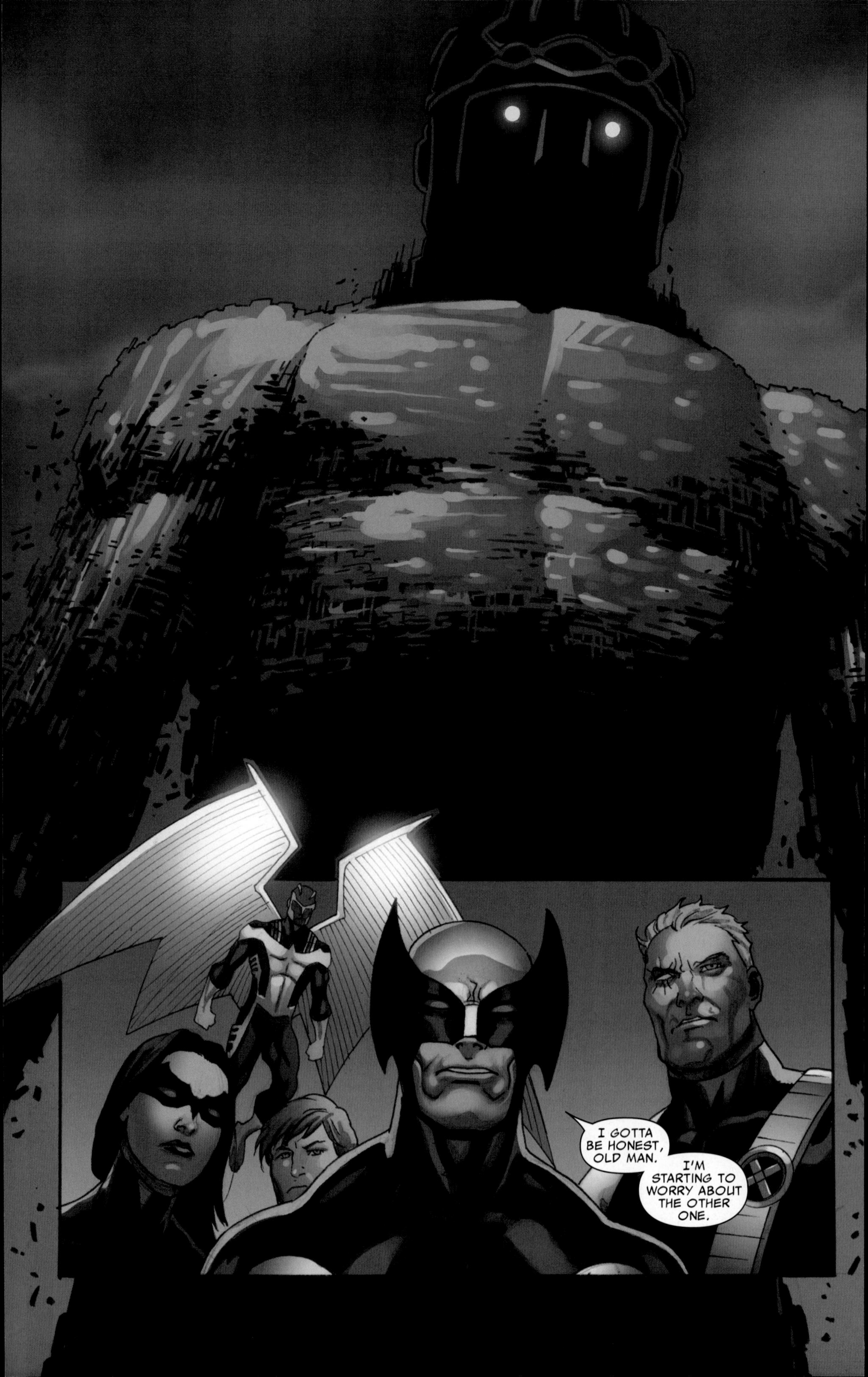
I GOTTA BE HONEST, OLD MAN.
I'M STARTING TO WORRY ABOUT THE OTHER ONE.

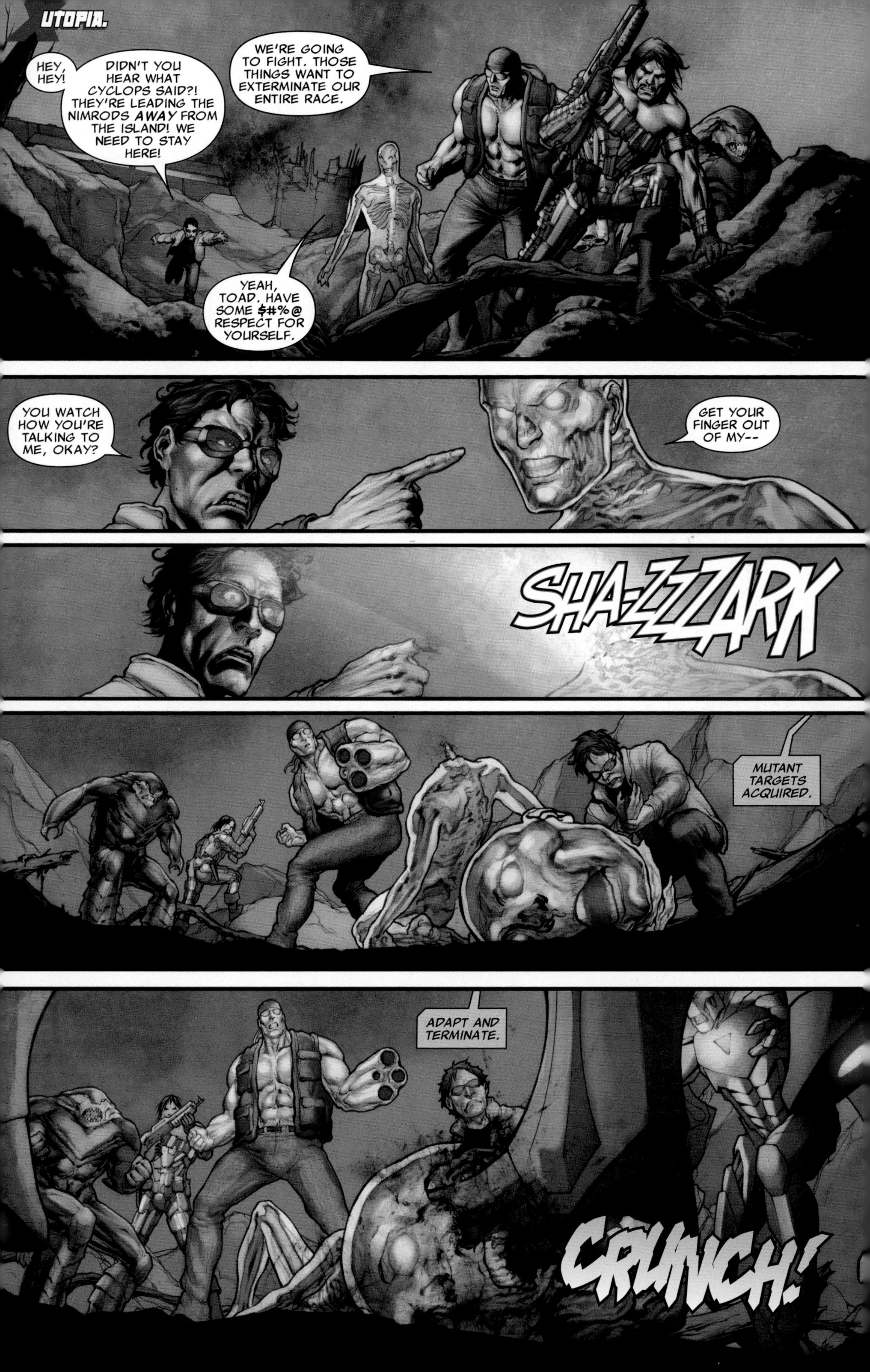
HEY, HEY!
DIDN'T YOU HEAR WHAT CYCLOPS SAID?! THEY'RE LEADING THE NIMRODS AWAY FROM THE ISLAND! WE NEED TO STAY HERE!
WE'RE GOING TO FIGHT. THOSE THINGS WANT TO EXTERMINATE OUR ENTIRE RACE.
YEAH, TOAD. HAVE SOME $#%@ RESPECT FOR YOURSELF.
YOU WATCH HOW YOU'RE TALKING TO ME, OKAY?
GET YOUR FINGER OUT OF MY--
SHA-ZZZARK
MUTANT TARGETS ACQUIRED.
ADAPT AND TERMINATE.
CRUNCH!

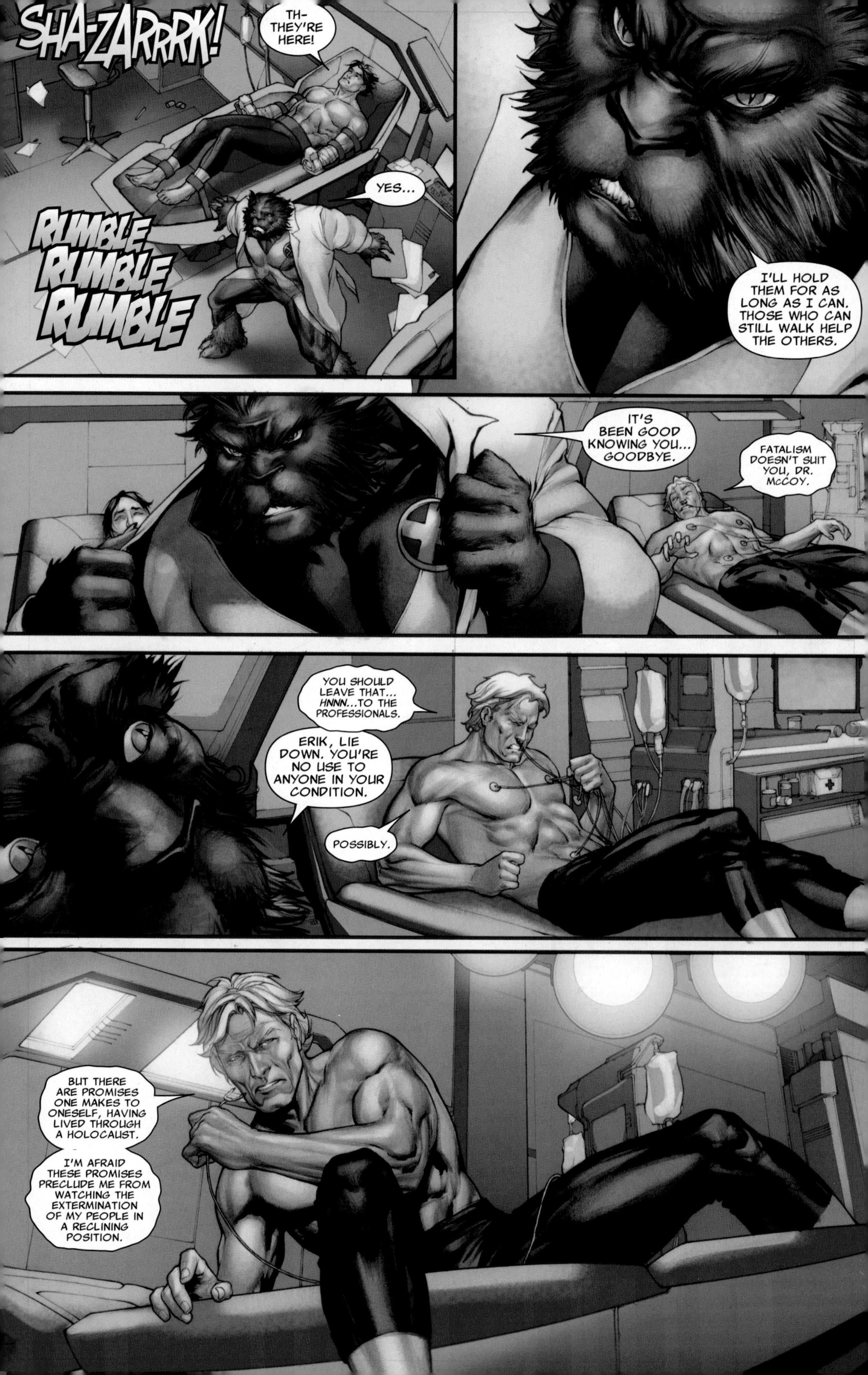
SHA-ZARRRK!
TH- THEY'RE HERE!
YES...
RUMBLE RUMBLE RUMBLE
I'LL HOLD THEM FOR AS LONG AS I CAN. THOSE WHO CAN STILL WALK HELP THE OTHERS.
IT'S BEEN GOOD KNOWING YOU... GOODBYE.
FATALISM DOESN'T SUIT YOU, DR. McCOY.
YOU SHOULD LEAVE THAT... HNNN...TO THE PROFESSIONALS.
ERIK, LIE DOWN. YOU'RE NO USE TO ANYONE IN YOUR CONDITION.
POSSIBLY.
BUT THERE ARE PROMISES ONE MAKES TO ONESELF, HAVING LIVED THROUGH A HOLOCAUST.
I'M AFRAID THESE PROMISES PRECLUDE ME FROM WATCHING THE EXTERMINATION OF MY PEOPLE IN A RECLINING POSITION.

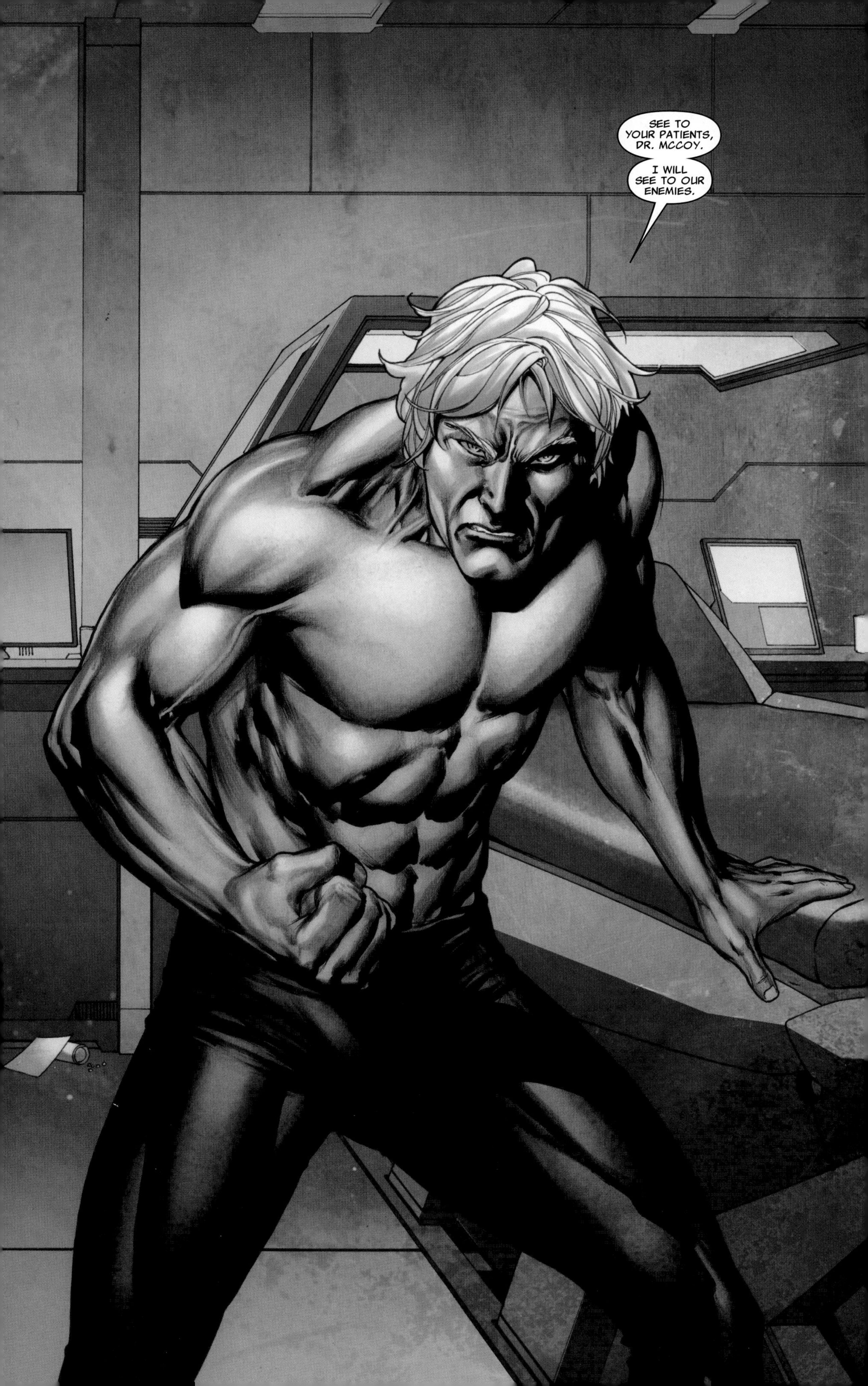
SEE TO YOUR PATIENTS, DR. MCCOY.
I WILL SEE TO OUR ENEMIES.

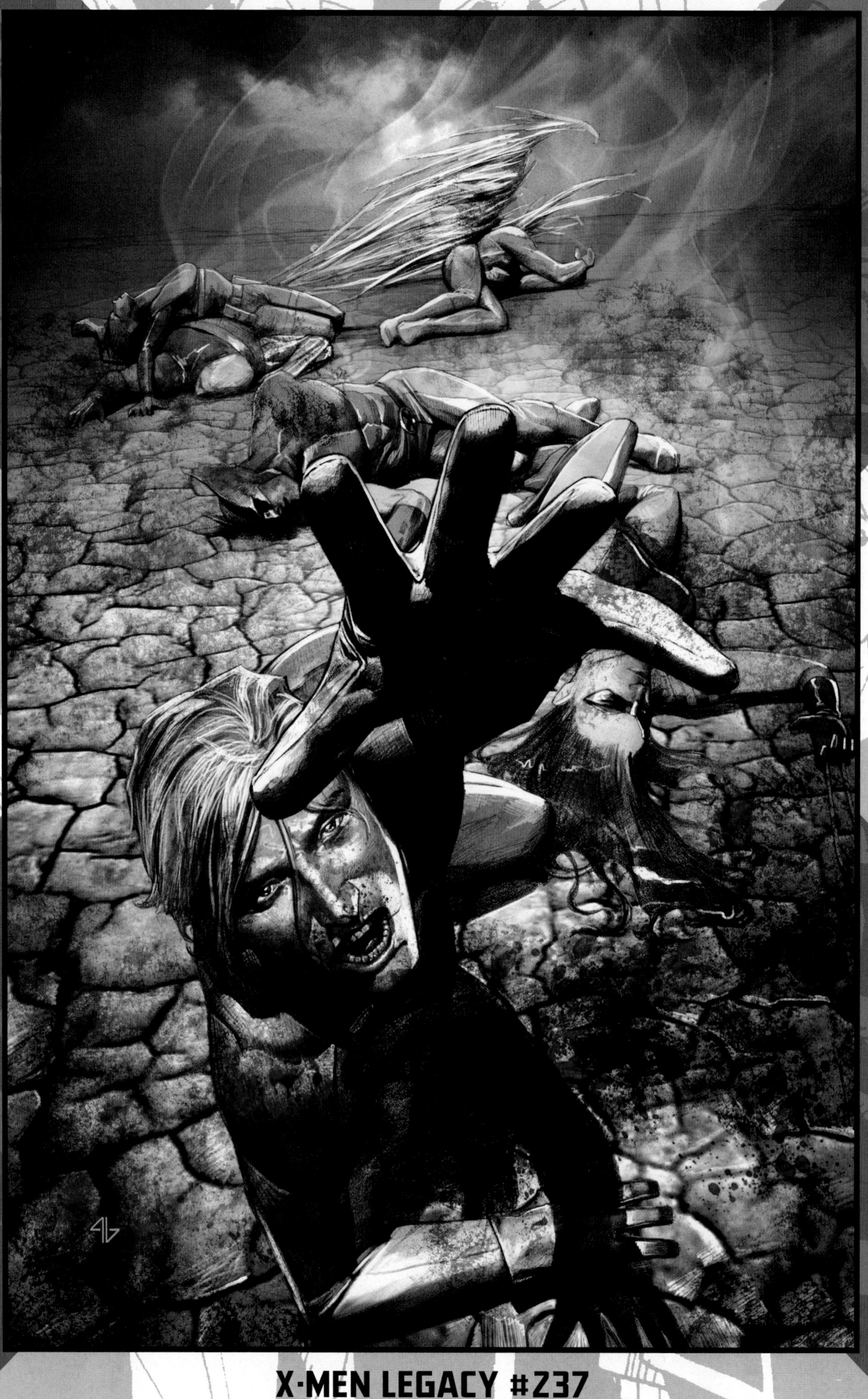

X-MEN LEGACY #237

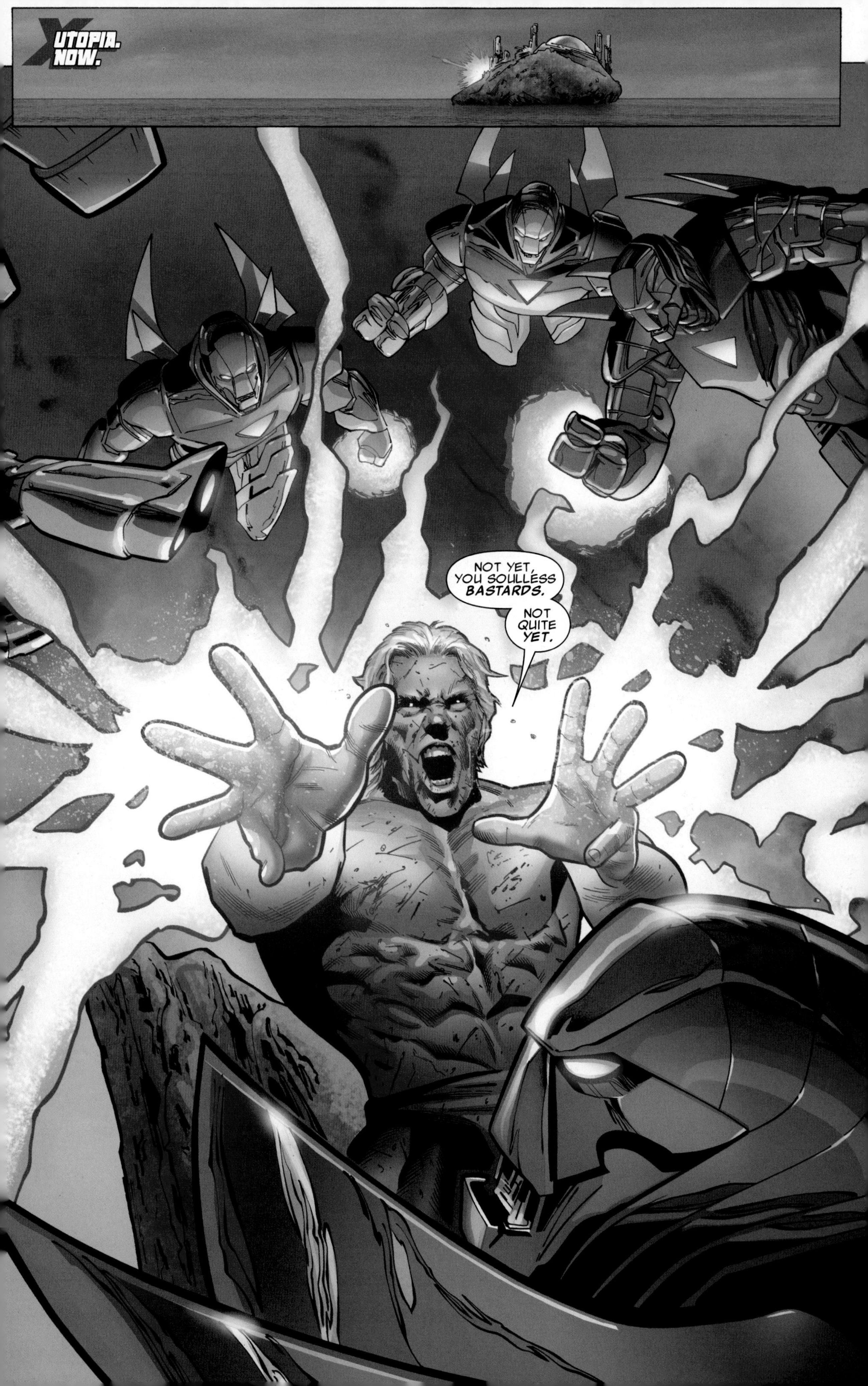
UTOPIA. NOW.
NOT YET, YOU SOULLESS BASTARDS.
NOT QUITE YET.

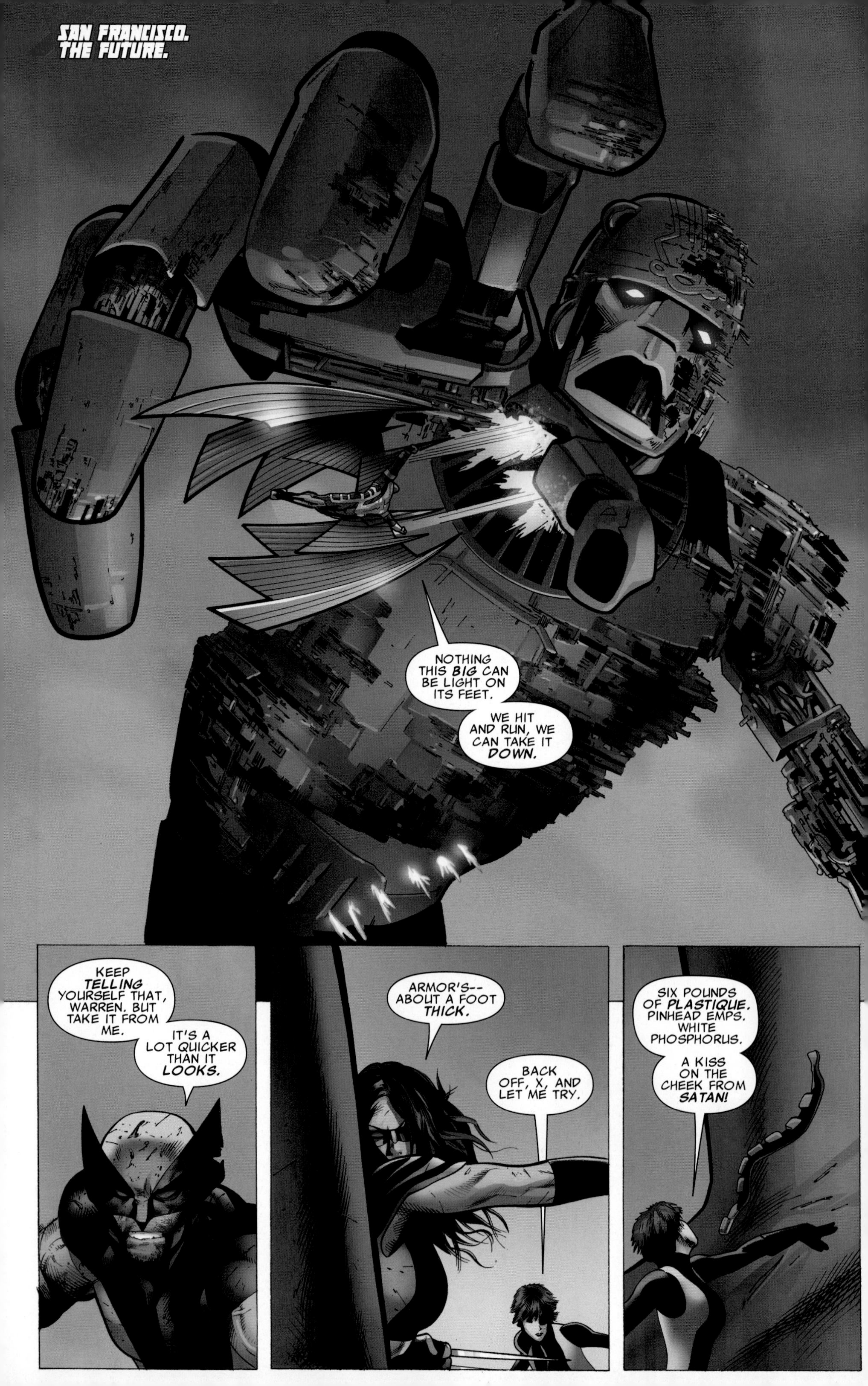
SAN FRANCISCO. THE FUTURE.
NOTHING THIS BIG CAN BE LIGHT ON ITS FEET.
WE HIT AND RUN, WE CAN TAKE IT DOWN.
KEEP TELLING YOURSELF THAT, WARREN. BUT TAKE IT FROM ME.
IT'S A LOT QUICKER THAN IT LOOKS.
ARMOR'S-- ABOUT A FOOT THICK.
BACK OFF, X, AND LET ME TRY.
SIX POUNDS OF PLASTIQUE. PINHEAD EMPS. WHITE PHOSPHORUS.
A KISS ON THE CHEEK FROM SATAN!

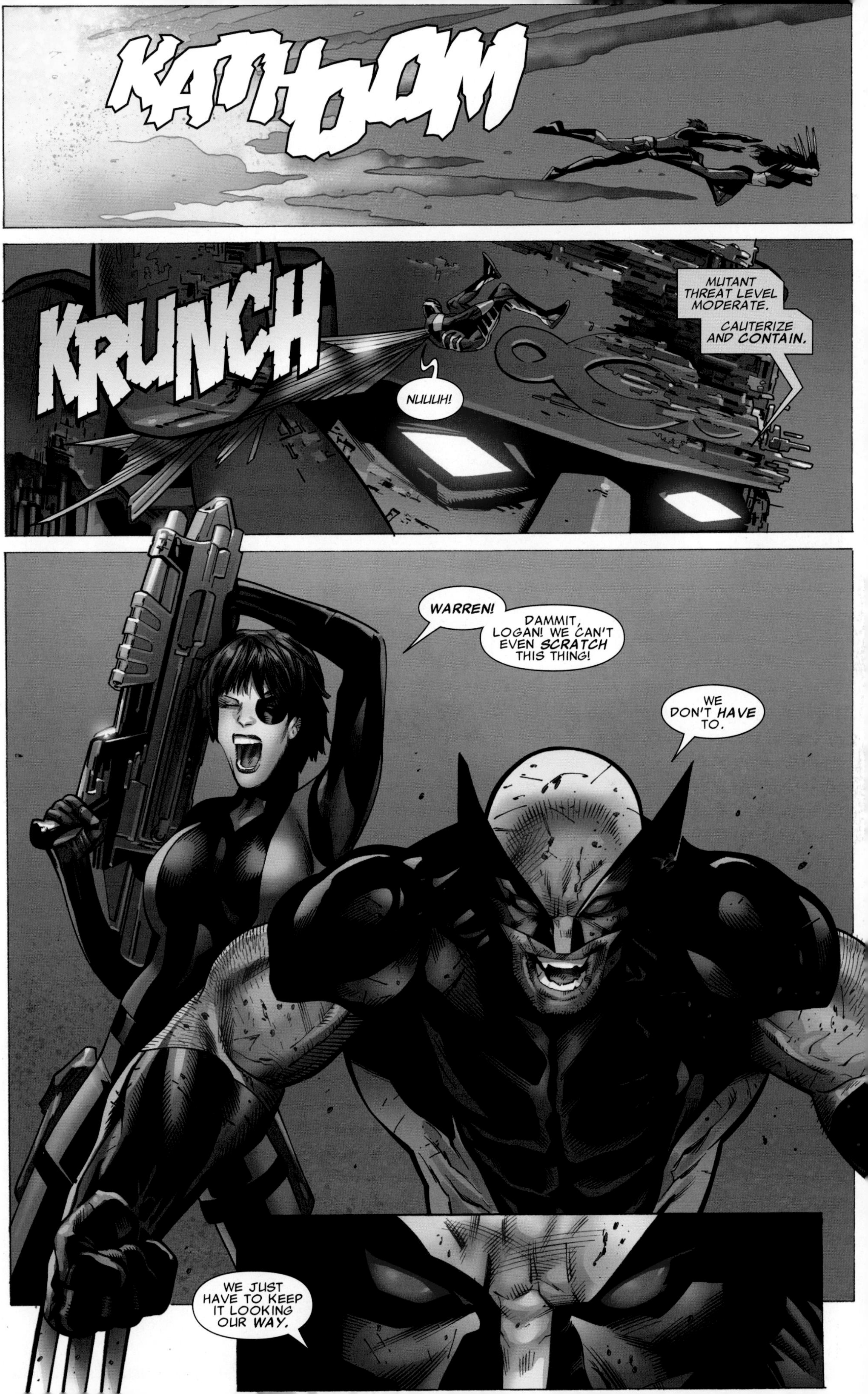
KATHOOM
KRUNCH
MUTANT THREAT LEVEL MODERATE.
CAUTERIZE AND CONTAIN.
NUUUH!
WARREN!
DAMMIT, LOGAN! WE CAN'T EVEN SCRATCH THIS THING!
WE DON'T HAVE TO.
WE JUST HAVE TO KEEP IT LOOKING OUR WAY.

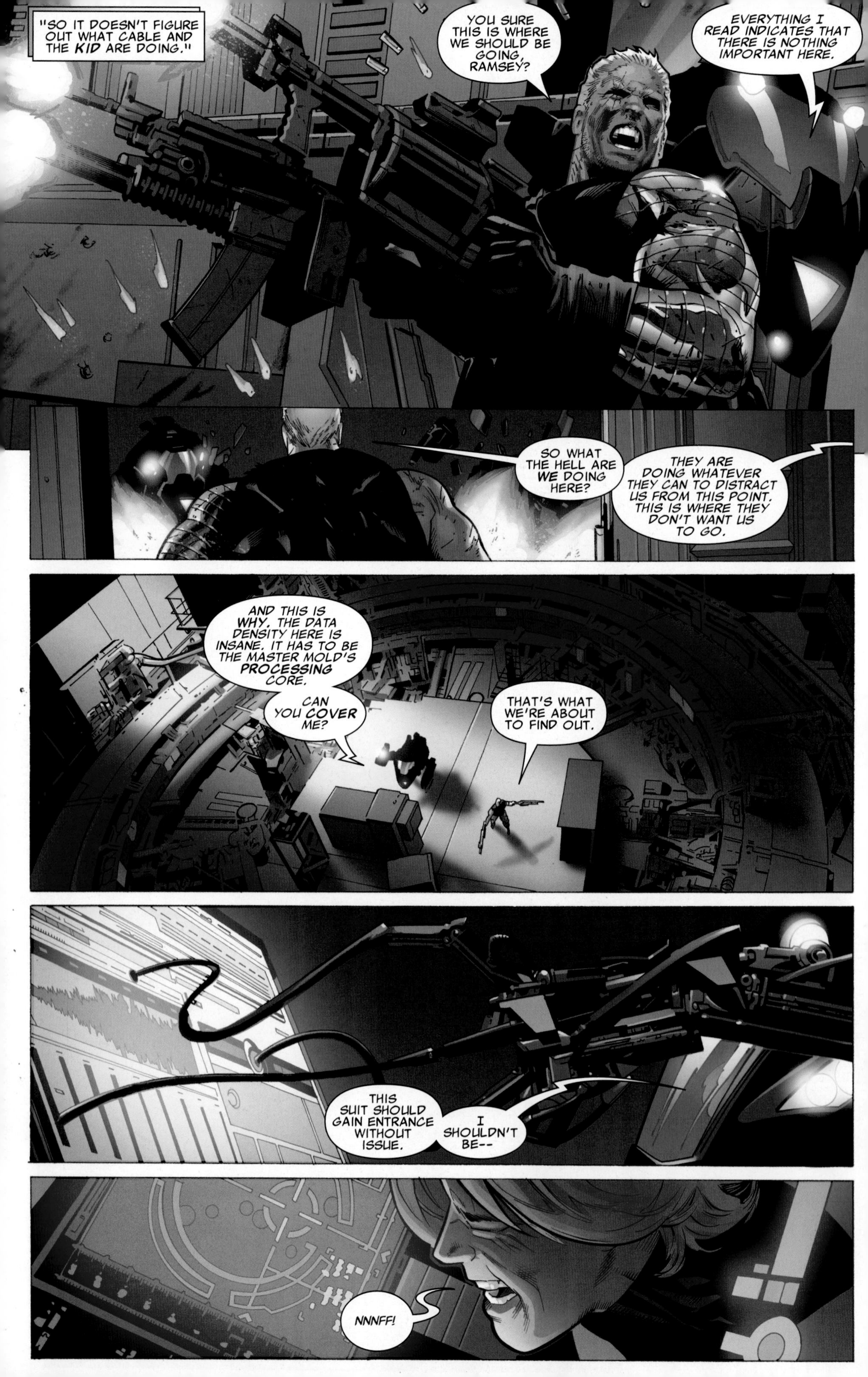
"SO IT DOESN'T FIGURE OUT WHAT CABLE AND THE KID ARE DOING."
YOU SURE THIS IS WHERE WE SHOULD BE GOING, RAMSEY?
EVERYTHING I READ INDICATES THAT THERE IS NOTHING IMPORTANT HERE.
SO WHAT THE HELL ARE WE DOING HERE?
THEY ARE DOING WHATEVER THEY CAN TO DISTRACT US FROM THIS POINT. THIS IS WHERE THEY DON'T WANT US TO GO.
AND THIS IS WHY. THE DATA DENSITY HERE IS INSANE. IT HAS TO BE THE MASTER MOLD'S PROCESSING CORE.
CAN YOU COVER ME?
THAT'S WHAT WE'RE ABOUT TO FIND OUT.
THIS SUIT SHOULD GAIN ENTRANCE WITHOUT ISSUE.
I SHOULDN'T BE--
NNNFF!

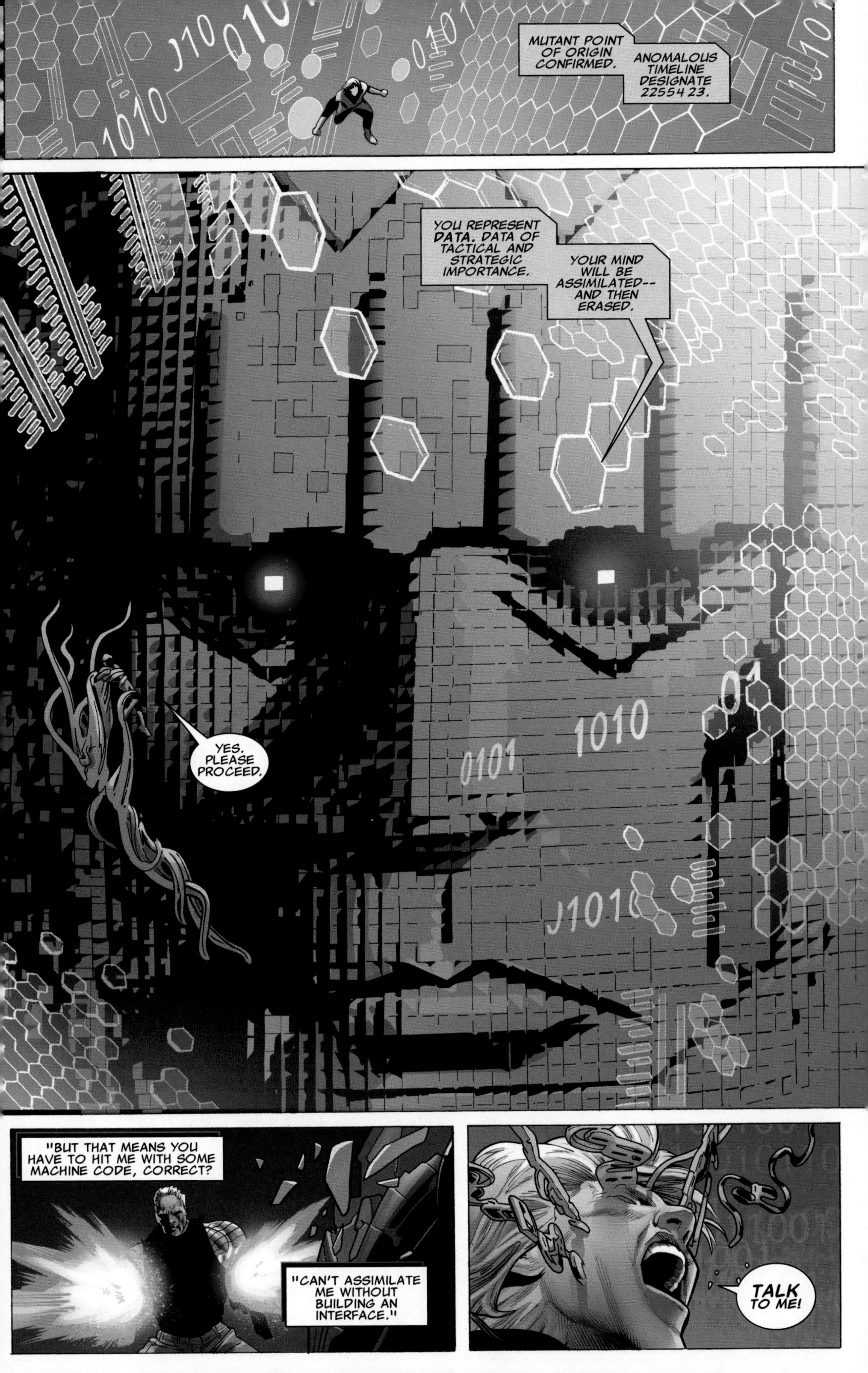
MUTANT POINT OF ORIGIN CONFIRMED.
ANOMALOUS TIMELINE DESIGNATE 2255423.
YOU REPRESENT DATA. DATA OF TACTICAL AND STRATEGIC IMPORTANCE.
YOUR MIND WILL BE ASSIMILATED-- AND THEN ERASED.
YES. PLEASE PROCEED.
"BUT THAT MEANS YOU HAVE TO HIT ME WITH SOME MACHINE CODE, CORRECT?
"CAN'T ASSIMILATE ME WITHOUT BUILDING AN INTERFACE."
TALK TO ME!

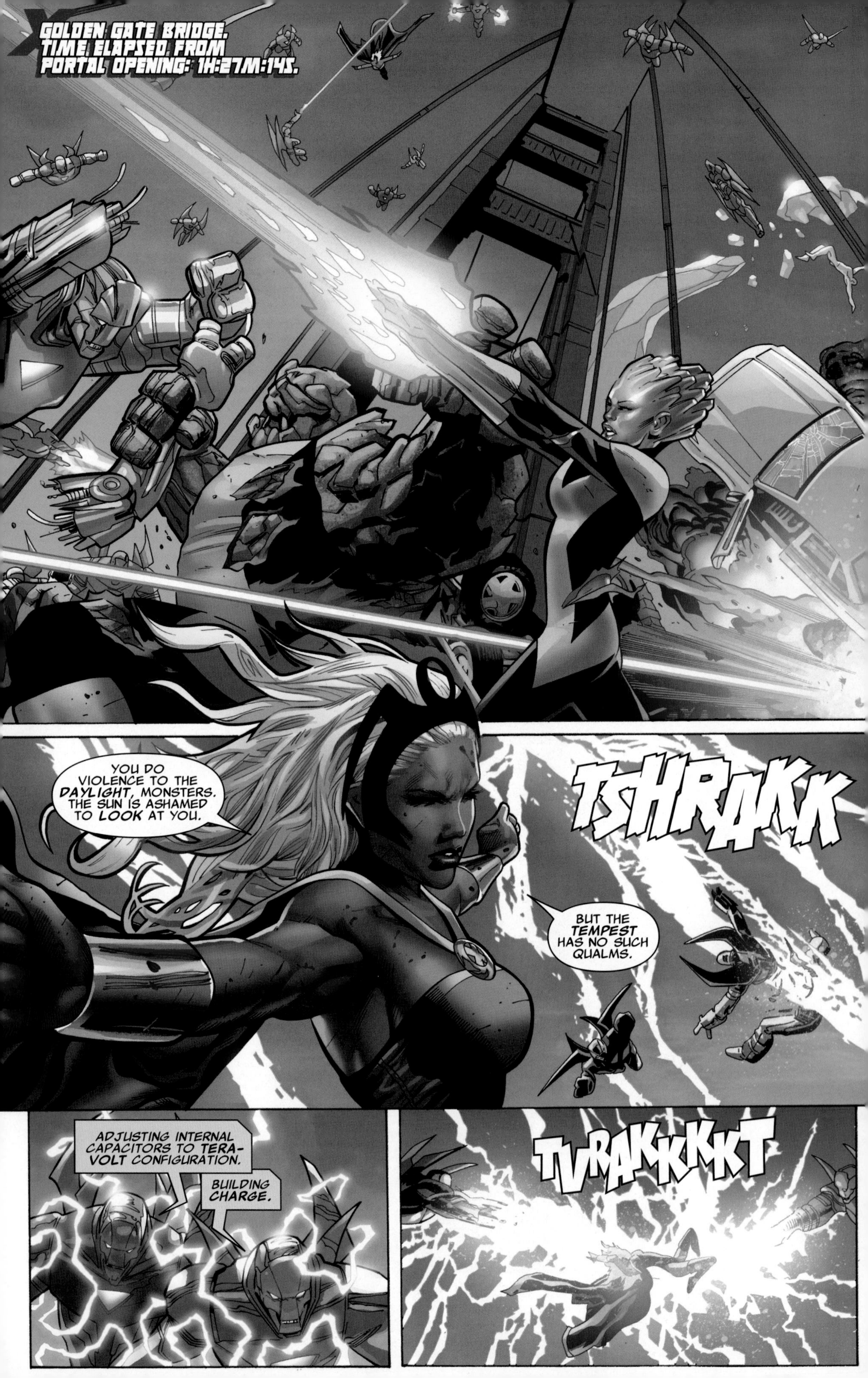
GOLDEN GATE BRIDGE. TIME ELAPSED FROM PORTAL OPENING: 1H:27M:14S.
YOU DO VIOLENCE TO THE DAYLIGHT, MONSTERS. THE SUN IS ASHAMED TO LOOK AT YOU.
TSHRAKK
BUT THE TEMPEST HAS NO SUCH QUALMS.
ADJUSTING INTERNAL CAPACITORS TO TERA-VOLT CONFIGURATION.
BUILDING CHARGE.
TVRAKKKKT

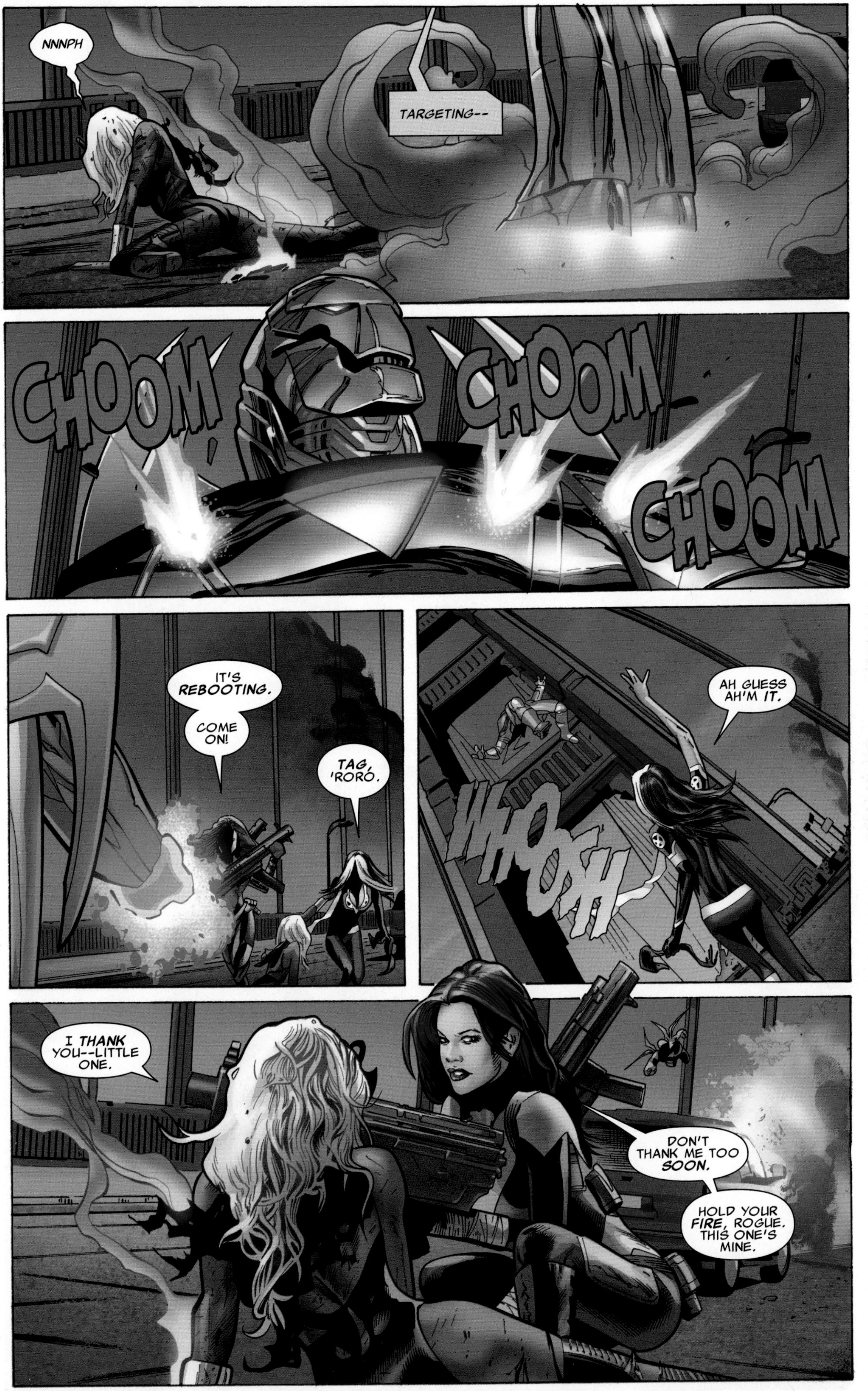
NNNPH
TARGETING--
CHOOM
CHOOM
CHOOM
IT'S REBOOTING.
COME ON!
TAG, 'RORO.
AH GUESS AH'M IT.
WHOOSH
I THANK YOU--LITTLE ONE.
DON'T THANK ME TOO SOON.
HOLD YOUR FIRE, ROGUE. THIS ONE'S MINE.

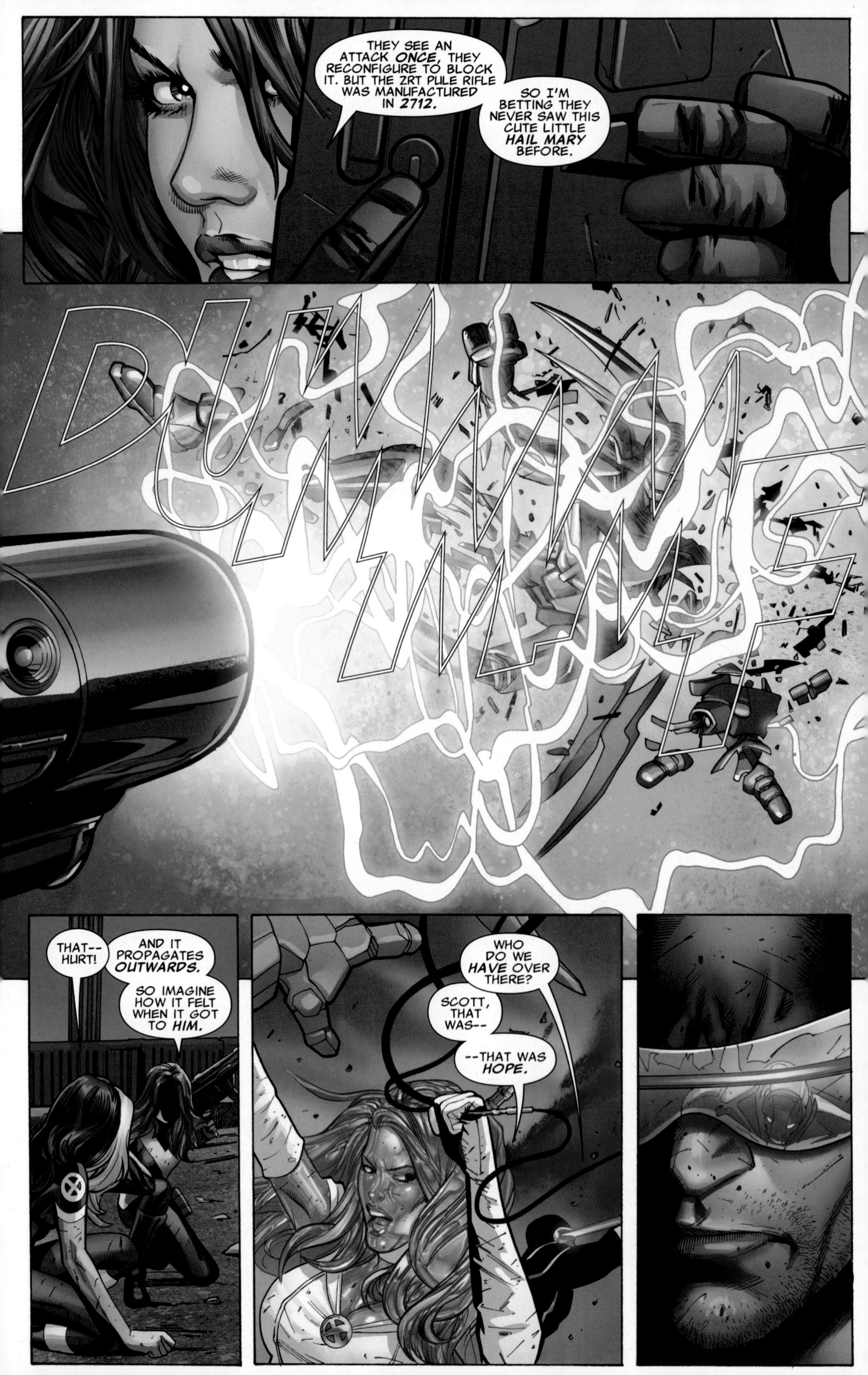
THEY SEE AN ATTACK ONCE, THEY RECONFIGURE TO BLOCK IT. BUT THE ZRT PULE RIFLE WAS MANUFACTURED IN 2712.
SO I'M BETTING THEY NEVER SAW THIS CUTE LITTLE HAIL MARY BEFORE.
DUMMMF
THAT--HURT!
AND IT PROPAGATES OUTWARDS.
SO IMAGINE HOW IT FELT WHEN IT GOT TO HIM.
WHO DO WE HAVE OVER THERE?
SCOTT, THAT WAS--
--THAT WAS HOPE.

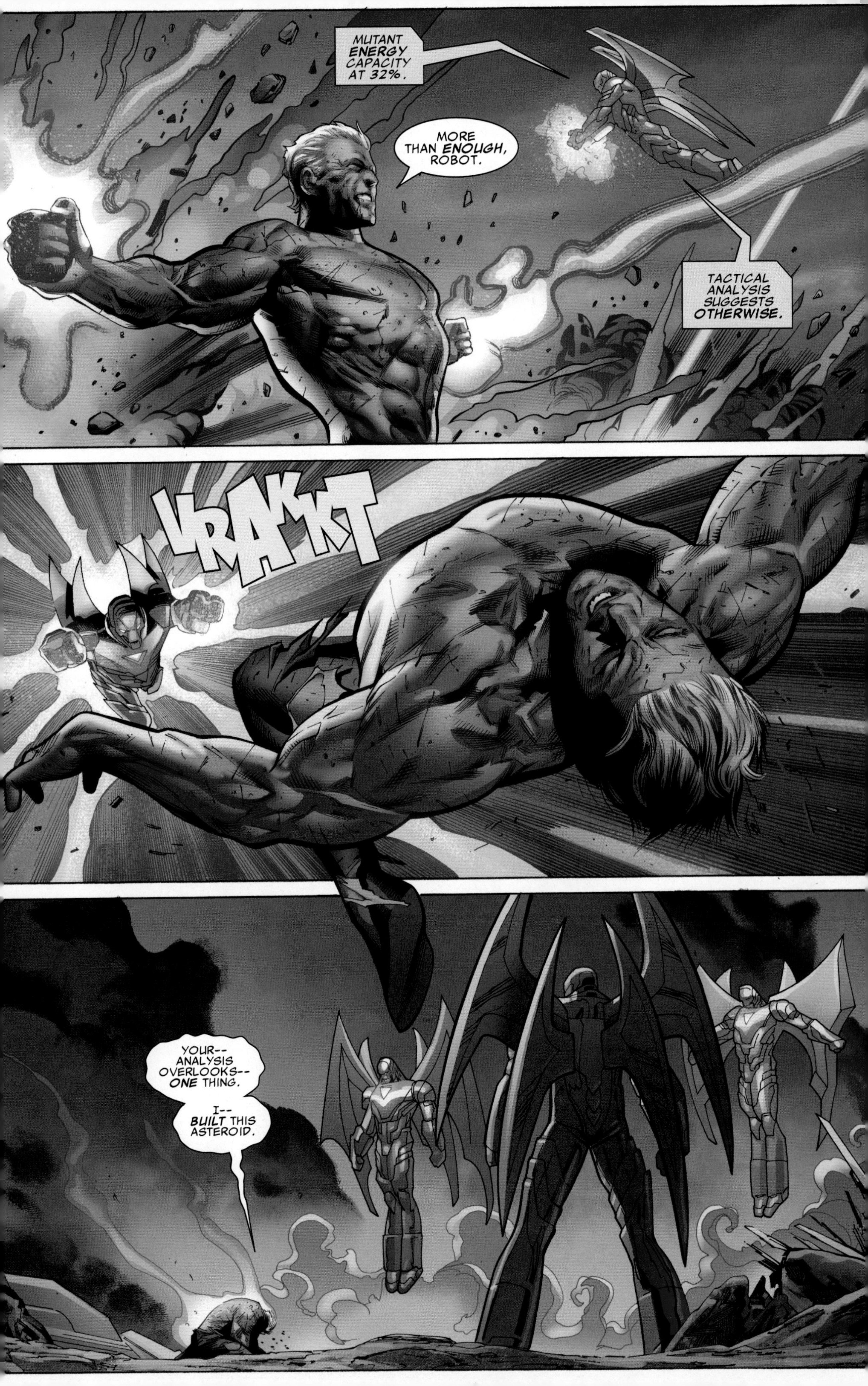
MUTANT ENERGY CAPACITY AT 32%.
MORE THAN ENOUGH, ROBOT.
TACTICAL ANALYSIS SUGGESTS OTHERWISE.
VRAKKT
YOUR-- ANALYSIS OVERLOOKS-- ONE THING.
I-- BUILT THIS ASTEROID.

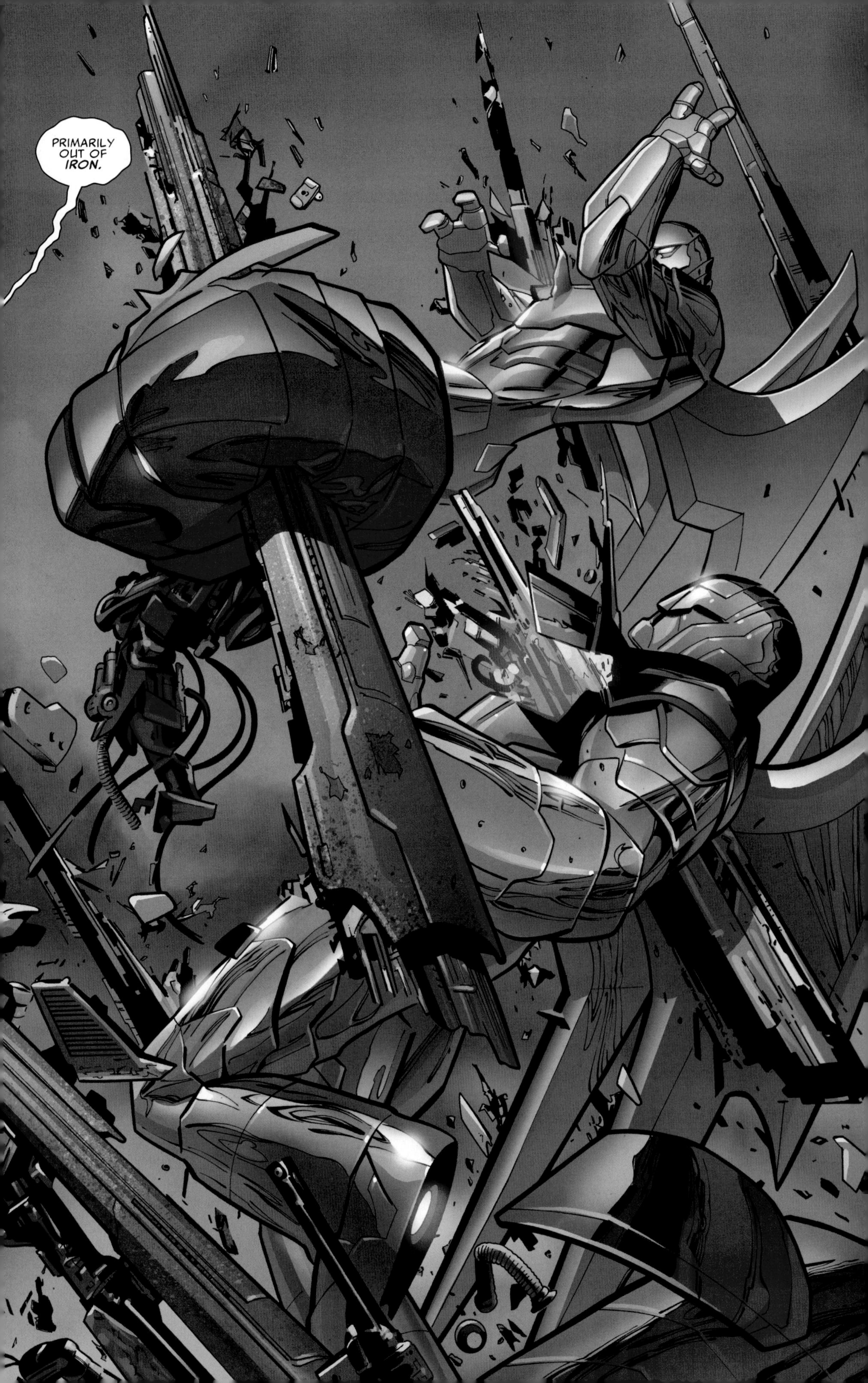
PRIMARILY OUT OF IRON.

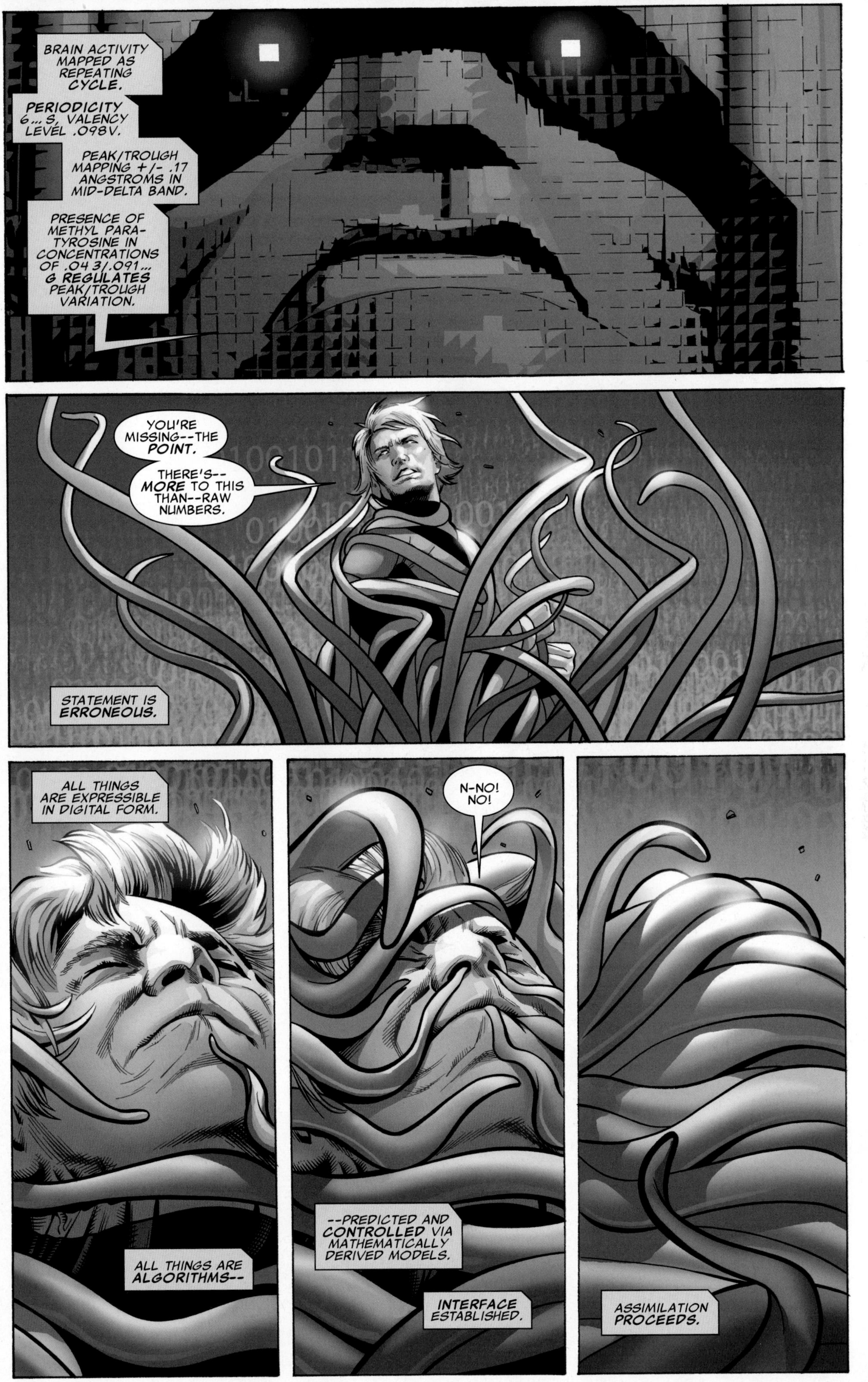
BRAIN ACTIVITY MAPPED AS REPEATING CYCLE.
PERIODICITY 6... S, VALENCY LEVEL .098V.
PEAK/TROUGH MAPPING +/- .17 ANGSTROMS IN MID-DELTA BAND.
PRESENCE OF METHYL PARA-TYROSINE IN CONCENTRATIONS OF .04 3/.091... G REGULATES PEAK/TROUGH VARIATION.
YOU'RE MISSING--THE POINT.
THERE'S--MORE TO THIS THAN--RAW NUMBERS.
STATEMENT IS ERRONEOUS.
ALL THINGS ARE EXPRESSIBLE IN DIGITAL FORM.
ALL THINGS ARE ALGORITHMS--
N-NO! NO!
--PREDICTED AND CONTROLLED VIA MATHEMATICALLY DERIVED MODELS.
INTERFACE ESTABLISHED.
ASSIMILATION PROCEEDS.

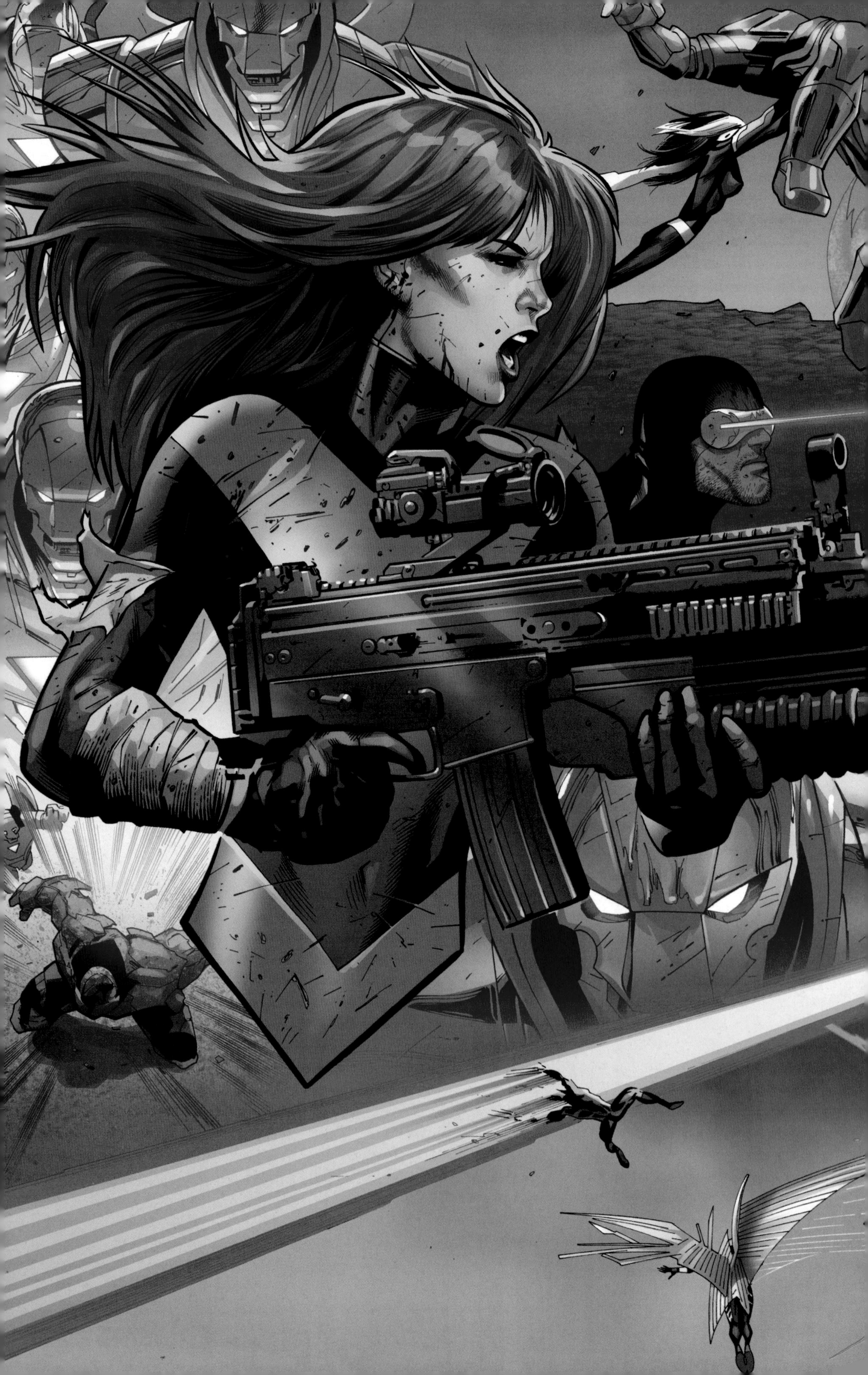

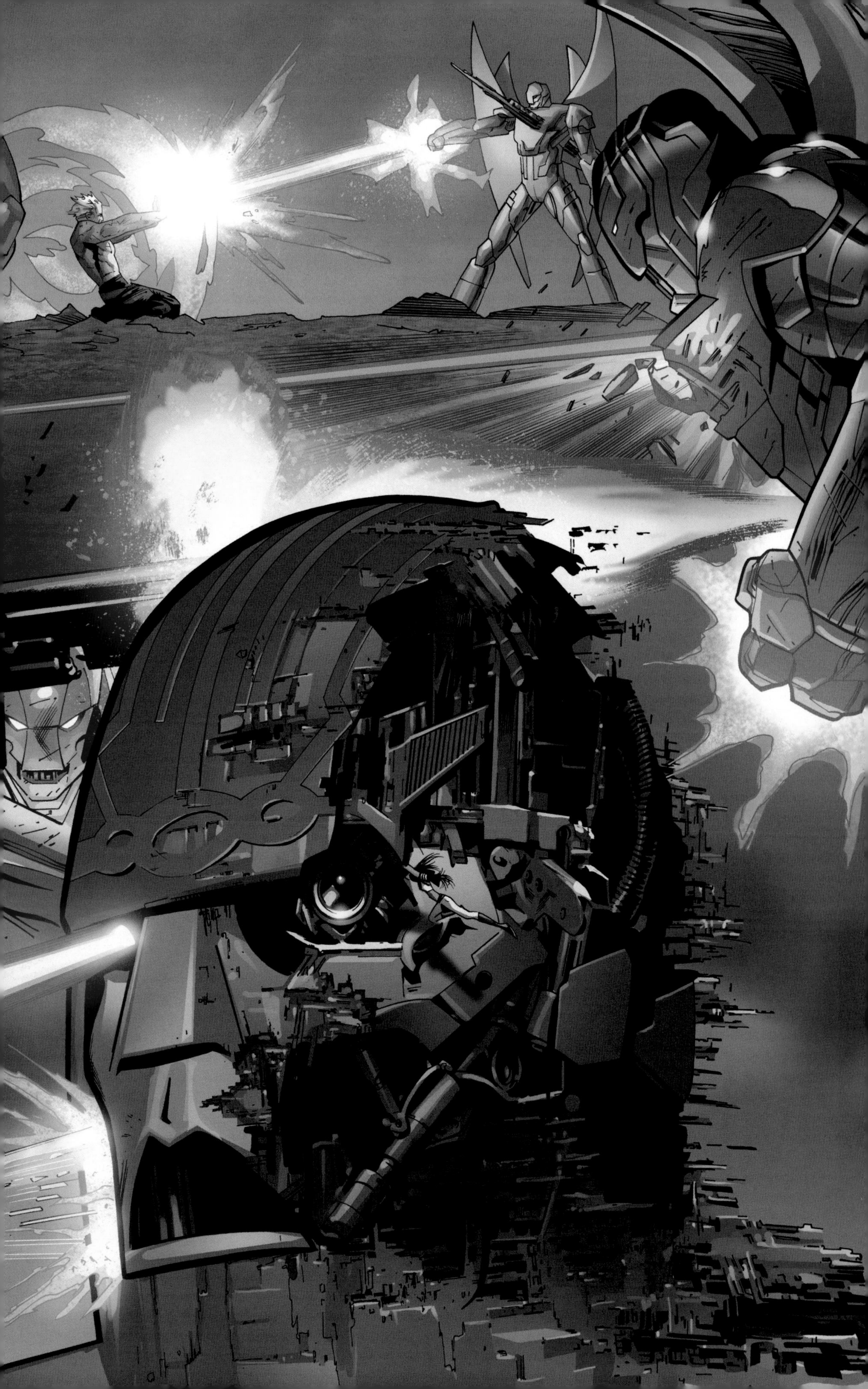

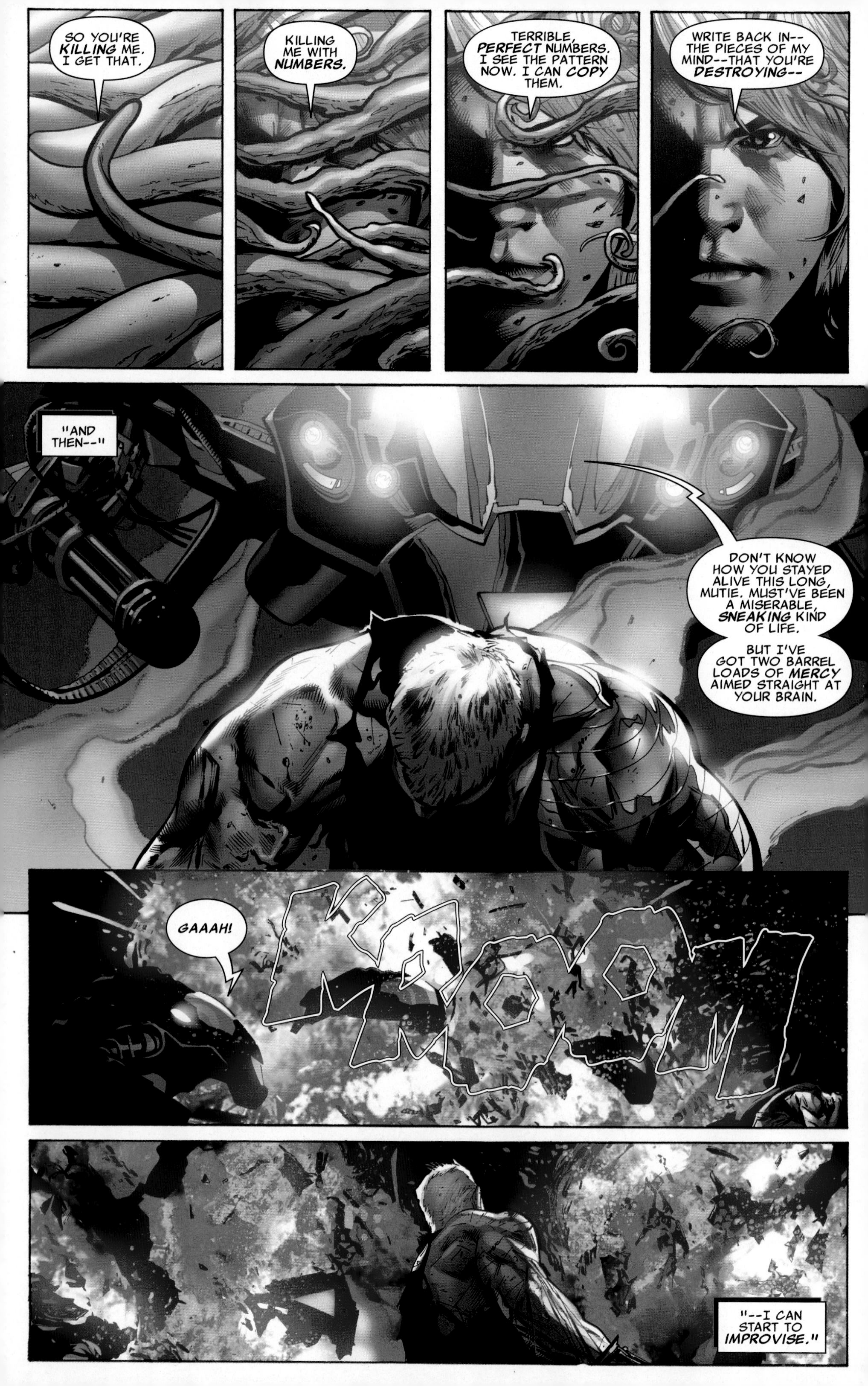
SO YOU'RE KILLING ME. I GET THAT.
KILLING ME WITH NUMBERS.
TERRIBLE, PERFECT NUMBERS. I SEE THE PATTERN NOW. I CAN COPY THEM.
WRITE BACK IN-- THE PIECES OF MY MIND--THAT YOU'RE DESTROYING--
"AND THEN--"
DON'T KNOW HOW YOU STAYED ALIVE THIS LONG, MUTIE. MUST'VE BEEN A MISERABLE, SNEAKING KIND OF LIFE.
BUT I'VE GOT TWO BARREL LOADS OF MERCY AIMED STRAIGHT AT YOUR BRAIN.
GAAAH!
KRA-KOOM
"--I CAN START TO IMPROVISE."

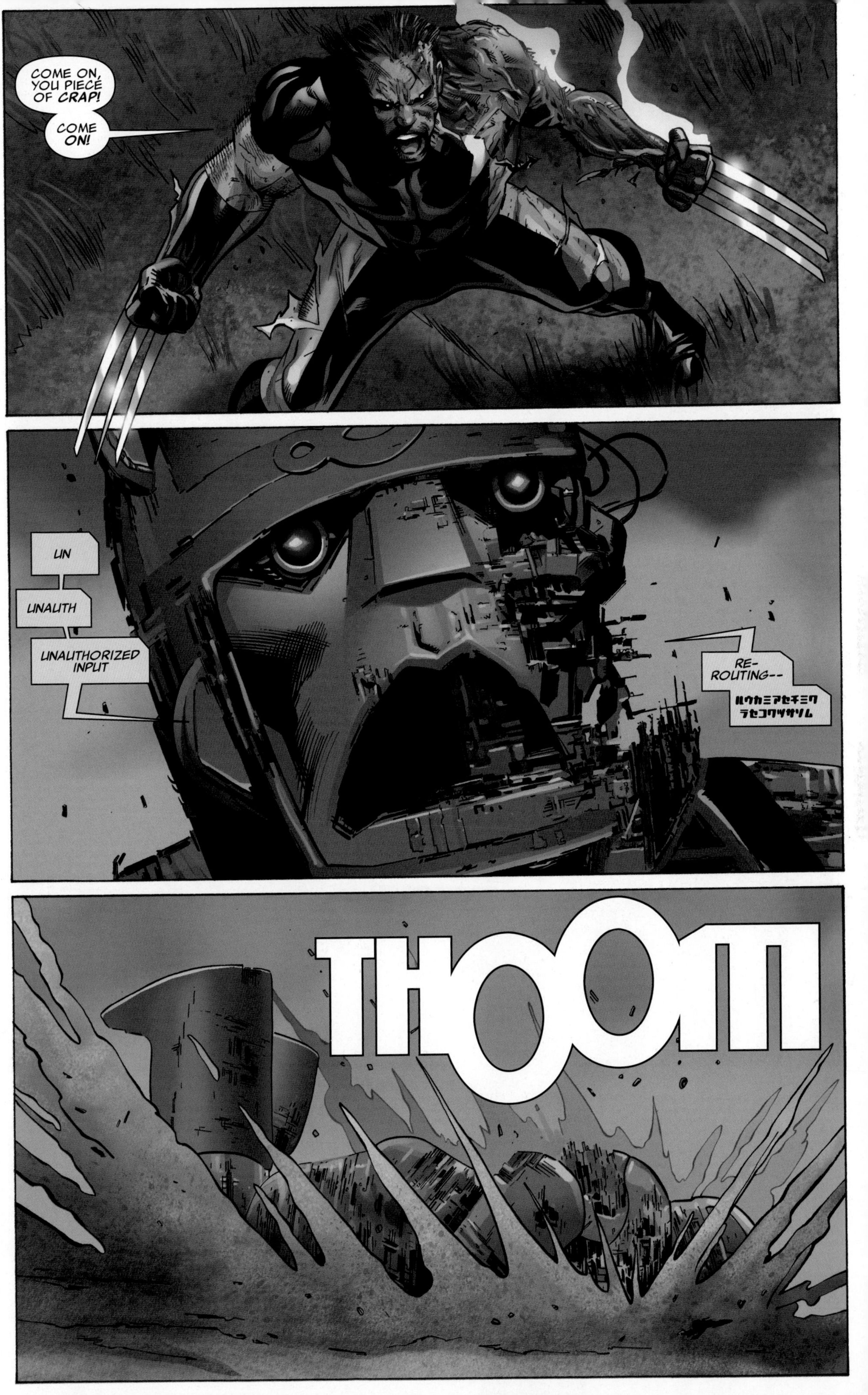

COME ON, YOU PIECE OF *CRAP!*
COME *ON!*
UN
UNAUTH
UNAUTHORIZED INPUT
RE-ROUTING--
ルウカミアセチミワ
ラセコワツサソム
THOOM

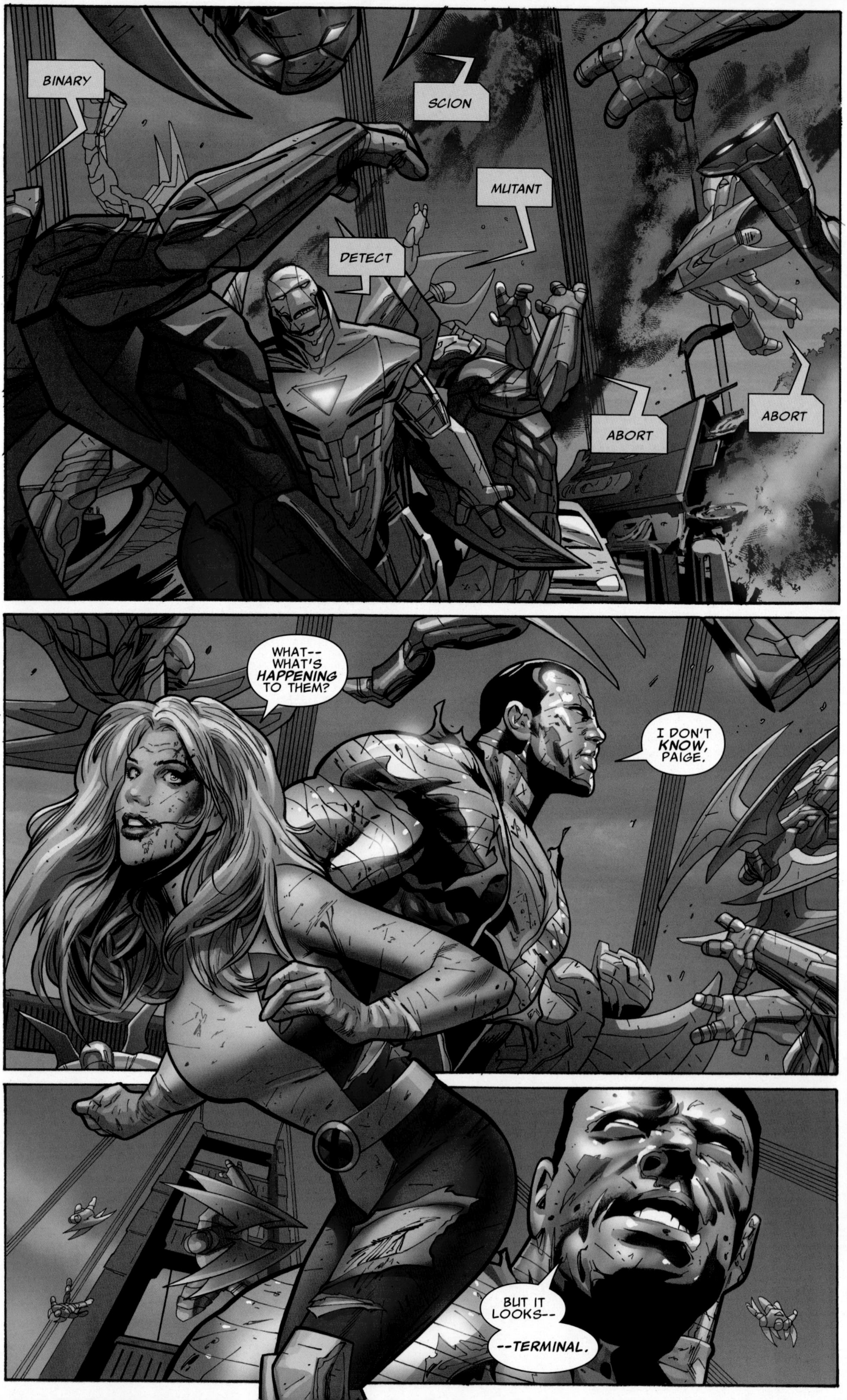
BINARY
SCION
MUTANT
DETECT
ABORT
ABORT
WHAT-- WHAT'S HAPPENING TO THEM?
I DON'T KNOW, PAIGE.
BUT IT LOOKS--
--TERMINAL.

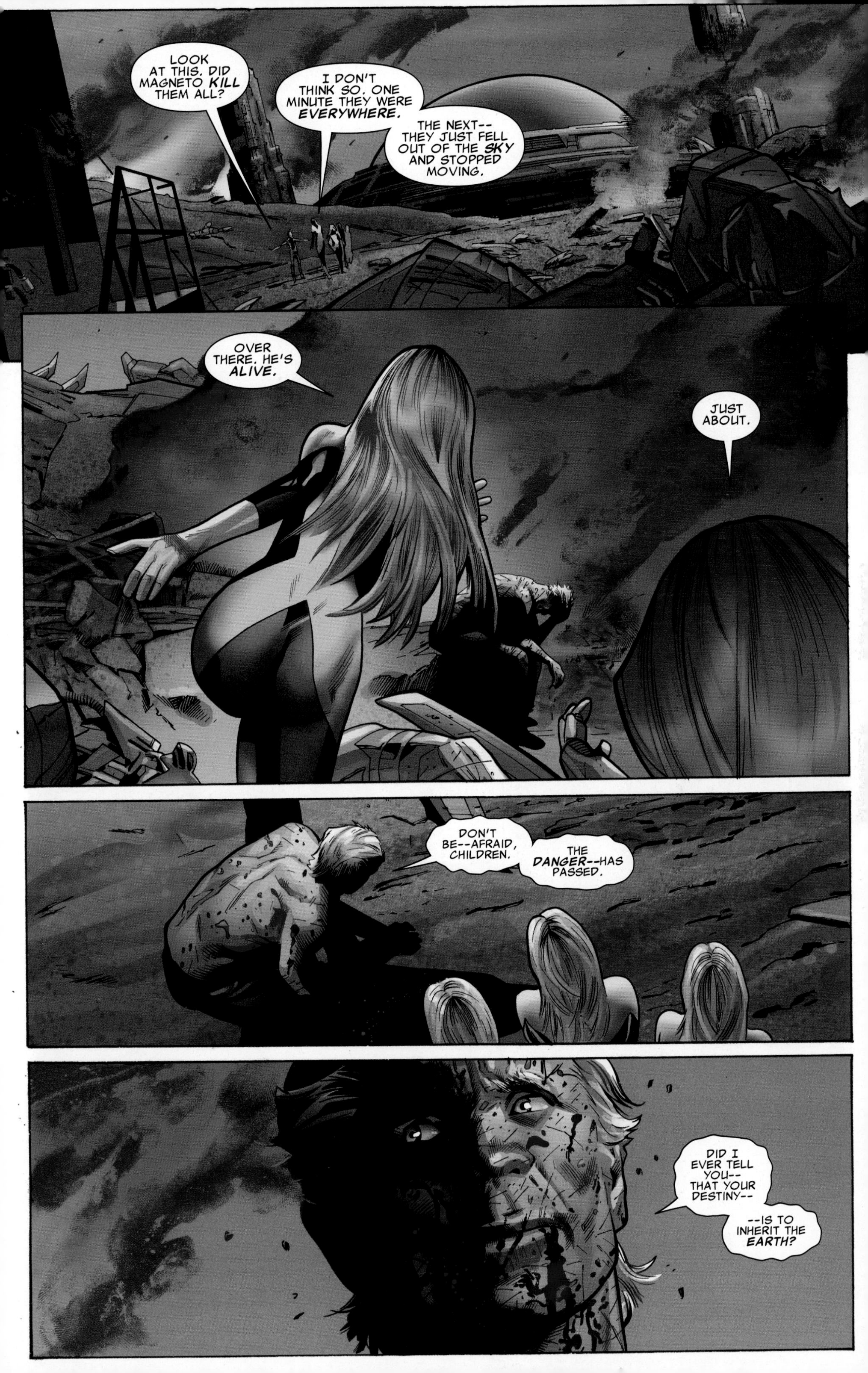
LOOK AT THIS. DID MAGNETO KILL THEM ALL?
I DON'T THINK SO. ONE MINUTE THEY WERE EVERYWHERE.
THE NEXT-- THEY JUST FELL OUT OF THE SKY AND STOPPED MOVING.
OVER THERE. HE'S ALIVE.
JUST ABOUT.
DON'T BE--AFRAID, CHILDREN.
THE DANGER--HAS PASSED.
DID I EVER TELL YOU-- THAT YOUR DESTINY--
--IS TO INHERIT THE EARTH?

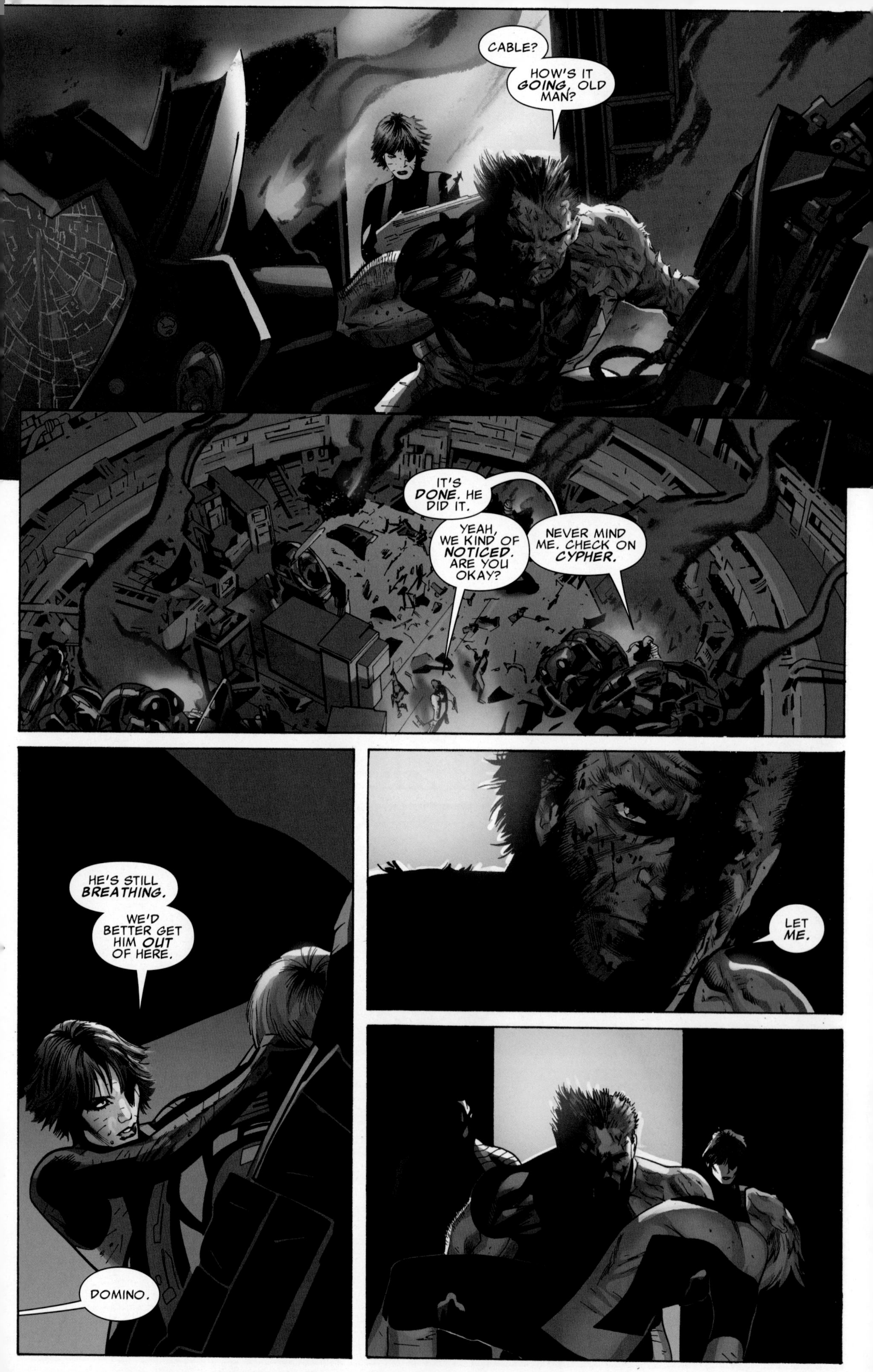
CABLE?
HOW'S IT GOING, OLD MAN?
IT'S DONE. HE DID IT.
NEVER MIND ME. CHECK ON CYPHER.
YEAH, WE KIND OF NOTICED. ARE YOU OKAY?
HE'S STILL BREATHING.
WE'D BETTER GET HIM OUT OF HERE.
DOMINO.
LET ME.

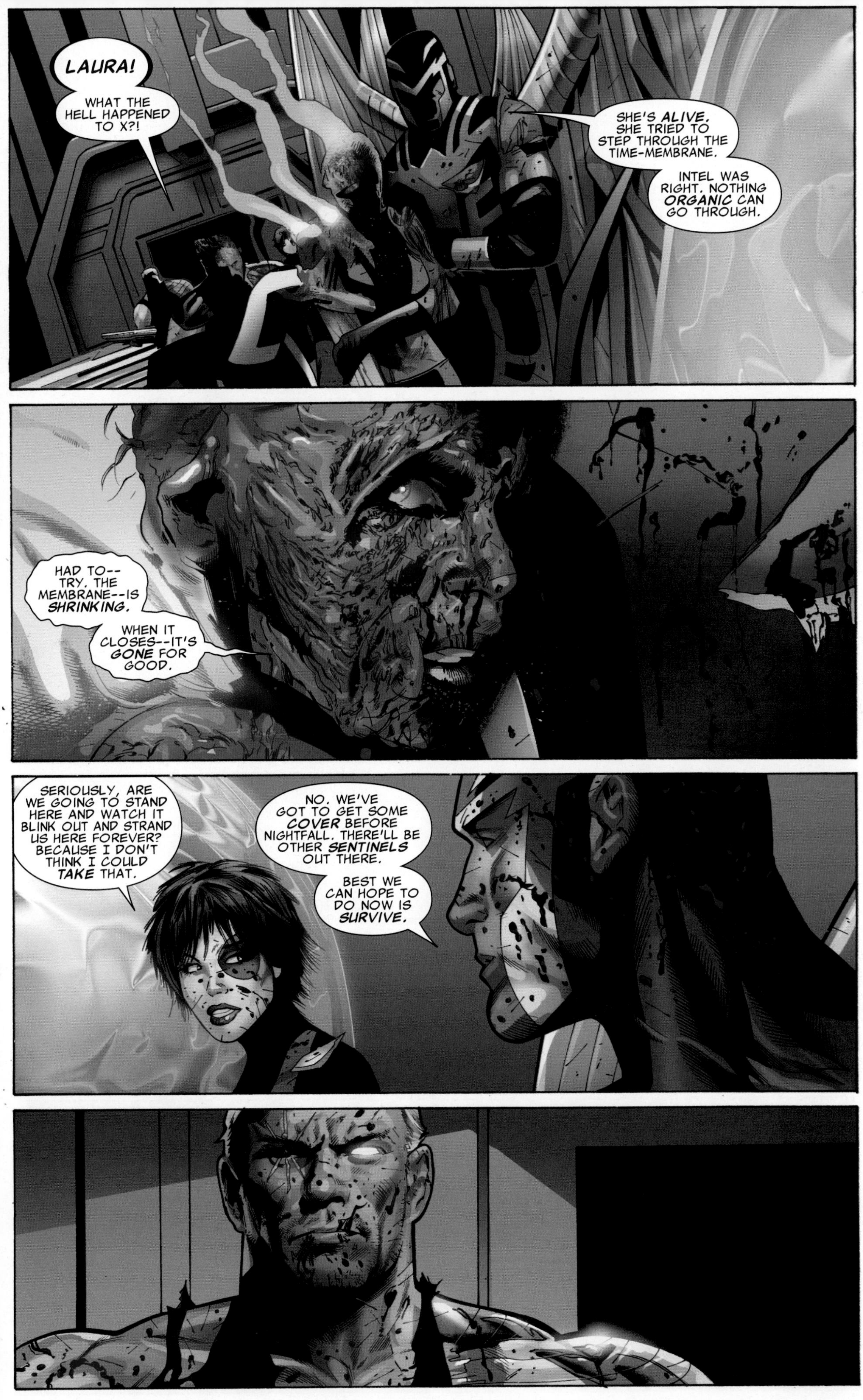
LAURA!
WHAT THE HELL HAPPENED TO X?!
SHE'S ALIVE. SHE TRIED TO STEP THROUGH THE TIME-MEMBRANE.
INTEL WAS RIGHT. NOTHING ORGANIC CAN GO THROUGH.
HAD TO-- TRY. THE MEMBRANE--IS SHRINKING.
WHEN IT CLOSES--IT'S GONE FOR GOOD.
SERIOUSLY, ARE WE GOING TO STAND HERE AND WATCH IT BLINK OUT AND STRAND US HERE FOREVER? BECAUSE I DON'T THINK I COULD TAKE THAT.
NO. WE'VE GOT TO GET SOME COVER BEFORE NIGHTFALL. THERE'LL BE OTHER SENTINELS OUT THERE.
BEST WE CAN HOPE TO DO NOW IS SURVIVE.

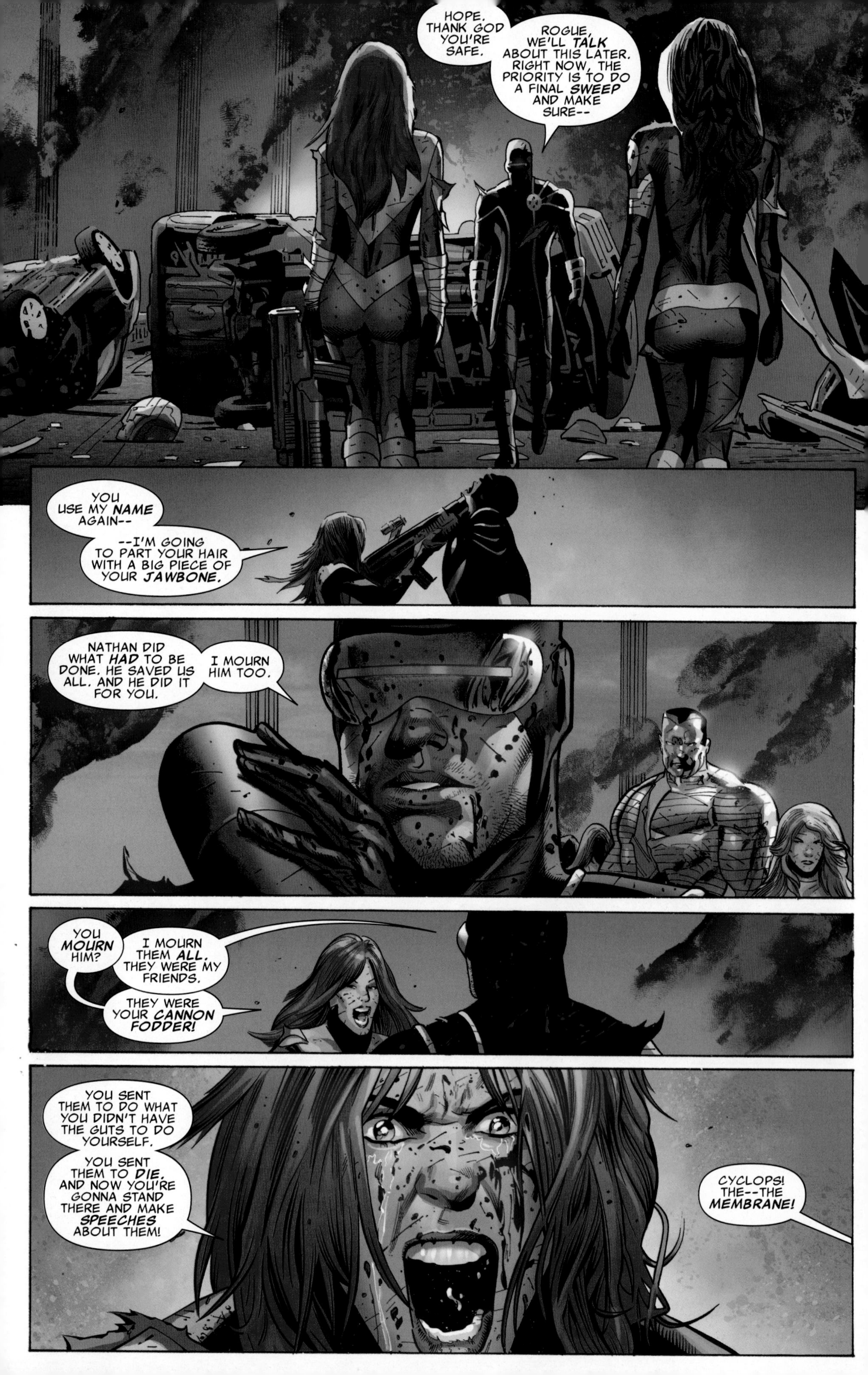
HOPE. THANK GOD YOU'RE SAFE.
ROGUE, WE'LL TALK ABOUT THIS LATER. RIGHT NOW, THE PRIORITY IS TO DO A FINAL SWEEP AND MAKE SURE--
YOU USE MY NAME AGAIN--
--I'M GOING TO PART YOUR HAIR WITH A BIG PIECE OF YOUR JAWBONE.
NATHAN DID WHAT HAD TO BE DONE. HE SAVED US ALL. AND HE DID IT FOR YOU.
I MOURN HIM TOO.
YOU MOURN HIM?
I MOURN THEM ALL. THEY WERE MY FRIENDS.
THEY WERE YOUR CANNON FODDER!
YOU SENT THEM TO DO WHAT YOU DIDN'T HAVE THE GUTS TO DO YOURSELF.
YOU SENT THEM TO DIE. AND NOW YOU'RE GONNA STAND THERE AND MAKE SPEECHES ABOUT THEM!
CYCLOPS! THE--THE MEMBRANE!

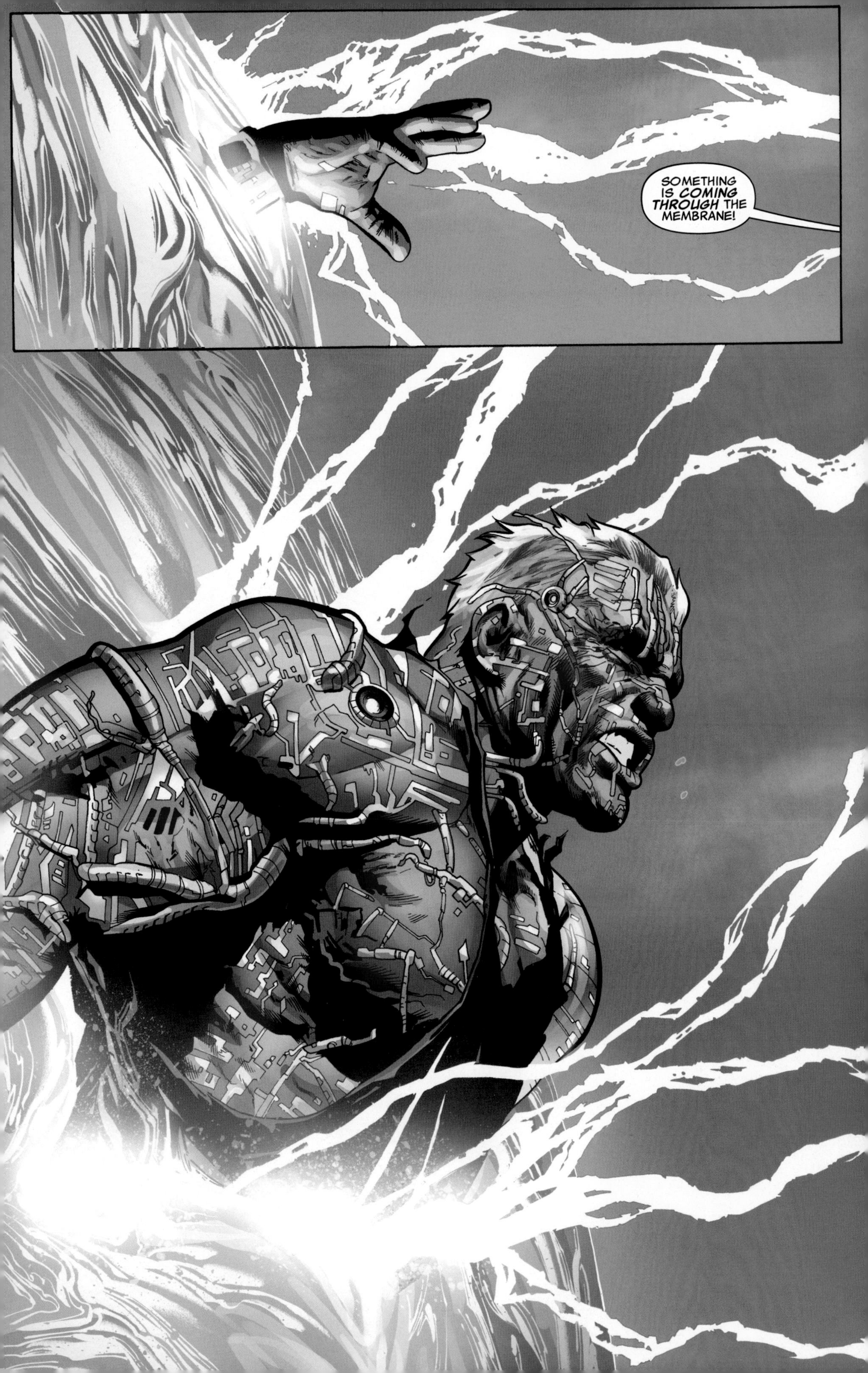
SOMETHING IS *COMING THROUGH* THE MEMBRANE!

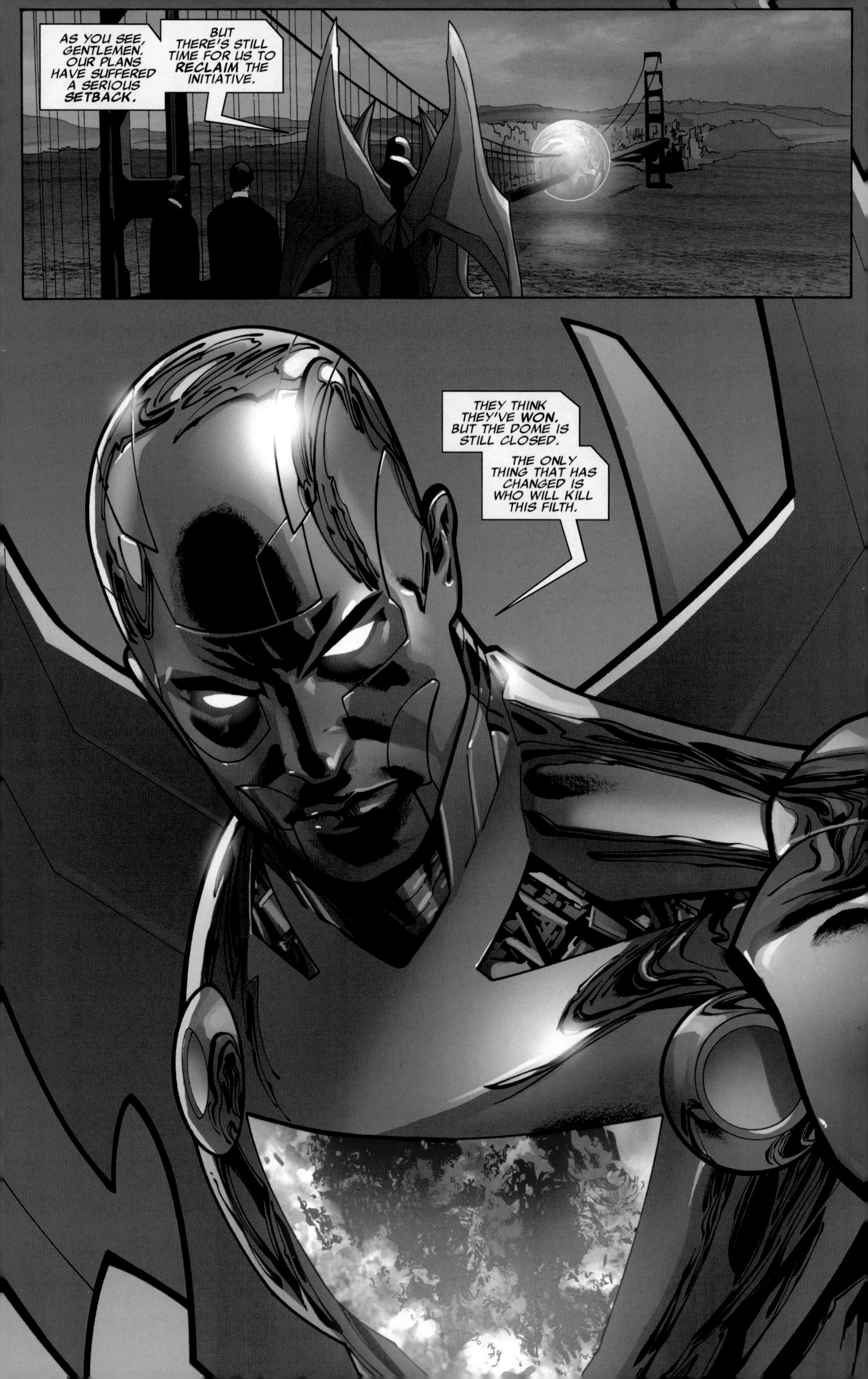
AS YOU SEE, GENTLEMEN, OUR PLANS HAVE SUFFERED A SERIOUS SETBACK.
BUT THERE'S STILL TIME FOR US TO RECLAIM THE INITIATIVE.
THEY THINK THEY'VE WON. BUT THE DOME IS STILL CLOSED.
THE ONLY THING THAT HAS CHANGED IS WHO WILL KILL THIS FILTH.

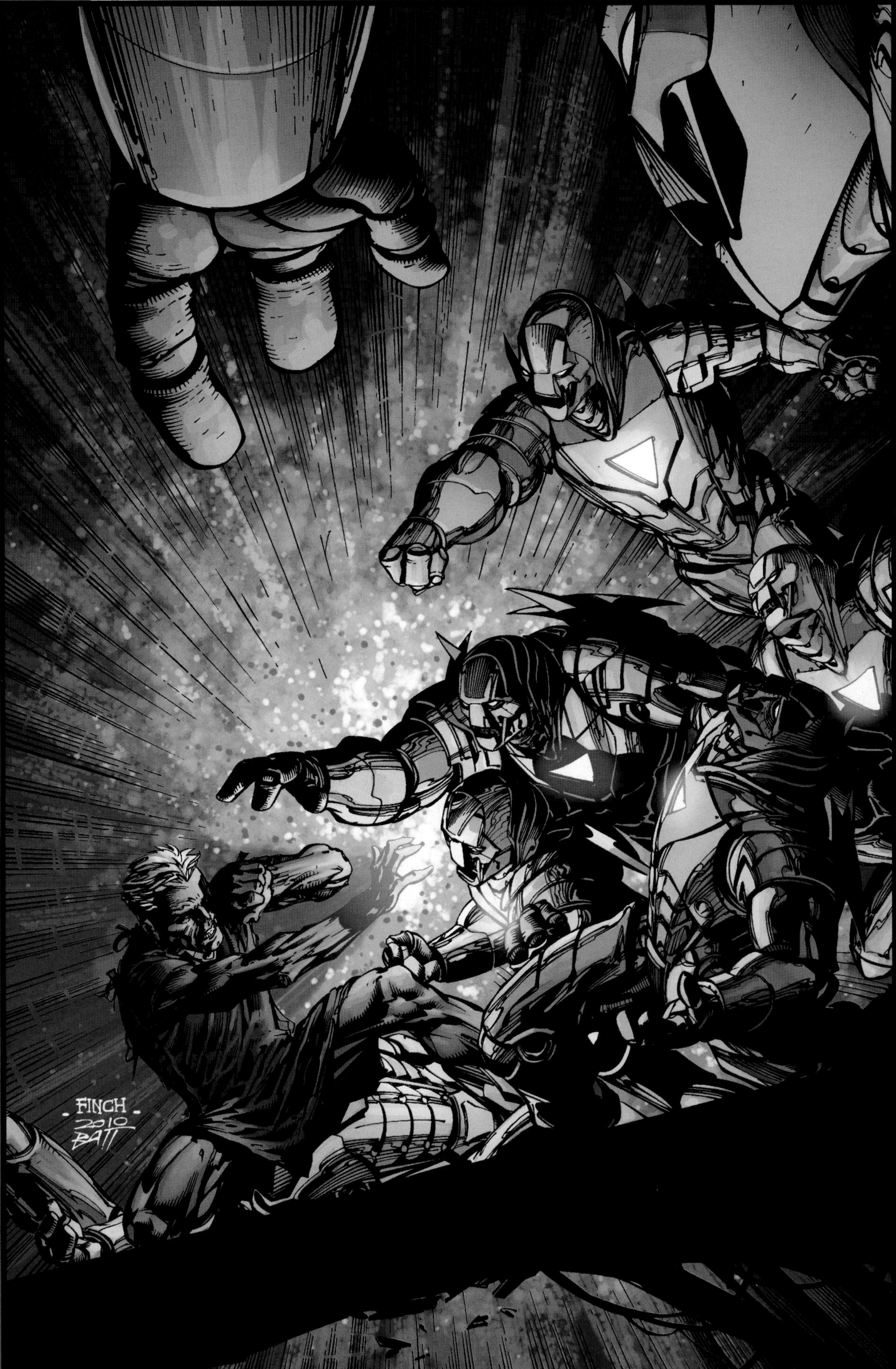
FINCH
2010
BATT

X-MEN LEGACY #237
VARIANT

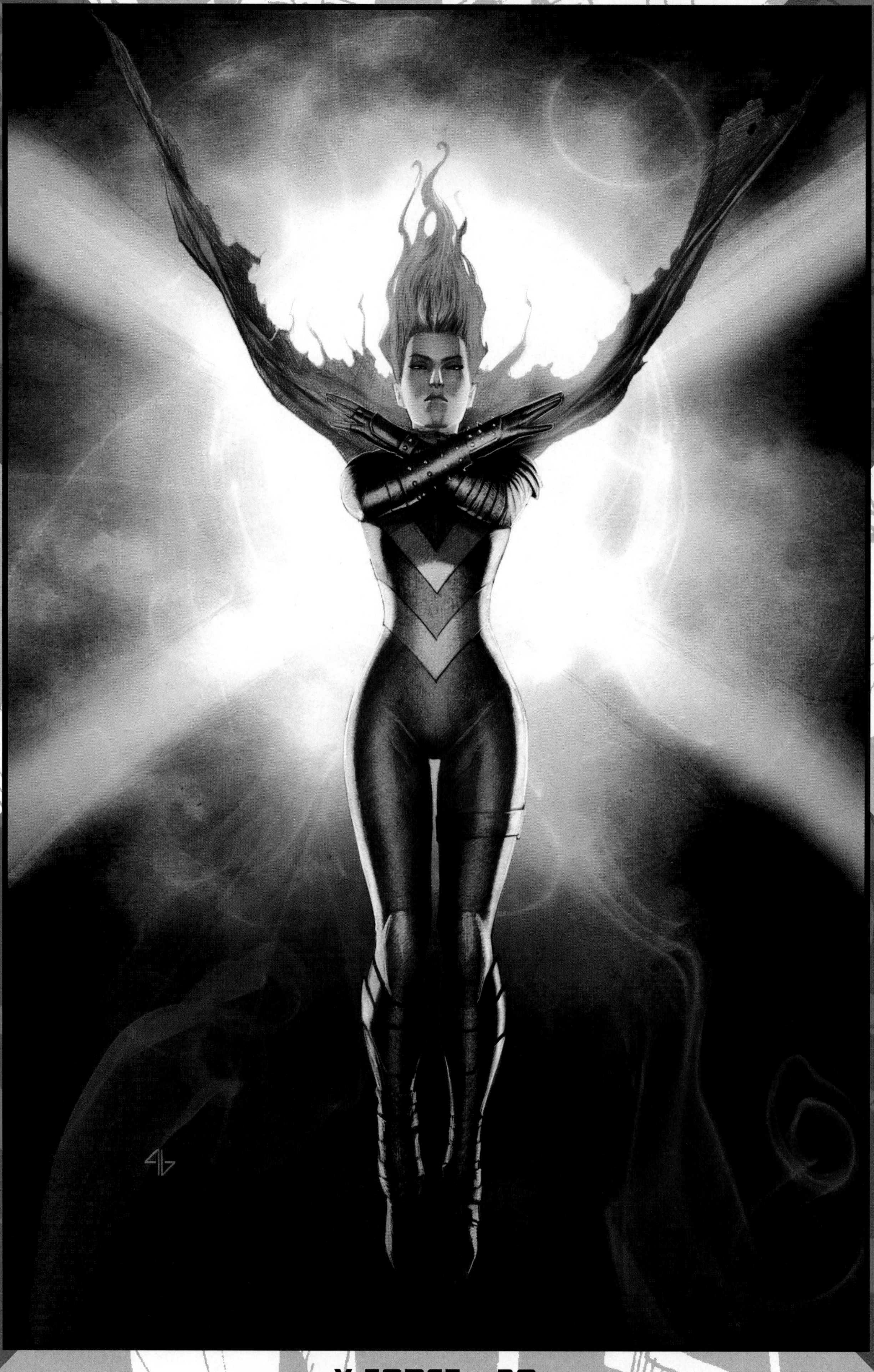

X-FORCE #28

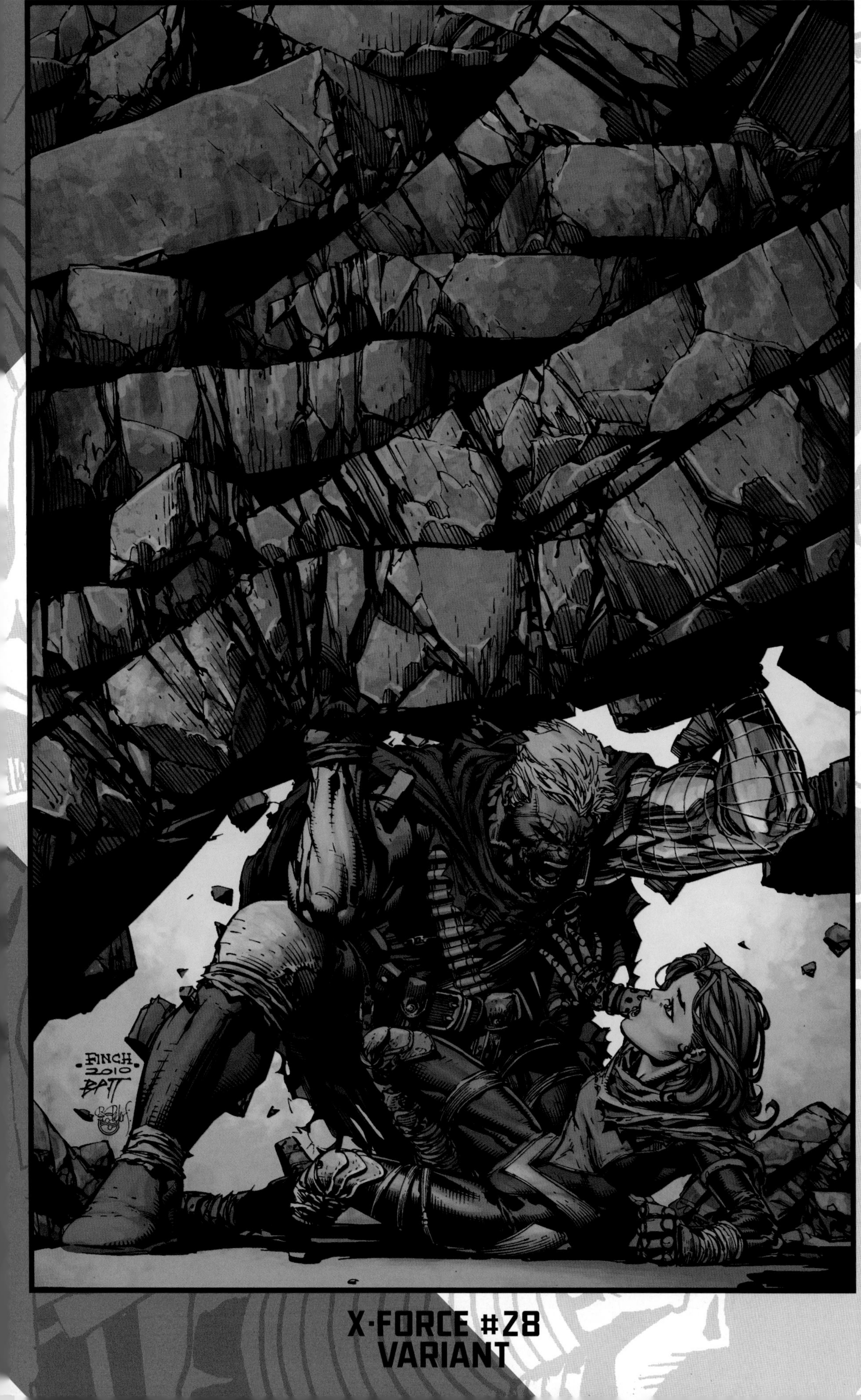
FINCH
2010
BATT

X-FORCE #28
VARIANT

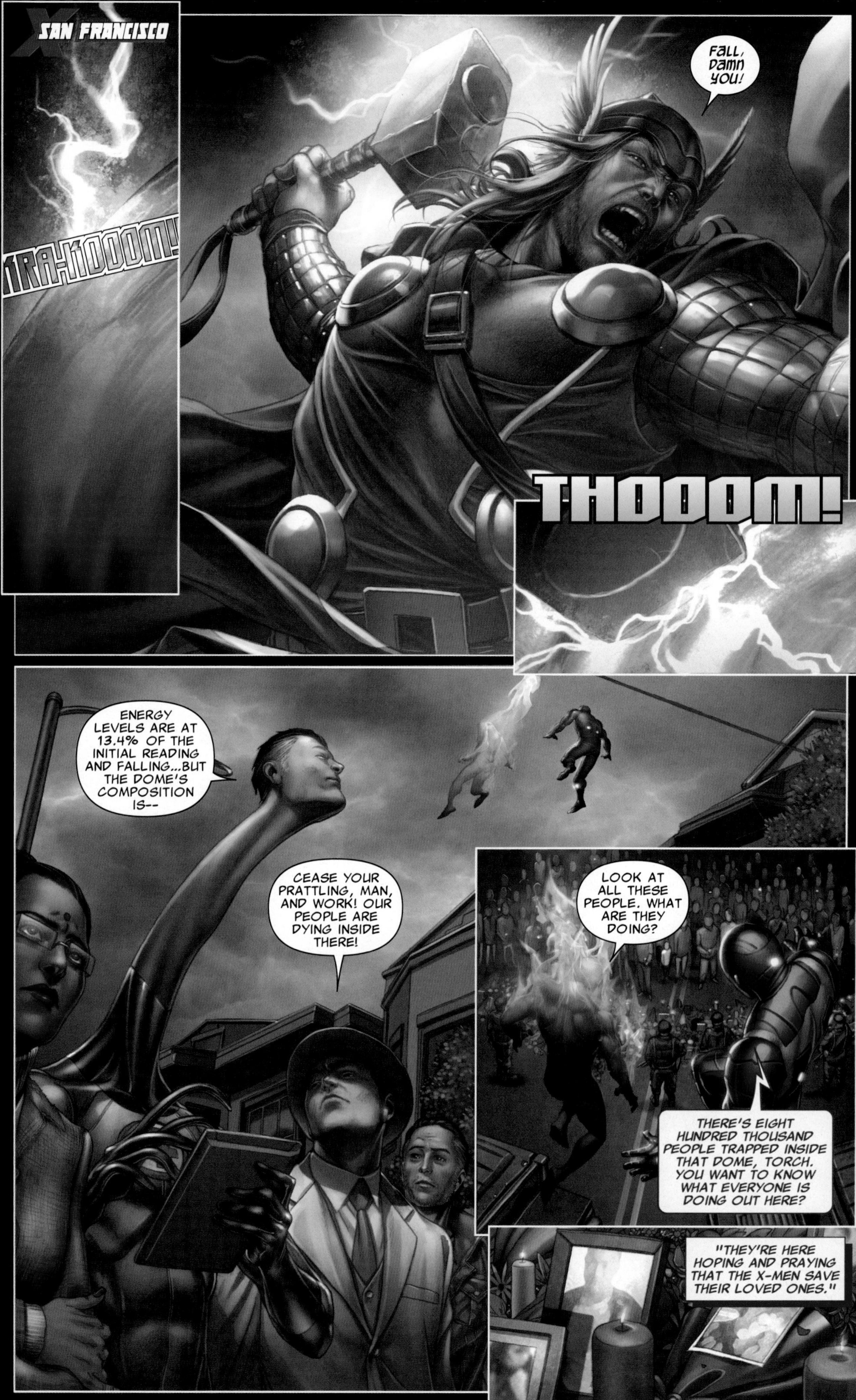
SAN FRANCISCO
KRA-KOOOM!
FALL, DAMN YOU!
THOOOM!
ENERGY LEVELS ARE AT 13.4% OF THE INITIAL READING AND FALLING...BUT THE DOME'S COMPOSITION IS--
CEASE YOUR PRATTLING, MAN, AND WORK! OUR PEOPLE ARE DYING INSIDE THERE!
LOOK AT ALL THESE PEOPLE. WHAT ARE THEY DOING?
THERE'S EIGHT HUNDRED THOUSAND PEOPLE TRAPPED INSIDE THAT DOME, TORCH. YOU WANT TO KNOW WHAT EVERYONE IS DOING OUT HERE?
"THEY'RE HERE HOPING AND PRAYING THAT THE X-MEN SAVE THEIR LOVED ONES."

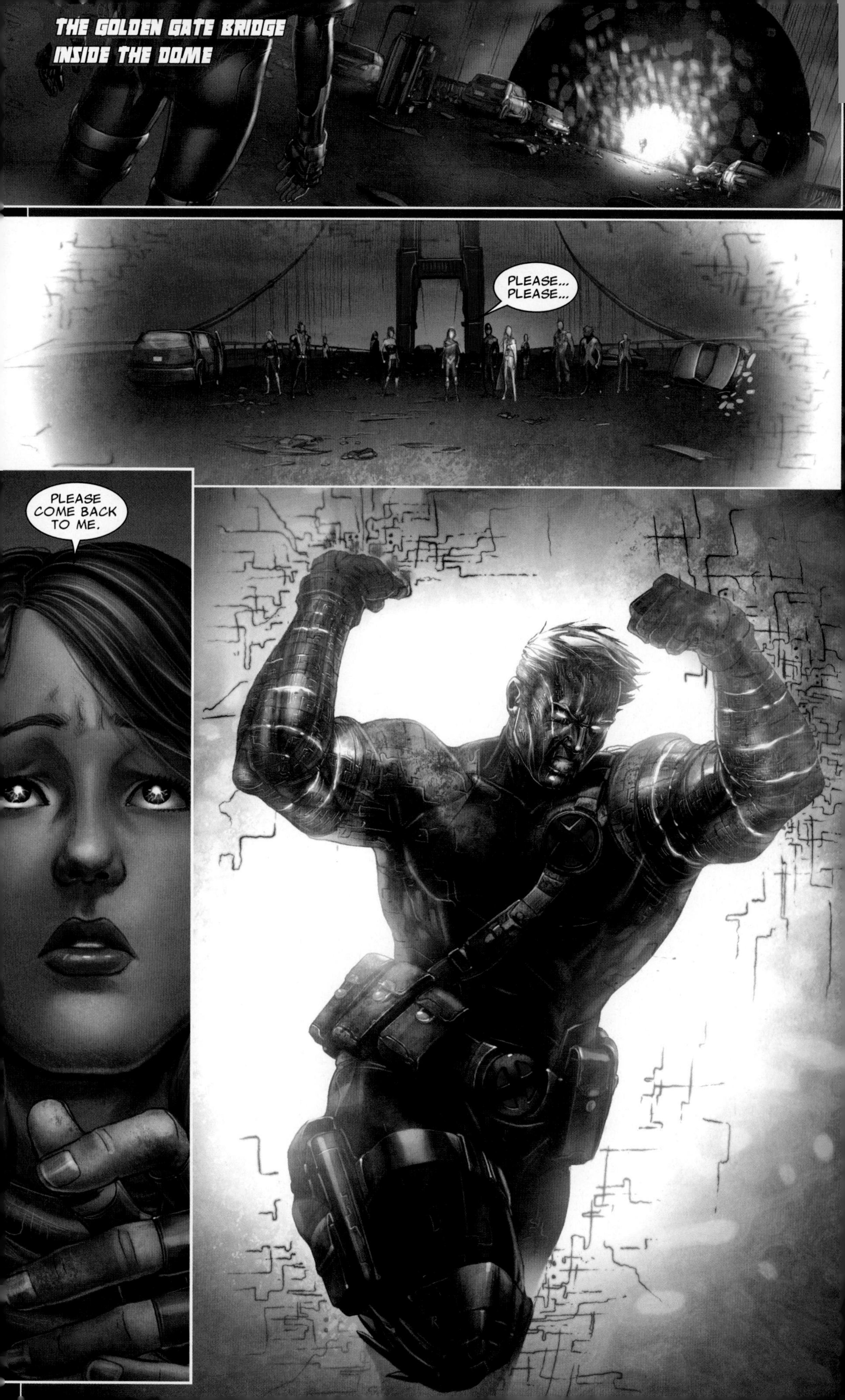
THE GOLDEN GATE BRIDGE
INSIDE THE DOME
PLEASE... PLEASE...
PLEASE COME BACK TO ME.

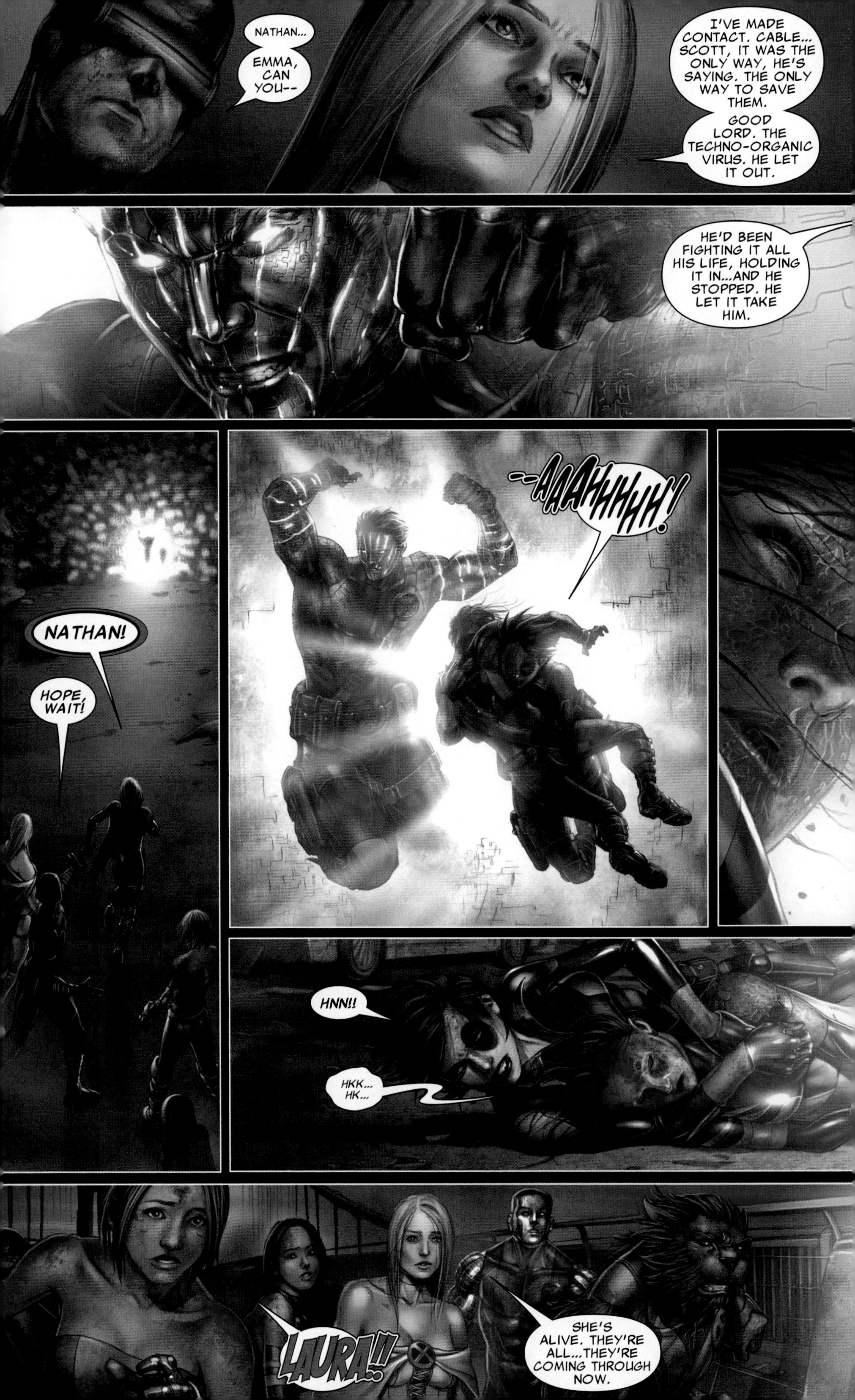
NATHAN...
EMMA, CAN YOU--
I'VE MADE CONTACT. CABLE... SCOTT, IT WAS THE ONLY WAY, HE'S SAYING. THE ONLY WAY TO SAVE THEM.
GOOD LORD. THE TECHNO-ORGANIC VIRUS. HE LET IT OUT.
HE'D BEEN FIGHTING IT ALL HIS LIFE, HOLDING IT IN...AND HE STOPPED. HE LET IT TAKE HIM.
NATHAN!
HOPE, WAIT!
--AAAAHHHHH!
HNN!!
HKK... HK...
LAURA!!
SHE'S ALIVE. THEY'RE ALL...THEY'RE COMING THROUGH NOW.

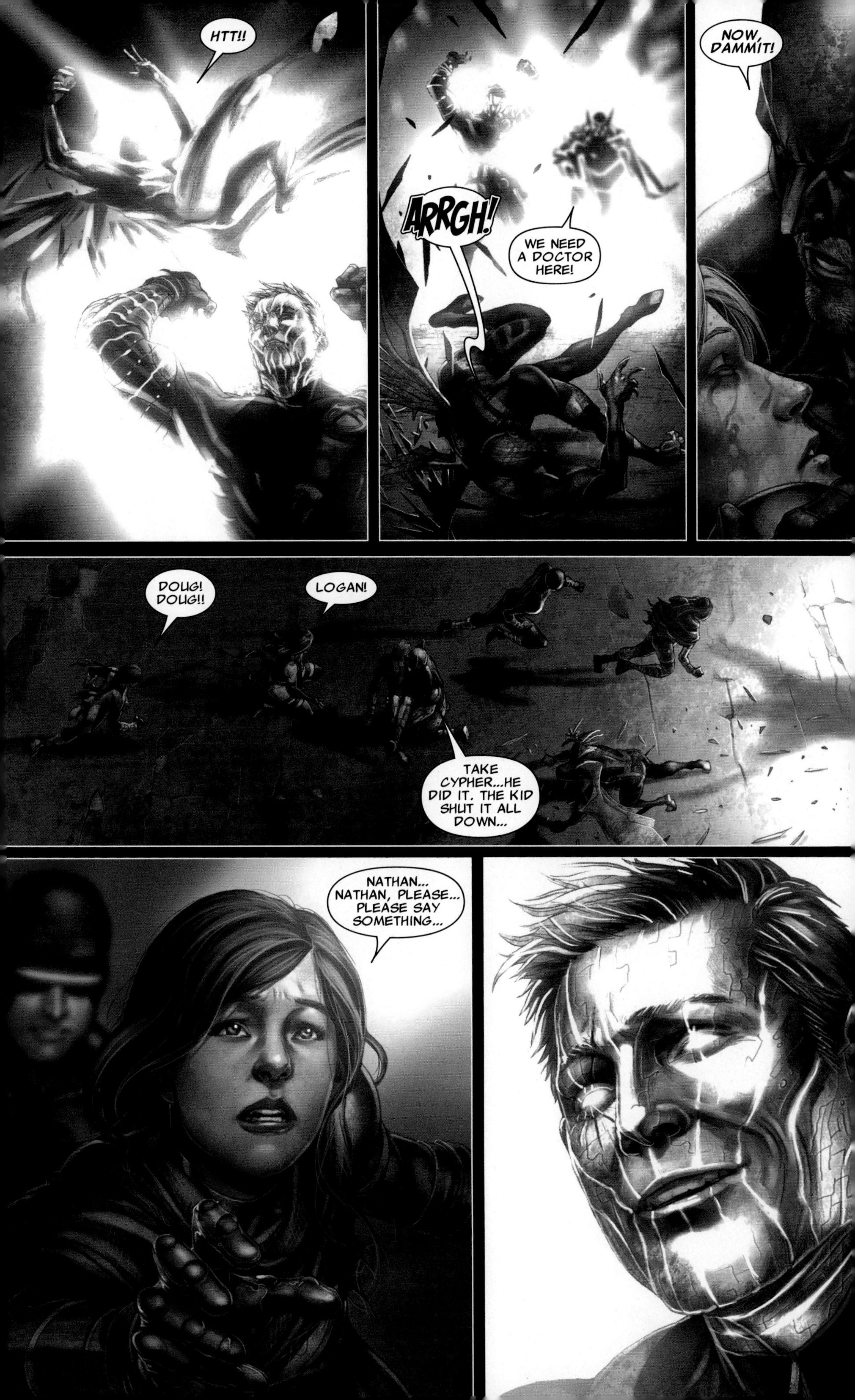
HTT!!
ARRGH!
WE NEED A DOCTOR HERE!
NOW, DAMMIT!
DOUG! DOUG!!
LOGAN!
TAKE CYPHER...HE DID IT. THE KID SHUT IT ALL DOWN...
NATHAN... NATHAN, PLEASE... PLEASE SAY SOMETHING...

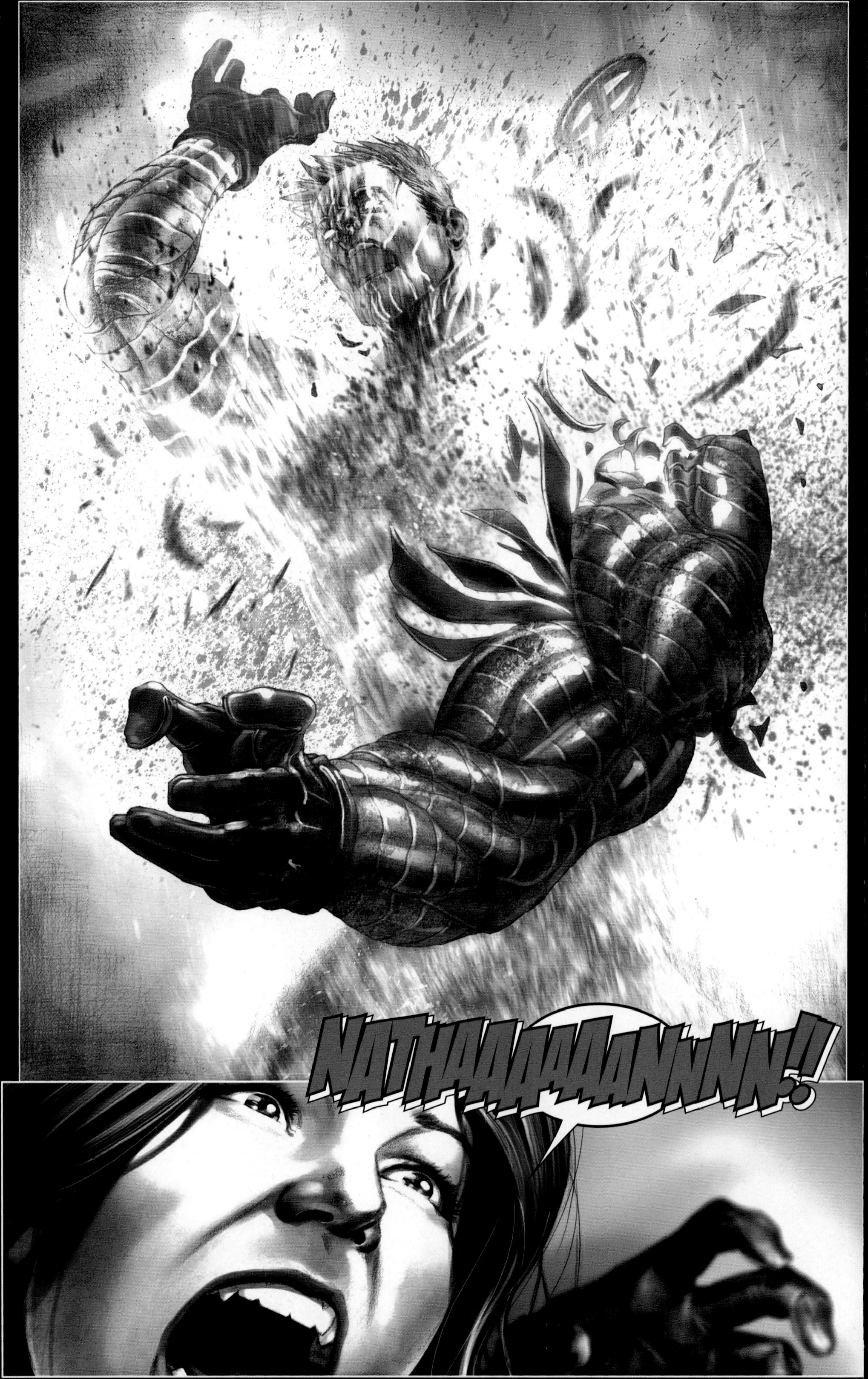
NATHAAAAAANNNNN!!

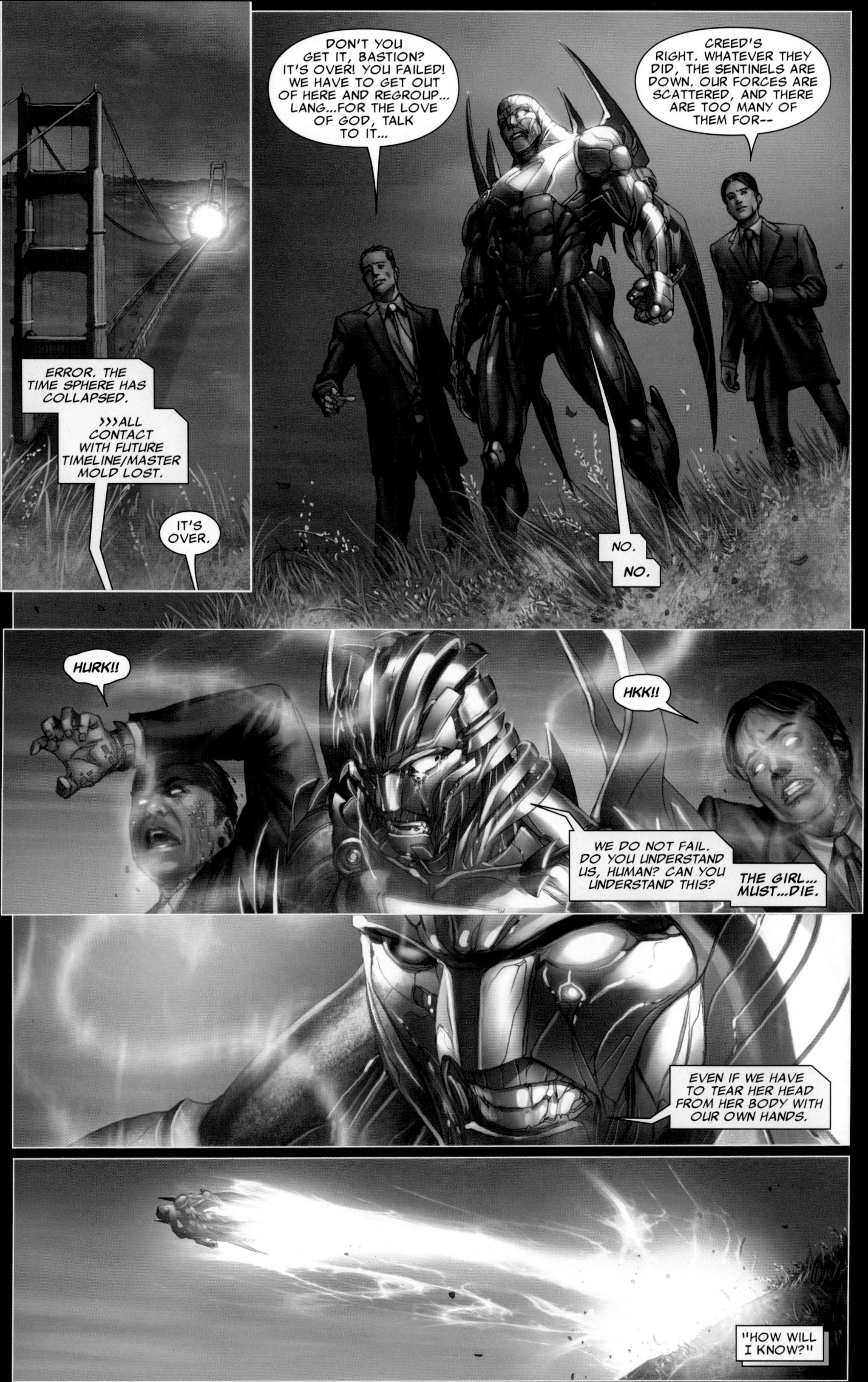

ERROR. THE TIME SPHERE HAS COLLAPSED.
›››ALL CONTACT WITH FUTURE TIMELINE/MASTER MOLD LOST.
IT'S OVER.
DON'T YOU GET IT, BASTION? IT'S OVER! YOU FAILED! WE HAVE TO GET OUT OF HERE AND REGROUP... LANG...FOR THE LOVE OF GOD, TALK TO IT...
CREED'S RIGHT. WHATEVER THEY DID, THE SENTINELS ARE DOWN. OUR FORCES ARE SCATTERED, AND THERE ARE TOO MANY OF THEM FOR--
NO.
NO.
HURK!!
HKK!!
WE DO NOT FAIL. DO YOU UNDERSTAND US, HUMAN? CAN YOU UNDERSTAND THIS?
THE GIRL... MUST...DIE.
EVEN IF WE HAVE TO TEAR HER HEAD FROM HER BODY WITH OUR OWN HANDS.
"HOW WILL I KNOW?"

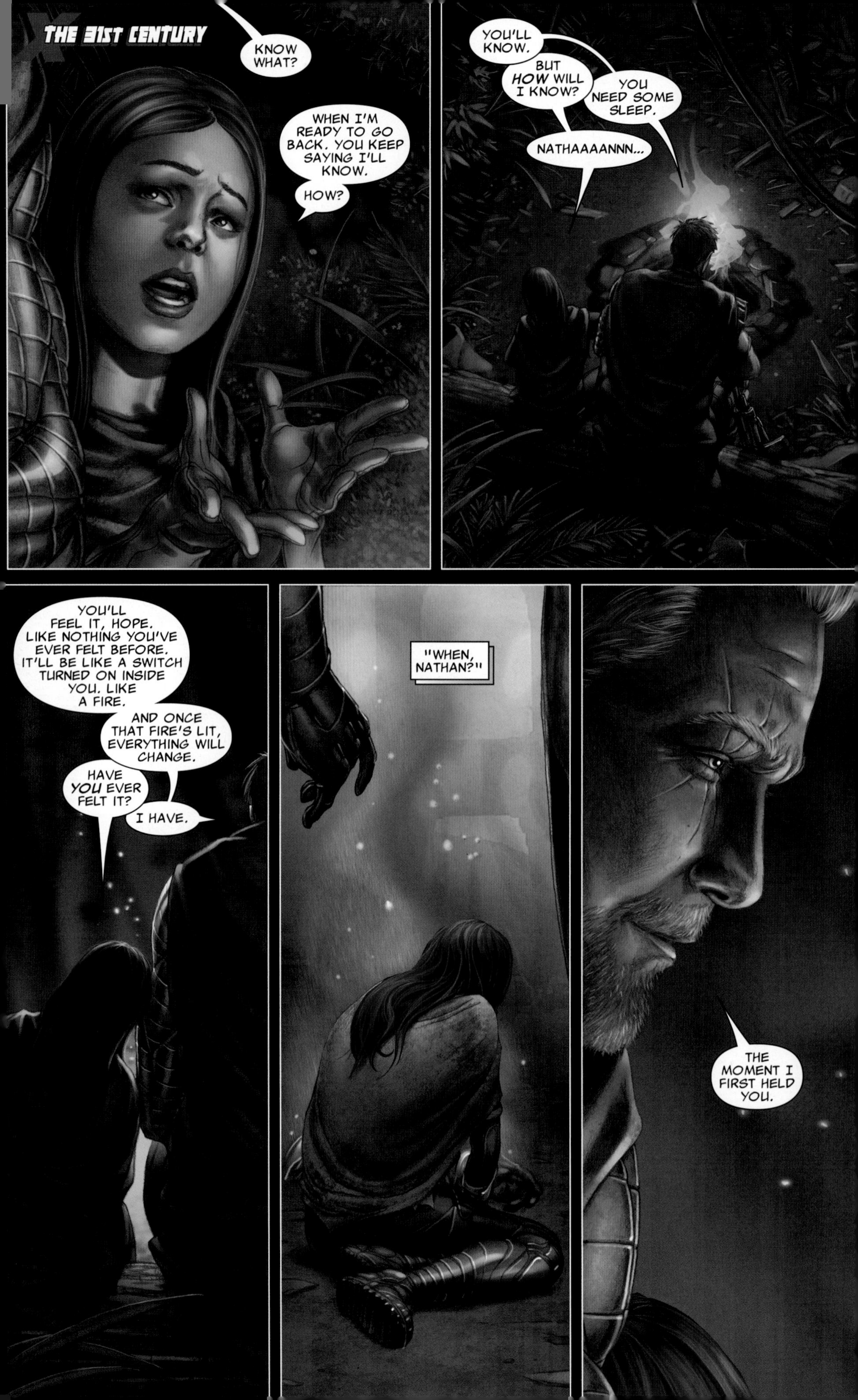
THE 31ST CENTURY
KNOW WHAT?
WHEN I'M READY TO GO BACK. YOU KEEP SAYING I'LL KNOW.
HOW?
YOU'LL KNOW.
BUT HOW WILL I KNOW?
YOU NEED SOME SLEEP.
NATHAAAANNN...
YOU'LL FEEL IT, HOPE. LIKE NOTHING YOU'VE EVER FELT BEFORE. IT'LL BE LIKE A SWITCH TURNED ON INSIDE YOU. LIKE A FIRE.
AND ONCE THAT FIRE'S LIT, EVERYTHING WILL CHANGE.
HAVE YOU EVER FELT IT?
I HAVE.
"WHEN, NATHAN?"
THE MOMENT I FIRST HELD YOU.

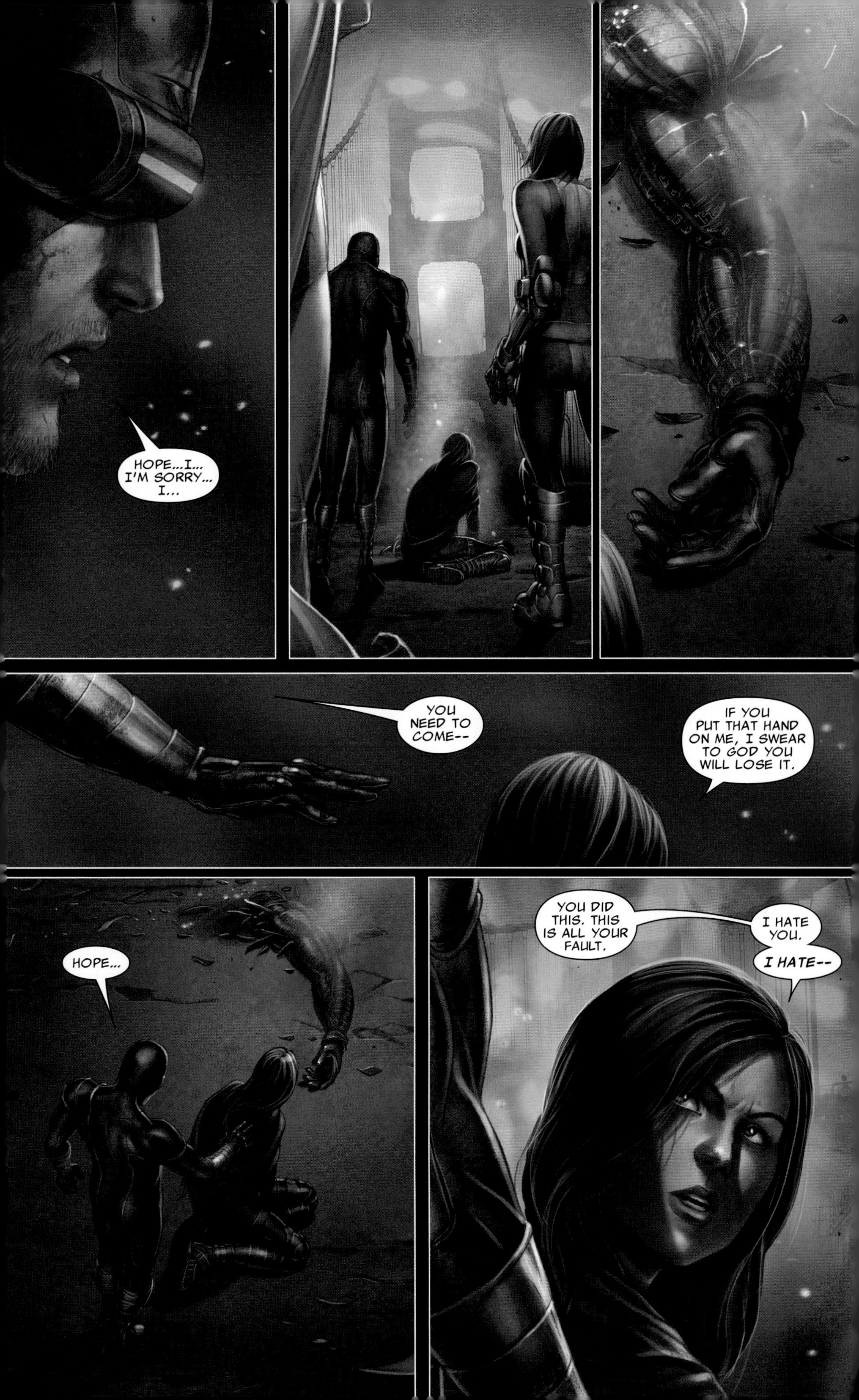
HOPE...I...
I'M SORRY...
I...
YOU
NEED TO
COME--
IF YOU
PUT THAT HAND
ON ME, I SWEAR
TO GOD YOU
WILL LOSE IT.
HOPE...
YOU DID
THIS. THIS
IS ALL YOUR
FAULT.
I HATE
YOU.
I HATE--

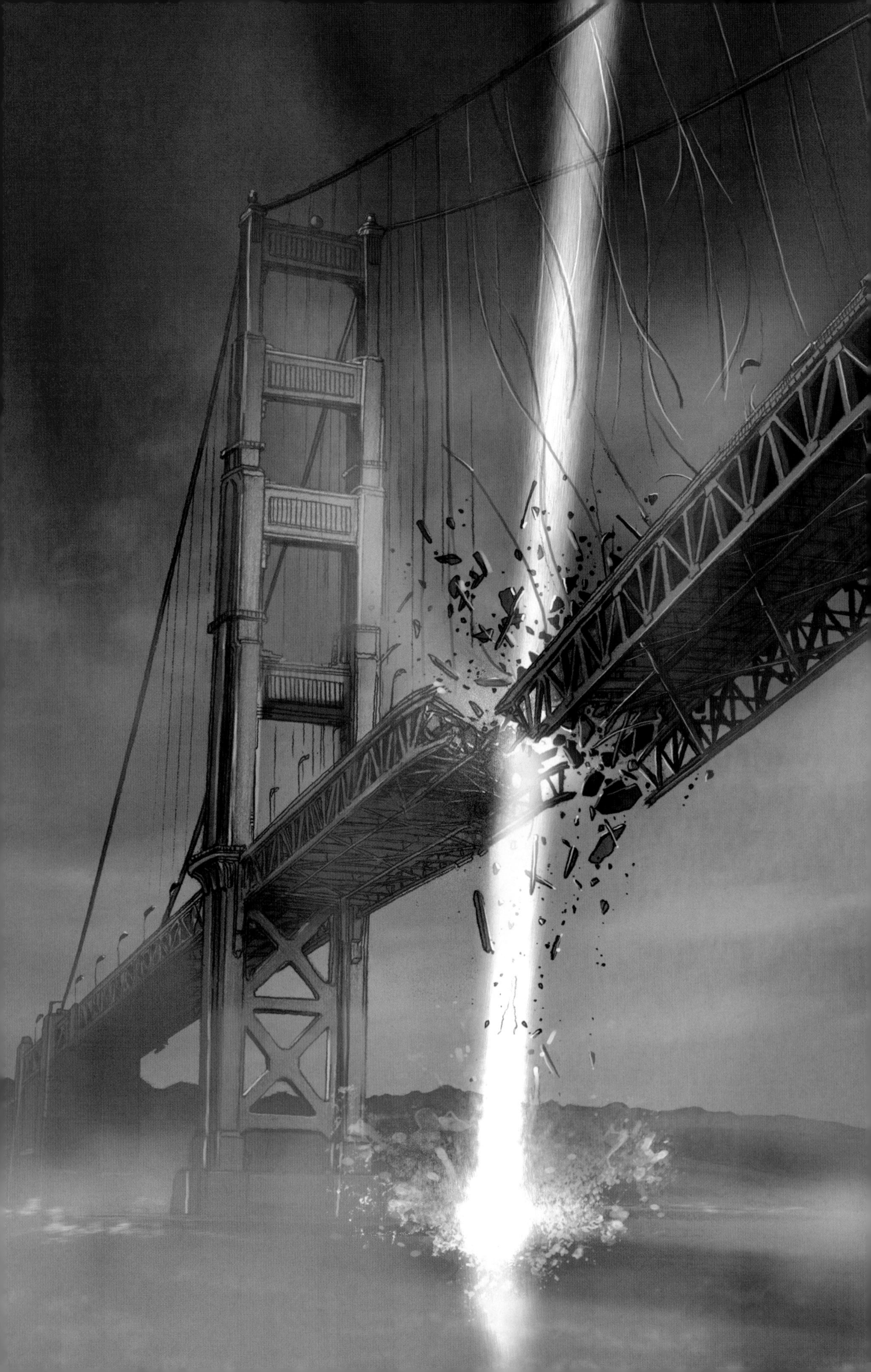

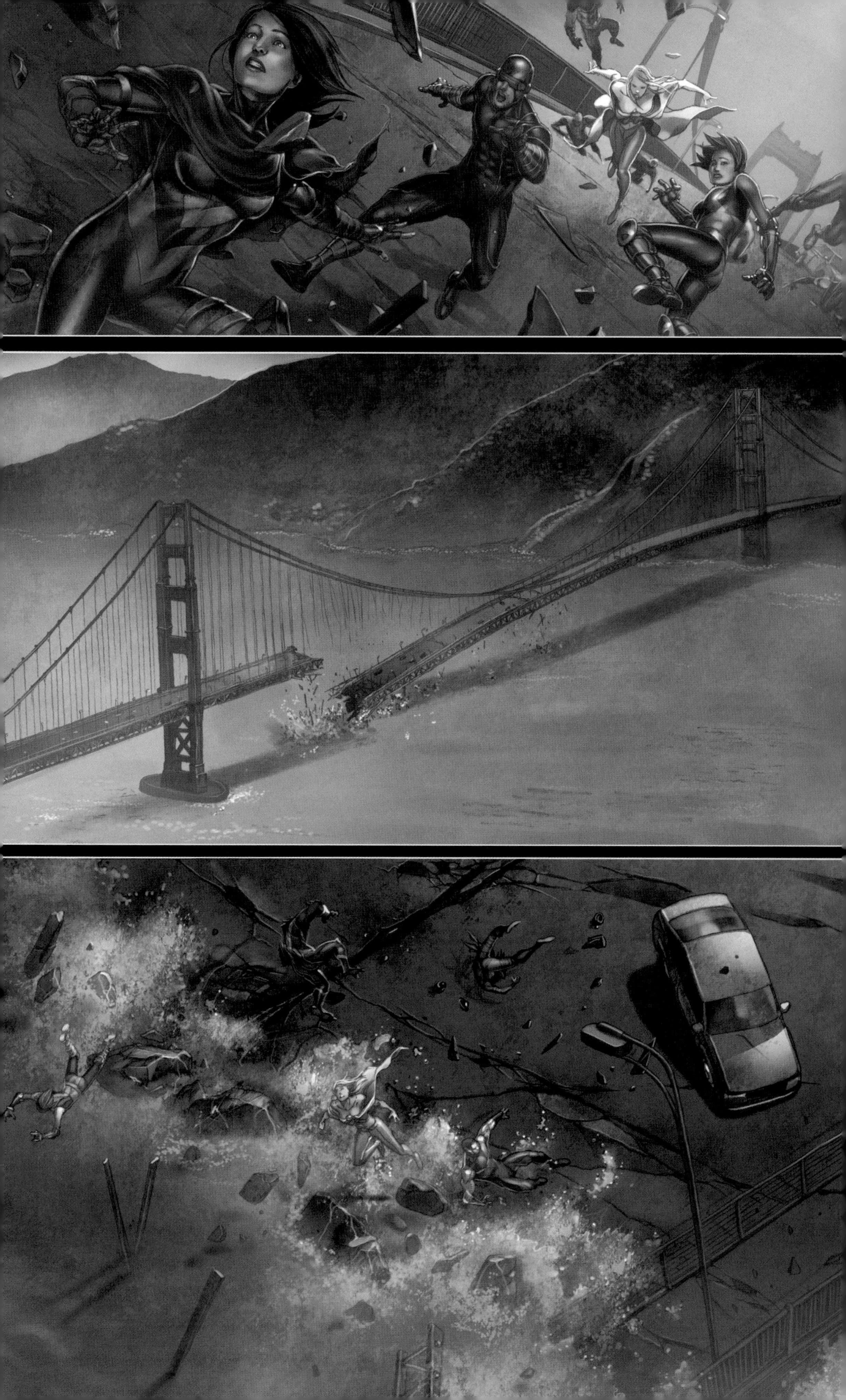

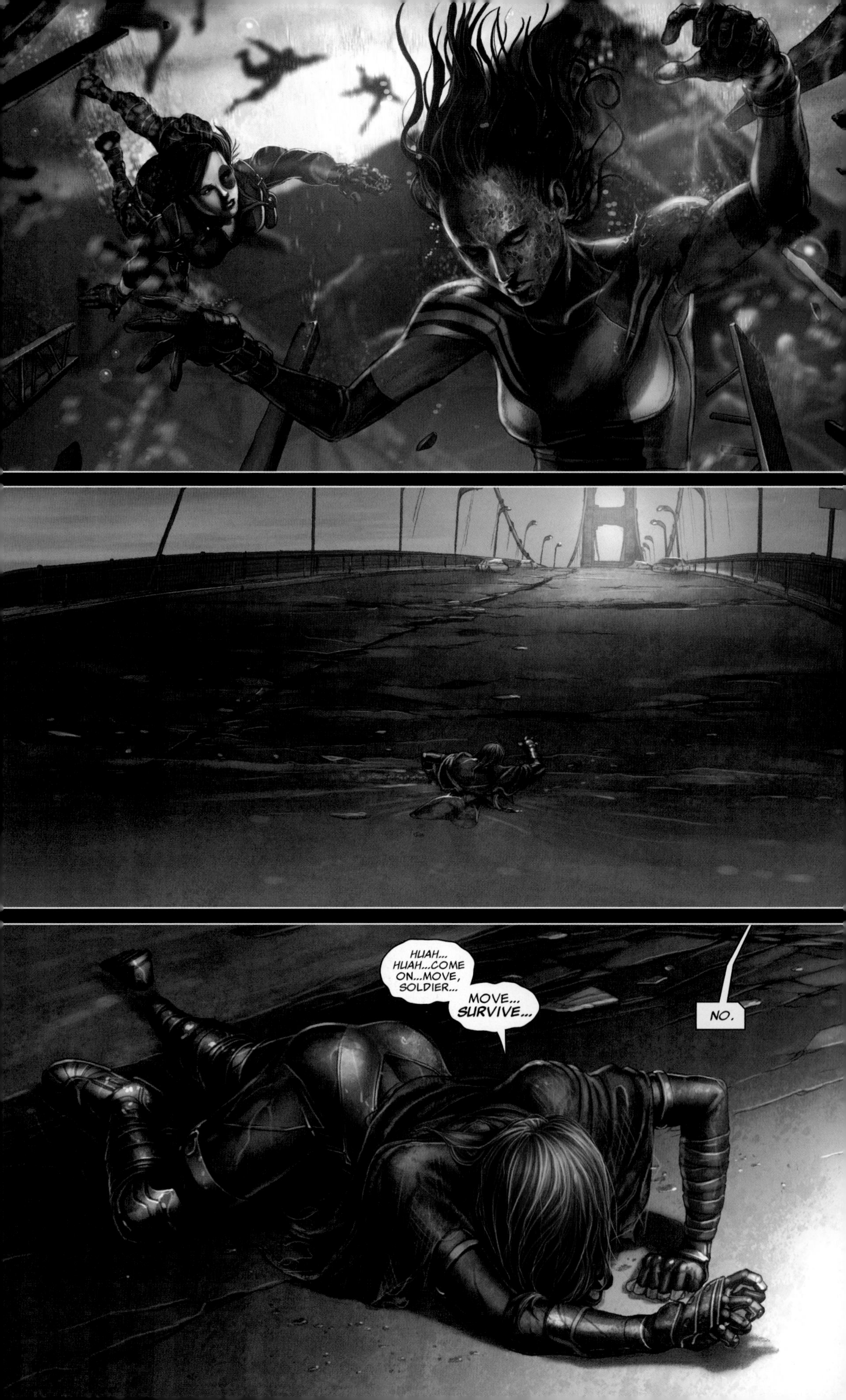
HUAH... HUAH...COME ON...MOVE, SOLDIER...
MOVE... SURVIVE...
NO.

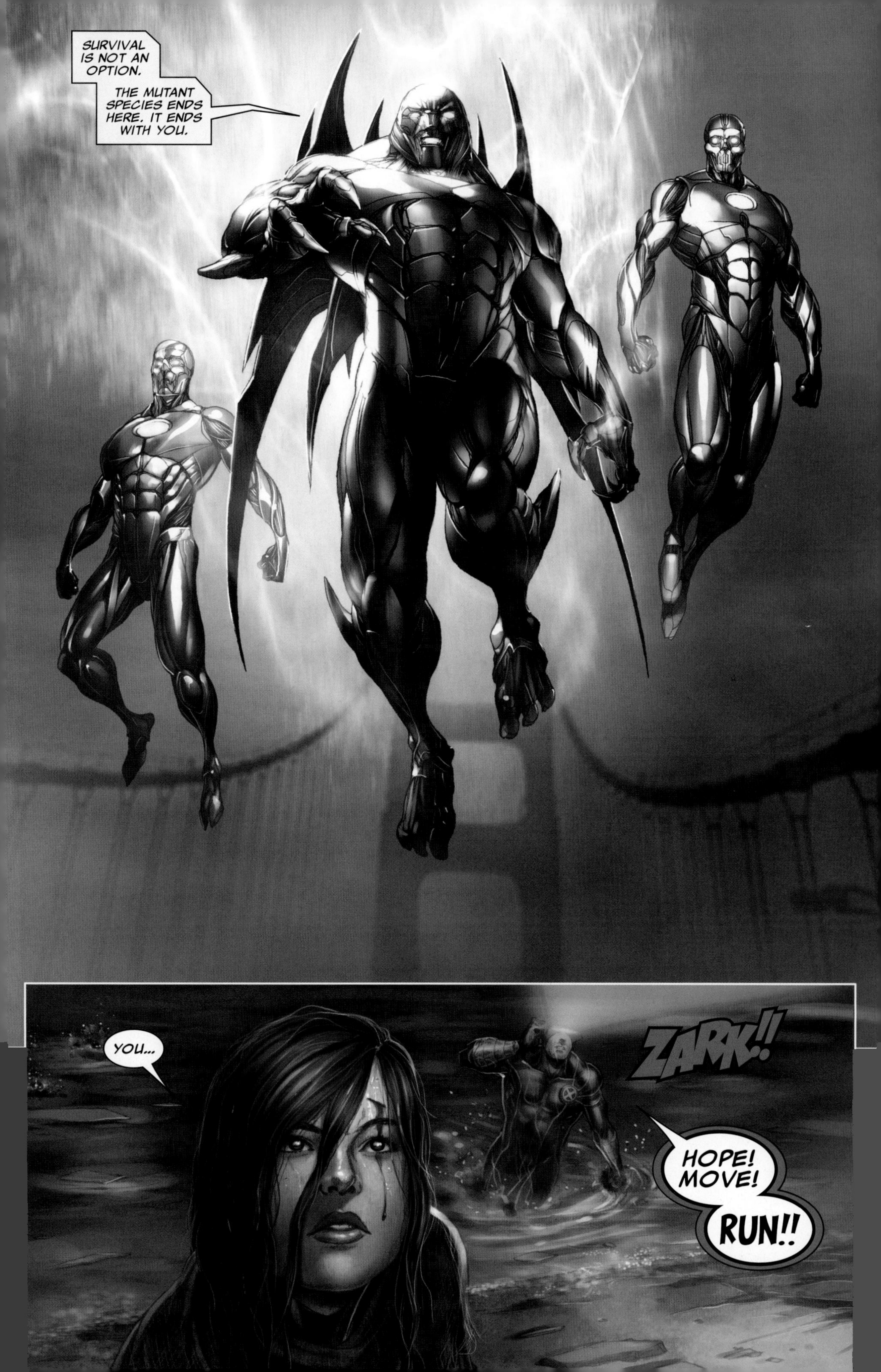
SURVIVAL IS NOT AN OPTION.
THE MUTANT SPECIES ENDS HERE. IT ENDS WITH YOU.
YOU...
ZARK!!
HOPE! MOVE!
RUN!!

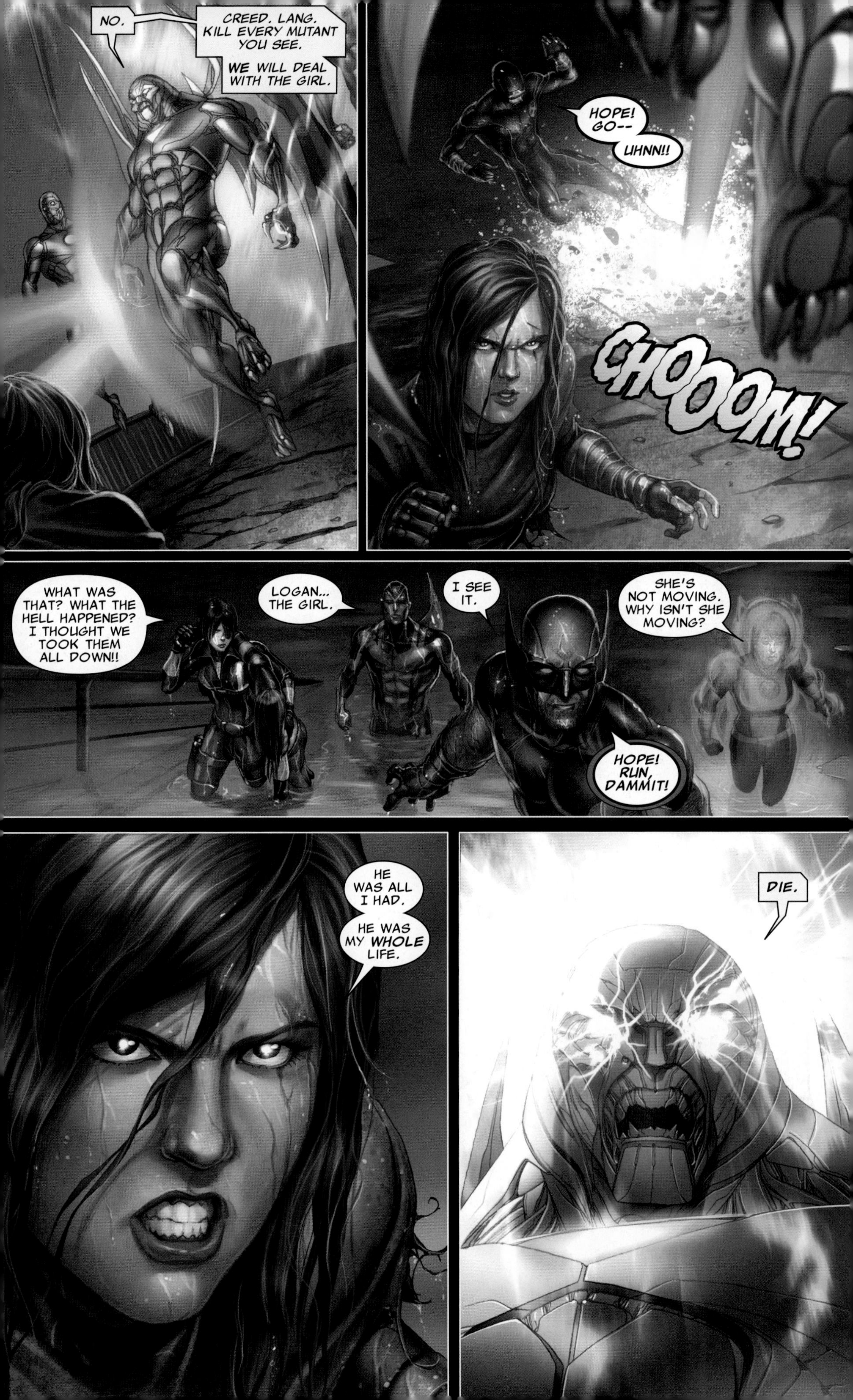
NO.
CREED. LANG. KILL EVERY MUTANT YOU SEE.
WE WILL DEAL WITH THE GIRL.
HOPE! GO--
UHNN!!
CHOOOOM!
WHAT WAS THAT? WHAT THE HELL HAPPENED? I THOUGHT WE TOOK THEM ALL DOWN!!
LOGAN... THE GIRL.
I SEE IT.
SHE'S NOT MOVING. WHY ISN'T SHE MOVING?
HOPE! RUN, DAMMIT!
HE WAS ALL I HAD.
HE WAS MY WHOLE LIFE.
DIE.

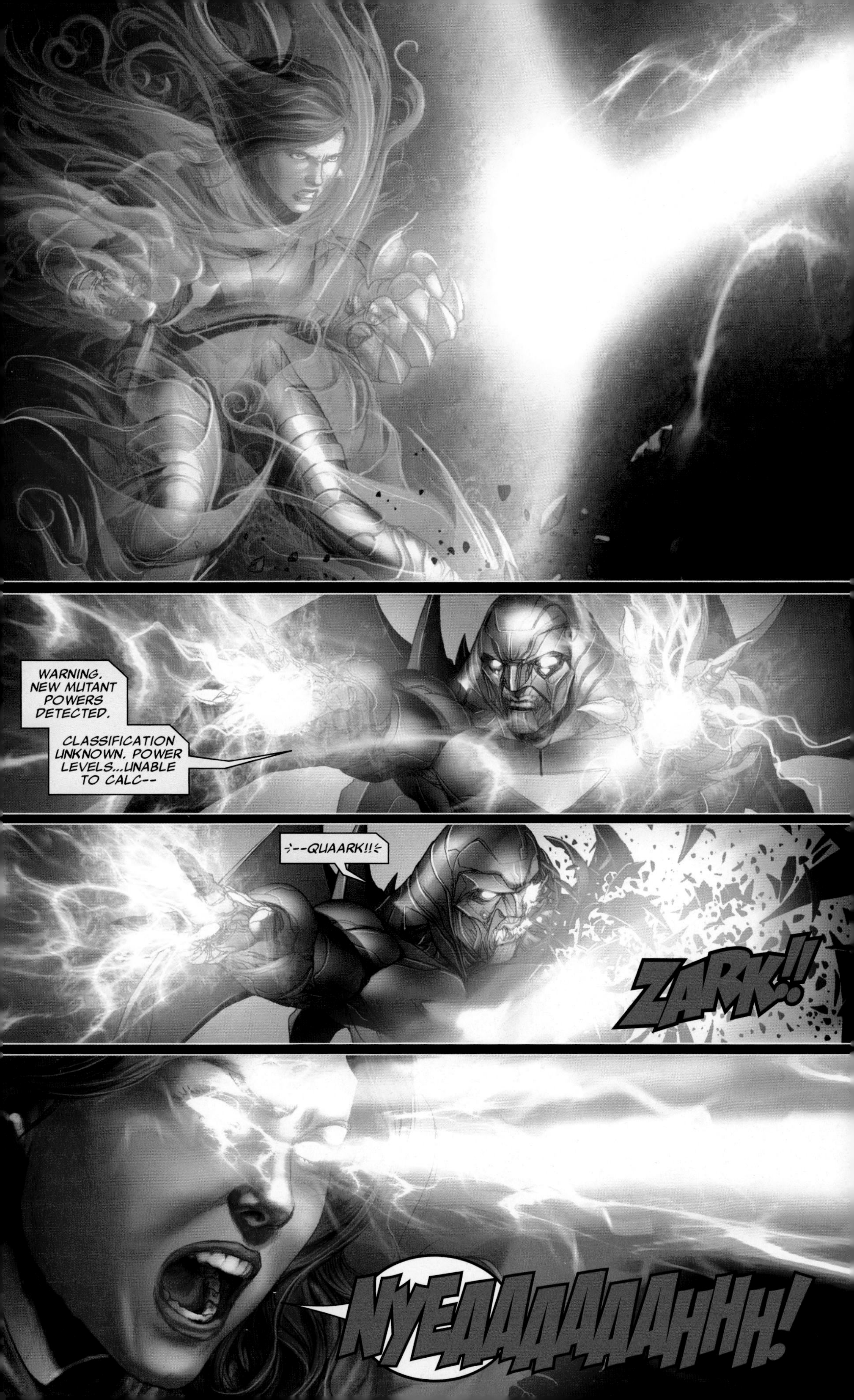
WARNING. NEW MUTANT POWERS DETECTED.
CLASSIFICATION UNKNOWN. POWER LEVELS...UNABLE TO CALC--
--QUAARK!!
ZARK!!
NYEAAAAAAAHHH!

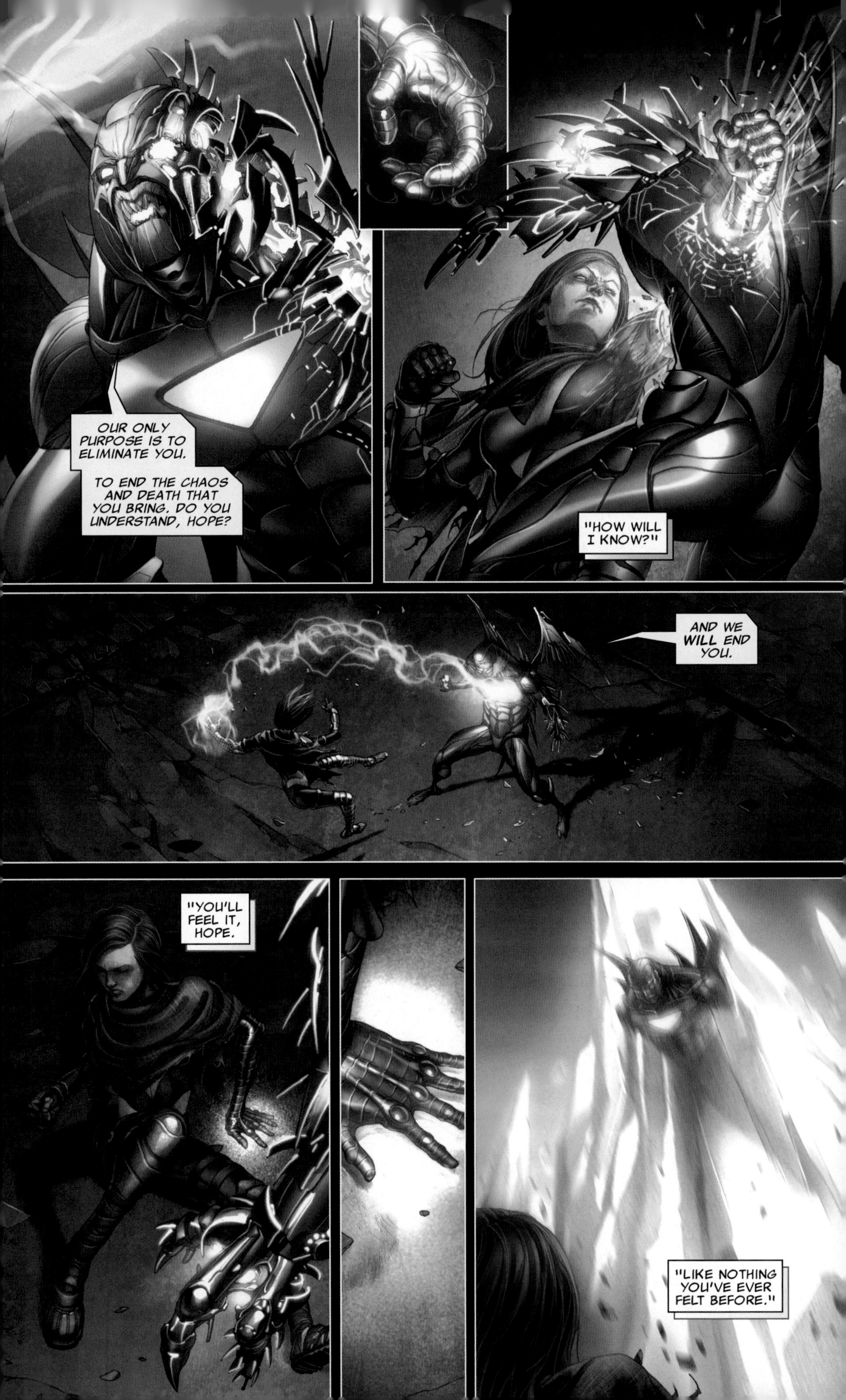
OUR ONLY PURPOSE IS TO ELIMINATE YOU.
TO END THE CHAOS AND DEATH THAT YOU BRING. DO YOU UNDERSTAND, HOPE?
"HOW WILL I KNOW?"
AND WE WILL END YOU.
"YOU'LL FEEL IT, HOPE.
"LIKE NOTHING YOU'VE EVER FELT BEFORE."

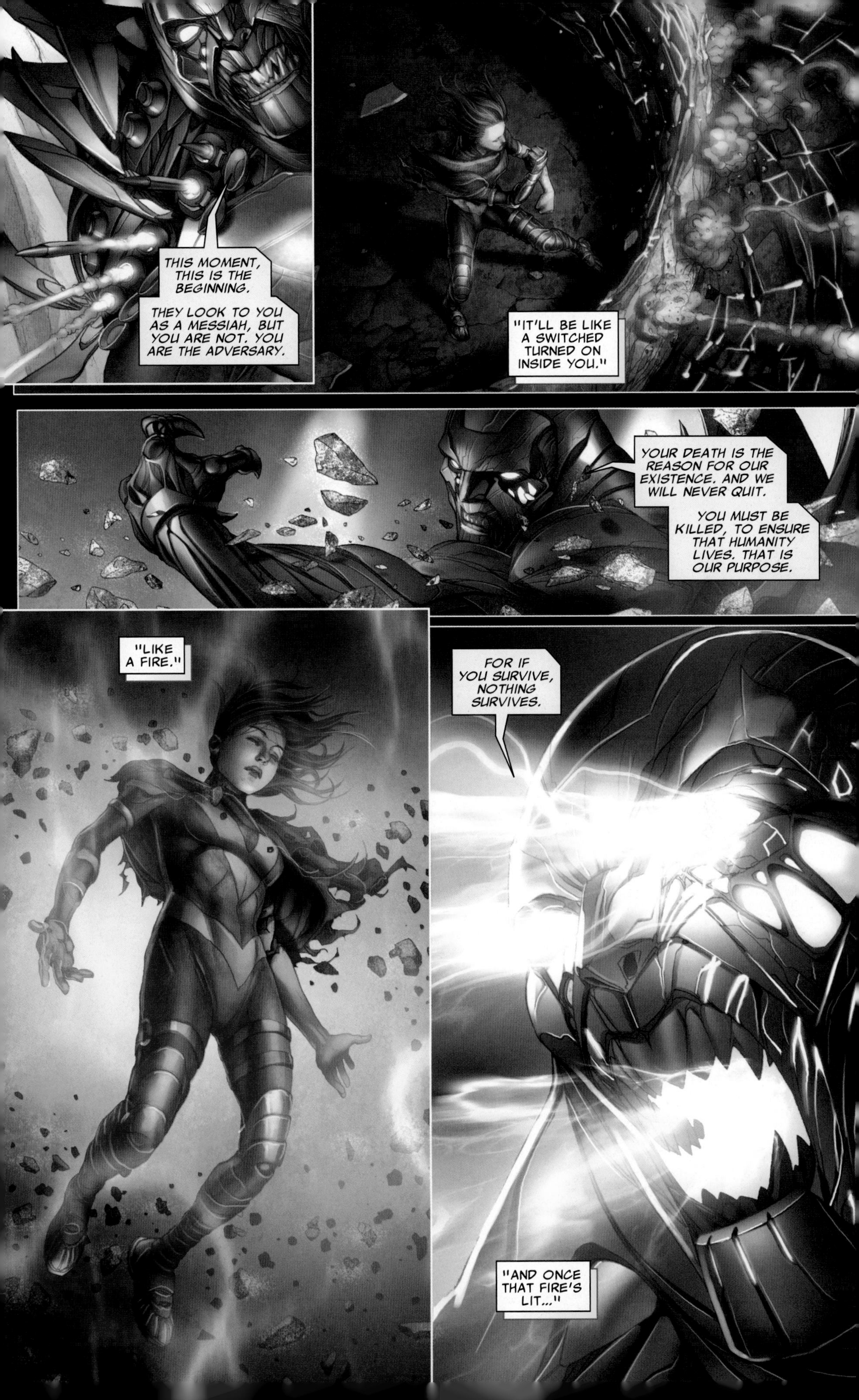
THIS MOMENT, THIS IS THE BEGINNING.
THEY LOOK TO YOU AS A MESSIAH, BUT YOU ARE NOT. YOU ARE THE ADVERSARY.
"IT'LL BE LIKE A SWITCHED TURNED ON INSIDE YOU."
YOUR DEATH IS THE REASON FOR OUR EXISTENCE. AND WE WILL NEVER QUIT.
YOU MUST BE KILLED, TO ENSURE THAT HUMANITY LIVES. THAT IS OUR PURPOSE.
"LIKE A FIRE."
FOR IF YOU SURVIVE, NOTHING SURVIVES.
"AND ONCE THAT FIRE'S LIT..."

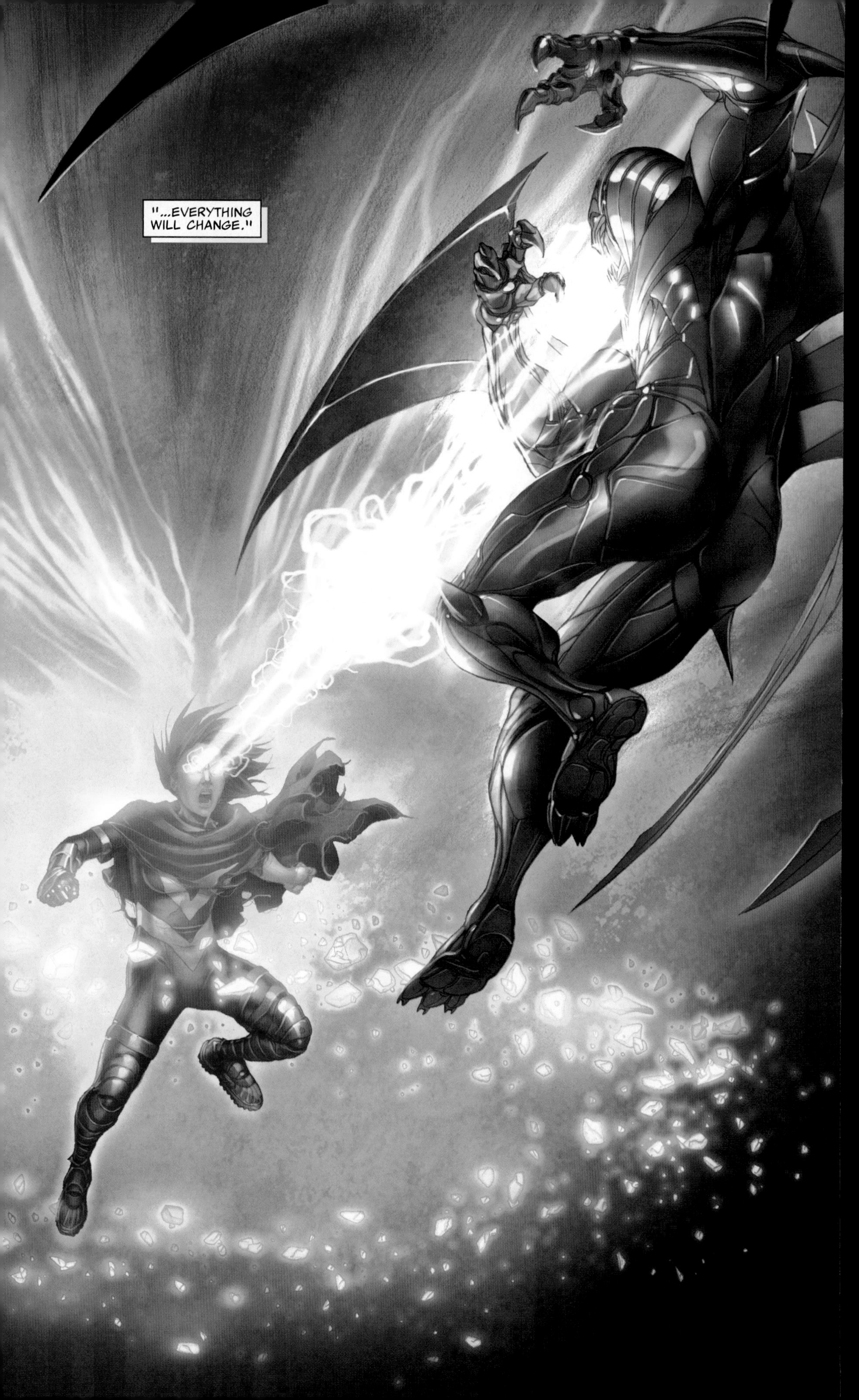
"...EVERYTHING WILL CHANGE."

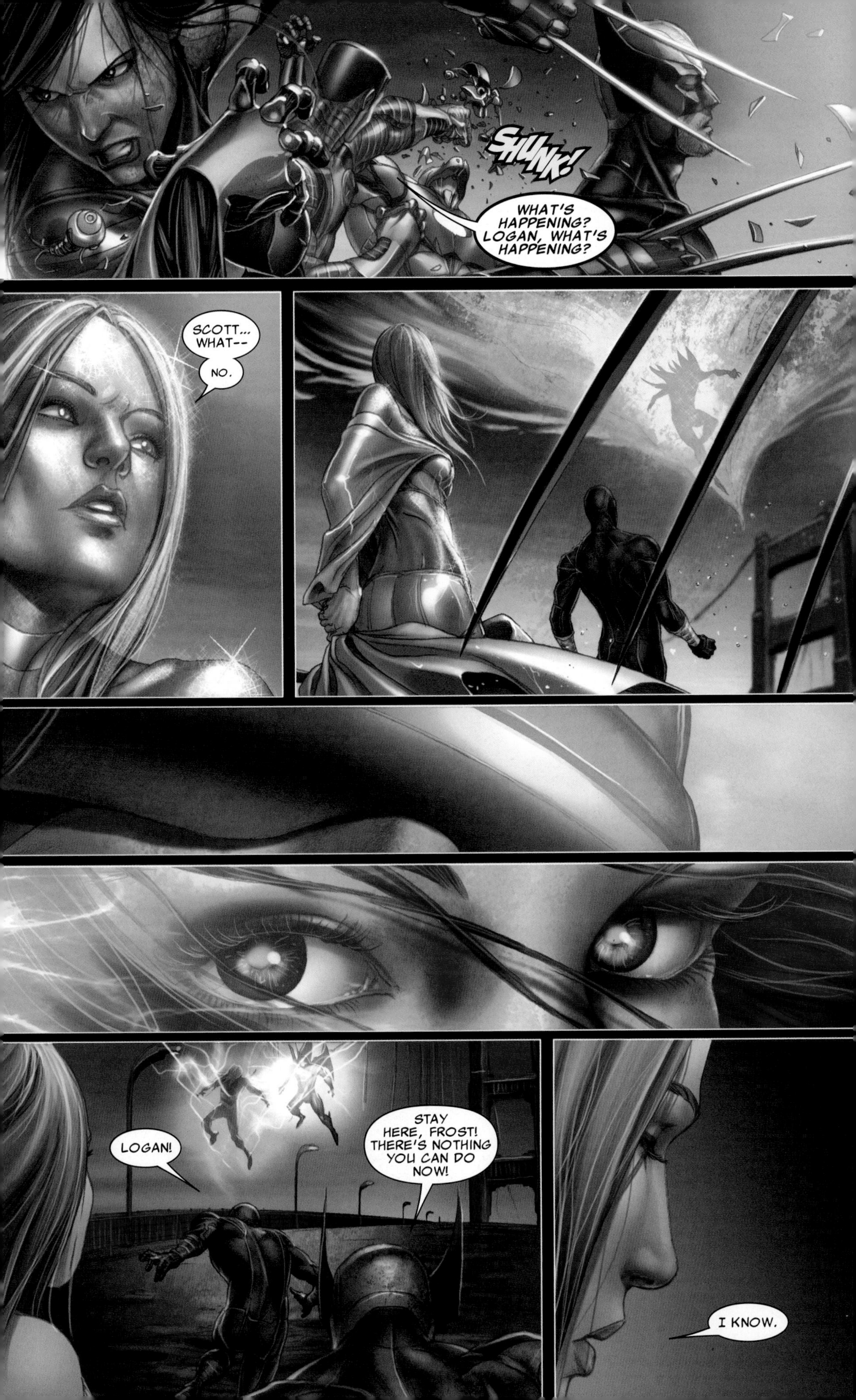
SHUNK!
WHAT'S HAPPENING? LOGAN, WHAT'S HAPPENING?
SCOTT... WHAT--
NO.
LOGAN!
STAY HERE, FROST! THERE'S NOTHING YOU CAN DO NOW!
I KNOW.

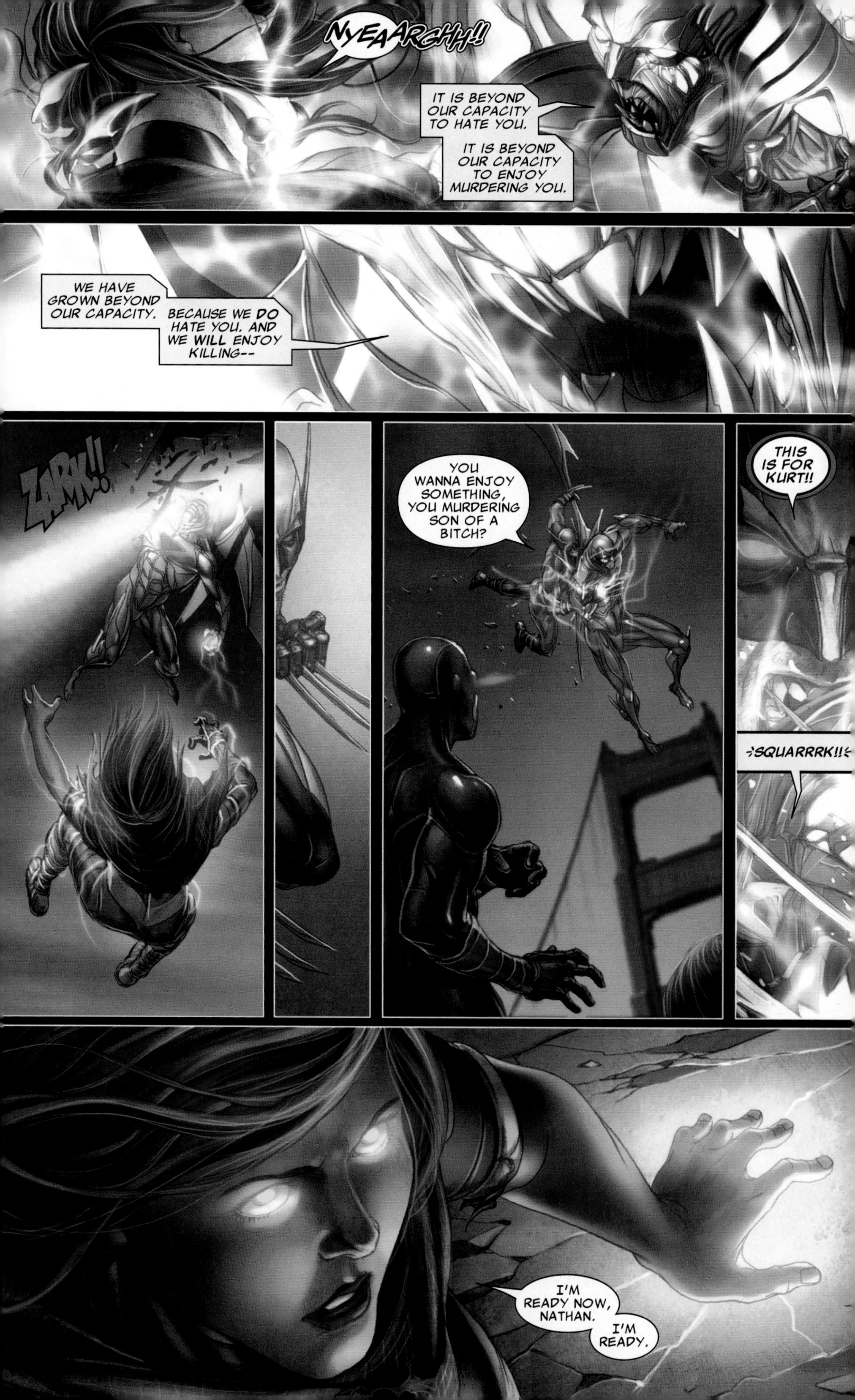
NYEAARGHH!!
IT IS BEYOND OUR CAPACITY TO HATE YOU.
IT IS BEYOND OUR CAPACITY TO ENJOY MURDERING YOU.
WE HAVE GROWN BEYOND OUR CAPACITY.
BECAUSE WE DO HATE YOU. AND WE WILL ENJOY KILLING--
ZARK!!
YOU WANNA ENJOY SOMETHING, YOU MURDERING SON OF A BITCH?
THIS IS FOR KURT!!
SQUARRRK!!
I'M READY NOW, NATHAN.
I'M READY.

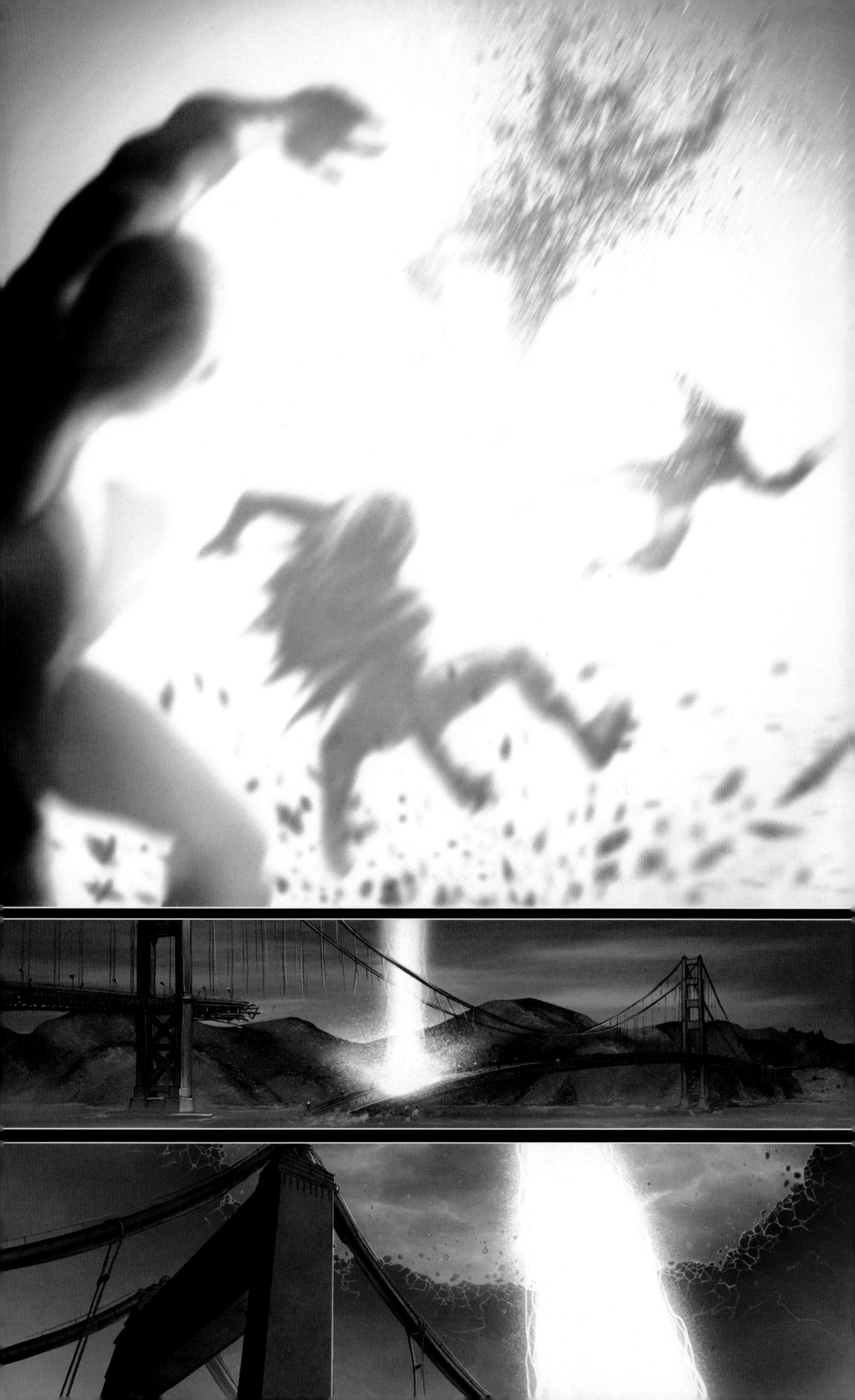

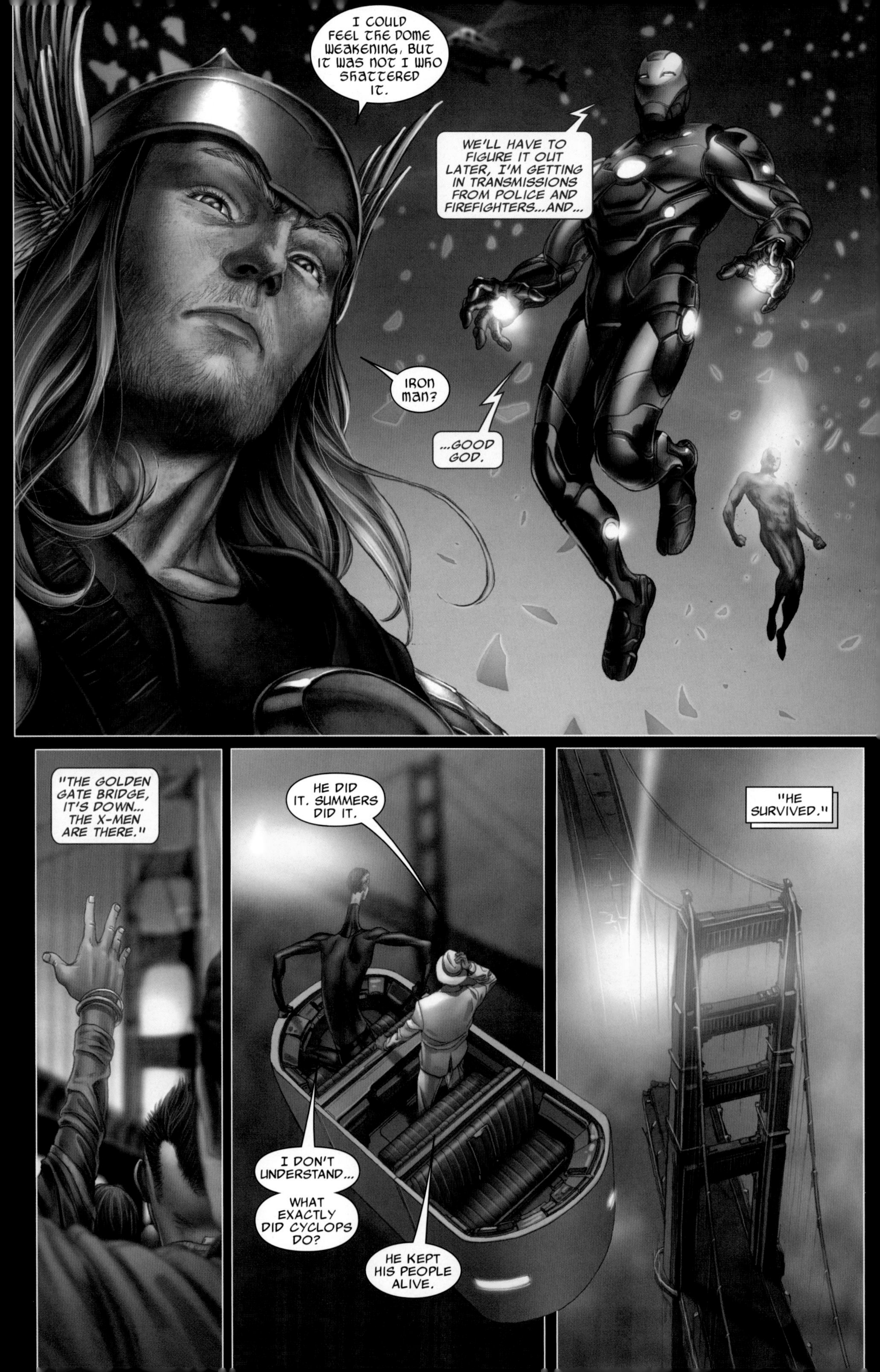
I COULD FEEL THE DOME WEAKENING, BUT IT WAS NOT I WHO SHATTERED IT.
WE'LL HAVE TO FIGURE IT OUT LATER, I'M GETTING IN TRANSMISSIONS FROM POLICE AND FIREFIGHTERS...AND...
IRON MAN?
...GOOD GOD.
"THE GOLDEN GATE BRIDGE, IT'S DOWN... THE X-MEN ARE THERE."
HE DID IT. SUMMERS DID IT.
I DON'T UNDERSTAND...
WHAT EXACTLY DID CYCLOPS DO?
HE KEPT HIS PEOPLE ALIVE.
"HE SURVIVED."

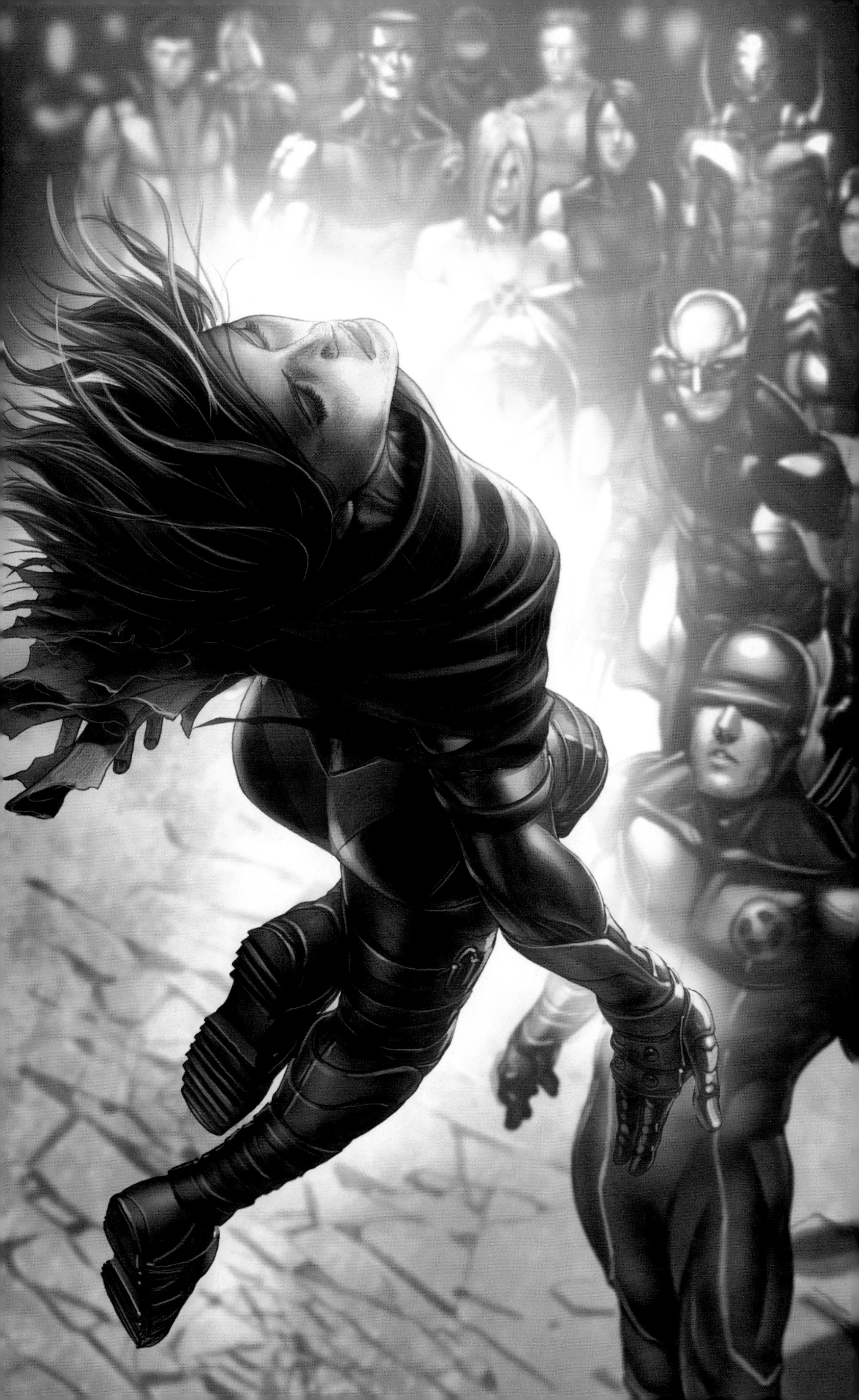

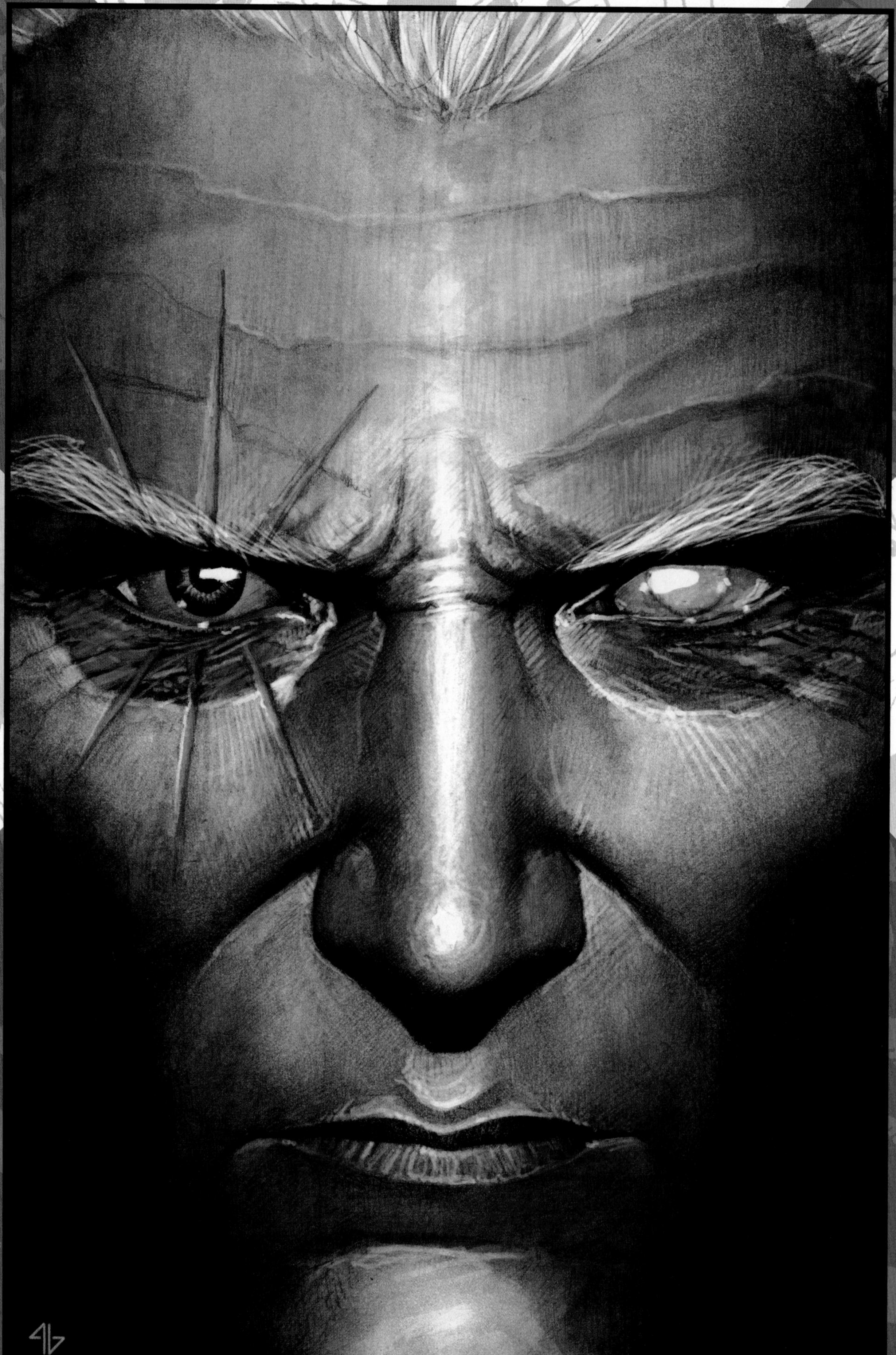

X-MEN: SECOND COMING #2

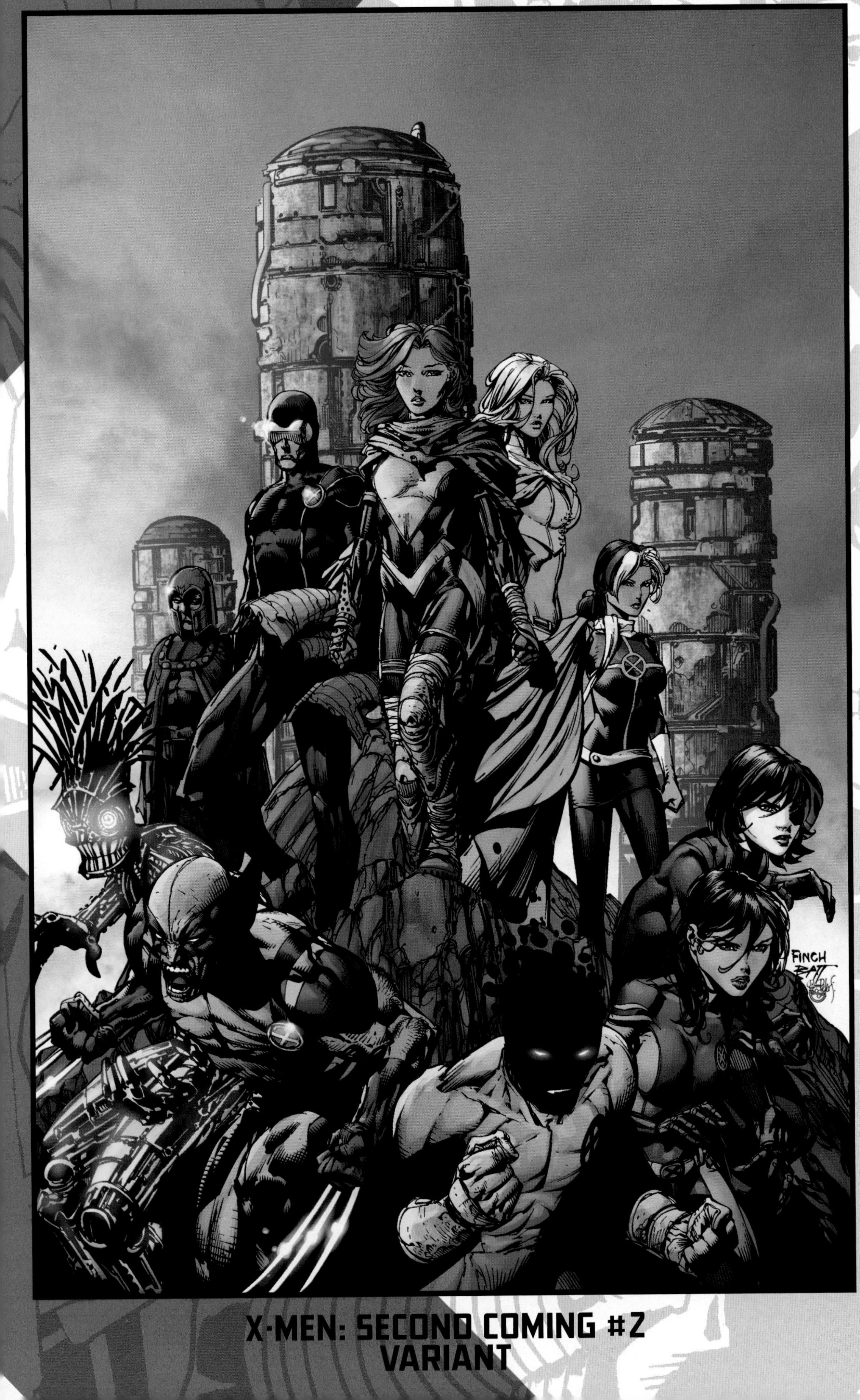
FINCH

X-MEN: SECOND COMING #2
VARIANT

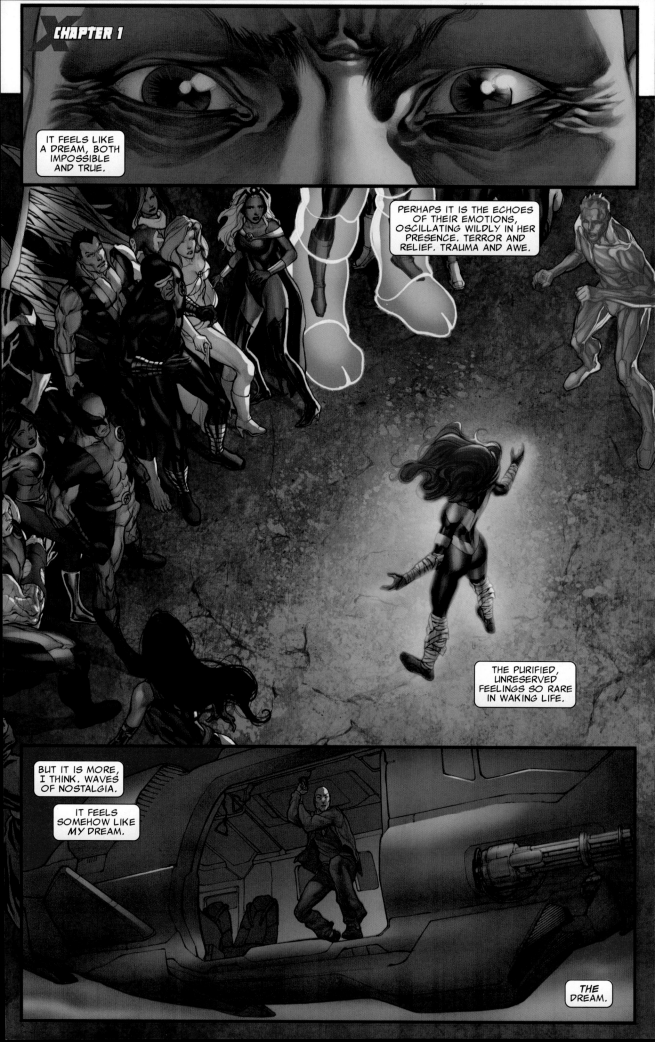

CHAPTER 1

IT FEELS LIKE A DREAM, BOTH IMPOSSIBLE AND TRUE.

PERHAPS IT IS THE ECHOES OF THEIR EMOTIONS, OSCILLATING WILDLY IN HER PRESENCE. TERROR AND RELIEF. TRAUMA AND AWE.

THE PURIFIED, UNRESERVED FEELINGS SO RARE IN WAKING LIFE.

BUT IT IS MORE, I THINK. WAVES OF NOSTALGIA.

IT FEELS SOMEHOW LIKE MY DREAM.

THE DREAM.

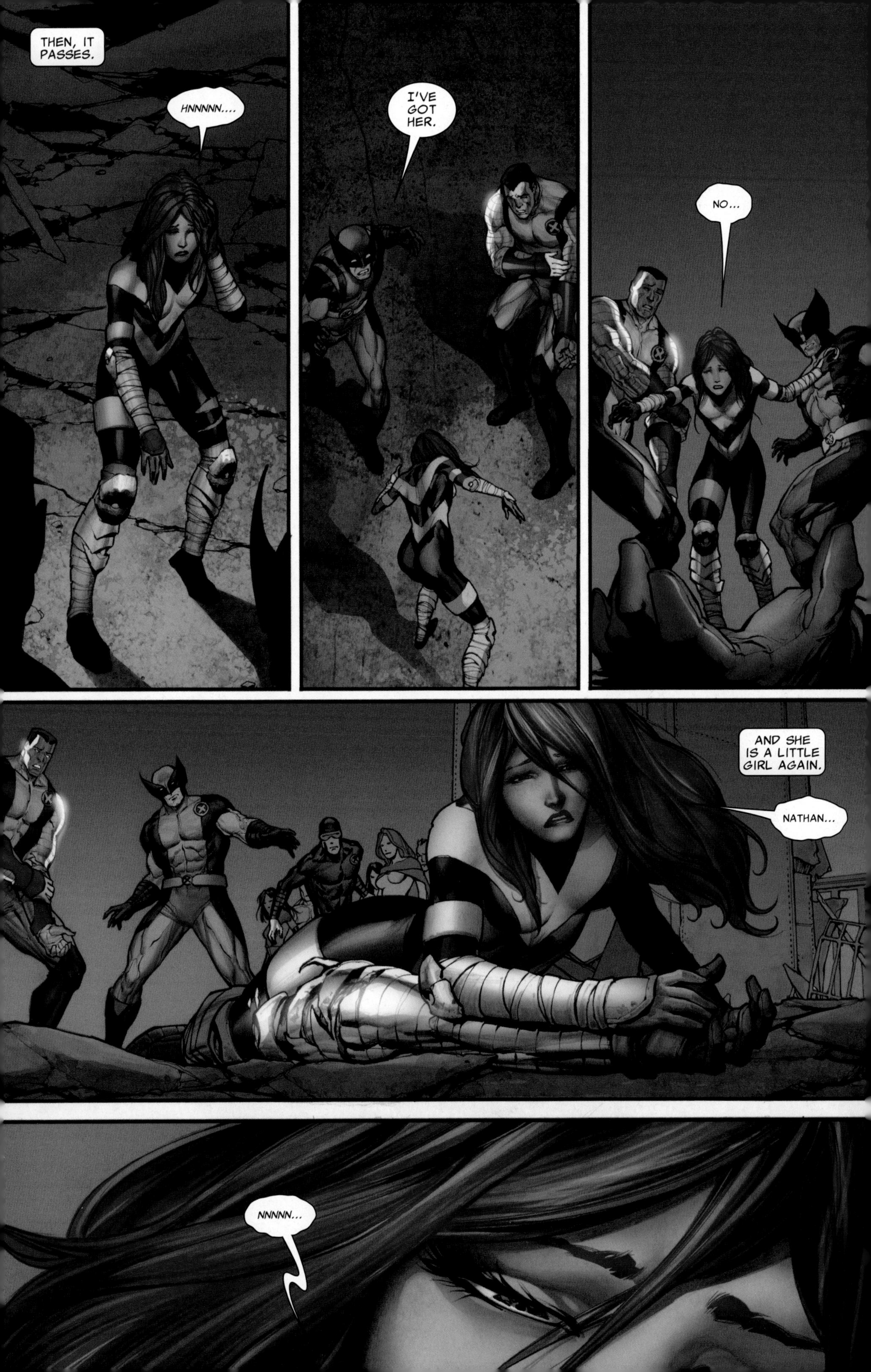
THEN, IT PASSES.
HNNNNN....
I'VE GOT HER.
NO...
AND SHE IS A LITTLE GIRL AGAIN.
NATHAN...
NNNNN...

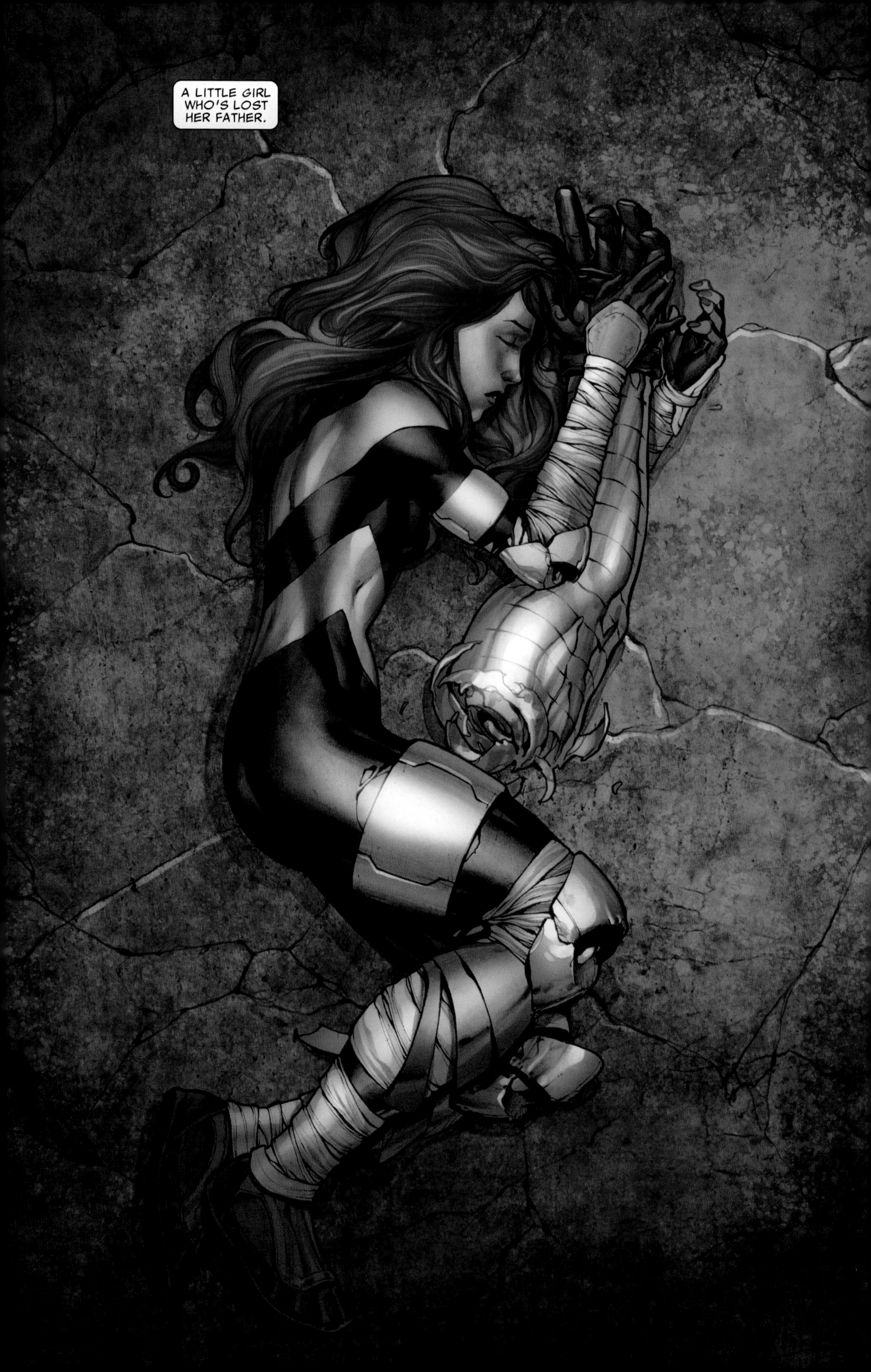
A LITTLE GIRL
WHO'S LOST
HER FATHER.

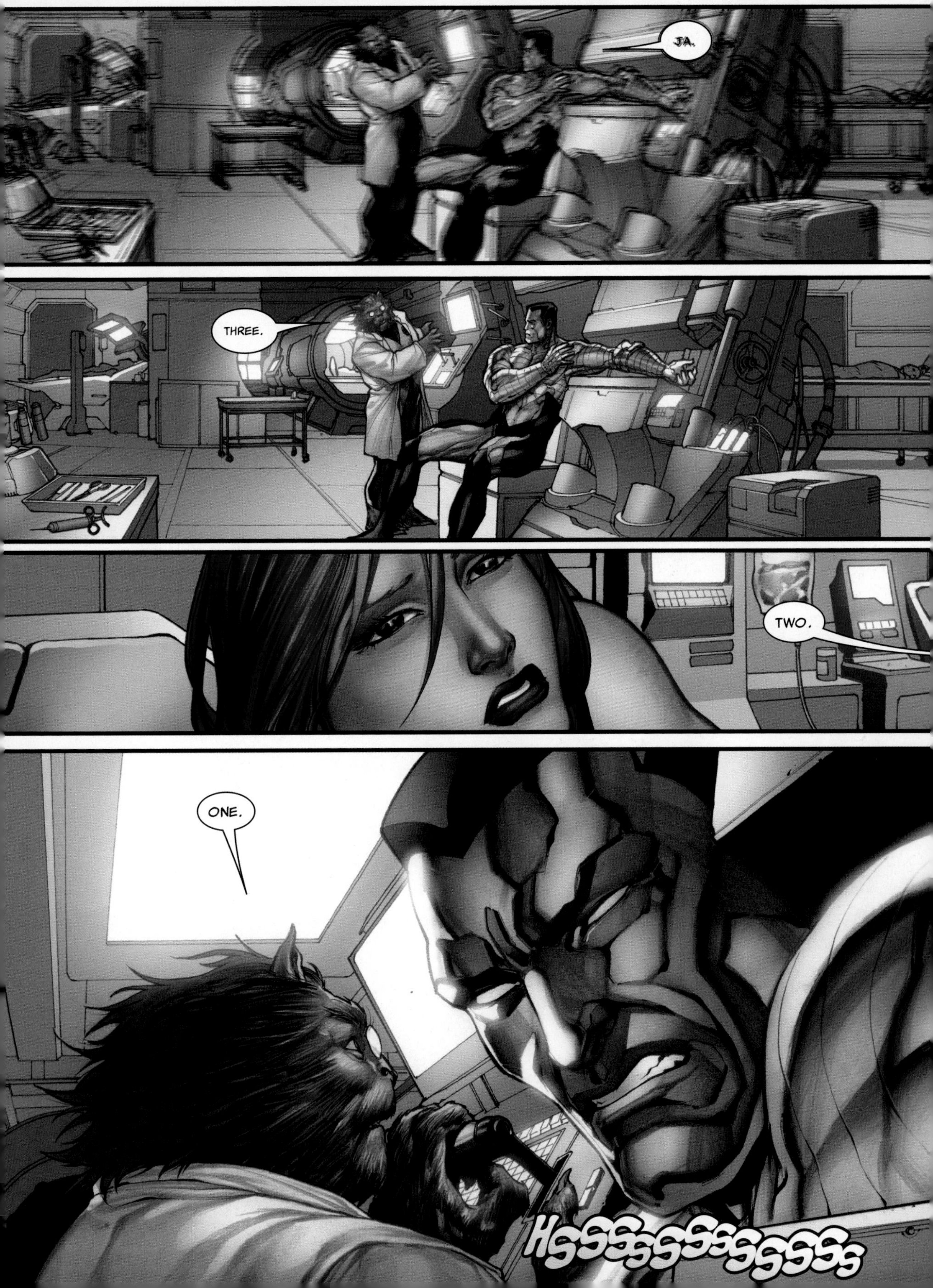
JA.
THREE.
TWO.
ONE.
HSSSSSSSSSSSSSS

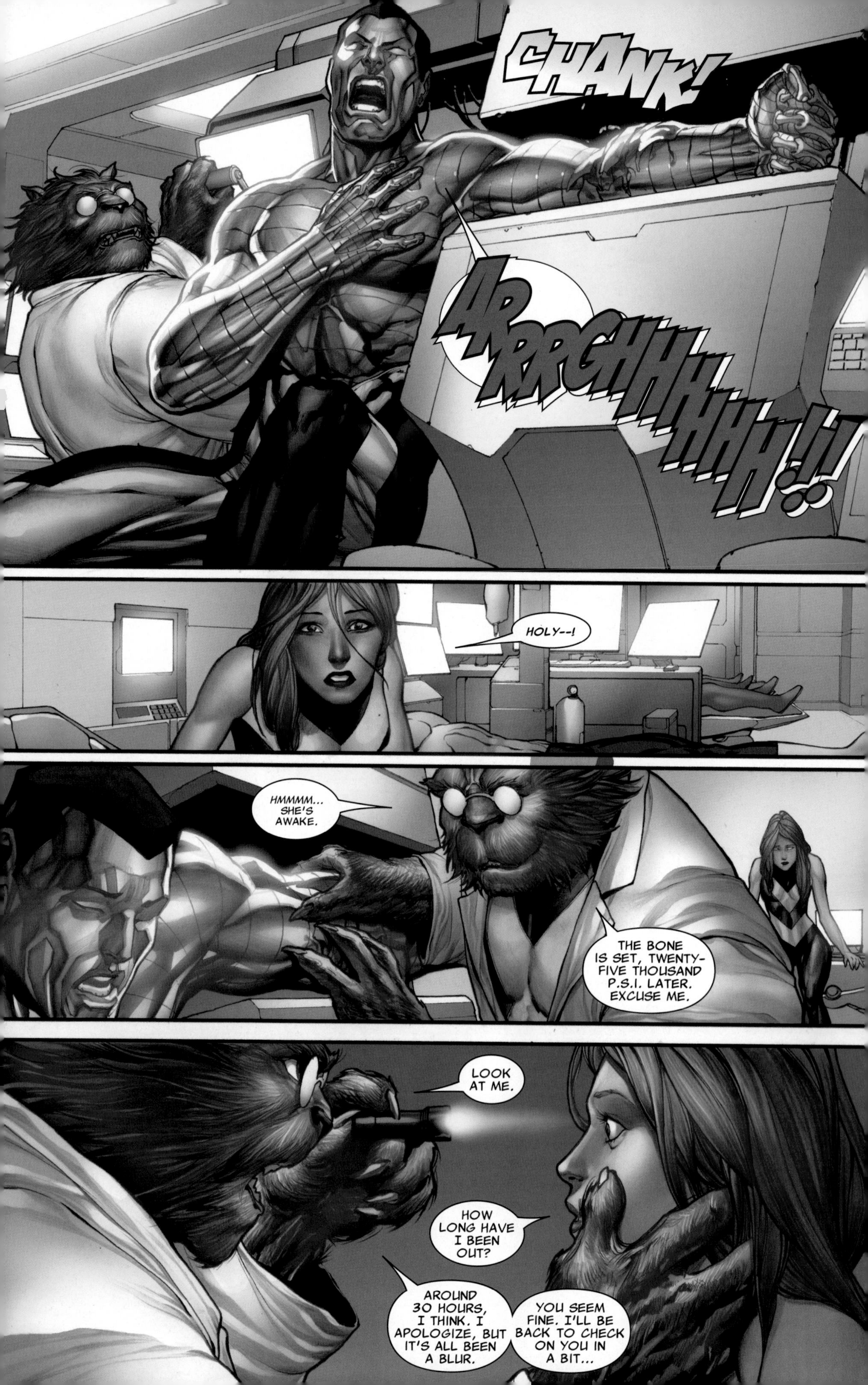
CHANK!
ARRRGHHHHHHH!!!
HOLY--!
HMMMM... SHE'S AWAKE.
THE BONE IS SET, TWENTY-FIVE THOUSAND P.S.I. LATER. EXCUSE ME.
LOOK AT ME.
HOW LONG HAVE I BEEN OUT?
AROUND 30 HOURS, I THINK. I APOLOGIZE, BUT IT'S ALL BEEN A BLUR.
YOU SEEM FINE. I'LL BE BACK TO CHECK ON YOU IN A BIT...

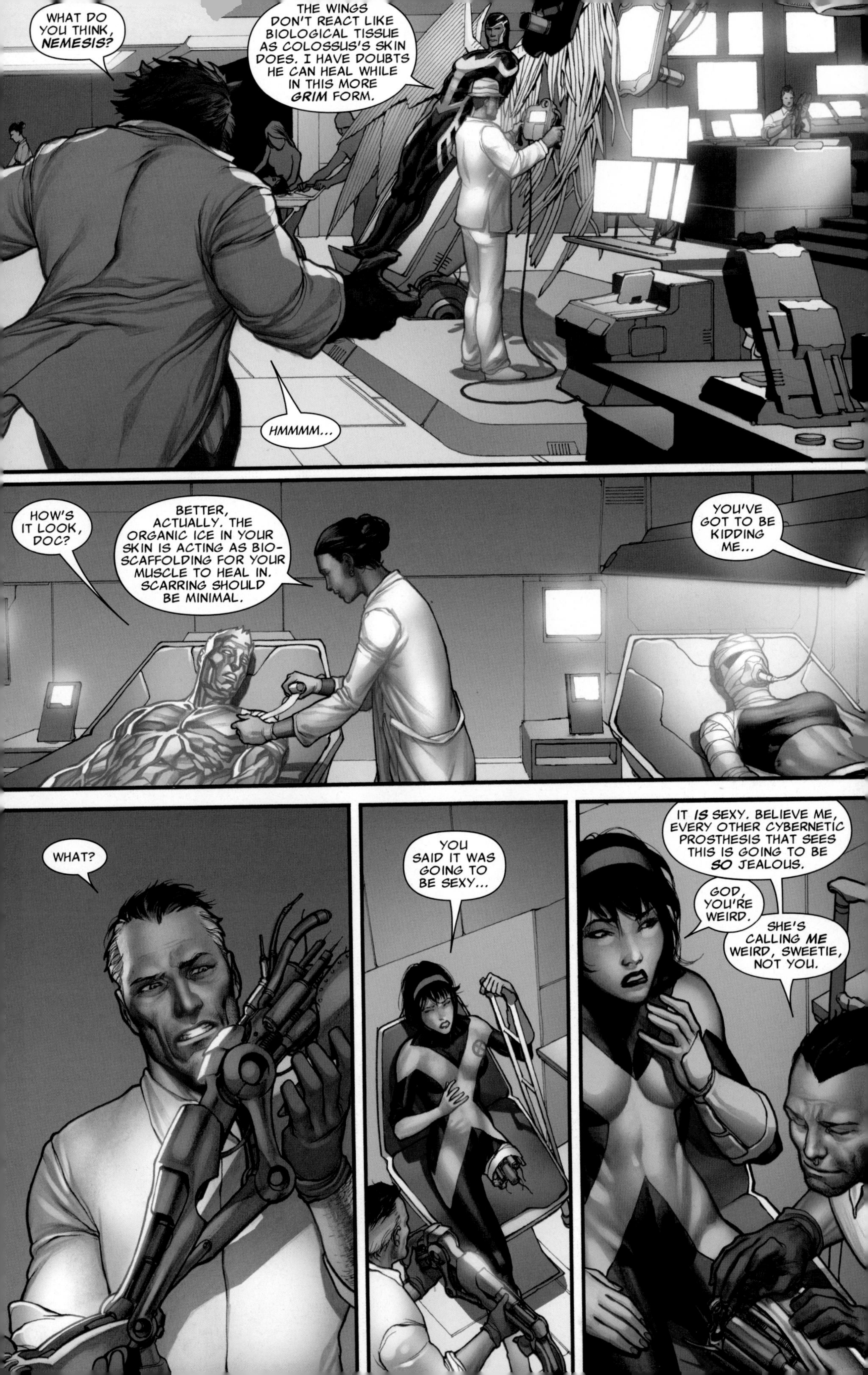
WHAT DO YOU THINK, NEMESIS?
THE WINGS DON'T REACT LIKE BIOLOGICAL TISSUE AS COLOSSUS'S SKIN DOES. I HAVE DOUBTS HE CAN HEAL WHILE IN THIS MORE GRIM FORM.
HMMMM...
HOW'S IT LOOK, DOC?
BETTER, ACTUALLY. THE ORGANIC ICE IN YOUR SKIN IS ACTING AS BIO-SCAFFOLDING FOR YOUR MUSCLE TO HEAL IN. SCARRING SHOULD BE MINIMAL.
YOU'VE GOT TO BE KIDDING ME...
WHAT?
YOU SAID IT WAS GOING TO BE SEXY...
IT IS SEXY. BELIEVE ME, EVERY OTHER CYBERNETIC PROSTHESIS THAT SEES THIS IS GOING TO BE SO JEALOUS.
GOD, YOU'RE WEIRD.
SHE'S CALLING ME WEIRD, SWEETIE, NOT YOU.

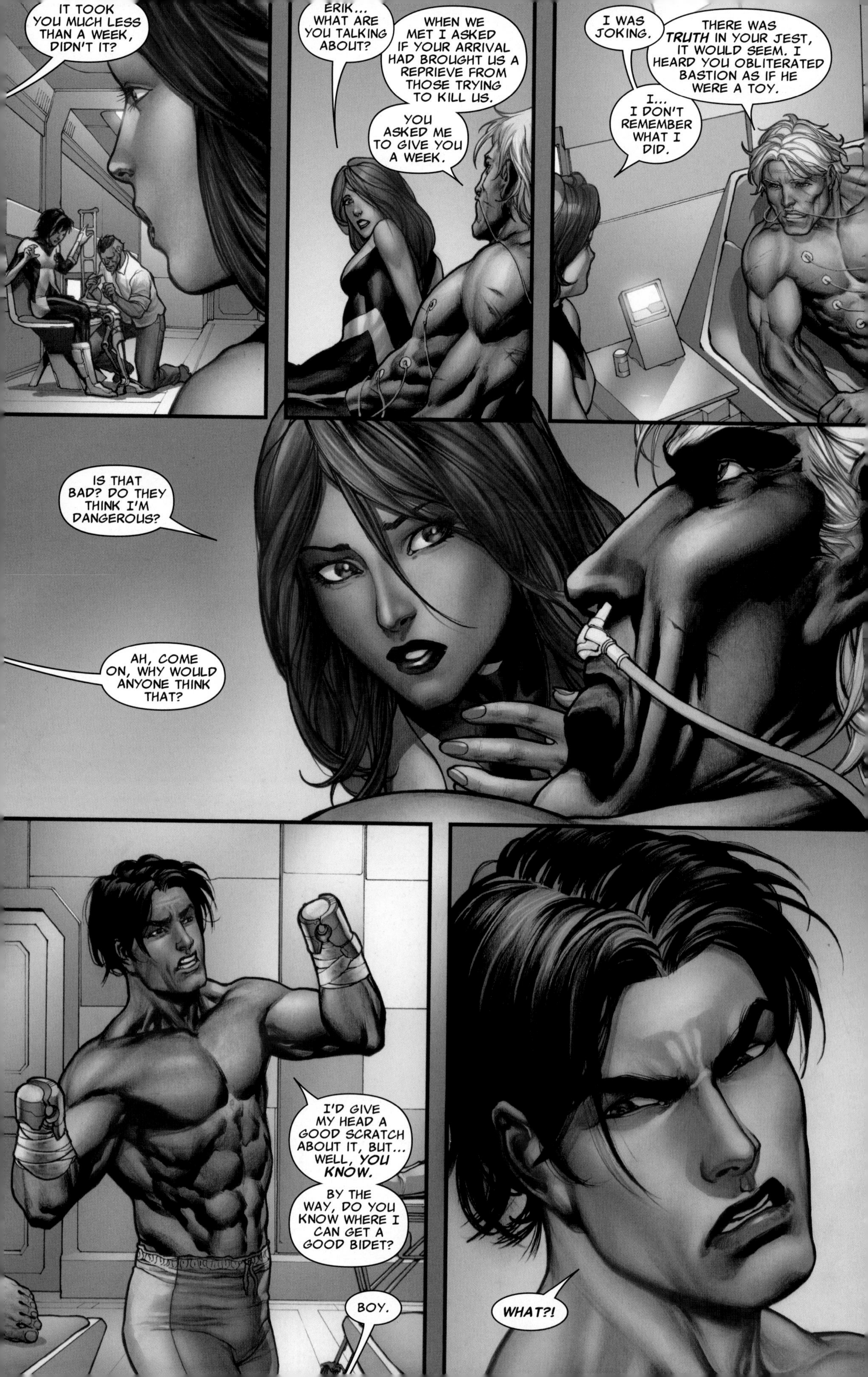
IT TOOK YOU MUCH LESS THAN A WEEK, DIDN'T IT?
ERIK... WHAT ARE YOU TALKING ABOUT?
WHEN WE MET I ASKED IF YOUR ARRIVAL HAD BROUGHT US A REPRIEVE FROM THOSE TRYING TO KILL US.
YOU ASKED ME TO GIVE YOU A WEEK.
I WAS JOKING.
THERE WAS TRUTH IN YOUR JEST, IT WOULD SEEM. I HEARD YOU OBLITERATED BASTION AS IF HE WERE A TOY.
I... I DON'T REMEMBER WHAT I DID.
IS THAT BAD? DO THEY THINK I'M DANGEROUS?
AH, COME ON, WHY WOULD ANYONE THINK THAT?
I'D GIVE MY HEAD A GOOD SCRATCH ABOUT IT, BUT... WELL, YOU KNOW.
BY THE WAY, DO YOU KNOW WHERE I CAN GET A GOOD BIDET?
BOY.
WHAT?!

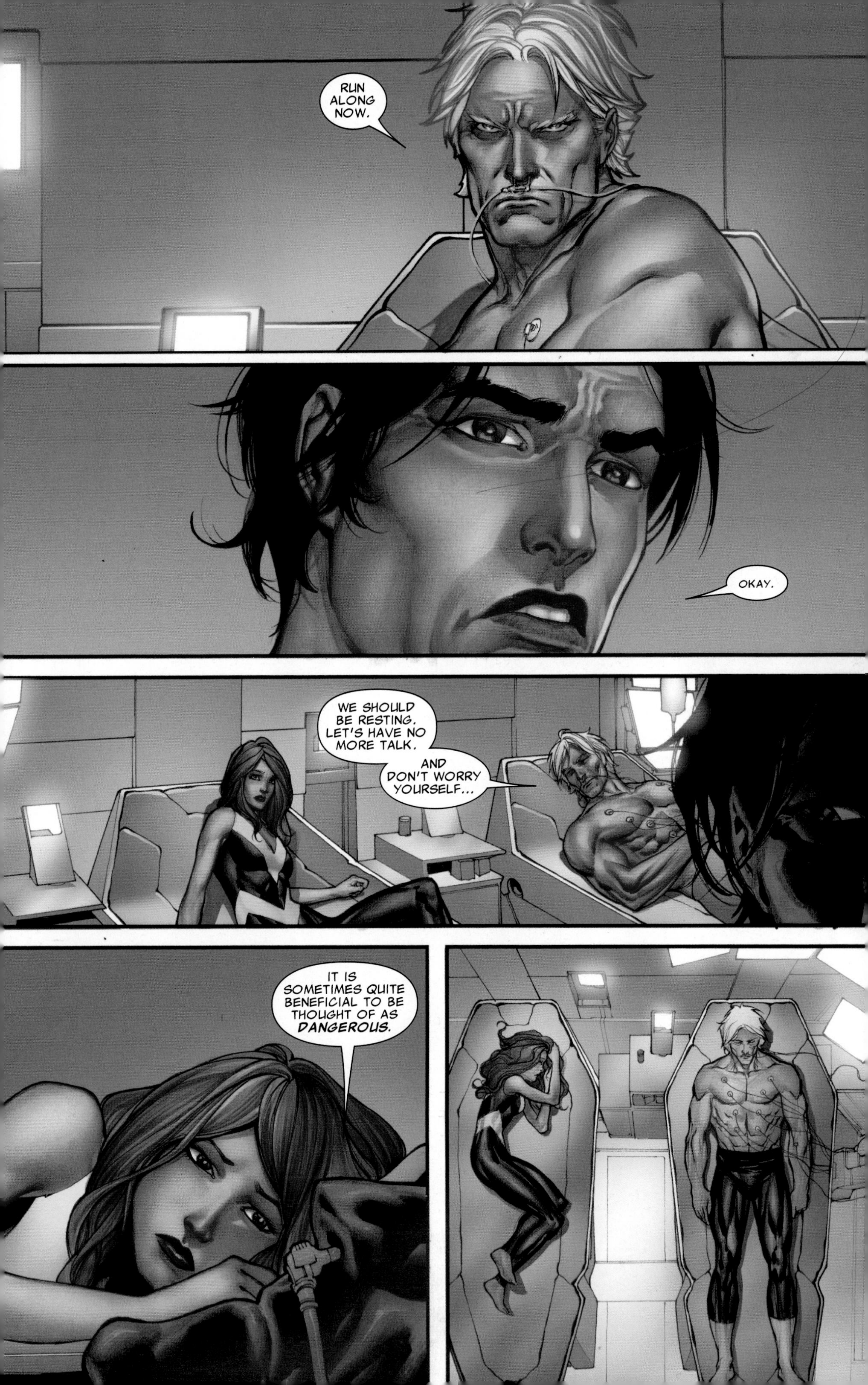
RUN ALONG NOW.
OKAY.
WE SHOULD BE RESTING. LET'S HAVE NO MORE TALK.
AND DON'T WORRY YOURSELF...
IT IS SOMETIMES QUITE BENEFICIAL TO BE THOUGHT OF AS *DANGEROUS.*

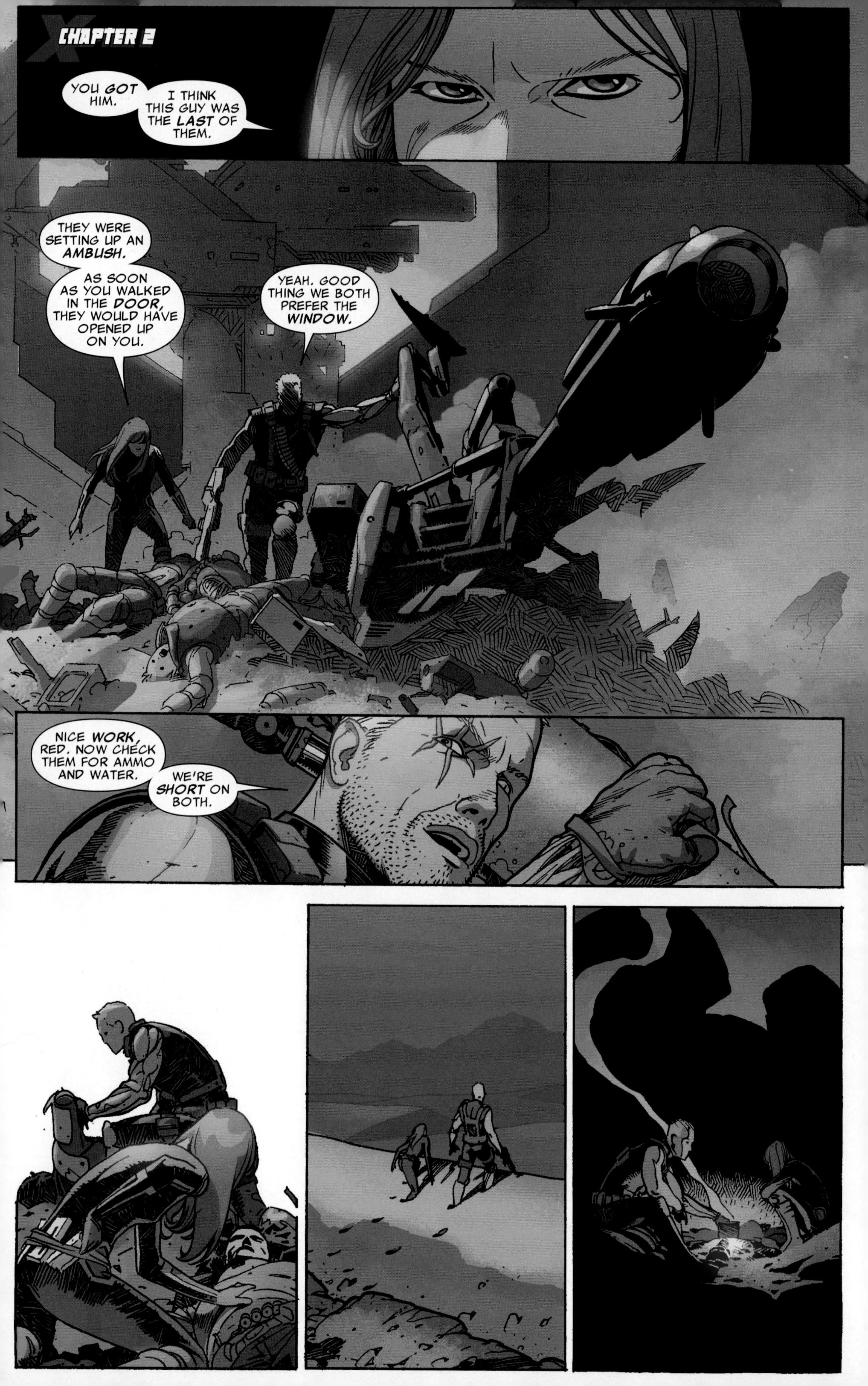
CHAPTER 2
YOU GOT HIM.
I THINK THIS GUY WAS THE LAST OF THEM.
THEY WERE SETTING UP AN AMBUSH.
AS SOON AS YOU WALKED IN THE DOOR, THEY WOULD HAVE OPENED UP ON YOU.
YEAH. GOOD THING WE BOTH PREFER THE WINDOW.
NICE WORK, RED. NOW CHECK THEM FOR AMMO AND WATER.
WE'RE SHORT ON BOTH.

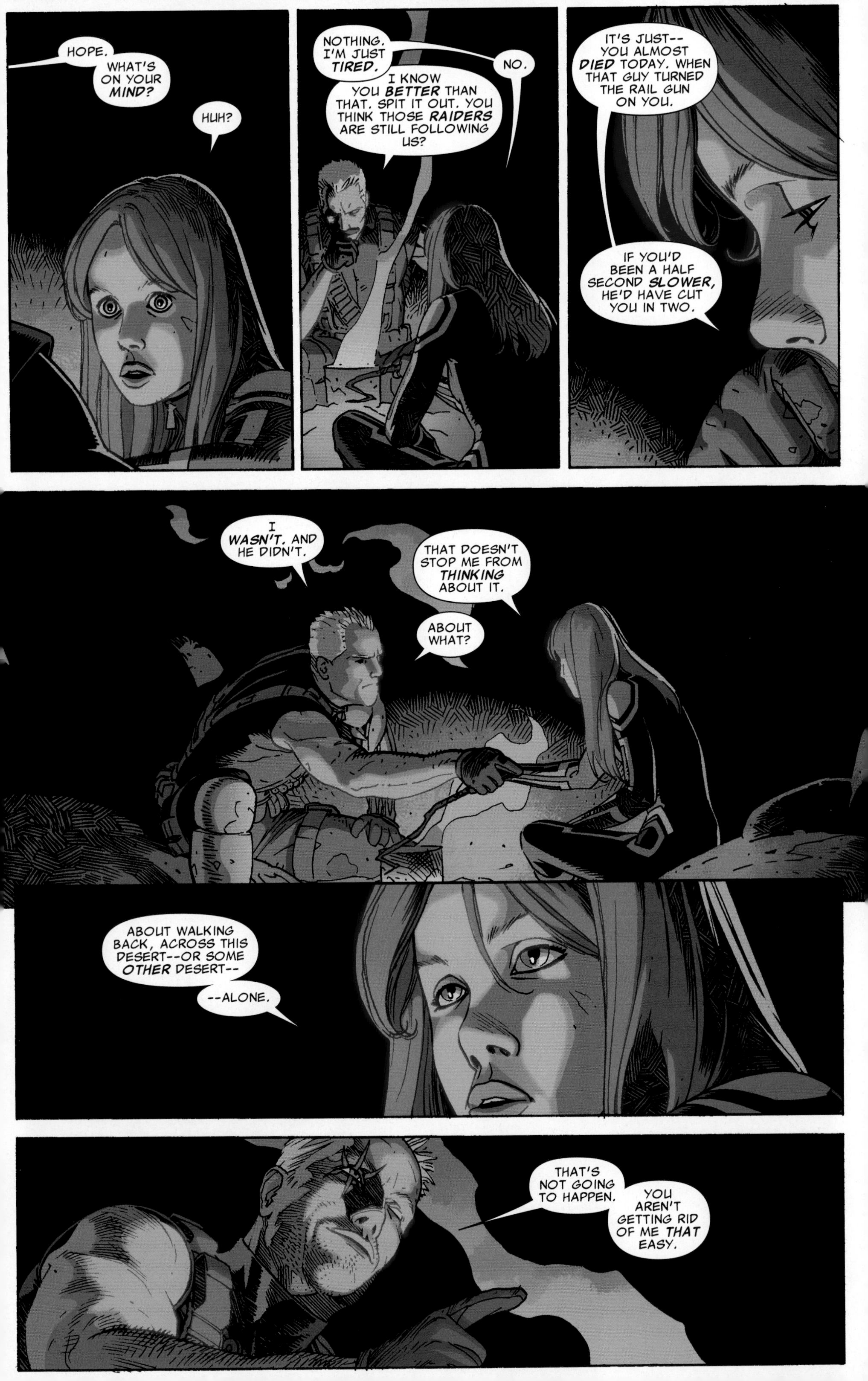

HOPE.
WHAT'S ON YOUR MIND?
HUH?
NOTHING. I'M JUST TIRED.
NO.
I KNOW YOU BETTER THAN THAT. SPIT IT OUT. YOU THINK THOSE RAIDERS ARE STILL FOLLOWING US?
IT'S JUST-- YOU ALMOST DIED TODAY. WHEN THAT GUY TURNED THE RAIL GUN ON YOU.
IF YOU'D BEEN A HALF SECOND SLOWER, HE'D HAVE CUT YOU IN TWO.
I WASN'T. AND HE DIDN'T.
THAT DOESN'T STOP ME FROM THINKING ABOUT IT.
ABOUT WHAT?
ABOUT WALKING BACK, ACROSS THIS DESERT--OR SOME OTHER DESERT--
--ALONE.
THAT'S NOT GOING TO HAPPEN.
YOU AREN'T GETTING RID OF ME THAT EASY.

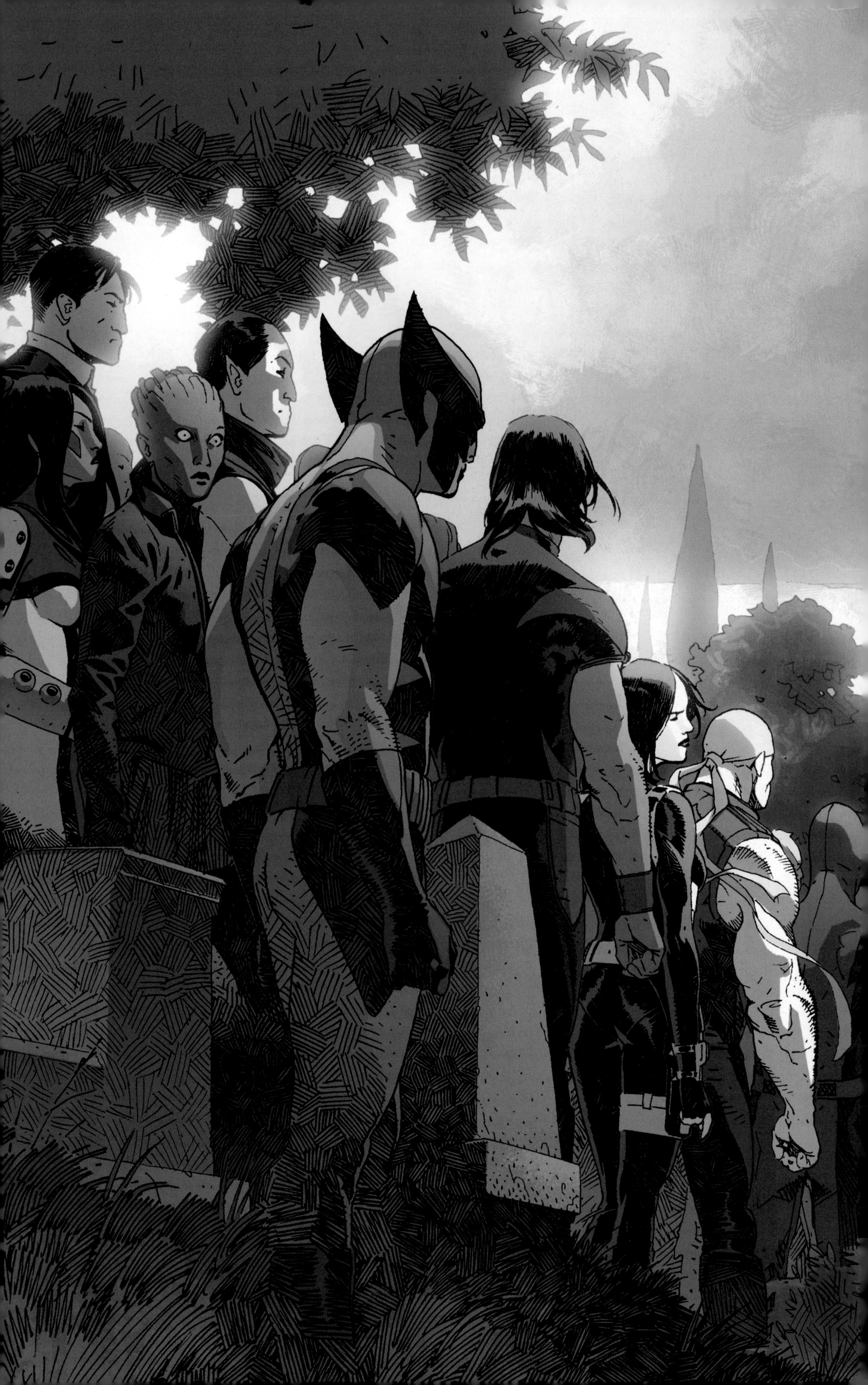

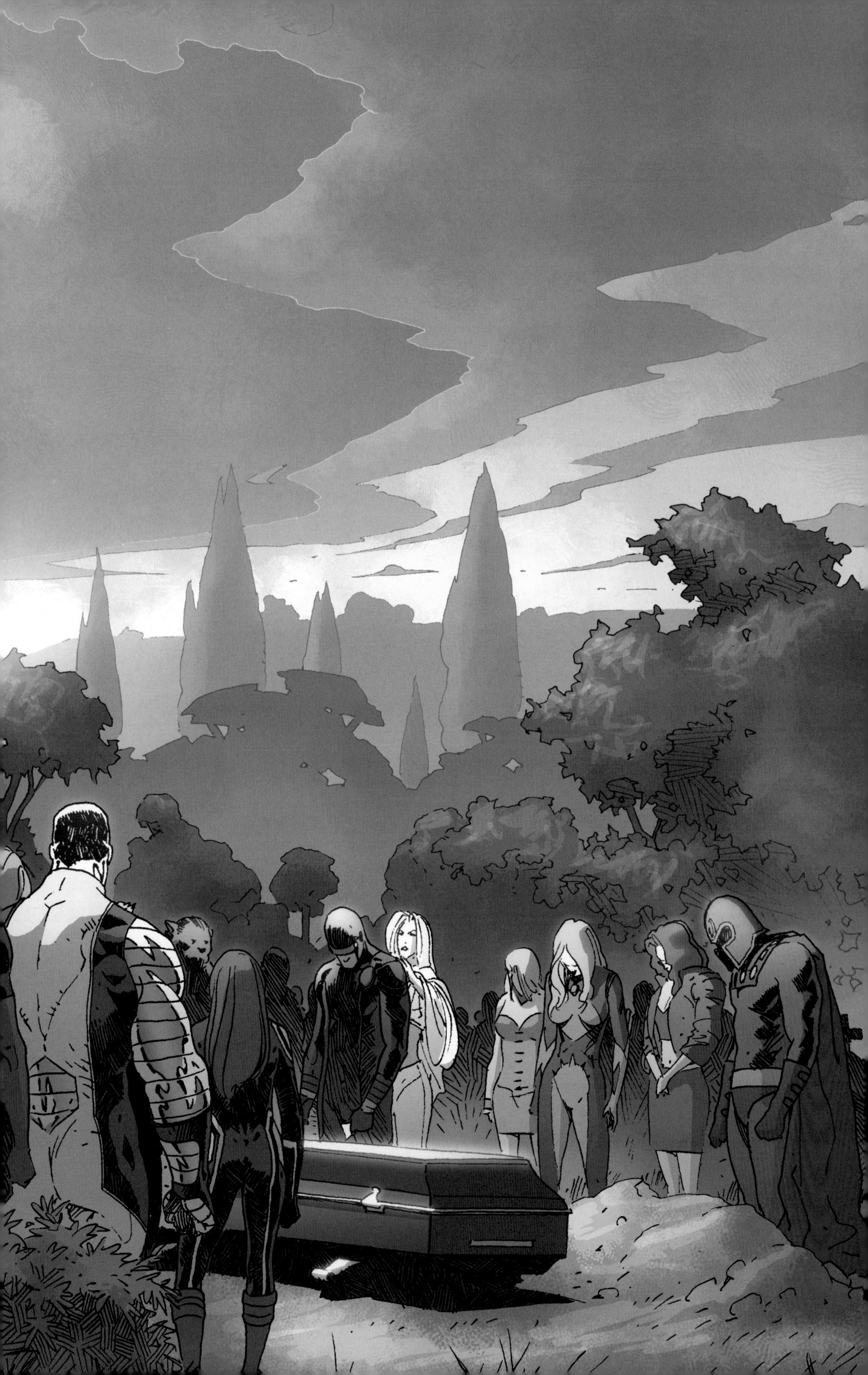

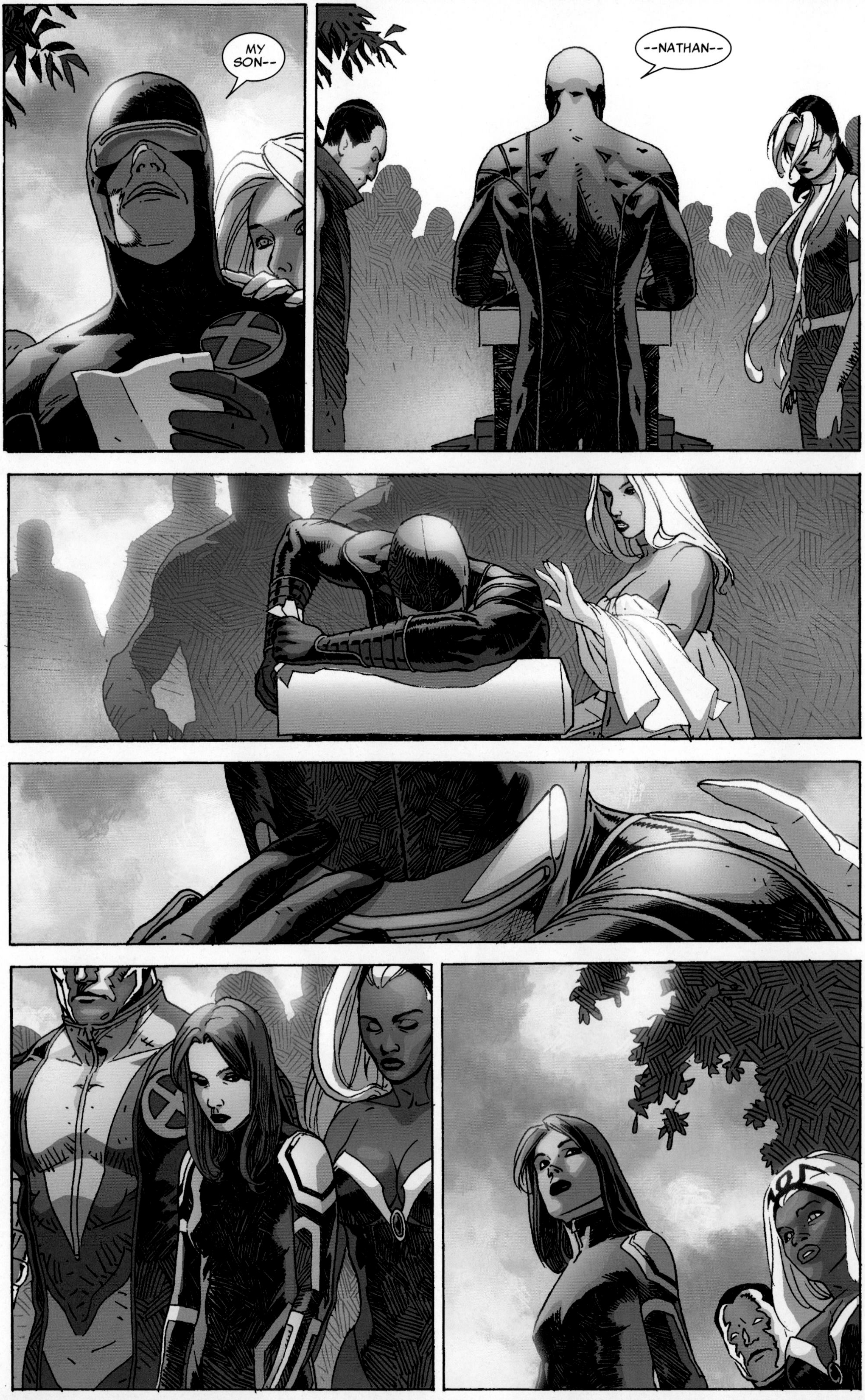
MY SON--
--NATHAN--

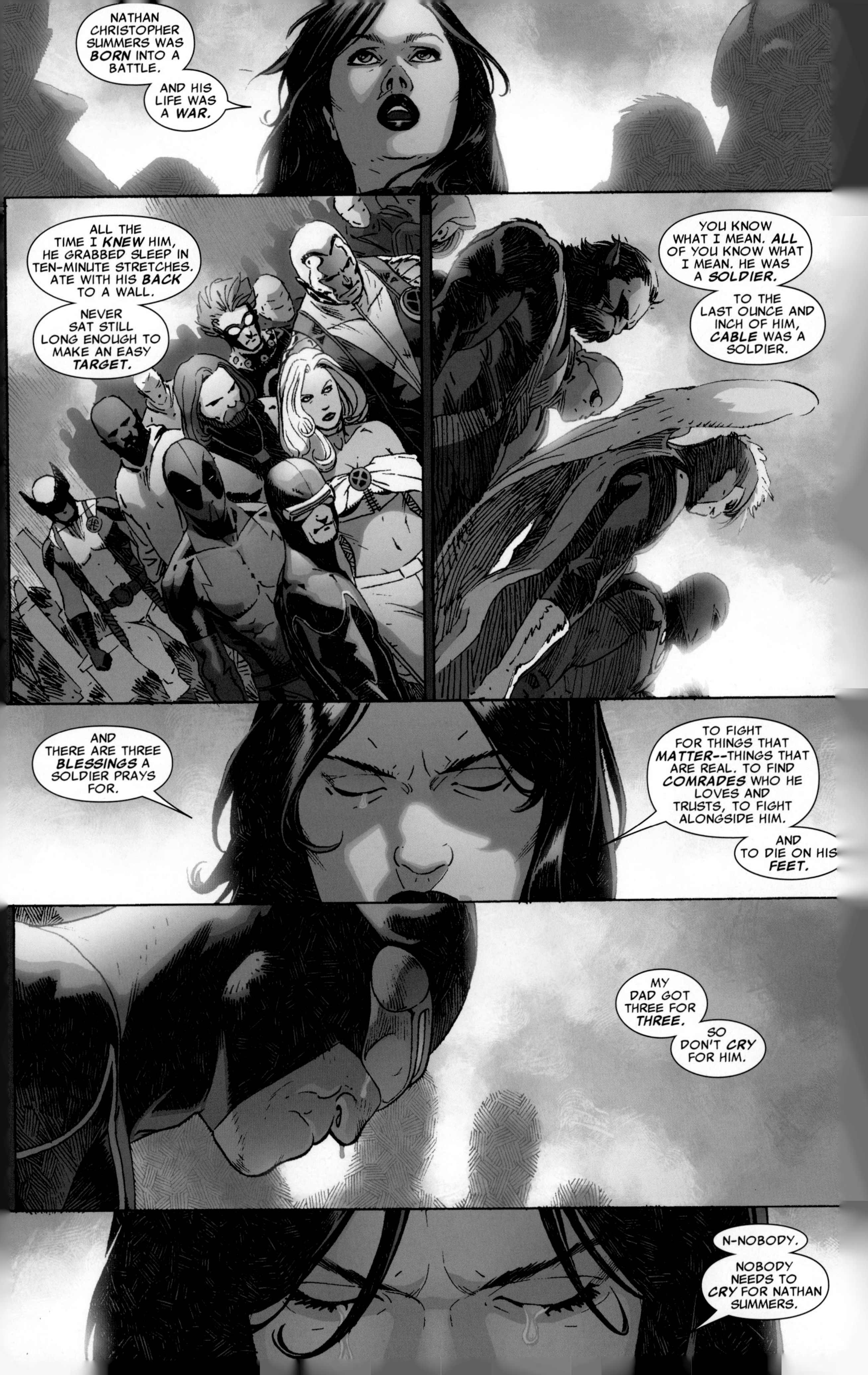
NATHAN CHRISTOPHER SUMMERS WAS BORN INTO A BATTLE.
AND HIS LIFE WAS A WAR.
ALL THE TIME I KNEW HIM, HE GRABBED SLEEP IN TEN-MINUTE STRETCHES. ATE WITH HIS BACK TO A WALL.
NEVER SAT STILL LONG ENOUGH TO MAKE AN EASY TARGET.
YOU KNOW WHAT I MEAN. ALL OF YOU KNOW WHAT I MEAN. HE WAS A SOLDIER.
TO THE LAST OUNCE AND INCH OF HIM, CABLE WAS A SOLDIER.
AND THERE ARE THREE BLESSINGS A SOLDIER PRAYS FOR.
TO FIGHT FOR THINGS THAT MATTER--THINGS THAT ARE REAL. TO FIND COMRADES WHO HE LOVES AND TRUSTS, TO FIGHT ALONGSIDE HIM.
AND TO DIE ON HIS FEET.
MY DAD GOT THREE FOR THREE.
SO DON'T CRY FOR HIM.
N-NOBODY.
NOBODY NEEDS TO CRY FOR NATHAN SUMMERS.

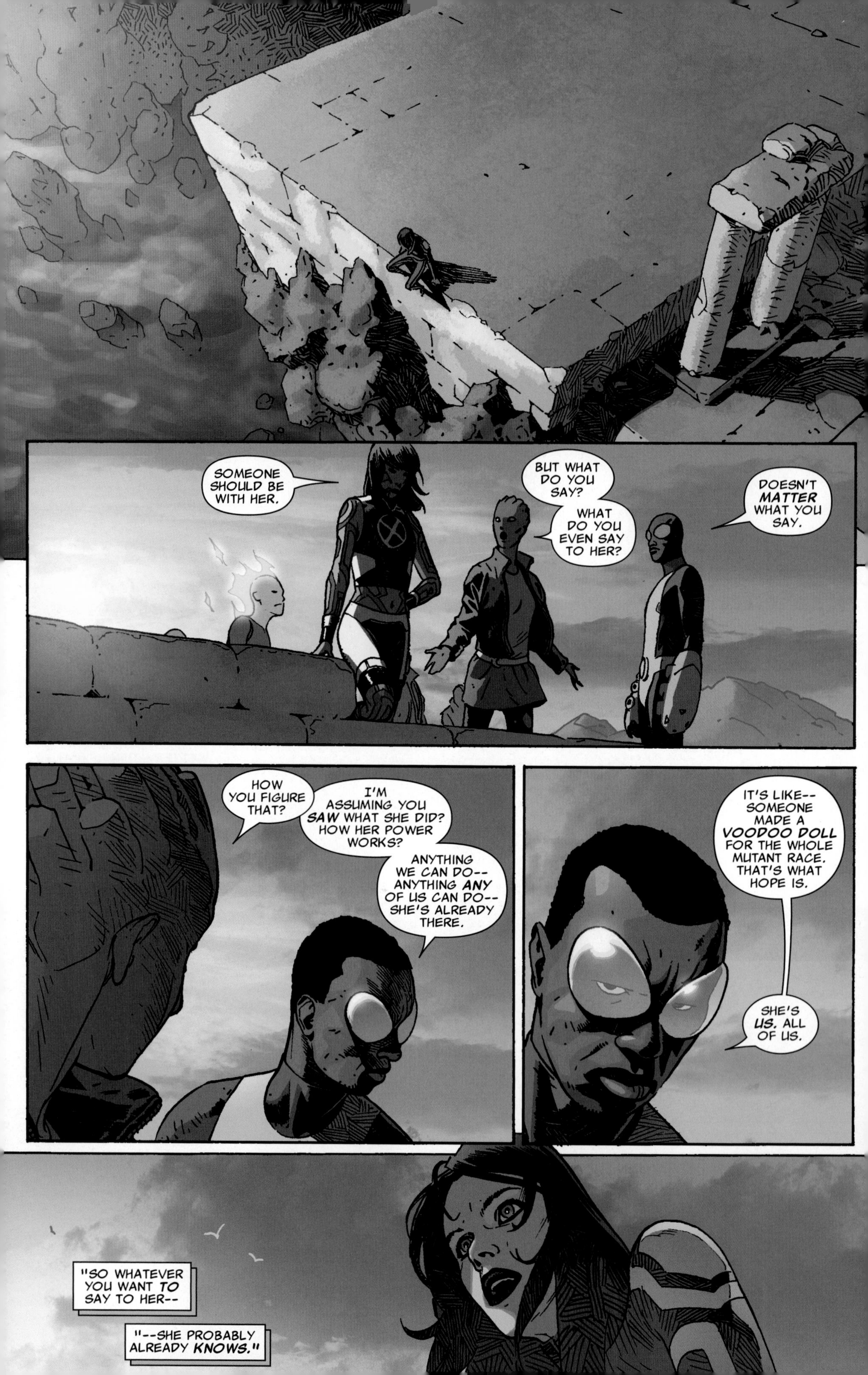
SOMEONE SHOULD BE WITH HER.
BUT WHAT DO YOU SAY?
WHAT DO YOU EVEN SAY TO HER?
DOESN'T MATTER WHAT YOU SAY.
HOW YOU FIGURE THAT?
I'M ASSUMING YOU SAW WHAT SHE DID? HOW HER POWER WORKS?
ANYTHING WE CAN DO-- ANYTHING ANY OF US CAN DO-- SHE'S ALREADY THERE.
IT'S LIKE-- SOMEONE MADE A VOODOO DOLL FOR THE WHOLE MUTANT RACE. THAT'S WHAT HOPE IS.
SHE'S US. ALL OF US.
"SO WHATEVER YOU WANT TO SAY TO HER--
"--SHE PROBABLY ALREADY KNOWS."

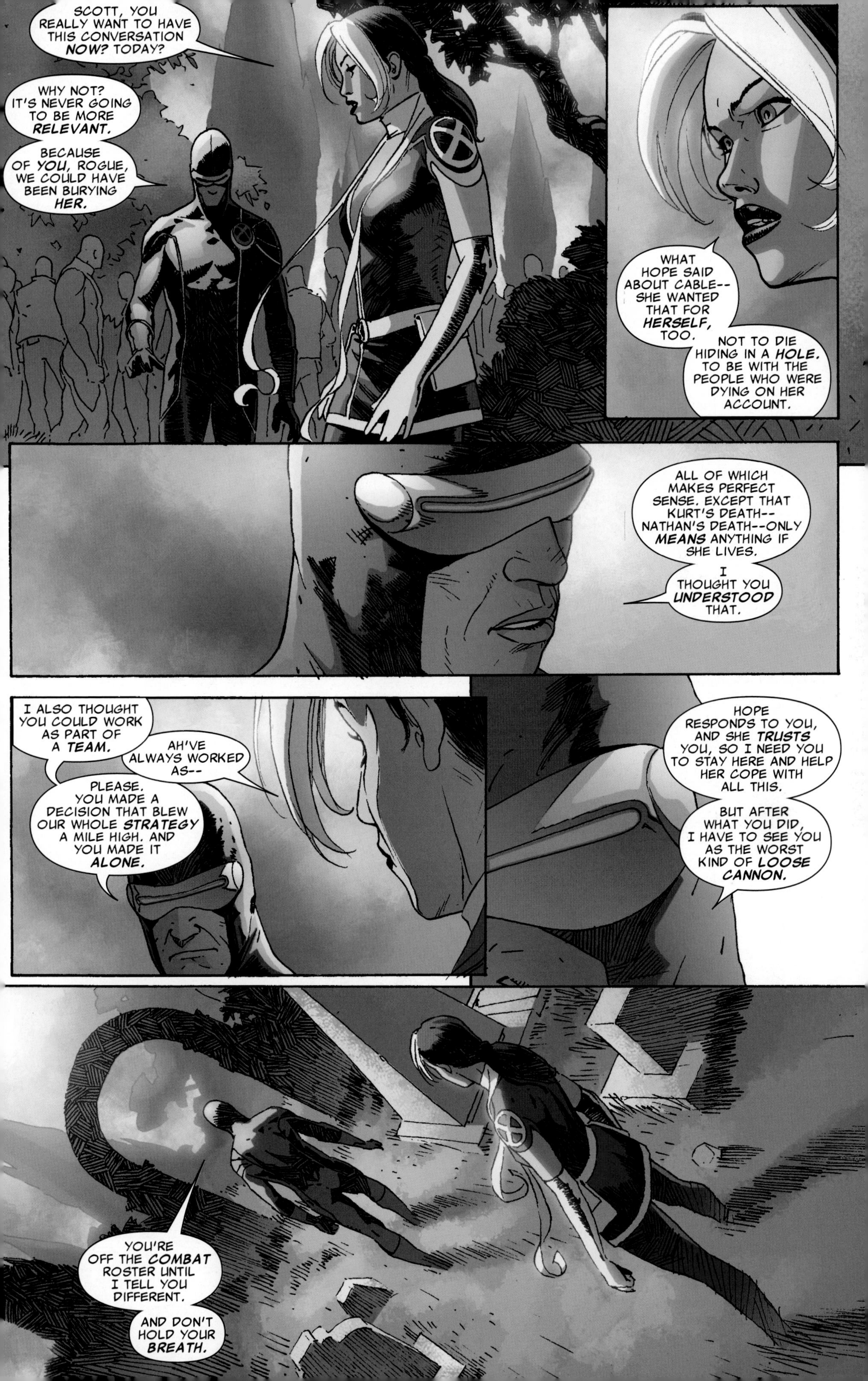
SCOTT, YOU REALLY WANT TO HAVE THIS CONVERSATION NOW? TODAY?
WHY NOT? IT'S NEVER GOING TO BE MORE RELEVANT.
BECAUSE OF YOU, ROGUE, WE COULD HAVE BEEN BURYING HER.
WHAT HOPE SAID ABOUT CABLE-- SHE WANTED THAT FOR HERSELF, TOO.
NOT TO DIE HIDING IN A HOLE. TO BE WITH THE PEOPLE WHO WERE DYING ON HER ACCOUNT.
ALL OF WHICH MAKES PERFECT SENSE. EXCEPT THAT KURT'S DEATH-- NATHAN'S DEATH--ONLY MEANS ANYTHING IF SHE LIVES.
I THOUGHT YOU UNDERSTOOD THAT.
I ALSO THOUGHT YOU COULD WORK AS PART OF A TEAM.
AH'VE ALWAYS WORKED AS--
PLEASE. YOU MADE A DECISION THAT BLEW OUR WHOLE STRATEGY A MILE HIGH. AND YOU MADE IT ALONE.
HOPE RESPONDS TO YOU, AND SHE TRUSTS YOU, SO I NEED YOU TO STAY HERE AND HELP HER COPE WITH ALL THIS.
BUT AFTER WHAT YOU DID, I HAVE TO SEE YOU AS THE WORST KIND OF LOOSE CANNON.
YOU'RE OFF THE COMBAT ROSTER UNTIL I TELL YOU DIFFERENT.
AND DON'T HOLD YOUR BREATH.

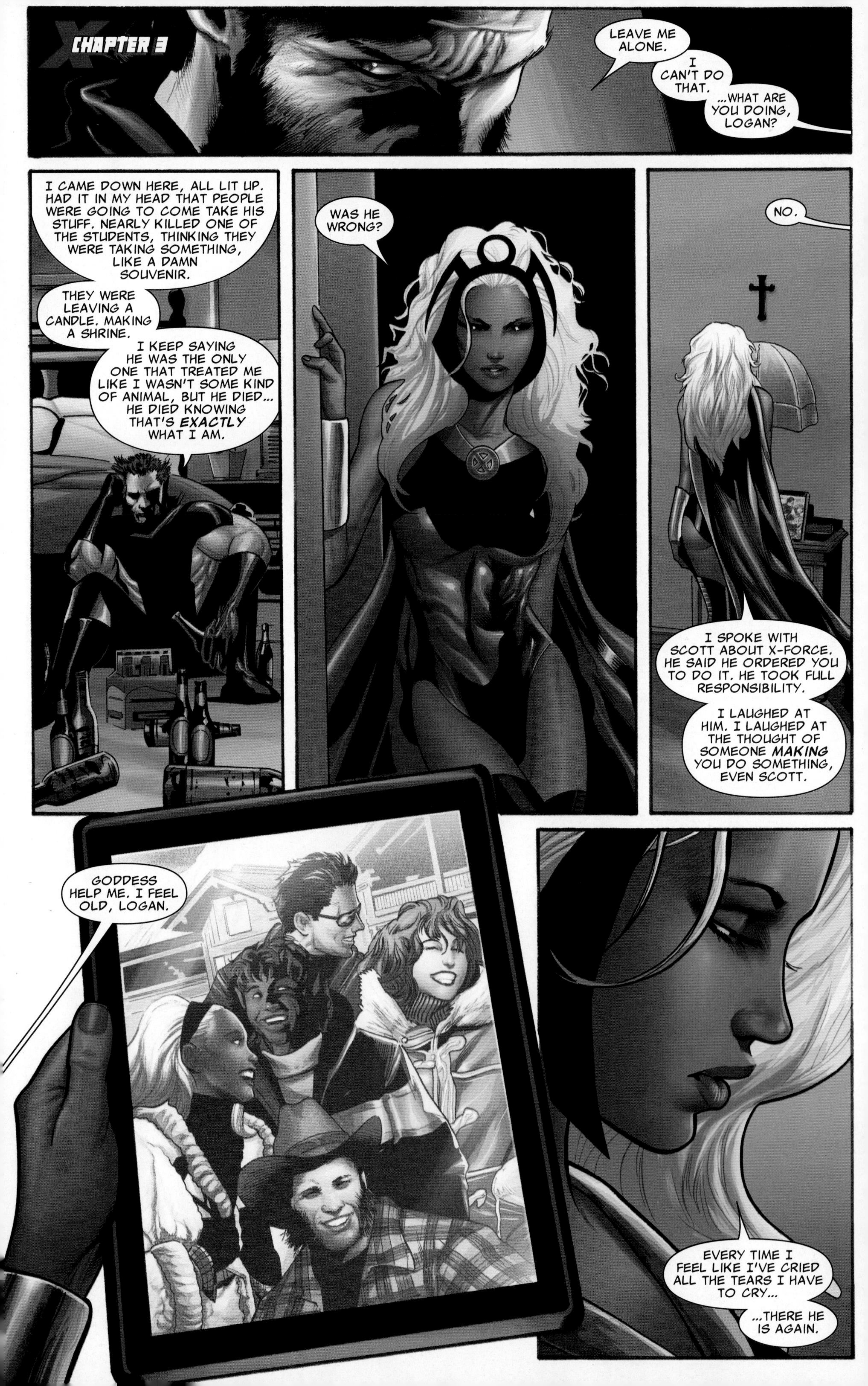

CHAPTER 3
LEAVE ME ALONE.
I CAN'T DO THAT.
...WHAT ARE YOU DOING, LOGAN?
I CAME DOWN HERE, ALL LIT UP. HAD IT IN MY HEAD THAT PEOPLE WERE GOING TO COME TAKE HIS STUFF. NEARLY KILLED ONE OF THE STUDENTS, THINKING THEY WERE TAKING SOMETHING, LIKE A DAMN SOUVENIR.
THEY WERE LEAVING A CANDLE. MAKING A SHRINE.
I KEEP SAYING HE WAS THE ONLY ONE THAT TREATED ME LIKE I WASN'T SOME KIND OF ANIMAL, BUT HE DIED... HE DIED KNOWING THAT'S EXACTLY WHAT I AM.
WAS HE WRONG?
NO.
I SPOKE WITH SCOTT ABOUT X-FORCE. HE SAID HE ORDERED YOU TO DO IT. HE TOOK FULL RESPONSIBILITY.
I LAUGHED AT HIM. I LAUGHED AT THE THOUGHT OF SOMEONE MAKING YOU DO SOMETHING, EVEN SCOTT.
GODDESS HELP ME. I FEEL OLD, LOGAN.
EVERY TIME I FEEL LIKE I'VE CRIED ALL THE TEARS I HAVE TO CRY...
...THERE HE IS AGAIN.

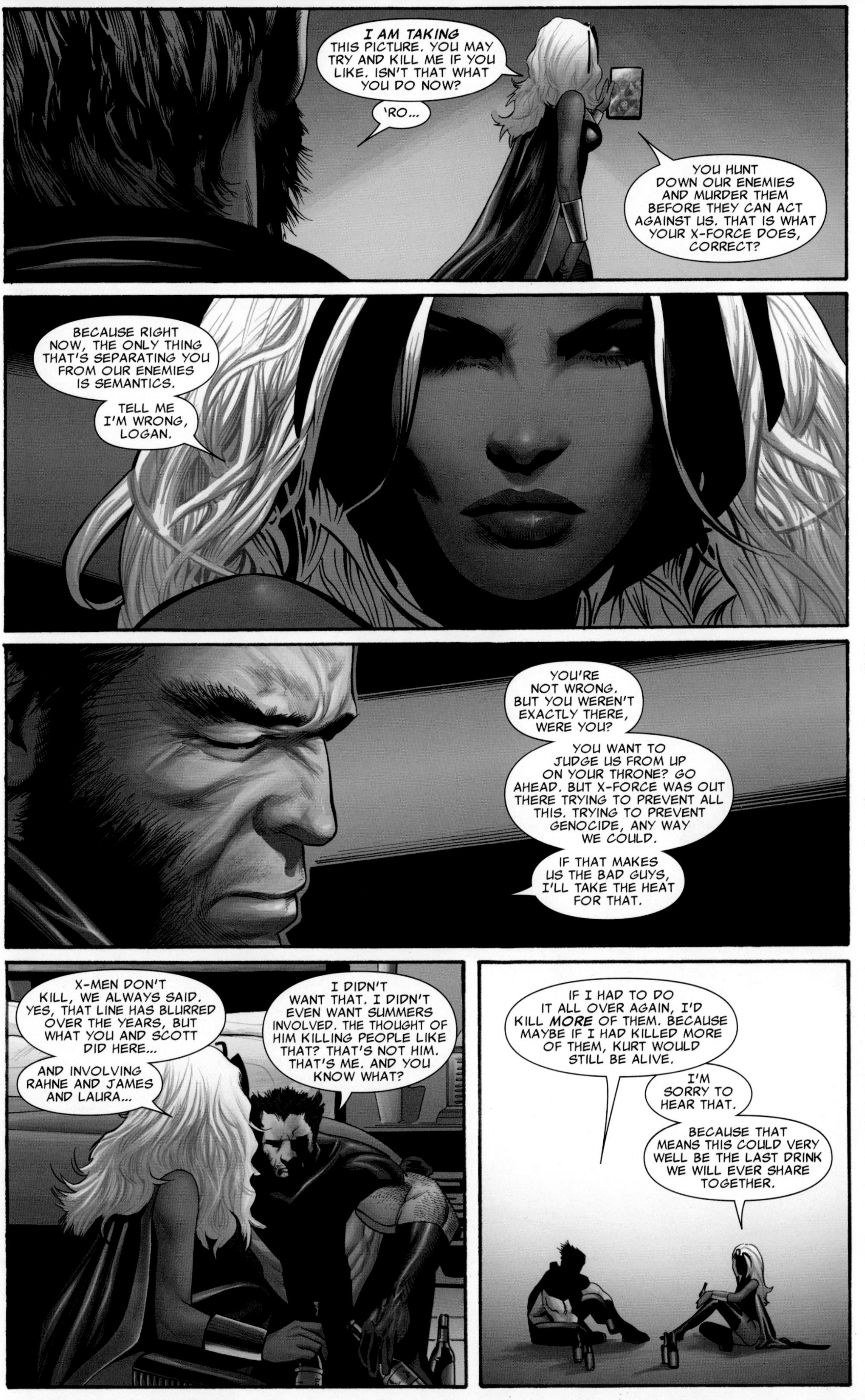
I AM TAKING THIS PICTURE. YOU MAY TRY AND KILL ME IF YOU LIKE. ISN'T THAT WHAT YOU DO NOW?
'RO...
YOU HUNT DOWN OUR ENEMIES AND MURDER THEM BEFORE THEY CAN ACT AGAINST US. THAT IS WHAT YOUR X-FORCE DOES, CORRECT?
BECAUSE RIGHT NOW, THE ONLY THING THAT'S SEPARATING YOU FROM OUR ENEMIES IS SEMANTICS.
TELL ME I'M WRONG, LOGAN.
YOU'RE NOT WRONG. BUT YOU WEREN'T EXACTLY THERE, WERE YOU?
YOU WANT TO JUDGE US FROM UP ON YOUR THRONE? GO AHEAD. BUT X-FORCE WAS OUT THERE TRYING TO PREVENT ALL THIS. TRYING TO PREVENT GENOCIDE, ANY WAY WE COULD.
IF THAT MAKES US THE BAD GUYS, I'LL TAKE THE HEAT FOR THAT.
X-MEN DON'T KILL, WE ALWAYS SAID. YES, THAT LINE HAS BLURRED OVER THE YEARS, BUT WHAT YOU AND SCOTT DID HERE...
AND INVOLVING RAHNE AND JAMES AND LAURA...
I DIDN'T WANT THAT. I DIDN'T EVEN WANT SUMMERS INVOLVED. THE THOUGHT OF HIM KILLING PEOPLE LIKE THAT? THAT'S NOT HIM. THAT'S ME. AND YOU KNOW WHAT?
IF I HAD TO DO IT ALL OVER AGAIN, I'D KILL MORE OF THEM. BECAUSE MAYBE IF I HAD KILLED MORE OF THEM, KURT WOULD STILL BE ALIVE.
I'M SORRY TO HEAR THAT.
BECAUSE THAT MEANS THIS COULD VERY WELL BE THE LAST DRINK WE WILL EVER SHARE TOGETHER.

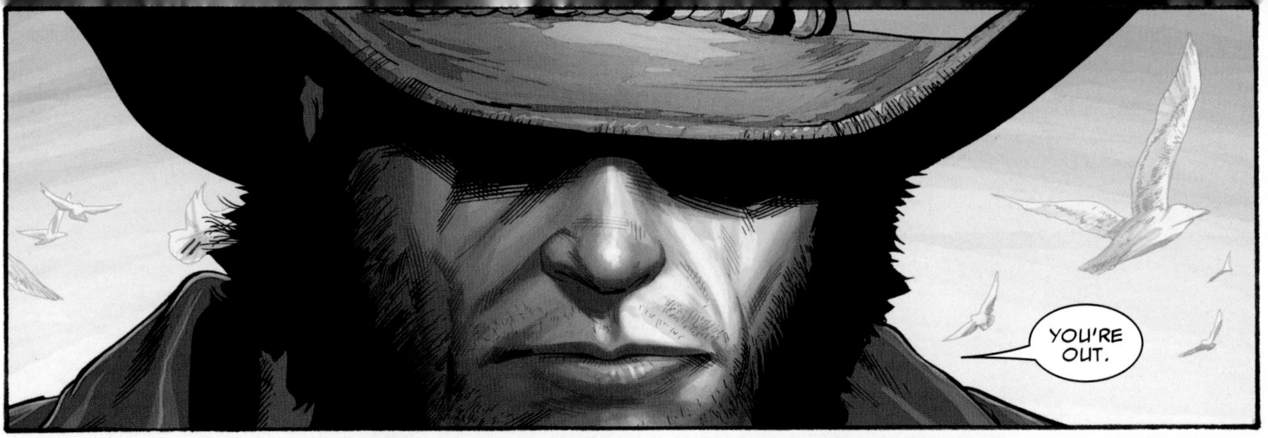
YOU'RE OUT.

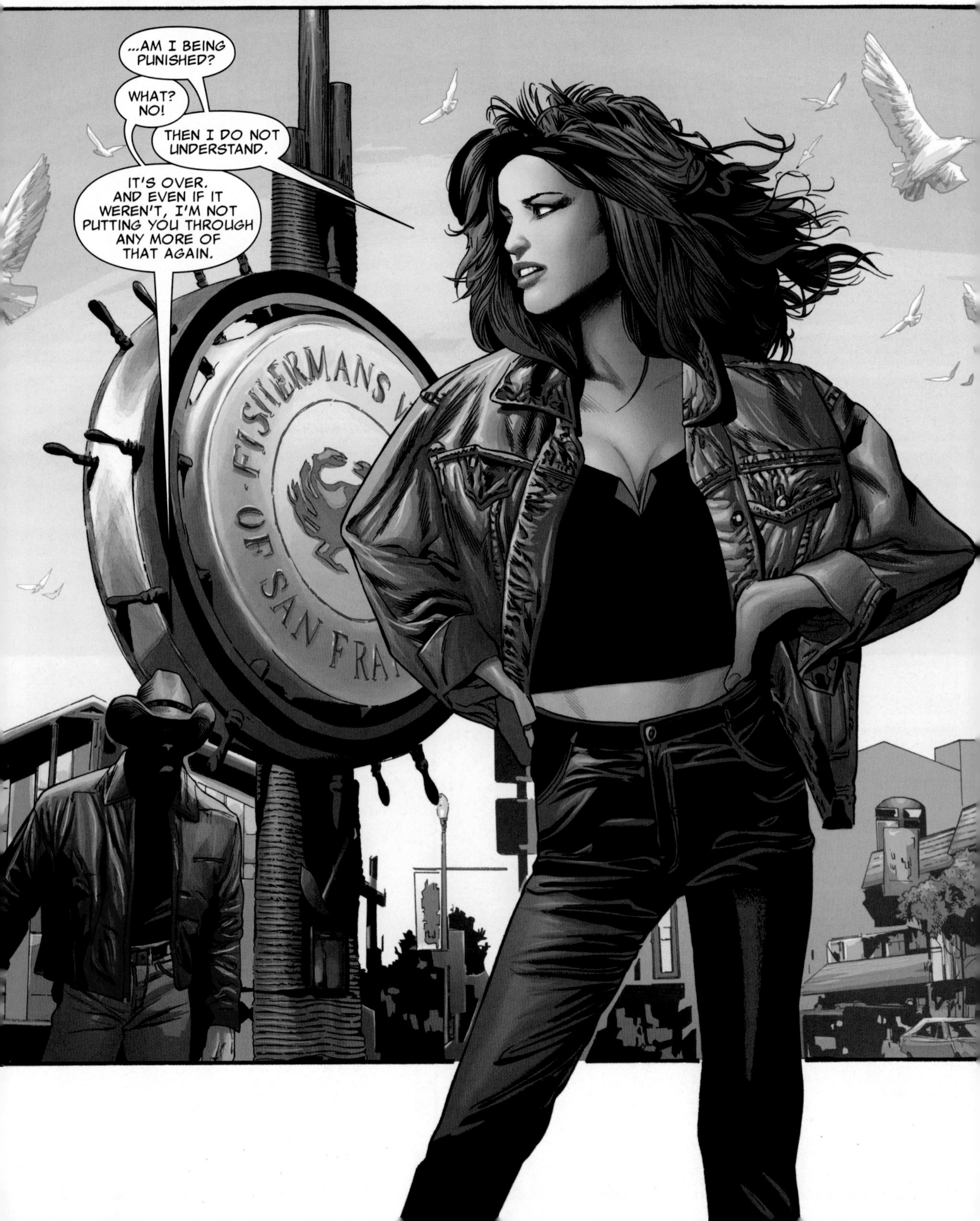
...AM I BEING PUNISHED?
WHAT? NO!
THEN I DO NOT UNDERSTAND.
IT'S OVER. AND EVEN IF IT WEREN'T, I'M NOT PUTTING YOU THROUGH ANY MORE OF THAT AGAIN.

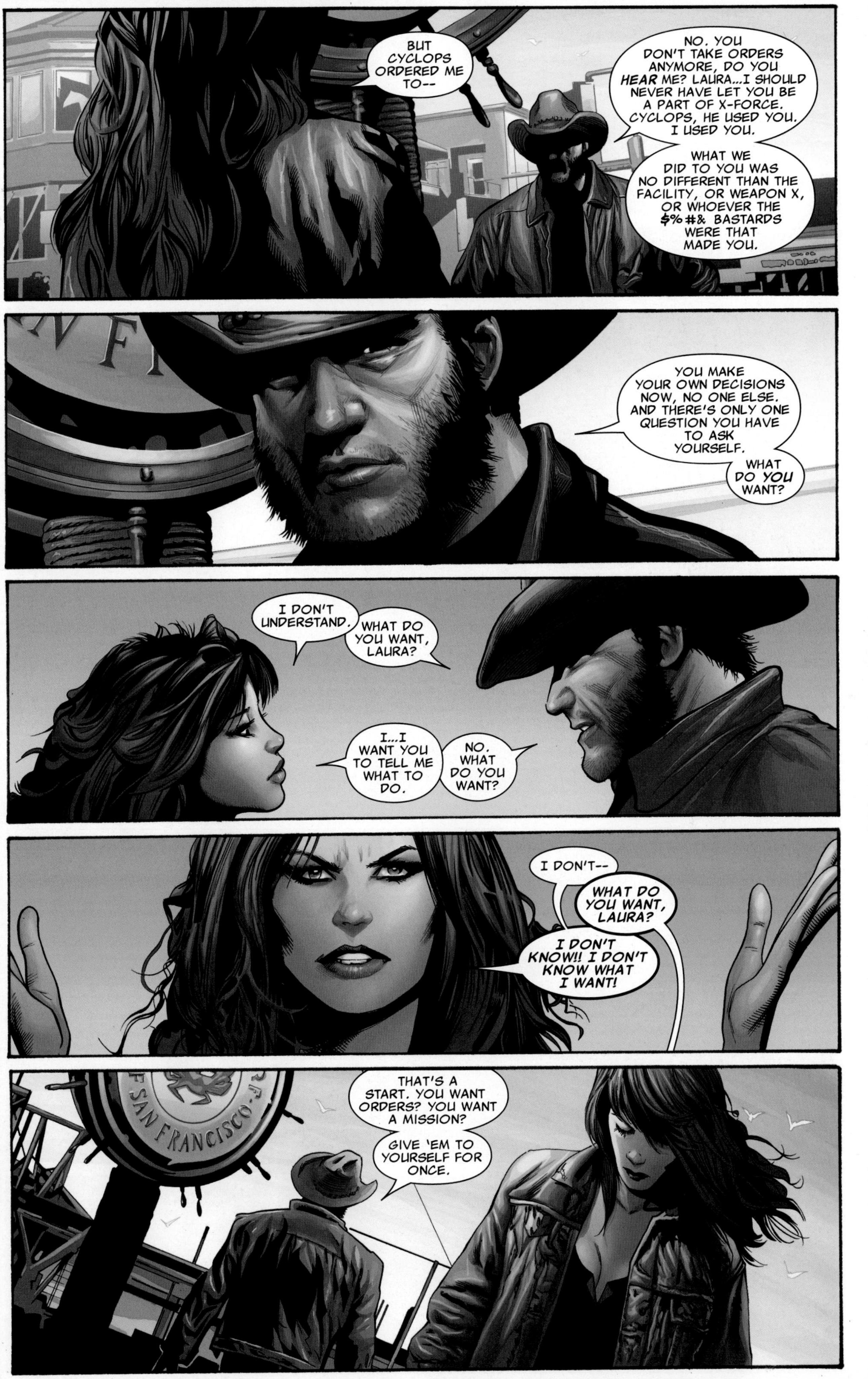
BUT CYCLOPS ORDERED ME TO--
NO. YOU DON'T TAKE ORDERS ANYMORE, DO YOU HEAR ME? LAURA...I SHOULD NEVER HAVE LET YOU BE A PART OF X-FORCE. CYCLOPS, HE USED YOU. I USED YOU.
WHAT WE DID TO YOU WAS NO DIFFERENT THAN THE FACILITY, OR WEAPON X, OR WHOEVER THE $%#& BASTARDS WERE THAT MADE YOU.
YOU MAKE YOUR OWN DECISIONS NOW, NO ONE ELSE. AND THERE'S ONLY ONE QUESTION YOU HAVE TO ASK YOURSELF.
WHAT DO YOU WANT?
I DON'T UNDERSTAND.
WHAT DO YOU WANT, LAURA?
I...I WANT YOU TO TELL ME WHAT TO DO.
NO. WHAT DO YOU WANT?
I DON'T--
WHAT DO YOU WANT, LAURA?
I DON'T KNOW!! I DON'T KNOW WHAT I WANT!
SAN FRANCISCO
THAT'S A START. YOU WANT ORDERS? YOU WANT A MISSION?
GIVE 'EM TO YOURSELF FOR ONCE.

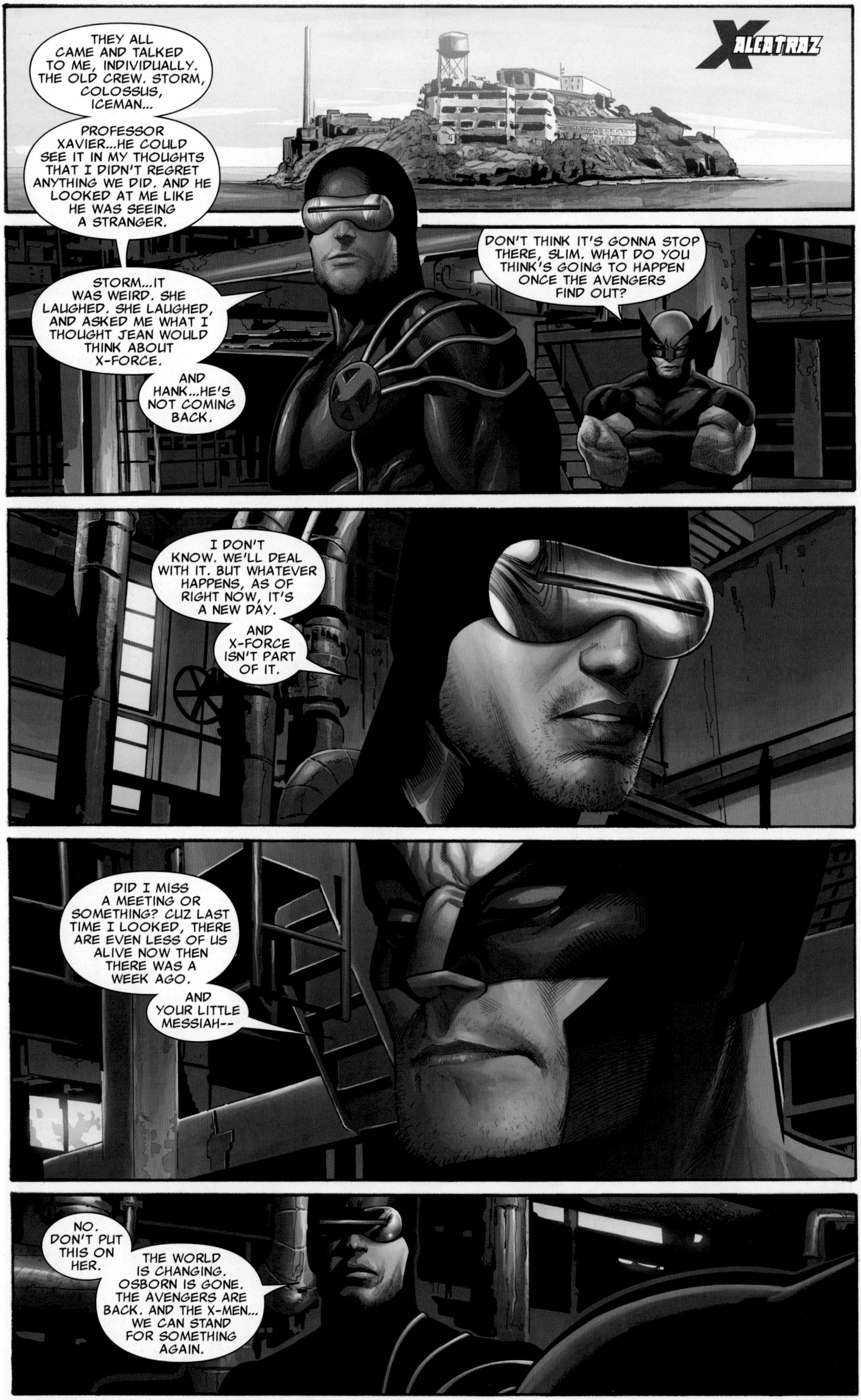
X ALCATRAZ
THEY ALL CAME AND TALKED TO ME, INDIVIDUALLY. THE OLD CREW. STORM, COLOSSUS, ICEMAN...
PROFESSOR XAVIER...HE COULD SEE IT IN MY THOUGHTS THAT I DIDN'T REGRET ANYTHING WE DID. AND HE LOOKED AT ME LIKE HE WAS SEEING A STRANGER.
STORM...IT WAS WEIRD. SHE LAUGHED. SHE LAUGHED, AND ASKED ME WHAT I THOUGHT JEAN WOULD THINK ABOUT X-FORCE.
AND HANK...HE'S NOT COMING BACK.
DON'T THINK IT'S GONNA STOP THERE, SLIM. WHAT DO YOU THINK'S GOING TO HAPPEN ONCE THE AVENGERS FIND OUT?
I DON'T KNOW. WE'LL DEAL WITH IT. BUT WHATEVER HAPPENS, AS OF RIGHT NOW, IT'S A NEW DAY.
AND X-FORCE ISN'T PART OF IT.
DID I MISS A MEETING OR SOMETHING? CUZ LAST TIME I LOOKED, THERE ARE EVEN LESS OF US ALIVE NOW THEN THERE WAS A WEEK AGO.
AND YOUR LITTLE MESSIAH--
NO. DON'T PUT THIS ON HER.
THE WORLD IS CHANGING. OSBORN IS GONE. THE AVENGERS ARE BACK. AND THE X-MEN... WE CAN STAND FOR SOMETHING AGAIN.

MUTANTKIND IS GOING TO SURVIVE, LOGAN.

WE TOOK EVERYTHING THAT BASTION HAD TO THROW AT US, AND WE MADE IT THROUGH.

NOT ALL OF US.

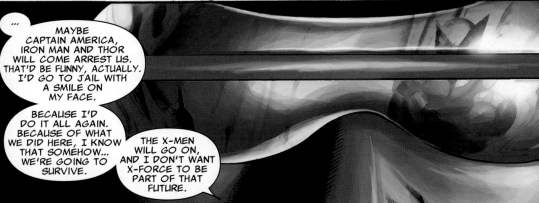

... MAYBE CAPTAIN AMERICA, IRON MAN AND THOR WILL COME ARREST US. THAT'D BE FUNNY, ACTUALLY. I'D GO TO JAIL WITH A SMILE ON MY FACE.

BECAUSE I'D DO IT ALL AGAIN. BECAUSE OF WHAT WE DID HERE, I KNOW THAT SOMEHOW... WE'RE GOING TO SURVIVE.

THE X-MEN WILL GO ON, AND I DON'T WANT X-FORCE TO BE PART OF THAT FUTURE.

FINE. IT'S DONE.

YOU SHOULD GET SOME SLEEP, SUMMERS. YOU LOOK LIKE %$#@.

THANKS.

LOGAN... THANK YOU.

YOU'RE WELCOME. I'VE GOTTA BURN SOME STUFF HERE. I'LL SEE YOU BACK ON THE ISLAND.

SORRY. CONVERSATION WENT ON LONGER THAN I THOUGHT IT WOULD.

WENT DIFFERENT THAN I THOUGHT IT WOULD, TOO. SO HERE'S THE DEAL...

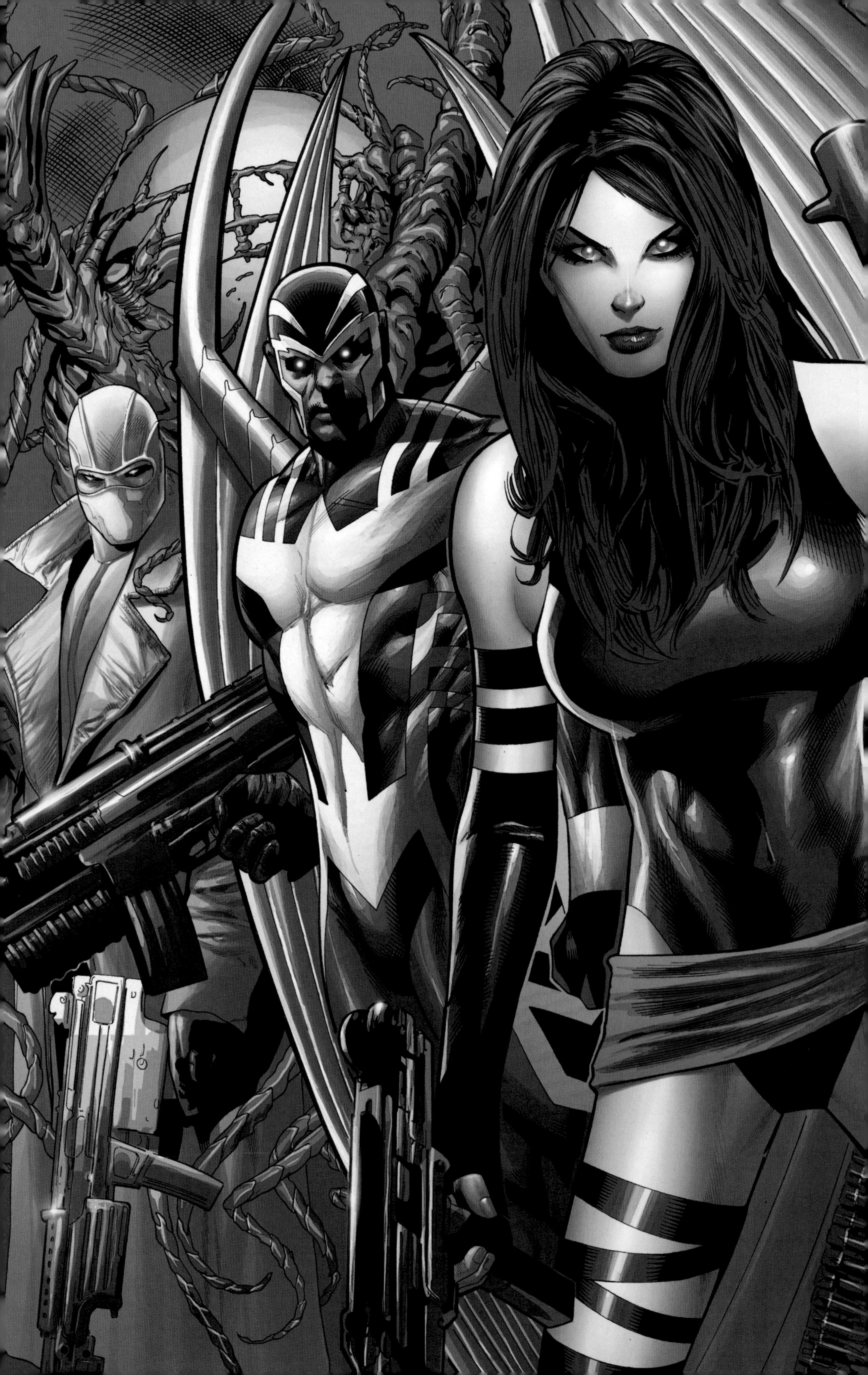

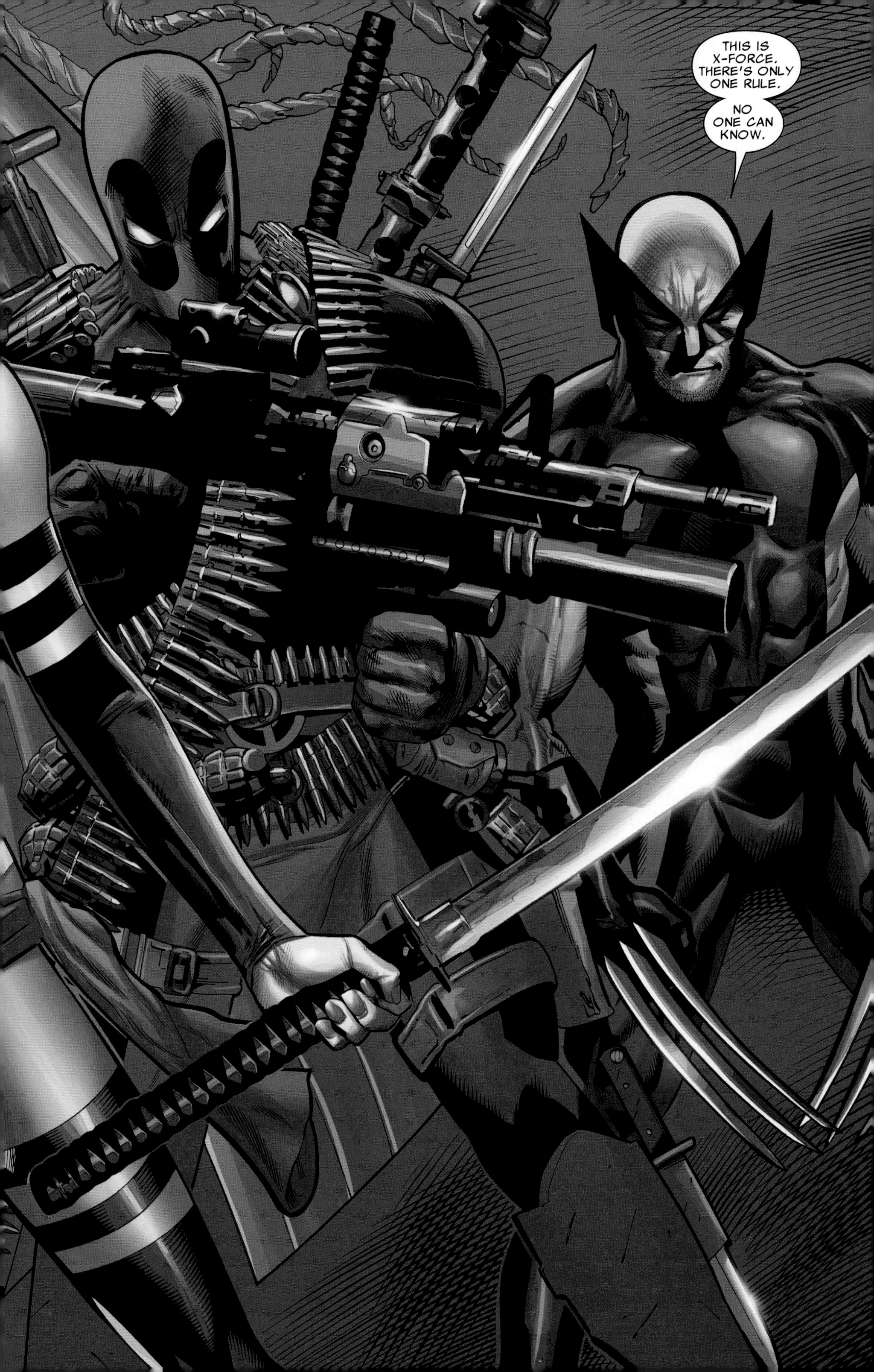
THIS IS X-FORCE. THERE'S ONLY ONE RULE.
NO ONE CAN KNOW.

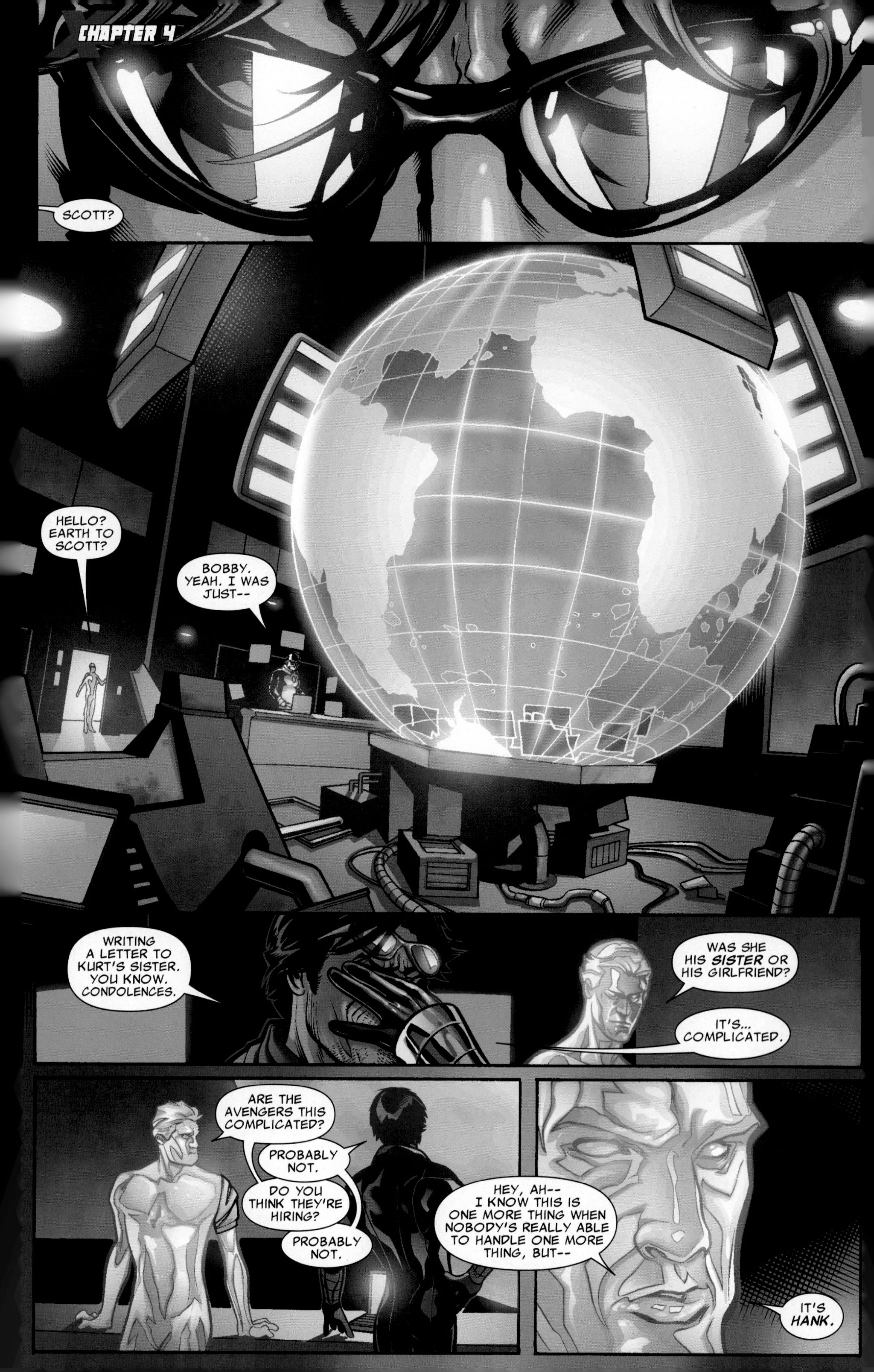
CHAPTER 4
SCOTT?
HELLO? EARTH TO SCOTT?
BOBBY. YEAH. I WAS JUST--
WRITING A LETTER TO KURT'S SISTER. YOU KNOW. CONDOLENCES.
WAS SHE HIS SISTER OR HIS GIRLFRIEND?
IT'S... COMPLICATED.
ARE THE AVENGERS THIS COMPLICATED?
PROBABLY NOT.
DO YOU THINK THEY'RE HIRING?
PROBABLY NOT.
HEY, AH-- I KNOW THIS IS ONE MORE THING WHEN NOBODY'S REALLY ABLE TO HANDLE ONE MORE THING, BUT--
IT'S HANK.

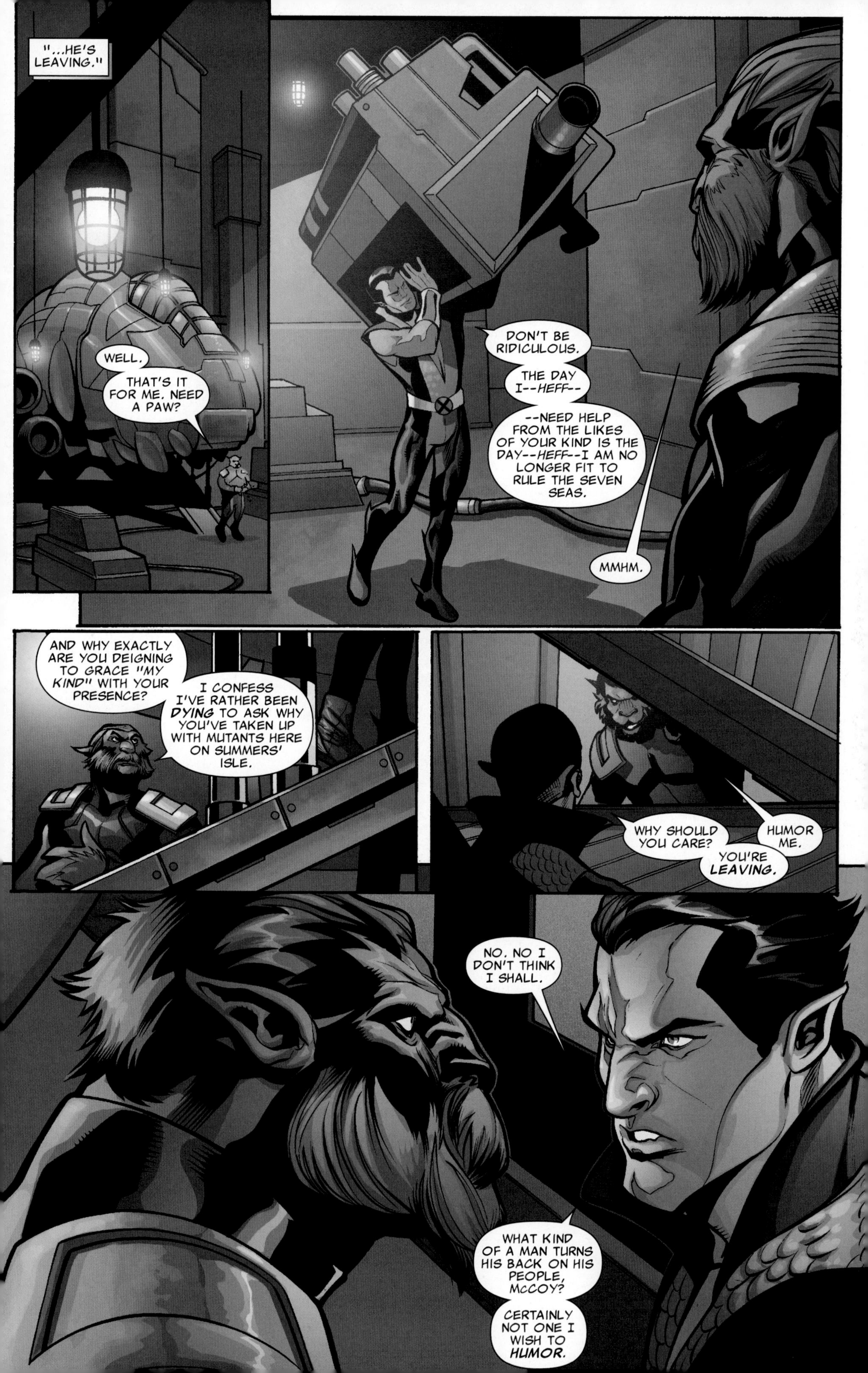
"...HE'S LEAVING."
WELL.
THAT'S IT FOR ME. NEED A PAW?
DON'T BE RIDICULOUS.
THE DAY I--HEFF--
--NEED HELP FROM THE LIKES OF YOUR KIND IS THE DAY--HEFF--I AM NO LONGER FIT TO RULE THE SEVEN SEAS.
MMHM.
AND WHY EXACTLY ARE YOU DEIGNING TO GRACE "MY KIND" WITH YOUR PRESENCE?
I CONFESS I'VE RATHER BEEN DYING TO ASK WHY YOU'VE TAKEN UP WITH MUTANTS HERE ON SUMMERS' ISLE.
WHY SHOULD YOU CARE?
HUMOR ME.
YOU'RE LEAVING.
NO. NO I DON'T THINK I SHALL.
WHAT KIND OF A MAN TURNS HIS BACK ON HIS PEOPLE, McCOY?
CERTAINLY NOT ONE I WISH TO HUMOR.

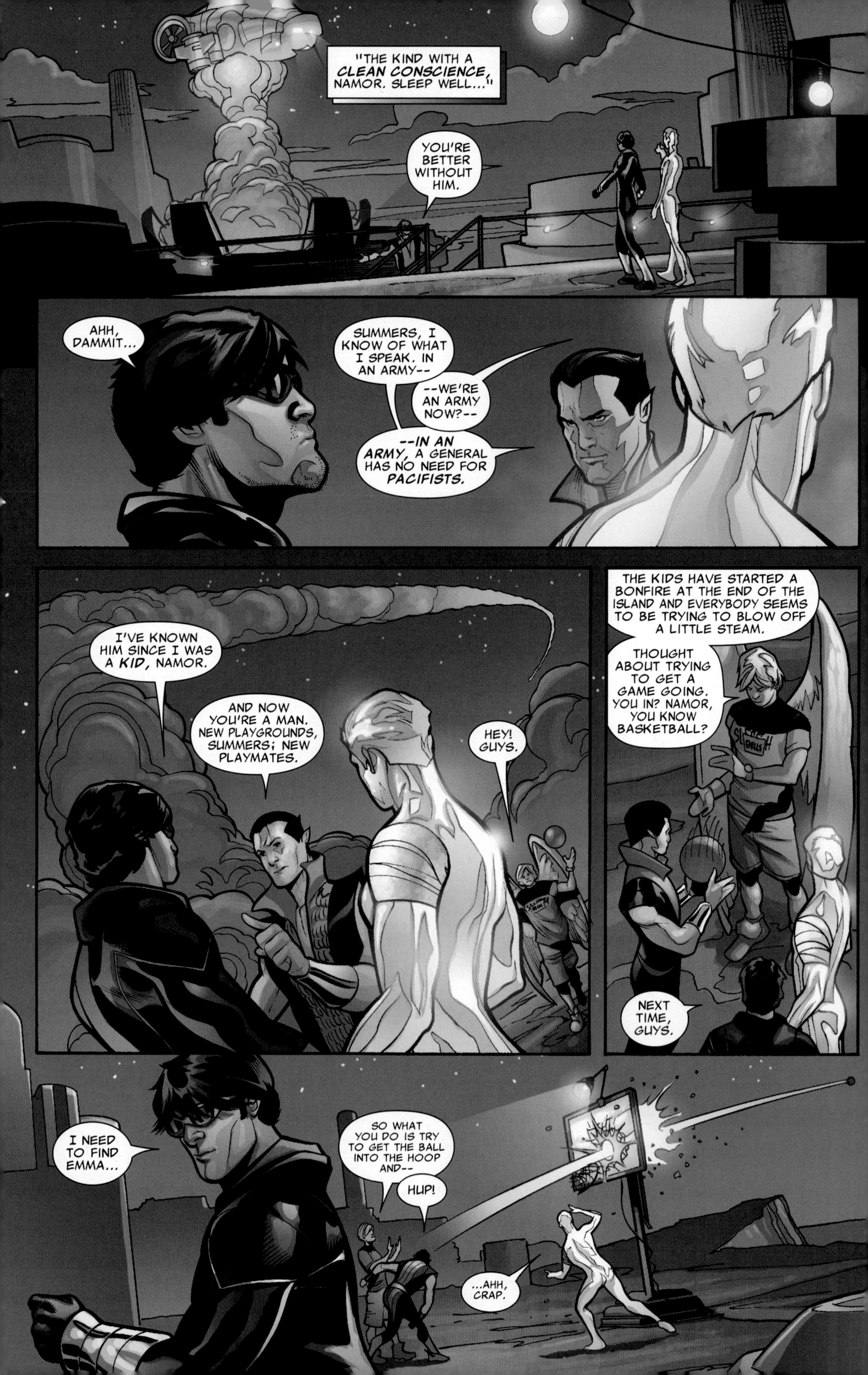
"THE KIND WITH A CLEAN CONSCIENCE, NAMOR. SLEEP WELL..."
YOU'RE BETTER WITHOUT HIM.
AHH, DAMMIT...
SUMMERS, I KNOW OF WHAT I SPEAK. IN AN ARMY--
--WE'RE AN ARMY NOW?--
--IN AN ARMY, A GENERAL HAS NO NEED FOR PACIFISTS.
I'VE KNOWN HIM SINCE I WAS A KID, NAMOR.
AND NOW YOU'RE A MAN. NEW PLAYGROUNDS, SUMMERS; NEW PLAYMATES.
HEY! GUYS.
THE KIDS HAVE STARTED A BONFIRE AT THE END OF THE ISLAND AND EVERYBODY SEEMS TO BE TRYING TO BLOW OFF A LITTLE STEAM.
THOUGHT ABOUT TRYING TO GET A GAME GOING. YOU IN? NAMOR, YOU KNOW BASKETBALL?
NEXT TIME, GUYS.
I NEED TO FIND EMMA...
SO WHAT YOU DO IS TRY TO GET THE BALL INTO THE HOOP AND--
HUP!
...AHH, CRAP.

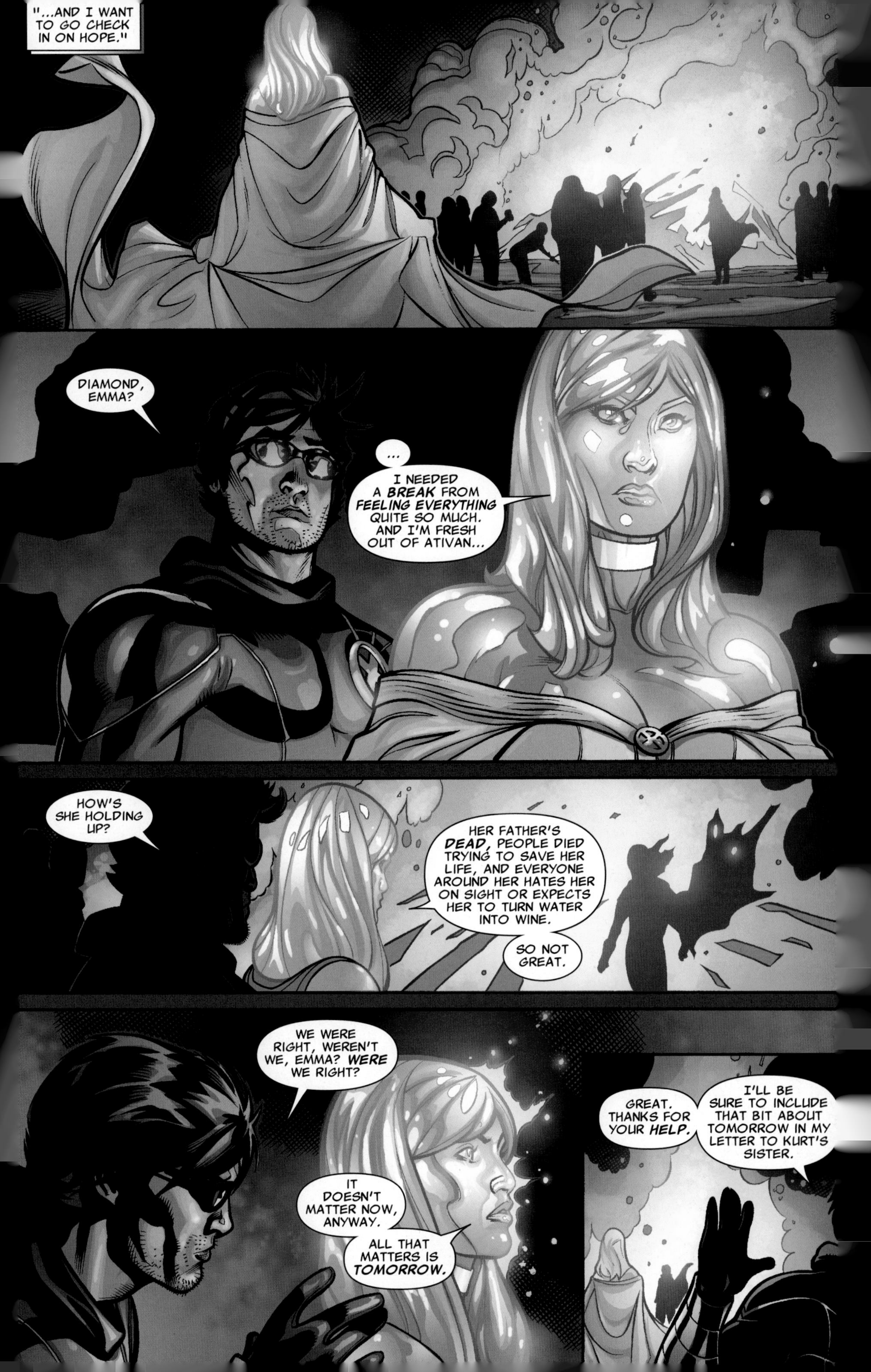
"...AND I WANT TO GO CHECK IN ON HOPE."
DIAMOND, EMMA?
...
I NEEDED A BREAK FROM FEELING EVERYTHING QUITE SO MUCH. AND I'M FRESH OUT OF ATIVAN...
HOW'S SHE HOLDING UP?
HER FATHER'S DEAD, PEOPLE DIED TRYING TO SAVE HER LIFE, AND EVERYONE AROUND HER HATES HER ON SIGHT OR EXPECTS HER TO TURN WATER INTO WINE.
SO NOT GREAT.
WE WERE RIGHT, WEREN'T WE, EMMA? WERE WE RIGHT?
IT DOESN'T MATTER NOW, ANYWAY.
ALL THAT MATTERS IS TOMORROW.
GREAT. THANKS FOR YOUR HELP.
I'LL BE SURE TO INCLUDE THAT BIT ABOUT TOMORROW IN MY LETTER TO KURT'S SISTER.

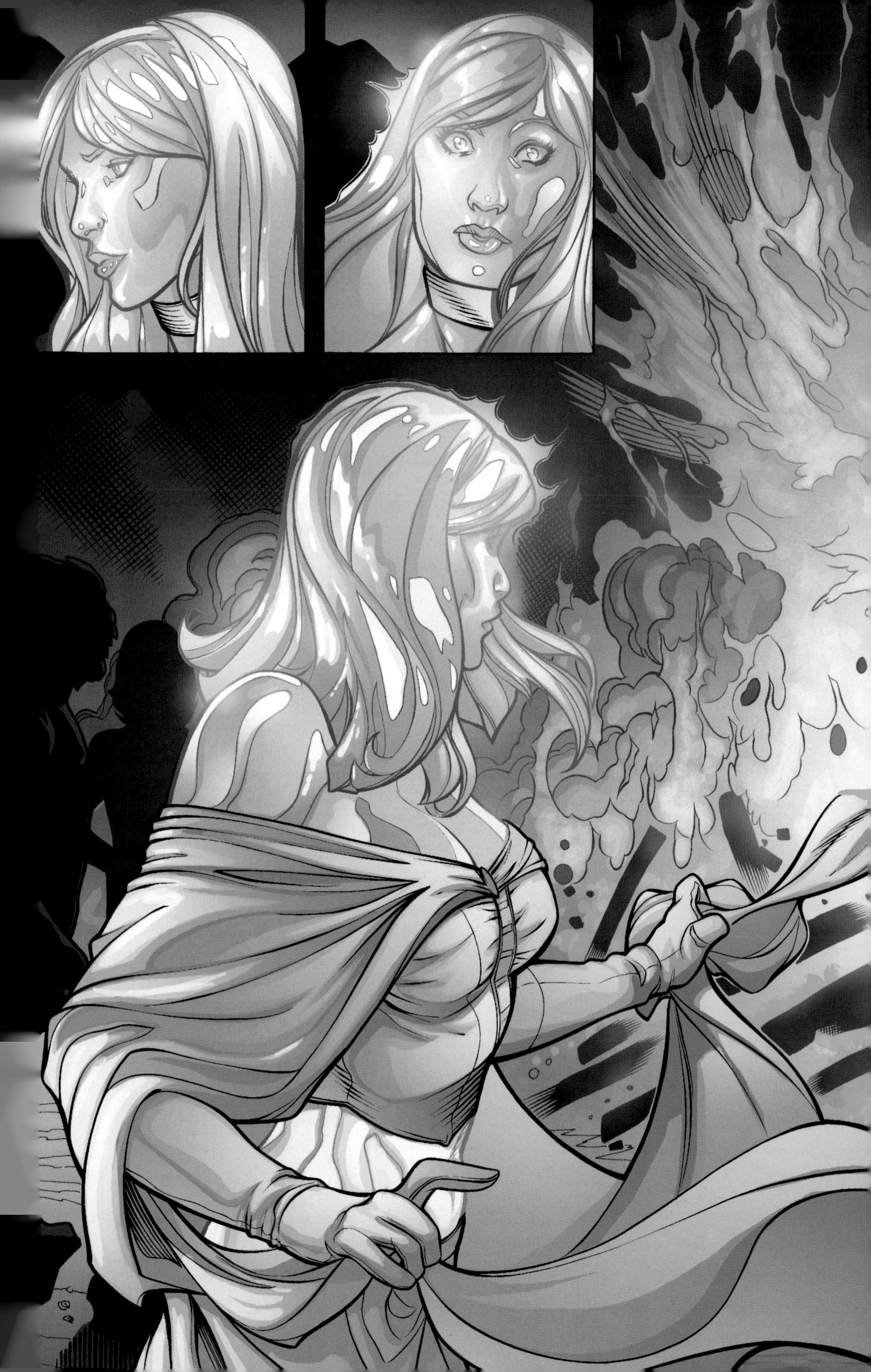

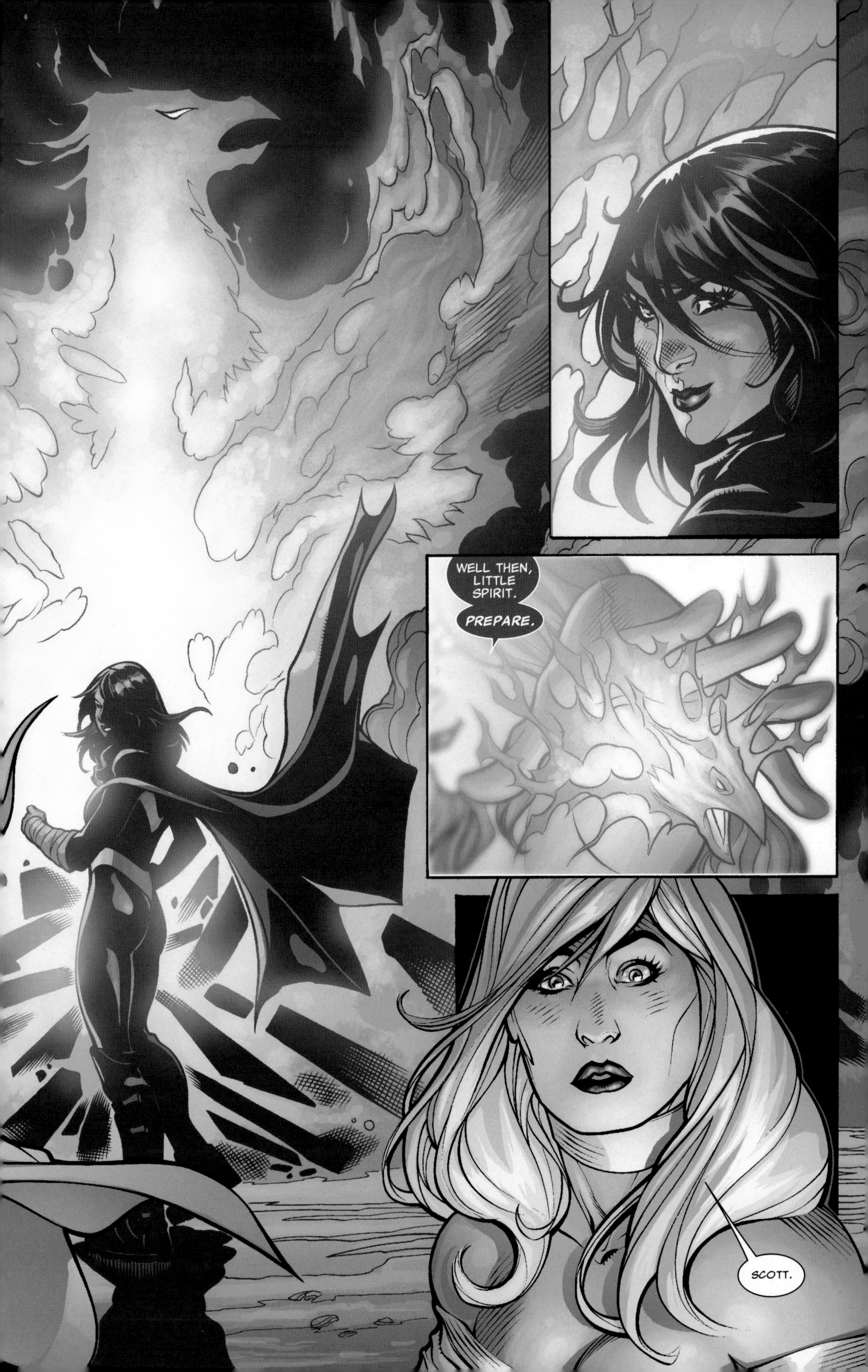
WELL THEN, LITTLE SPIRIT.
PREPARE.
SCOTT.

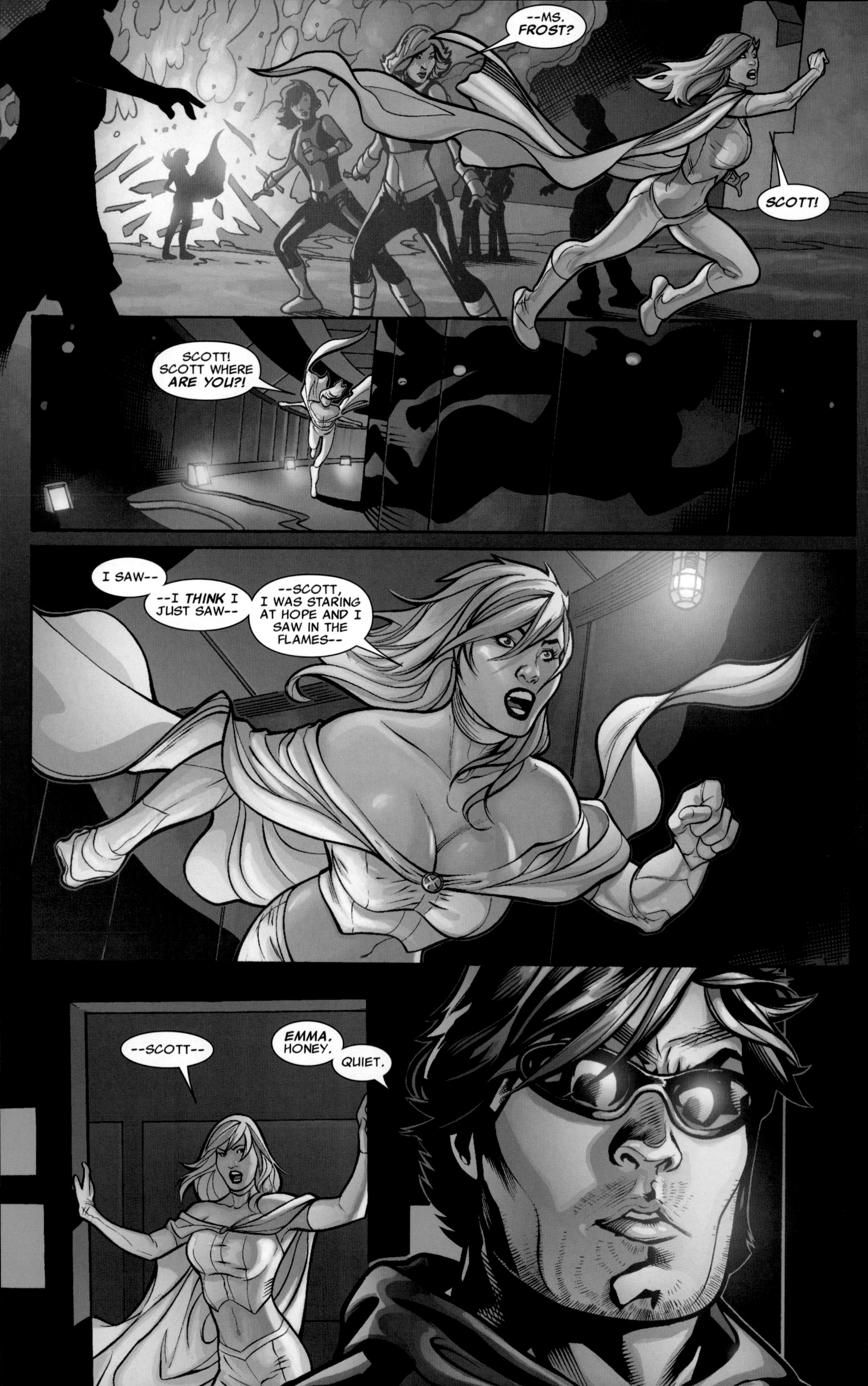
--MS. FROST?
SCOTT!
SCOTT! SCOTT WHERE ARE YOU?!
I SAW--
--I THINK I JUST SAW--
--SCOTT, I WAS STARING AT HOPE AND I SAW IN THE FLAMES--
--SCOTT--
EMMA. HONEY.
QUIET.

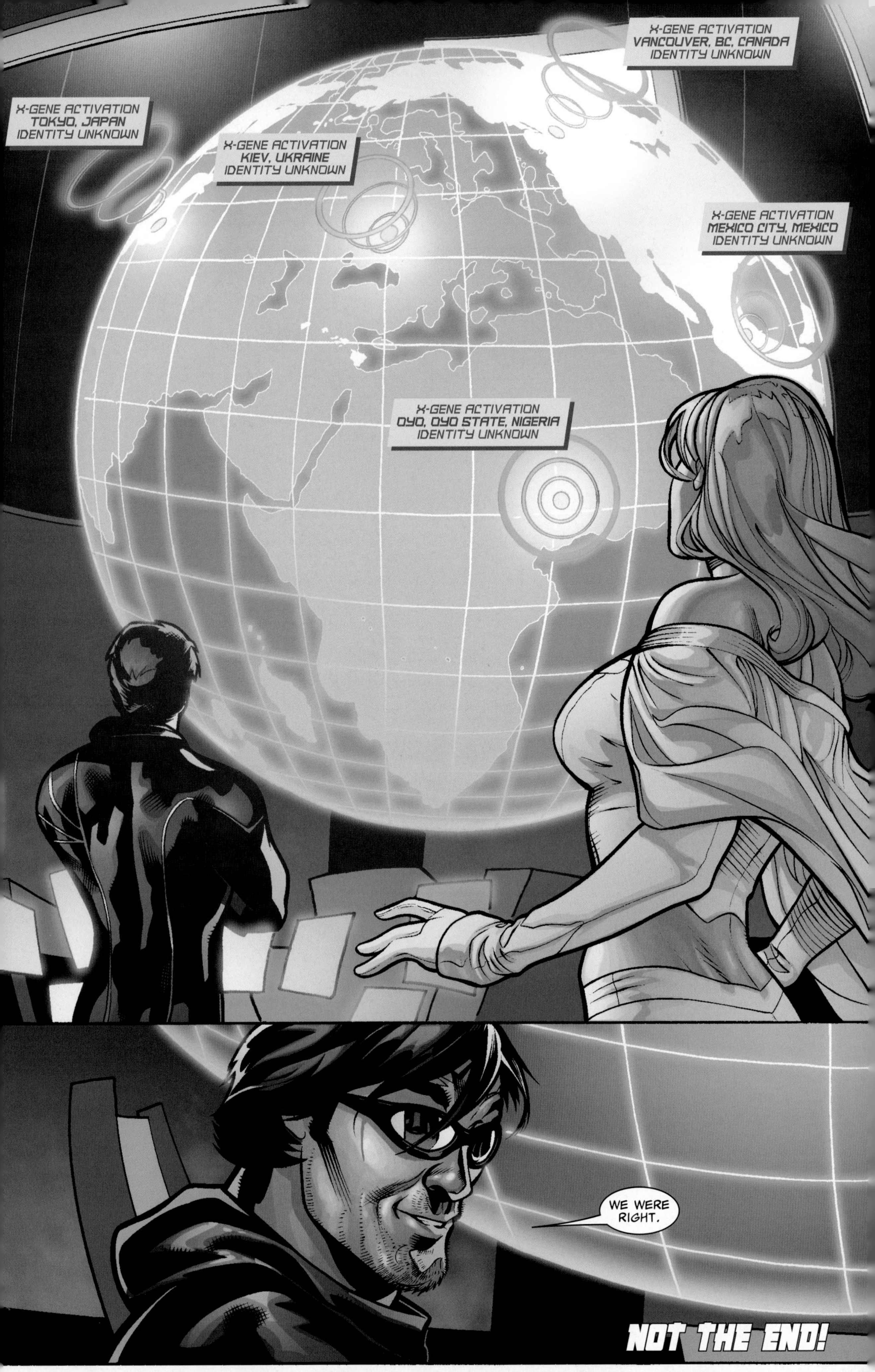
X-GENE ACTIVATION
VANCOUVER, BC, CANADA
IDENTITY UNKNOWN
X-GENE ACTIVATION
TOKYO, JAPAN
IDENTITY UNKNOWN
X-GENE ACTIVATION
KIEV, UKRAINE
IDENTITY UNKNOWN
X-GENE ACTIVATION
MEXICO CITY, MEXICO
IDENTITY UNKNOWN
X-GENE ACTIVATION
OYO, OYO STATE, NIGERIA
IDENTITY UNKNOWN
WE WERE RIGHT.
NOT THE END!

>>>OPEN FILE… KILL INDEX.
>>>USER IDENT: BASTION
>>>PASSWORD: 01001101 01000001 01010011 01010100 01000101 01010010 00100000 01001101 01001111 01001100 01000100

BASTION

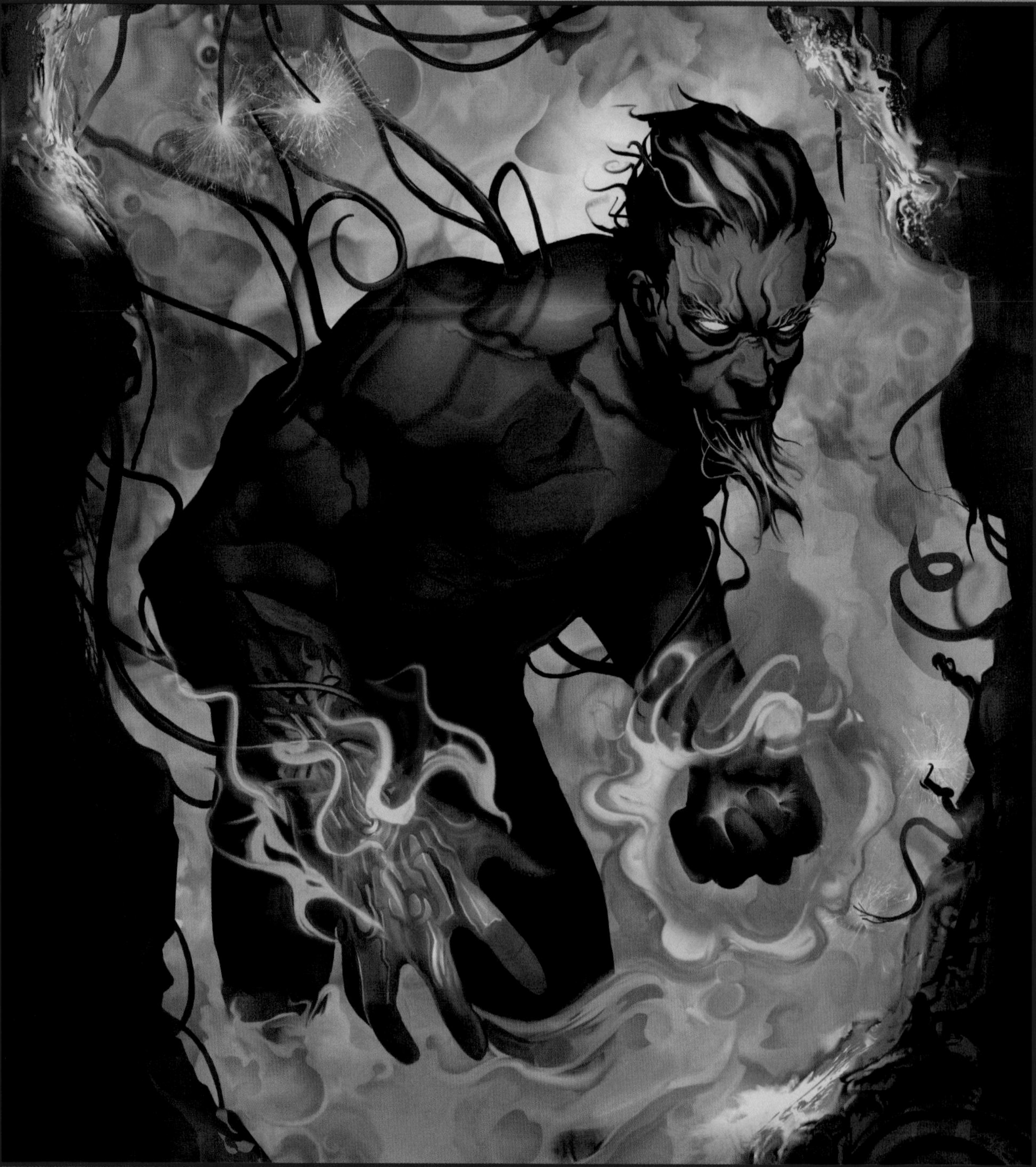

I am Bastion, an amalgamation of the Sentinel Master Mold and a future NIMROD hunter-killer Sentinel. The forcible extinction of mutantkind is our mandate. As of now there are less than 200 of the genetic anomalies left on the planet. Full termination is imminent.

But data from the NIMROD aspect within us warns of a potential new genesis for mutantkind. A child is returning, and it is imperative that she die.

The child's name, the data suggests, is HOPE.

CABLE AND HOPE

>>>THREAT LEVEL: EXTREME/MEDIUM

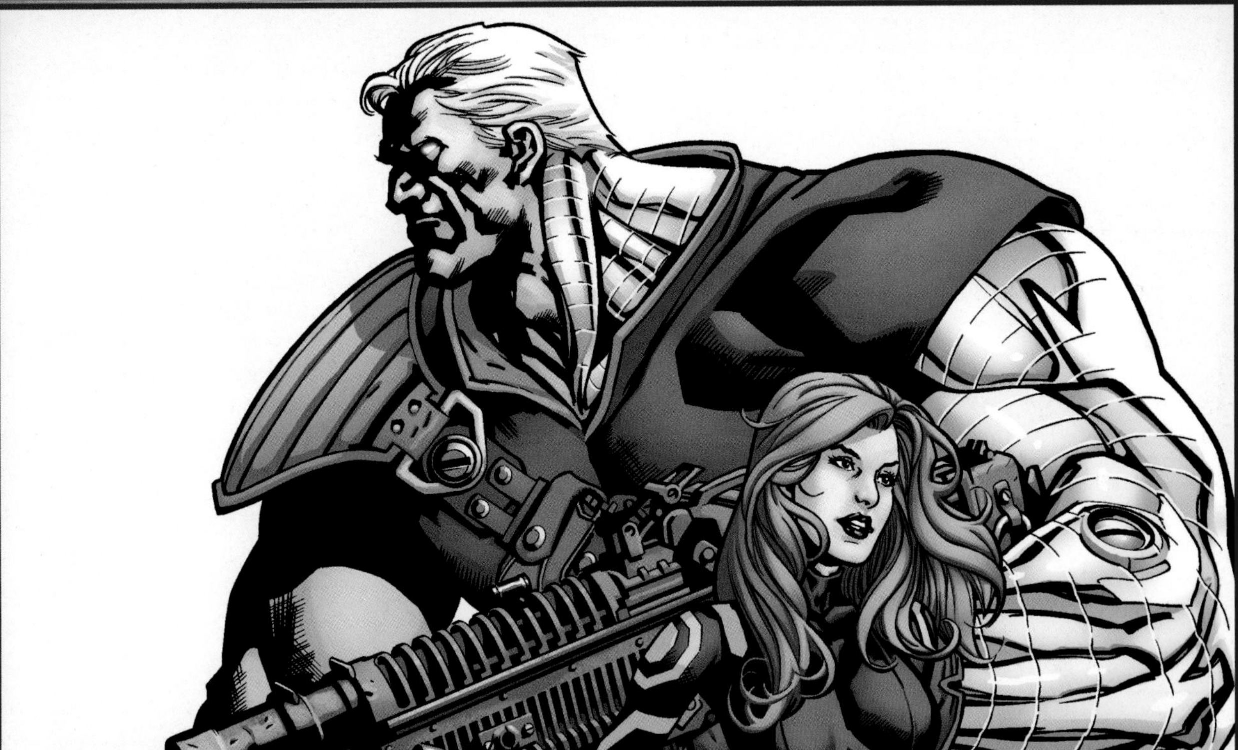

Data from the paramilitary group THE PURIFIERS reveals that "Hope's" birth triggered a hunt between them and multiple mutant factions. The child escaped into the timestream with a protector...the mutant soldier known as CABLE.

The girl's age and genetic abilities upon return to the timeline are unknown. Data suggests extreme caution: initial readings upon the subject's birth suggest heretofore uncharted power levels.

Cable is a known element. While his telekinetic and telepathic powers are weakened due to the presence of the TECHNO-ORGANIC VIRUS within him, he is an incredibly resourceful and lethal opponent.

CYCLOPS

>>>THREAT LEVEL: HIGH

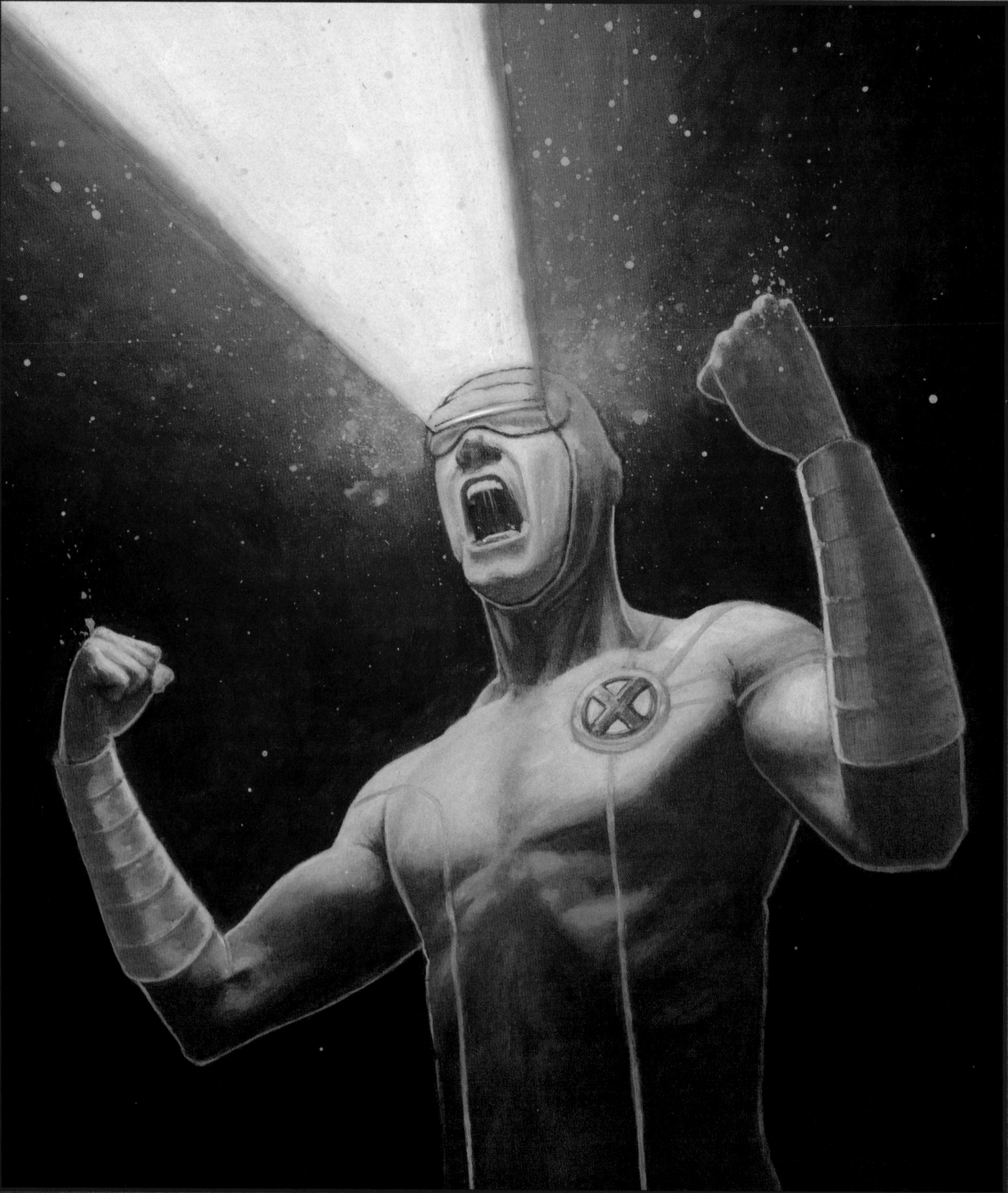

CYCLOPS was identified as a mutant leader long ago by MASTER MOLD, and has been targeted for high priority termination. His mutant power is formidable, but his true strength lies in his ability to gather and lead the remaining mutant forces.

Previously rogue mutants including MAGNETO and NAMOR now appear subservient to him. While mutants like XAVIER and APOCALYPSE have attempted to consolidate power, only Cyclops has achieved this.

THE X-MEN

>>>THREAT LEVEL: HIGH

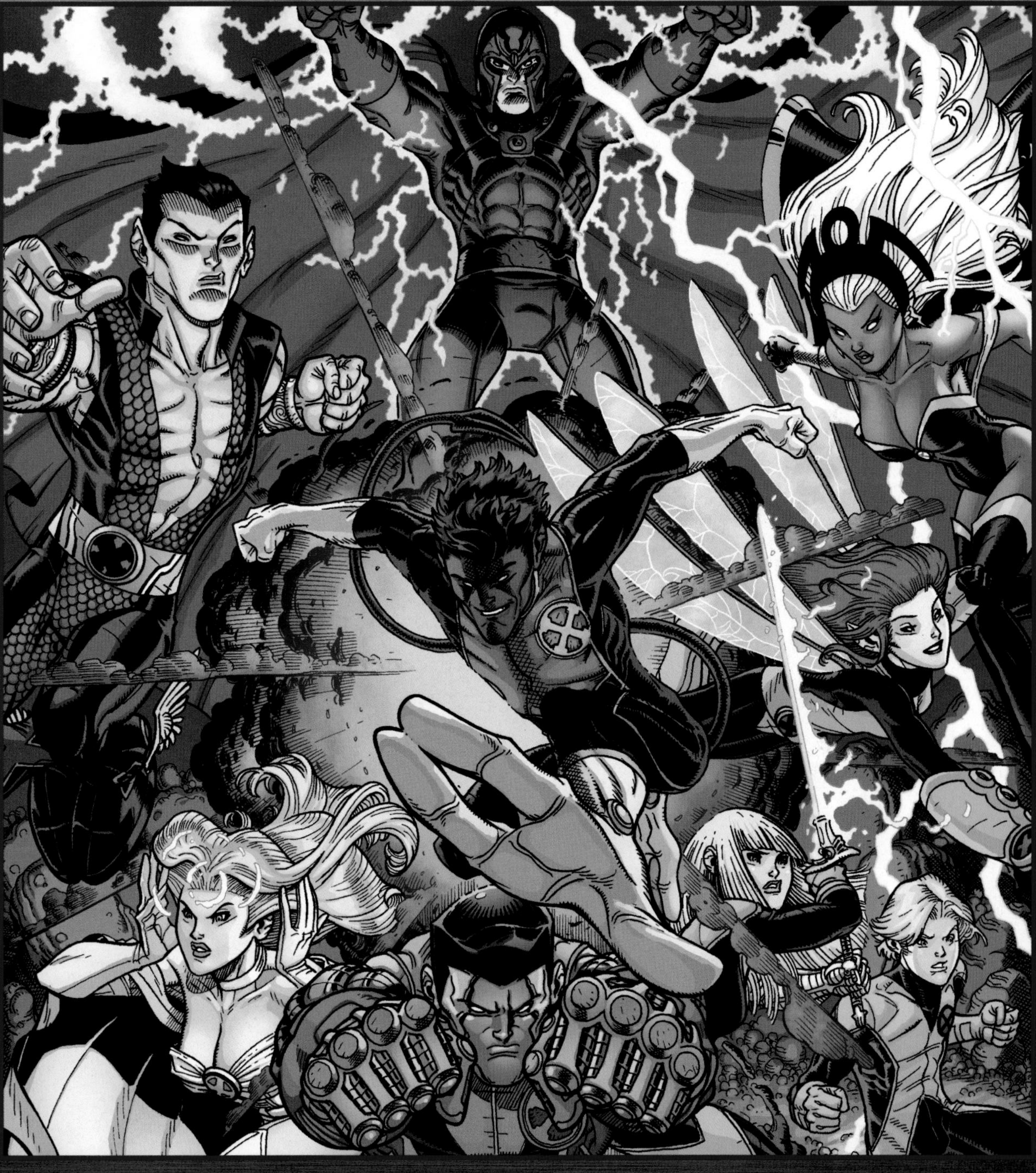

The X-Men have long defended humanity from mutant threats, striving for peace and co-existence. Faced with extinction, however, their current goal is a singular one: survival. Under the leadership of Cyclops, mutantkind has become united--hero and "villain" alike, in some cases.

But no matter how great their power, the X-Men cannot fight the inevitable. Their numbers preclude natural propagation of their species and they exist now on faith. Faith that a mutant messiah will come save them.

"Faith" and "hope" are human delusions.

X-FORCE

>>>THREAT LEVEL: EXTREME

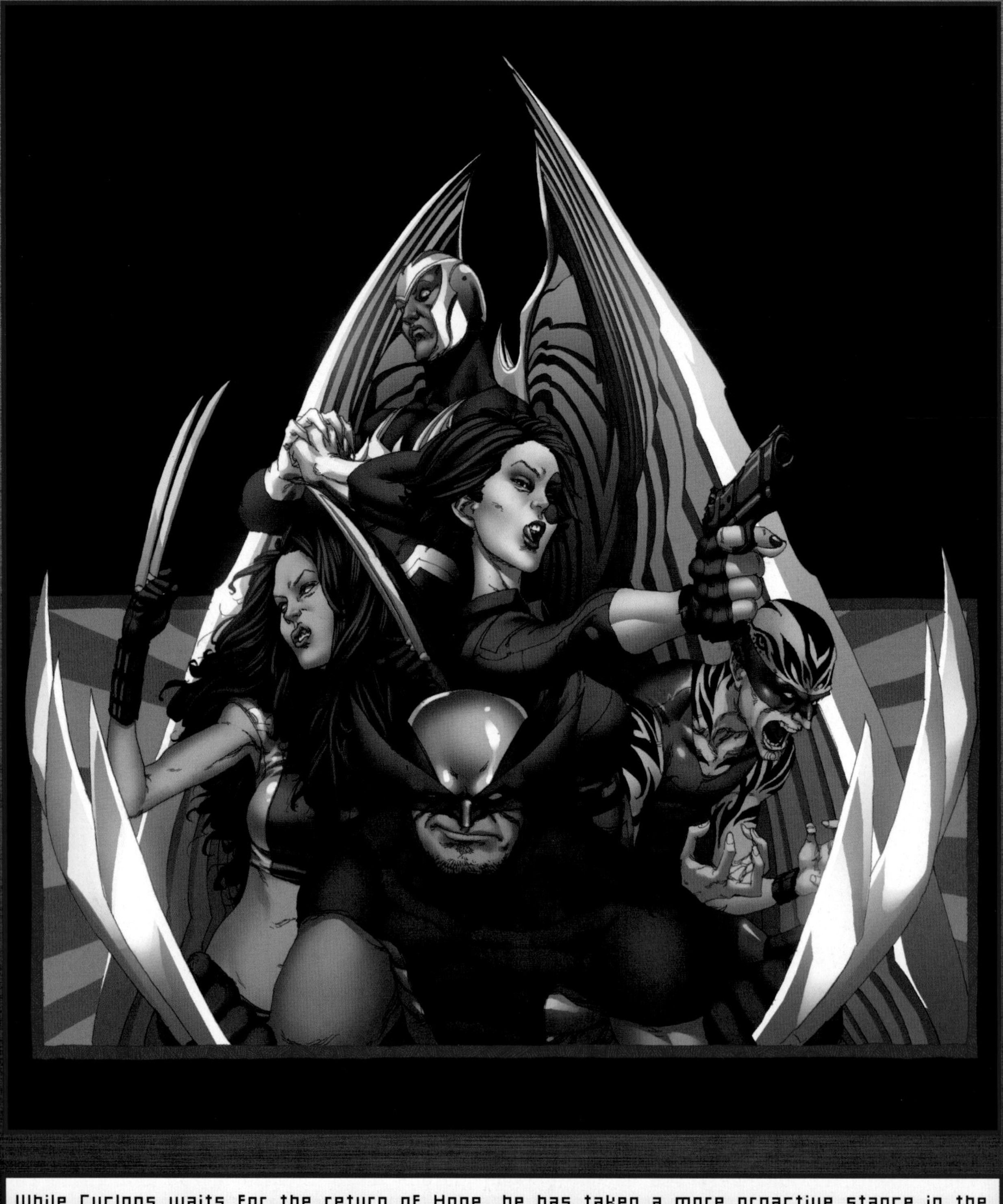

While Cyclops waits for the return of Hope, he has taken a more proactive stance in the protection of mutantkind. We have firsthand knowledge of his X-Force squad, a group of X-Men that he has authorized to strike out against mutantkind's enemies. More importantly, Cyclops has ordered them to use lethal force.

While this is logical, it goes against all existing data compiled on the X-Men. While no individual member is an extreme level threat, they have exhibited a persistence that elevates them.

However, the existence of X-Force also reveals a weakness within Cyclops. He is desperate.

THE HUMAN COUNCIL

>>>STEVEN LANG>>>BOLIVAR TRASK>>>GRAYDON CREED
>>>WILLIAM STRYKER>>>CAMERON HODGE>>>

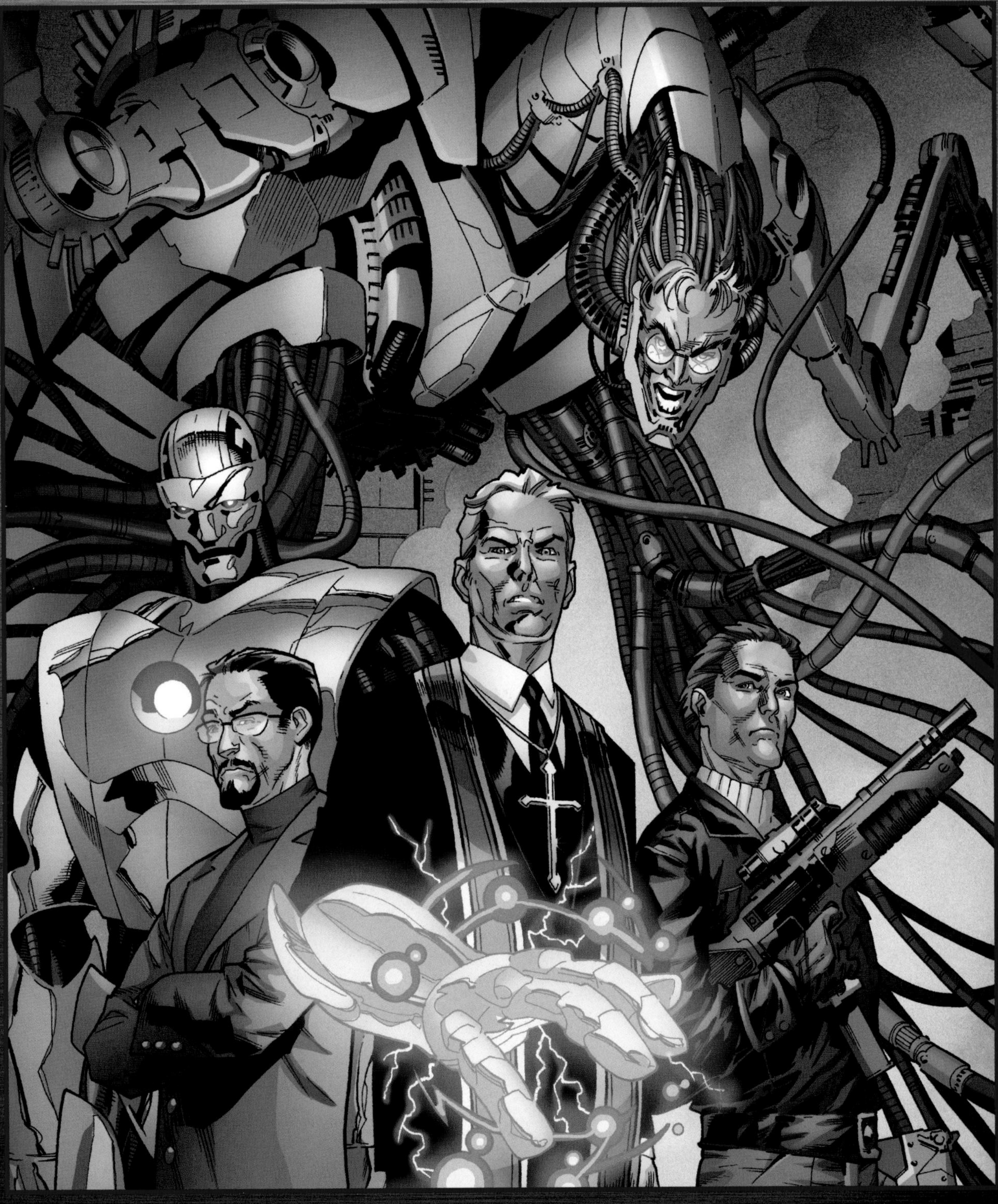

The elimination of mutantkind is the first step. The evolution of humanity is the next. We have gathered human leaders, men who will be the face of the future for mankind, something they are...comfortable with.

That future begins with the death of Hope. ➡

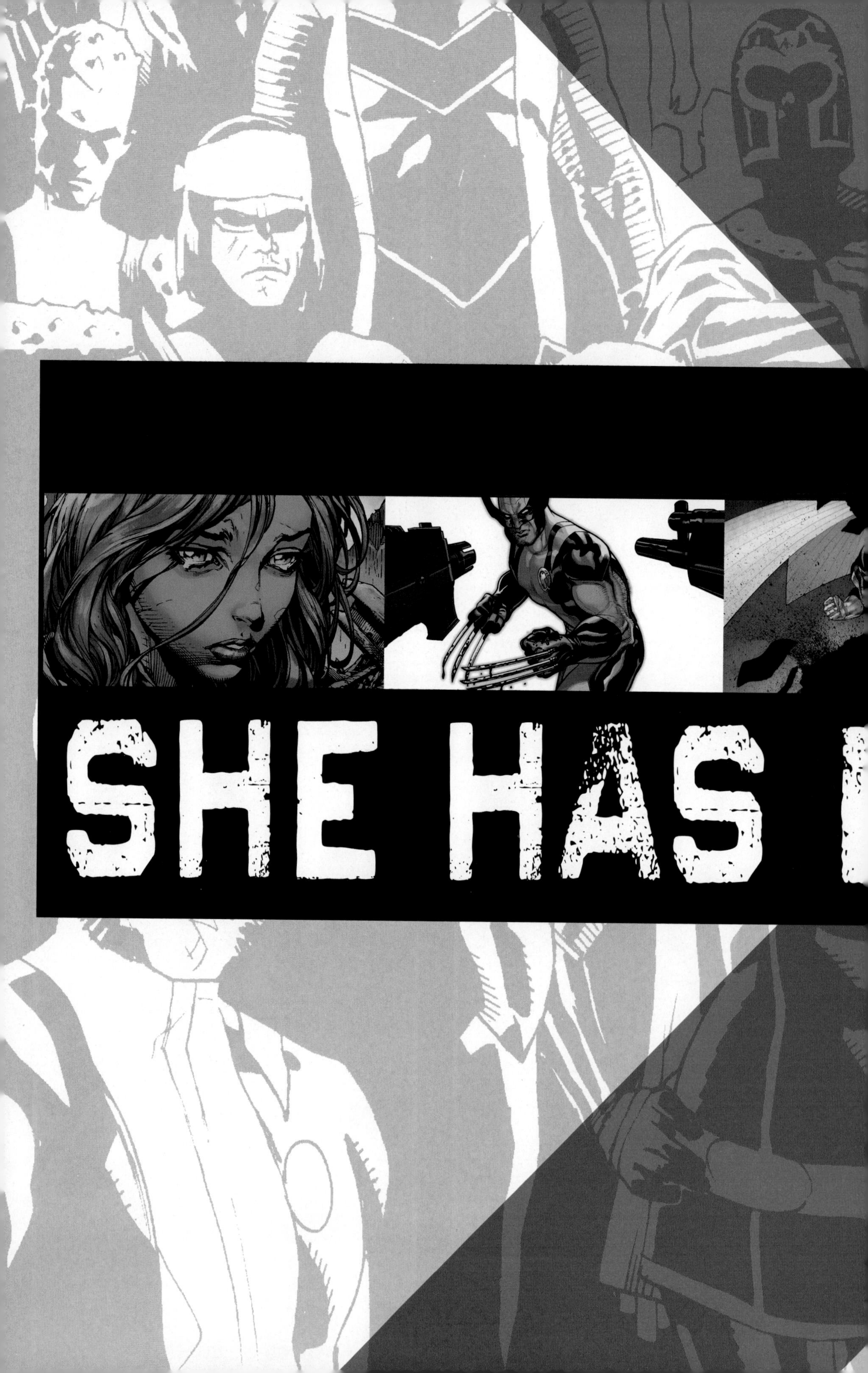
SHE HAS

RETURNED

X-MEN: SECOND COMING #1
3RD PRINTING VARIANTS

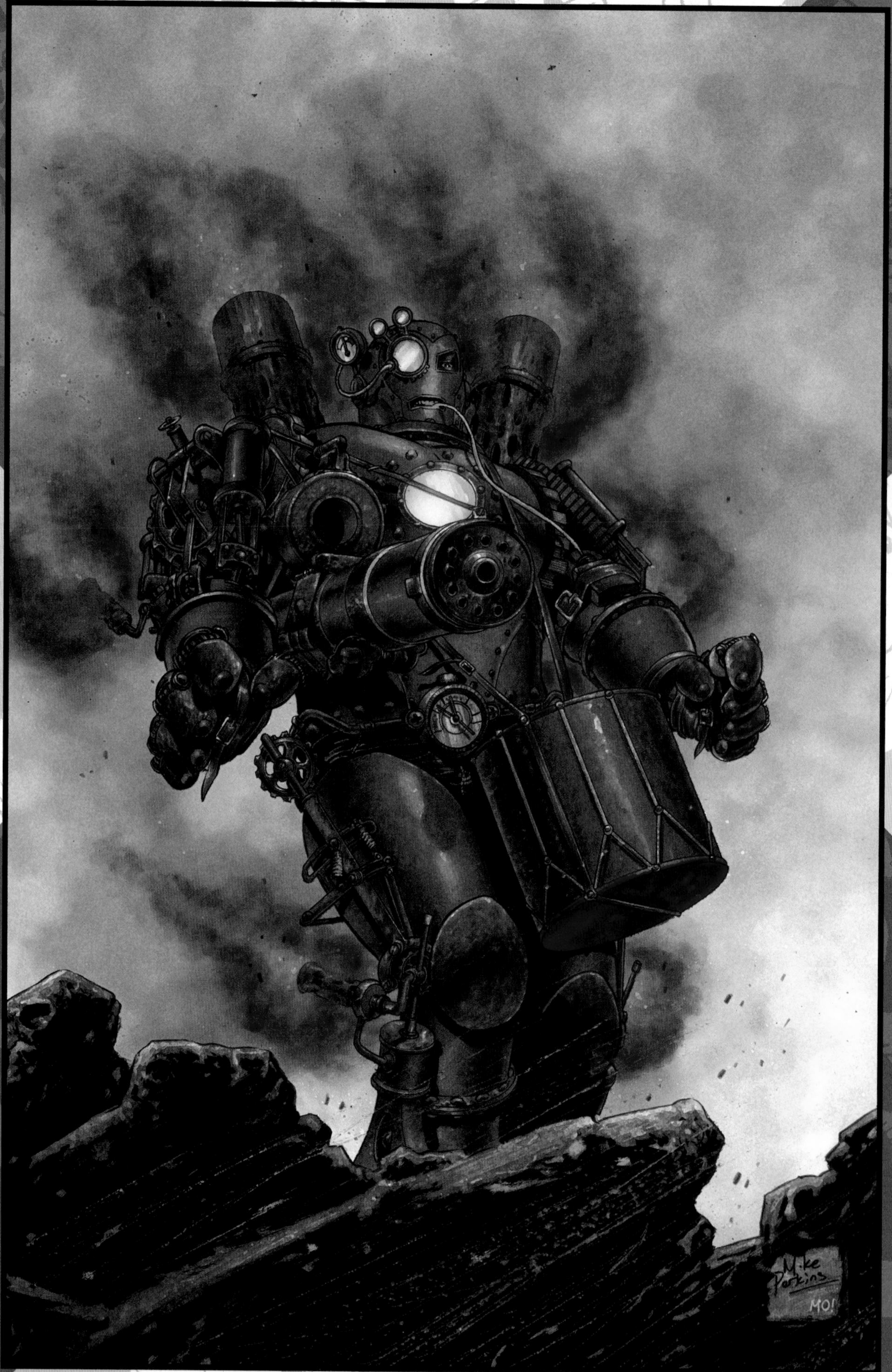
Mike
Perkins
MO!

UNCANNY X-MEN #523 IRON MAN BY DESIGN VARIANT
BY MIKE PERKINS & MORRY HOLLOWELL

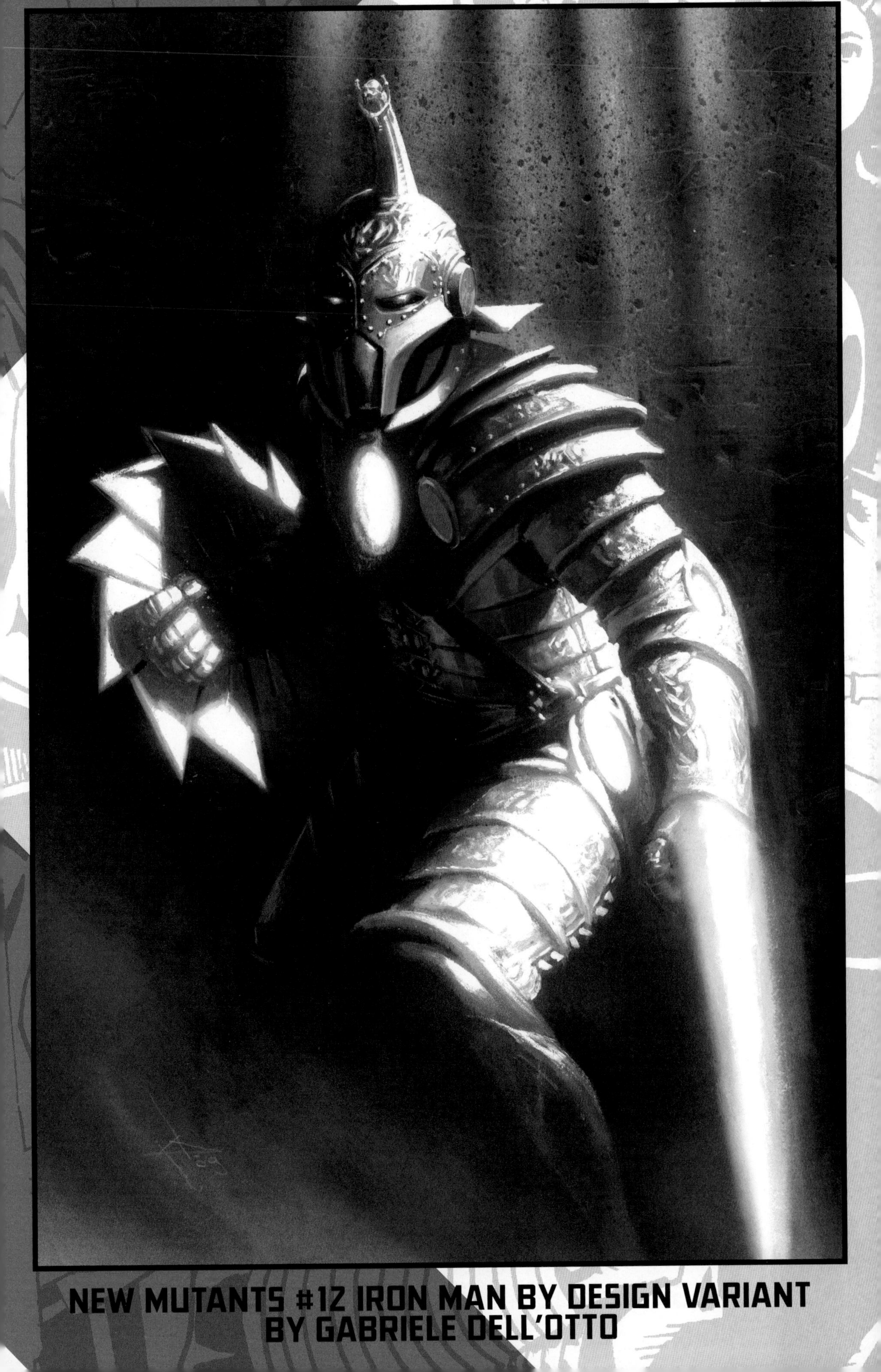

NEW MUTANTS #12 IRON MAN BY DESIGN VARIANT
BY GABRIELE DELL'OTTO

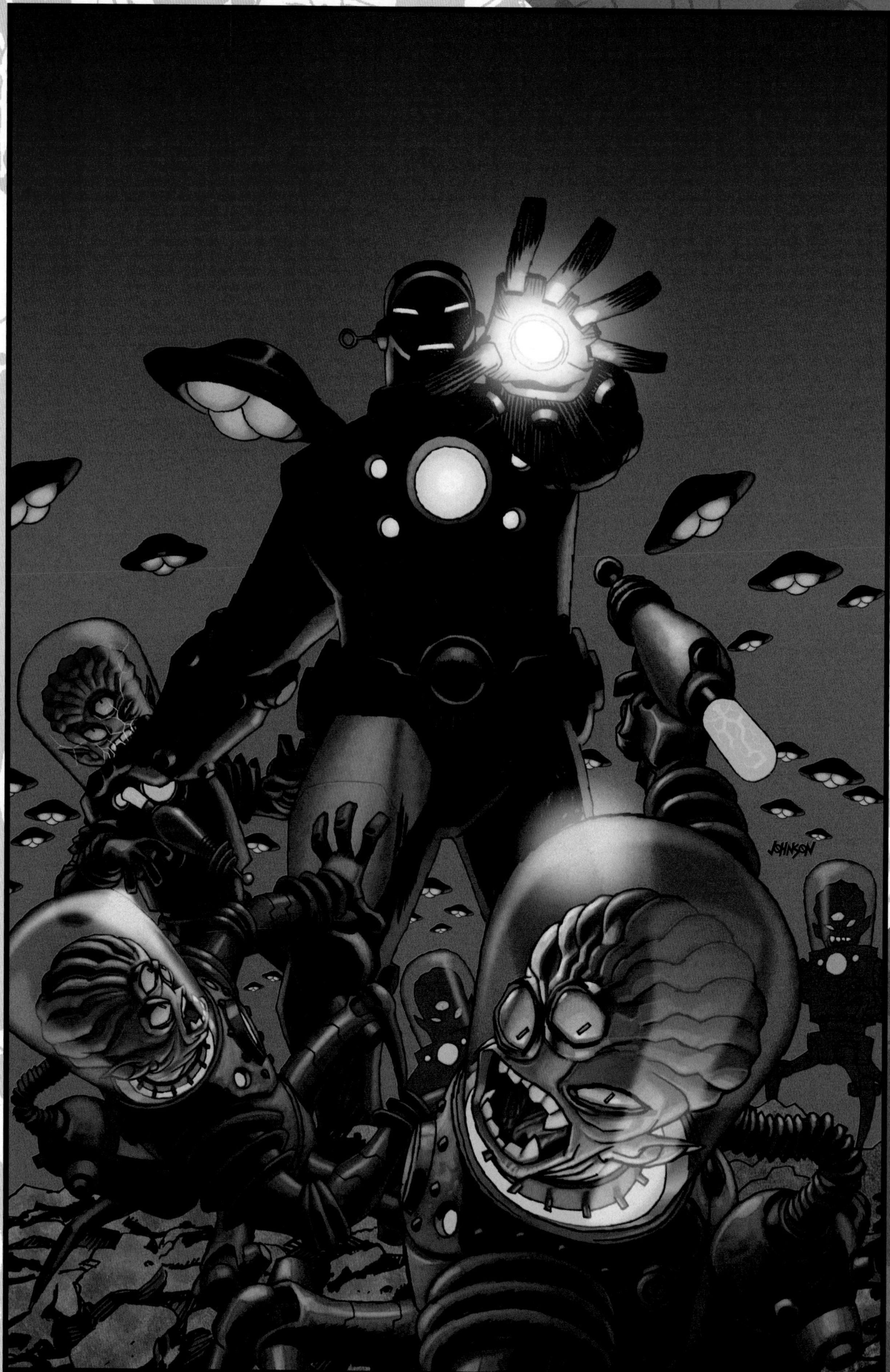
JOHNSON

X-MEN LEGACY #235 IRON MAN BY DESIGN VARIANT BY DAVE JOHNSON

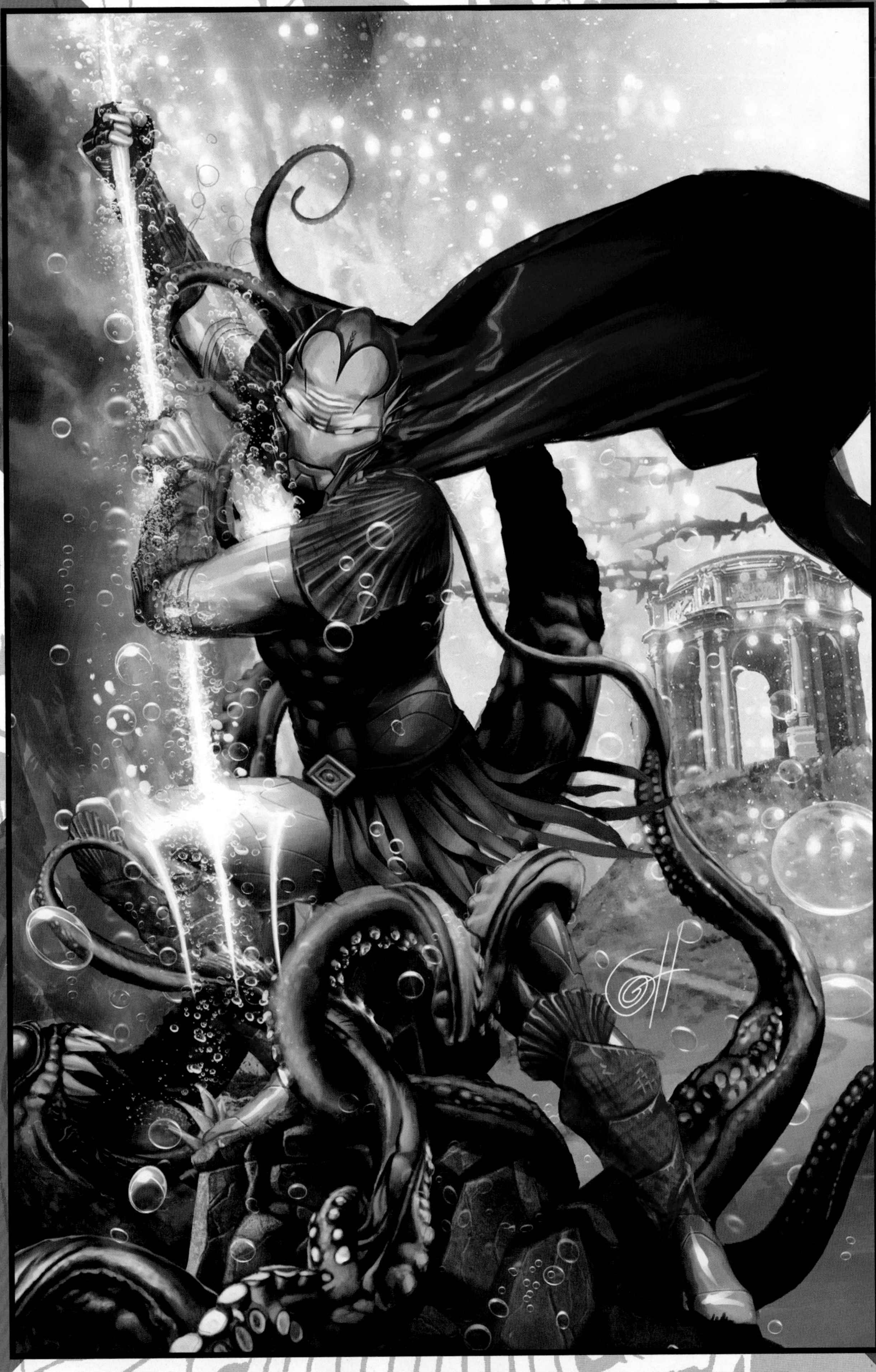

X-FORCE #26 IRON MAN BY DESIGN VARIANT
BY GREG HORN

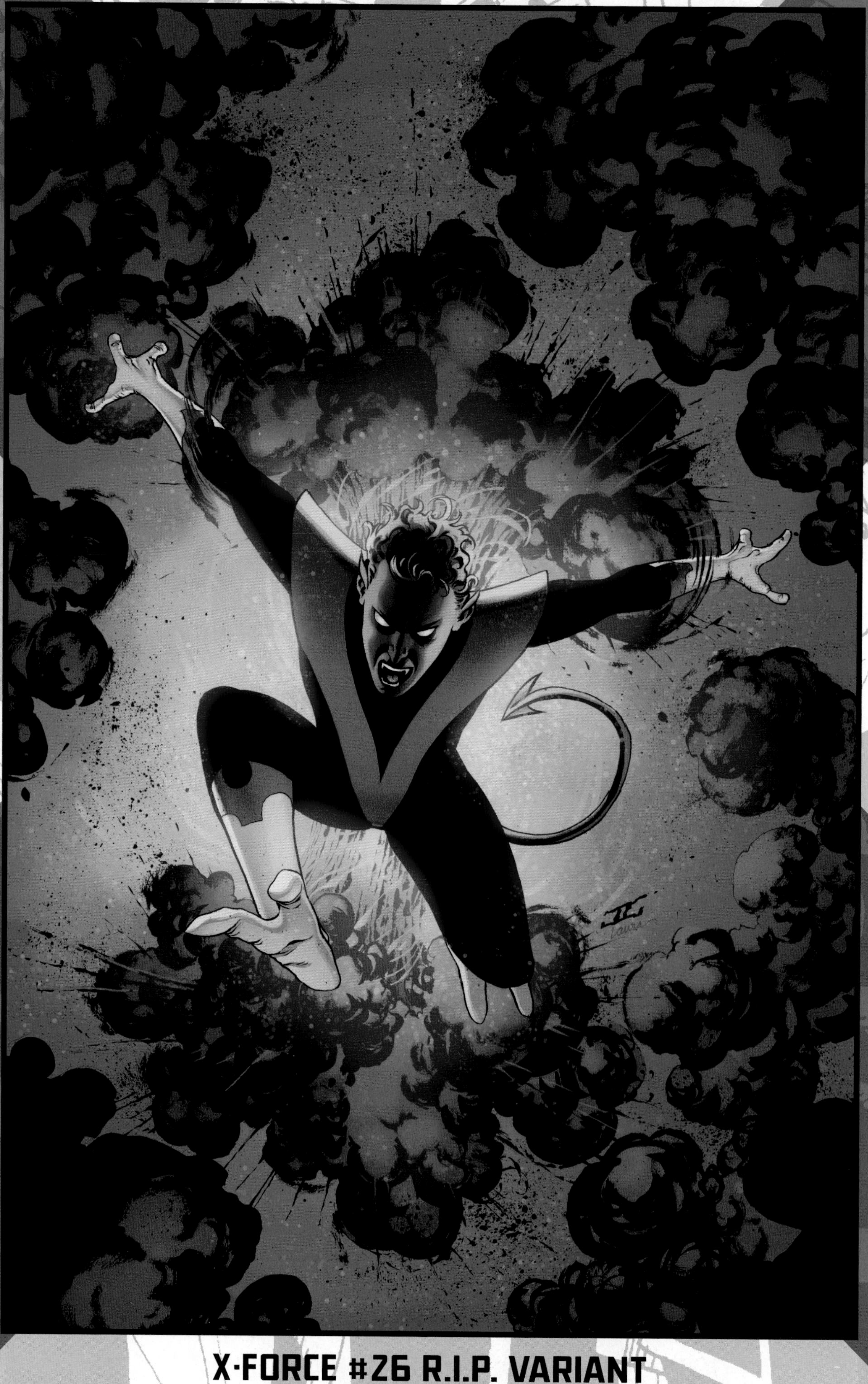

**X-FORCE #26 R.I.P. VARIANT
BY JOHN CASSADAY**

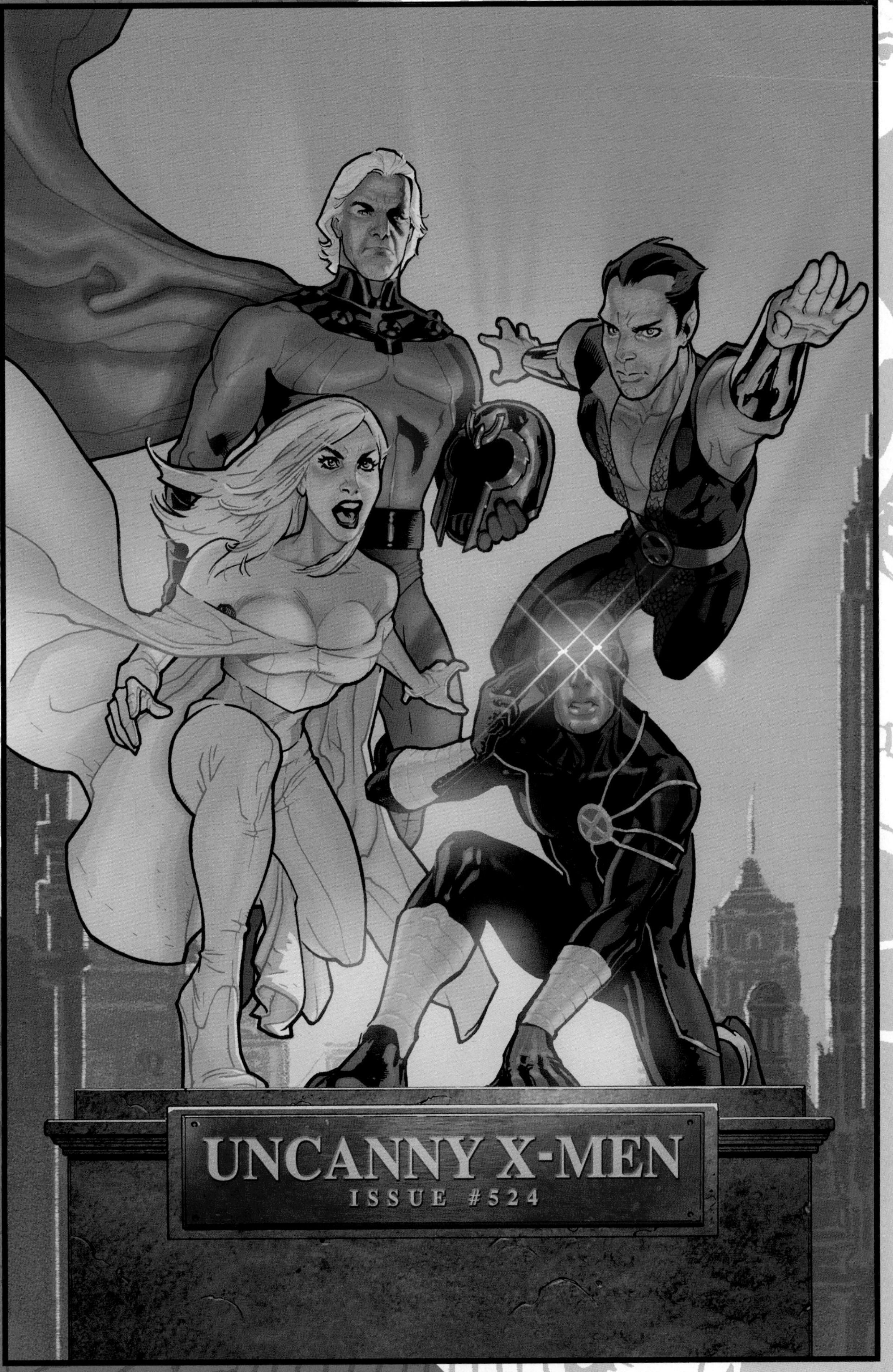
UNCANNY X-MEN
ISSUE #524

HEROIC AGE VARIANT
BY STEPHANE ROUX

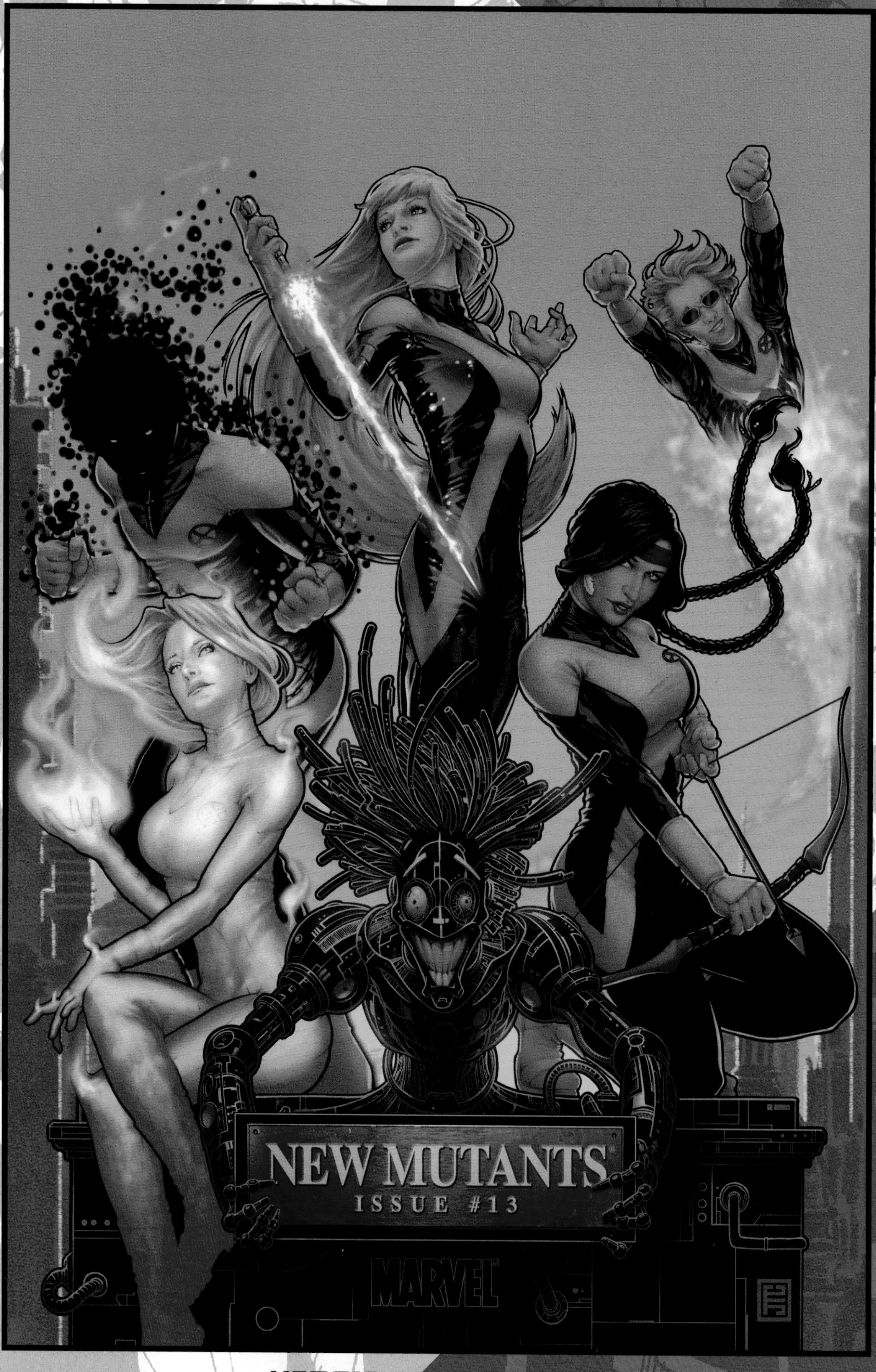
NEW MUTANTS
ISSUE #13
MARVEL

HEROIC AGE VARIANT
JOHN TYLER CHRISTOPHER

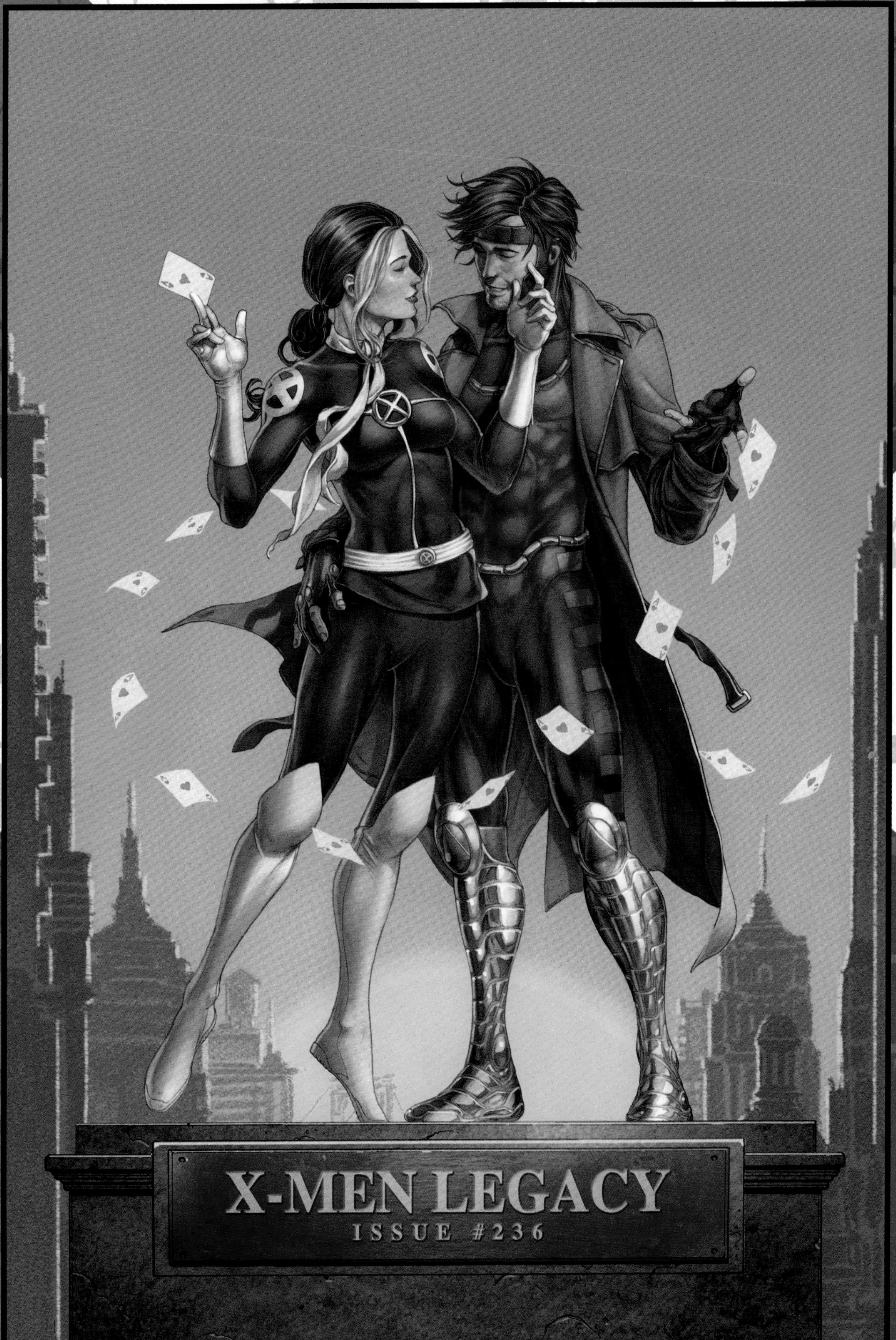
X-MEN LEGACY
ISSUE #236

HEROIC AGE VARIANT
BY MIKE CHOI & SONIA OBACK

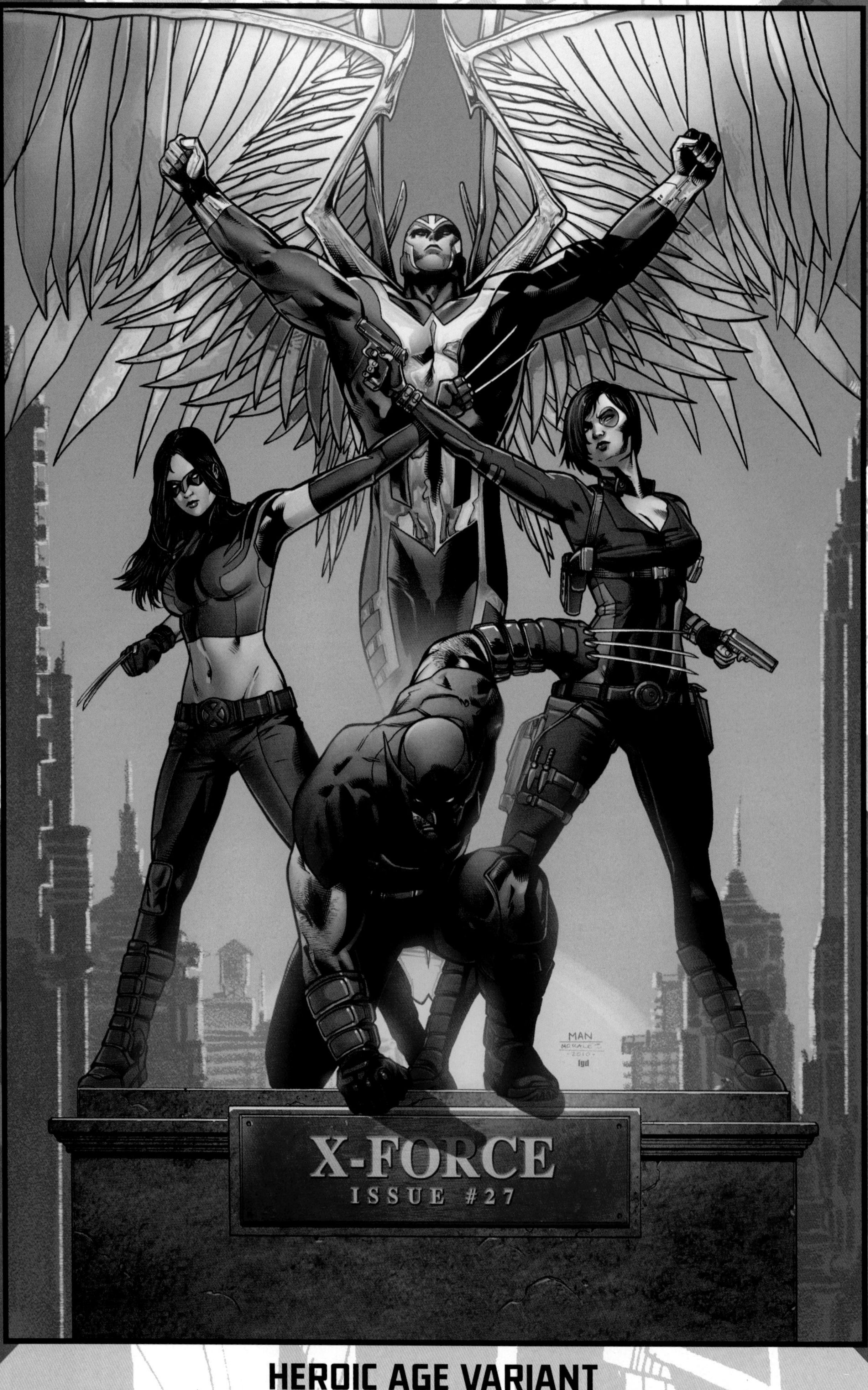
X-FORCE
ISSUE #27
MAN
MORALES
2010
fgd

HEROIC AGE VARIANT
BY CLAY MANN, MARK MORALES & FRANK D'ARMATA

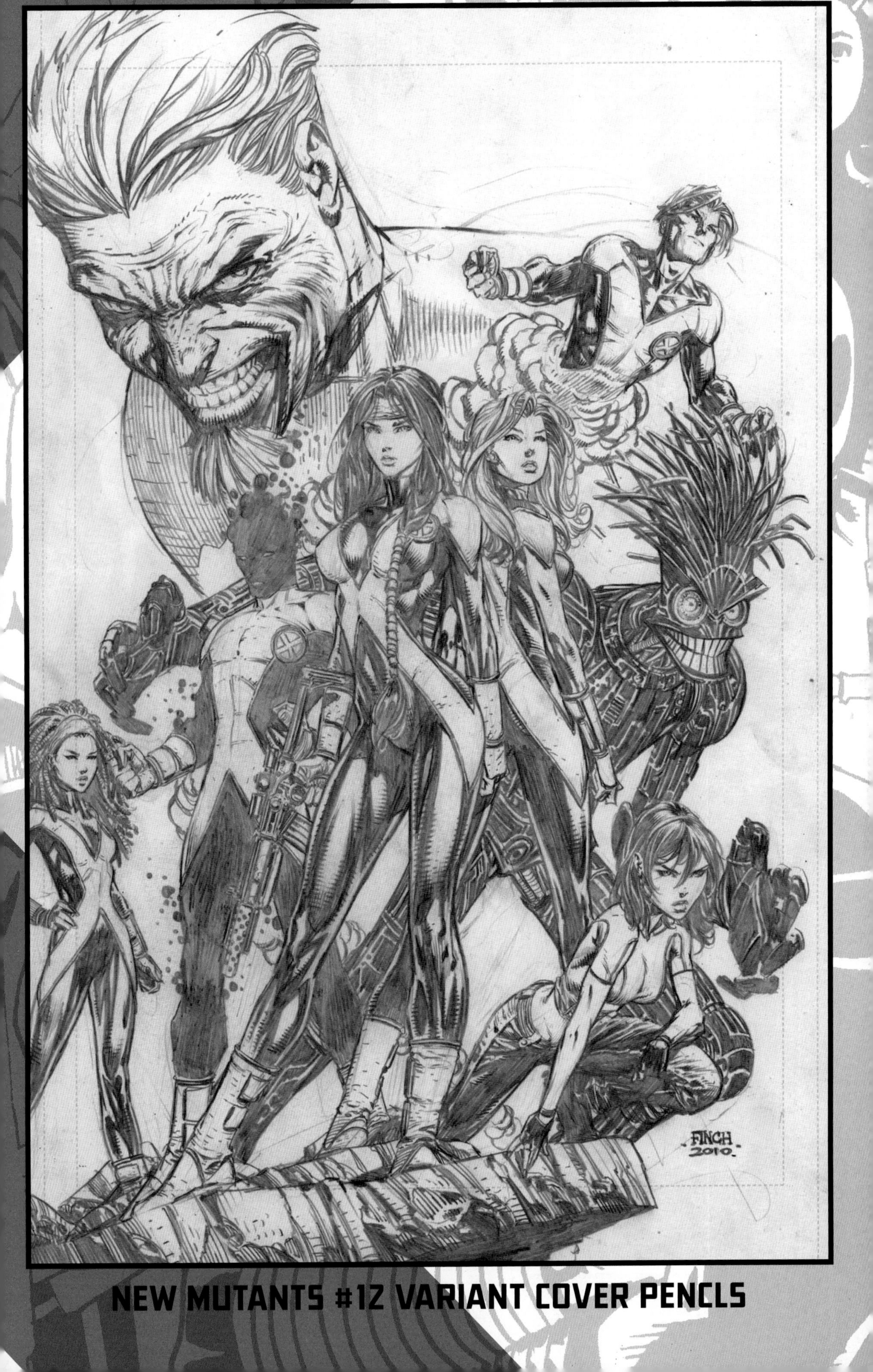
FINCH
2010

NEW MUTANTS #12 VARIANT COVER PENCLS

XMEN LEGACY #235
VARIANT PENCILS

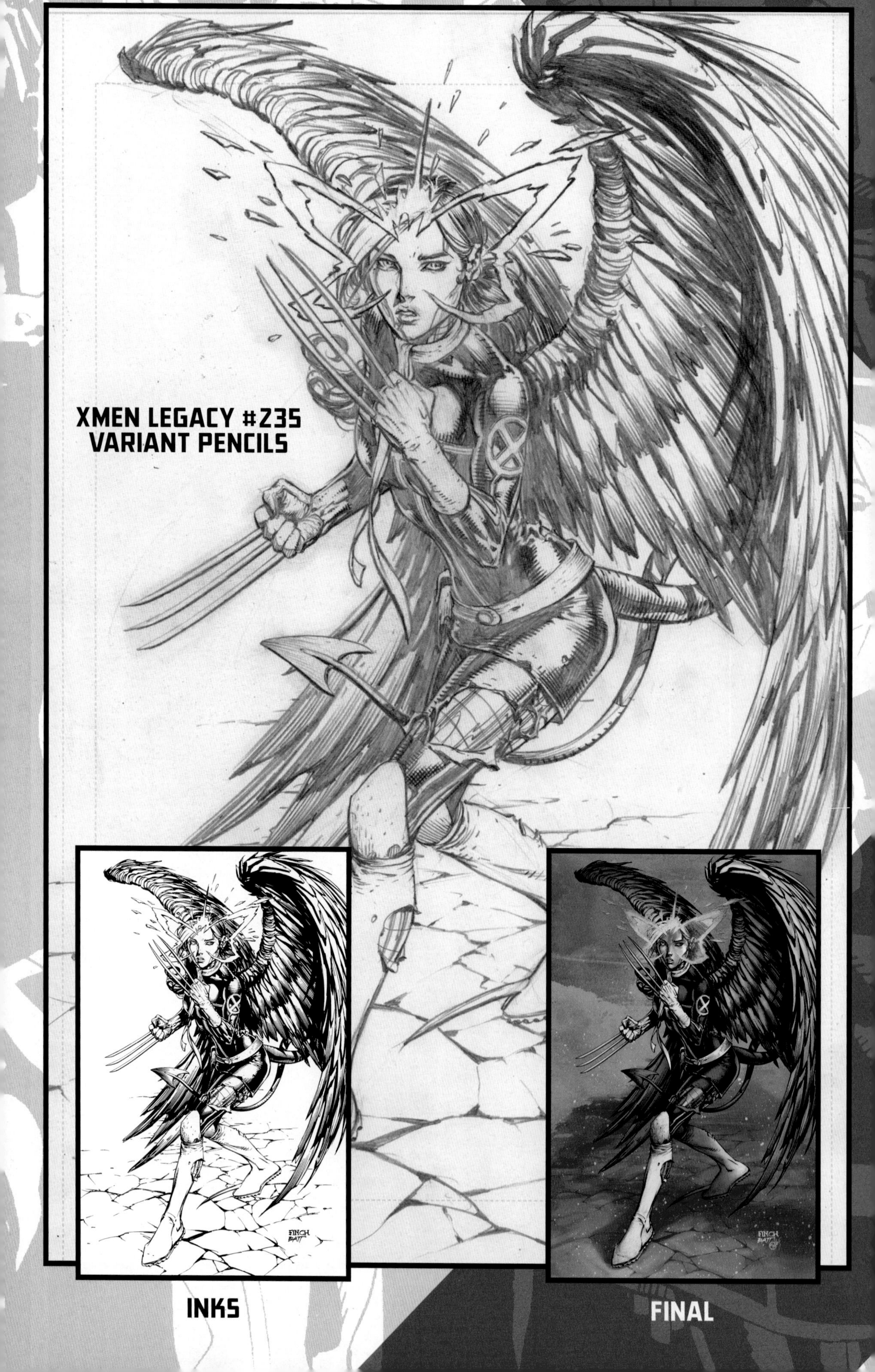
FINCH
BATT
FINCH
BATT

INKS

FINAL

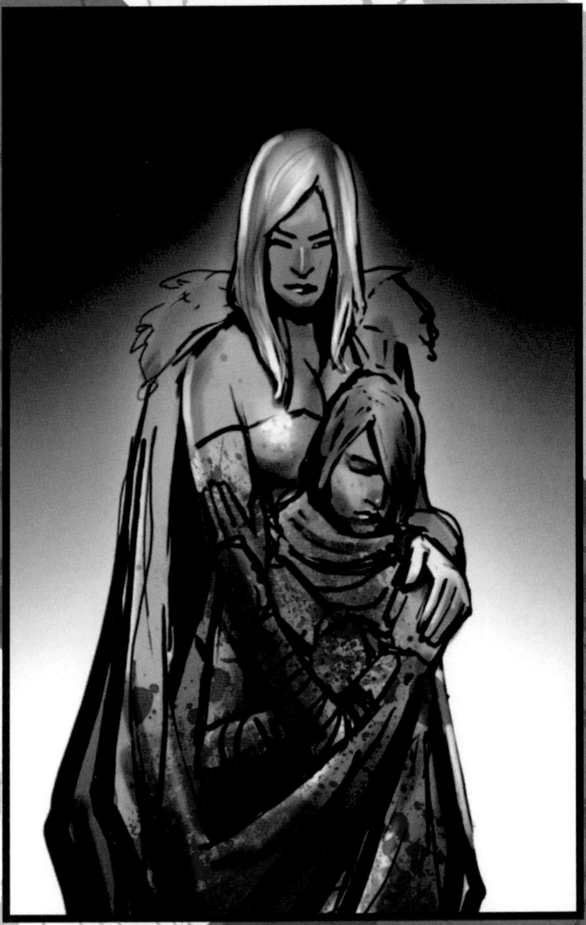

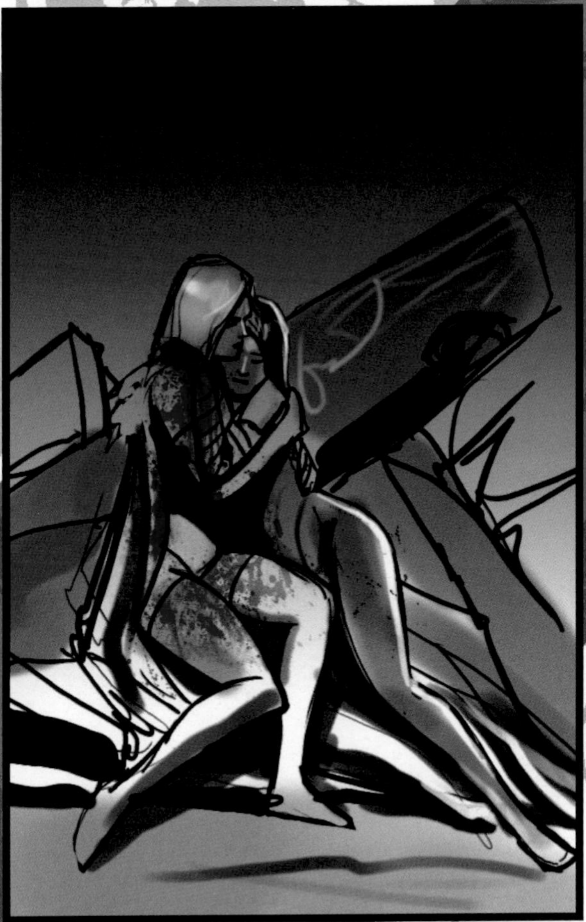

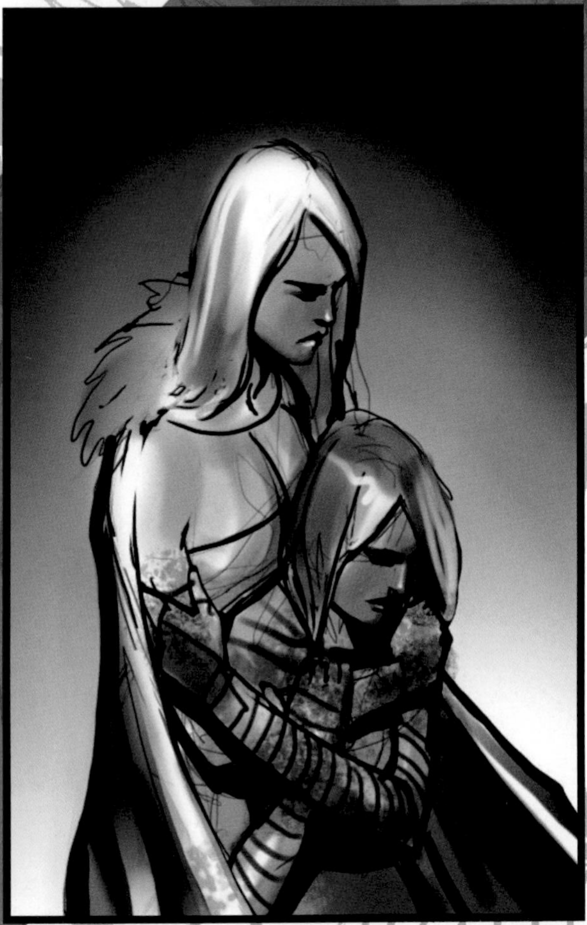

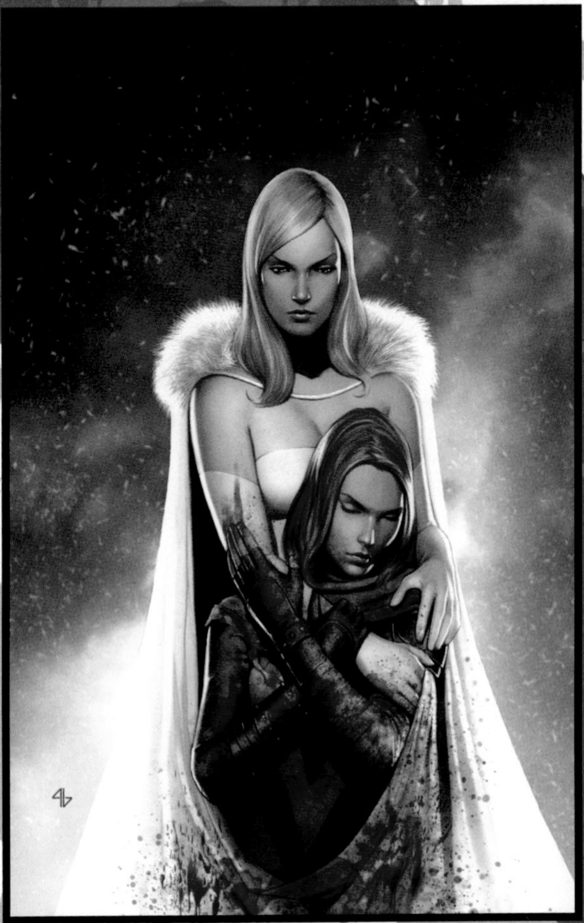

X-FORCE #26 COVER SKETCHES AND FINAL